AMERICAN SOCIAL WELFARE POLICY

A STRUCTURAL APPROACH

HOWARD J. KARGER
University of Missouri

DAVID STOESZ
San Diego State University

Longman
New York & London

American Social Welfare Policy: A Structural Approach

Longman, 10 Bank Street, White Plains, N.Y. 10606

Associated companies:
Longman Group Ltd., London
Longman Cheshire Pty., Melbourne
Longman Paul Pty., Auckland
Copp Clark Pitman, Toronto

HJK
For Aaron and Saul, two budding and intrepid warriors for social justice

D.S.
For Marc, Darcy, and Tim

Executive editor: David J. Estrin
Production editor: Camilla T.K. Palmer
Cover design: Susan J. Moore
Production supervisor: Priscilla Taguer

Library of Congress Cataloging in Publication Data
Karger, Howard Jacob
    American social welfare policy: a structural approach / Howard
  Jacob Karger, David Stoesz.
        p.   cm.
    Includes index.
    ISBN 0-8013-0193-9
    1. Public welfare—United States. 2. United States—Social
  policy. 3. Welfare state. I. Stoesz, David. II. Title.
  HV95.K35 1990
  361'.973—dc19   88-27131
                                                      CIP

6 7 8 9 10-DO-95949392

Contents

Preface   *ix*

PART 1.   AMERICAN SOCIAL WELFARE POLICY   **1**

1. Social Policy and the American Welfare State   3

    Definitions of Social Welfare Policy   4
    Social Problems and Social Welfare Policy   5
    Values Within Social Welfare Policy   6
    Ideology and the Welfare State   7
    The Political-Economy of American Social
        Welfare   9
    The Diversity of American Social Welfare   15
    Interest Groups within Social Welfare   18
    Diversity and Recent Changes in Social Welfare   21

2. A Framework for Social Policy Analysis   24

    A Proposed Model for Policy Analysis   26
    The Incompleteness of Policy Analysis   30

3. The Origins of the American Social Welfare State   32

    The English Poor Laws   32
    The Poor in Colonial America   33
    Social Welfare in the Civil War Era   34
    Industrialization and the Voluntary Sector   35
    The Great Depression and the Modern Welfare
        State   45
    The Contemporary Social Welfare State   48

4. The Making of Governmental Policy   53

    Social Stratification   53
    The Policy Process   54
    Implications for Social Welfare   63

5. Social Stigma in the American Social Welfare
        State   68

    Racism   68
    Legal Attempts to Remediate the Effects of
        Racism   75
    Sexism: How Do We Know That It Exists?   77
    Gays and Lesbians: Two Populations at Risk   83
    Ageism   84
    The Disabled   85
    Social Stigma and Oppression   87

6. Poverty in America   92

    Who Make Up the Poor?   93
    Income Distribution and Inequality   97
    Some Characteristics of Poverty   102
    Work and Poverty   102
    Some Theoretical Formulations About Poverty   103
    A Note on Strategies Developed to Combat
        Poverty   107

PART 2.   THE VOLUNTARY AND FOR-PROFIT
           SOCIAL WELFARE SECTOR   113

7. The Voluntary Sector Today   115

    The "Forgotten Sector"   115
    Advancing Social Justice   118
    Contemporary Nonprofit Human Service
        Organizations   119
    The Declining Fiscal Capacity of the Voluntary
        Sector   122

8. The Corporate Sector   126

    History of the Corporate Sector   127
    Corporate Social Responsibility   130
    Corporate Influence on Social Welfare Policy   132
    The Future of Corporate Involvement in Social
        Welfare   137

9.   Human Service Corporations   143

   The Scope of Human Service Corporations   144
   The New Human Service Markets   145
   Implications for Social Workers   148

10.   Private Practice   152

   The Sociology of Professions   153
   The Political Economy of Private Practice   154
   Private Practice in Social Work   156
   Issues in Private Practice   158
   The Business of Private Practice   159
   The Future of Private Practice   161

PART 3.   THE GOVERNMENT SECTOR   **165**

11.   Social Insurance and Income Maintenance
         Programs   167

   Definition of Social Insurance   167
   The Background of Social Insurance   168
   Key Social Insurance Programs   169
   Issues in Social Insurance   175
   Income Maintenance Programs   176
   Some Assumptions that Underlie the AFDC
         Program   181
   Issues in AFDC   184
   Supplemental Security Income   188
   General Assistance   189
   Summary   190

12.   The American Health Care System   192

   The Organization of Medical Services   192
   The Major Health Programs: Medicaid and
         Medicare   193
   Medicare   199
   Cutting Federal Health-Care Costs: The
         Diagnostic Related Groups (DRGs)   200
   Other Governmental Health Services   202
   A Comparative Analysis: Health Care in
         Scandinavia and Britain   202
   The Crisis in Medical Care   207

13.   Mental Health Policy   216

      Mental Health Reform   217
      The Community Mental Health Centers Act   218
      Deinstitutionalization   219
      The Revolving Door   221
      CMHCs Under Siege   222
      Alcoholism and Substance Abuse   223
      The Future of Mental Health Policy   226

14.   Child Welfare Policy   231

      History of Child Welfare Policy   231
      Protective Services for Children   233
      Foster Care for Children   235
      Adoption   236
      Emerging Issues in Child Welfare   238
      The Future of Child Welfare   241

15.   The Crisis in Housing   243

      Issues in Housing Policy   245
      Homelessness   254
      Housing Reform   257

16.   Food Policy and Politics   261

      Governmental Food Programs   261
      The Farm Crisis   264

17.   Employment Policies   273

      History of Employment Policy   274
      Job Training Programs   276
      Dual Labor Markets   277
      Workfare   278
      The Underclass   280

PART 4.   THE FUTURE OF AMERICAN SOCIAL
           WELFARE   285

18.   The Fragmentation of Welfare State Ideology   287

      Ideology and the Welfare State   288
      Voices From the Left   289
      Conceptions of Social Welfare   290
      The Future of American Social Welfare   293

19. Welfare Reform   298

     Neoconservatism   299
     Neoliberalism   301
     The New Welfare Reform Initiative   302
     Reforming the Welfare State   304
     Toward a New Welfare Agenda   306

20. Privatization: Issues for the Voluntary and
          Corporate Sectors   310

     Commercialization   311
     Preferential Selection   313
     Cost-Effectiveness   314
     Standardization   316
     Oligopolization   317
     The Challenge of Privatization   318

21. Issues in Social Service Delivery   321

     Bureaucracy and the Delivery of Social Services   321
     Social Workers and Unions   326
     Self-Determination in the Social Service
          Workplace   332

22. Social Work and the Future of American Social
          Welfare   337

     Leaders in Social Welfare   338
     Political Practice   340
     Advocacy Organizations   342
     The New Welfare Institutes   342
     Social Work and the Future of Social Welfare
          Policy   344
     Radical Social Work   345
     Conclusion   346

Glossary   348

Index   355

Preface

In American social welfare, a wide gulf separates social welfare policy from social work practice. It is commonplace for students entering the human service professions to focus on intervention with clients around discrete problems, or "direct" practice. Occasionally, students understand that their professional careers will lead to responsibilities of an administrative nature, but rarely do they express an interest in social policy. Over the years welfare institutions have come to reflect these preferences. The result is not without considerable cost to welfare professionals who find themselves having to work by— and frequently around—social policies that have little consonance with the needs of the practitioner or client.

When institutional practices are so out of line with human requirements, momentum builds to change social programs. This seems to have taken two forms in relation to social welfare in the United States. On the one hand, many human service professionals have left traditional settings of welfare practice—the voluntary and governmental sectors—in favor of new settings, the corporate sector and private practice. On the other hand, pressure to reform government welfare programs has increased, as evident in the number of "welfare reform" proposals introduced in Congress. These proposals are of particular interest because much of the welfare reform legislation penalizes disenfranchised populations— women, racial minorities, the aged, children, the handicapped—that have been a traditional concern of welfare professionals. As a result, much of what we understand to be social welfare in America is in flux, yet welfare professionals are exerting little influence in redefining this important social institution.

The failure of welfare professionals to act effectively in this area of social welfare policy is troubling to us. It is difficult to imagine changes in health policy around which physicians do not flock, or alterations in legal policy that do not convene a gaggle of attorneys. Yet, social workers have not played prominent roles in welfare policy for some time. Such has not always been the case. Mary Richmond proved instrumental in the Charity Organization Society movement, Jane Addams became a heroine through her work in the settlement movement, and Harry Hopkins championed programs pioneered by the New Deal. More recently, Wilbur Cohen engineered important parts of the programs that comprised the War on Poverty. But few social workers of national prominence have emerged since the Great Society programs.

Fortunately, this omission is being addressed— albeit in somewhat haphazard fashion. The National Association of Social Workers (NASW) has mobilized a political action committee and recently established a policy institute to press for social welfare policies congruent with NASW priorities. In 1984, Barbara Mikulski, a social worker from Maryland, was elected to the United States Senate, joining Ron Dellums, a Representative from California, and "Ed" Towns, a Representative from New York, as the only Congresspersons who are social workers. It remains to be seen whether the large mass of welfare professionals will become accustomed to thinking about social welfare policy. We hope so. This book is a result of our belief that social welfare policy has an immediate and profound effect on the work of welfare professionals, and our conviction is that welfare programs could be made more adequate and humane if these professionals were more actively engaged in setting social policy.

In trying to bridge this gap, we have adopted a "structural approach" to social welfare policy. In doing so, the book has been organized around the primary sectors that have evolved in American social welfare: the voluntary sector, the governmental sector and, more recently, the corporate sector, and private practice. These sectors have addressed problems presented at different periods in our national life. Today, these sectors of American social welfare coexist, reflecting a diversity that is as characteristic of American pluralism as it is sometimes maddening to the student of welfare policy analysis.

The rationale for our approach is straightforward. First, social welfare encompasses, in the American experience, a complicated arrangement of policies and programs. A structural approach helps sort out the major institutional actors, introducing a measure of order to what otherwise appears to be institutional anarchy. Second, many welfare professionals (and, for that matter, nonprofessionals) begin their careers in agencies of the voluntary sector. Unfortunately, these agencies are not always given the credit they deserve. In our judgment, the voluntary sector is an integral component of social welfare in the United States, even if it relates to policy with a small "p." Our emphasis on the voluntary sector is based on the belief that as public policy shifts, more of the welfare burden will be transferred from the government to the private sector. Third, a proprietary, corporate sector has rapidly emerged during the last two decades, providing a substantial volume of services and a corresponding number of employment opportunities for human service professionals. Failure to recognize the importance of this sector is tantamount to ignoring what is probably the most important development in social welfare since the War on Poverty, and possibly even the New Deal. Finally, many social workers have found private practice, independent of the organizational restraints associated with the voluntary, governmental, and corporate sectors, an attractive method of service delivery. The popularity of private practice among human service professionals justifies its inclusion in any discussion of social welfare policy. Through an examination of these sectors we hope to acquaint students with the central structures and processes that shape American social welfare.

In order to facilitate the comprehension of material, we have used Part I to focus on basic concepts underlying social policy analysis. This segment also includes a historical survey of social welfare in the United States, and a discussion of the values, social forces, and theoretical assumptions which affect the creation, operation, and implementation of social policies. In much of this we have borrowed heavily from economics, as well as political and social theory. Because of the disparity between the intentions of policymakers and the program realities facing welfare professionals, we have examined in a critical manner the legislative, judicial, and administrative processes which influence the design and implementation of social welfare policy. A special focus is placed on the interactional effects of social policies and programs on vulnerable groups: the aged, minorities, women, homosexuals, the poor, as well as children and families. This segment of the book also provides students with a framework for understanding the complex nature of American social welfare. Throughout the book, essential social policy terms are referenced in a glossary located at the end of the text. With basic conceptual tools at hand, students will find the descriptive material of Parts II and III—the voluntary, governmental, corporate, and private practice—less overwhelming. Familiarity with these analytic concepts will also make the discussion of the future of American social welfare—Part IV—more stimulating.

Because of our emphasis on institutional transformation, we have included what we suspect are developments likely to become more prominent in the future, among them privatization, unionization in social work, and welfare reform. The inclusion of these factors necessitates that we risk being out of date because current policies can change so swiftly. In these instances we have tried to outline the general trend, and we beg the reader's forgiveness for any change in events. Such is the price of relevance. We have also omitted some of the details about program specifications that appear in some treatments of welfare policy. In doing so, we are less concerned about program detail—which practitioners become acquainted with during their first day on the job—than we are on defining the themes around which welfare policy is constructed. Given political developments since the mid-1970s, we believe this corrects an error on the part of many liberal analysts. Specifically, while preoccupied with program intricacies, many welfare professionals have found, much to their chagrin, that ideologues of the political right had commanded public attention, attained positions in high public office, and used that power effectively to alter the rules of the game, thereby executing punishing cuts in social programs in the processs. If welfare professionals are to reinstate a liberal direction to social welfare policy, they will have to temporarily abandon questions of program "puzzle solving" and return to defining the paradigm of social programs.[1] In other words, social workers need to play more than the notes—they also need to play the music.

Social work students often ask why they are required to study social policy. Some believe that they entered social work to help people and thus their sole concern is with the provision of direct services. As experienced clinicians we recognize the distance between social welfare policy and direct practice; and we have come to appreciate the difficulties that clients and practitioners encounter because of social welfare policy. Accordingly, we insist that direct service is inextricably linked to policy. Clients exist in a society and are continually influenced by social forces. The more disenfranchised the clients, the more exposed they are to the maelstrom of social forces swirling about them. Social work helps clients not only by working with them individually, but by protecting the collective interests of vulnerable populations—children, the aged, racial and ethnic minorities, the handicapped, and the poor, among others. There are many ways of helping and social workers must try to learn all of them.

One of the major goals we had in writing this book was to encourage students to think critically about social policy. We hope that students and instructors will argue about and critique the ideas in the book. For us, that is part of the joy of policy analysis. Unfortunately, the student of policy analysis will soon find that few things are carved in stone. Although sometimes frustrating, these "gray areas" can provide an exciting challenge. Because social policy is not rigid in its method, it demands creative ideas and solutions. The "openness" of policy requires that each student come up with his or her own answers for the major social policy questions of our times.

American Social Welfare is the product of two authors, both of the same mind. Over the years we have collaborated on enough work that it is sometimes unclear as to who originated what. The interaction that has led us this far is what scholarship is all about, and we have found it immensely gratifying. There is a strange convention in publishing about junior and senior authors. In this regard we note that the listing of the authors on the cover is alphabetical. Both authors contributed equally, and no author was more "senior" than the other in the preparation of this book.

To our associates of policy America, a nonprofit research group established in 1985 to develop innovations in social welfare policy, we owe a special thanks. This band of intellectual guerrillas not only critiqued parts of the book, but also convinced us that thinking about social welfare policy and dancing to zydeco music were not mutually exclusive. Ten percent of the royalties from the sales of this book are contributed to policy America.

We also extend our deep-felt appreciation to our colleagues at Longman. As senior editor, David Estrin showed confidence in us by accepting the idea for this book on face value, thus obviating the detail demanded by most editors. The manner in which he has directed this publication is a model for editorial coordination. Victoria Mifsud, Editorial Assistant, helped keep the book on track by efficiently handling our requests and the details involved in the preparation of a manuscript. Camilla Palmer was more than gracious in trying to track us down during our semester break.

Special thanks is also offered to Steve McMurtry and Thomas Watts for a thorough and systematic critique of the manuscript. Thanks also to Larry Litterst, a good friend and a fine economist. His thorough critique of economic principles helped strengthen the book, especially in areas where his advice was heeded. A deep appreciation is offered to Stephen J. Boland, computer wizard, Paul Michalewicz, data cruncher, Debbie Dycaico, "sleuth"-reader, and Lucinda Roginske and Suzanne Cooper, table and glossary compilers, for their assistance in assembling technical materials. Appreciation is ex-tended to Michael Kelly for his generosity in sharing high tech equipment, and to Karen Stout, Mary Ann Reitmeir, Joanne Melmelstein, Paul Sundet and Roland Meinert, as well as other people too numerous to mention. The students who sat through our policy classes deserve special credit for their patience, insight, and ideas.

H.J.K.
Columbia, Missouri
January, 1989

D.S.
San Diego, California
January, 1989

H.J.K.

A profound debt is owed to Connie for tolerating my self-absorption and complaining, and for doing more than her share of everyday work. An apology is offered to Aaron and Saul for having to put up with a moody and often distracted daddy. Lastly, a long overdue thank you is offered to Samuel Karger for having tried to teach me to question and to see beyond the obvious choices.

D.S.

A warm and special thanks is extended to Martha Joseph for her patience and thoughtful suggestions.

1   Thomas Kuhn, *The Structure of Scientific Revolutions* (Chicago: University of Chicago Press, 1956).

PART ONE

American Social Welfare Policy

CHAPTER 1

Social Policy and
the American Welfare State

American social welfare is in a period of transition. Since the Social Security Act of 1935, advocates of the unfortunate have held that federal social programs were the best way to help the disadvantaged. Now, after a half-century of experimentation with the "welfare state," a discernible shift has occurred. As a result of the increasing conservatism of American culture, private institutions are being called upon to shoulder more of the welfare burden. Meanwhile, many government social programs have been reduced or eliminated. For proponents of social justice, the suggestion that the private sector should be the basis for welfare represents a retreat from hard-won governmental social legislation that has provided essential benefits to millions of Americans— children, the aged, racial minorities, veterans, farmers, the poor, women, ethnic groups, and the handicapped. Justifiably, these groups fear the loss of basic goods and services during the transition in American social welfare.

At the same time, the pluralistic nature of American culture must be acknowledged in social welfare as it has been recognized in other institutions, such as education, in which private institutions exist alongside those of the public sector. American social welfare has a noble tradition of voluntary groups of citizens taking the initiative to solve local problems. Today, private voluntary groups are providing important services to patients with Acquired Immune Deficiency Syndrome (AIDS), the homeless, and refugees. While voluntary activities represent the historical contribution by the private sector to American social welfare, a more

recent development within the private sector raises fundamental questions for the future provision of human services. Social welfare has become big business. During the last twenty-five years the number of human service corporations—for-profit firms providing social welfare through the marketplace—has increased dramatically. Human service corporations are prominent in long-term nursing care, health maintenance, child day care, psychiatric and substance abuse services, even corrections. For many welfare professionals, the proprietary provision of human services is troubling since it occurs at a time when government is reducing its commitment to social programs. Yet, human service corporations are likely to be prominent players in the shaping of the nation's social welfare policies. So long as American culture is open, democratic, and capitalistic, groups will be free to establish social welfare services in the private sector, both as nonprofit agencies and for-profit corporations.

The pluralism of American social welfare—in which the voluntary, governmental, and corporate sectors coexist—poses important questions for social welfare policy. To what extent can voluntary groups assume responsibility for public welfare when their fiscal resources are limited? For which groups, if any, should government divest itself of responsibility? Can human service corporations be induced to care for poor and multi-problem clients while continuing to generate profits? Equally important, how can welfare professionals shape coherent social welfare policies given the fragmentation that is inherent in such pluralism? Clearly, the answers to these questions have much to say about how social welfare programs are perceived by human service professionals, their clients, and the taxpayers who continue to subsidize social programs.

The multitude of questions posed by the transition of American social welfare is daunting in itself. Moreover, the interaction of ideological, political, social, and economic factors has exacerbated the problem to the extent that "the welfare mess" has become a fixture in contemporary folklore. Yet, past advocates of social justice—Jane Addams, Whitney Young, Jr., and Wilbur Cohen, to name a few—interpreted the inadequacy of social provision and the confusion of their times as an opportunity to further social justice. It remains for another generation of welfare professionals to demonstrate the imagination, perseverance, and courage to advance social welfare in the future. Those accepting this challenge will need to be familiar with the various meanings of social welfare policy, differing political and economic explanations for social welfare, and the various interest groups that have emerged within American social welfare.

DEFINITIONS OF
SOCIAL WELFARE POLICY

Social welfare policy is a subset of social policy, which may be defined as the formal and consistent ordering of human affairs. Beyond this, social welfare policy is influenced to a large extent by the context in which benefits are provided to people. For example, social welfare policy is often associated with governmental programs which are mandated by legislation, as in the case of Aid to Families with Dependent Children (AFDC). In the instance of AFDC, social welfare policy consists of the rules by which the state apportions benefits to an economically disadvantaged population by taxing citizens who are better off. Benefits provided through governmental social welfare

policy are generally of two types: cash benefits and in-kind benefits. Cash benefits are further divided into social insurance and means-tested grants.

In-kind benefits (meaning benefits that are provided instead of cash) include a variety of social services (family, mental health, and child welfare), and vouchers (such as Food Stamps and Medicaid). While this classification of social welfare policy is complicated, it reflects a common theme, the redistribution of resources from those who are well-off to those who are comparatively disadvantaged. This redistributional aspect of social welfare policy is typical of those who view social welfare as a function of the state. Richard Titmuss, for example, defined social services as "a series of collective interventions that contribute to the general welfare by assigning claims from one set of people who are said to produce or earn the national income to another set of people who may merit compassion and charity."[1] This form of governmental social welfare policy is often referred to as "public" policy because it is the result of decisions reached through a process that involves a legislature which is representative of the entire population.

But social welfare is also provided by entities that are nongovernmental, in which case social welfare policy is not a manifestation of public policy, but of "private" policy. For example, a nonprofit agency that is beset with limited resources but increased demand for services may establish a waiting list as agency policy. As other agencies in similar circumstances adopt the same strategy for rationing services, clients begin to pile up on waiting lists. Eventually, some clients are denied services because private agencies have established waiting lists. In this case, the policies of independent private agencies have a significant effect on the welfare of clients. Or consider the practice of "dumping," when private health care providers have established policies through which uninsured patients are abruptly transferred to public hospitals even though they suffer from traumatic injuries. In some instances, patients have died as a result of a policy that is essentially a private social welfare policy.

Because American social welfare has been shaped to a great extent by policies of the government and nonprofit agencies, a good deal of confusion has occurred with the emergence of for-profit firms which provide human services. Traditionally, the distinction between the "public" and "private" sectors was marked by the boundary between government and nonprofit agencies. However, for-profit firms are also "private" in that they are nongovernmental entities; but they differ from the traditional private voluntary agencies which are not-for-profit. Consequently, it is important to distinguish within private social welfare those policies of for-profit as opposed to nonprofit organizations. A logical way to redraw the social welfare map is to adopt the following usage: governmental social welfare policy refers to decisions established by the state; voluntary social welfare policy refers to those created by nonprofit agencies; corporate social welfare policy refers to decisions by for-profit firms. Whether the product of governmental, voluntary, or corporate institutions, *social welfare policy regulates the provision of benefits to people who require assistance in meeting basic needs in living, such as employment, income, food, housing, health care, and relationships.*[2]

A final point of clarification is necessary to describe the context of social welfare policy. With the renaming of the federal Department of Health, Education and Welfare to the Department of Health and Human Services, the term "human services" has become prevalent. For all practical purposes, human services refers to the welfare programs administered by the federal government so that the terms are interchangeable. Because of the stigma associated with "welfare," some analysts prefer the term "human services" to describe social welfare. For those concerned about guilt by association, "human services" provides some distance from the negative connotations of "welfare"—human services, in other words, represents sanitized social welfare.

SOCIAL PROBLEMS AND SOCIAL WELFARE POLICY

Social problems often provide the rationale for social welfare policy. The massive social and economic dislocation caused by the Great Depression provided the justification for the first generation of federal welfare legislation. As part of the New Deal, the Social Security Act was passed in 1935, addressing the problems of a family's loss of income due to retirement, unemployment, disability, and widowhood. The second generation of federal welfare legislation was passed during the period of the Civil Rights Movement. The War on Poverty, usually marked by the enactment of the Economic Opportunity Act of 1964, addressed problems of poverty and discrimination through a wide range of programs. The 1970s and 1980s saw no new welfare initiatives on the scale of the New Deal or the War on Poverty, but social problems continued to serve as the justification for social welfare programs. Problems of child abuse, substance abuse, AIDS, and welfare dependency led to social welfare policies designed to remedy these problems. The relationship between social problems and social welfare policy is not simple, however. Not all social problems generate social welfare policies.

Millions of undocumented workers and their families are in need of social welfare services, yet the United States has no coherent policy for addressing their needs. While many European countries have "guest worker" policies, the closest the United States has come to recognizing the needs of foreign workers is the Immigration Reform and Control Act of 1986 which established strict requirements for obtaining legal residence status—a provision that covered only a minority of alien workers and which had expired by 1988. In other instances, social welfare policies exist, but are funded at such inadequate levels that they are ineffectual. The Child Abuse Prevention and Treatment Act of 1974, for example, introduced standards that should have contended with the problem of child abuse, yet underbudgeting left Child Protective Service (CPS) workers in a "Catch 22." The act required that CPS workers investigate complaints of child abuse shortly after receiving them, yet agencies had inadequate staff resources to deal with the number of complaints, which had skyrocketed. Caught in a resources crunch, CPS workers were unable to properly investigate allegations of abuse, and thus many children were seriously injured or died as a result of abusive adults. Eventually, the Supreme Court agreed to determine whether governments were liable for the poor performance of CPS workers in cases where abused children received injuries after being placed under the care of child welfare personnel. As this example might suggest, social welfare policies sometimes aggravate social problems. For decades, states authorized mental hospitals to warehouse the mentally disturbed, a practice that further handicapped mental patients. To replace state mental hospitals, the federal Community Mental Health Centers (CMHC) Act of 1963 authorized the creation of community-based facilities. This reform proved short lived and was subverted by lack of support for CMHCs. Now, with a substantial number of the homeless having been hospitalized for mental illness in the past, the CMHC Act is associated with a worsening of care for the seriously mentally ill. What had once been mental health reform seems to have exacerbated a social problem.

As the relationship between social problems and social welfare policy suggests, social welfare is not merely an expression of social altruism—it contributes to the maintenance, indeed the survival, of society. In this respect, social welfare policy can be instrumental in helping hold together a society that tends to fracture along social, political, and economic stress lines. Social welfare policy can thus be useful in enforcing social control, especially as a proxy for other coercive forms of societal control, such as law enforcement and the courts.[3] By providing a minimum of basic needs, the disadvantaged are less inclined to revolt against the unequal distribution of resources. A population that has nothing to lose is highly volatile. Social welfare policies also subsidize the marketplace. Public social welfare benefits often supplement wages that are so low that people could not survive without them. Such wage supplements benefit employers who would have otherwise to raise wages. Social welfare also subsidizes important industries, such as agriculture, housing, and health care. Indeed, if social welfare benefits were eliminated, a substantial segment of American business would collapse. In addition, social welfare redistributes income from one segment of the population to another, allowing the disadvantaged essential income and services. Without such social benefits, fundamental questions would arise about the moral, spiritual, and ethical quality of American society. Moreover, social welfare policies relieve social and economic dislocations caused by the uneven nature of economic development. Finally, social welfare policies are a means for rectifying past injustices. For example, affirmative action is intended to remedy historic racist and sexist practices that have denied blacks and women access to economic opportunities and positions of power.

VALUES WITHIN SOCIAL WELFARE POLICY

If social welfare policy were a simple matter of social engineering, arriving at objectives and methods of achieving them which are optimal for societal functioning would be relatively easy. But social welfare policies are not created in a vacuum; they are shaped by a set of social and personal values that reflect the preferences of those in decision-making capacities. According to veteran policy analyst, David Gil, "choices in social welfare policy are heavily influenced by the dominant beliefs, values, ideologies, customs, and traditions of the cultural and political elites recruited mainly from among the more powerful and privileged strata."[4] Yet, even if social welfare policies were established through a more representative process, the odds are high that the result would not be straightforward. Charles Prigmore and Charles Atherton list no fewer than fifteen values that influence social welfare policy: achievement and success, activity and work, public morality, humanitarian concerns, efficiency and practicality, material comfort, equality, freedom, external conformity, science and secular rationality, nationalism and patriotism, democracy and self-determination, individualism, racism and group superiority, and belief in progress.[5]

How these values are played out in the world of social welfare is the domain of the policy analyst. It goes without saying that, despite the best of intentions, social welfare policy is not always based on a rational series of assumptions and research. The Pareto Optimality maintains that for a social policy to be worthwhile, it should leave no one worse off and at least one person better off, at least as each person judges his or her wants. In the real world of policy that is rarely the case. More often, the policy game is played as a zero-sum game, where some people are advantaged at the expense of others. When value-laden stereotypes about welfare "cheats," insensitive bureaucrats, and "greedy" professionals are added to the script, social welfare policy begins to resemble a morality play. In fact, some analysts believe that the value dimension is the most important element in determining social welfare policy. Alfred Kahn, for example, believes that major social policy changes are made in relation to values, not through the careful consideration of effectiveness of alternative policies.[6]

Of course, there are serious consequences when social welfare policy is determined to a high degree by values. Since 1980, social welfare policy has been shaped largely by values that emphasize individualism, self-sufficiency, and work. Since the disadvantaged were expected to be more independent, supports from government social programs were cut significantly. While these reductions in social programs saved substantial sums in the short run, they were predicated on assumptions that were not well founded. Most of the beneficiaries of social programs that fell to the budget ax were children. Eventually, cuts in social programs are likely to lead to greater expenditures as the generation of children who went without essential services begins to require programs to remedy problems associated with poor maternal and infant health care, poverty, illiteracy, and family disorganization, among others.

IDEOLOGY AND THE WELFARE STATE

Ideology is the framework of commonly held beliefs through which we view the world. In other words, ideology is a set of assumptions about how the world works: what has value, what is worth living and dying for, what is good and true, and what is right. For the most part, these assumptions are rarely examined and are assumed to be true, a priori. When widely held ideological beliefs are questioned, society often reacts with strong sanctions. The core of ideological tenets around which society is organized exists as a collective social consciousness that defines the world for its members. All societies reproduce themselves, in part, through reproducing ideology. In this way each generation believes the basic ideological suppositions of the preceding generation.

In the United States, the primary ideologies are liberalism and conservatism. One need only watch a political campaign to appreciate the historical significance of these ideological traditions—Democrats invoke the names of liberal presidents, such as Franklin Delano Roosevelt or John F. Kennedy, when they wish to trace the source of their ideas; Republicans can go back further, citing Abraham Lincoln. That ideology is associated with political parties—Democrats tending to be liberal, Republicans conservative—does not mean that there is no overlap. Nor does it mean that ideologies are fixed. During the last decade important variations of the basic American ideological conventions have appeared in the forms of *neo*liberalism and *neo*conservatism. Essentially, neoliberals are liberals who have had second thoughts about some of the basic assumptions of liberalism, such as expensive social programs, government regulation of the economy, and reallocating defense expenditures for domestic purposes. For neoliberals the New Deal orientation to social welfare is too expensive and too unpopular to address current problems. This neoliberal idea that traditional liberalism is outmoded has led some neoliberals to label old-school liberals as *paleo*liberals. Neoconservatives, on the other hand, are conservatives who have come to appreciate the fact that some issues associated with liberalism, such as social welfare, are too important to ignore, and they have given serious thought to dealing with social problems.

Ideology influences social welfare in two important ways. First, the basic American ideologies, liberalism and conservatism, hold vastly different views of social welfare. Liberals have tended to view government as the only institution capable of bringing a measure of social justice to the millions of Americans who cannot participate in the social mainstream because of societal obstacles—racism, poverty, and sexism, among others. As a result, liberals have favored government social welfare programs. Conservatives, by contrast, prefer that individuals and families meet their welfare needs by participating in the marketplace, primarily through work. According to conservatives, government has only a minimal and temporary role—the "safety net"—in assuring the social welfare of citizens. Accordingly, conservatives have preferred private sector approaches to

social welfare, while advocating smaller government social welfare programs. These ideological trends influence social welfare directly when adherents to one ideological orientation hold a majority in decision-making bodies, such as the state or national legislature. From the mid-1930s to the mid-1970s, government social programs expanded because to a great extent liberal Democrats controlled Congress. In 1980, further growth of government social programs was abruptly halted when conservative Republicans gained the White House and the Senate.

Second, ideology shapes social welfare during periods of social and economic instability. The steady continuity of American history has been shattered intermittently when groups that have been victims of oppression have reasserted their rights in the face of mainstream norms. Too easily forgotten, perhaps, are the egregious conditions that provided justification for the militancy of workers during the Labor Movement, of women during the Suffrage Movement, and of blacks during the Civil Rights Movement. Periods of social unrest strain the capacity of conventional ideologies to explain social problems and pose solutions. Sometimes social unrest is met with force, as during the Great Upheaval of 1877. In other instances, as in the Great Depression, social unrest is met with the expansion of social welfare programs. Frances Fox Piven and Richard Cloward have attributed the cyclical nature of social welfare programs to periods of social unrest.

> Relief arrangements are ancillary to economic arrangements. Their chief function is to regulate labor, and they do that in two general ways. First, when mass unemployment leads to outbreaks of turmoil, relief programs are ordinarily initiated or expanded to absorb or control enough of the unemployed to restore order; then, as turbulence subsides, the relief system contracts, expelling those who are needed to populate the labor markets.[7]

Louis Althusser has described two functions of ideology as the Ideological State

Apparatus (ISA), a set of ideological means which include education, the print media, the family, television, and tradition; and the Repressive State Apparatus (RSA), including courts, police, jails, and so on.[8] In most stable societies the ISA is sufficient to ensure order, stability, and the reproduction of ideological "stories." Through the family, media, religion, and so forth, most people become convinced that a given society is far better than radically different social models. When the ISA breaks down and social instability results, the RSA becomes activated. For example, one need only look to Chile, Cuba, El Salvador, and South Africa to see the power of the RSA. Virtually all societies have powerful RSA apparatuses that lurk near the surface.

The RSA is a trigger mechanism that is usually activated only when a group or individual refuses to act in accordance with generally held social norms. Should a powerful insurgency movement arise in the United States—as it did in the late 1960s and early 1970s—it is possible that the omnipresent repressive state apparatuses would be activated. In fact, many groups including the American Indian Movement (AIM) and the once popular Black Panthers found that the RSA was—and in the case of AIM, still is—directed against them. Continual—and often illegal—covert operations of the Federal Bureau of Investigation, against groups perceived to be a threat to American security, attest to the presence of a powerful RSA in the United States.

In American political economy, the ISA and RSA can be understood in the context of the tension between liberal and conservative paradigms. While Americans are assured of their political rights through a Constitution that delineates a representative democracy, there is no corresponding document to guarantee economic rights. For adherents to a capitalistic market economy, such a document would be undesirable, because it would allow government to interfere in the operations of a free market. Largely as a result of this absence of economic rights, large numbers of Americans have found that the economy is not responsive to their needs and that the political system is the only vehicle through which to seek redress. But because access to the political system often presupposes wealth and status, it is a less than optimal method for achieving social justice for many citizens. The political-economy of the United States, then, increases the likelihood that disruptions in the social order will occur. Social welfare programs are one method for compensating for deficiencies in the American "political-economy" by appeasing dissident groups. This role of social welfare is well established within the ISA; both political parties recognize the importance of social programs in American culture. When advocates of the disadvantaged are unable to seek necessary concessions through manipulating the ISA, they occasionally resort to tactics that deliberately provoke the RSA. For example, the Civil Rights Movement gained much public sympathy when the national news broadcast film clips of police dogs turned loose among freedom marchers. Savvy proponents of social welfare initiatives, then, often demonstrate a willingness to use both the ISA and the RSA to advance their ends.

THE POLITICAL-ECONOMY OF AMERICAN SOCIAL WELFARE

The term "political-economy" refers to the interaction of political and economic institutions in the society. The political-economy of the United States has been labeled as "democratic-capitalist," reflecting an open, representative form of government coexisting with a market economy. As noted above, this interaction of political and economic institutions is frequently irregular, and social welfare functions to make the society more stable. The main function of social welfare is to modify the play of market forces and ameliorate the social and economic inequities the market generates.[9] In order to accomplish that end, two sets of activities are necessary: state provision of social services (benefits of cash and in-kind services) and state regulation of private activities to alter (but not necessarily improve) the lives of citizens. In short, social welfare augments ideology by helping to remedy the problems associated with economic dislocation, thereby allowing a society to remain in a state of more or less controlled balance.

An understanding of political-economy is important because of the breadth of social welfare, and because of the intense disagreement about the most desirable way to enhance the general welfare. Federal expenditures for health and welfare claim 45 percent of the federal budget, more than any other category, including defense.[10] In 1985, social welfare expenditures by the federal government totaled $727.9 billion, or 18.4 percent of the gross national product.[11] Yet, despite such enormous expenditures, there is no common understanding about how American political-economy *does* work, or how it *should* work. Instead, several competing schools of thought have emerged which purport to explain not only how the political-economy functions, but also the best way that it should be deployed to solve new problems. The stakes are clearly high, since major institutions—government, corporations, organized labor, social programs—stand to lose or gain greatly when one school of thought has gained public confidence. Invariably, any given explanation of political-economy benefits some institutions over others. Since social welfare is advantaged or disadvantaged according to which school of political-economy holds sway for a given moment, social welfare policy analysts pay close attention to the most important schools of thought.

Keynesian Economics

Sometimes called demand or consumer side economics, Keynesian economics emerged from a model developed in 1936 by John Maynard Keynes in *The General Theory of Employment, Interest and Money*. Keynes took the classical model of economic analysis (self-regulating markets, perfect competition, the laws of supply and demand, etc.) and added the insight that macroeconomic stabilization by government is necessary to keep the economic clock operating smoothly.[12] Keynes rejected the classical idea that, since a perfectly competitive economy tended toward a balance of full employment automatically, the government should not interfere with the process ("laissez faire"). Keynes observed that, instead of a self-correcting economy that pulled itself from recessions easily, the modern economy was quite recession prone and the attainment of full employment was problematic. Periodic volatile economic situations during which unemployment peaked were primarily caused by an instability in investment expenditures. The government could stabilize—i.e., correct recessionary or inflationary trends—by increasing or decreasing total spending on output. This could be accomplished by the government increasing or decreasing taxes, thereby increasing or decreasing consumption as well as the transfer of public goods or services. For Keynes, the "good" government was an activist government in economic matters, especially when the economy got out of a full employment mode.

Keynesian economics posits that increased consumption through government subsidies (welfare payments, public jobs, unemployment compensation, social security, and so forth) will result in increased production. If people have more income, especially the poor, they will purchase more goods and thus stimulate the economy. Keynesians believe that government and business have a joint responsibility for creating a healthy economy, and they must engage in a kind of partnership. In addition, Keynesians believe that social welfare expenditures augment the national income by increasing human potential, providing jobs, and creating a more humane environment. Keynesians hypothesize that social welfare expenditures are investments in human capital which ultimately increase national wealth and therefore boost everyone's net income.

Because Keynesian economics forms the basis and rationale for the American and western European welfare states, a more specific analysis is helpful. The world was in the midst of a profound depression when Keynes wrote *The General Theory of Employment, Interest and Money*. Radicals on both the left and right of the political spectrum were gaining power, and their arguments greater currency. Moreover, capitalism was being attacked at its roots —its inability to provide for the welfare of its citizens. Keynes maintained that government must become a major actor through its ability to regulate the money flow and, more importantly, through the economic power inherent in its ability to spend. In that sense, Keynesian economics is concerned with reducing the often harsh effects of capitalist cycles of prosperity and recession. For example, Keynesians maintain that in a recession the government must spend money on goods, public transfers, public employment, and cash welfare benefits. This increased spending allows consumers to continue spending and therefore consume the surplus of economic goods. In addition, this spending also permits the economy to return to an equilibrium which is at or near full employment. When the economic crisis is over, government must diminish its spending and repay the deficit accrued during the crisis. Affluent economic times allow government to generate budget surpluses that can pay off prior deficits through increased taxation or wider tax bases. As such, government has the fiscal responsibility for fine-tuning the economy as well as the obligation to provide for the needs of different constituencies. According to Keynesians, government must become the economic conscience of a nation, assuming responsibility for (1) stable growth, (2) stable price levels, and (3) full employment. Unfortunately, many economists argue that these goals are not economically consistent, as illustrated by the economic

conditions of the 1970s and early 1980s, where inflation and unemployment were high and economic stagnation the dominant trend.

Supply-Side Economics

Supply-side economics is a school of political and economic thought that gained considerable currency during the 1980s. Although some supply-siders would prefer to think of it as pure economics, it contains enough political implications (both covert and overt) to qualify as a political as well as an economic theory. Popularized by ardent supporters such as Jack Kemp and later Ronald Reagan, supply-side economics provided the major rationale for cuts in federal social programs executed during the Reagan administration. Supply-side economics stresses the concept of a self-regulating economy and posits an economic system based on "perfect competition." Transactions in the economy are likened to those that occur in simple marketplaces; the rationality of supply and demand serves to provide the market with a "general equilibrium" which characterizes the entire economy.[13] This model emphasizes the efficiency of markets and focuses on the supplier (hence the term "supply-side economics").

Supply-side adherents maintain that large social welfare programs—including unemployment benefits and public service jobs—are detrimental to the society in two ways. First, government social programs erode the work ethic by supporting those who do not work. Secondly, public sector social welfare programs divert money away from the private sector because they are funded by taxes—diverted income that could otherwise be invested in capital formation. Supply-siders believe that when government alters the patterns of rewards to favor work over leisure, and investment over consumption, it fosters the expansion of real economic demand. Supporters of supply-side economics believe that economic growth helps everyone because overall prosperity creates more jobs, income, and goods which eventually filter down to the poor. Investment is the key to prosperity for supply-siders—it is the raw fuel that feeds the economic machine, and without it the economy is frozen. It is this investment in capital that creates the economic growth that results in more jobs, income, and goods. Accordingly, supply-siders favor tax breaks for the wealthy. The more disposable after-tax income that is available, the more is freed up for investment. High taxes are therefore an impediment to economic progress because they channel money away from "private" investment into "public" investment.

The difference between private capitalization and public investment (social welfare programs and other public services) results in a vastly different form of economic growth and mix of goods and services. The agenda advocated by supply-siders is decidedly conservative and includes: (1) major cuts in taxes (exemplified by the huge tax cuts enacted in 1981) or, at least, no tax increases; (2) reduction of government controls and regulations which are expensive not only for business (which must absorb costs of compliance) but also for government, which must fund regulatory agencies; and (3) major cuts in the federal budget (particularly in social programs) to decrease governmental spending. This agenda has direct implications for social welfare. Supply-siders allege that government should have little direct responsibility for people's welfare. Instead, welfare ought to be a private matter; and when help is needed, it should be provided on a neighborly basis or through churches, private social service agencies, and so forth. Private charitable giving should form the economic basis for social welfare, with more responsibility for provision of service transferred to the voluntary sector. Adherents to supply-side economics claim that welfare programs create dependency and a disincentive for recipients to engage in productive work. The disincentive to work, in large part, is due to the fact that welfare programs bring people too far above the poverty level. Stricter eligibility requirements and "workfare" pro-

grams (required work for welfare recipients) are necessary to combat the deleterious effects of public welfare on work effort. Ultimately, the supply-side school holds that the best anti-poverty measure is a thriving economy—if the economy does well, everyone benefits.

Despite its popularity during the early years of the Reagan administration, supply-siders fell out of favor when it became clear that massive tax cuts for the wealthy and corporations did not result in increased capital formation and economic activity. Rather, the wealthy spent their tax savings on luxury items, and corporations used their tax rebates to purchase other companies in a "merger mania" that took even Wall Street by surprise. Many corporations took advantage of temporary tax savings to transfer operations abroad, further reducing the supply of higher-paying industrial jobs in the United States. For these and other reasons, the budget deficit in the Reagan administration grew at an unprecedented rate (from about $50 billion a year in the Carter term to between $145 and $200 billion a year in the 1980s). This contradiction was explained away by a belief that sound economic growth would result in a larger tax base, which would then yield more federal taxes without a tax increase. In short, the Reagan rationale was based on the premise that the tax base would eventually meet and exceed the current tax shortfall. Some critics, including George Bush, have called this idea "voodoo economics." Today, the central idea of supply-side economics, that tax decreases bring forth such massive relative growth as to more than replenish lost government tax revenues, is in disrepute among many mainstream economists. Nevertheless, supply-side economics continues to provide a compelling economic and political theory for many conservative thinkers.

The major difference between supply-side and Keynesian economics is in the focus of economic policy. Keynesians emphasize the need to encourage production by increasing the demand side through stimulating consumer buying and government spending on goods. Supply-siders focus on stimulating supply-side growth at a rate as fast as that of demand. Both schools are committed to the need for an energized and vigorous economy through increased production. Keynesians and supply-siders differ in other substantial ways. The Keynesian perspective, clearly more supportive of the welfare state than the conservative one, stresses the issue of equity. While conservatives maintain that equity should be based solely on one's ability to produce and consume, Keynesians believe that equity can be realized through redistributive mechanisms (i.e., welfare state programs) and that it can be encouraged through increasing the ability of more people to consume. Moreover, the role of government is perceived differently by each school: supply-siders see little government responsibility for welfare, while the Keynesians define the social contract as containing a strong governmental commitment to social welfare. Keynesian economics and supply-side theories have been the two most important concepts affecting the American welfare state since its inception in the middle 1930s.

Socialism

Socialism differs from both Keynesian and supply-side theories. In fact, the above schools have more in common with each other than with a radical, leftist perspective. According to Jeffry Galper, one of social work's most articulate proponents of a radical perspective, socialists see social problems as a logical consequence of an unjust society.[14] Galper and other left-wing theorists maintain that the failure of capitalism has led to political movements that have pressured institutions to respond with increased social welfare services. For socialists, social welfare is an ingenious arrangement on the part of business to get the public to assume the costs incurred by the social and economic dislocations attributable to capitalism.

Social welfare, then, serves both the needs of people and the needs of capitalist expansion and production. According to socialists, social welfare expenditures "socialize" the costs of capitalist production—they make public the costs of private enterprise. In the final analysis, social welfare programs do respond to human needs, but they do so in a way that supports an unjust economic system which continues to generate problems requiring social programs.

Socialists believe that real social welfare is structural and can only be accomplished through a redistribution of resources. In a just society—where all goods, resources, and opportunities are made available to everyone—all but the most specific forms of welfare (health care, rehabilitation, counseling, and so forth) are unnecessary. In the context of a radical framework, poverty is inextricably linked to structural inequality. Therefore, people need welfare because they are exploited and denied opportunity to resources. In an unjust society, welfare functions as a substitute, albeit a puny one, for social justice.

Radicals maintain that social welfare programs function like "junk food" for the impoverished: they provide just enough subsistence to discourage revolution, but not enough to make a real difference in the lives of the poor. Moreover, according to Frances Fox Piven and Richard Cloward, social welfare programs have been used by capitalists to control insurgency.[15] When mass protests arise and people demand economic justice, the state (acting as an agent for the capitalists), attempts to buy off discontent with the palliative of social welfare reforms. Within the radical framework, then, social welfare is seen as a form of social control. In place of liberal social welfare reforms, the radical vision requires that the entire social, political, and, especially, the economic system undergo a major overhaul. In short, the radical position informs us that real welfare reform—complete redistribution of goods, income, and services—can occur only in the context of a socialist system.

Other Schools of Thought

While the Keynesian, supply-side, and socialist schools represent the major themes of political and economic thought in the United States, they do not reflect all of it. As the aforementioned schools illustrate, explanations of the best way to address questions of political-economy change over time. These newer schools of thought deserve attention because they may become prominent in the future. One school of thought that is having an impact on American social welfare is the *traditionalist* school. Following a Christian religious orientation to social policy, exemplified by evangelical groups such as the Moral Majority, traditionalists emphasize the moral relationship between politics and religion. According to traditionalists, God's laws must be translated into politics and "higher laws" must become the laws of the state. Because this group presumes the United States to be, for all practical purposes, a Christian nation, the separation of church and state is seen as unnatural. Apart from the belief in a strong military defense, this group emphasizes the Christian value of hard work and proposes little welfare, except for the most needy. Traditionalists have been highly critical of governmental social programs which they associate with a liberal social philosophy (secular humanism)—a philosophy which has eroded traditional social institutions, particularly the family and the church. Lightning-rod issues for traditionalists have been abortion, prayer in school, affirmative action, and school integration—all associated with the increasing liberalism of society. Traditionalists have been among the most severe critics of governmental social programs.

Another perspective can be found among *libertarians*. This relatively small—but increasingly influential—group believes in virtually no government regulation. Libertarians hold that the smaller the government the better, since government grows invariably at the expense of individual freedom. The libertarian view proposes that the only proper role for government is to provide a police force and a military. Moreover, the only weapons that the military should possess are defensive. Libertarians are highly critical of taxation, recognizing that government is dependent on tax revenues. Aside from advocating minimal taxation earmarked for military and police activities, libertarians oppose the income tax. Due to their emphasis on individual freedom, and therefore individual responsibility, libertarians advocate the decriminalization of narcotics. Government should intercede in social affairs only when the behavior of an individual threatens the safety of another. The libertarian critique of social welfare is based on the belief that the state should not be involved in social and economic activities save for very limited and extreme circumstances.

The *self-reliance* school is a newly emerging perspective, gaining adherents in economically distressed areas of the United States as well as third-world countries.[16] This school maintains that industrial economic models are irrelevant to the economic needs of poor communities and are often damaging to the spiritual life of their peoples.[17] Adherents of self reliance repudiate western economic philosophies that stress economic growth and a belief that the quality of life can be measured by the material acquisitions of citizens. These economists stress a balanced economy based on the needs of people, production designed for internal consumption rather than export, productive technologies that are congruent with the culture and background of the population, the use of appropriate and manageable technologies, and a small scale and decentralized form of economic organization.[18] Simply put, proponents of self reliance postulate that more is less and less is more. The objective of self reliance is the creation of a no-poverty society where economic life is organized around issues of subsistence rather than trade and economic expansion. Accepting a world of finite resources and inherent limitations to economic growth, the true question of social and economic development is not what people think they want or need, but what people must have for survival. The self-reliance school accepts the need for social welfare programs to ameliorate the social and economic dislocations caused by industrialization, but prefers low-technological and local solutions to social problems. This is in contrast with the conventional meaning of the welfare state which describes a set of programs on a national scale, administered by large bureaucracies through sophisticated management systems.

Lastly, the *public choice* school has become more prominent among conservative analysts, particularly as faith has ebbed in the supply-side school. The public choice school was not widely known beyond academic circles until its major proponent, James Buchanan, was awarded the Nobel Prize for economics in 1986. According to this school, a political-economy with a large number of interest groups tends to generate budget deficits. As a result, government must be vigilant and be very selective about making concessions to interest groups or their demands will eventually destabilize the economy. Briefly, the public choice model states that there are strong incentives for interest groups to make demands on government since the concessions flow directly to the group while the cost of these concessions is spread to all taxpayers. Initial concessions lead to demands for further concessions, which are likely to be forthcoming so long as the interest group is vociferous in its demands. Under such an incentive system, interests are also encouraged to band together to make demands since there is no reason for an interest group to oppose the demands of others. But while demands for goods and services increase, revenues tend to decrease. This is because interest groups resist paying taxes directed toward them specifically, and because "no interest groups will have much individual incentive to support general taxes." The result of such a scenario is predictable: irresistible demands for government benefits accompanied by declining revenues leads to government borrowing to finance programs, resulting in large budget deficits.[19] While the public choice school is critical of demands posed by any interest group, it has been adopted by conservatives to explain the gradual expansion of government social programs. As a result, adherents to public choice theory view social welfare as a series of concessions to disadvantaged groups that could be endless, eventually bankrupting government. On the other hand, it is just as logical to apply public choice analysis to interest groups related to the defense industry which make similar demands on government while not paying corresponding taxes. Despite such contradictions in its application, the public choice school is likely to be more influential in shaping future social welfare policy by calling for further reductions in public expenditures for social programs.

THE DIVERSITY
OF AMERICAN SOCIAL WELFARE

Consistent with the pluralism of thought evident in the various schools of political-economy, social welfare in the United States is characterized by a high degree of diversity. American social welfare is not a monolithic, highly centralized, and well-coordinated system of programs. Rather, a great variety of organizations provide a wide range of benefits and services to different client populations. The vast array of social welfare organizations contributes to what is commonly called "the welfare mess." As the term suggests, different programs, serving different groups through still different procedures, become part of an impenetrable tangle of institutional red tape that often functions poorly for administrators, human service professionals, and their clients.

The complexity of social welfare can be attributed to several cultural influences, some of which are peculiar to the American experience. Our Constitution outlines a federal system of government through which the states vest certain functions in a national government. Although the states have assumed primary responsibility for social welfare through much of the history of the United States, this changed with the New Deal of Franklin Delano Roosevelt, which ushered in a raft of federal programs. Over the subsequent decades federal social welfare initiatives took on a dominant role in the nation's social welfare effort. Still, states continued to manage important social welfare programs, such as mental health and social services. Over time, then, the relationship between the federal government and the states has changed. From the New Deal of the 1930s through the Great Society of the 1960s, federal welfare programs expanded, forming the American version of the "welfare state." During the 1980s, however, the Reagan administration sought to return more responsibility for welfare to the states, a process called "devolution."[20]

A second confounding element can be attributed to the relatively open character of American society. Often called the "melting pot," the national culture is a protean brew of groups immigrating to the United States, then competing with each other to become an established part of our national life.[21] An enormous immigration of Europeans during the last century has given way to waves of Hispanics and Asians entering the United States a century later.[22] Historically, social welfare programs have been an important part of the acculturation process of these groups. At the same time, many ethnic groups bring with them their own fraternal and community associations that not only provide welfare benefits to members of the community, but also serve to maintain its norms. Other groups that have exerted important influences on American social welfare are blacks, the aged, women, and American Indians. The very pluralism of American society —a diverse collection of peoples, each with somewhat different needs—contributes to the complexity in social welfare.

The American economic system is another reason why social welfare is complex. With some important exceptions, the economy of the United States is predominantly capitalist— most goods and services are owned, produced, and distributed through the marketplace. In a capitalist economy, people are expected to meet their basic needs through the marketplace, and they ordinarily do this through participation in the labor market. When groups are unable to participate fully in the labor market because they are unable to work—the aged and handicapped—or because they do not earn enough as a result of discrimination—women and blacks—programs are deployed to support these groups. These programs take on a variety of forms. Many are governmental programs which are "mandated" by legislation. Private sector programs often complement those of the public sector. Within the private sector, two organizational forms are common—nonprofit organizations and for-profit corporations. Sometimes public and both forms of private sector organizations coexist, approximate to one another.[23] In many communities, family planning services are provided by the public health department (a governmental agency), Planned Parenthood (a private, nonprofit agency), or Maxicare (a private, for-profit health maintenance company).

Finally, various religious organizations have influenced social welfare. This is most clearly articulated by a range of sectarian agencies that appear in most American cities: Jewish Family Services, Lutheran Social Services, Catholic Charities, and the Salvation Army, among others. Because of the American tradition of the separation of church and state, these nongovernmental agencies are vehicles for providing services to groups that would not otherwise get them because government does not support religious activities or because corporations do not find them profitable. However, this is not to say that there is no relationship between government and sectarian agencies. During the 1970s, the federal government experimented with contracting out some services to the private sector, and sectarian agencies frequently competed for these contracts. Today, many sectarian agencies receive federal funds for particular services they provide to the public. A more recent illustration of the influence of religion on social welfare has been the religious right which has sought to curtail the reproductive rights of adults through opposing federal funding of family planning programs and abortion services.

The pluralism of American culture is of recent interest to social welfare policy analysts as the influence of the federal government in social policy has diminished. With reductions in many federal social programs and calls for the private sector to assume more responsibility for welfare, the prospect of molding the diverse entities involved in American social welfare into one unified whole under the auspices of a central authority—the federal government— seems remote. This vision is often implicit in proposals of advocates for nationalized programs that assure basic goods and services— food, housing, education, health, income—to all as a right of citizenship. While programs of this nature have been integral to the welfare states of northern Europe for decades, there is a serious question about how plausible they are for a nation, such as the United States, with so much complexity built into social welfare.[24]

Questions about the correct role of the federal government in social welfare reached controversial proportions by the late 1980s. Proponents of a strong federal role conceded that the American welfare state was, by European standards, incomplete. For these analysts, the "reluctant welfare state"[25] or the "semi-welfare state"[26] required further elaboration through social programs in primary areas of need—income, health, and employment. The principle that social welfare should be a "national effort on behalf of those in need," noted Harvard's Robert Reich, has been central to American social welfare for a half-century. "The theme permeated Roosevelt's New Deal, Truman's Fair Deal, Johnson's Great Society:

America is a single, national community, bound by a common ideal of equal opportunity, and generosity toward the less fortunate. E Pluribus Unum."[27] To proponents of more state intervention in social welfare, advocates of nongovernmental initiatives represented the abandonment of the most effective method for assuring protection of vulnerable populations. "Conservatives," some observed, "continually assert than many social services in the public sector can be transferred to the voluntary sector."[28]

Advocates of more nongovernmental activity in social welfare trace their argument to the colonial era of America. Daniel Boorstin, former Librarian of Congress, has written passionately about the unique role played by voluntary organizations in the United States. Boorstin maintains that voluntary organizations "have many unique characteristics and a spirit all their own." Voluntary organizations are no less than

> monuments to what in the Old World was familiar neither as private charity nor as governmental munificence. They are monuments to community. They originate in the community, depend on the community, are developed by the community, serve the community, and rise or fall with the community.[29]

But can problems of postmodern America be addressed adequately without massive federal social programs? Daniel Patrick Moynihan, the most distinguished authority on welfare in Congress, claims there is no choice but to begin thinking about new ways to solve social problems. "*The issues of social policy the United States faces today have no European counterpart nor any European model of a viable solution*," Moynihan maintained. "*They are American problems, and we Americans are going to have to think them through by ourselves*."[30] To the extent that Moynihan is correct, future welfare initiatives are increasingly likely to reflect the diversity of American social welfare.

INTEREST GROUPS WITHIN SOCIAL WELFARE

Differences on how best to promote the general welfare also exist within the social welfare community. Considering the scope of social welfare in a postindustrial society, the divisive influences attributable to our national culture, and the ideologies that frequently guide social policy, it is not surprising that human service professionals should have varying ideas about the best way to address human need. Four such groups can be identified within American social welfare: traditional providers, welfare bureaucrats, clinical entrepreneurs, and human service executives.[31]

Traditional Providers

Traditional providers are both professionals and laypersons who seek to maintain and enhance traditional relations, values, and structures in their communities. Traditional providers hold an organismic conception of social welfare, seeing it tightly interwoven with other community institutions. According to traditional providers, voluntary nonprofit agencies offer the advantages of neighborliness, a reaffirmation of community values, a concern for community as opposed to personal gain, and freedom to alter programming so as to conform to changes in local priorities. Their base of influence consists of the private, nonprofit agencies, often referred to as the voluntary sector.

Much of the heritage of social welfare can be traced to this interest (e.g., Mary Richmond of the Charity Organization Society movement, and Jane Addams of the Settlement House movement). Charity Organization Societies and settlement houses were transformed by two influences: the need for scientifically based treatment techniques and the socialization of charity. Together, these factors functioned as an anchor for the social casework agencies in American industrial society. The agency provided the grist for scientific casework which was instrumental in the emergence of the social work profession. The new schools of social work, in turn, relied on casework agencies for internship training, a substantial portion of professional education. Once graduated, many professionals elected to work in the voluntary sector, assuring agencies of a steady supply of personnel.

Voluntary agencies routinized philanthropic contributions by socializing charity. Beginning with Denver's Associated Charities in 1887, the concept of a community appeal spread so rapidly that by the 1920s over 200 cities had community chests. The needs of workers for effective treatment techniques and the economic imperatives for organizational survival functioned together to standardize the social agency. Perhaps the best description of the casework agency is found in the Milford Conference of 1923. The Milford Conference Report, *Social Casework: Generic and Specific*, comprehensively outlined the organization through which professional caseworkers delivered services.[32] By the 1940s, the social casework agency had become a predominant form of service delivery. Today, much social service provision exists in the form of United Way subsidized sectarian and nonsectarian agencies, whose member groups collected $2.4 billion in 1986.[33]

Welfare Bureaucrats

Welfare bureaucrats are public functionaries who maintain the welfare state in much the same form in which it was conceived during the New Deal. "Their ideology stresses a rational, efficient, cost-conscious, coordinated ... delivery system."[34] They view government intervention vis-à-vis social problems as legitimate and necessary, considering the apparent lack of concern by the private sector and local government. Moreover, they contend that government intervention is more effective because authority is centralized, guidelines are standardized, and benefits are allocated according to principles of equity and equality.

The influence of welfare bureaucrats grew as a result of the Social Security Act of 1935. To a limited extent, the larger community chests "exerted a pressure toward rationalization of the professional welfare machinery,"[35] but this did not diminish the effect of the federal welfare bureaucracy, which soon eclipsed the authority of traditional providers. Actually, a unilinear evolution between these interests could have occurred had Harry Hopkins, head of the Federal Emergency Relief Administration, not prohibited states from turning federal welfare funds over to private agencies.[36] Denied the resources to significantly address the massive social problems caused by the Great Depression, private agencies lapsed into a secondary role while federal and state agencies ascended in importance. An array of welfare legislation followed, including the Social Security Act of 1935, the Housing Act of 1937, the G.I. Bill of 1944, the Community Mental Health Centers Act of 1963, the Civil Rights Act of 1964, the Food Stamp Act of 1964, the Economic Opportunity Act of 1964, the Elementary and Secondary Education Act of 1965, the Medicare and Medicaid Acts of 1965, Supplemental Security Income in 1974, Title XX of the Social Security Act of 1975, and the Full Employment Act of 1978.

The flourishing of bureaucratic rationality, concomitant with this legislative activity, represented the institutionalization of liberal thought which sought to control the caprice of the market, assure a measure of equality among widely divergent economic classes, and establish the administrative apparatus which would assure continuity of these principles. Confronted with a rapidly industrializing society lacking basic programs for ameliorating social and economic catastrophes, progressives perceived the state as a vehicle for social reform. Their solu-

tions focused on "coordinating fragmented services, instituting planning, and extending public funding."[37] Implicit in the methods advocated by welfare bureaucrats is an expectation, if not an assumption, that social welfare administration should be administratively centralized, that eligibility of benefits should be universalized, and that social welfare should be firmly anchored in the institutional fabric of society.

The influence of welfare bureaucrats had been curtailed by the mid-1980s. The Reagan administration all but capped the growth of welfare programs, and Democrats who smarted from election losses in 1980, 1984 and 1988, began to voice preference for private sector solutions to social problems. Still, the volume of resources and the number of people dependent on public welfare assure welfare bureaucrats of a dominant and continuing role in the near future.

Clinical Entrepreneurs

Clinical entrepreneurs are professional service providers, chiefly social workers, psychologists, and physicians, who work for themselves instead of being salaried employees. Important to clinical entrepreneurs is the establishment of a professional monopoly, the evolution of which represents a concern on the part of practitioners that their occupational activity not be subject to political interference from the state or the ignorance of the lay public. In the United States, the professions found that a market economy was conducive to occupational success. In the most fundamental sense, private practice reconciles the desire for autonomy by professionals with the imperatives of a market economy. The transition from entrepreneur to professional monopolist is a matter of obtaining legislation restricting practice to those duly licensed by the state. "Professionalism provides a way of preserving monopolistic control over services without the risks of competition."[38] As an extension of the entrepreneurial model of service delivery, professional monopoly offers privacy in practice, freedom to valuate one's worth through setting fees, and the security assured by membership in the professional monopoly.

The social worker as clinical entrepreneur is a relatively recent phenomenon and the National Association of Social Workers (NASW) did not officially sanction this form of service delivery until 1964. Prior to that, privately practicing social workers identified themselves as psychotherapists and lay analysts. Typically, they relied on referrals from physicians and psychiatrists and, after World War II, they began to establish "flourishing and lucrative" practices.[39] By the 1970s, private practice in social work was developing as an important form of service delivery. In 1975, NASW estimated that from 10,000 to 20,000 social workers were engaged in private practice. By 1983, Dr. Robert Barker, author of *Social Work in Private Practice* and a column on private practice in *NASW News*, speculated that about 30,000 social workers, or 32 percent of all social workers, engaged in private practice on a full- or part-time basis.[40] By 1985, a large portion of psychotherapy was being done by social workers, and the *New York Times* noted that "growing numbers of social workers are treating more affluent, private clients, thus moving into the traditional preserve of the elite psychiatrists and clinical psychologists...."[41]

Clinical entrepreneurs are an emerging interest in social welfare. Continued growth of this group is likely for several reasons. Through local and state chapters NASW has been effective in expanding the scope of its professional monopoly. In 1983, 31 states had passed legislation regulating the practice of social work; by 1986 the number had increased to 45. At the same time, professional groups have lobbied for vendorship privileges which allow them more regular income through insurance held by clients. Finally, a large number of students entering graduate schools of social work do so with the expressed intent of setting up a private practice.[42] Thus, clinical entrepreneurs are

likely to become a more influential interest in the future.

Human Service Executives

Human service executives share an important characteristic with clinical entrepreneurs: both represent ways of organizing service delivery in the context of the market. However, in some important ways they differ. Unlike clinical entrepreneurs, human service executives are salaried employees of proprietary firms and, as such, they have less autonomy. The administrators or chief executive officers of large corporations, human service executives advance market strategies for promoting social welfare. This differs from the ideology of welfare bureaucrats which emphasizes the planning and regulatory functions of the state, while human service executives favor the rationality of the marketplace in allocating resources and evaluating programs. In the present circumstance, human service executives advocate market reform of the welfare state—the domain of welfare bureaucrats—and thus are in a position to challenge this interest.

For-profit firms became prominent in American social welfare during the 1960s, when Medicaid and Medicare funds were paid to proprietary nursing homes and hospitals.[43] Since then, human service executives have been rapidly creating independent, for-profit human service corporations that provide an extensive range of nationwide services. Human service corporations have established prominent—if not dominant—positions in several human service markets, including nursing home care, hospital management, health maintenance, child care, home care, and corrections. In 1981, 34 human service corporations reported annual revenues above $10 million; by 1985, the number of firms had increased to 66. Several corporations reported revenues above the total contributions to the United Way of America.[44]

As the proprietary sector expands to dominate different human service markets, oligopolies emerge and a fundamental change occurs. No longer passively dependent on government appropriations, proprietary firms are in a strong position to shape the very markets they serve, influencing not only consumer demand, but also government policy. It is this capacity to determine or control a market that qualitatively distinguishes corporate welfare from the earlier form of business involvement in social welfare, i.e., philanthropic contributions to nonprofit agencies of the voluntary sector. For these reasons, human service executives are well positioned to influence welfare bureaucrats.

The history of American social welfare shows that interest groups within social welfare vary in their methods for addressing social problems. Differences of ideology on the part of groups within social welfare, of course, can complement different schools of political-economy. The ideologies within social welfare interact with the ideologies external to social welfare so that supply-side and public choice theories complement the ideologies of traditional providers, clinical entrepreneurs, and human service executives. On the other hand, the ideologies of Keynesian economics and socialism are more consistent with welfare bureaucrats. The dynamic relationship between groups within social welfare and the prevailing political-economic philosophy helps explain how different preferred solutions to social problems evolve over time. Thus, thinking about social welfare changes as one particular group, promoting an ideology that has gained currency, ascends while others lapse in significance.

DIVERSITY AND RECENT CHANGES IN SOCIAL WELFARE

The complexity of American social welfare helps account for changes in welfare policies and programs. Since 1980, for example, a convergence of social, political, and economic forces led to a reappraisal of welfare in the United States. Both liberal and conservative

scholars had begun to question the dominance of government programs in welfare provision. At the same time, a firestorm of fundamentalism swept across the nation, attracting the allegiance of groups associated with the evangelical church. The "traditionalist movement" flexed its muscle through the elections of Ronald Reagan and George Bush, the installation of a Republican Senate during the early 1980s, and an effective grass-roots mobilization that challenged government policies on issues that ranged from the family to affirmative action.

By the mid-1980s the influence of conservatism had begun to influence leaders of the Democratic party, a traditional supporter of government welfare programs. This became more pronounced with the sound defeat of the Walter Mondale–Geraldine Ferraro presidential ticket, widely interpreted as a referendum on liberal designs in social policy. The 1984 and 1988 presidential elections provided momentum to a new generation of Democratic leaders who identified themselves as "neoliberals." In order to reestablish credibility in an increasingly conservative political climate, neoliberals distanced themselves from the large-scale government welfare programs with which Democrats had been associated since the New Deal. In their place, neoliberals called for a reliance on personal responsibility, work, and thrift. Accordingly, proposals for welfare reform advanced by neoliberal Democrats emphasized participation in the labor market (workfare), meeting family obligations (child support enforcement), and fiscal frugality (modest budget appropriations).

The consequences of the conservative tilt in public sentiment are significant for social welfare policy.[45] The classic trinity of liberal welfare reform—full employment, a guaranteed income, and national health care—have virtually disappeared from public debate. The interest groups within social welfare have keenly felt the conservative shift. Welfare bureaucrats have braced themselves against repeated blows to programs for which they are responsible. As more of the responsibility for welfare is shifted to private institutions, the voluntary sector has been called upon to expand its programs, such as by establishing emergency shelters and soup kitchens. At the same time, the voluntary sector has struggled to maintain conventional programs while government support for its welfare activities has diminished. Meanwhile, programs of the human service executives have prospered, as have clinical entrepreneurs. The consequences of the conservative movement in social policy have also been felt by disadvantaged groups. Government programs that benefited blacks, women, and the poor have been severely cut, leaving these groups more vulnerable. Approaching the end of the century, a formidable challenge is posed for the community of welfare professionals: How can basic goods and services be assured to vulnerable populations within a context of complexity and uncertainty?

NOTES

1. Richard Titmuss, *Essays on the Welfare State* (Boston: Beacon Press, 1963), p. 16.
2. Education would logically be included here, except that in the American experience it has been treated separately.
3. Frances Fox Piven and Richard Cloward, *Regulating the Poor* (New York: Vintage, 1971).
4. David Gil, *Unraveling Social Policy* (Boston: Schenkman, 1981), p. 32.
5. Charles Prigmore and Charles Atherton, *Social Welfare Policy* (Lexington, Mass.: D. C. Heath, 1979), pp. 25–31.
6. Alfred Kahn, *Social Policy and Social Services* (New York: Random House, 1979).
7. Piven and Cloward, *Regulating the Poor*, pp. 3–4.
8. Louis Althusser, *Lenin and Other Essays* (London: N. B. Books, 1974).
9. Claus Offe, *Contradictions of the Welfare State* (Cambridge, Mass.: The MIT Press, 1984).
10. Diana DiNitto and Thomas Dye, *Social Welfare: Politics and Public Policy* (Englewood Cliffs, N.J.: Prentice-Hall, 1987), p. 27.
11. *Social Security Bulletin: Annual Statistical Sup-*

plement, *1987* (Washington, D.C.: U.S. Government Printing Office, 1987), p. 67.
12. John Maynard Keynes, *The General Theory of Employment, Interest and Money* (London: Macmillan, 1936).
13. Robert Kuttner, "The Poverty of Economics," *The Atlantic Monthly* (February 1985), p. 74.
14. Jeffry Galper, "Introduction of Radical Theory and Practice in Social Work Education: Social Policy." Mimeographed paper, Michigan State University School of Social Work, circa 1978.
15. Piven and Cloward, *Regulating the Poor*.
16. Bruce Stokes, *Helping Ourselves: Local Solutions to Global Problems* (New York: W. W. Norton, 1981).
17. Sugata Dasgupta, "Towards a No-Poverty Society," *Social Development Issues* 12 (Winter 1983).
18. Some of these economic principles were addressed by E. F. Schumacher, *Small Is Beautiful* (New York: Harper and Row, 1973).
19. *Privatization: Toward More Effective Government* (Washington, D.C.: U.S. Government Printing Office, 1988), pp. 233–34.
20. Domestic Policy Council, *Up from Dependency* (Washington, D.C.: White House Domestic Policy Council, December 1986).
21. For a classic description of the assimilation phenomenon, see Nathan Glazer and Daniel Patrick Moynihan, *Beyond the Melting Pot* (Cambridge, Mass.: MIT Press, 1970).
22. Thomas Muller et al., *The Fourth Wave* (Washington, D.C.: Urban Institute, 1985).
23. The three auspices of social welfare in the United States have been termed the "mixed economy of welfare." Sheila Kamerman, "The New Mixed Economy of Welfare," *Social Work* 28 (January–February 1983).
24. Marc Bendick, *Privatizing the Delivery of Social Welfare Service* (Washington, D.C.: National Conference on Social Welfare, 1985).
25. Bruce Jansson, *The Reluctant Welfare State* (Belmont, Calif.: Wadsworth, 1988).
26. Michael Katz, *In the Shadow of the Poorhouse* (New York: Basic Books, 1986).
27. Robert Reich, *Tales of a New America* (New York: Vintage, 1987), p. 11.
28. Robert Schilling, Steven Schinke, and Richard Weatherly, "Service Trends in a Conservative Era: Social Workers Rediscover the Past,"

Social Work 33, no. 1 (January–February 1988), p. 7.

29. Daniel Boorstin, *Hidden History* (New York: Harper and Row, 1987), p. 194.

30. Original emphasis, Daniel Patrick Moynihan, *Came the Revolution* (New York: Harcourt Brace Jovanovich, 1988), p. 291.

31. David Stoesz, "A Structural Interest Theory of Social Welfare," *Social Development Issues* 10, no. 1 (Winter 1985).

32. National Association of Social Workers, *Social Casework: Generic and Specific* (Silver Spring, Md.: NASW, 1974).

33. As per conversation with United Way of America staff, Washington, D.C., April 15, 1986.

34. Robert Alford, *Health Care Politics* (Chicago: University of Chicago Press, 1975), p. 204.

35. Roy Lubove, *The Professional Altruist* (New York: Atheneum, 1969), p. 197.

36. Walter Trattner, *From Poor Law to Welfare State* (New York: Macmillan, 1974), p. 237; and "The First Days of Social Security," *Public Welfare* 43, no. 4 (Fall 1985).

37. Alford, *Health Care Politics,* p. 2.

38. Ibid., p. 199.

39. Trattner, *From Poor Law to Welfare State,* p. 250.

40. Robert Barker, "Private Practice Primer for Social Work," *NASW News* (October 1983), p. 13.

41. D. Goleman, "Social Workers Vault Into a Leading Role in Psychotherapy," *New York Times*, April 3, 1985, p. C1.

42. Maryann Mahaffey, "Fulfilling the Promise," *Proceedings*, Fifth Annual Association of Baccalaureate Program Directors Conference, Kansas City, 1987.

43. Donald Light, "Corporate Medicine for Profit," *Scientific American* 255, no. 6 (December 1986).

44. David Stoesz, "Human Service Corporations and the Welfare State," *Society/Transaction* (forthcoming, 1989).

45. For further details, see David Stoesz, "The Functional Conception of Social Welfare," *Social Work* (March, 1989).

CHAPTER 2

A Framework
for Social Policy Analysis

This chapter will examine one of the major tools used by the policy researcher—a structured framework for policy analysis. The chapter will also explore the common components of a policy framework, and the authors will propose their own model for policy analysis.

The previous chapter examined how ideology, economic theories, and interest groups influence the social welfare state, and the role that concepts such as social justice and equity play in the formation of social welfare policy. A policy framework—in other words, a systematic means for examining a specific social welfare policy or a series of policies—is one means for evaluating the congruence of a policy with the mission and goals of the social welfare state. Policy frameworks also assess whether key social welfare values (e.g., social justice, redistribution, equity, and so forth) are incorporated within a given policy. Moreover, policy frameworks are useful in determining whether a policy fits within the theoretical guidelines of social welfare activities, and whether a policy is consistent with established social welfare foundations, i.e. its fit with historical precedents which guide social welfare initiatives. For example, let us consider the proposal that AIDS testing should be made mandatory for everyone, and that those found to be AIDS positive should be quarantined. The use of a policy framework would show that this proposal represents a clear break with the general drift of late twentieth-century social policy and, moreover, that it repudiates general social welfare values which stress self-determination, justice, equity, and compassion. In addition, a systematic analysis would show that this policy is neither economically, politically, nor socially feasible.

Apart from examining a given policy, an analytic framework is also useful for comparing existing policies. For example, comparing the mental health policies of Missouri with those of Massachusetts and Minnesota would yield valuable information for all three states. A comparative analysis of the health systems of the United States, Canada, and Sweden would also provide useful information for decision makers. Lastly, analytic frameworks can be used to evaluate competing policies. Given alternative policies, the analytic framework could be used to help the analyst make a recommendation as to which policy would most effectively solve a problem or remediate a need.

Social welfare policies and programs are complex phenomena. For example, it is easy to propose a social policy such as mandatory drug testing for all federal employees. On the surface it may appear that the policy is simple: drug users are discovered by the tests and are then forced to seek treatment. On closer scrutiny, however, the hidden issues appear more problematic. Is it constitutional to require drug treatment if a positive result is found? Is occasional use of marijuana sufficient grounds for mandatory drug treatment? Because it is a legal substance, tests do not measure the appearance of alcohol. Is alcohol therefore less debilitating than marijuana? Can the policy of mandatory drug testing be misused by supervisors to harass employees? Will the policy produce the intended results? Although the above questions must be addressed, without a way to systematically analyze the effects of an intended policy, decisions become arbitrary and may produce side effects worse than the original problem.

All well-designed policy frameworks contain key elements:

1. Policy frameworks attempt to *systematically* analyze a social policy or program.
2. Policy frameworks reflect an understanding that social policy is not created in a vacuum—social policy is context-sensitive and policy options usually contain a set of competing priorities.
3. Policy frameworks employ rational methods for inquiry and analysis. The evidence used for the analysis of a policy is derived from scientific inquiry, and all data must be collected from reliable and legitimate sources. Furthermore, the data should be interpreted and analyzed in an objective manner.
4. Although open to interpretation, the analytic method is explicit, and all succeeding analysts should be able to approximate the same conclusion.
5. The objectives of policy analysis reflect a belief in deriving the largest possible social benefit at the least possible social cost. Thus, a good social policy is one that benefits at least one person (as that person perceives his or her own best self-interest), while at the same time hurting no one. In the real world of finite resources—and a proliferating claim upon them—that goal is rarely achieved. Nevertheless, analysts should strive to approximate that aim.
6. Policy frameworks should take into account the unintended consequences of a particular policy or program.
7. Policy frameworks examine a particular policy in the context of alternatives, i.e., alternative social policies or alternative uses for the resources allocated to a given policy.
8. Policy frameworks examine the potential impact of a policy (or series of policies) on other social policies, social problems, and the public.

In the end, the analysis of social policy—often through utilizing a policy framework—provides decision makers and the general public with information, an understanding of the possible ramifications of the policy on the target problem as well as on other problems and policies, and a series of alternative policies that could be more effective in dealing with the problem. Untoward costs and injuries are more likely to result when a systematic framework for policy analysis is not used.

History is replete with examples of well-intentioned policies that proved to be catastrophic. For example, the prohibition of alcohol from 1919 to 1932 was enacted by the U.S. Congress in order to deter crime, familial instability, unemployment, and a myriad of social problems. Proponents of Prohibition, including many social workers, touted the end of alcohol as a major step forward in the social evolution of the United States. However, when Prohibition was repealed 13 years later, most of the original supporters did not vigorously argue for its continuance. Despite the hopes of its backers, Prohibition did not decrease crime, familial instability, or encourage social order; instead, Prohibition encouraged the growth of an organized crime industry that fed the ongoing taste of Americans for alcohol. Instead of eliminating an alcohol-related night life, Prohibition fostered the growth of illegal but well-attended speakeasies. Even many supporters conceded that alcohol was almost as abundant as before Prohibition. Had a systematic policy analysis of Prohibition been undertaken, good policy analysts might have demonstrated the futility of the measure. However, social policy is often driven by politics, and is rarely, if ever, systematically analyzed. Policy analysis often occurs only after a bill or policy is enacted, and analysts are occasionally asked to perform an autopsy to determine why a specific bill or policy failed.

The purpose of a policy framework is to provide the analyst with a model—a set of questions—for systematically analyzing a policy.[1] As such, the choice of a framework must fit the requirements of the project as well as those of the analyst. Every existing policy framework can either be fine-tuned or substantially modified. In fact, the best policy framework may result from a synthesis of existing models. In short, a policy framework is simply a set of questions that is systematically asked of a past, present, or future policy to determine its desirability.

A PROPOSED MODEL FOR POLICY ANALYSIS

The policy analyst is expected to evaluate a policy and make recommendations. In order to succeed in this charge, the analyst must accept his or her own values while, at the same time, basing the analysis on objective criteria. The policy framework proposed by the authors is divided into five sections: (1) the historical background of the policy, (2) the description of the problem that necessitated the policy, (3) the description of the policy, (4) the policy analysis, and (5) the summary and conclusions.

Policy Framework

I. The Historical Background of the Policy. Understanding the historical antecedents of a particular policy is important to the policy analyst for two reasons: the analyst needs to know the historic problems that led to the creation of the policy, and he or she needs to know the historical background of the policy under consideration. Questions that are addressed should include: What historical problems led to the creation of the policy? How important have these problems been historically? How was the problem previously handled? What is the his-

torical background of the policy? When did the policy originate? How has the original policy changed over time? In addition, the policy analyst must examine similar policies that were adopted in the past and their disposition.

Apart from providing continuity, a historical analysis helps to curb the tendency of decision makers to reinvent the wheel. Policies that were previously unsuccessful may continue to be so, or the analyst may come to realize that historical circumstances have changed, thus creating a climate in which a previously failed policy might now be viable. In addition, a historical analysis helps the analyst to understand the forces that were previously mobilized to support or oppose a given policy. In short, a historical analysis locates a particular policy within a historical fabric, thus helping to explicate the often evolutionary nature of a specific social policy or a series of policies.

II. Description of the Problem That Necessitated the Policy. The second major step in analyzing a policy addresses the problem(s) that led to the creation of the policy. In order to assess the ability of a policy to successfully remediate a social problem, the analyst must understand the parameters of the problem. Furthermore, the analyst must be familiar with the nature, scope, magnitude, and populations affected by the problem. In this way, the policy analyst is able to discern early the appropriateness of the policy for tackling the problem it is expected to ameliorate. Specific questions that the policy analyst might ask include: What is the nature of the problem? How widespread is the problem? How many people are affected by the problem? Who is affected and how? What are the causes of the problem? How will the policy help to address the problem?

III. Description of the Policy. The next step in this policy framework is the description of the policy. This section requires a detailed explanation of the policy, including a description of: (1) the way the policy is intended to work; (2)

the resources or opportunities the policy is expected to provide (i.e., power, cash, economic opportunity, in-kind services, status redistribution, goods and services, and so forth); (3) who will be covered by the policy and how (e.g., universal versus selective entitlement, means testing, and so forth); (4) how the policy will be implemented, including means for coordination; (5) the intended short- and long-term goals and outcomes of the policy; (6) the administrative auspices under which the policy will be lodged, including the roles of the private sector, and the local, state and federal government in the development and implementation of the policy; (7) the funding mechanism for the policy, including long- and short-term funding commitments; (8) the agencies or organizations that have overall responsibility for overseeing, evaluating, and coordinating the policy; (9) the criteria that will be used—formal or informal—to determine the effectiveness of the policy and its appropriateness; (10) the length of time the policy is expected to be in existence—e.g., is it a "Sunshine law"?; and (11) the knowledge base or scientific grounding upon which the policy rests.

IV. Policy Analysis.   In this section, the policy analyst goes beyond a simple description of the policy and engages in a *systematic* analysis of the policy (the heart of any good policy analysis).

Policy Goals—The goals of the policy are the criteria by which all else is measured. Oftentimes the goals of a policy are not overtly stated, and the analyst must tease out or conjecture on the overall goals of the policy. The following represents a series of questions that help to explicate the goals of a particular policy.

Are the goals of the policy legal?
Are the goals of the policy just and democratic?
Do the goals of the policy contribute to greater social equality?

Do the goals of the policy positively affect the redistribution of income, resources, rights, entitlements, rewards, opportunities, and status?
Do the goals of the policy contribute to a better quality of life for the target population? Will the goals adversely affect the quality of life for the target group?
Does the policy contribute to positive social relations between the target population and the overall society?
Are the goals of the policy consistent with the values of professional social work (i.e., self-determination, client rights, self-realization, and so forth)?

Other, perhaps more difficult, questions should also be asked of the policy. Analysts must understand the value premises of the policy as well as the ideological assumptions that underlie it. Several questions should be asked, including: What are the hidden ideological suppositions contained within the policy? How is the target population viewed in the context of the policy? What social vision, if any, does the policy contain? Does the policy encourage the continuation of the status quo or does it represent a radical departure? Who are the major beneficiaries of the policy—the target population or another group? In whose best interest is the policy? Is the policy designed to foster real social change or merely placate a potentially insurgent group? Uncovering the hidden ideological dimensions of a policy is often the most difficult task for the policy analyst.

Feasibility—Despite the good intentions of a prospective policy, its goals must be achievable for it to be successfully implemented. American history is littered with good policies that were simply not viable at the time they were proposed. For example, during the middle 1930s (at the height of the Depression), a California physician named Francis Townsend proposed that all citizens over the age of 65 be given a flat governmental pension of $200 per month.

While in affluent times this proposal might have been given at least a cursory hearing, in the midst of one of the greatest depressions in American history, policymakers summarily dismissed the proposal as not viable. The overall feasibility of a policy is based on three factors: political feasibility, economic feasibility, and administrative feasibility.

Political Feasibility of a Policy

The political feasibility of a particular policy is always a judgment call. In order to evaluate a policy, the analyst must assess which groups will oppose and which groups will support a particular policy, as well as estimate the constituency and power base of each group. In American politics, however, the size of the constituency base and its relative power are sometimes unrelated. For example, despite its relatively small numbers, the American Medical Association (AMA) is a powerful lobby in American politics. Conversely, although over 30 million people in the United States are poor, their political clout at this point is negligible. Hence, the analyst must carefully weigh the political salience of each side in the policy struggle.

The political viability of a policy is always subject to the public's perception of its feasibility. In other words, for a policy to be feasible, it must be *perceived* as being feasible by the public. For example, although some observers maintain that a sizable portion—if not the majority—of the public would like to see some form of National Health Insurance (NHI), none exists. In part, an NHI plan has not been enacted because the public believes that it cannot happen, in part because of the power of the medical lobby, particularly the AMA. Therefore, the U.S. lacks NHI not because the public rejects it, but because we believe that it cannot occur. Thus is born a public myth around what is possible and impossible. Many good policy options are not enacted because of the public mythology around what is feasible.

To assess the political feasibility of a policy, the analyst must also examine the public sentiment toward it. Is a large segment of the public concerned about the policy? Do they feel as if they will be directly affected by the policy? Does the policy address a problem which is considered to be a major political issue? Does the policy threaten fundamental social values? Is the policy compatible with the present social and political climate? What is the general public sentiment toward the policy? What is the possibility that either side will be able to marshal public sentiment for or against the policy? The answers to these questions help the policy analyst determine the political feasibility of the policy.

The politics of political feasibility also encompasses a smaller, but no less important, dimension. In order to do a thorough assessment, the analyst must understand the relationship between the policy and external actors in agencies and institutions. For example, which social welfare agencies, institutions, or organizations support or oppose the policy? What is the relative strength of each group? How strong is their support or opposition to the policy? Who are the major federal, state, or local agencies affected by this policy? How are they affected? The world of social policy is heavily political, with some governmental and private social welfare agencies having political power that is on par with that of elected decision makers. These groups often coalesce around issues, problems, or policies that directly affect them, and through their lobbying strength, they have the ability to defeat legislation. In cases where they cannot defeat a policy outright, these administrative institutions can choose to implement a policy in such a way as to ensure its failure. The analyst must therefore take into account whether these administrative organs support or oppose a proposed or existing social policy.

Economic Feasibility of a Policy

Many, if not most, social policies require some form of direct or indirect funding. In assessing the economic feasibility of a policy, the analyst must ask several hard questions: What is the minimum level of funding required for the successful implementation of the policy? Does adequate funding for the policy currently exist? If not, what is the public sentiment toward reallocating resources for the policy? Is the funding called for in the policy adequate? What are likely to be the future funding needs of the policy?

Given the magnitude of the current federal deficit, it appears unlikely that new social policy initiatives requiring large revenues will be successful. Perhaps new policy legislation necessitating additional revenues will be based on the reallocation of existing resources rather than on new revenue sources, a situation which may result in taking money away from one program to fund another. The inherent danger in this approach is that by thinning out fiscal resources among many programs, none will be adequately funded. The analyst must therefore decide whether a new policy initiative should be recommended regardless of the funding prospects. The positive and negative aspects of this decision are complex. If a new policy is recommended, despite insufficient resources, the chances for its failure are greater. However, if a policy is not recommended, the possibility exists that adequate fiscal resources might be allocated in the future. Many policy analysts lean toward incremental approaches, thus tending to recommend policies in the hope that suitable funding will become available in the future.

Administrative Feasibility of a Policy

The analyst must also be concerned with the administrative viability of the policy. Despite the potential value of the policy, responsible administrative agencies must be capable of effectively implementing it. As such, administrative and supervisory agencies must possess the necessary personnel, resources, skills, and expertise to effectively implement the policy. If the requisite personnel are absent, agencies must have the fiscal resources necessary to hire qualified employees. In addition, directors and supervisors must be sympathetic to the goals of the policy, have the expertise and skill necessary to implement or oversee the policy, and possess an understanding of the fundamental objectives of the policy initiative.

Effectiveness—refers to the likelihood that the policy can meet its stated objectives. In short, is the policy likely to accomplish what its creators intended? The answer to this encompasses several questions: Is the policy broad enough to accomplish its stated goals? Will the benefits of the policy reach its target group? Are the side effects of the policy likely to cause other social problems? What ramifications does the policy have on the non-target sector (e.g., higher taxes, reduced opportunity, diminished freedom, less resources, and so forth)?

An important question facing policy analysts involves the nature and extent of the unintended consequences of a policy. Virtually all policies have certain consequences that are unforeseen. An example of the unforeseeable consequences of a social policy is illustrated in the case of methadone, a drug legally given to addicts as a substitute for heroin. When introduced in the 1960s, methadone was thought to be a safe way to wean addicts away from heroin. By the middle 1970s, health experts realized that methadone was almost as addictive as heroin, and that some addicts were selling their methadone as a street drug. Despite this outcome, some addicts were able to withdraw from heroin and, in hindsight, the methadone program was probably a positive development. Because policy analysts cannot see into the future, they only make their recommendations based on available data. Nevertheless, an attempt must be made to predict possible adverse future consequences.

Efficiency and Alternative Policies—refers to the cost-effectiveness of the proposed policy compared to alternative policies, no policy, or the present policy. Social policy is always a trade-off. Even in the best of economic times, societal resources are always inadequate compared to the breadth of human need. For example, virtually everyone could benefit from some form of free social welfare allocation, i.e., counseling services, food stamps, free health care, and so forth. Because resources are finite, society must choose the main beneficiaries of social allocations. Publicly financed services are often awarded based on two criteria: provision of service to those who require the allocation most (severity of problem), and providing services to those who can least afford it (means tests). As a result of finite resources, the adequate funding of one policy often means denying or curbing allocations to another. This is the essential trade-off in social welfare policy. When an analyst evaluates a policy, he or she must be cognizant that promoting one policy means that needs in other areas may go unmet. Thus, a primary question remains: "Is this policy important enough to justify the expenditure of scarce resources?" Moreover, are there other areas where resources could be better used?

The policy analyst is also concerned with the cost effectiveness of a given policy compared to alternative policies and the present one. Given the additional expenditure of money, will the new policy provide results that are better than either the present policy or no policy at all? Is it advantageous to enlarge or modify the present policy as opposed to creating a new one? Can an alternative policy provide better results at lower cost? What alternative policies could be created to achieve the same results? How do these alternative policies compare with each other and with the proposed policy? These questions must be answered in any thorough policy analysis.

In conclusion, the policy analyst must address several key questions: Is the proposed policy workable and desirable? What, if any, modifications should be made in the policy?

Does the policy represent a wise use of resources? Are there alternative policies that would be preferable? How feasible is the implementation of the policy? What barriers, if any, exist regarding the full implementation of the policy? The above questions represent the core of policy analysis.

THE INCOMPLETENESS OF POLICY ANALYSIS

The choice of a framework for policy analysis is dependent upon a number of considerations, including: (1) the kind of problem or policy that must be analyzed; (2) the available resources of the policy analyst, including time, money, staff, facilities, availability of data, and so forth; (3) the requirements of the decision maker requesting the analysis; and (4) the time frame in which the analysis must be completed.

No policy analysis is ever complete. Because it is impossible to discover *all* of the data (data are essentially infinite) and to ask *all* of the possible questions, policy analysis is never complete nor is it ever perfect. Policy analysis is always an approximation of the ideal and, as such, decisions are always made based on incomplete data. How incomplete the data are and how good an approximation of a rational decision is provided to decision makers are contingent upon the skills of the analyst, the available resources, and the time allotted for the project.

Despite the reliance on an analytic framework, social policy analysis is to some degree subjective. Because humans analyze policy, it is always done through the lens of the analyst's value system and his or her understanding of the goals and purposes of social welfare. Subjectivity may occur by the omission (conscious or otherwise) of facts or questions, or it may occur by the relative weight given to one variable at the expense of others. Subjectivity may also be expressed by asking the wrong questions of the policy, evaluating it based on expectations that it cannot meet, and by expecting it to tackle a problem that it was not designed to address. Lastly, political pressure may be put on the policy analyst to come up with recommendations that are acceptable to a certain interest group. Regardless of the causes for subjectivity, policy analysis is always an approximation—an informed hunch as to effects of a policy or a set of policies.

NOTE

1. Many social policy writers, including Elizabeth Huttman, *Introduction to Social Policy* (New York: McGraw-Hill, 1981); Neil Gilbert and Harry Specht, *Dimensions of Social Welfare Policy*, 2nd Edition (Englewood Cliffs, N.J.: Prentice-Hall, 1986); Gail Marker, "Guidelines for Analysis of a Social Welfare Program," in John E. Tropman et al., *Strategic Perspectives on Social Policy* (New York: Pergamon Press, 1976); David Gil, *Unraveling Social Policy* (Boston: Schenkman, 1981); and Charles Prigmore and Charles Atherton, *Social Welfare Policy* (New York: D. C. Heath, 1979), have developed excellent policy frameworks.

CHAPTER 3

The Origins of the American Social Welfare State

The American social welfare state did not emerge in a vacuum. To grasp its complexity, the student of social welfare policy must understand the historical foundation upon which it has been built. As such, this chapter examines the historical antecedents of the American social welfare state, and will take the reader from its immediate roots—the English Poor Laws—to the recent developments that mark the emergence of modern social welfare.

THE ENGLISH POOR LAWS

The English Poor Laws, in many ways, functioned as an early model for American social welfare. Early social welfare relief in England was considered a private and church matter. For example, individual benefactors took responsibility for building almshouses, hospitals, and even bridges and roads. Despite private philanthropy, the main burden for the poor rested on the shoulders of the Church. Most European governments, including that of England, assumed little responsibility to care for the poor. This fact, however, would change with the emergence of industrialization and its stark realities.

As a result of rapid industrialization and the transformation of farmland into more profitable pasture areas for sheep—a transformation that was necessary to feed the hungry wool mills of England—the resulting urban migration of displaced and impoverished peasants produced untoward social consequences, including begging and vagrancy. In 1349, after the Black Death drastically reduced the population of England, King Edward III created the Statute of Laborers which fixed maximum wages, placed travel restrictions on unemployed persons, forced the jobless to work for any employer willing to hire them, and outlawed giving alms to the able-bodied.[1] In 1531 the English Parliament outlawed begging for the able-bodied. Although repressive, the act also instructed local officials to seek out the worthy poor and to assign them areas where they could beg.[2]

The passage of the Act for the Punishment of Sturdy Vagabonds and Beggars in 1536—the Poor Law—further mandated the English government to take limited responsibility for the poor. Although this act increased the punishment for begging, it also ordered officials to obtain resources—through voluntary church donations—to care for the poor, the sick, the lame, and the aged. In addition, the statute required local officials to locate work for the able-bodied and to arrange for the apprenticeship of poor children aged five to fourteen. In 1572 the English Parliament enacted yet another poor law, this time requiring local officials to implement a mandatory tax for the provision of economic relief to the poor.[3]

In 1601 the English government established the Elizabethan Poor Laws. These laws were developed primarily to control those poor who were unable to obtain employment in the new industrial sector, and who, because of that, might become disruptive. Taxes were levied to finance the law, but the rules were, by our standards, harsh. Again a primary theme of the law was to distinguish the "deserving" from the "undeserving" poor. The worthy poor were the lame, the blind, orphaned children, and those unemployed through no fault of their own. The unworthy poor were vagrants, drunkards, and those considered slothful. The Elizabethan Poor Laws—which with minor modifications were to stand for 250 years—contained positive and repressive features. For example, parents with means were legally responsible for supporting their children and grandchildren. Children were responsible for supporting their parents and grandparents. On the repressive side, the unworthy poor were sent to workhouses and forced to do menial work for the minimum necessities of life. Poor people who refused to work could be sent to jail, or, in some cases, executed. In addition, the English Poor Laws established the principle of "less eligibility"—the idea that welfare will be less than the lowest prevailing wage.

In essence, these laws established the responsibility of the English government to provide relief to the needy. Furthermore, the laws decreed that the needy had a legal right to receive governmental assistance. In order to define the boundaries of government help, the law distinguished among three classes of dependents and proposed remediative measures: needy children were given apprenticeships, the able-bodied were given work, and the worthy poor were provided either indoor (institutional) or outdoor (home) relief. Lastly, the law ordered local governments to assume responsibility for the needy.[4] The English Poor Laws formed the basis for statutes that were enacted in both colonial and post-colonial America.[5]

THE POOR IN COLONIAL AMERICA

Many aspects of the Elizabethan welfare system were adopted by the American colonists. Like its English corollary of the parish, the town was responsible for its residents. Up to about 1700, when almshouses began to appear, cases of pauperism were handled on an individual basis in town meetings. When the number of poverty cases increased as a result of indentured servants and abandoned children, the English system of overseers was introduced.

Most settlers in colonial America were poor.[6] However, unlike their European ancestors, they were not destitute. Therefore, despite the poverty in colonial America, pauperism and dependency on outside relief was not widespread. According to Morris, less than 1 percent of American colonists received help from outside sources.[7]

In smaller towns unable to support an almshouse, it was not uncommon for the town council to auction off the poor to neighboring farmers, apprentice out children, place the poor in private homes at public expense, or send them to privately operated almshouses. Settlers believed that children should be part of a family unit and thus the practice of indenture became widespread. However, by the end of the colonial period, the locus of responsibility for the poor began to shift from the town to the province.[8]

While the settlers had compassion for indigent townspeople, considerably less compassion was shown for destitute strangers. As the numbers of poor increased, some communities enacted laws of settlement. Residency requirements were strictly enforced through the policies of "warning out" or "passing on." The former term meant that newcomers were urged to move on if they appeared to be indigent. Passing on meant returning the transient poor to their former counties of residence. In addition to "warning out practices," some colonies established residency requirements to determine eligibility for public assistance. The "fit" poor in Colonial America were treated harshly. Idleness was regarded as a vice and the able-bodied loafer was either indentured, expelled from town, whipped, or jailed. By the eighteenth century the able-bodied unemployed were either placed in workhouses or almshouses.[9]

By the early 1800s the process for helping the poor radically changed. The quasi-benevolence of the town council was replaced by a reliance on workhouses. In some areas, the use of outdoor relief was all but abandoned in favor of institutional care. Moreover, it was not until the middle 1800s that the national government conceded even limited responsibility for the poor. Local government activities were based on a belief that poverty was a consequence of moral weakness—a theory linked to Puritan values and hence more prevalent in the New England rather than Middle-Atlantic states—and thus demanded reeducation and an economical system of relief.[10]

SOCIAL WELFARE IN THE CIVIL WAR ERA

Historically, the federal government's role in providing relief has been a contentious issue. This question, however, was to be advanced by the reform activities of Dorothea Dix, a name that has become synonymous with the movement for the humane care of the mentally ill. As a result of volunteering as a Sunday school teacher for an insane asylum in 1841, Dix went through a kind of emotional conversion. Appalled by the conditions she saw at the asylum, Dix committed herself to fighting for reform in the care of the mentally ill.

The majority of mentally ill people in the 1840s were placed in public mental institutions, jails, or almshouses. Their treatment was often brutal and consisted of beatings, being chained, or being sequestered in cages or pens. Dix decided that neither private philanthropy nor local action could remedy the problem. For Dix, the solution to caring for the insane lay in state and federal intervention.

After having successfully lobbied for state action, Dix decided that because of the large expenditures required, federal intervention was necessary. With the support of well-known clergymen, prominent citizens, newspapermen,

and public and private organizations, a bill was passed in 1854 by both houses of Congress which provided federal support for the mentally ill. Unfortunately, President Franklin Pierce vetoed the bill in 1854 claiming that, "If Congress has the power to make provisions for the indigent insane ... it has the same power for the indigent who are not insane ... I cannot find any authority in the Constitution for making the Federal Government the great almoner of public charity throughout the United States."[11] Pierce's veto was in large part based on his belief in "states' rights," but, more importantly, for the next seventy-five years his veto provided the rationale for the federal government's refusal to provide social welfare services.[12]

The Civil War ushered in a new period for relief activities. Families who lost a breadwinner, or who had a breadwinner return from the war permanently disabled, could not be blamed for their own misfortune. As a response to the hardship created by the Civil War, localities passed laws which raised funds for the sick and needy and, in some instances, for the founding of homes for disabled soldiers.

Other welfare issues in the Civil War included the disease and filth rampant in army camps and hospitals as well as the shortage of trained medical personnel. In an effort to remedy this situation, in 1861 a group of citizens (composed mainly of women) organized the U.S. Sanitary Commission, the first important national public health group. Functioning as a quasi-governmental body, the Commission was financed and directed by the private voluntary sector. Working initially in the area of preventive health education, the Commission eventually became involved in a variety of direct and indirect avenues for serving the needs of soldiers.[13]

Another social welfare development that emerged from the Civil War was the Freedmen's Bureau. By the close of the Civil War political leaders realized that the emancipation of millions of slaves would create serious social problems. Former slaves having no occupational training, land, or jobs would require assistance. In 1865 Congress established the Bureau of Refugees, Freedmen, and Abandoned Lands. The Freedmen's Bureau, as it was commonly called, was responsible for directing a program of temporary relief for the duration of the war and one year afterward. After a bitter struggle, Congress extended the Freedmen's Bureau for an additional six years.

The Bureau, under General Oliver Howard, performed a variety of services designed to help blacks make the transition from freedom to slavery. For example, the Bureau served as an emergency relief center which distributed 22 million rations to needy Southerners. The Bureau also functioned as a black employment agency, a settlement agency, a health center which employed doctors and operated hospitals, an educational agency which encouraged the funding of black universities and provided financial aid, and finally, as a legal agency which maintained courts where civil and criminal cases involving blacks were heard. The Freedmen's Bureau set a crucial precedent for federal government involvement in a variety of human services. In 1872 the Bureau was dissolved by Congress.[14]

INDUSTRIALIZATION AND THE VOLUNTARY SECTOR

Private efforts to enhance the welfare of the community have been a prominent part of social welfare throughout the history of the United States. During his travels through the young nation early in the nineteenth century, Alexis de Tocqueville commented on the proclivity of Americans to voluntarily band together to solve problems besetting their communities.

> Americans of all ages, all conditions, and all dispositions, constantly form associations. They have not only commercial and manufacturing companies, in which all take part, but associa-

tions of a thousand other kinds,—religious, moral, serious, futile, extensive or restrictive, enormous and diminutive. The Americans make associations to give entertainments, to found establishments for education, to build inns, to construct churches, to diffuse books, to send missionaries to the antipodes; and in this manner they found hospitals, prisons, and schools. If it be proposed to advance some truth, or to foster some feeling of encouragement of a great example, they form a society. Wherever, at the head of some new undertaking, you see the Government of France, or a man of rank in England, in the United States you will be sure to find an association.[15]

Reliance on voluntary associations to solve problems corresponded with the nature of the community of that era. Prior to industrialization, most people lived in communities with an array of institutions that afforded a high degree of self-sufficiency. Survival necessitated a degree of solidarity, or interdependence, that was taken as a law of nature. Cohesiveness of this kind can still be found among certain religious sects, such as the Amish, which manage human need through the voluntary impulses of residents who see good deeds as a normal extension of daily activities.

With industrialization, however, this method of managing welfare proved inadequate for most groups, and special entities became designated to provide for social welfare.[16] The fact that institutions specializing in welfare would emerge at this time is related to the industrial revolution and the subsequent social dislocation that resulted in the relocation of millions of families. From 1890 to 1920, 22 million immigrants came to the United States. At the same time, the American people became more urban. Seventy-five percent of foreign immigrants stayed in cities; and, during the decade following 1920, 6 million people moved from farms to cities.[17]

Life in late nineteenth-century America was hard. The dream of "milk and honey" that motivated many immigrants to leave their homeland became, for many, a nightmare. The streets of American cities were not paved in gold; instead, they were overcrowded, rampant with disease and crime, and economically destitute. Many tenement houses in some of the larger cities contained neither windows nor indoor plumbing. Tuberculosis was rampant and, among some groups, infant mortality ran as high as 50 percent. Scant medical care existed for the poor; there was no public education, and insanity and prostitution rates among immigrants were high.[18] The industrial and economic prospects were equally bleak. Factory conditions were abominable: workers were expected to labor six or seven days a week (often on Sunday), and eighteen-hour days were not unusual, especially in summer.[19] Factories were poorly lit, contained little sanitation, were fire traps, and offered almost no job security. Moreover, homework (taking piecework home, usually for assembly by whole families in one- or two-room tenements) was common. Women were forced to work night shifts and then take care of their homes and children during the day.[20] No special protective legislation for women existed until the early 1900s, and child labor was legal. According to Hofstadter, industrial accidents affected one out of ten to twelve workers, and employees had neither worker's compensation nor disability insurance.[21] When these conditions are added to the fact that every fifteen or twenty years there was another depression, it is obvious that the lot of the immigrant and the working-class American was marked by hardship. The extent of this suffering is evident in a description of New York City.

> With the shift of population from the grange to the tenement house came a degree of over expansion and under management that brought large cities to the crisis point: sanitation and health were plainly inadequate; there was a constant fear of rioting and crime; the police used their night sticks against the people they were sworn to protect. Fed by immigrants streaming through Castle Garden and, after 1891, Ellis Island, New York's East Side was the end point of all cities. With over 500 people for each acre, nearly five times the average for the rest of Manhattan, the Tenth Ward was the most densely settled area in the world, and its ghetto was larger than Warsaw's. It was "the suicide ward" and "the typhus ward," and the breeding place of the "white plague" of tuberculosis, epidemics of all kinds, crime, pauperism, alcoholism, sweated labor, hopelessness, and a frightful mortality rate.[22]

Faced with this dilemma a growing middle class struggled to explain and cope with the mounting social debris in American cities. There was an urgency to this task. Through the germ theory, medical science had identified the cause of many contagious diseases, but had yet to develop preventive vaccines or cures. Thus, it was no accident that Charles Loring Brace, a pioneer of child welfare, entitled his book *The Dangerous Classes of New York*. Moreover, graft and corruption became rife as urban immigrants competed for scarce food, housing, and jobs, eking out marginal existences in squalid city tenements. Eventually, political machines emerged which converted city governments into fiefdoms of patronage. In an exposé of graft in New York City, Jacob Riis, a muckraking journalist, alleged that the political machine of "Boss" Tweed's Tammany Hall was nothing more than "a band of political cutthroats." Not particularly surprising, Riis noted that Tweed was the product of a Fourth Ward tenement.[23] Yet, even when muckrakers uncovered abuses and railed against them in banner headlines, political bosses were so confident of the indispensability of "the machine" that they responded to accusations with defiance. For example, upon hearing of an exposé by Lincoln Steffens, George Washington Plunkett, a Tammany Hall crony, quipped: "Steffens means well but, like all reformers, he don't know how to make distinctions. He can't see no difference between honest graft and dishonest graft and, consequently, he gets things all mixed up."[24]

Social Darwinism

Many people looked to the developing social sciences for guidance in redefining social policy. There, prominent scholars drew lessons from the natural sciences which could be used for purposes of social engineering. Borrowing from the natural sciences, some American proponents of the new science of sociology applied the idea of natural selection to social affairs.

Social Darwinism was a bastard outgrowth of Charles Darwin's theory of evolution as described in his 1859 classic, *The Origin of Species*.[25] Social theorists such as Herbert Spencer and America's William Graham Sumner reasoned that if Darwin's laws of evolution determined the origin and development of the species, then they also might be applied to understanding the laws of society.[26]

Applying Darwin's rules to society, and then adopting laissez faire principles of economics to sociology, led to a problematic set of assumptions. For one, if the "survival of the fittest" (a term coined by Spencer) is a law governing the lower species, then it must also govern the higher species. Therefore, subsidizing the poor allows them to survive, which then circumvents the law of nature. Because the poor reproduce more rapidly than the middle classes, society is thus subsidizing its own demise. Social Darwinists believed essentially that the poor would eventually overrun society and bring down the general level of civilization.

Secondly, if as Darwin maintains, competition for resources is the law of life, then the poor are impoverished because they cannot compete. Conversely, the economic elite are entitled to their spoils because of their "fitness" and their competitive abilities. In any case, by subsidizing the poor—thus allowing them to reproduce—society artificially alters the laws of nature, and, in doing so, weakens the human gene pool.

Lastly, Social Darwinists believed that albeit unfortunate, the poor must pay the price of nature and be allowed to die out. According to the Social Darwinists, social welfare thwarts nature's plan of evolutionary progress toward higher forms of social life. Speaking for many intellectuals, the British theorist Herbert Spencer concluded that:

> It seems hard that widows and orphans should be left to struggle for life or death. Nevertheless, when regarded not separately but in connexion with the interests of universal humanity, these harsh fatalities are seen to be full of beneficence—the same beneficence which brings to early graves the children of diseased parents, and singles out the intemperate and the debilitated as the victims of an epidemic.[27]

While some thinkers promoted the harsh strictures of Social Darwinism, and socialists saw poverty as a manifestation of an unjust class society, Christianity provided yet another answer.

Religion and Social Welfare

Religion and social welfare in nineteenth-century America were inextricably linked. Almost all forms of relief emanated from church groups, and all major denominations had some mechanism for providing social welfare.[28] For example, as early as 1880 there were 500 private, church-related social welfare organizations in New York City alone, with the largest network for social services provided by Protestant churches.

Poverty was seen as a moral failing in the context of orthodox Protestant theology. Martin Luther viewed work as a responsibility to God. Furthermore, work contained dignity and was a "calling" by God. In Luther's view, a person served God by doing the work of his vocation. Therefore, those who are able-bodied and unemployed are sinners. John Calvin took Luther's argument one step further and claimed that work carried out the will of God and, as such, work would ultimately help to create God's kingdom on earth. According to both Luther and Calvin, God-fearing people must work regardless of their wage or type of work.[29]

Because the command to work came from God, economic success was seen as a sign of favor. Poverty, therefore, was also a sign of God's will. This Protestant ethic fueled the creation of a work-oriented society and placed a religious base under the indifference of the elite classes toward the poor. In addition, by adding a religious dimension to poverty, conservative Protestantism more sharply focused the distinction between the worthy and unworthy poor.[30]

Conservative theologians used a religious framework to connect poverty and improvidence: people were poor because they engaged in drinking, slothfulness, licentious behavior, gambling, and so forth. Some critics have argued that despite the social welfare services provided by churches, in the final analysis, Protestant theology contained a basically antisocial welfare stance.[31]

It was thought that in order to reclaim providence, the poor must be taught to live a moral and self-disciplined life. While early religious social workers clung tenaciously to their desire to teach the moral life, they also understood the need to provide material assistance.[32] The major concern of the early social worker was, however, more often on spiritual guidance rather than material aid.

The relief assistance provided by these evangelical social workers was often linked to harsh criteria. For example, it was not uncommon for social workers to appraise the worth of the family's possessions and then instruct them to sell off everything in order to qualify for relief. Nor was it uncommon for social workers to deny relief because they felt that the poor family was intemperate and not sufficiently contrite. And, if the family refused to accept moral guidance, they could be deemed ineligible for relief. Despite the fact that these social workers dispensed relief, they were basically opposed to the concept of it. They believed that distributing relief was imprudent, because a reliance on

charity would weaken the moral fabric of the poor and provide a disincentive for work.

The reign of conservative Protestant theology was not without opposition. In the late nineteenth and early twentieth century, a movement emerged known as the Social Gospel, composed of theologians concerned with the abuses created by industrialization and the excesses of capitalism. Social Gospelists, such as Josiah Strong, Graham Taylor, and others, believed that the church should recapture the militant spirit of Christ by concerning itself with issues of social justice and poverty. The critique posed by the Social Gospelists called for fair play and simple justice for the worker.[33]

Proponents of the Social Gospel movement maintained that churches wrongfully stressed spirituality rather than morality.[34] The condemnation of classical economics, business ethics, and the lawlessness of the plutocracy was centered on a moral rather than a spiritual plane. For the Social Gospelists, social reformation could not occur without a regeneration of character.[35] Although the movement contained degrees of radicalism, all Social Gospelists were moved by a sense of social crisis, and all believed in the necessity of a Christian solution.[36] The legacy of the Social Gospel movement is evident in the current rise of "Liberation Theology," a grass-roots movement of progressive theologians that is gaining strength in many Latin American and African nations.

In any case, the combination of Social Darwinism and Christian charity suffused the organizations which assumed a major share of responsibility for social welfare during the industrial era—Charity Organization Societies and Settlement Houses.

Charity Organization Societies

First evident in the 1870s, Charity Organization Societies (COSs) had offices in most American cities by 1900.[37] With the exception of meager state-sponsored indoor and outdoor relief, the COS movement was a major provider of care to the destitute. COSs varied in their structures and methods. In general they coordinated relief giving by operating community-wide registration bureaus, providing direct relief, and "educating" both the upper and lower classes on their mutual obligations.

The work of the COS was carried out by a committee of volunteers and agency representatives who examined "cases" of needy applicants and decided on a course of action. The agent of the COS was the "friendly visitor," whose task was to conduct an investigation of the circumstances surrounding the "cases" and to instruct the poor in ways to better manage their lives. Friendly visitors, drawn from the upper classes, often held a morally superior attitude toward their clientele and their intervention into the lives of the poor was interpreted by some observers as a form of social control[38] as well as a means of providing assistance. In any case, the charity provided by these organizations was often less than generous. Leaders of the movement drew an important lesson from Social Darwinism—beneficent charity was counterproductive because it contributed to sloth and dependency. Josephine Shaw Lowell, President of the New York Charity Organization Society, believed that charity should be dispensed "only when starvation was imminent."[39]

To be sure, it was difficult for friendly visitors to maintain a sense of Christian duty in the midst of immoral behavior. In such instances, when some wretched souls seemed beyond instruction and charity, more radical measures were in order. Charles Loring Brace, head of the New York Children's Aid Society, described his approach to dealing with a German mother who worked as a "swill-gatherer" in "Dutch Hill."

On the eastern side of the city, in the neighborhood of Fortieth Street, is a village of squatters, which enjoys the title of "Dutch Hill." The inhabitants are not, however, "Dutch," but mainly poor Irish, who have taken temporary possession of unused sites on a hill, and have erected shanties which serve at once for pig-pens, hen-coops, bed-rooms, and living-rooms. They enjoy the privilege of squatters in having no rent to pay; but they are exposed to the penalty of being at any moment turned out from their dens, and losing land and house at once.... The village is filled with snarling dogs, which aid in drawing the swill or coal carts, for the children are mainly employed in collecting swill and picking coals through the streets.

[An] old rag-picker I remember whose shanty was a sight to behold; all the odds and ends of a great city seemed piled up in it,—bones, broken dishes, rags, bits of furniture, cinders, old tin, useless lamps, decaying vegetables, ribbons, cloths, legless chairs, and carrion, all mixed together, and heaped up nearly to the ceiling, leaving hardly room for a bed on the floor where the woman and her two children slept. Yet all these [children] were marvels of health and vigor, far surpassing most children I know in the comfortable classes. The woman was German, and after years of effort could never be induced to do anything for the education of her children, until finally I put the police on their track as vagrants, and they were safely housed in the "Juvenile Asylum."[40]

And, what happened to the children who had been placed in the "Juvenile Asylum"? Brace's solution was as ingenious as it was compatible with the tenets of Social Darwinism and Christian charity. The Children's Aid Society transported between 50,000 and 100,000 "orphans" westward by train, where they were placed with farm families.[41] The advertisement in Figure 3.1, posted in McPherson, Kansas, provides some detail on the procedures devised by Brace and his associates.[42]

Settlement Houses

The settlement house movement, which began in the 1880s and emerged in most of the big cities over the next two decades, was also a response to the urban conditions of the times.

Homes For Children
=== WANTED ===

A Company of Homeless Children from the East Will
Arrive at

McPherson, Friday, September 15.

These children are of various ages and of both sexes, having been thrown friendless upon the world. They come under the auspices of the Children's Aid Society, of New York. They are well disciplined, having come from various orphanage. The citizens of this community are asked to assist the agent in finding good homes for them. Persons taking these children must be recommended by the local committee. They must treat the children in every way as members of the family, sending them to school, church, Sabbath school and properly clothe them until they are 18 years old. Protestant children placed in Protestant homes and Catholic children in Catholic homes. The following well known citizens have agreed to act as a local committee to aid the agents in securing homes:

| Dr. Heaston | H. A. Rowland | C. W. Bachelor |
| F. A. Vaniman | W. J. Krehbiel | K. Sorensen |

Applications must be made to and endorsed by the local committee.

An address will be given by the agents. Come and see the children and hear the address. Distribution will take place at

Opera House, Friday, September 15
at 10:00 a. m. and 2:00 p. m.

Miss A. L. HILL and MISS C. B. COM STOCK, Agents, 105 East 22nd Street, New York City. W. W. BUGBEE, Eldorado, Kansas, State Agent.

Handbills promoted the orphan trains. This one is for McPherson, KS, in 1911.

Figure 3.1. Reprinted from Martha Nelson Vogt and Christina Vogt, *Searching for Home* (Martha Nelson Vogt and Christina Vogt, 1062 Edison N. W., Grand Rapids, Michigan, 1979)

Settlement houses were primarily set up in immigrant neighborhoods by wealthy people, college students, unattached women, teachers, doctors, and lawyers, who themselves moved into the slums as residents. Rather than simply engaging in friendly visiting, the upper- and middle-class settlement leaders tried to bridge class differences and to develop a less patronizing form of charity. They sought to help the people in the neighborhoods organize themselves, rather than coordinate existing charities as had the COSs. Because they actually lived in the same neighborhoods as the impoverished immigrants, settlement workers could provide fresh and reliable knowledge about the social and economic conditions of American cities.

Jane Addams established Hull House in 1889. She approached the project—and the Chicago ethnic community where it was based —with a sense of Christian Socialism that was derived from a "rather strenuous moral purgation,"[43] rather than a sense of *noblesse oblige*. The co-founder of Hull House, Ellen Gates Starr, described the values of the settlement house worker.

> After we had been here long enough and people see that we don't catch diseases and that vicious people do not destroy us or our property ... we have well founded reason to believe that there are at least half a dozen girls in the city who will be glad to come and stay a while and learn to know the people and understand them and their ways of life; to give out of their culture and leisure and overindulgence and to receive the culture that comes from self-denial and poverty and failure which these people have always known.[44]

By 1915 this altruism was shared by enough settlement workers that over 300 settlements had been established, and most larger American cities could boast of at least one or more settlement houses.[45]

While providing individual services to the poor, the larger settlements were essentially reform oriented. These reforms were achieved not only by organizing the poor to press for change, but often by using interest groups formed by elite citizens, as well as the formation of national alliances. Settlement-pioneered reforms included tuberculosis prevention, the establishment of well-baby clinics, the implementation of housing codes, the construction of outdoor playgrounds, the enactment of child labor and industrial safety legislation, and the promotion of some of the first studies of the urban Negro in America, such as W. E. B. Du Bois's *The Philadelphia Negro*. Many of the leaders of the New Deal had worked in settlements. For example, alumnae of Hull House included Edith Abbott, drafter of the Social Security Act; her sister, Grace Abbott, and Julia Lathrop, who became directors of the U.S. Children's Bureau; and Frances Perkins, Secretary of Labor and the first woman to be appointed to a cabinet post.[46]

Black Associations

If the conditions of immigrants were difficult, those of blacks were that much more trying. In the absence of government programs, blacks had to rely on private sources of welfare, even though many of those voluntary agencies frequently discriminated against them. Consequently, a number of fraternal and benefit associations emerged within the black community, such as the Knights of Tabor, the Knights of Pythias, the Ancient Sons of Israel, and the Grand United Order of True Reformers.[47] These indigenous organizations were instrumental in binding the fabric of a community that suffered from continual distress compounded by limited resources. As an example, consider some of the constitutional provisions of one health and burial society:

> Sec.1. This society shall be known as the Sons and Daughters of Zion.
> Sec.2. The object of this society shall be to care for its sick and bury its dead members, and all moneys paid therein shall be expended for same. By a two-thirds vote,

however, of all the active members, money may be expended for other purposes.

Sec.5. The monthly fee of all members in Sons and Daughters of Zion shall be 25 cents.

Sec.17. The Society shall not employ more than three doctors, who shall be elected annually, and shall purchase all medicine from one drug store.

Sec.18. The burial expenses shall in no case exceed $25.00, and in all cases the hearse shall be used in conveying the body to the cemetery.

Rule 19. The chairman of the sick and burial committee shall summon as many male members as are necessary to dig a grave. In his absence the male messenger shall discharge this duty. Members who fail to assist in digging a grave after having been appointed, and who do not get anyone in their place, shall pay a fine of 75 cents or be suspended for six months.

Rule 26. The society shall not be responsible for the following bills: Bills caused from accident or death in disreputable places, self-abuse among men as diseases brought on by lewd habits, women confined, accident or death from stealing or anything dishonorable.[48]

Before government played a prominent role in guaranteeing the basic rights of citizens, important events in the history of black Americans were often connected with voluntary associations that arose within the black community. Talladega College, the first distinguished liberal arts college serving rural blacks, had its origin in a carpenter shop where David White, Sr., a freedman, and Leonard Johnson, "a black man who had in some way acquired the rudiments of learning," began a school.[49] Morehouse College, the alma mater of Martin Luther King, Jr., began in 1867 as a night school in the Springfield Baptist Church of Augusta, Georgia.[50] When it appeared that the industrial education approach of Booker T. Washington would not assure blacks of full citizenship, W. E. B. Du Bois galvanized a group of reformers, among them social workers such as Ida B. Wells, Mary White Covington, and Jane Addams, into the Niagara Movement. Marshaling support through meetings at centers of abolitionist sentiment, the Niagara Movement became the National Association for the Advancement of Colored People. Meanwhile, a concern for economic justice led George Edmund Haynes, a Columbia University graduate student, to write *The Negro at Work in New York City*. The attention attracted by this study contributed to the formation in 1911 of the National Urban League on Urban Conditions. Using philanthropic assistance from foundations, the League established a program for social work training which "made possible the education of many of America's most distinguished social work leaders in the next generation."[51]

Prior to World War I, social welfare in the United States consisted almost exclusively of private agencies voluntarily established by groups for the purpose of enhancing the public welfare. Indeed, many of the community agencies with which most Americans are familiar were established at this time, as shown in the following list of the founding dates of selected organizations.

1851—Young Men's Christian Association
1858—Young Women's Christian Association
1880—Salvation Army
1881—American Red Cross
1896—Volunteers of America
1902—Goodwill Industries
1907—Boys' Clubs of America
1910—Boy Scouts of America
1910—Catholic Charities
1911—Family Service Association of America
1912—Girl Scouts of America

The Social Casework Agency

Charity Organization Societies and Settlements served as models for the delivery of social welfare services in the voluntary sector organizations that emerged during the Progressive Era. Similar in many respects, their commonalities evolved to form the social casework agency. Both were of modest size in terms of the number of staff, they were located in the communities of the clientele that they served, they served a predominantly poor population, and they relied on contributions from a variety of sources—private donations, the Community Chest, and foundations.[52] Typically, workers in these agencies were female volunteers. COS techniques for investigation were refined, with their aim being the identification of a "social diagnosis" as the basis for case intervention.[53] Subsequently, these activities, along with the community-oriented work of the settlement reformers, gave birth to the profession of social work.

Despite the efforts of these early women of social work, their professional stature was not highly esteemed. At the time, the caricature of the journalist H. L. Mencken was perhaps typical of public sentiment.

> The social worker, judging by her own pretensions, helps to preserve multitudes of persons who would perish if left to themselves. Thus her work is clearly dysgenic and anti-social. For every victim of sheer misfortune that she restores to self-sustaining and social usefulness, she must keep alive scores of misfits and incompetents who can never, for all her help, pull their weight in the boat. Such persons can do nothing more valuable than dying.[54]

As predominant service delivery forms, COSs and Settlements were transformed by two influences: the need for scientifically based treatment techniques, and the socialization of charity. Together, these factors contributed to the emergence of the social casework agency. COSs and Settlements had provided meaningful activity for upper- and middle-class women who found it necessary to ground their work in treatment techniques which were derived from science. This necessity had been driven home

in 1915 during the National Conference of Charities and Correction, when Abraham Flexner, a renowned authority on professional graduate education, had been asked to address the question of whether social work was a profession. Much to the disappointment of the audience, Flexner judged that social work lacked all the requirements of a profession, particularly a scientifically derived knowledge that was transmittable.[55] Subsequently, the Milford Conference Report of 1923 underscored the importance of a scientific base for social work knowledge.

> The future growth of social casework is in large measure dependent upon its developing a scientific character. Its scientific character will be the result of a scientific attitude in social caseworkers towards their own problems, and as part of increasingly scientific adaptations from the subject matter of other sciences.[56]

Scientific social work served the manifest function of improving the effectiveness of social work practice, and thereby increasing the status of the new profession. At the same time, it served a latent function. Describing the social worker's client in scientific terms functioned to elevate the image of the client from one of an inept wretch to one characterized by specific afflictions which were mutable.

At the same time, the funding of COSs, Settlements, and other service organizations had proven undependable because of competition among agencies for donors' funds, and the fact that these gifts were dependent on a largesse which fluctuated with an unstable economy. The solution to this problem emerged in the form of a collective approach to philanthropic giving. As early as 1887, Denver's Associated Charities had pioneered the concept whereby a group of agencies appealed to the conscience of the community for operating funds. By the 1920s, over 200 cities had adopted community chests, reducing the need for the independent agency to curry favors on its own.[57] The socialization of charity provided agencies with a relatively steady income while demanding uniformity in operations. Uniformity was allied with efficiency, a guiding principle of the Progressive Era,[58] resulting in an organizational form that served to rationalize a previously haphazard array of social services.[59]

Together, the needs of workers for effective treatment techniques and the economic imperatives for organizational survival functioned to standardize the social casework agency.

Perhaps the best description of the casework agency evolved from the Milford Conference of 1923, when sixteen executives and board members from six national organizations drafted a document which endorsed agency-based service delivery. The Milford Conference Report provided a comprehensive outline of the organization through which professional caseworkers delivered services. The social casework agency was located in a community and derived its objectives and purposes from it. The agency was governed by a board of directors which hired the agency director and met monthly to monitor agency affairs. Caseworkers functioned under supervision, thus combining the need for administrative and professional accountability. Importantly, workers had a repertoire of over twenty-five methods—among them diagnosis, interviewing, prognosis, planning, treatment, and reeducation. Moreover, some or all of these methods were useful for countering a host of "deviations" from "normal social life"— alcoholism, delinquency, family antagonisms, mental ill health, pauperism, and vagrancy, to name a few. The social casework agency concept encompassed the fields of child welfare, family welfare, visiting teaching, medical social work, psychiatric social work, and probation work. They accomplished this charge within administrative procedures "in accordance with accepted business standards and practice, including audits of accounts at least annually by an accredited public accountant."[60]

This characterization of the social agency was prophetic and served as a model for human service delivery over the following decades. Child guidance clinics, probation departments, mental health clinics, family planning clinics, and public welfare offices resembled the casework agency envisaged by the Milford Conference Report. Despite differences in auspices and service mandate, the fundamental elements remained intact. The social casework agency provided a service delivery model through which the emerging profession of social work could apply its skills.

Economically, the social casework agency met accountability requirements of different funding sources. In the case of private donations—corporate, individual, and foundation—the casework agency was managed by an executive officer and operated in accordance with established business practices. In the case of other charities—the Community Chest and United Way—the casework agency was under the guidance of a board of directors which upheld the best interests of the community. In the case of public [governmental] funding, the casework agency was administered on the basis of governmental regulations by the executive director who was part of the government bureaucracy. According to the needs of the professional social work community and the fiscal requirements of philanthropic and governmental funding sources, the casework agency was perceived to be professionally managed and economically efficient. Through much of the twentieth century the social casework agency was a common setting for the provision of human services, reflecting the basic principles outlined in the Milford Conference of 1923.

The Progressive Movement

A reaction to the heartlessness that characterized a large segment of American society came in the form of the Progressive movement, a social movement that was popular from the early 1900s to the First World War.

Progressive Era philosophy, intended to introduce a measure of public credibility and

Christian morality into social, political, and economic affairs, was a unique blend of social reform which encompassed anti-big business attitudes, a belief that government should regulate the public good, a strong emphasis on ethics in business and personal life, a commitment to social justice, a concern for the "common man," a strong sense of paternalism and, not surprisingly, a tendency toward jingoism. Progressives believed the state had a responsibility for protecting the interests of the public, especially people who were vulnerable. The Progressive Party, supported by the nation's most respected social workers, including Jane Addams, Lillian Wald, and Paul U. Kellogg, presented a presidential ticket in 1912.

Impressive governmental reforms were enacted during the Progressive period. For example, President Theodore Roosevelt made great strides in the areas of natural resource conservation, civil service reform, and strengthening the power of the Interstate Commerce Commission. President Woodrow Wilson's administration made major reforms in the areas of tariffs, banking, and a curb on monopolistic practices through the Clayton Antitrust Act of 1914. Other reforms enacted during Wilson's administration included better credit facilities and agricultural education for farmers, better working conditions in the Merchant Marine, a worker's compensation law for all federal civil service employees, the establishment of the eight-hour day for all workers on interstate railroads, a law excluding the products of child labor from interstate commerce, and federal aid to states for highway construction.[61]

Progressive reformers also experienced limited successes in protecting the rights of working women. By 1912 eleven states had legislated a floor under which women's wages could not fall. In 1919, Massachusetts passed a bill which limited the maximum number of hours (for most classes of working women) to 44 per week. New York followed suit in 1919 with a 54-hour week for a limited number of women workers.[62] In addition to minimum wage and maximum hour legislation, many states had enacted laws prohibiting night work for women in certain industries, as well as lifting restrictions regulating the maximum weight a woman could be required to handle.[63]

The advent of World War I helped diminish the liberal fervor that characterized the Progressive Era of the late 1800s and early 1900s. In the wake of the disillusionment that followed the war, the mood of the country became conservative. Progressive ideas were treated skeptically in the 1920s; frequently the proponents of those ideas were accused of being Bolsheviks. By 1924 the situation grew even worse: Congress had curtailed immigration, the child labor amendment was all but defeated, political repression became commonplace, many foreign radicals were deported as a result of the raids conducted by Attorney General A. Mitchell Palmer, the Ku Klux Klan was gaining strength, labor unrest exploded everywhere, and corruption in high places was rampant.[64] Americanization and intolerance became operational concepts, and even the settlement houses lost much of their sway during the conservative, post-World War I era. Despite the suffrage movement which gave women the right to vote, the 1920s was an extremely conservative period in American history.

Although we think of the 1920s as a period of prosperity, over one-third of the American population lived in poverty.[65] Many of the reforms enacted during the Progressive Era of the early 1900s were rescinded in the "Roaring Twenties." By the end of the 1920s some states had enacted widows' pensions and workers' compensation laws, but most charity still occurred by way of private social service organizations.

THE GREAT DEPRESSION AND THE MODERN WELFARE STATE

In the election of 1928 Herbert Hoover ran for president against the Catholic and democratic governor of New York State, Alfred Smith. Known as a prohibitionist and a humanitarian (due to the relief activities he was involved in at the end of World War I), Hoover handily beat Smith. Based on his strong humanitarian record and his militant Prohibitionist stance, many social workers, including Jane Addams, supported Hoover.[66]

In October 1929 the stock market crashed. A year later, 6 million men and women walked the streets looking for work. By 1932, over 600,000 were jobless in Chicago, and a million in New York City. In Cleveland, 50 percent of workers were unemployed, in Akron 60 percent, and in Toledo 80 percent of the population was looking for work. Only three years after the crash, over 100,000 workers were being fired in an average week.[67] By the early 1930s the Gross National Product (GNP)—the sum total of all the goods and services produced in the society—had dropped to one-half of what it had been prior to the depression. The national income dropped from $81 billion in 1929 to $40 billion in 1932.[68] By 1932 manufacturing output had fallen to 54 percent of what it had been in 1929, a little less than the total production in 1913. In that same year the automobile industry was operating at only one-fifth of its 1929 capacity. Steel plants operated at only 12 percent of their potential and the output of pig iron was the lowest since 1896. In addition, factory wages shrank from $12 billion in 1929 to $7 billion in 1932. Unemployment reached a high of 24 percent and, for the first time, more people emigrated from America than migrated to it (in 1932, 35,329 people emigrated to America and 103,295 left). Even the birthrate was cut almost in half—from 30 births per thousand in 1929 to 18 births per thousand in 1940. By 1932, 20 million people were on the relief rolls.[69]

In search of work, or perhaps just motion, thousands of Americans aimlessly wandered the country. In 1929 the Missouri Pacific Railroad reported 13,745 migrants; in 1931, 186,028; and by 1932, between 1 and 2 million people roamed the country.[70] The unemployed who chose to stay close to home often frequented the thousands of soup lines that sprang up across the country.

Relief under the Hoover administration proved wholly inadequate. Private charities and local governments soon exhausted their coffers. Relief payments, which in 1929 totaled $5 per week for an entire family, were cut to $2.39 in New York, and still less elsewhere. Dallas and Houston refused relief to all Hispanic and black families. Detroit slashed its relief rolls by one-third. New Orleans refused all new relief applicants, and St. Louis cut its relief rolls in half. Except for New York, Illinois, Pennsylvania, New Jersey, and Wisconsin, state governments did almost nothing to aid the victims of the depression. More than 100 cities had no relief appropriations in 1932.[71]

Having seen little of the acclaimed prosperity of the 1920s, most farmers were devastated by the Depression. American foreign trade declined from $10 billion in 1929 to $3 billion in 1932. Crop prices registered new lows: wheat fell from $1.05 a bushel in 1929 to 39 cents in 1932, corn from 81 cents to 33 cents a bushel, cotton from 17 to 6 cents a pound, and tobacco from 19 to 10 cents a pound. As a result, gross farm income fell from nearly $12 billion in 1929 to only $5 billion in 1932.[72] Farmers responded to these economic conditions with angry protests. From Pennsylvania to Nebraska, farmers banded together to prevent banks and insurance companies from foreclosing on mortgages. When sheriffs attempted to break up those actions, some farmers brandished pitchforks and hangman's nooses to make their point.

Herbert Hoover's response to the Depression was for the most part inaction. Hoover opted to rely on the voluntary social welfare sector, justifying his position on the belief that federal relief would weaken the social and moral fiber of the society, impair the credit and solvency of the government, and delay the natural forces at work to restore the economy. Moreover, according to Hoover, federal relief was illegal and a violation of states' rights.[73]

The voluntary social welfare sector responded to the depression by organizing massive fund drives but, because of the sheer scope of the problem, they proved ineffective. Although a large segment of the social work community and most voluntary social welfare agencies agreed with Hoover in his opposition to federal aid, by 1932 he was forced to propose an unemployment assistance program in which the federal government paid 80 percent of the costs. By the time Hoover was defeated by Franklin Delano Roosevelt (FDR) in the election of 1932, Hoovervilles (shantytowns sarcastically named in Hoover's honor) were erected in most large cities. Soup lines became a part of the urban landscape, economically motivated suicides were commonplace, and legendary robbers (Dillinger, Baby Face Nelson, etc.) were the rage.

When FDR assumed the presidency in 1933 he faced a country increasingly divided between right- and left-wing political factions, an industrial system experiencing convulsions in the form of violent labor strikes, a class society at its breaking point, and a banking system on the verge of collapse. As one of his first acts, FDR declared a "bank holiday." While the banks were closed, FDR put in place the FDIC program (later called FSLIC) which guaranteed depositors that the federal government would insure their deposits (up to a certain dollar amount) if a member bank became insolvent. FDR's response to the Depression involved a massive social experiment whose objectives were relief, recovery, and reform.[74] Despite the accusations made by his critics, FDR was not a socialist. The philosophy of the New Deal was neither socialistic or Marxian. In the final analysis, FDR was not a proponent of radicalism, and his New Deal programs served to salvage capitalism. Faced with an economic system at the breaking point, Roosevelt plunged into relief activities to save capitalism. In that sense, FDR was the quintessential "liberal capitalist."

Roosevelt's first task was to alleviate suffering and provide food, shelter, and clothing for the millions of unemployed workers. In 1933 Congress established the Federal Emergency Relief Administration (FERA) which distributed over $5.2 billion of emergency relief to states and local communities. In 1933 FDR initiated the National Recovery Act (NRA) which provided a comprehensive series of public works projects. Under the umbrella of the NRA, Congress instituted the Public Works Administration (later changed to the Works Progress Administration—WPA) to coordinate the system of public works. Workers employed by this make-work program built dams, bridges, and other important public structures. In 1935 the WPA was expanded to provide more employment through an emphasis on long-range projects which had a positive value for the country. WPA projects employed white- and blue-collar workers as well as unskilled laborers. The WPA ultimately cost about $11.3 billion, employed 3.2 million workers a month by 1938, and produced roads, public parks, airports, schools, post offices, and various other public buildings. In addition, the white-collar division of the WPA provided work opportunities through the Federal Writers' Project, the Federal Arts Project, and the Federal Theater Project.[75]

FDR created the Civilian Conservation Corps (CCC) and the National Youth Administration (NYA) to address the problem of unemployed youth. The purpose of the CCC was to employ poor youths (ages 17 to 23) to replant forests and to help conserve the soil. Apart from obtaining employment, the 2.5 million young men served by the CCC received a leisure-time educational program as well as vocational and academic training. The NYA, on the other hand, was designed for young adults who wanted to stay at home, and for needy high school and college students. Begun in 1935, the NYA eventually provided part-time employment for over 1.7 million young people and assisted more than 1.8 million high school and college students.

Other experiments followed suit: Congress established the Tennessee Valley Authority (TVA) in 1933, a radical technological and social experiment which brought electricity to the South, helped control flooding, reclaimed land, improved river navigation, and produced nitrates; the Farm Security Administration aided farmers and migratory workers by attempting to raise prices of farm goods; and in 1934, Congress established the Federal Housing Administration, an agency designed to provide insurance to lenders against losses on secured and unsecured loans for repairs and improvements, and on first mortages for residential property. In addition, in 1937 Congress began a slum clearance and low-income housing program under the auspices of the WPA.[76]

In 1937 Congress passed the Fair Labor Standards Act (FLSA), which established a floor for minimum wage (25 cents an hour) and a maximum work week (44 hours, and then time-and-a-half for additional hours). The FLSA also abolished child labor for those under 16. In addition, the passage of the National Labor Relations Act (NLRA) gave private-sector workers the right to collectively bargain, organize, and strike.

The apogee of FDR's New Deal was the Social Security Act of 1935. This legislation included: (1) a national old-age insurance system; (2) federal grants to states for maternal and child welfare services, relief to dependent children (ADC), vocational rehabilitation for the handicapped, medical care for crippled children, aid to the blind, and a plan to strengthen public health services; and (3) a federal-state unemployment system. Conspicuously omitted was a national health insurance plan—a policy included in virtually every other social security plan adopted by nations in the industrialized world. The Social Security Act of 1935 was clearly the most enduring of all of FDR's programs.

Although the New Deal programs were important, some argue that they did not represent a real change of direction. Most of FDR's policies were based on past employment, and thus did not help the hard-core poor who had a meager work record, if any. FDR's policies had several major effects. Federal policy was used to make income more equal (e.g., minimum wage laws, right of workers to strike and collectively bargain, etc.). The New Deal programs, especially the Social Security Act, established the framework for the modern social welfare state.

THE CONTEMPORARY SOCIAL WELFARE STATE

The end of World War II brought with it a similar kind of repression as occurred after World War I. Progressive ideas were labeled as Communist inspired, and the House Un-American Activities Committee hearings, chaired by Martin Dies, frightened away all but the most intrepid social reformers. Welfare programs also suffered. The anti-welfare reaction was so strong that some major newspapers would publish a list of welfare recipients in an attempt to shame them off the rolls. Virtually no new welfare programs were proposed, and the existing ones were in constant jeopardy. Many political leaders balked at the need for welfare programs, given the relatively healthy economy of the period.

The 1950s were marked by a kind of smugness. Americans believed that for the most part poverty had been eradicated, and even though there were small pockets of poverty, we lived in an age of affluence. The concept of a poverty-free America was ruptured by several social reformers, including Michael Harrington, whose book *The Other America: Poverty in the United States*, became a classic. Harrington and others maintained that American society encompassed a subculture of poverty. These poor were hidden from the middle classes and, like specters, they wandered through the cities, towns, and villages. This poor subculture was composed of blacks, Indians, Mexicans, and whites.[77] Harrington and others were correct, since in 1959 about 22 percent of the nation lived below the poverty level.[78]

The relative quiet of the 1950s gave way to the quasi-revolutionary spirit of the 1960s. After John F. Kennedy was assassinated in 1963, President Lyndon Johnson exploited the sentiments of the nation and declared a "War on Poverty." This War on Poverty—later changed to the Great Society—comprised many social programs designed to cure poverty in America. Driven by massive urban riots in black communities during the middle and late 1960s, Johnson's programs were aimed at empowering poor communities to arrest poverty and increase economic opportunity within their own neighborhoods. Operating under the umbrella of the Office of Economic Opportunity (OEO), various programs were tried, including Volunteers in Service to America (VISTA), a domestic peace corps; Upward Bound, a program which encouraged poor and ghetto children to attend college; a Neighborhood Youth Corps for unemployed teenagers; Operation Head Start, a program which provided preschool training for lower income children; special grants and loans to rural families and migrant workers; a comprehensive Community Action Program (CAP) designed to mobilize community resources; Legal Services Corporation; the Model Cities Program; Job Corps, a manpower program which provided job training for disadvantaged youths from 16 to 21; and the Economic Development Act of 1965, which provided states with grants and loans for public works and technical assistance. The Economic Opportunity Act of 1964 (in 1973 it was incorporated under the Comprehensive Employment and Training Act [CETA]) emphasized education and job training.

A key phrase in Johnson's Great Society program was "the maximum feasible participation of the poor," a concept which informed poor communities that they should invoke self-determination in their attempt to politically and economically empower themselves. The major thrust of Johnson's War on Poverty was focused on the belief that job creation, education, and other incentives can alleviate poverty.

By 1968 the Great Society programs had become unpopular with the American public. Despite the huge amounts of money the Johnson administration spent on the poverty problem, critics and lay voices claimed the programs were ineffective. Several causes emerge as plausible explanations for this phenomenon. For one, Johnson was faced with a costly war in Vietnam at the same time he was constructing his war on poverty. Although America was wealthy, it became increasingly clear that it could not afford to conduct two wars. In addition, confusion in Washington, inexperienced personnel, delays in funding, corrupt local politicians, intransigent bureaucrats, and ineffective community leaders all contributed to massive problems in the programs. Despite the grim post-mortem offered by subsequent scholars, however, during the Great Society period the number of people below the poverty line was cut almost in half, from about 25 percent in the early 1960s to around 12 percent by 1969.

Richard Nixon assumed the presidency in 1969 and promptly began to dismantle the Great Society. As one of his first moves, he curbed the power of the then-influential OEO. Determined to clean up the "welfare mess," Nixon proposed another type of welfare reform in 1969—a guaranteed annual income for all poor persons. Under Nixon's Family Assistance Plan (FAP), every unemployed family of four would receive $2400 a year from the federal government. The working poor would be allowed a minimum of $1600 per year until their earned income reached $4000, after which time the payments would be discontinued. In order to be eligible for assistance, the able-bodied—including women with children over three years of age—would be required to work or to be enrolled in a job training program. The program was eventually to be turned over the states.[79] Although parts of his plan were adopted, notably the Supplemental Security Income (SSI) program in 1972, for the most part the concept of a guaranteed income was rejected by Congress. One of the biggest problems with this plan involved what the minimum income should be, as well as the forced work approach.

During the relative conservatism of the 1970s a major shift in national priorities occurred. From 1965 to 1975, America's national priorities became reversed: in 1965 defense expenditures accounted for 42 percent of the federal budget while social welfare expenditures accounted for only 25 percent; by 1975 defense expenditures accounted for only 25 percent of the federal budget while social welfare outlays accounted for 43 percent. Social welfare is currently the major expenditure in the federal budget. Even in Ronald Reagan's budget of 1986, characterized by large increases in defense spending, only 29 percent was so earmarked, while 41 percent was allocated to social welfare.[80]

Beginning with Reagan's election in 1980, the years of his presidency saw a reappraisal of the welfare state. Reagan's ideological stance assumed that (1) federal government expenditures for social welfare should be minimal, (2) only those who are "truly needy" should receive welfare, and (3) welfare should be provided only on a short-term basis. As a result of Reagan's position, the American social welfare state was marked, at best, by inattention. In terms of real dollars, benefits for those on public assistance fell precipitously. Uneven economic development accelerated: while some people found themselves better off, larger segments of American society experienced greater economic hardship. Homelessness grew at unprecedented rates for a non-depression period. Real income continued to fall as higher paying industrial jobs were replaced by jobs in a burgeoning and relatively low-paid service sector. At the same time, most redistributive mechanisms, including social welfare allocations, experienced cuts or freezes. This situation was complicated by enormous budget and trade deficits that justified curtailing the welfare functions of the federal government. The parsimony of the Reagan years has fostered a rise in the number of those in poverty and the buildup of extreme social pressures, a situation that President Bush will undoubtedly have to address.

The debate over the future of the welfare system is complex and multifaceted. In the end, the struggle exists between those who want a highly restrictive welfare system and those who want an open system based on a belief in the value of institutional social welfare.

NOTES

1. Robert Morris, *Rethinking Social Welfare* (New York: Longman, 1986), pp. 7–8.
2. Karl de Schweinitz, *England's Road to Social Security* (Philadelphia: University of Pennsylvania Press, 1943).
3. Ibid.
4. Ibid.
5. Walter Trattner, *From Poor Law to Welfare State* (New York: Free Press, 1974), p. 12.
6. David Rothman and Sheila Rothman, eds., *On Their Own: The Poor in Modern America* (Reading, Mass.: Addison-Wesley, 1972).
7. Morris, *Rethinking Social Welfare*, p. 143.
8. Nathan Edward Cohen, *Social Work in the American Tradition* (New York: Holt, Rinehart and Winston, 1958), pp. 23–24.
9. Trattner, *From Poor Law to Welfare State*.
10. Morris, *Rethinking Social Welfare*, p. 153.
11. Trattner, *From Poor Law to Welfare State*, p. 62.
12. Cohen, *Social Work in the American Tradition*, p. 36.
13. Trattner, *From Poor Law to Welfare State*.
14. Ibid.
15. Alexis de Tocqueville, *Democracy in America*,

vol. 2 (New Rochelle, N.Y.: Arlington House, 1966), p. 114.

16. Ibid.

17. June Axinn and Herman Levin, *Social Welfare* (New York: Dodd, Mead, 1975), p. 129.

18. Robert Bremner, *From the Depths: The Discovery of Poverty in the United States* (New York: New York University Press, 1956).

19. David Montgomery, *Workers' Control in America* (Cambridge: Cambridge University Press, 1979).

20. Ibid.

21. Richard Hofstadter, *The Age of Reform* (New York: Vintage Books, 1955), p. 242.

22. Justin Kaplan, *Lincoln Steffens* (New York: Simon and Schuster, 1974), pp. 50–51.

23. Jacob Riis, *How the Other Half Lives* (New York: Charles Scribner and Sons, 1890), p. 15.

24. Justin Kaplan, *Lincoln Steffens*, p. 51.

25. Charles Darwin, *On the Origin of Species* (London: Murray, 1859).

26. See Herbert Spencer, *An Autobiography*, 2 vols. (New York: D. Appleton, 1904); William Graham Sumner, *Social Darwinism* (Englewood Cliffs, N.J.: Prentice-Hall, 1963); and Richard Hofstadter, *Social Darwinism in American Thought* (Boston: Beacon Press, 1959).

27. Herbert Spencer, *An Autobiography*, p. 186.

28. David Macarov, *The Design of Social Welfare* (New York: Holt, Rinehart and Winston, 1978).

29. Ibid.

30. Ibid.

31. Herbert G. Guttman, *Work, Culture and Society* (New York: Vintage Books, 1977).

32. Roy Lubove, *The Professional Altruist: The Emergence of Social Work as a Career, 1880–1930* (New York: Atheneum Books, 1975).

33. Charles Howard Hopkins, *The Rise of the Social Gospel in American Protestantism, 1865–1915* (New Haven: Yale University Press, 1940).

34. Ibid.

35. Henry F. May, *Protestant Churches in Industrial America* (New York: Octagon Books, 1963).

36. Howard Jacob Karger, *The Sentinels of Order: A Study of Social Control and the Minneapolis Settlement House Movement, 1915–1950* (Lanham, Md.: University Press of America, 1987).

37. Lubove, *The Professional Altruist*, pp. 1–21.

38. Ibid., p. 14.

39. Axinn and Levin, *Social Welfare*, p. 100.

40. Charles Loring Brace, *The Dangerous Classes of New York* (New York: Wynkoop and Hallenbeck, 1872), pp. 151–52.

41. Jean Quam, "Charles Loring Brace," *Encyclopedia of Social Work*, 18th ed. (Silver Spring, Md.: NASW, 1987), p. 916.

42. Martha Nelson Vogt and Christina Vogt, *Searching for Home* (Martha Nelson Vogt and Christina Vogt, 1062 Edison N. W., Grand Rapids, Mich. 49504, 1979).

43. Hofstadter, *The Age of Reform*, p. 211.

44. Allen F. Davis, *American Heroine: The Life and Legend of Jane Addams* (New York: Oxford University Press, 1973), p. 57.

45. Ibid., p. 92.

46. "Biographies," *Encyclopedia of Social Work*, 18th ed. (Silver Spring, Md.: NASW, 1987), pp. 913–36.

47. John Hope Franklin, *From Slavery to Freedom* (New York: Knopf, 1979), p. 288.

48. *Constitution of the Sons and Daughters of Zion*, author's collection.

49. Addie Louise Joyner Butler, *The Distinctive Black College: Talladega, Tuskegee, and Morehouse* (Metuchen, N.J.: Scarecrow Press, 1977), pp. 17–18.

50. Ibid., p. 102.

51. John Hope Franklin, *From Slavery to Freedom*, pp. 318–321.

52. H. L. Weissman, "Settlements and Community Centers," *Encyclopedia of Social Work*, 18th ed. (Silver Spring, Md.: NASW, 1987).

53. Mary Richmond, *Social Diagnosis* (New York: Russell Sage Foundation, 1917).

54. H. L. Mencken, *Minority Report* (New York: Knopf, 1956), p. 153.

55. Maryann Syers, "Abraham Flexner," *Encyclopedia of Social Work,* 18th ed. (Silver Spring, Md.: NASW, 1987), p. 923.

56. National Association of Social Workers, *Social Casework: Generic and Specific* (Washington, D.C.: NASW, 1974), p. 27.

57. Walter Trattner, *From Poor Law to Welfare State*, pp. 221–22.

58. Larry Hirschhorn, "The Social Service Crisis and the New Subjectivity," (Berkeley, Calif.: University of California, Berkeley, Institute of

Urban and Regional Development, December 1974).

59. Roy Lubove, *The Professional Altruist*, pp. 172, 185.

60. National Association of Social Workers, *Social Casework*, pp. 16–50.

61. See Cohen, *Social Work in the American Tradition*; and William E. Leuchtenburg, *The Perils of Prosperity, 1914–32* (Chicago: University of Chicago Press, 1958).

62. Clarke A. Chambers, *Seedtime of Reform: American Social Service and Social Action, 1918–1933* (Ann Arbor, Mich.: University of Michigan Press, 1967).

63. Hofstadter, *Age of Reform*.

64. See Karger, *Sentinels*, and Chambers, *Seedtime*.

65. Chambers, idem.

66. Ibid.

67. Leuchtenburg, *Perils of Prosperity*, p. 247.

68. Cohen, *Social Work in the American Tradition*, p. 161.

69. Ibid., p. 162.

70. Leuchtenburg, *Perils of Prosperity*, p. 254.

71. Ibid., pp. 252–53.

72. Ibid., p. 248.

73. Trattner, *From Poor Law to Welfare State*, p. 230.

74. Cohen, *Social Work in the American Tradition*, p. 169.

75. Ibid.

76. Ibid.

77. Michael Harrington, *The Other America: Poverty in the United States* (New York: Penguin Books, 1962).

78. Robert Morris, *Social Policy of the American Welfare State* (New York: Longman, 1985), p. 63.

79. Trattner, *From Poor Law to Welfare State*.

80. Diane M. DiNitto and Thomas R. Dye, *Social Welfare: Politics and Public Policy* (Englewood Cliffs, N.J.: Prentice-Hall, 1987).

CHAPTER 4

The Making
of Governmental Policy

This chapter describes the process by which governmental policy is made, examines the influence of various social groups on the policy process, and explores the phases of the policy process with particular attention focused on the role of key organizations. The public policy process is important because many social welfare policies are established by government, and decisions by federal and state agencies have a direct bearing on the administration and funding of social welfare programs that assist millions of Americans.

In an open, democratic society, it is desirable that public policy reflect the interest of all citizens to the greatest extent possible. For a variety of reasons, however, this ideal is not evident in the making of governmental policy. While many Americans have the right to participate in the establishment of public policy, they often fail to do so. Governmental policy may be perceived as being too far removed from the daily activities of citizens, or too complicated, to warrant the type of coordinated and persistent efforts necessary to alter public policy. Moreover, many Americans are unable to directly affect governmental policy, as in the case of children and the emotionally impaired who must rely on others to speak on their behalf. Consequently, governmental policy does not necessarily reflect the interests—or for our purposes, the welfare—of the public even though it is intended for that purpose.

The extent to which governmental policy reflects the concerns of one group of citizens while neglecting others is ultimately a question of power and influence. Power is derived from several sources and these have attracted the attention of philosophers over the centuries. Plato questioned the organization and execution of civil authority of the state. Machiavelli focused on the limits of discretionary authority exercised by leaders of the state. During the Enlightenment, the social contract philosophers—Hobbes, Locke, and Rousseau—considered the moral obligation of the state toward its citizens. Later, as the industrial revolution proceeded unchecked, Karl Marx attributed inequities in influence to control over the means of production. Subsequently, as governmental authority expanded to ameliorate the economic and social dislocation brought on by industrial capitalism, Max Weber identified bureaucratic administrators as a pivotal group. As the postindustrial era unfolded, such social critics as Marshall McLuhan and Alvin Toffler emphasized how information can be processed and used as a source of power and influence.

Clearly, the moral, legal, economic, political, and technological components of influence make it a complicated subject. As these relate to governmental policy formation, however, three elements become evident: the social stratification of the society, the phases through which policy is formulated, and the organizational entities that have evolved as instrumental in the decision-making process. These will be described and charted as they pertain to social welfare policy.

SOCIAL STRATIFICATION

A variety of schemes have been presented to differentiate groups with influence from those lacking it. The most simple of these consists of a dual stratification, such as capitalists and the proletariat presented by Marx. A stratification common to Americans is in three parts: an upper class, a middle class, and a lower class. Placement of individuals in the appropriate class usually occurs on the basis of income, education, and occupational status. This three-part stratification is limited in its capacity to explain very much about American social welfare, however. If asked, most Americans identify themselves as middle class, even if by objective criteria they belong to another class. Further, the designation "lower class" is not particularly informative about the social conditions of a large portion of the population about which welfare professionals are concerned.[1] Finally, the term "*lower* class" is pejorative, connoting a social station that is valued less than others.

A more informative stratification has been developed by a social psychologist, Dexter Dunphy, who identified six social groups. Dunphy suggested that these groups differed according to several factors, the most important of which were wealth, internal solidarity, and the control over the environment. This stratification appears in Table 4.1.[2]

As this social stratification illustrates, some groups—executives and organizers—are much more able to influence the environment, while other groups—erratics and apathetics—have very little influence. This has important implications for social welfare, since those who are of lower status tend to be the recipients of welfare benefits, which are the product of a social policy process in which they do not participate. The way in which these groups influence the social policy process will be discussed in greater detail.

THE POLICY PROCESS

Questions of governmental decision making often focus on two aspects: the degree of change in policy represented by a decision and the rationality of the decision. Governmental policies vary in the extent to which they depart from the status quo. While it can be argued that, in the final analysis, there are no new ideas, there *are* new governmental policies which have enormous implications for certain groups. Few could dispute that the Social Security Act and the Civil Rights Act were radical departures from the status quo and substantially changed the circumstances of the aged and blacks. On the other hand, such radical departures are dependent on a relatively unique set of circumstances, and occur rarely. As Charles Lindblom has observed, the vast majority of decision making is "incremental," representing marginal improvements in social policy.[3] More recently, Amitai Etzioni has suggested the concept of "mixed-scanning" to describe how decisions are derived. According to Etzioni, decision makers take a quick overview of a situation, weigh a range of alternatives—some incremental, some radical—ultimately selecting the one that satisfies the most important factors impinging at the moment.[4] While significant changes in social policy are possible, they are infrequent: most social policy changes consist of relatively minor technical adjustments in program administration and budgeting.

The rationality of a decision refers to the degree of its internal coherence and the extent to which it accomplishes its intended objectives. Paradoxically, most governmental policy is irrational when evaluated by these standards. Inevitably, public policy is elaborated to take into account the interests of various groups that are concerned about its effects. It is not unusual for descriptions of governmental policy to require dozens of pages of text, and for its various provisions to be contradictory. For example, the 28-page Immigration Reform and Control Act of 1986 reflects the concerns of three groups: undocumented residents, most of whom are Hispanic; truck farmers who require migratory laborers; and, the Immigration and Naturalization Service (INS) which regulates immigration to the United States.[5] Because the

TABLE 4.1. Social Stratification

Name of Group	Examples	Characteristics
conservative groups (old wealth)	upper elites, the independently wealthy, large stockholders	ownership of resources is the main source of power; control over goals is very high, but control over means is through organizers
organizer groups (executives)	top administrators in business, government, the military	organizational solidarity facilitates effective policy implementation; some control over goals and a high degree of control over means
cabal groups (professionals)	middle-level managers, technical experts, private practitioners, community leaders	environment encourages limited solidarity; control over means is high, and goal setting can be influenced if collective action is undertaken
strategic groups (organized workers)	semiskilled workers, civic and political clubs, social action organizations	environment encourages solidarity, groups have some control over the means by which goals are realized
erratic groups (working/welfare poor)	temporary and part-time workers earning minimum wage and who use welfare as a wage supplement	a subjugated position with no control over the environment; frustration is shared and irrational, explosive behavior results
apathetic groups (underclass)	unemployables and illiterates; disabled substance abusers; itinerants, drifters, migrant workers	a subjugated position with no control over the environment; a sense of failure coupled with mobility reduces social interaction and leads to retreatism

Source: Dexter C. Dunphy, *The Primary Group: A Handbook for Analysis and Field Research*, © 1972, pp. 42–44. Reprinted by permission of Prentice-Hall, Inc. Englewood Cliffs, NJ.

interests of these groups differ greatly, various provisions of the Act are sometimes inconsistent. For example, in interpreting the Act, the INS has decided that children of families in which one parent failed to qualify for amnesty faced deportation, although single-parent families in which the parent qualified would be allowed to stay in the United States.[6] Hispanic groups were outraged at this interpretation since it encouraged families to break up in order for parents to qualify for amnesty. Because of the importance of the family in Hispanic culture, this interpretation contributed to the reluctance of undocumented workers to apply for the amnesty program. Meanwhile, some truck farmers watched crops go unharvested because migrant workers were not coming to the United States due to the confusion over the provisions of the Act.

Despite such irrationality, social policy does order human affairs and, to that extent, the logic of the policy is of great significance.

There are two basic forms of rationality that justify social policy: bureaucratic rationality and market rationality.[7] Bureaucratic rationality refers to the ordering of social affairs by governmental agencies. Since Max Weber's work on the modern bureaucracy, this form of rationality has been central to governmental policy. According to bureaucratic rationality, government civil servants can objectively define social problems, develop strategies to address them, and deploy programs in an equitable and nonpartisan manner. Bureaucratic rationality takes its authority from power vested in the state, and its bureaucracies have become predominant in social welfare at the federal (through the Department of Health and Human Services) and the state levels. A characteristic of bureaucratic rationality is a reliance on social planning. Several social planning methods have been developed to anticipate future problems and deal with existing ones. Generally, these can be classified under two headings: techno-methodological and sociopolitical.

Techno-methodological planning methods emphasize data bases from which projections about future program needs can be derived. Such methods place a premium on relatively sophisticated social research methods and work best with programs which can be quantified and routinized, as in the case of cash payments through the Social Security program. Sociopolitical approaches to planning are more interactive, involving groups likely to be affected by a program. Community development activities, for example, frequently feature planners bringing together neighborhood residents, businesspersons, and local officials to create a plan that is relevant to the needs of a particular area.[8] Regardless of planning method, it is important to recognize the power and influence that governmental agencies have assumed in social welfare policy, much of it by exercise of bureaucratic rationality.

Market rationality refers to reliance on the supply and demand of goods and services as a method of ordering social affairs. While this may appear on the surface to be antithetical to the meaning of rationality, in fact, a high degree of social ordering occurs within capitalism. Such organization is implicit in the very idea of a market, a large number of prospective consumers which business seeks to exploit. In a modern market economy, the very success of a business will depend on the ability of managers to survey the market, merchandise goods and services, shape consumer preferences through advertising, and reduce competition by buying or outmaneuvering competitors. Of course, market rationality is not a panacea for provision of social welfare because the marketplace is not particularly responsive to those who do not fully participate in it—racial minorities, women, children, the aged, and the handicapped. Yet, market rationality cannot be dismissed as a rationale for delivering social welfare benefits. Some 132 million Americans get their health and welfare needs met through employer-pro-

vided benefits that are ultimately derived from the market.[9] Another example of the market providing social welfare benefits is the practice by governmental jurisdictions of contracting out particular human services to private sector businesses, usually with the rationale of reducing costs by taking advantage of efficiencies associated with the market.[10]

As a result of differences between reliance on government or the market to assure social welfare, acrimony frequently accompanies the policy process. If the United States has a serious problem of unemployment among adolescents and young adults, for example, what is the most effective policy response? Proponents of market rationality prefer a market strategy that eliminates the minimum wage so that employers can hire more young workers for the same amount but at lower wage levels. Proponents of bureaucratic rationality opt for a governmental public works program that assures constructive activities at an adequate wage. In the absence of definitive data on the most desirable course of action, decisions are often made on the basis of some loosely defined, intended outcome. And rationality—of a bureaucratic or market nature—often features prominently in establishing a policy that intends a particular outcome.

With these clarifications in mind, the policy process can be divided into four stages—formulation, legislation, implementation, and evaluation. While these terms are somewhat self-explanatory, during the decision-making process different organizational entities exert their influence, making the process an uneven one which is frequently characterized by fits of starts and stops. Organizations correspond to the stratification groups that figure prominently in their organizational activities and thereby in the policy process.

Formulation

Prior to the nineteenth century it would have been accurate to state that policy formulation began with the legislative phase. Clearly this was intended by the drafters of the Constitution, but theirs was an agricultural society with comparatively little institutional specialization. With industrialization, many complexities were injected into the society and eventually, special institutions emerged to assist the legislature in evaluating social conditions and preparing policy options. Eventually, even Constitutionally-established bodies, such as Congress, lapsed into a reactive role, largely responsive to other entities that formulated policy.[11] Initially, institutions of higher education provided this technical intelligence to assist the legislative branch, and some still do. For example, the University of Wisconsin Institute for Research on Poverty provides analyses on important welfare policies.[12]

That legislators at the federal level—as well as those in larger states—would rely on experts to assess social conditions and develop policy options is not surprising, given that each legislator must attend to multiple committee and subcommittee assignments that require expertise in particular matters, at the same time contending with the general concerns of a large constituency. A typical day in the life of a legislator has been reconstructed by Charles Peters, a long-time Washington observer:

> The most striking feature of a congressman's life is its hectic jumble of votes, meetings, appointments, and visits from folks from back home who just drop by. From an 8 A.M. breakfast conference with a group of union leaders, a typical morning will take him to his office around 9, where the waiting room will be filled with people who want to see him. From 9 until 10:30 or so, he will try to give the impression that he is devoting his entire attention to a businessman from his state with a tax problem; to a delegation protesting their town's loss of air or rail service; to a constituent and his three children, who are in town for the day and want to say hello; and to a couple of staff members whose morale will collapse if they don't have five minutes alone to go over es-

> sential business with him. As he strives to project one-on-one sincerity to all these people, he is fielding phone calls at the rate of one every five minutes and checking a press release that has to get out in time to make the afternoon papers in his district.

> He leaves this madhouse to go to a committee meeting, accompanied by his legislative aide, who tries to brief him on the business before the committee meeting begins. The meeting started at 10, so he struggles to catch the thread of questioning, while a committee staff member whispers in his ear. And so the day continues.

> The typical day...usually ends around 11:30 P.M., as the congressman leaves an embassy party, at which he has been hustling as if it were a key precinct on election eve. He is too tired to talk about any but the most trivial matters, too tired usually to do anything but fall into bed and go to sleep.[13]

As a result of competing demands, legislators pay somewhat less attention to the policy process than may be their public image, leaving much to their staffs. Even then, public policy tends to get short shrift. Because reelection is a primary concern for legislators, their staffs are frequently assigned to solve the relatively minor problems presented by constituents. In fact, placating unhappy constituents had become so prominent a concern that one legislative observer noted that constituency services had become "more important than issues" for representatives.[14]

Gradually, institutions have begun to specialize in providing the social intelligence necessary for policy formulation. These policy institutes, or "think tanks" as they are sometimes called, now wield substantial influence in the social policy process. Not unlike prestigious colleges, think tanks maintain multidisciplinary staffs of scholars who prepare position papers on a range of social issues. With multimillion dollar budgets and connections with national and state capitals, think tanks are well positioned to shape social policy. Generally, finan-

Institute for Policy Studies	Urban Institute	Brookings Institution	American Enterprise Institute	Hoover Institution	Heritage Foundation

←———→
liberal   conservative
(left)   (right)

Figure 4.1. Ideological Continuum

cial support is derived from wealthy individuals and corporations which have a particular ideological inclination, a fact which is evident in the types of think tanks they support. Several of the prominent policy institutes are located on the ideological continuum in Figure 4.1.

Within policy institutes, prominent scholars, usually identified as senior fellows, hold endowed chairs, having often served in cabinet level positions within the executive branch. When Republican administrations come into power, large numbers of senior fellows from conservative policy institutes assume cabinet appointments, while their Democratic counterparts return to liberal institutes where senior chairs await them. For junior staff, an appointment in a think tank can provide invaluable experience in how the governmental policy process actually works. It is, however, important to recognize that think tanks are private, nongovernmental institutions that influence public policy.

Through most of this century, a generation of largely liberal policy institutes—such as the Brookings Institution—contributed to the formulation of governmental welfare policy. Their role was essentially passive in that they provided technical expertise to legislators and governmental agencies upon request. By the mid-1970s, however, a second generation of conservative policy institutes—such as the American Enterprise Institute and the Heritage Foundation—moved aggressively forward, shaping a public philosophy more consistent with their values. The elections of Ronald Reagan and George Bush did much to further the influence of these organizations, and the works of scholars from these policy institutes became important to the implementation and continuation of the "Reagan revolution."[15] A third generation of policy institutes has emerged more recently to promote programs for the poor. The Children's Defense Fund, the Center on Budget and Policy Priorities, and the National Center on Policy and Practice (associated with NASW) are efforts to reassert the needs of the disadvantaged in social welfare policy.[16] Their success in this regard remains to be seen.

Legislation

The legislative phase involves two primary groups: the legislature and special interest groups (often called advocacy groups in social welfare). The interaction of these groups is frequently intriguing, as Eric Redman's *The Dance of Legislation* portrays so well. With the exception of Nebraska, which has a unicameral legislature, all states and the federal government have a legislature composed of two chambers. Legislators are appointed to committees and subcommittees usually according to their particular interests. An important and often unappreciated component of the legislative phase is the role played by the staffs of committees and subcommittees. Legislative staffers are definitive experts in the subject area of a committee and are highly prized as lobbyists for special interest groups.[17] As a result of increasing complexity in the policy process, the number of legislative staff has multiplied; 24,000 staff members now serve Congress, more than double the number a decade earlier.[18] Committees are the loci of testimony on issues, and legislative hearings provide official (and sometimes the only) input from the public on some matters. Accordingly, representatives of advocacy groups make it a point to testify before certain committees in order to assure that their views are heard. At the federal level, the primary committees dealing with social welfare in 1988, along with the names of their chairpersons, are listed below.[19]

Senate

- Finance Committee—Lloyd Bentsen
  Subcommittees: Health; Social Security; Family Policy
- Agriculture, Nutrition and Forestry— Patrick Leahy
  Subcommittees: Nutrition; Investigations
- Appropriations—Quentin Burdick
  Subcommittees: Labor; Human Services; Education
- Labor and Human Resources—Ted Kennedy
  Subcommittees: Aging; Children; Family; Drugs and Alcoholism; Employment and Productivity; Handicapped; Labor
- Special Aging—John Melcher

House of Representatives

- Ways and Means—Dan Rostenkowski
  Subcommittees: Health; Public Assistance and Unemployment Compensation; Social Security
- Education and Labor—Augustus Hawkins
  Subcommittee: Human Resources
- Appropriations—Jamie Whitten
  Subcommittees: Labor; Health and Human Service; Education
- Aging—Edward Roybal
- Children, Youth, and Families—

George Miller
Hunger—Mickey Leland

The process by which an idea becomes legislation is complex. The concern of a legislator is first developed into a legislative proposal and usually printed in the *Congressional Record*. Because legislators have a party affiliation and a constituency, their proposals reflect their priorities. Usually, several legislators will prepare proposals that are important to similar constituencies, assuring that all sides of an issue are aired. Through subtle interaction of ideas, the media, and legislative leadership, one proposal—usually a synthesis of several—is presented as a policy alternative. Other legislators are asked to sign on as cosponsors and the measure is officially introduced. After it is assigned to the appropriate committee, hearings are held, and the committee convenes to "mark up" the legislation so that it incorporates the concerns of committee members who have heard public testimony. Under propitious circumstances, the legislation is forwarded to the full body of the chamber which must approve it. While being approved by the full body of one chamber, a similar bill is often introduced in the other where it begins a parallel process. Differences in the legislation approved by each chamber are ironed out in a conference committee. The proposed legislation becomes law after it is signed by the chief executive, or by a two-thirds vote of each legislative chamber, if the executive vetoes the bill. This process is always tortuous and usually unsuccessful. During each of the past several Congresses, about 20,000 bills have been introduced in the House of Representatives and, of that number, fewer than 5 percent have become law.[20] The eventual enactment of legislation under these conditions is a true testament to legislative leadership.

Throughout the process, advocacy groups attempt to shape the proposal so that it is more congruent with their interests. Large interest groups can exert almost continuous pressure on legislators by establishing political action committees (PACs). Through PACs, campaign contributions are funneled to candidates who reflect the priorities of the interest group—a legal exercise of influence that has increased dramatically. In 1974, 608 PACs contributed $8.5 million to congressional campaigns; but by 1986, 4157 PACs were showing their muscle by donating $132.2 million. Most PACs are established by the corporate sector and reflect policy preferences that are relatively conservative.[21] Less well-funded are PACs established by labor and welfare-advocacy groups. In conjunction with the National Association of Social Workers, Political Action for Candidate Election (PACE) makes contributions to candidates for national office who profess positions similar to those of the social work professional association. In 1984 PACE distributed over $250,000 to candidates for national office.[22]

Lest legislators become forgetful of the concerns of specific interest groups, many organizations hire career lobbyists to represent them. By 1987 some 23,011 lobbyists had registered, as required by law, to work the halls of Congress.[23] Limited by meager resources, social welfare advocacy groups usually rely on volunteer lobbyists. In addition to NASW, there are several advocacy groups within social welfare which have been instrumental in advancing legislation to assist vulnerable populations— among them, the National Conference on Social Welfare, the American Public Welfare Association, the Child Welfare League of America, the National Association for the Advancement of Colored People, the National Urban League, the National Assembly of Voluntary Health and Welfare Associations, the American Association of Retired Persons, and the National Organization for Women. Despite the number of welfare advocacy organizations and their successful record in evolving more comprehensive social legislation, changes in the policy process are making their work more difficult. Increases in the number of governmental agencies as well as their staffs make it difficult to track policy developments in addition to changes in administrative procedures. Worse, the escalating cost of influencing social policy, evident in the number of paid lobbyists and the contributions lavished about by PACs, is simply beyond the means of welfare advocacy organizations. As one Democratic candidate for the Senate lamented, "only the well-heeled have PACs— not the poor, the unemployed, the minorities, or even most consumers."[24]

This is not to say that proponents of social justice are ineffectual. Despite their disadvantageous status, welfare advocacy groups were able to mobilize grass-roots support to beat back some of the more regressive proposals of the Reagan presidency. In the early 1980s, for example, scholars from the conservative Cato Institute and the Heritage Foundation proposed cutting the Social Security program. They were trounced by an effective lobbying campaign by the American Association of Retired Persons and the leadership of octogenarian Congressman Claude Pepper. Unfortunately, other social welfare programs did not fare as well. At the same time as Social Security was spared from budget cuts, social programs for the poor were reduced by significant margins.

Implementation

Simply because a policy has been enacted does not necessarily mean it will be implemented. Often governmental policy fails to include adequate authority, personnel, or funding to accomplish its stated purpose. This is a chronic problem for social welfare programs. It is also possible that governmental policy is not enforced even after it has been established. Many states have correctional and mental health institutions operating under court supervision because judges have agreed with social advocates that institutions are not in compliance with state or federal law. In another instance, full compliance with the civil rights and affirmative action policies was not sought during the Reagan presidency because the Justice Department found these policies disagreeable.

Under the best of circumstances, implementation is problematic. In a book with a telling subtitle—*Implementation: How Great Expectations in Washington are Dashed in Oakland: Or, Why It's Amazing that Federal Programs Work at All. This Being a Saga of the Economic Development Administration as Told by Two Sympathetic Observers Who Seek to Build Morals on a Foundation of Ruined Hopes*—Jeffrey Pressman and Aaron Wildavsky recount an endeavor to reconstruct the inner city of Oakland, California. The Oakland Project was a collaborative effort involving the Economic Development Administration (EDA), city officials, and faculty of the University of California.

> Congress appropriated the necessary funds, the approval of city officials was obtained, and the program was announced to the public amidst the usual fanfare. Yet, years later, construction had been partially completed, business loans had died entirely, and the results in terms of minority employment were meager and disappointing.[25]

Of $23 million appropriated for the Oakland Project, only $3 million had been spent within the first three years—and that for an overpass to the coliseum and architect's fees. Ironically, the project encountered no extraordinary obstacles. "If one is always looking for unusual circumstances and dramatic events," the authors concluded, "he cannot appreciate how difficult it is to make the ordinary happen."[26]

If implementation is trying in the normal course of events, it is that much more difficult given the disaffection of the public for governmental institutions. The episodic nature of public endorsement of governmental institutions has been studied by Albert O. Hirschman, who investigated the relationship between "private interest and public action" in *Shifting Involvements*. According to Hirschman, public endorsement of governmental institutions is a fundamental problem for industrialized capitalist societies which emphasize individual competitiveness, while generating social and economic dislocations that require collective action. "Western societies appear to be condemned to long periods of privatization during which they live through an impoverished 'atrophy of public meanings,'" Hirschman observes, "followed by spasmodic outbursts of 'publicness' that are hardly likely to be constructive."[27] Disenchantment with governmental solutions to social problems makes public welfare programs vulnerable to their critics, leading to reductions in staff and fiscal support, often followed by an escalation in the social problem for which the social program was initially designed. Thus, the episodic nature of public support for programs designed to alleviate social problems further impedes effective implementation. A classic example of the cyclical nature of public policy appears in immigration legislation. In response to the estimated 12 million undocumented workers in the United States, the Immigration Reform and Control Act of 1986 allowed aliens who had been in the country before January 1, 1982, to apply for amnesty. Significantly, the amnesty provision was open for only one year, during which but half of the 4 million aliens thought eligible for amnesty applied. By the summer of 1988, hundreds of amnesty processing offices established by the Immigration and Naturalization Service (INS) were closed, not only leaving a large number of aliens ineligible for amnesty, but also further contributing to the gradual buildup of the undocumented population. As the number of undocumented workers swells, Congress will once again be faced with the legalization problem and, in all likelihood, will authorize the INS to reopen amnesty processing offices. To many welfare advocates, this opening and closing of immigration processing facilities is not only inhumane, but also a foolish waste of administrative resources.

In some instances, public dissatisfaction with governmental programs has been exploited by astute politicians to virtually paralyze welfare activities. Richard Nixon attempted to cut welfare expenditures by impounding federal funds. Although the Supreme Court ruled this unconstitutional, the move effectively stymied programs for months. Taking a lesson from this, Ronald Reagan appointed cabinet level officers who attempted to eliminate the very departments for which they had responsibility. In some instances, they reduced their department's influence by decimating programs through substantial reductions in funding and staff requests submitted to Congress. The politicization of the higher levels of government service represents a departure from a long-standing tradition. Until very recently, a high-level appointment in government service was viewed as a public service and an obligation owed the society for success in private life. The stewardship implied by this tradition acknowledged the validity of programs even though they may be personally distasteful, because they were established through the legislative process. Under these circumstances, implementation was more feasible than under conditions where the executive branch has polemicized the administration to such a degree that legislative intent is disregarded. Thus, appointed bureau heads have substantial influence over social policy through their control over the means by which programs are implemented.

Evaluation

The expansion of governmental welfare policies has spawned a veritable industry in program evaluation. Stung by abuses of the executive branch during Watergate and the Vietnam War, Congress established additional oversight agencies to review federal programs.[28] As a result, multiple units within the executive and legislative branches of government have the evaluation of programs as their primary mission. At the federal level, the most important of these include the Government Accounting Office (GAO), the Office of Management and Budget (OMB), the Congressional Budget Office (CBO), and the Congressional Research Service (CRS). State governments have similar units. In addition, departments have evaluation units that monitor program activities for which they are responsible. Finally, federal and state levels of government commonly contract with non-governmental organizations for evaluations of specific programs. As a result, many universities provide important research services to government. More recently, private consulting firms have entered the field, often hiring former governmental officials and capitalizing on their connections in order to secure research contracts. Of course, any politicization of the research process is frowned upon because it raises questions about the impartiality of evaluations. Is a former governmental official willing to assess rigorously a program that is part of an agency in which he or she was employed in the past, or would like to be employed in the future? Questions about the validity of evaluation studies because of the closeness between governmental agencies and research firms have become so common that the consulting firms located near the expressway surrounding Washington, D.C., are known as "the beltway bandits."

Investigations by program evaluation organizations can be characterized as applied research (as opposed to "pure" research) with the objective being to optimize program operations. As a result of this emphasis on the function of programs, evaluation studies frequently focus on waste, cost-effectiveness, and goal attainment. Due to the contradictory objectives of many welfare policies, the constant readjustments in programs, and the limitations in the art of evaluation research, evaluations frequently conclude that any given program has mixed results. Rarely does a program evaluation provide a clear indication for future action. Often the results of program evaluations are used by critics and defenders alike to either dismantle or advance programs. The very inconclusiveness of program evaluation contributes to the partisan use to which evaluation research can be put. It is not uncommon for decision makers to engage in statistical arguments that have a great influence in social welfare policy. Of the recent "stat wars," several relate directly to social welfare. One example is whether underemployed and discouraged workers should be included in the unemployment rate. Currently, the Department of Labor defines as unemployed only those who are out of work and looking for jobs, and considers part-time workers as employed. As a result, many blacks, Hispanics, young adults, and women are not considered unemployed even though advocates for these groups contend that they are not fully employed. Liberals argue that by including the underemployed and discouraged workers in the unemployment rate, it would become a more accurate measure of the employment experience of disadvantaged groups. Conservatives argue that the employment rate is not a good indicator of employment opportunity, citing the millions of undocumented workers who come to the United States every year illegally to take menial jobs. Further, including underemployed and discouraged workers would increase the unemployment rate by as much as fifty percent, and would prove unacceptably expensive since extensions in the number of quarters during which workers are eligible for unemployment compensation are tied to the unemployment rate.

IMPLICATIONS FOR SOCIAL WELFARE

If the governmental decision-making process is somewhat irregular and irrational, it is also unrepresentative. As Figure 4.2 illustrates, groups in the upper levels of the social stratification populate the institutions through which policy is made. In the case of welfare policy, welfare beneficiaries must adjust to rules established by other social groups.

The primary players in the social policy game are organizers (executives) and cabals (professionals). Conservatives (old wealth) are able to opt out, leaving their social obligations in the hands of organizers. As the social stratification is descended, the remaining groups have less influence on governmental policy. The interests of these groups is left in the hands of maverick professionals who work through advocacy organizations, although occasional unrest on the part of erratic (working/welfare poor) groups results in increased welfare benefits.

The lack of influence on the part of lower socioeconomic groups in the social policy process is virtually built into governmental decision making. The term "non-decision-making" has been coined to describe this phenomenon—the capacity to keep the interests of some groups off the decision-making agenda.[29] Non-decision-making has a long history in the United States; generations of blacks and women were legally excluded from decision making prior to emancipation and suffrage. More recent attempts to increase the influence of disadvantaged groups in decision making have not been well received. Perhaps the best known example of this occurred during the War on Poverty when poor people were to be assured "maximum feasible participation" in the Community Action Program (CAP). Even though this was interpreted to mean that one-third of the members of CAP boards of directors must be poor people—a seemingly reasonable expectation—the militancy of poor people in some cities at the time led to utter chaos in many CAPs. As a result of pressure from mayors and other officials, this requirement was rescinded in order to make CAPs more compliant.[30] Since then, the representation of lower socioeconomic groups in decision making has been limited, for all practical purposes, to an advisory capacity —if it is incorporated at all.

The governmental policy process also poses problems for administrators and practitioners. Policies frequently reflect assumptions about the human condition that may be reasonable to the upper socioeconomic groups that make them, but bear little resemblance to the reality of the lower socioeconomic groups that are supposed to be beneficiaries. For example, child support enforcement policy assumes that fathers of children on the Aid to Families with Dependent Children program have the kind of regular, well-paying jobs that would allow them to meet the amounts of their court orders, when often their jobs are intermittent and low-wage. Consequently, support payments to children who are dependent on welfare are below the collection level (15.7 percent of cases in 1986) preferred by policy makers.[31] To cite another example, workfare programs assume that youths want to complete their education and gain meaningful employment, when their socialization often insists that school and work are irrelevant, and having a child may be the most meaningful thing they can do.

It is not surprising, then, that welfare programs are not well received by many of the people who depend on them. Instead of being grateful, beneficiaries are frequently resentful. In turn, upper-income taxpayers find this apparent ingratitude offensive and are inclined to make programs more punitive. Ironically, beneficiaries of welfare programs tend to respond to punitive policies with indifference and defiance because, for many of them, welfare programs have never been particularly helpful. This perception is occasionally validated when—due to exceptional circumstances—someone from an upper socioeconomic group falls into the social safety net and suddenly appreciates the importance of many welfare programs for daily survival.

Not all welfare programs are perceived in such a negative light. Generally, programs that benefit persons solidly in the working class fare better. The social insurance programs, such as Social Security, Unemployment Compensation, and Medicare are usually regarded more highly by beneficiaries. Of course, the insurance programs require prior payment into the program in order to claim benefits later, so they are designed to be different from the means-tested programs intended for the poor.

A particular consequence of governmental policy making falls on the shoulders of welfare professionals. "Workers on the front lines of the welfare state find themselves in a corrupted world of service," wrote Michael Lipsky in his award-winning *Street-Level Bureaucracy*. According to Lipsky, "Workers find that the best way to keep demand within manageable proportions is to deliver a consistently inaccessible or inferior product."[32] In response to the irrelevance often characteristic of governmental welfare policies, personnel in public welfare offices frequently deny benefits to people who are eligible for them, a process labeled "bureaucratic disentitlement."[33] It should come as no surprise, then, that public welfare programs mandated by governmental policy have acquired an undesirable reputation within the professional community. The Executive Director of the California Chapter of NASW candidly stated that "Public social services are being abandoned by MSW social workers. It seems to be employment of last resort."[34] Another veteran observer was even more graphic: "To work in a public agency today is to work in a bureaucratic hell."[35] Within the context of public welfare it is not surprising to find that "burnout" has become pervasive among welfare professionals. The inadequacy of public welfare policies for beneficiaries and professionals is an unfortunate consequence of the governmental policy process as it is currently structured.

Making the process by which public policy is made more representative is a primary concern of welfare advocates. Since the Civil Rights Movement, blacks and the poor have recognized the power of the ballot, and voter registration has become an important strategy for advancing the influence of these groups. Following this strategy, the Center for Participation in Democracy set as its goal the registration of 1 million voters in California prior to the 1988 national election.[36] The registration of Hispanics in the Southwest has been the mission of the Southwest Voter Research Institute, founded by the late Willie Velasquez.

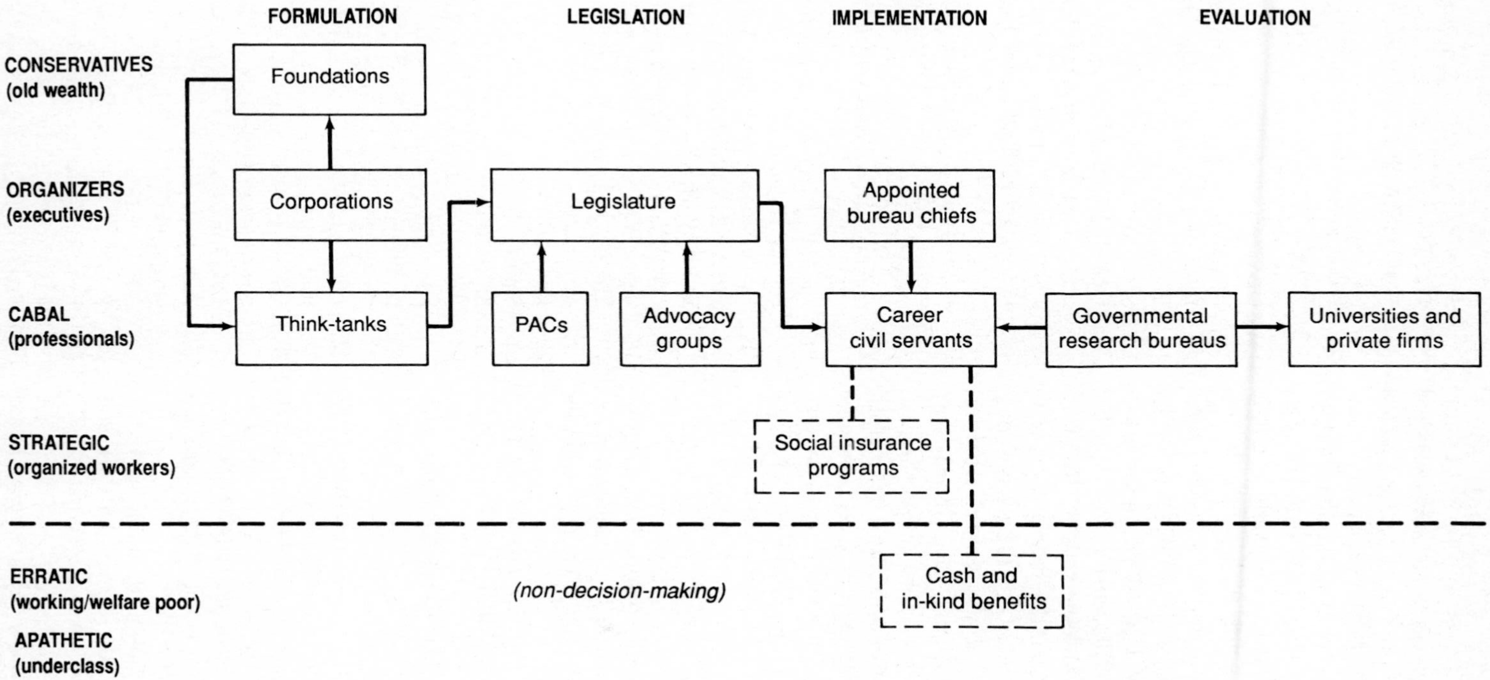
FORMULATION
LEGISLATION
IMPLEMENTATION
EVALUATION
CONSERVATIVES
(old wealth)
ORGANIZERS
(executives)
CABAL
(professionals)
STRATEGIC
(organized workers)
ERRATIC
(working/welfare poor)
APATHETIC
(underclass)
Foundations
Corporations
Think-tanks
Legislature
PACs
Advocacy groups
Appointed bureau chiefs
Career civil servants
Governmental research bureaus
Universities and private firms
Social insurance programs
Cash and in-kind benefits
(non-decision-making)

Figure 4.2. Governmental Policy Process

Under the visionary leadership of Velasquez, Latino voter registration grew steadily, reflected in an increase in the number of Chicano elected officials. Fifteen years of voter registration campaigning by the Institute contributed to a doubling of the number of Hispanic elected officials in the Southwest.[37] The most visible example of political empowerment of those usually excluded from decision making was Jesse Jackson's 1988 campaign for presidential nomination by the Democratic party. Expanding on the grassroots political base built during his 1984 bid for the nomination, Jackson's 1988 "Rainbow Coalition" demonstrated the support of a wide spectrum of disenfranchised Americans. Thus, mobilization of the working- and welfare-poor, as Velasquez and Jackson have shown, can make the policy process more representative. Assuring that public policy is more democratic in origin is a continuous struggle and one that is supported by welfare advocacy organizations.

NOTES

1. Even Marx, who used a two-part classification, conceded the existence of a "lumpen proletariat," although he did little to develop the concept.
2. Dexter Dunphy, *The Primary Group* (New York: Appleton-Century-Crofts, 1972), pp. 42–44.
3. Charles Lindblom and David Braybrooke, *Strategy of Decision* (New York: The Free Press, 1970).
4. Amitai Etzioni, *The Active Society* (New York: The Free Press, 1968), pp. 282–88.
5. "Conference Report on Immigration Reform and Control Act of 1986," *Congressional Record*, October 14, 1986, pp. H10068–95.
6. "An INS Recipe for Family Separation," *The San Diego Tribune*, October 24, 1987, p. B3.
7. For a description of these forms of rationality, see Robert Alford, "Health Care Politics," *Politics and Society* 2 (Winter 1972), pp. 127–64.
8. Neil Gilbert and Harry Specht, *Dimensions of Social Welfare Policy* (Englewood Cliffs, N.J.: Prentice-Hall, 1986), pp. 206–10.
9. "Nuking Employee Benefits," *Wall Street Journal*, August 29, 1988.
10. For example, see Harry Hatry, *A Review of Private Approaches for Delivery of Public Services* (Washington, D.C.: Urban Institute, 1983).
11. Charles Peters, *How Washington Really Works*, Revised Edition (Reading, Mass.: Addison-Wesley, 1983), p. 112.
12. See, for example, Sheldon Danziger and Daniel Weinberg, *Fighting Poverty* (Cambridge, Mass.: Harvard University Press, 1986).
13. Peters, *How Washington Really Works*, pp. 101–2, 116.
14. Hedrick Smith, *The Power Game: How Washington Works* (New York: Random House, 1988), p. 152.
15. David Stoesz, "Policy Gambit: Conservative Think Tanks Take On the Welfare State," *Journal of Sociology and Social Welfare* (forthcoming, 1989).
16. David Stoesz, "The New Welfare Policy Institutes." Unpublished manuscript, School of Social Work, San Diego State University.
17. Peters, *How Washington Really Works*, p. 114.
18. Smith, *The Power Game*, p. 24.
19. *The U.S. Congress Handbook 1987* (McLean, Va.: Barbara Pullen, 1987).
20. Ibid., p. 146.
21. Smith, *The Power Game*, p. 252.
22. Steve Burghardt, "Community-Based Social Action," *Encyclopedia of Social Work*, 18th ed., (Silver Spring, Md.: NASW, 1987), p. 297.
23. Smith, *The Power Game*, p. 238.
24. Ibid., p. 254.
25. Ibid.
26. Jeffrey Pressman and Aaron Wildavsky, *Implementation* (Berkeley, Calif.: University of California Press, 1974), p. xii.
27. Albert O. Hirschman, *Shifting Involvements* (Princeton, N.J.: Princeton University Press, 1982), p. 132.
28. Peters, *How Washington Really Works*, p. 111.
29. Peter Bachrach and Morton S. Baratz, *Power and Poverty* (New York: Oxford University Press, 1979), p. 7.

30. For a review of the CAP experience, see Daniel Patrick Moynihan, *Maximum Feasible Misunderstanding* (New York: Random House, 1973).

31. Marcia Slacum Greene, "Crackdown Vowed on Child Support," *The Washington Post*, January 24, 1987.

32. Quoted in Robert Kuttner, *The Economic Illusion* (Boston: Houghton Mifflin, 1984), p. 86.

33. Michael Lipsky, "Bureaucratic Disentitlement in Social Welfare Programs," *Social Service Review* 33, no. 4 (March 1984), pp. 81–88.

34. Ellen Dunbar, "Future of Social Work," *NASW California News* 13, no. 18 (May 1987), p. 3.

35. Harris Chaiklin, "The New Homeless and Service Planning on a Professional Campus," University of Maryland, Chancellor's Colloquium, Baltimore, December 4, 1985, p. 7.

36. Sharon Griffin, "Voter-Registration Drive Well on Way to Goal," *San Diego Union*, September 3, 1988.

37. "Willie's Vision for Chicano Empowerment," *Southwest Voter Research Notes* 2, no. 3 (June 1988), p. 1.

CHAPTER 5

Social Stigma in the American Social Welfare State

Social stigma and poverty are inextricably linked to the fabric of American social welfare. As manifested in economic, social, and political discrimination, social stigma ultimately leads to poverty for most of its vulnerable victims and, in turn, results in income maintenance and poverty programs designed to address the effects of poverty. Realizing that social stigma encourages poverty, some policymakers have attempted to address this cycle of misery by attacking discrimination, one of its core components. In the end, these policymakers hope that by curtailing discriminatory practices and attitudes, vulnerable populations will be given equal opportunities for achievement and success, thereby reducing the need for expensive and often inadequate social welfare programs. This chapter will probe discrimination based on race, gender, affectional preference, disability, and age.

RACISM

Racism refers to the discrimination against and prejudicial treatment of a racially different minority group. This prejudicial treatment may take the form of differential hiring and firing practices, promotions, resource allocations in education, the structure of transportation systems, segregation and housing policies, health care, behavior of the judicial and law enforcement systems, media images of the minority group, and so forth. A pattern of racial discrimination that is strongly entrenched in a society is sometimes called institutional racism.

A question that has plagued contemporary social scientists is, "Why have blacks remained consistently poor when other groups, such as the Irish, Jews, and Poles, have been able to climb out of poverty?" Several attempts have been made to answer this question, running the gamut from the alleged genetic deficiency of blacks, to the difficulty of blacks to assimilate because of the color barrier. Cultural, racial, and family explanations have all been touted as the correct answer at some time in contemporary social science history.

One of the most controversial answers to the above question has been offered by Daniel Patrick Moynihan, now a U.S. Senator from New York. In his book, *Maximum Feasible Misunderstanding*, Moynihan stated that:

> At the heart of the deterioration of the fabric of Negro society is the deterioration of the Negro family. It is the fundamental source of weakness for the Negro community at the present time.... The white family has achieved a high degree of stability. By contrast, the family structure of lower class Negroes is highly unstable, and in many centers is approaching a complete breakdown! ... the circumstances of the Negro community in recent years have been probably getting worse, not better ... the fundamental problem, in which this is most clearly the case, is that of family structure ... so long as this structure persists, the cycle of poverty and disadvantage will continue to repeat itself.... A national effort is required that will give a unity of purpose to the many activities of the federal government in this area, directed to a new kind of goal: the establishment of a stable Negro family structure.[1]

Moynihan maintained that the black family was ruptured both during slavery and at the beginning of the twentieth century, when the large migration of blacks to the urban areas of the North occurred.[2] Prompted by the intense debate over the Moynihan report, Herbert Guttman demonstrated that the black family was not profoundly disrupted either during slavery or urban migration; instead, the problems of the contemporary black family were associated with modern forces.[3] In any case, Moynihan's perspective clearly located the problem of poverty within the fabric of black family life. For Moynihan, the problem of poverty lay in the matriarchal black family: the supposed emasculation of the black male by a strong matriarch coupled with the absence of powerful black men as role models for black youngsters contributed to an identity problem for black male teenagers, a problem that would play out in terms of crime and violence. Outraged by Moynihan's analysis, black leaders launched an attack on his pseudo-psychoanalytic explanation of black family life. What emerges from the speculation about the causes of black poverty is an understanding that its causes are complex and rooted in the social, political, and economic realities of contemporary America.

Black Poverty

Individual and institutional racism often manifests itself as impoverishment. Blacks comprise 11.7 percent of the U.S. population (26.4 million out of a total population of 226.5 million). The black population is primarily urban, with over 85 percent of blacks living in cities. Thirty-four percent of all blacks live in only seven cities: New York, Los Angeles, Washington, D.C., Philadelphia, Baltimore, Chicago, and St. Louis. In 1980, 57 percent of all poor black children lived in central cities compared to 27.1 percent of poor white children. Only 26.2 percent of poor black children lived in non-metropolitan areas.[4]

In recent years, many blacks have not only improved their socioeconomic position, but have done so at a relatively faster rate than comparable whites. The most noticeable gains have occurred in the areas of professional employment, the incomes of two-earner families, higher education, and home ownership. For example, the number of blacks in technical, professional, and managerial positions increased by 57 percent (from just under 1 million to over 1.5 million) from 1973 to 1982. In comparison, the number of whites in such positions increased by only 36 percent. In black households where couples were between the ages of 24 and 35, and where both the husband and wife were employed, the difference in the annual income between blacks and whites was less than $3,000, a significant improvement over earlier decades. The fraction of black families earning $25,000 a year or more (calculated in 1982 dollars) increased from 10.4 percent in 1960 to 24.5 percent in 1982. Furthermore, blacks recorded a 47 percent increase in home ownership during the 1970s, compared to a 30 percent increase for whites.[5] Despite this relative improvement, millions of blacks did not experience progress during the last decade, but instead, a significant erosion in their standard of living.

Racism rears its head in all sectors of social, political, and economic life. For example, although blacks constitute 11 percent of the population, they account for 26 percent of all arrests, and 51 percent of all violent crime arrests. Moreover, they are 8.5 times more likely than whites to go to prison.[6] In 1984, close to 42 percent of all prisoners facing the death sentence were either black or members of another minority group.

Racism also influences health. On the average, blacks live six years less than whites. Black men are six times as likely to die from homicide (and legal intervention) than white males. The black infant mortality rate in 1982 was almost twice that for whites—20 deaths per 1,000 births compared to 10.5 deaths per 1,000 births for white babies.[7] The differential in white and black infant mortality was the same in 1980 as in 1965. Moreover, there is no indication that the black infant mortality rate is falling fast enough to converge with white levels.[8]

Blacks have the highest infant mortality rate for any group in the United States. While the definitive cause is unknown, what is clear is that a low birth weight in babies increases the chances of infant death during the first year by forty times. Also known is that low birth weight is often correlated with inadequate nutrition in mothers during pregnancy. Overall, black children in 1980 were 68.6 percent more likely to die between ages 1 and 4 than were white children, 46.8 percent more likely to die between ages 5 and 9, and 22.8 percent more likely to die between ages 10 and 14.[9] Black mothers are four times more likely to die in childbirth than white mothers.[10] Higher mortality rates for black mothers may be correlated to the fact that in 1981 only 62.4 percent of black mothers received early prenatal care.[11] Infant health care is equally gloomy. In 1982, only 48.4 percent of black children were fully immunized with three doses of DPT, and 39.1 percent of black children 1 to 4 years old had received three doses of polio vaccine.[12]

Racism also has a profound impact on the family life of minorities. From 1960 to 1982, black teenage births dropped from 156.1 per thousand to 97 per thousand. The birthrate for white teenagers dropped from 79.4 per thousand in 1960 to 44.6 per thousand in 1982. In 1982, 87 percent of births to black teenagers and 37 percent of births to white teenagers were to unwed mothers. In 1970 the percentages were 44 for blacks and 17.5 for whites. Teenage mothers are now more likely to keep their children, regardless of their income.[13] The out-of-wedlock birthrate for black teenagers aged 15 to 19 doubled from 1940 to 1972; by 1977 it was over six times the rate for white teenagers.[14] During the 1970s the birth rate for black unmarried adolescents dropped significantly. Even given the drop, the rate for out-of-wedlock black births is still close to three times that for whites.[15] More than half (55.3 percent) of all black children are born to a single mother.[16]

Apart from the moral connotations, out-of-wedlock births contain profound economic implications. For example, teenage mothers are twice as likely to be poor as non-teen mothers, and a teenage mother earns half the lifetime wage of a woman who waits until 20 to have her first child.[17] A strong correlation also exists between single, young mothers and high welfare dependency. In 1984, 44.6 percent of never-married mothers ages 16 to 19 received public welfare; for whites that number was 35.7 percent and for blacks it was 50.7 percent.[18] Although the absence of economic opportunities for young blacks makes childbirth and the welfare system seem more appealing than a dead-end, minimum wage job, 51.7 percent of black female-headed families fell below the poverty line in 1984,[19] and more than half of all black children born in 1982 were poor.[20]

The high incidence of out-of-wedlock births creates a unique family landscape for blacks. Black families are twice as likely to be living with grandparents, grandchildren, or brothers or sisters than white families.[21] Female-headed families doubled for both whites and blacks from 1970 to 1980, and almost 60 percent of black children under three do not live with both parents. Black children under three are four times as likely to live with only one parent, and five times as likely to live with neither parent, as their white counterparts.[22]

Welfare dependency may also be construed as one indicator of racism, because it is directly correlated to the economic conditions of blacks. Although blacks comprise only 11.7 percent of the U.S. population, they make up 44 percent of all AFDC recipients, 35 percent of all food stamp recipients, and 27 percent of SSI beneficiaries.[23]

Education is believed to have a major influence in determining poverty, as is shown

TABLE 5.1. White, Black, and Hispanic Households below Poverty Level by Educational Level, 1986

* Education of Householder	White		Black		Hispanic		All Races	
	Number (in thousands)	%**	Number	%	Number	%	Number	%
Elementary School:								
Less than 8 years	771	24.1%	262	33.8%	374	36.2%	1068	26.2%
8 years	456	13.9	119	32.7	111	34.7	592	15.9
High School:								
1–3 years	904	15.0	489	39.4	185	30.2	1429	19.4
4 years	1498	7.9	584	25.0	145	15.0	2163	9.9
College:								
1 year or more	637	3.1	234	13.7	67	8.6	921	4.0

* Percent refers to percentage below the poverty line. **Householders includes persons 25 years or older. Source: Bureau of the Census, *Statistical Abstract of the United States,* Vol. 107 (Washington, D.C., U.S. Government Printing Office, 1987), p. 445.

in Tables 5.1 and 5.2. The high school dropout rate for blacks and whites is similar: 17 percent for blacks and 12 percent for whites.[24] However, white high school dropouts had an unemployment rate of 29.2 percent in 1984, while black high school dropouts reported an unemployment rate of 71.4 percent.[25]

Although education improves the relative economic standing of blacks, its effect on whites is greater. For example, 14 percent of whites with an eighth grade education have incomes below the poverty line, while for blacks that rate is 32 percent. These differences also persist at the high school and college levels, and more than four times as many black high school graduates are poor as white graduates.[26] College graduation does not eradicate the difference in earnings potential. Forty percent of blacks with four or more years of college earned $20,000 to $40,000 a year; the same percentage as whites with only a high school education.[27] Despite this differential, education does have a bearing on poverty ratios. Forty percent of black families with less than three years of high school

TABLE 5.2. 1985 Yearly Mean Income of Black, Hispanic, and White Families by Educational Level (in Thousands)

	White	Black	Hispanic	Mean Income (All Races)
Elementary School:				
Less than 8 years	$14,501	$11,321	$15,219	$13,854
8 years	$17,002	$12,164	$16,288	$16,577
High School:				
1–3 years	$19,594	$14,041	$17,061	$18,849
4 years	$26,541	$18,427	$23,429	$25,698
College:				
1–3 years	$32,215	$21,700	$27,261	$29,344
4 years	$43,642	$32,057	$37,339	$42,938

Source: Bureau of the Census, *Statistical Abstract of the United States,* Vol. 107 (Washington, D.C.: U.S. Government Printing Office, 1987), p. 433.

education are poor. When high school is completed that number falls to 26 percent, and where some college training is received, that number drops to 12 percent.

Because of civil rights legislation and other variables, such as increased student aid, 50 percent of all black high school graduates attended college in 1977, compared to 51 percent of white high school graduates.[28] In 1978 the number of black undergraduates peaked at 10.4 percent.[29] By 1982, however, the proportion of black high school graduates attending college dropped to 36 percent; at the same time the proportion of white students remained steady at 52 percent.

While the educational strides made by blacks appear promising, the overall economic picture is bleak. The black unemployment rate is consistently over twice that for whites. In 1984 black median income was $15,432 compared to $27,686 for whites, and $18,833 for Hispanics.[30] The median black family income in 1987 was about 56 percent of their white counterpart. Ten percent of black families earned less than $7,500 per year in 1984 (the poverty line was $10,626 for a family of four), compared to 8.1 percent for Hispanics, and 3.7 percent for whites. White families are twice as likely as black families to earn between $35,000 and $50,000 per year.[31] In addition, blacks earn less than whites irrespective of household composition, education, region, or religion.

Hispanics and Poverty

Because of the large number of undocumented aliens coming from Latin America and Mexico, the Hispanic population of the United States is difficult to ascertain. Approximately 2.3 million legal immigrants entered the U.S. from 1961 to 1980, most from Mexico and Latin America.[32] According to the Census Bureau, over 14.6 million people of Spanish origin lived in the United States in 1980. This number represented an increase of 61 percent from 1970 to 1980.[33] The Hispanic population is highly concentrated

geographically. For example, just over 60 percent of Hispanics live in three states: California, Texas, and New York. Eighty-five percent of all Hispanics live in nine states, and 88 percent live in urban areas (a figure 13 percent higher than the national average).[34]

According to the Center on Budget and Policy Priorities, the overall poverty situation for Hispanics has been worsening in the last few years.[35] In 1984, about 28 percent of Hispanic families—approximately 60 percent of whom were Mexican-Americans—were below the poverty line. That rate was double the overall U.S. poverty rate of 14.4 percent. In 1985, 5.2 million Hispanic children were living in poverty (39.9 percent of all Hispanic children), the highest level ever recorded since the Census Bureau began keeping data on Hispanics in 1973.[36] Furthermore, the per capita income for Hispanics actually dropped below black per capita income in 1985. This translates into the fact that the median Hispanic family income actually dropped $478 in 1985 after adjusting for inflation. All told, Hispanic family income has dropped more than $2,000 since 1973. Poverty also rose for the Hispanic elderly, and in 1985 their poverty rate climbed to 23.9 percent.

Although for statistical purposes the Hispanic population is often considered as a single group, the distinct social and historical background of each subgroup may lead to misconceptions. For example, Cuban-Americans living in Florida may have little in common both historically and politically with Mexican-Americans living in California. Moreover, Puerto Ricans living in New York may have little understanding of the culture of either Cuban-Americans or Mexican-Americans.

According to the Bureau of the Census, in 1980 there were over 8.7 million Mexican-Americans in the U.S., a 93 percent increase over the 1970 census. Mexican-Americans constitute almost 60 percent of all Hispanics in this country and are the fastest growing of the Spanish-speaking subgroups. Moreover, the continuation of this rate of growth will place the Mexican-American population at about 16.9 million by the early 1990s, and by the year 2000, they are expected to be the largest minority group in the United States.[37]

The poverty of Mexican-Americans is correlated, at least in part, to deficits in educational attainment. Although they have made educational gains, in 1980 the median attendance in school was 9.8 years, the lowest of any Hispanic subgroup. Moreover, they have the highest dropout rate in the United States. In 1980, almost 58 percent of those 25 years or older had less than a high school education, and only 7.7 percent had finished four or more years of college.[38]

One of the most impoverished groups in America are the migrant and seasonal farm workers, a group heavily composed of Mexican-Americans. Working six to eight months a year, migrants travel in family groups, and virtually all family members—including children—work in the fields. Working under extremely difficult and hazardous conditions, migrants face dangers from both powerful pesticides and complicated farm equipment, thus making these people highly vulnerable to health problems. For example, the infant mortality rate for migrants is 25 percent higher than the national average; the death rate from influenza is 20 percent higher than in the general population; poor nutrition causes higher instances of pre- and post-natal deaths; and parasitic infections affect 27 to 45 percent of migrant children.[39] Taken together, these health problems result in a life expectancy of only 49 years for migrant farm workers. Educational prospects for migrant children are equally bleak: 9 out of 10 migrant children never enter high school and, of those, only 3 out of 10 graduate.[40]

In the 1960s the deplorable conditions faced by farm workers led to the emergence of the United Farm Workers Association (UFW) in California, a movement led by the charismatic Cesar Chavez. Initiating a grape and lettuce boycott, the UFW was able to raise the wages of farm workers and lobby for protective legislation. However, despite the limited victories of the UFW, the plight of many migrant farm workers remains desperate at best.

Puerto Ricans constitute 14 percent of all Hispanics in the U.S. and less than 1 percent of the total population. In the last 25 years, Puerto Ricans have steadily lost ground in labor force participation, earnings of family heads, and poverty status. By 1980 Puerto Ricans had one of the lowest family incomes of any minority group in the United States, $20,951 a year for a married couple. From 1960 to 1980 Puerto Rican family income dropped relative to other minority groups, and 34.9 percent of all Puerto Rican families presently live under the poverty line.[41] If current poverty trends continue, Hispanics will replace blacks as the most impoverished group by 1999.

At least some of the Hispanic poverty is attributable to the large numbers of illegal immigrants entering the United States, and the low-paying, menial jobs they occupy. In 1986 Congress passed the Immigration Reform and Control Act, allowing at least some illegal immigrants to apply for temporary resident status.

The Act is a mixed blessing for undocumented Hispanic workers. For one thing, the Act includes an employer sanction provision which specifies imprisonment and fines of up to $10,000 per worker for employers who knowingly hire undocumented workers. In a controversial approach, the Immigration and Naturalization Service (INS) will rely on employers to determine the legitimacy of each worker, thereby making it more risky for employers to hire alien workers. Under the amnesty provision of the Act, undocumented persons who can prove they entered the U.S. before 1982 are eligible to apply for temporary resident status. After eighteen months they may apply for permanent resident status. Provided they have no criminal record, and do not apply for benefits from a federally subsidized welfare program for the next five years, they may stay in the United States. After that, they could apply for citizenship. There lies the hitch. Forced to accept low-paying jobs because of language and educational deficits, these workers become banished to the netherworld of minimum-wage employment. These immigrants will thus be forced to rely on family or nongovernmental aid, deprived of the welfare safety net guaranteed to most Americans.[42] The United States may therefore be forcing prospective citizens to become second-class citizens in order to qualify for citizenship.

American Indians and Poverty

Oppression and exploitation are by no means limited to blacks and Hispanics. In some ways the most destitute group in the United States, American Indians experience the same intensity of oppression as other disenfranchised populations.

The history of American Indians is marked by hardship, deprivation, and gross injustice. Before the arrival of Christopher Columbus, estimates of the Indian population in the territorial United States ranged from 900,000 to 12 million.[43] As a result of the westward expansion of whites—and the wars and genocidal activities that ensued—the indigenous Indian population was almost decimated. By 1880 the census reported the existence of only 250,000 Indians.[44] From 1970 to 1980, the American Indian population increased from 574,000 to almost 1.4 million—an increase of 72 percent.[45] This population rise was due to a lower infant mortality rate, a high birthrate, and the fact that more individuals of mixed Indian descent reported their race as Indian. This last factor may be correlated to the resurgence of Indian pride that marked the period of the 1970s.

In 1980, about 25 percent of American Indians (400,000) lived on 278 federal and state reservations. However, because of the federal policy of selling or leasing reservation land, only 49 percent of the inhabitants of reservations are American Indians, the rest being non-

Indian spouses, ranchers, merchants, teachers, doctors, and government employees. With the exception of the Navaho nation (containing over 100,000 Indians), most reservations are small, having under 1,000 Indian residents.[46] Sixty-three percent of all Indians live away from the reservations, and almost 600,000 live in urban areas. Thus, almost half of the American Indian population is now urban.

American Indians often experience severe social and economic problems. For example, only 56 percent of Indian children graduate high school, and in 1980, 20.5 percent of American Indian families fell below the poverty line. The median family income in 1980 was $24,919 per year, only slightly above that of black families.[47] It is estimated that about 38,000 Indian homes lack safe water and adequate sanitation. Moreover, 43 percent of Indians who live beyond infancy die before age 55, compared to just over 16 percent of the total population. Indians have a maternal death rate 20 percent higher than the national rate. Other health indicators for Indians are equally dismal. The Indian death rate for tuberculosis is six times that of the population as a whole; the death rate for chronic liver disease is four times the norm; for accidents, three times; for diabetes, influenza, and pneumonia, two times; and Indian suicide rates are twice the national average, with rates tending to be highest among young people. Moreover, American Indians have the highest rate of alcoholism of any ethnic group in the U.S.

Caught in the paternalistic and authoritarian web of the Bureau of Indian Affairs (BIA), American Indians struggle both for their identity and their survival. Having been robbed of their land, murdered indiscriminately by encroaching white settlers (as well as the U.S. Cavalry), and treated alternately as children and pests by the federal government, Indians were further oppressed by having their children removed from their homes by welfare officials. This widespread abuse by welfare workers—who evaluated Indian child-rearing practices in the context of white middle-class family life—was partially remedied by the Indian Child Welfare Act of 1978 that restored child-placement decisions to the individual tribes. As a result of this Act, priority for the placement of Indian children is now given to tribal members rather than white families. In an attempt to remedy historical injustices, the Indian Self-Determination Act of 1975 emphasized tribal self-government, self-sufficiency, and the establishment of independent health, education, and welfare services. Despite these limited gains, the plight of American Indians exists as a reminder of the mistakes made by America in its past and present policy toward disenfranchised minority groups.

LEGAL ATTEMPTS TO REMEDIATE THE EFFECTS OF RACISM

Concerted attempts to eliminate racism are relatively recent phenomena. While the Fourteenth Amendment of the Constitution guaranteed all citizens equal protection under the law, it was also used to perpetuate discrimination by forming the grounds for "separate but equal." In fact, complete segregation was condoned until the middle of the twentieth century, and separate but [supposedly] equal public facilities characterized much of the social and economic activity of America. This extensive system of segregation included public transportation, schools, private economic activities, and even public drinking fountains. It was not until the mid-1950s that the U.S. Supreme Court overturned the *Plessy v. Ferguson* (1896) decision which had justified the separate but equal doctrine.

In 1954 the Supreme Court, in a landmark decision in *Brown v. Board of Education of Topeka, Kansas*, ruled that "separate but equal" facilities in education were not equal. The court ruled that separating the races was a way of denoting the inferiority of the black race. In addition, the court stated that segre-

gation retarded the educational and mental development of black children. Although the Supreme Court ruled against officially sanctioned segregation in public schools, *de facto* segregation was not addressed until the *Swann v. Charlotte–Mecklenburg Board of Education* ruling in 1971. This ruling approved court-ordered busing to achieve racial integration of school districts that had a history of discrimination. In 1974 the Supreme Court flip-flopped and ruled in *Milliken v. Brady* that mandatory school busing across city–suburban boundaries to achieve integration was not required, unless the segregation had resulted from an official action. In effect, this ruling allowed *de facto* segregated schools in the white suburbs that surround black inner cities. School busing designed to achieve integration continues to be a controversial issue.

The legal gains made by blacks were won through considerable struggle. Up to the middle 1960s, Southern blacks enjoyed few rights, with total segregation enforced in almost all spheres of social, economic, political, and public activity. (Segregation in the North occurred through *de facto* [unofficial] rather than *de jure* [legal] means, although the net effect was in many ways the same). In 1955, Rosa Parks, ostensibly too tired to move to black seating in the back of a bus in Montgomery, Alabama, sparked a nonviolent bus boycott led by Martin Luther King, Jr. Still another protest was begun when black students in North Carolina were refused service at an all-white lunch counter. The civil rights movement grew and resulted in widespread demonstrations (in Selma, Alabama, one march drew over 100,000 people), picket lines, sit-ins, and other forms of political protest. Gaining international publicity, the protests attracted northern religious leaders, students, and liberals—some of whom would lose their lives. By the time that Reverend Martin Luther King, Jr., was assassinated in 1968, many of the demands of the civil rights movement had been incorporated into the Civil Rights Act of 1964.

The Civil Rights Act of 1964 is the single most important reform act for racial equality since *Brown v. Board of Education*. In summary form the Act states that:

1. Voter registration is a legal right and must not be tampered with.
2. It is unlawful to discriminate or segregate persons on the grounds of race, color, religion, or national origin in any public accommodation, including hotels, motels, theaters, and other public places that offer to serve the public.
3. The attorney general shall undertake civil action on the part of any person who is denied access to a public accommodation. If the owner continues to discriminate, a court fine and imprisonment will result.
4. The attorney general is mandated to represent anyone who undertakes the desegregation of a public school.
5. Each federal department shall take action to end discrimination in all programs or activities receiving federal assistance.
6. It shall be unlawful for any employer or labor union with 25 or more persons to discriminate against an individual in any fashion because of their race, color, religion, national origin, or sex. An Equal Opportunity Commission shall be established to enforce this provision.

In 1968 an amendment to this Act prohibited discrimination in housing.

The 1964 Civil Rights Act did not live up to its implicit promise. The balance of racial power did not shift, and for the most part, blacks continued to be economically and politically disenfranchised. It soon became clear that other remedial methods were required, one of those being affirmative action, a set of policies designed to achieve equality in admissions and employment opportunities for minorities. Affirmative action tactics represent an aggressive step beyond the largely reactive stance taken by simple nondiscrimination policies. The intent of affirmative action is to right a historical wrong by aggressively recruiting minorities and other disenfranchised groups. In addition, rigorous affirmative action policies may also give preferential treatment to minority applicants, and often will include a quota system that favors historically disenfranchised groups.

Critics of affirmative action charge that it violates equal protection under the laws provided in the Fourteenth Amendment and that it sets up a process of reverse discrimination. Moreover, these critics argue that rights inhere in individuals, not in groups. On three separate occasions, the U.S. Supreme Court upheld the opinions of affirmative action critics. In the Marco DeFunis, Jr. case, the Supreme Court ruled that Washington University Law School must admit DeFunis, who claimed he was denied admission even though his grades and test scores were higher than those of blacks who were accepted. In another case, the Supreme Court ruled that Alan Bakke was unfairly denied admission to the University of California–Davis Medical School. Bakke maintained that his qualifications were stronger than those of many of the minority candidates that were admitted. In 1984 the U.S. Supreme Court (*Memphis Firefighters v. Stotts*) ruled that an employer may use bona fide seniority rules in laying off employees, even when those rules adversely affect the percentage of minority employees. The Court ruled that employers are permitted to use seniority rules for layoffs when individual members of minority groups are not directly victims of discrimination. This ruling was a blow to affirmative action because it perpetuated the minority dilemma—minorities are the last to be hired and the first to be fired.

At best, affirmative action policies were only passively enforced by the Justice Department under the Reagan administration. The resistance of the Reagan administration to enforcing affirmative action guidelines, and its relaxation of former federal initiatives, was based on the ideological predilection that these policies benefit minorities who are not victims of discrimination and disadvantage whites who are innocent of any wrongdoing. Despite its power, the Justice Department had only limited success in promoting its argument and, in general, affirmative action initiatives have withstood attacks by critics.

Attacks on affirmative action have also come from liberal quarters. For example, William Julius Wilson, a progressive black sociologist, criticizes the ability of affirmative action strategies to help the most disadvantaged members of society:

> Programs based solely on...[race-specific solutions] ... are inadequate ... to deal with the complex problems of race in America.... This is because the most disadvantaged members of racial minority groups, who suffer the cumulative effects of both race and class subjugation ... are disproportionately represented amongst the segment of the general population that has been denied the resources to compete effectively in a free and open market.
>
> On the other hand, the competitive resources developed by the *advantaged minority members* [original emphasis]—resources that flow directly from the family stability, schooling, income and peer groups that their parents have been able to provide—result in their benefiting disproportionately from policies that promote the rights of minority individuals by removing artificial barriers to valued positions....
>
> Thus, if policies of preferential treatment ... are developed in terms of racial group membership rather than real disadvantages suffered by individuals, then these policies will further improve the opportunities of the advantaged without necessarily addressing the problems of the truly disadvantaged such as the ghetto underclass.[48]

Wilson goes on to observe that:

> Although present-day discrimination undoubtedly has contributed to the increasing social and economic woes of the ghetto under-class...these problems have been due far more to a complex web of other factors that include shifts in the American economy—which has produced extraordinary rates of black joblessness that have exacerbated other social problems in the inner city—the historic flow of immigrants, changes in the urban minority age structure, population changes in the central city, and the class transformation of the inner city.[49]

In short, Wilson maintains that, "The problems of the truly disadvantaged may require *nonracial* [original emphasis] solutions such as full employment, balanced economic growth, and manpower training and education...."[50]

Despite *Brown v. the Board of Education*, the Civil Rights Act of 1964, and widespread affirmative action programs, the situation for most blacks and other minorities has improved only marginally, if at all. The current economic picture for minorities is bleak. Perhaps one of the most significant indictments of the failure of civil rights programs can be seen in the 98th Congress, where only 21 U.S. Representatives were black, and there were no black U.S. Senators.

Discrimination based on race is not the only form of prejudice that exists in America—gender discrimination represents a major obstacle to the social, political, and economic well-being of a major segment of society.

SEXISM: HOW DO WE KNOW THAT IT EXISTS?

Sexism is a term that denotes the discriminatory and prejudicial treatment of women based solely upon their gender. It is a problem that this society has wrestled with since the beginning of the republic. Moreover, sexism is widespread and permeates every aspect of social and political life in America. The fact that women more often than men have to resort to public welfare programs has led some scholars to coin the term "feminization of poverty." Advocates of this idea maintain that the feminization of poverty is evident if one examines the poverty demographics. For example, the number of female-headed households with children under 18 increased by 120.3 percent from 1970 to 1987; the poverty rate for female-headed households climbed to 34.6 percent in 1986.[51] Moreover, the number of poor families headed by women increased 54 percent by 1981, while at the same time the number of poor families headed by men dropped nearly 50 percent. The combined effects of the dual labor market, occupational segregation, and sex discrimination and racism, have resulted in the 1983 median income for women being a scant $6,320 a year compared to $14,630 for men. In any case, two out of three poor adults are women, and the economic status of families headed by women is declining.[52] Not surprisingly, the "feminization of poverty" has led to a high dependence of women on the welfare system. This pattern of dependency is illustrated by the huge increase in the welfare rolls from 1960 (3 million recipients) to 1975 (11.4 million).[53]

The causes of the "feminization of poverty" are complex. When women are deserted or divorced, many have to find jobs immediately or go on welfare. Those who choose welfare are held in poverty by the low benefits, and those women who opt to work are kept in poverty by the low wages that tend to characterize service jobs. These low-paying service jobs, such as servers in fast-food restaurants and sales clerks, make the paltry benefits of welfare seem attractive, because at least there are no child care costs incurred if one stays at home.

When one examines the entrance of women into the marketplace, the door used most often is through the service and retail trades—clerical, cleaning, food, personal service work, auxiliary health service work, and so forth. These occupations are characterized by low pay, a low level of union organization, little status, meager work benefits, and limited prospects for job advancement. Many of these same service jobs were previously held by blacks and other minorities. Thus, much of the entrance of women into the work force has been in the secondary labor market, a marginal area of employment which provides few work benefits and little hope for economic betterment. When supporters of the status quo refer to the millions of jobs that were created in the 1980s, much of what they refer to (44 percent) has been in this secondary labor market, the underbelly of the work world.

Some critics suggest that women are increasingly becoming a surplus army of temporary and part-time workers, a function that used to be reserved exclusively for the poorest of minorities. In effect, this scenario suggests that women are now pitted against blacks for the lowest paying jobs in the service sector. In part, this may explain some of the reservations that many poorer blacks have toward the feminist movement. In the end, patriarchal societies have structured and defined the work of women, and the cultural view of them is reflected in the workplace.

The economics of low-paying service work are gloomy. For example, if a single mother with two children chooses to avoid the stigma of welfare and finds work at minimum wage, her prospects of survival are dismal. Let us assume that this single mother finds full-time employment at $3.75 an hour (above the minimum wage). Before taxes her monthly wage would total $600. Out of that sum she would have to pay at least $400 a month for day care for two children (a conservative estimate), leaving her $200 for rent, food, transportation, clothing, and so forth. That budget is an impossibility, because rent alone would cost more than her remaining income. Thus, work at minimum or close to the minimum wage becomes infeasible, and the economic choices of the unskilled female-headed household are limited.

In some measure, welfare dependency is influenced by the refusal of fathers to pay child support. In 1983 there were 8.7 million single women raising children. Of those women, 58 percent had court orders for child support and 42 percent did not. Of the 58 percent awarded child support, only half received the full amount; a quarter received partial payment; the rest received nothing. If the 42 percent of mothers who received no child support is added to the equation, the statistics become even more startling: 29 percent of all single mothers received full payment, 14 percent got partial payment, and 56 percent collected nothing.[54] Another study reported similar findings, and according to Bell, only 34.6 percent of all women with children under 21 received child support payments in 1979; moreover, a year or two after a divorce, refusal to comply with child support payments becomes the rule rather than the exception.[55] Refusal to pay child support characterizes both poor and nonpoor fathers. One study reported that 58 percent of nonpoor unwed fathers aged 19 to 56 reported paying child support—the average payment amounting to $2,492. Forty-two percent of these fathers, although not poor, reported paying no child support.[56] Increased welfare dependency only mirrors the reality of American society. In 1984 median income for married couples was $29,612; for male-headed households it was $23,325, and for female-headed households it was only $12,803.[57] Even for singles the poverty rate is higher for women: 19 percent for males and 24 percent for females.[58]

Inequities in public transfer programs exacerbate the economic problems of low-income women. For example, Social Security and public assistance are often the only viable options for women, and about eight out of ten female-headed families rely on public cash transfers through public welfare programs.[59] Although median transfers to women are lower, they constitute a higher share of their total income, about one-third for female-headed households as compared with one-tenth for male-headed households. Moreover, Social Security is the only source of income for 60 percent of elderly women, and in 1984, 15 percent of these women were in poverty as compared to 9 percent for men.[60] Like other public transfer programs, Social Security is riddled with pitfalls. In large part, many problems with Social Security are based on the assumptions that all families are nuclear in character, and that families with young children need more per capita income than aged couples.

Some women have argued that Social Security has mistreated them for a number of reasons:

1. Because women's wages are lower than those of men, their retirement benefits also tend to be lower.
2. Married female workers fare better on Social Security than those who are single. Individuals who have never worked can benefit from Social Security payments made by a spouse.
3. Couples in which one worker earned most of the wages may fare better than couples where a husband and wife earned equal wages.
4. Homemakers are not covered on their own unless they held a job in the past.
5. Widows do not qualify for benefits unless they are 60 years old or have a minor in the house.
6. Regardless of how long they were married, divorced women are only entitled to one-half of their ex-husband's benefits. If this partial payment is the only income of a divorced woman, it is usually inadequate. Furthermore, divorced women must have been married to the beneficiary of Social Security for at least ten years to qualify for his benefits.
7. Because women are less likely to spend as much time in the work force as men—due to child responsibilities—their benefits are usually lower.[61]

As result of the Social Security Amendments of 1983, several sex-based qualifications were eliminated: divorced persons were able to qualify for benefits at age 62 (even if the ex-spouse has not yet claimed benefits), and divorced husbands could claim benefits based on the earnings record of their ex-wives.[62]

Work and Gender

Excuses have abounded in attempts to explain why women have been consistently paid less than men. These explanations include:

1. Women have inferior job performance compared to men.
2. Women have always been disinclined to get into a male-dominated occupation. They preferred low-level employment because of the characteristics they associated with femininity (i.e., lack of competitiveness, aggressiveness, etc.).[63]
3. Women's wages were secondary to their spouses', and often they worked for "pin money."
4. Women were thought of as temporary workers who would quit their jobs when they got married, became pregnant, or when their husbands were transferred.
5. Women were thought to find employment only in jobs that would not conflict with their husbands' work, or their housework or childrearing duties.[64]

The reality of why women work is at odds with the myths that have been created. Of the over 53 million households in America, 15 percent are headed by women. By 1981, close to 70 percent of all divorced women and 60 percent of all single or separated women were in the work force.[65] Moreover, one-third of women who worked in 1984 had a spouse who earned less than $15,000 per year.[66] Women presently make up over 44 percent of the total U.S. work force, and nine out of ten women will work at some time in their lives.[67] Women's labor force participation grew from 37.7 percent in 1960 to 55.3 percent in 1986. This rise accounted for 60 percent of the total growth in

the work force.[68] More than two-thirds of women aged 25 to 54 are employed, as are three out of every five women with children.[69]

The largest growth in women entering the work force is attributable to the increase in working mothers. From 1940 to 1970 the number of working mothers rose from 9 percent to 42 percent. In 1986, 72 percent of mothers with children aged 6 through 17 were in the labor force, up from 55 percent in 1975. In that same year, 54 percent of mothers with children under the age of 6 were in the labor force, up from 39 percent in 1975.[70] In other words, by 1984, 9.3 million children under age 6, and 14.7 million children from 6 to 13 had mothers in the labor force.[71] Many of these mothers, however, do not work full-time, year round.

Unfortunately, great disparities exist with regard to women and work. While women make up 44 percent of the total labor force, they hold 62 percent of the service industry jobs.[72] In 1980 only 15.9 percent of all working women were in the professions and technical fields, 33.7 percent had clerical jobs, 18.8 percent were in the service sector, and less than 7 percent were managers or administrators.[73] In 1986 women earned only 64 percent of what men did. Although there has been a decrease in the wage gap, about 25 percent of the reduction has occurred not because women are making more, but because men are making less. As a result of declining employment in high-wage industries since 1973, full-time, year-round male earnings have dropped by 9.2 percent.[74] The income disparity between men and women translates into the fact that median income for female-headed families is 43 percent less than that of males. For example, in 1986 the median income for female-headed households was $13,500 compared to $28,300 for two-parent families, and $23,000 for families headed by a single man.[75]

Some of this income disparity can be traced to female occupational clusterings. Roughly half of all working women are employed in occupations where 80 percent of the other workers are women.[76] Nevertheless, both within and outside of these clusterings, women consistently earn less than men. For example, professional and technical female workers earned 64.3 percent of their male counterparts' wages in 1981; for managers and administrators that number dropped to 57.9 percent; for salesworkers it dropped to 51.4 percent; and for service workers the ratio was 60.5 percent.[77]

Although women are attending college at rates higher than men (by 1979 women outnumbered men, but not as full-time students), the average female college graduate fares worse. In 1980 the average female college graduate earned only 57.6 percent ($16,417) of a male college graduate's salary ($28,306). In fact, the average female college graduate earned only slightly more than a male with an eighth grade education ($15,709). This discrepancy exists even for graduate education. In 1980 women with five-plus years of college earned only 59 percent ($19,520) of the salary of males ($33,085) with a similar education. Moreover, women with five-plus years of college earn less than a male high school graduate.[78]

Day Care: A Barrier to Female Employment

A major barrier to female employment involves the problem of day care and subsidized childcare leaves. For many working families child care has become a necessity. A 1982 Census Bureau survey found that 45 percent of single mothers would seek employment if quality and affordable child care were available. Serious shortages of quality child care exist, and when it can be found, the costs average about $3,000 a year for each child.[79]

Day care has historically been a service geared toward the working and middle classes. The first day-care center was begun in 1854 with the establishment of the Nursery for Children of Poor Women. The goal of this Nursery was to prevent child neglect in families of working mothers. An alternate model was a nursery school designed to address middle-class concerns. A group of faculty wives at the University of Chicago organized the first cooperative nursery in 1915, with the express purpose of providing middle-class women with a respite from child care.[80]

Federally funded day care grew rapidly because of the need for women to fill the industrial jobs vacated by men during World War II. However, when the men returned from the war, women were vigorously encouraged to leave their jobs and return to homemaking. Despite this discouragement, women continued to enter the work force in growing numbers from 1940 to 1971. In 1971 Congress passed the Comprehensive Child Care Act, later vetoed by former president Richard Nixon.

Title XX is the largest federal program for child-care services. However, as a result of the budget cuts enacted in the first three years of the Reagan administration, its funds were cut by 21 percent. Thirty-two states provided less care to poor children in 1983 than in 1981,[81] and the group hurt most by these cutbacks was poor female-headed families. Moreover, many of the working poor have been eliminated from the welfare rolls and have thus lost their eligibility for publicly funded day care.

The lack of subsidized child care leaves poses a major problem for American working women. Sheila Kammerman reported on a study of working mothers in five industrialized countries—Sweden, East and West Germany, Hungary, and France.[82] In all countries, except for West Germany, a higher proportion of women were employed than in the U.S. All nations, except the U.S., provided a tax-free family allowance that ranged from $300 to $600 yearly. Guaranteed maternity leave (in Sweden the leave also pertained to fathers) ranged from fourteen weeks in West Germany to eight months in Sweden. Guaranteed maternity leave also included full pay in most places. No guaranteed maternity leave exists in the United States.

The child-care system in the United States is two tiered: those with adequate incomes can afford to purchase first-rate child care or, if they desire, they can stay at home; those with low wages are at the mercy of the ebb and flow of political support for publicly supported day care.[83]

Fighting Back: The Equal Rights Amendment and Comparable Worth

In 1920 the Nineteenth Amendment to the Constitution gave women the right to vote. That, however, did not seem to obviate their economic and social plight, and shortly after winning the vote the Women's Party proposed the first Equal Rights Amendment (ERA). Although at first glance a good idea, progressive social workers such as Jane Addams, Florence Kelley, and Julia Lathrop, among others, saw the ERA as endangering the hard-fought protection won for women workers. For example, reformers successfully fought for a maximum weight limit on lifting for women workers, the establishment of maximum work-day laws in many states, and mandatory work breaks. These social workers saw the ERA as having the potential to eradicate protective legislation for women workers. Moreover, these reformers saw the ERA as mainly benefiting middle-class professional women at the expense of poor, working-class women. Many female trade unionists continued to oppose the ERA well into the 1970s.

In 1972 the Congress passed the ERA and set a 1979 date for state ratification. When the ERA had not been ratified by 1978, Congress extended the deadline to June 30, 1982. Despite the endorsement of 450 organizations representing 50 million members, opponents of the ERA were able to defeat the amendment in 1982, just three states short of the 38 required for ratification.

Cutting through the controversy surrounding the ERA, the Act reads as follows: "Equality of rights under the law shall not be denied or abridged by the United States or any other State on account of sex.... The Congress shall have the power to enforce, by appropriate legislation, the provisions of this article.... This amendment shall take effect two years after the date of ratification."[84]

Contrary to the myths surrounding it, the ERA would not have nullified all laws distinguishing on the basis of sex; instead, it would have required that men and women be treated equally. Most alimony, child support, and custody laws would not have been invalidated, although laws giving preference to one sex would have been struck down. On the other hand, special restrictions on property rights of married women would have been invalidated; married women would have been free to manage their own separate finances and property. Again, contrary to popular myth, the ERA would have only affected public employment; private employment practices would not have been changed. In the areas of military service and jury duty, women would have been subject to participation under the same conditions as men. Like men, women would have been eligible for the draft.[85]

Shrouded in fear and misinformation—much of it purposeful—the ERA became a symbolic struggle. Opponents feared what *might* happen if the ERA were passed. These fears—often couched in hyperbolic language—suggested that the passage of the ERA would result in men and women being forced to share the same bathrooms, the drafting of women to serve on the front line, and granting women the legal right to refuse to cook for their husbands. If not for the seriousness of the ERA, the dialogue and the subsequent intellectual gyrations could have made a slapstick comedy. More importantly, the struggle around the ERA was a conflict about the future of gender relations in America.

Another front for fighting sexism has been the issue of comparable worth—the idea that workers should be paid equally when they do *different* types of work requiring the same level of skill, education, knowledge, training, responsibility, and effort.

An illustration of the debate around comparable worth is provided in Table 5.3, comparing jobs typically occupied by women with those held by men. Although a controversial notion, 20 states have already passed laws making comparable worth a requirement or goal of state employment. While in theory a good idea, comparable worth brings up a difficult problem: namely, "What criteria do we use to determine comparable but different jobs?"

Legal protection for women workers is not a recent phenomenon. As early as the turn of the century, protective legislation restricted the amount of weight a woman was allowed to lift, mandated rest and lunch periods, prohibited hours of work beyond a specified number, regulated night work, and prohibited employment in particular occupations. In 1963 the Equal Pay Act was passed, that required employers to compensate male and female workers equally for performing the same job under the same conditions (although a progressive bill, not all jobs were covered). Another protective measure was Title VII of the Civil Rights Act of 1964, which prohibited sex discrimination in employment practices and provided the right of court redress. In 1972, Presidential Executive Order 11375 mandated that employers practicing sexual discrimination be prohibited from receiving federal contracts. Title IX of the Educational Amendments of 1972 prohibited discrimination in educational institutions receiving federal funds. And lastly, the Equal Credit Act of 1975 prohibited discrimination by lending institutions based on sex or marital status.

To compound the problem, the political process has not been responsive to the needs of women. In 1985 women comprised only 14.8 percent of state legislators, 9.6 percent of the mayors (in cities of 30,000 or more), two out of the 100 U.S. Senators, and only 23 of the 435 U.S. Representatives.[86] In short, sexual dis-

TABLE 5.3. Comparable Worth and Average Annual Income, 1981

	1981 Average Annual Income
Teacher's Aide	$ 8,632
Truck Driver	$16,380
Secretary	$11,908
Warehouse Laborer	$14,040
Pre-kindergarten and Kindergarten Teacher	$13,728
Mail Carrier	$21,216
Registered Nurse	$17,212
Brick Layer	$20,852
Bank Teller	$ 9,776
Stock Clerk	$15,086

crimination appears to be tied into all areas of social, political, and economic life.

GAYS AND LESBIANS: TWO POPULATIONS AT RISK

A group that can lay claim to being historically scorned is homosexuals. Forced to live in the "closet," gays and lesbians have been compelled to conceal their sexual preferences in order to to survive in a hostile world. Often the objects of ridicule, homosexuals have been beaten, killed, assaulted, denied employment, and harassed on the job because of their sexual preference. In many states homosexuality is still considered a criminal or felony offense, and in some of those states, the police systematically raid homosexual bars and randomly arrest the patrons. In 24 states women risk prosecution for being in a lesbian relationship.[88]

Represented in all occupations and socioeconomic strata, gays and lesbians make up about 10 percent of the general population.[89] Despite their numbers, when gays and lesbians have decided to "come out of the closet" and demand equal rights under the law, the result has been mixed, although generally negative. During the 1970s Miami gays tried to pass a civil rights amendment which would have pre-

vented discrimination based on sexual preference. The referendum failed in Miami, and
similar ones were defeated in St. Paul and other
cities. In 1986 Houston voters defeated two gay
rights proposals, one calling for an end to discrimination based on sexual preference in city
employment practices, and the other proposing
to stop the city from maintaining sexual orientation data in city employment records.[90] For
almost twenty years the Supreme Court refused
to hear cases of gay rights, but in 1985 it decided
to hear the case of *Oklahoma City Board of
Education v. the National Gay Task Force*. The
Supreme Court decided that public school
teachers cannot be forbidden to advocate homosexuality (e.g., public demonstrations), but
they can be prohibited from engaging in homosexual activity in public. In a major setback for
gay rights, the Supreme Court in 1986 refused
to strike down laws in Georgia and Texas that
forbid homosexuals from engaging in similar
types of activity. Despite these setbacks, 26
states had implemented decriminalization by
1984. Seven other states prohibit discrimination
in public employment, and some form of protection is provided for gays and lesbians in 51
municipalities and 12 counties nationwide.[91]

Homophobia—the irrational fear of
homosexuality—is a social phenomenon which
has resulted in attempts to limit the civil rights
and legal protection of gays and lesbians. Justifications for this attitude have been found in
traditional religious dogma which treats homosexuality as a sin against God, and in psychological explanations which view homosexuality
as a disease—a symptom of an arrested developmental process or a fear of intimacy.
Nevertheless, in the last 15 years the self-
perception of gays and lesbians has undergone
a dramatic change. Gays and lesbians have
begun to identify themselves as members of an
oppressed minority, similar in many ways to
other oppressed minority groups. As they have
become more visible, gays and lesbians have
organized support groups, religious groups
(Dignity [Roman Catholics], Integrity [Epis-

copalians], Mishpachat Am [Jews], and Lu-
therans Concerned [Lutherans]), social service
organizations, sub-chapters of professional associations, and political action groups. The
political power of gays and lesbians has grown
to the point that in 1984 they succeeded in
inserting a gay civil rights plank in the platform
of the Democratic party.

Homophobic attitudes have been given
increased expression as a result of the AIDS
crisis. Predominantly a disease that affects
selected population groups—gays and bisexual
men (73 percent of its victims), intravenous
drug users, and hemophiliacs—the movement
of AIDS into the heterosexual community has
fueled both criticism and fear of the gay population. Manipulated by anti-gay groups, the fear
of AIDS has led to suggestions for quarantining
AIDS victims, renewed attempts at punishing
homosexual behavior, increased job discrimination, and a generally hostile climate for both
gays and lesbians.

On the other hand, the AIDS crisis has led
some people to better understand the suffering
of the gay community. There are few gays in
larger cities that have not lost either a lover or
friend to the disease. This suffering, combined
with AIDS education, has led to a galvanizing
of the gay community that is unprecedented.
Comprehensive medical and support services
have been developed in several of the larger
cities, and many members of the gay community
are exercising increased caution in the choice
of sexual partners and in the sexual act itself.
As a result of these measures, there has been a
decrease in the numbers of AIDS cases in some
cities. Despite these advances, AIDS remains
one of the most significant problems facing
both gay and heterosexual communities.

AGEISM

Ageism—the discrimination against older persons—is a significant problem in a consumer-
oriented society which idolizes youth. Unlike

other cultures, the aged in America are not often revered and respected for their wisdom and experience. Nor do they occupy an elevated social position protected by tradition. Instead, usually devoid of earning potential, the aged are often perceived as a financial albatross around the neck of an economically productive society. A youth-oriented society which values consumption and economic productivity above all else and in which people's worth is determined by their economic contribution, tends to isolate the older member who is thought to be no longer productive and thus an economic drain. Socially isolated in retirement communities, low-income housing, or other old-age ghettos, the aged become invisible.

Due to medical advances, the population of elderly persons is growing dramatically. However, as the elderly increase in both age and numbers, their demands on society for housing, health, and recreational services become more pronounced. Because the elderly vote in large numbers, their demands have been heard more clearly by politicians than those of blacks and other minorities. In the 1960s, policymakers began to respond to the needs of the elderly and passed the Older Americans Act (OAA) of 1965. The objectives of the OAA include: (1) An adequate retirement income that corresponds to the general standard of living; (2) the achievement of good physical and mental health, regardless of economic status; (3) the provision of centrally located, adequate, and affordable housing; (4) the necessity of meaningful employment, with the elimination of age-specific and discriminatory employment practices; (5) the pursuit of meaningful activities in the area of civic, cultural, and recreational opportunities; and (6) adequate community services, including low-cost transportation and supported living arrangements.[92]

Despite attempts made by the American Association of Retired Persons (AARP) and other advocacy groups, such as the Grey Panthers, problems still persist. Negative stereotypes of elderly persons continue to dominate the media; the availability of quality health care for the aged is still sporadic. The elderly continue to the victimized by violence and abuse, and for many of the elderly, especially minorities, their economic well-being is precarious.

The obvious way ageism is expressed is through employment policies. The Age Discrimination in Employment Act (ADEA) of 1967 protects most workers from ages 40 to 69 from discrimination in job retention, promotion, and hiring. However, for most workers the protection of the ADEA stops when they reach age 70. Legislation to remove the "70" cap has consistently failed in Congress, as employer lobbies have persuasively argued that they require a free hand in personnel policies. Like race, gender, and sexual preference, age is a liability which makes populations vulnerable to oppression and injustice.

THE DISABLED

Disabled persons represent another group that experiences the effects of discrimination. About 8 to 17 percent of the population between the ages of 20 and 64 have disabilities that limit their ability to work, and about half of that number are disabled to the point that they cannot work, or work only irregularly.[93]

Disability is a difficult concept to define. The medical definition is based on the assumption that it is a chronic disease requiring various forms of treatment. Another definition derived from the medical model—also used as a basis for determining eligibility in the Social Security Disability Insurance program—sees disabled people as unable to work (or unable to work as frequently) in the same range of jobs as non-disabled people.[94] Disabled people are thus viewed as inherently less productive than the able-bodied. A third model defines disability in terms of what the disabled person cannot do, seeing the disabled in terms of their inability to perform certain functions expected of the able-bodied population. As William Roth maintains: "The functional limitation, economic, and medical models all define disability by what a person is not—the medical model as not healthy, the economic model as not productive, the functional limitation model as not capable."[95]

A newer definition—the psychosocial model—views disability as a socially defined category. In other words, disabled persons constitute a minority group, and if the disabled person is poor, it is less a result of personal inadequacy than of a discriminatory society. This definition situates the problem of disability in the interaction between the person and the social environment. Therefore, the adjustment to disability is not merely a personal problem, but one requiring the adjustment of society to the disabled. This definition requires that society adjust its attitudes and, as such, remove the barriers it has placed in the way of self-fulfillment for the disabled—i.e., architecture and transportation systems designed for the able-bodied, and subtle stereotypes that impugn the competence of the disabled. In part, this newer definition of disability has been expressed in Section 504 of the Rehabilitation Act of 1973 (P.L. 93–112), sometimes called a civil rights act for the disabled.

While the range of disabilities is great, the disabled share a central experience rooted in stigmatization, discrimination, and oppression. Like other stigmatized groups, the disabled experience poverty and destitution in numbers proportionately larger than the general population. Perhaps not surprisingly, rates of disability are greatest among the aged, blacks, the poor, and blue-collar workers.[96] Compared to the able-bodied, the disabled tend to be more frequently unemployed and underemployed and, as a consequence, often fall below the poverty line. Moreover, because disability is often correlated to poor education, age, and poverty, it is not surprising that blacks are twice as likely to be disabled as whites (their representation is even greater in the fully disabled population), and that more women are disabled than men.

The problems of low wages and unemployment are exacerbated because the disabled often need more medical and hospital care than others, are less likely to have health insurance, and spend three times more of their own money on medical care than the able-bodied.[97]

Although discrimination continues to exist, major strides have been made in the integration of disabled people within the social mainstream. These advances have often resulted from organized political activity on the part of the disabled and their families. For example, an outgrowth of this political activity is Title V of the Rehabilitation Act of 1973, which mandates the following rules for all programs and facilities that receive federal funds:

1. Federal agencies must have affirmative action programs designed to hire and promote disabled people.
2. The Architectural and Transportation Barriers Compliance Board must enforce a 1968 rule mandating that all buildings constructed with federal funds—including buildings owned or leased by federal agencies—be accessible to disabled persons.
3. All businesses, universities, and other institutions having contracts with the federal government must implement affirmative action programs targeted for the disabled.
4. Discrimination against disabled persons is prohibited in all public and private institutions receiving federal assistance.[98]

Despite federal laws discouraging discrimination, prejudice against the disabled is still widespread. For example, most buildings still do not meet the needs of the disabled in terms of access, exits, rest rooms, parking lots, warning systems, and so forth. Many apartment complexes and stores continue to be built without recognition of the needs of disabled people. The struggle of disabled people for full integration is an ongoing social, political, and economic battle.

SOCIAL STIGMA AND OPPRESSION

Although discrimination exists in American society, the causes are complex and elusive. An impressive range of literature attempts to explicate the motives for discrimination. Broken down, these theories fit into three broad categories—psychological, normative cultural, and economic.

Psychological interpretations attempt to explain discrimination in terms of intrapsychic variables.[99] A theory called the frustration-aggression hypothesis, formulated by J. Dollard, maintains that discrimination is a form of aggression that is activated when individual needs become frustrated.[100] According to Dollard, when people cannot direct their aggression at the actual sources of their rage, they seek a substitute target. Thus, relatively weak minority groups become an easy and safe target for the aggression and frustration of stronger discontented groups. For example, poor whites have often been one of the most racist groups in Southern society. Although exploited by the rigid economic and social class system of the old South, poor whites often focused their rage on blacks, a group that was even weaker than they. Blacks have thus had a twin function for poor whites: on the one hand, they formed a lower socioeconomic group which made poor whites feel better about their own standing; and on the other hand, they functioned as a scapegoat for the frustrations of poor whites. Women, racial minorities, homosexuals, and other disenfranchised groups serve the same function for those on a slightly higher social rung.

The "authoritarian personality" theory, developed by Theodore Adorno and other psychoanalytic authors, posited that discriminatory behavior is determined by personality traits that involve a reaction to authority.[101] Persons who exhibit the traits of irrationality, rigidity, conformity, xenophobia, and so forth, are more likely to discriminate against minorities. Other authors, such as Wilhelm Reich, argued that discriminatory attitudes emanate from a sense of deep insecurity, self-hatred, deep-seated fears, and unresolved childhood needs and frustrations.[102]

The normative-cultural explanation suggests that individuals hold prejudicial attitudes because of their socialization. Through covert and overt messages, a society teaches discrimination and rewards those who conform to prevailing attitudes and behaviors. Because societal pressures to conform to established norms are great, resistance to discriminatory practices becomes difficult.[103] For example, particular wrath in the old South was reserved for liberal whites who broke the norms regarding interaction with blacks. It is perhaps axiomatic that societies are more tolerant of norms that are broken by "outsiders" than "insiders." In any case, this theory suggests that as the social and institutional norms which support discriminatory practices change, individual attitudes will follow suit.

The economic argument contends that dominant groups discriminate to maintain their economic and political advantage. This theory is grounded in the belief that relative group advantages are gained from discrimination. For example, male workers might discriminate against women because they perceive that they are encroaching on their employment prospects. In short, male workers fear that they might be replaced by a female worker who would be satisfied with lower wages. On the other hand, employers might uphold discriminatory attitudes because as long as women workers are stigmatized, they will command a lower salary, thereby proving to be a cheap pool of labor. In that sense, the increasing racial tensions in American society can be partly understood as a reaction to the job advancements made by blacks, and the fears of whites that this may affect their promotions, and even their jobs. Regardless of the causes of discrimination, the net effect is to transform disenfranchised groups into the lower class.

All forms of stigma, including race, gender,

affectional preference, and age, are connected to oppression to form the complex mosaic of American society. Sexism, racism, homophobia, and other forms of discrimination are present, in large part, because of their economic usefulness. Industrialization requires a mobile labor force willing to relocate to available employment. Perhaps inadvertently, discrimination has resulted in disenfranchised groups being forced to relocate (usually westward) in order to flee persecution based on ethnic, religious, or racial differences. Capitalism also requires a marginal and unskilled labor pool willing to take jobs refused by economically franchised groups. The use of stigma reduces the economic currency of whole populations and thus creates an underclass forced to take whatever jobs are available at whatever wages are offered. Furthermore, by threatening relatively well-paid workers with replacement by a stigmatized group, employers are able to force wage concessions. By manipulating stigmatized groups against each other, employers can keep wage demands in these groups relatively low. Moreover, because stigmatized groups are often employed in unstable jobs, they can be moved around as the economy requires. Paradoxically, the reduction in the economic currency of disenfranchised groups increases their value to the economic order.

In order for discrimination to maintain an air of legitimacy, it must have a moral, social, and theological underpinning. To that end, ultraconservatives have used the Bible to explain the inferiority of women, the "sin" of homosexuality, and the necessity of separating the races. To augment or replace Biblical interpretations, spurious scientific explanations have been developed which are rooted in quasipsychoanalytic theory, Social Darwinism, and pseudomedical "insights" concerning the attributes of stigmatized groups. For example, some people maintain that menstrual cycles cause severe mood swings that make women incapable of being in positions of power. Others believe that blacks originated from Ham and have thus committed Biblical sins that justify discrimination. Some members of the Ku Klux Klan argue that blacks are racially inferior based on theories grounded in shaky anthropological research confirmed by even more dubious intelligence testing. Without the legitimation offered by moral, religious, social, and theological sources, discrimination becomes devoid of social validity and becomes mere exploitation.

Out of the insidious brew of prejudice comes oppression—the enforcement of discrimination and unequal power relationships. It is perhaps a truism that oppression flows from prejudice in the same way that opportunity flows from tolerance. Discrimination is a likely manifestation for a society which breeds an individualistic and competitive ethos, status fears among marginal groups, and the need for visible scapegoats on which to blame the alienating quality of life. In the final analysis, social stigma and discrimination invariably lead to poverty and destitution.

NOTES

1. Daniel Patrick Moynihan, *Maximum Feasible Misunderstanding* (New York: The Free Press, 1969).
2. Daniel Patrick Moynihan, *The Negro Family: The Case for National Action* (Washington, D.C.: Office of Policy Planning and Research, U.S. Department of Labor, 1965).
3. Herbert G. Guttman, *The Black Family in Slavery and Freedom, 1750–1925* (New York: Pantheon, 1976).
4. U.S. Bureau of the Census, *Money Income and Poverty Status of Families and Persons in the United States, 1982*, Current Population Reports, series P–60, no. 140 (Washington, D.C.: U.S. Government Printing Office, 1982).
5. William Julius Wilson, *The Truly Disadvantaged: The Inner City, the Underclass, and Public Policy* (Chicago: The University of Chicago Press, 1987), p. 109.

6.   Robert Elias, *The Politics of Victimization* (New York: Oxford University Press, 1986), p. 56.

7.   U.S. Bureau of the Census, *Statistical Abstract of the U.S., 1984* (Washington, D.C.: U.S. Government Printing Office, 1984).

8.   National Center for Health Statistics, "Advance Report of Final Mortality Statistics, 1980," *Monthly Vital Statistics Report*, 32, no. 4, Washington, D.C., 1980.

9.   Marian Wright Edelman, "The Sea Is So Wide and My Boat Is So Small," in Harriet Pipes McAdoo and John Lewis McAdoo, *Black Children* (Beverly Hills, Calif.: Sage, 1985), p. 77.

10. Council on Interracial Books for Children, Inc., "Fact Sheets on Institutional Racism," (New York: Council on Interracial Books, November 1984).

11. Department of Health and Human Services, "U.S. Health and Human Services" (Washington, D.C.: U.S. Government Printing Office, 1984).

12. Edelman, "The Sea Is So Wide," p. 78.

13. "Teenaged Childbearing and Welfare Policy," *Focus* 10, no. 1 (Spring 1987), p. 16.

14. Ruth Sidel, *Women and Children Last* (New York: Penguin Books, 1986), p. 18.

15. Children's Defense Fund, *A Children's Defense Budget* (Washington, D.C.: Children's Defense Fund, 1986), pp. 3–65.

16. Edelman, "The Sea Is So Wide," p. 75.

17. Michael Harrington, with the assistance of Robert Greenstein and Eleanor Holmes Norton, *Who are the Poor?* (Washington, D.C.: Justice for All, 1987).

18. "Teenaged Childbearing and Welfare Policy," p. 18.

19. See Sidel, *Women and Children Last*, pp. 3 and 18; and *A Children's Defense Budget*, p. 388.

20. Edelman, "The Sea Is So Wide," p. 74.

21. Robert B. Hill, *The Strength of Black Families* (New York: Emerson Hall Publishers, 1972), pp. 5–6.

22. Edelman, "The Sea Is So Wide," p. 75.

23. *Statistical Abstract of the U.S.*, pp. 373, 393, 396.

24. *U.S. News and World Report*, December 19, 1983.

25. *Digest of Education Statistics, 1983–84.*

26. Diane M. DiNitto and Thomas R. Dye, *Social Welfare: Politics and Public Policy* (Englewood Cliffs, N.J.: Prentice-Hall, 1987), pp. 246–47.

27. Council on Interracial Books, p. 27.

28. Edelman, "The Sea Is So Wide," p. 79.

29. Council on Interracial Books, p. 28.

30. U.S. Bureau of the Census, 1985, p. 9.

31. Ibid.

32. F. Bean et al., "Generational Differences in Fertility Among Mexican Americans," *Social Sciences Quarterly*, 65, no. 2 (Spring 1984), pp. 573–82.

33. U.S. Bureau of the Census, *1980 Census Population Reports—Provisional Estimates of Social, Economic and Housing Characteristics* (Washington, D.C.: U.S. Government Printing Office, 1982).

34. U.S. Bureau of the Census, *General Social and Economic Characteristics: U.S. Summary* (Washington, D.C.: U.S. Government Printing Office, 1981).

35. Center on Budget and Policy Priorities, "Hispanic Rise in Poverty in 1985 Sets New Records," Washington, D.C., September 2, 1986.

36. Ibid.

37. Guadalupe Gibson, "Mexican Americans," *Encyclopedia of Social Work*, 18th edition, (Silver Spring, Md.: NASW, 1987), p. 139.

38. Ibid., p. 140.

39. V. A. Wilk, *The Occupational Health of Migrant and Seasonal Farmworkers in the United States* (Washington, D.C.: Farmworkers Justice Fund, 1985).

40. Juan Ramos and Celia Torres, "Migrant and Seasonal Farm Workers," *Encyclopedia of Social Work*, 18th edition, (Silver Spring, Md.: NASW, 1987), p. 151.

41. "The Declining Economic Status of Puerto Ricans," *Focus*, 10, no. 2 (Summer 1987), pp. 25–26.

42. David Stoesz, "What Amnesty Means to All of Us," *Newsday*, May 18, 1987, p. 77.

43. H. F. Dobyns, *Native American Historical Demography: A Critical Bibliography* (Bloomington, Ind.: Indiana University Press, 1976).

44. H. E. Fey and D. McNickle, *Indians and Other Americans: Two Ways of Life Meet* (New

York: Harper and Row, 1970), pp. 9–12.

45. Evelyn Lance Blanchard, "American Indians and Alaska Natives," *Encyclopedia of Social Work*, 18th ed. (Silver Spring, Md.: NASW, 1987), p. 61.

46. Ibid.

47. "The Declining Economic Status of Puerto Ricans," p. 26.

48. Wilson, *The Truly Disadvantaged*, pp. 146–47.

49. Ibid., p. 62.

50. Ibid., p. 147.

51. Harrington, *Who are the Poor?*

52. Sidel, *Women and Children Last*.

53. See John L. Palmer, and Isabel Sawhill, eds., *The Reagan Record* (Cambridge, Mass.: Ballinger Publishing Company, 1984), p. 363; and Blanche Bernstein, "Welfare Dependency," in Lee D. Bawden, ed., *The Social Contract Revisited* (Washington, D.C.: The Urban Institute Press, 1984), p. 128.

54. *Congressional Record*, Senate, 133, no. 120 (Washington, D.C., July 21, 1987), pp. S10400–404.

55. Winifred Bell, *Contemporary Social Welfare* (New York: Macmillan, 1983), pp. 131–33.

56. *Congressional Record*, Senate, 1987.

57. U.S. Bureau of the Census, *Money Income and Poverty Status of Families and Persons in the United States, 1984*, Current Population Reports, series P-60, no. 149, Washington, D.C., 1985, p. 2.

58. Ibid.

59. Bell, *Contemporary Social Welfare*, 129.

60. U.S. Bureau of the Census, 1984.

61. Martha N. Ozawa, "Gender and Ethnicity in Social Security," *Conference Proceedings*, Gender and Ethnicity in Social Security, Nelson A. Rockefeller Institute of Government, State University of New York at Albany, November 1985, pp. 2–6.

62. Ibid.

63. DiNitto and Dye, *Social Welfare: Politics and Public Policy*, p. 235.

64. Ibid.

65. Howard Hayghe, "Marital and Family Patterns of Workers: An Update," *Monthly Labor Review*, 105 (May 1982), pp. 53–56.

66. Nina Totenberg, "Why Women Earn Less," *Parade*, June 10, 1984, p. 5.

67. Social Security Administration, "Notes and Brief Reports," *Social Security Bulletin*, 48, no. 2 (February 1985), p. 27.

68. Harrington, *Who are the Poor?*

69. Sidel, *Women and Children Last*, p. 60.

70. *Congressional Record*, Senate, 1987.

71. Children's Defense Fund.

72. Harrington, *Who are the Poor?*

73. National Commission on Working Women, "Women's Work: Undervalued, Underpaid," (Washington, D.C.: National Commission on Working Women, 1982).

74. Harrington, *Who are the Poor?*

75. Stephen J. Rose, *The American Profile Poster* (New York: Pantheon Books, 1986), p. 7.

76. Bell, *Contemporary Social Welfare*, p. 126.

77. Nancy Rytina, "Comparing Annual and Weekly Earnings from the Current Population Survey," *Monthly Labor Review* (April 1983), p. 35.

78. Nijole V. Benokraitis, and Joe R. Feagin, *Modern Sexism: Blatant, Subtle, and Covert Discrimination* (Englewood Cliffs, N.J.: Prentice-Hall, 1986), p. 55.

79. Children's Defense Fund.

80. Sidel, *Women and Children Last*.

81. Ibid.

82. Sheila B. Kammerman, "Child Care and Family Benefits: Policies of Six Industrialized Countries," *Monthly Labor Review*, 103 (November 1980), pp. 23–28.

83. Sidel, *Women and Children Last*.

84. Jim Harris, *The Complete Text of the Equal Rights Amendment* (New York: Ganis and Harris, 1980), p. 7.

85. "Fighting Discrimination," *The Legal Advisor* (Spring 1982), pp. 457–58.

86. National Commission on Working Women.

87. National Women's Political Caucus, *National Directory of Women Elected Officials, 1985* (Washington, D.C.: National Women's Political Caucus, 1985).

88. Natalie Jane Woodman, "Homosexuality: Lesbian Women," *Encyclopedia of Social Work*, 18th ed. (Silver Spring, Md.: NASW, 1987), p. 809.

89. A. P. Bell and M. S. Weinberg, *Homosexualities: A Study of Diversity Among Men and Women* (New York: Simon and Schuster, 1978).

90. DiNitto and Dye, *Social Welfare*.
91. National Gay Task Force, *Legal Rights of Gays and Lesbians*, Washington, D.C., 1984.
92. Ibid., p. 155.
93. L. D. Haber, "Trends and Demographic Studies on Programs for Disabled Persons," in L. G. Perlman and G. Austin, eds., *A Report of the Ninth Annual Mary E. Switzer Memorial Seminar* (Alexandria, Va.: 1985), pp. 27–40. See also Bell, *Contemporary Social Welfare*, p. 174.
94. William Roth, "Disabilities: Physical," *Encyclopedia of Social Work*, 18th ed. (Silver Spring, Md.: NASW, 1987), p. 86.
95. Ibid.
96. Haber, "Trends and Demographic Studies on Programs for the Disabled," p. 32.

97. Bell, *Contemporary Social Welfare*, p. 174.
98. DiNitto and Dye, *Social Welfare: Politics and Public Policy*, p. 104.
99. Billy J. Tidwell, "Racial Discrimination and Inequality," *Encyclopedia of Social Work*, 18th ed. (Silver Spring, Md.: NASW, 1987), p. 450.
100. J. Dollard et al., *Frustration and Aggression* (New Haven, Conn.: Yale University Press, 1939).
101. Theodore W. Adorno et al., *The Authoritarian Personality* (New York: Harper and Row, 1950).
102. Wilhelm Reich, *Listen Little Man* (Boston: Beacon Books, 1971).
103. Tidwell, "Racial Discrimination and Inequality," p. 450.

CHAPTER 6

Poverty in America

This chapter will examine the characteristics of poverty in America. Particular attention will be focused on the definition of terms and concepts used in the study of poverty, the examination of its demographic aspects, and the relationship between poverty and income distribution. This chapter will also provide an overview of strategies developed to combat poverty.

Poverty is at once both a complex and simple phenomenon. It can be defined as deprivation and, in particular, as absolute and relative deprivation (or poverty). Absolute poverty refers to an unequivocal standard necessary for survival (i.e., caloric intake necessary for physical maintenance, shelter adequate for protection against the elements, clothing that provides enough warmth, and so on). Those people who fall below that absolute standard of poverty are considered poor.

Relative poverty refers to the idea that deprivation is relative to the standard of living enjoyed by other members of society. Although their basic needs are met, a segment of the population may be considered poor because they possess fewer resources, opportunities, or goods than their fellow societal members. For example, if most families in a society have two cars and a particular family can afford only one, they are relatively poor. Relative poverty (or deprivation) can be understood as inequality in the distribution of income, goods, or opportunities. In our current political climate little attention is being focused on relative deprivation.

Absolute deprivation in the United States is based on a poverty line drawn at a given income set by the Social Security Administra-

tion (SSA). Formally adopted by the SSA in 1969, this official measure provides a set of income cutoffs adjusted for the size of the household, the number of minor children (those under age 18), and the age of the household head. In order to ensure the same purchasing power each year, the SSA adjusts the poverty threshold by using the Consumer Price Index (CPI). Through use of the CPI, the SSA estimates the yearly cash income required for individuals and families to satisfy their basic survival (food, clothing, medical, and shelter) needs. This absolute figure, known as the poverty index or poverty line, is calculated by making an estimate of the food costs for a household (based on the Thrifty Food Plan designed by the Department of Agriculture) and multiplying that figure by three. (It is assumed that one-third of an average household budget is, or should be, spent on food).

In 1987 the federal poverty index for a family of four was set at $11,629 per year.[1] Looking at the poverty line in five-year increments (for a family of four), in 1970 the poverty index was set at $3,968, in 1975 it rose to $5,500, and in 1980 it rose again, this time to $8,414 (see Table 6.1).[2] For the most part, these increases do not represent a liberalization of the poverty index, but instead, are due almost solely to the effects of inflation. Moreover, poverty is assumed to be eliminated when the income of a family exceeds the poverty line, regardless of the changes occurring nationally in the average household income.

Although attempts have been made to make it objective, the poverty index is plagued with severe structural problems that make it the subject of controversy. In recent years there

TABLE 6.1. Changes in Poverty Levels Based on Income and Family Size, 1970–1985

| Family Size | Income | | | |
| | Selected Years | | | |
	1970	1975	1980	1985
1	$1,954	$2,724	$4,190	$5,250
2	2,525	3,506	5,363	7,050
3	3,099	4,293	6,565	8,850
4	3,968	5,500	8,414	10,650
5	4,680	6,499	9,966	12,450
6	5,260	7,316	11,269	14,250
7	6,468	9,022	13,955	16,050

Source: U.S. Bureau of the Census, *Statistical Abstract of the United States*, Vol. 103 (Washington, D.C.: U.S. Government Printing Office, 1984); *Federal Register*, March 1985 (Washington, D.C.: U.S. Government Printing Office, 1985).

has been a heated debate over the poverty count. Households which are under the poverty line because they do not have adequate income from private market sources are considered the pre-transfer poor. However, after receiving Food Stamps, housing assistance, and so forth, many of these families are raised above the poverty line. Some critics argue that the value of noncash benefits (e.g., Food Stamps, Medicaid, Medicare) should be counted as income. If those benefits were counted, fewer people would be classified as poor. These criticisms have validity—Food Stamps do indeed raise the purchasing power of a family. However, placing a value on noncash benefits produces a new set of problems; namely, how much should noncash benefits be worth? Some critics who favor placing a dollar value on noncash benefits (the "market value" approach) believe these benefits should be valued highly. For example, under this approach elderly persons with no cash income could be considered as living above the poverty line simply because they possess a Medicare card (assumed to have greater monetary value than the poverty line figure).

Another problem with the poverty index occurs in relation to the dollar threshold. While the poverty line is calculated by multiplying the Thrifty Food Plan by three, and although food has jumped in price, it has not escalated as high

as rent, home heating fuel, and medical care. Consequently, these necessities now comprise a larger share of the family budget than they did twenty years ago when the USDA devised the poverty index. Thus, while food costs may still constitute one-third of the family budget, other costs appear to consume a greater share of the remainder.

Lastly, the Thrifty Food Plan is based on an emergency diet and assumes the existence of an educated consumer able to discern nutritious and inexpensive foods. Obviously not every consumer is exemplary. Moreover, regional economic differences are overlooked. One is hard-pressed to imagine that the costs of food and, especially, housing are similar in New York City and Boonville, Missouri. Despite the SSA's calculations, reason suggests that $11,629 is simply not enough for the survival of either an urban or rural family of four, particularly if they are renters.

WHO MAKE UP THE POOR?

Before entering into a discussion of the theories and causes surrounding the study of poverty, it is necessary to ask the question "Who is poor in America?" (See Tables 6.2 and 6.3.) In 1987, over 32.5 million Americans were poor, an increase of almost 8 million above the 1978

TABLE 6.2. Persons Below the Poverty Line, Selected Years and Characteristics, 1969–1986*

Categories	Total Persons in Poverty	Persons Over Age 65 in Poverty	Total Children in Poverty
All Groups			
1986	32,570	3,477	12,876
Rate	13.6%	12.4%	20.5%
1980	29,720	3,871	11,543
Rate	13.0	15.7	18.3
1978	24,497	3,233	9,931
Rate	11.4	14.0	15.9
1969	24,147	4,972	9,501
Rate	12.1	25.3	13.8
White			
1986	22,955	2,689	8,209
Rate	11.0	10.7	16.1
1980	19,699	3,042	7,181
Rate	10.2	13.6	13.9
1975	17,770	2,634	6,937
Rate	9.7	13.4	12.7
1969	16,659	2,322	5,667
Rate	9.5	23.3	9.7
Black			
1986	9,629	722	4,148
Rate	31.1	31.0	43.1
1984	9,490	710	4,413
Rate	33.8	31.7	46.6
1980	8,579	783	3,961
Rate	32.5	38.1	42.3
1975	7,545	652	3,925
Rate	31.3	36.3	41.7
1969	7,095	689	3,677
Rate	32.2	50.2	39.6
***Hispanic*			
1986	5,600	204	2,507
Rate	37.7	22.5	37.7
1984	4,806	176	2,376
Rate	28.4	21.5	39.2
1980	3,491	179	1,749
Rate	25.7	30.8	33.2
1975	2,991	137	1,619
Rate	26.9	32.6	33.1

* Numbers are in thousands. **Hispanic persons may be of any race. Sources: Compiled from: U.S. Bureau of the Census, "Money, Income and Poverty Status of Families and Persons in the United States—1984," *Current Population Reports*, Series P-60, No. 149, August 1985 (Washington, D.C.: U.S. Government Printing Office, 1985); U.S. Bureau of the Census, "Poverty in the United States, 1986" *Current Population Reports*, Series P-60, No. 160 (Washington, D.C.: U.S. Government Printing Office, 1986), pp. 7–8.

TABLE 6.3. Percentage of Families Below Poverty Level by Age, Race and Family Size, 1985

Characteristic	All Races	White	Black	Spanish Origin
Total	**11.4%**	**9.1%**	**28.7%**	**25.5%**
Age of Householder:				
15–24 years old	30.2%	24.7%	62.1%	40.2%
25–44 years old	13.1	10.5	30.3	28.5
45–54 years old	7.9	6.1	20.3	16.3
55–64 years old	8.2	6.8	22.5	17.1
65 years and older	7.0	5.6	22.0	16.6
Size of Family:				
2 persons	9.1	7.6	24.8	18.8
3 persons	11.1	8.9	27.5	26.0
4 persons	11.3	9.1	29.0	24.2
5 persons	14.9	11.9	30.0	28.7
6 persons	19.0	15.2	35.6	30.3
7 persons or more	32.1	25.0	49.7	46.2
Mean number of children per family with children	2.23	2.14	2.39	2.57

Source: U.S. Bureau of the Census, *Statistical Abstract of the United States*, Vol. 107 (Washington, D.C.: U.S. Government Printing Office, 1987), p. 445.

figure of 24.5 million. The overall poverty rate in 1987 was 13.6 percent—higher than that of any year of the 1970s, including the recession years of 1974 and 1975. While poverty occurs across a wide spectrum, several groups are hit the hardest. Not surprisingly, in absolute numbers, more whites than blacks are poor. In 1985, of the 32 million poor people in America, roughly 23 million were white and over 9.5 million were black. In 1987 whites represented 69 percent of the poor, blacks 28 percent, and other races 3 percent. Blacks are almost three times as likely to experience poverty as whites: the poverty rate for blacks in 1987 was 33.1 percent compared to 10.5 percent for whites and 28.2 percent for Hispanics.[3]

Perhaps the hardest hit of any group in America are single female-headed families. In 1985 the poverty rate for families headed by couples was 7 percent, for male head of households 13 percent, and for female-headed households 35 percent. When disaggregated the figures become even more astounding: for families headed by white women the poverty rate was 28.2 percent; for families headed by black and Hispanic women, the rate was 50.2 and 51.2 percent, respectively.[4]

Children are some of the main victims of poverty, being twice as likely to be poor as adults. In 1987 there were over 13 million poor children in America (an increase of 3 million over 1978), or about 20.6 percent of all children under age 18. For children under five the poverty rate was even higher (23 percent). In 1987, the poverty rate for black children under age six reached the highest level ever recorded, 49 percent, an increase of 3.5 percent over 1986. In short, almost one out of every two black children under age six is poor. For Hispanic children the poverty rate stood at 39.8 percent, up sharply from 27.6 percent just nine years earlier.[5] The probability of children growing up poor is strongly correlated to family circumstances. The Census Bureau estimates that 61 percent of children born in 1987 will spend some part of their childhood in single-parent families, which are five times more likely to be poor than a two-parent family.[6]

The poverty picture appears less bleak for the elderly, once the poorest group in America. In 1959 the poverty rate for those over 65 stood at 35.2 percent, in 1970 that number was reduced to 24.5 percent, and in 1973 it further decreased to 16.3 percent. Although financially better off, the elderly still have a poverty rate of 12.4 percent. Despite economic gains, almost 3.5 million senior citizens still live in poverty, with many more hovering around the poverty line. Moreover, elderly women experience a disproportionate share of poverty: in 1986, 71.8 percent of the elderly poor were women. A further disaggregation of the poverty statistics reveals that the elderly of color also experience a greater share of poverty. In 1986 the poverty rate for elderly blacks was 31.0 percent; for Hispanics it was 22.5 percent. In addition, 8 percent of elderly whites received no Social Security, compared to 14 percent of blacks and 25 percent of Hispanics.[7]

Poverty occurred unequally in urban and rural areas in 1986, with a poverty rate of 19.6 percent in farming areas and 13.6 percent in nonfarm areas. In comparison, the suburban poverty rate was considerably less, registering only 10 percent.

The demographics of poverty show some interesting twists and turns. In 1962 about 20 percent of the population was poor; as a result of increased AFDC rolls, by 1969 that number had dropped to 12.1 percent, and by 1979 it had dropped even further to 11 percent. For blacks, especially black children, the progress made in the 1960s was dramatic. In 1959, 65.5 percent of all black children were poor, but by 1969 that number plummeted to 39.6 percent. By 1979 the gains started to reverse, and by 1986 the poverty rate for black children was over 43 percent.

Overall poverty rates declined from 1965 to 1978. According to Sheldon Danziger, much of this decline occurred between 1965 and the mid 1970s when real expenditures for cash and in-kind transfers outpaced the real increase in general household income, a development that would slow in the 1980s. From 1978 to 1982, the average cash transfer to a poor household declined by 5 percent—for non-aged women heading households that decline was 10 percent.[8] From 1978 onward the poverty rate has generally increased. In 1984, as a consequence of Reagan's economic policies and large social welfare cuts, the poverty rate increased to 15.3 percent, then dropped to 14.4 percent in 1985. Except for 1982 and 1983, the poverty rate of 14.4 percent was the highest since 1966.

Paradoxically, the drop in the poverty level (from 15.3 percent to 14.4 percent) was especially disappointing because it came on the heels of a major reduction in unemployment (from a high of 11 percent in 1979 to 6 percent in 1987). Thus, even though unemployment dropped by 5 percent, the level of poverty was reduced only minimally. This phenomenon suggests that at least a portion of those who were economically displaced by the high unemployment in the late 1970s and early 1980s either have not reentered the work force, or have reentered it at significantly reduced wages.

From 1979 to 1983 poverty rose at a steady rate. This period was marked by high inflation, high unemployment, and large budget cuts for social programs serving low-income people. This situation was exacerbated by the fact that almost 40 percent of non-aged poor households received no income transfers, and even many of those who received transfers did not get enough to lift their families out of poverty.[9] Although there was a modest economic recovery in the middle 1980s, the levels of poverty did not correspond to the increased affluence. For example, in 1976 and 1977—before the rise in poverty began—unemployment levels were at the same point as in 1984, yet the poverty rate was almost three percentage points lower. Those three percentage points translated into 6 million Americans. The paradox involving the economic recovery of the middle 1980s and the elevated poverty levels can be understood by examining income distribution trends.

TABLE 6.4. **Percentage Share of Aggregate Pretax Family Income Received by Each Fifth of Families, and Family Income at Selected Levels, 1950–1984**

	Percentage of Aggregate Income Received by					
	Lowest 5th	**Second 5th**	**Middle 5th**	**Fourth 5th**	**Highest 5th**	**Top 5%**
1984	4.7	11.0	17.0	24.4	42.9	16.0
1980	5.1	11.6	17.5	24.3	41.6	15.3
1975	5.4	11.8	17.6	24.1	41.1	15.5
1970	5.4	12.2	17.6	23.8	40.9	15.6
1965	5.2	12.2	17.8	23.9	40.9	15.6
1960	4.8	12.2	17.8	24.0	41.3	15.9
1955	4.8	12.3	17.8	23.7	41.3	16.4
1950	4.5	12.0	17.4	23.4	42.7	17.3

Income at Selected Positions (Current Dollars)

		Upper Limit of Each Fifth				
	Mean Income for All Families	**Lowest 5th**	**Second 5th**	**Middle 5th**	**Fourth 5th**	**Lower Limit of Top 5%**
1984	$31,052	$12,489	$21,709	$31,500	$45,300	$73,230
1980	23,974	10,286	17,390	24,630	34,534	54,060
1975	15,546	6,914	11,465	16,000	22,037	34,144
1970	11,106	5,100	8,320	11,299	15,531	24,250
1965	7,704	3,500	5,863	7,910	10,800	16,695
1960	6,227	2,784	4,800	6,364	8,800	13,536
1955	4,962	2,221	3,780	5,082	6,883	10,605
1950	3,815	1,661	2,856	3,801	5,283	8,615

Source: U.S. Bureau of the Census, "Consumer Income 1984," *Current Population Reports*, Series P-60, No. 151, Table 12 (Washington, D.C.: U.S. Government Printing Office, 1985).

INCOME DISTRIBUTION AND INEQUALITY

In large part, poverty can be understood as inequality in the distribution of income (see Table 6.4). By examining the distribution of wealth in society, it becomes obvious why poverty rates have not declined and why social welfare programs have only managed to keep poverty constant rather than alleviate it. Current data show that the economic gap between upper- and lower-income American families was wider in 1987 than at any time since the Census Bureau began collecting this data in 1947. When breaking the population down into fifths, the poorest fifth in 1987 received just 4.6 percent of the national income, while the upper fifth received 43.7 percent. The top two-fifths

of the population (40 percent) received 67.8 percent of the national income, the highest ever recorded by the Census Bureau.[10] This 67.8 percent stands in sharp contrast to the 15.4 percent of the national income received by the bottom 40 percent (the lowest ever recorded). The middle fifth of the population received 16.9 percent of the national income, also the lowest since the Census Bureau began collecting this data.

The income data becomes even more stunning when the top quintile is disaggregated. In 1977 the wealthiest 1 percent of the population took in 9.2 percent of all pretax income; by 1988 that increased to 12.5 percent. In 1977 the average member of the richest 1 percent had an annual income of $301,000 (calculated in 1988 dollars); in 1988 that group averaged

TABLE 6.5. Median Incomes of Rich and Poor Families (Constant 1987 Dollars)

	Median Family Income		
Year	Bottom 40%	Top 40%	Top 10%
1987	$14,450	$52,910	$86,300
1986	$14,393	$52,211	$85,279
1980	$14,187	$47,631	$74,562
1978	$15,191	$48,879	$78,181

Source: Reprinted from Center on Budget and Policy Priorities, "Analysis of Poverty in 1987." Washington, D.C., 1988, p. 15.

$452,000 per year.[11] In 1972 the richest 1 percent of the population held 20.7 percent of all household wealth. Moreover, more than 75 percent of the wealth of the top 1 percent was held by the top .5 percent, a group whose net worth in 1972 was $721.7 billion. The wealth of this elite group translates into power, and the richest 1 percent of the population controls 30 percent of total business claims.[12] According to Winifred Bell, the richest 1 percent hold: (1) 15.5 percent of all real estate, (2) 56.5 percent of all corporate stock, (3) 60 percent of bonds, (4) 13.5 percent of cash deposits, (5) 52.7 percent of debt instruments such as notes and mortgages, (6) 7 percent of life insurance (cash surrender value), (7) 89.9 percent of all trusts, and (8) 9.8 percent of all miscellaneous assets.[13]

While the rich are getting richer, real earnings for most Americans have either stagnated or fallen during the past decade. From 1978 to 1987 the median income for the wealthiest 40 percent (after adjusting for inflation) of the population grew by $3,031; for the wealthiest 10 percent it grew by $8,119 (see Table 6.5). On the other hand, median income for the poorest 40 percent of the population (after adjusting for inflation) was actually $741 *lower* in 1987 than in 1978.[14]

Lower-income families with children also fared worse. From 1979 to 1984, average family income for the poorest fifth dropped almost 24 percent (after adjusting for inflation). For the next poorest fifth it dropped 14 percent. Only families in the wealthiest fifth came out ahead. If we examine this data over an eleven-year period, the figures are even bleaker. From 1973 to 1984 the incomes of the poorest fifth with children fell 34 percent (after adjusting for inflation). It is estimated that from 1980 to 1984, there was a net transfer of $25 billion in disposable income from poor and middle-income families to the richest fifth of the population.[15]

The income of the typical poor family fell further below the poverty line than at any time since the Census Bureau began collecting those data in 1959 (see Table 6.6). In particular, the income of the typical poor family was $4,165 below the poverty line in 1987, the largest poverty deficit on record.[16] Lastly, the poorest of the poor, those with incomes of less than $5,000 per year have become more numerous since 1976. Two out of five poor families fell into the "poorest of the poor" category in 1987. Five percent of all families had incomes of less than $5,000 a year in 1984, a 43 percent increase since 1977.[17]

According to Robert McIntyre, director of Citizens for Tax Justice, a Washington-based research and lobbying group, federal tax policy has played a major role in promoting income inequality. A Congressional Budget Office study released in October 1987 estimated that 95 percent of American families were paying a higher share of their income in taxes than in 1977. Only the richest 5 percent of the population received real tax cuts, with the largest share going to the richest 1 percent. The wealthiest 1 percent in 1987 had a tax cut that amounted to $44,750, a 25 percent tax reduction since 1977.

TABLE 6.6. Trends in the Distribution of Income for Families and Children 1968–1983

Percentage Shares of Cash Family Incomes That Went to Each Fifth of
Total Families with Children

Calendar Year	Lowest Fifth	Second Fifth	Third Fifth	Fourth Fifth	Highest Fifth	Total
1968	7.4	14.8	19.5	24.5	33.8	100
1969	7.4	14.7	19.6	24.6	33.7	100
1970	7.2	14.7	19.4	24.7	34.0	100
1971	7.0	14.5	19.5	24.7	34.4	100
1972	6.8	14.2	19.5	25.1	34.5	100
1973	6.8	14.4	19.5	25.0	34.4	100
1974	6.4	14.3	20.6	25.1	34.6	100
1975	6.3	13.9	19.6	25.3	34.9	100
1976	6.4	13.9	19.7	25.3	34.7	100
1977	6.1	13.7	19.5	25.5	35.2	100
1978	6.1	13.7	19.5	25.4	35.4	100
1979	6.0	13.7	19.5	25.3	35.5	100
1980	5.6	13.3	19.5	25.5	36.1	100
1981	5.4	13.0	19.4	25.8	36.5	100
1982	4.9	12.7	19.1	25.9	37.5	100
1983	4.8	12.3	18.9	26.0	38.1	100

Source: *The American Profile Poster* by Stephen J. Rose. Copyright © 1986 by Social Graphics Co. Reprinted by permission of Pantheon Books, a division of Random House, Inc.

As a consequence of tax and economic changes, real after-tax income of typical middle-class families grew by only 1 percent from 1977 to 1987; the average after-tax income of the richest 1 percent grew by 74 percent.[18] According to McIntyre, supply-side tax policy lowered federal taxes for the richest 5 million American families (including their share of corporate tax reductions) by almost $370 billion during the 1981–88 period, more than double the 1987 annual budget deficit. Conversely, supply-side tax policies increased the federal tax burden sixfold on poverty-level families of four, from 1.8 percent of their income in 1979 to 10.8 percent in 1986.[19]

In 1986 Congress passed a major tax reform act. Although this bill decreased the tax load on the working poor back to 1979 levels, and took back 25 percent of the tax cuts previously awarded to the richest 5 percent of the population, tax cuts for the wealthy are still expected to cost the federal treasury $60 billion in 1989. Moreover, the richest 1 percent is

expected to amass $452 billion in pretax income in 1988, more than the total income of the bottom 40 percent of all families.

The poor also experience the unequal burden of taxation through often ill-conceived and regressive state and local taxation policies (see Table 6.7). In 1986, close to 38 percent of all state tax revenues were collected from individual and corporate income taxes. About half of state revenues were collected from general and selective sales taxes. Income and corporate taxes are generally thought to be progressive, because the tax received from the individual or corporation is based on the extent of income or profit. At least theoretically, the rich pay more and the poor less. On the other hand, general and selective sales taxes are regressive, because they are not based on the ability of people to pay, but based solely on purchases. Therefore, an affluent family that purchases $75 worth of clothing will pay the same amount of sales tax as a poor family, even though that purchase represents a greater share of the poor family's income. For example, a purchase of $75 worth of clothing may represent 1 percent of the monthly income of a wealthy family, whereas it may represent 10 percent of the monthly income of a poor family. As a general rule, the poor—when compared to the wealthy—spend a larger proportion of their income on items subject to sales tax. Although the burden of sales tax can be partially relieved by exempting certain necessity items, of the 46 states that have a general sales tax, only 29 exempt most grocery purchases, and 32 states exempt sales tax paid on utilities.[20] To help rectify this problem, 7 states have instituted a tax rebate pro-

TABLE 6.7. State Sales Taxes and Exemptions, 1987

		Exemptions		
	Sales Tax Rate*	Consumer Electric and Gas Utilities	Food	Low Income Sales Tax Credit
Alabama	4.0%	no	no	no
Alaska	no sales tax			
Arizona	5.0	no	yes	no
Arkansas	4.0	yes	no	no
California	4.8	yes	yes	no
Colorado	3.0	yes	yes	no
Connecticut	7.5	yes	yes	no
Delaware	no sales tax			
Dist. of Col.	6.0	no	yes	no
Florida	5.0	yes	yes	no
Georgia	3.0	no	no	no
Hawaii	4.0	no	no	yes
Idaho	5.0	yes	no	yes
Illinois	5.0	no	yes	no
Indiana	5.0	no	yes	no
Iowa	4.0	no	yes	no
Kansas	4.0	yes	no	yes
Kentucky	5.0	yes	yes	no
Louisiana	4.0	yes	yes	no
Maine	5.0	yes	yes	no
Maryland	5.0	yes	yes	no
Massachusetts	5.0	yes	yes	no
Michigan	4.0	no	yes	no
Minnesota	6.0	yes	yes	no
Mississippi	6.0	no	no	no
Missouri	4.2	yes	no	no
Montana	no sales tax			
Nebraska	3.5	no	yes	no
Nevada	5.8	yes	yes	no
New Hampshire	no sales tax			
New Jersey	6.0	yes	yes	no
New Mexico	4.8	no	no	yes
New York	4.0	yes	yes	no
North Carolina	3.0	yes	no	no
North Dakota	5.5	yes	yes	no
Ohio	5.0	yes	yes	no
Oklahoma	4.0	yes	no	no
Oregon	no sales tax			

TABLE 6.7. (cont.)

		Exemptions		
	Sales Tax Rate*	Consumer Electric and Gas Utilities	Food	Low Income Sales Tax Credit
Pennsylvania	6.0	yes	yes	no
Rhode Island	6.0	yes	yes	no
South Carolina	5.0	yes	no	no
South Dakota	5.0	no	no	yes
Tennessee	5.5	yes	no	no
Texas	6.0	yes	yes	no
Utah	5.1	yes	no	no
Vermont	4.0	yes	yes	yes
Virginia	3.5	yes	no	no
Washington	6.5	yes	yes	no
West Virginia	5.0	yes	yes	no
Wisconsin	5.0	yes	yes	no
Wyoming	3.0	no	no	yes
U.S. Median Rate	5.0	—	—	—
Number with Provision	46	32	29	7

* This represents only state sales tax rates. Counties or cities may levy additional sales taxes.
Source: Advisory Commission on Intergovernmental Relations, *Significant Features of Fiscal Federalism, 1987*; National Association of State Budget Officers and National Governors' Association, *Fiscal Survey of the States*, September 1987.

gram which provides poor households with a rebate check (or a credit against income tax liabilities) to defray the cost of sales tax.

Although income taxes tend to be less regressive than general sales taxes, a majority of the states have failed to follow the federal government's lead in eliminating poor families from the tax rolls. For example, in 13 states (Alabama, Arkansas, Hawaii, Illinois, Indiana, Iowa, Kansas, Kentucky, Michigan, Montana, New Jersey, North Carolina, and Pennsylvania), working four-person families who earned more than $10,000 a year paid over $100 in state income tax in 1988. Four of those states (Indiana, Kentucky, North Carolina, and Pennsylvania) required that same family to pay over $200 per year in income tax. Eight states in 1988 required working four-person families to pay taxes on earnings of less than $6,000 a year. Apart from paying state income taxes, some of these same families also had to pay local income, sales, wage, or property taxes. Twenty-eight of the 41 states with income taxes required payment from some four-person working families who had incomes below the poverty line. In 9 states (Alabama, Arkansas, Illinois, Indiana, Kansas, Kentucky, New Jersey, North Carolina, and Virginia), working families of four with incomes below *half* of the poverty level paid state income taxes in 1988.[21]

Although income distribution is a good indicator of social equity, in the United States it reveals a highly stratified economic system where the rich are getting richer while the poor are getting poorer. Given this income disparity, it is not surprising that welfare programs appear to be losing the battle to contain poverty. In some measure, welfare programs release the pressure on the system by subsidizing income to compensate for its skewed distribution. However limited, without the redistributive function of welfare, the economic stratification in American society would undoubtedly be worse.

SOME CHARACTERISTICS OF POVERTY

There are three general categories of poverty: people making only minimum wage (the working poor), the unemployed, and people who have an occupational disability or poor health (a deficit in human capital—e.g., poor education, a deficit in the quality and quantity of their training and skills, and so forth).

Data from the Panel Study of Income Dynamics (PSID), a study conducted at the University of Michigan which followed 5,000 American families for ten years (1969–1978), found that only 2 percent of the families were persistently poor—that is, poor throughout the entire period.[22] This finding suggests that poverty is a fluid rather than static condition. The data show that as people gain (or lose) jobs, as marriages are created (or dissolved), or as offspring are born (or leave home)—people are either pushed into or escape from poverty.

Further research on the PSID data conducted by Greg Duncan and his colleagues at the University of Michigan shows that most of the people who are poor in a given year have not been poor (and probably will not remain poor) for an extended period of time.[23] In fact, Duncan found that about one-third of the individuals who were poor in any given year escaped from poverty the following year, and only about one-third of the poor families in any given year had been poor for at least eight of the preceding years. Duncan and his colleagues also discovered that family composition, and especially divorce or separation, was the leading cause of poverty. Conversely, spells of poverty were most often ended by family reconstitution (i.e., remarriage).

WORK AND POVERTY

Labor force participation is a key variable in determining poverty. Over two-thirds of the poor in the United States are children, the aged, or the disabled. Apart from these groups—who for the most part are unable to work—poverty is also evident within the work force. The number of working individuals (aged 22 to 64) who are poor has escalated sharply, increasing more than 60 percent since 1978. Forty-nine percent of all poor people heading families now work some time during the year. Moreover, the number of poor people who are employed full-time on a year-round basis stands at two million, an increase of over two-thirds since 1978.

This rise in the number of the working poor is attributable to several factors, chief among them being the replacement of high-paying industrial jobs with low-paying service jobs. Almost 20 percent of jobs will not support a worker and two dependents. In 1986, 34.9 percent of all people who worked part- and full-time earned less than $8,500 a year. Moreover, according to the Joint Economic Committee, about 44 percent of the new jobs created between 1979 and 1985 paid less than $7,400 a year.[24]

The freezing of the minimum wage since 1981 is also related to the increase in poverty rates for the working poor. Throughout the 1960s and 1970s, a three-person family in which one person worked full-time at the minimum wage realized enough income to raise his or her family to the poverty line. However, since 1981 the minimum wage has been frozen, while at the same time the cost of living has increased 27 percent. Consequently, that same family now earns only enough income to raise themselves to 77 percent of the poverty line.[25]

Another major factor in determining poverty is under- and unemployment. Between 1981 and 1986, 10.8 million workers lost their jobs because of plant shutdowns, layoffs, or other forms of job terminations. Five million of those workers had been at their jobs for at least three years.[26] From 1979 to 1984 the Department of Labor conducted a special study of 5.1 million workers whose jobs were abolished between January 1979 and January 1984. This study reported in 1984 that 40 percent of the workers were still unemployed or out of the work force. Of the remainder, close to half of these workers were employed at either part-time jobs or jobs with lower weekly earnings, and the majority of these workers experienced significant economic losses for a lengthy time after their jobs were terminated.[27]

Unemployment benefits reflect the nature of a selective recession which is disproportionately felt by the poor and lower-middle class. Throughout most of the 1970s the majority of unemployed workers received unemployment benefits each month. For example, in 1975, 75 percent of the jobless received benefits. By 1986, the percentage of unemployed workers receiving benefits dropped to the lowest levels in the history of the program, with only 32.9 percent of jobless workers receiving benefits in a given month. In other words, some 5.5 million unemployed people went without benefits in an average month in 1986.[28]

Moreover, as the coverage has declined, so too have the benefits. In 1986 the total insurance benefits were 59 percent lower than in 1976 (after adjusting for inflation). The above figures are complicated by the fact that from 1980 to 1986 the number of long-term unemployed (those looking for work for more than a year) rose from 820,000 to 1.2 million. These factors, coupled with federal budget cuts in 1981 that largely eliminated unemployment benefits for those unemployed more than six months, contributed to the falling rates of unemployment coverage and the subsequent increase in poverty rates for the unemployed.

SOME THEORETICAL FORMULATIONS ABOUT POVERTY

In a tongue-in-cheek fashion, Herbert Gans lists thirteen reasons for the existence of poverty in the United States: (1) The poor are expected to do the menial, dangerous, and dirty work that no one else wants to do; (2) the poor do the kind of work (domestic labor) that allows others to pursue more rewarding activities; (3) poverty creates jobs for the middle class—e.g., social workers, law officers, and so forth; (4) the poor buy old, defective, and used merchandise that no one else wants; (5) the poor are used as an object lesson to teach middle-class values—e.g., the poor are called lazy because the general society values hard work; (6) the poor allow the rest of society to live vicariously, i.e., the larger society is able to fantasize about the supposed world of the poor—free sex, drugs, alcoholic behavior, and so forth; (7) the poor often contribute to unique cultural events such as music and dance; (8) the existence of poverty allows the upper classes to maintain their higher status in society; (9) the poor provide a lucrative market for illegal activities, thereby profiting some of the wealthy who are engaged in that business; (10) the poor provide a cause for the affluent who desire to pursue charity; (11) the poor bear the burden of economic growth—e.g., razing of the slums to make way for urban renewal; (12) the poor serve political functions—e.g., without the poor vote the Democratic party would lose much of its power; (13) the poor function as a target for social criticism, thereby deflecting criticism away from the more affluent.[29]

The Culture of Poverty

Several schools of thought have attempted to explain poverty. One such school is composed of the Culture of Poverty (COP) theorists who maintain that poverty—more specifically, poverty traits—are transmitted intergenerationally. These theorists, led by Edward Banfield and Oscar Lewis, maintain that poverty is a way of life passed on from generation to generation in a self-perpetuating cycle. The COP, according to this theory, transcends regional, rural-urban, and national differences, and shows striking similarities in family structure, interpersonal relations, time orientation, value systems, and patterns of spending.[30]

Oscar Lewis maintains that the COP flourishes in societies where (1) there is a cash economy, wage labor, and production for profit; (2) a high rate of under- and unemployment exists for unskilled workers; (3) low wages are common; (4) there is a failure to provide low-income groups with social, political, and economic organization, either on a voluntary basis or by government imposition; (5) a bilateral kinship system exists rather than a unilateral one; (6) a set of values held by the dominant class stresses the accumulation of wealth and property, the possibility of upward mobility, thrift, and an ideological explanation of low economic status as a result of personal inadequacy.

According to Lewis, the COP is characterized by: (1) hopelessness, indifference, alienation, apathy, and a lack of effective participation and integration of the poor in the social and economic fabric of society; (2) a present-tense time orientation; (3) a cynicism and mistrust of those in authority; (4) strong feelings of marginality, helplessness, dependence, and inferiority; (5) a high incidence of maternal deprivation, orality, and a weak ego structure; (6) confusion of sexual identification; (7) lack of impulse control and the inability to defer gratification; (8) a sense of resignation and fatalism; (9) a widespread belief in male superiority; (10) a high tolerance for psychological pathology of all kinds; (11) a provincialism coupled with little sense of history; (12) the absence of childhood as a protected and a specially prolonged state, and thus early initiation into free sexual unions or consensual marriages; (13) a high incidence in the abandonment of wives and children; (14) a matriarchal family structure containing an emphasis on family solidarity which is never achieved because of sibling rivalry and competition for maternal affection; (15) a proclivity toward authoritarianism; and (16) a minimum level of organization beyond the nuclear or extended family, a low level of community organization, and a strong sense of territoriality.

Adherents of the COP theory believe that simply being poor does not initiate one into the Culture of Poverty. Banfield and Lewis both believe that most people who experience poverty through the loss of a breadwinner, involuntary unemployment, illness and so forth, are able to overcome their impoverishment. The poverty that these people endure is not the squalid, degrading, or self-perpetuating kind found among COP victims. Lewis suggests that only 20 percent of people living under the poverty line are actually ensconced in the COP. Nevertheless, according to Banfield, those in the COP will be poor regardless of their external circumstances, and improvements in their environment will only superficially affect their poverty.

Some opponents of the COP argue that this theoretical orientation diverts attention from the real factors that cause poverty. These critics maintain that an unjust society encourages the attitudes that Lewis and Banfield observe. Other critics argue that many of Lewis's observations about the COP are also evident in the middle and upper classes. For example, the inability to defer gratification underlies many credit card purchases. Free sexual unions and consensual (non-legal) marriages are a common occurrence among the middle classes, and especially publicized in Hollywood. A lack of community and provincialism are earmarks of the modern suburb as well as the slum. The inability to achieve family solidarity, feelings of indifference, helplessness, alienation, and dependence probably afflict the modern middle-class person as often as the slum dweller. Consequently, either a COP does not exist, or it has been usurped by the middle classes in the same way as marijuana and jazz.

Eugenics and Poverty

Eugenic theories, based on a belief that poverty is grounded in genetic inferiority, have periodically surfaced as plausible explanations for poverty, crime, and disease. In 1877 Richard Dugdale wrote *The Jukes*, a study of the New

York penal system which found that crime, pauperism, and disease were transmitted intergenerationally and were closely related to prurient behavior, feeblemindedness, intemperance, and mental disorder.[31] A second major book of the eugenics movement was Henry Goddard's *The Kallikak Family*, an account of a Revolutionary War soldier who had an affair with a feebleminded servant girl before his marriage to a "respectable woman."[32] As part of his analysis, Goddard meticulously listed the disreputable descendants of the servant girl and compared them to the respectable achievers who emerged from the wife's descendants. Dugdale's and Goddard's findings were reaffirmed by similar pseudoscientific research which further established poverty as an inherited characteristic. Generations of students were taught the irrefutable dogma of eugenics.

The eugenics movement went into remission when it became obvious how racial and genetic theories had formed the groundwork for Hitler's genocidal policies. However, the movement has reemerged after close to forty years—albeit, in a modified form—with the publication in 1969 of Arthur Jensen's article, "How Much Can We Boost IQ and Scholastic Achievement."[33] Jensen concluded that compensatory education was doomed to failure since 80 percent of intelligence (as measured by intelligence tests) was inherited. He pointed to the fact that the average IQ scores of blacks were 15 points lower than their white counterparts, and therefore, money spent on compensatory education was wasted.[34]

Jensen's theories were taken one step further by William Shockley, a Nobel Laureate in physics, who became interested in genetics in 1974. Shockley advocated paying the "unfit poor" (those who paid no income taxes) $1,000 for each point they fell below 100 IQ, if they agreed to be sterilized. The money they received would be placed in a trust fund and dispensed to them throughout their lives.[35] To encourage the propagation of brilliant people like himself, Shockley invited other Nobel Laureates to follow his lead and contribute to a sperm bank.[36]

Richard Herrnstein, a Harvard psychologist and a colleague of Shockley and Jensen, claimed that income and wealth are distributed among Americans based on their abilities, which, in the final analysis, are connected to their IQ scores. Herrnstein maintained that America was becoming a "hereditary meritocracy," and the most capable citizens should receive the greatest rewards, thereby forming an incentive to take the responsibility of leadership.[37]

The theories of Shockley, Jensen, and Herrnstein have been repudiated by dozens of educators, psychologists, sociologists, and anthropologists. Critics claim that IQ scores do not guarantee success in life and, in fact, many incarcerated criminals have high IQ scores. Moreover, several studies have shown that compensatory education does significantly raise IQ scores.[38] Lastly, a variety of studies have found that IQ tests are biased in favor of middle-class and upper socioeconomic level students. In short, assertions about genetic inferiority fail to hold up under scrutiny.

The Radical School and Poverty

Another school of thought is the radical approach. Radicals define poverty as the result of exploitation by the ruling or dominant class. According to Marxians, one function of poverty is to provide the capitalists with an army of surplus laborers who are used as a means to depress the wage structure of society. For example, the law of supply and demand also pertains to the wage marketplace—an oversupply of workers means that employers can bid with wages, knowing quite well that there is an abundance of takers. Moreover, when there is an oversupply of labor, employers can threaten recalcitrant workers with dismissal more easily because the worker is aware of the competition for his or her job. The oversupply of workers is inextricably linked to the fabric of poverty and, as such, poverty inadvertently becomes a way to discipline the labor force, thereby forcing concessions that might otherwise not be made.

A second function of poverty is to increase the prestige of the middle class by having a class directly below them. As long as an underclass exists, the middle class has a group they can feel superior to. The superiority felt by the middle class encourages a bond with the upper class around the issue of social stability, because both classes fear the loss of their social position. Inadvertently, the existence of the poor obscures the class tensions between the upper and the middle class around resource distribution. In that sense, the best way to galvanize two potential enemies is to create a third enemy (the poor), one that appears to threaten both parties.

According to David Gil, poverty can also be understood in another light: status and resource allocation and the division of labor.[39] Most developed societies must perform several universal processes. For one, a society must develop resources—symbolic, material, life-sustaining, and life-enhancing goods and services. Moreover, most complex societies must develop a division of labor which is usually connected to the allocation of statuses, as well as assigning individuals or groups to specific tasks related to developing, producing, or distributing the resources of a society. The division of labor is used as the basis for assigning statuses to individuals and groups—that is, the more highly the society prizes the function the individual or group is expected to perform, the higher the status and the reward. By manipulating the division of labor a society is able to assign individuals to specific statuses within the total array of statuses and functions available. These status allocations involve corresponding roles and prerogatives.

Complementing the assignment of status roles is the issue of rights distribution. Higher status roles implicitly demand greater compensation than lower-status roles, and those rewards come in the distribution of rights.

Therefore, higher-status groups are rewarded by a substantial and liberal distribution of specific rights to material and symbolic resources, goods, and services through general entitlements. Conversely, lower-status groups are denied these resources by formal and informal constraints. The entire process is couched in the language of the marketplace. This form of status and goods allocation is rationalized by a belief in the omniscient quality of the marketplace, and, to appear rational, the market is mystically imbued with an internal sense of reason and logic. The implicit ideology is so well masked that it often appears fail-safe, and its rationality is rarely questioned.

Although it often appears inequitable, society must allocate goods and statuses because all valuable resources are finite, with their worth judged by the available quantity. For example, gold is a valuable commodity because its quantity is limited. In that sense, opportunity is a valuable commodity because it, too, is limited. Harvard is a prestigious institution partly because it only accepts a certain number of students yearly, and its policy of admissions is thought to be stringent. Should Harvard adopt an open-door admissions policy, one might expect its prestige to plummet. High status occupations or social positions are also a scarce commodity and thus are socially distributed.

The question remains as to how those statuses are distributed and how the division of labor is determined. In American society the division of labor and status allocation—and their by-product, the distribution of rights—are differentially determined by sex, race, and social class. In large part, those occupying high status positions determine their successors and, more often than not, the heir-apparents belong to their same social class.

Poverty is a logical outgrowth of an inequitable system of resource, status, and rights distribution. Those who live in poverty have been assigned specific social tasks and roles, and the status of the group often corresponds to the nature of the task. Through the assignment of status, role, and rights distribution, societies attempt to reproduce themselves and the ideologies which justify them. In the end, the main job of any society is to reproduce itself and, in doing so, it often reproduces the relations of production and power.

Although on the surface this argument appears to explain social inequity, it does not necessarily explain poverty. For example, is it possible for status allocation to be based on the need for a society to reproduce itself, and for that society to still obviate poverty? Adherents to the radical approach argue that as long as society reproduces itself based on the private ownership of the means of production, poverty will be omnipresent. Moreover, many radical theorists argue that even though status must be allocated, poverty can still be eliminated through the equitable distribution of goods and resources. Although it may be possible to eradicate poverty and, at the same time, allocate status, most radicals doubt that it can be done under the aegis of capitalism.

According to radical critics, the social function of the poor cannot be altered without a basic rearrangement in the social fabric of American society. In short, poverty is an immutable reality in a society marked by discrimination and the inequitable distribution of resources.

A NOTE ON STRATEGIES DEVELOPED TO COMBAT POVERTY

Social scientists and policy analysts have identified three basic strategies for combating poverty. The first strategy, used by Lyndon Johnson in the War on Poverty and Great Society programs, was an attempt to apply a curative approach to the problems of the poor. The curative strategy aims to end the cycle of poverty by allowing the poor to become self-supporting through bringing about changes in their personal lives as well as their environment. By breaking the self-perpetuating cycle

of poverty, the poor are initiated into the working class and later the middle class. The goal of the curative perspective is rehabilitation rather than relief, and its target is the causes of poverty, not the consequences.

The second antipoverty strategy is the alleviative approach. This perspective is best exemplified by public assistance programs which attempt to ease the suffering of the poor rather than ameliorate the causes of poverty.

The third approach is the preventive strategy, best exemplified by the nation's social insurance programs (Social Security). In this approach, people are required to save money to insure their future against accidents, sickness, death, old age, unemployment, and disability. The preventive strategy sees the state as a large insurance company whose umbrella shelters its productive members against the vicissitudes of life.

In 1958 John Kenneth Galbraith, later to become one of John F. Kennedy's principal economic advisors, wrote *The Affluent Society*. In this landmark book, Galbraith identified two kinds of poverty: case poverty and area poverty. According to Galbraith, case poverty was a product of a personal deficiency, or a deficit in human capital. Area poverty was related to economic problems endemic to a region. "Pockets of poverty" or "depressed areas" resulted from a lack of industrialization in a region, or the inability of an area to adjust to technological change. This kind of poverty was a function of the changing nature of the marketplace.[40]

One example of a case poverty approach is the federal government's attempts to encourage education as a means to increase human capital. Poverty is highly correlated with educational deficits, and adolescent parenthood is strongly associated with low levels of basic skills and high dropout rates. For example, youths with the weakest reading and math skills are eight times as likely to have children out of wedlock and seven times as likely to drop out of high school compared to students with above-average skills.[41] To help address the educational deficits of the poor, the federal government instituted the Head Start program that was targeted for poor children aged three to five and their families. The High/Scope Educational Research Foundation's 20-year follow-up study of Head Start (and similar pre-school) graduates found that they were more likely to complete high school, receive additional vocational or academic training, be employed, be self-supporting, have less problems with the law, have lower instances of teenage pregnancy, and be less likely to become public assistance recipients.[42]

The reality of area poverty becomes obvious when examining the poverty demographics on a state by state basis (Table 6.8). In 1985 the poverty rate for all persons in the United States was 14 percent. Some states, however, had much higher poverty rates, including the District of Columbia (20.4 percent), West Virginia (22.3 percent), Alabama (20.6 percent), Mississippi (25.1 percent), and Arkansas (22.9 percent). On the other hand, states such as New Hampshire (6.0 percent), Connecticut (7.6 percent), and New Jersey (8.3 percent) had poverty rates below the national norm.[43] Depressed states such as Arkansas, Mississippi, Alabama, and West Virginia, among others, traditionally experience a recession regardless of the economic prosperity enjoyed by the rest of the nation.

TABLE 6.8. State Poverty Rates (1979 and 1985) and Per Capita Income

	1979	1985	Percentage Point Difference	Per Capita Income (1986)	Rank (Per Capita Income, 1986)
State					
Alabama	22.0	20.6	−1.4	$11,115	45
Alaska	10.8	8.8	−2.0	17,744	4
Arizona	10.1	10.7	0.7	13,220	31
Arkansas	21.1	22.9	1.8	10,773	48
California	10.2	13.6	3.4	16,778	7
Colorado	7.2	10.3	3.1	15,113	12
Connecticut	5.9	7.6	1.7	19,208	1
Delaware	9.0	11.4	2.4	15,010	14
Dist. of Col.	16.1	20.4	4.3	18,980	2
Florida	14.6	13.4	−1.2	14,281	20
Georgia	15.0	17.7	2.7	13,224	29
Hawaii	9.1	10.7	1.6	14,691	16
Idaho	11.3	16.0	4.7	11,432	42
Illinois	11.8	15.6	3.8	15,420	10
Indiana	9.8	12.0	2.2	12,944	33
Iowa	7.9	18.0	10.1	13,322	30
Kansas	8.3	13.8	5.5	14,379	19
Kentucky	12.0	19.4	7.4	11,129	44
Louisiana	18.5	18.1	−0.4	11,227	43
Maine	12.0	11.9	−0.1	12,709	35
Maryland	6.4	8.7	2.3	16,588	8
Massachusetts	8.9	9.3	0.4	17,516	5
Michigan	8.9	14.5	5.6	14,064	21
Minnesota	7.4	12.6	5.2	14,737	15
Mississippi	19.9	25.1	5.2	9,552	51
Missouri	11.2	13.7	2.5	13,657	26
Montana	14.2	16.1	1.9	11,904	39
Nebraska	9.8	14.8	5.0	13,377	24

TABLE 6.8. (cont.)

	1979	1985	Percentage Point Difference	Per Capita Income (1986)	Rank (Per Capita Income, 1986)
Nevada	7.0	14.4	7.4	15,074	13
New Hampshire	7.0	6.0	−1.0	15,922	9
New Jersey	10.8	8.3	−2.5	18,284	3
New Mexico	18.5	18.5	0.0	11,037	47
New York	12.5	15.8	3.3	17,118	6
North Carolina	13.6	14.2	0.6	12,245	38
North Dakota	13.1	15.9	2.8	12,284	37
Ohio	9.8	12.8	3.0	13,743	25
Oklahoma	12.8	16.1	3.3	12,368	36
Oregon	9.0	11.9	2.9	13,217	32
Pennsylvania	9.0	10.5	1.5	13,944	22
Rhode Island	7.5	9.0	1.5	14,670	17
South Carolina	20.2	15.2	−5.0	11,096	46
South Dakota	14.5	17.3	2.8	11,850	40
Tennessee	16.2	18.1	1.9	11,831	41
Texas	15.1	15.9	0.8	13,523	27
Utah	8.1	11.1	3.0	10,743	49
Vermont	13.2	9.2	−4.0	12,845	34
Virginia	11.0	10.0	−1.0	15,374	11
Washington	9.6	12.0	2.4	14,498	18
West Virginia	14.3	22.3	8.0	10,530	50
Wisconsin	7.1	11.6	4.5	13,796	23
Wyoming	6.4	12.0	5.6	13,230	28

Sources: Adapted from Christine M. Ross and Sheldon Danziger, "Poverty Rates by State, 1979 and 1985: A Research Note," *Focus*, Vol. 10, No. 3 (Fall 1987); and U.S. Department of Commerce *News*, April 16, 1987.

The above approaches to poverty are not merely hypothetical formulations, they have formed the foundation for social welfare policy throughout much of the 1960s and beyond. Between 1965 and 1980, social welfare policies were grounded in the view that public expenditures should be used as a direct means to stimulate opportunities for the poor. As a result, major social welfare legislation was enacted and billions of dollars earmarked for the remediation of poverty. Beginning with the Reagan administration in 1980, there was a move away from reliance on social welfare expenditures and to an emphasis on ending poverty through economic growth. Consequently, public expenditures for poverty programs decreased while tax cuts to provide incentives to work and save money increased. The Reagan approach assumed that it would be in the best interests of the poor to wait for gains realized through increased economic activity, rather than to rely on welfare programs. This perspective assumed that the trickle-down effect of economic growth would benefit the poor more than direct economic subsidies. Nevertheless, despite the emphasis on eradicating poverty through market incomes, the major factors influencing the general decrease in poverty from the 1960s to the late 1970s were governmental cash and in-kind transfers.[44]

Because poverty is a political as well as a social issue, the policies surrounding it are often less than objective. For example, one can cut the rate of poverty in half simply by redefining the poverty index. Conversely, one can swell the ranks of the poor by moving the poverty line upward; that is, by increasing the income level at which people are defined as poor. Poverty can also be technically eliminated by placing a high dollar value on in-kind benefits such as Food Stamps and Medicaid. Like all social policies, poverty-related policies exist in a context marked by political exigencies, public opinion, the economic health of a society, and the complex mask of ideology.

NOTES

1. *Federal Register*, vol. 53, no. 46 (Washington, D.C.: U.S. Government Printing Office), March 20, 1987, p. 9518.
2. U.S. Bureau of the Census, *Statistical Abstract of the United States*, (Washington, D.C.: U.S. Government Printing Office, 1984), p. 447.
3. Michael Harrington, with the assistance of Robert Greenstein and Eleanor Holmes Norton, *Who Are the Poor?* (Washington, D.C.: Justice for All, 1987), pp. 3–4. See also Center on Budget and Policy Priorities, "Analysis of Poverty in 1987," Washington, D.C., 1988, p. 8.
4. Ibid., p. 17.
5. Center on Budget and Policy Priorities, "Poverty Rate Shows Disappointing Drop; Income Inequality Widens," Washington, D.C., August 27, 1988.
6. *Congressional Record*, Senate, vol. 133, no. 120 (Washington, D.C.: U.S. Government Printing Office, July 21, 1987), pp. S10400–S10404.
7. Harrington, *Who Are the Poor?*, p. 9.
8. Sheldon Danziger, "Poverty," *Encyclopedia of Social Work*, 18th Edition (Silver Spring, Md.: NASW, 1987), pp. 295, 297.
9. Sheldon Danziger and David Feaster, "Income Transfers and Poverty in the 1980s," in J. Quigley and D. Rubinfeld, eds., *Agenda for Metropolitan America* (Berkeley, Calif.: University of California Press, 1985), p. 126.
10. See U.S. Bureau of the Census, "Money, Income, and Poverty Status of Persons and Families in the United States, 1984" (Washington, D.C.: U.S. Government Printing Office), August 27, 1985. See also Center on Budget and Policy Priorities, "Analysis of Poverty in

1987," p. 11.
11. Robert S. McIntyre, "The Populist Tax Act of 1986," *The Nation*, 246, no. 13 (April 2, 1988), p. 445.
12. Winifred Bell, *Contemporary Social Welfare* (New York: Macmillan, 1983), p. 65.
13. Ibid.
14. Center on Budget and Policy Priorities, "Analysis of Poverty in 1987," p. 14.
15. Ibid.
16. Center on Budget and Policy Priorities, "Poverty Remains High Despite Economic Recovery," Washington, D.C., 1988, p. 1.
17. Ibid.
18. McIntyre, "The Populist Tax Act of 1989," p. 462.
19. Ibid.
20. Isaac Shapiro and Robert Greenstein, *Holes in the Safety Nets* (Washington, D.C.: Center on Budget and Policy Priorities, 1988), pp. 27–28.
21. Ibid., pp. 25–27.
22. Blanche Bernstein, "Welfarë Dependency," in Lee D. Bawden, ed., *The Social Contract Revisited* (Washington, D.C.: Urban Institute Press, 1984), p. 129.
23. Greg J. Duncan et al., *Years of Poverty, Years of Plenty* (Ann Arbor, Mich.: Institute for Social Research, 1984).
24. Harrington, *Who Are the Poor?* p. 10.
25. Ibid., p. 11.
26. Ibid., p. 10.
27. Center on Budget and Policy Priorities, *Smaller Pieces of the Pie*.
28. Center on Budget and Policy Priorities, "Left Out: The Plight of the Jobless Workers in 1986," Washington, D.C., March 1987.
29. Herbert J. Gans, "The Uses of Poverty: The Poor Pay All," *Social Policy* 2, no. 2 (July–August 1971), pp. 20–24.
30. See Edward C. Banfield, *The Unheavenly City* (Boston: Little, Brown, 1966); and Oscar Lewis, *La Vida* (New York: Harper and Row, 1965).
31. Richard Dugdale, *The Jukes*, New York, 1877.
32. Henry Goddard, *The Kallikak Family*, New York, 1911.
33. Arthur R. Jensen, "How Much Can We Boost IQ and Scholastic Achievement," *Harvard Educational Review*, 39 (Winter 1969), pp. 1–23.

34. Bell, *Contemporary Social Welfare*.

35. William Shockley, "Sterilization: A Thinking Exercise," in Carl Bahema, ed., *Eugenics: Then and Now* (Stroudsburg, Pa.: Doidon, Hutchinson and Ross, 1976).

36. Bell, *Contemporary Social Welfare*.

37. Richard Herrnstein, *IQ and the Meritocracy* (Boston: Little, Brown, 1973).

38. Bell, *Contemporary Social Welfare*.

39. David Gil, *Unraveling Social Policy* (Boston: Schenkman, 1981).

40. John Kenneth Galbraith, *The Affluent Society* (Boston: Houghton Mifflin, 1958).

41. Harrington, *Who Are the Poor?*, p. 17.

42. Ibid., p. 22.

43. Christine M. Ross, "Poverty Rates by State, 1979 and 1985: A Research Note," *Focus* 10, no. 3 (Fall 1987), pp. 1–5.

44. Danziger, "Poverty," pp. 301–2.

PART TWO

The Voluntary and For-profit Social Welfare Sector

CHAPTER 7

The Voluntary Sector Today

This chapter describes the voluntary sector—those private, nonprofit organizations that are important in American social welfare. Prominent human service agencies—such as the Red Cross, the Family Service Association of America, and the Salvation Army—are identified. In addition, the role of voluntary agencies in advocating social justice is described. The fiscal crisis of the voluntary sector is discussed.

Approaching the twenty-first century, welfare professionals are reassessing the capacity of the voluntary sector to meet the nation's social welfare needs. The primary reason for renewed interest in the voluntary sector is the reluctance of taxpayers and politicians to authorize major new governmental welfare initiatives. As governmental expenditures for social welfare fail to increase in the face of rising demand for human services, the voluntary sector has been called upon to shoulder more of the welfare burden. This has been stated explicitly by President Reagan who appealed to the charitable impulses of Americans as a way to address human need while reducing federal appropriations to social programs and restated by George Bush in his now-famous reference to "a thousand points of light" during the 1988 presidential campaign.

While many liberals were skeptical about the sincerity of the Reagan and Bush administrations in this regard—suspecting it was a ruse to gut governmental social programs—other events conspired to focus attention on the voluntary sector. A wave of conservative populism, most evident in the religious right, helped to effectively halt the introduction of liberally inspired social legislation. Conservative populists challenged welfare programs on the basis that they divided the family, eroded the work ethic, and subverted communal norms. A widely distributed monograph by analysts from the American Enterprise Institute criticized social "megastructures," which contributed to alienation among Americans, while calling for stronger "mediating structures"—voluntary entities—to empower people.[1] Reacting to these conservative trends, Democrats jettisoned traditional welfare planks from their party platform—i.e., full employment, national health care, and a guaranteed income—for the first time since the New Deal. Finally, welfare advocates established a new organization, Independent Sector, to promote the interests of voluntary sector organizations. By 1986, six years after its inception, Independent Sector was able to boast more than 650 corporate, foundation, and voluntary organization members.

THE "FORGOTTEN SECTOR"

Despite this recent flurry of activity, the voluntary sector is neither fully appreciated nor well understood in American social welfare.[2] Following the triumph of the New Deal, leading welfare theoreticians expected government to dominate in the creation and administration of the welfare state. In fact, so complete was the expectation that the government-driven welfare state would dominate social welfare in the United States that reference to private voluntary agencies became scant in the professional literature. There was little room within welfare state ideology for a dynamic voluntary sector, and references to private, nonprofit agencies virtually disappeared from discussions about American social welfare. When discussed at all, voluntary agencies were viewed as quaint and residual organizations from an earlier time.

To the extent that the voluntary sector was considered within the context of the governmental welfare state, it was considered a subcontractor of social service. This role was made possible through an amendment to the Social Security Act, Title XX, which allowed for the "purchase of service" from private providers. Under purchase of service contracts, government could avoid the costs and responsibilities of administering programs directly. Because of an open-ended funding formula, however, federal costs for Title XX services escalated sharply. Congress later capped Title XX expenditures, initially at $2.5 billion, in order to contain program costs, and later the Reagan administration was successful at having the program placed under a Social Services Block Grant, with further funding restrictions.[3] Consequently, in response to Title XX, many voluntary social service agencies secured purchase of service contracts, the funding for which allowed nonprofit agencies to expand programs in the late 1960s and early 1970s. However, when funding was reduced, voluntary sector agencies were heavily penalized. Federal expenditures for Title XX fell from $2.8 billion in 1980 to $2.6 billion in 1986, a significant reduction since it occurred at a time during which demand for service rose sharply.[4] As a result, voluntary social welfare agencies were hard pressed to maintain such services as home-based care, child day care and protective services, self-support education, adoption and family counseling services, among others. Although federal assistance to voluntary sector social service agencies became critically important to them, accounting for up to half of agency funding, purchase of service continued to be a relatively minor portion of governmental welfare expenditures. In 1986, for example, Title XX accounted for only about 2 percent of all federal expenditures

for welfare programs benefiting low-income people.[5]

Consequently, when policymakers turned to the voluntary sector in the 1980s to compensate for reductions in the governmental welfare effort, little was known about nonprofit social service agencies. Lester Salamon and Alan Abramson, authorities on the voluntary sector, observed that, "despite their importance, these organizations have tended to be ignored in both public policy debates and scholarly research."[6] As government assumed a dominant role in American social welfare, the voluntary sector receded in importance. Now, after half a century of neglect, the "forgotten sector" is being called upon to assume new responsibilities in caring for the needy.

Only in recent times have researchers begun to investigate the scope of the voluntary sector. Their task has not been without difficulty. The voluntary sector is composed of tens of thousands of organizations, many of which are not associated with a national umbrella association. The picture that is emerging from these preliminary investigations reveals a sector that, if small by economic standards, is extraordinarily rich socially. Perhaps the most convenient measure of the scale of the voluntary sector is to count those voluntary and philanthropic associations that have received tax-exempt status from the Internal Revenue Service—821,000 in 1984.[7] Despite the large number of voluntary sector organizations, they account for only 6 percent of the national income, compared to 79 percent attributed to commerce and 15 percent to government.[8] Indeed, the strength of the voluntary sector lies in its incorporation into the social fabric of American life. Nearly half of all Americans 14 years or older (89 million) volunteered in 1985.[9] A substantial majority of Americans (89 percent in 1984) made charitable contributions to voluntary sector agencies, averaging $650.[10] Contrary to popular assumption, the voluntary sector is not bankrolled by wealthy philanthropists and their foundations. Foundations and

TABLE 7.1. Primary Sources of Income for Voluntary Services, 1982, 1984

	1982	1984
Federal, state, and local government	48.1%	43.9%
Fees for service	12.4%	12.6%
Private giving	34.1%	37.4%
Other	6.1%	5.4%

Source: Virginia Hodgkinson and Murray Weitzman, *Dimensions of the Independent Sector* (Washington, D.C.: Independent Sector, 1986), p. 119. Reprinted with permission.

corporations account for only 10 percent of voluntary sector contributions; "about half of all charitable dollars comes from families with incomes under $25,000."[11]

Of all nonprofit organizations, approximately 130,000 were active in social welfare in 1984.[12] Funds allocated for social welfare in 1982—i.e., social services, community development, legal services, and certain health programs—totaled $27.3 billion.[13] Significantly, voluntary sector agencies providing social services fared poorly compared to voluntary sector organizations in fields such as education, arts and culture, and religion. While social service agencies comprise 40 percent of all voluntary sector entities, they claim only 12 percent of the resources.[14] The primary sources of in-

come for voluntary social service agencies are identified in Table 7.1.[15]

These data reveal two developments influencing voluntary social service agencies. First, governmental and private giving account for about 80 percent of revenues. Second, governmental support declined sharply during the early 1980s. The significance of this will be addressed later in the chapter. Perhaps most importantly, fees charged to clients of voluntary social service agencies account for about 12 percent of revenues, dispelling any thought that these organizations as a group could become self-sufficient through collection of client fees. While some organizations are able to derive more of their revenues from fees, most social service agencies depend on other revenue sources, as Table 7.2 illustrates.[16]

Proponents of private, nonprofit organizations contend that economic measures do not adequately represent the significance of the voluntary sector in the national culture. Consistent with the label "voluntary," nonprofit social service agencies attract the commitment of millions of volunteers who see human service organizations as a vehicle for improving the quality of life in their communities. During 1984, volunteers in social service agencies put in enough time to equal a million paid full-time

TABLE 7.2. Agency Funding Sources, 1986

	Private Support	Government	Fees and Dues	Other*
Boys Clubs	66%	7%	8%	19%
Catholic Charities	21	47	12	19
Child Welfare Agency	15	65	6	14
Family Service Agency	28	46	17	9
Goodwill Industries	29	19	19	33
Jewish Community Centers	16	7	54	23
Salvation Army	57	14	10	20
Volunteers of America	13	45	8	34
YMCA, YMCA-YWCA	17	4	67	12
YWCA	29	21	36	14

* Other includes such sources of income as bequests, investment income, sale of capital goods and sale of merchandise. The relatively high percentage of support in the "other" category for Goodwill Industries, the Salvation Army, and Volunteers of America comes from sales of donated merchandise. Source: Virginia Hodgkinson and Murray Weitzman, *Dimensions of the Independent Sector* (Washington, D.C.: Independent Sector, 1986), p. 21. Reprinted with permission.

employees, the cash value of which was $15.2 billion. Significantly, volunteering increased in the early 1980s, to some extent compensating for reductions in governmental support. While social service agency volunteers donated about 10 percent of their time in 1981, by 1985 this had increased to 15 percent.[17] Despite this outpouring of support for voluntary social service agencies, a question remains concerning the degree to which nonprofit social service agencies should have to rely on volunteers when nonprofit organizations in education and the arts are more likely to have employees providing services.

ADVANCING SOCIAL JUSTICE

In addition to providing social services, the voluntary sector has been important in American social welfare because it has been the source of events that have advanced the rights of disenfranchised populations. In this respect, the voluntary sector is essential to American culture since it is a correcting influence to the indifference often shown to minority populations by governmental and corporate bureaucracies. This case has been argued vigorously by John W. Gardner, former Secretary of Health, Education, and Welfare; President of the Carnegie Corporation; and now Chairperson of the Board of Independent Sector. According to Gardner, the voluntary sector fosters much of the pluralism in American life, taking on those concerns that do not attract the broad spectrum of public support necessary for the legislation that mandates governmental programs—or concerns that do not represent the commercial prospects necessary to attract the interests of the business community. In other words, the voluntary sector serves as the best—and in some cases, the only—vehicle for addressing certain social needs. Indeed, much of what Americans would identify as central to their culture is attributed to organizations of the voluntary sector: hospitals, schools, religious institutions, welfare

agencies, fraternal associations, symphonies and museums, as a partial list. According to Gardner:

> Institutions of the nonprofit sector are in a position to serve as the guardians of intellectual and artistic freedom. Both the commercial and political marketplaces are subject to leveling forces that may threaten standards of excellence. In the non-profit sector, the fiercest champions of excellence may have their say. So may the champions of liberty and justice.[18]

Gardner's last reference here is not merely rhetorical, but has its basis in history. As Alexis de Tocqueville observed over a century earlier, Americans have depended on voluntary organizations to solve communal problems. In doing so, the voluntary sector has claimed an impressive list of positive additions to American life. Those seeking solutions to present problems often find inspiration in voluntary sector initiatives of the past. Gardner noted that, "At a time in our history when we are ever in need of new solutions to new problems, the private sector is remarkably free to innovate, create, and engage in controversial experiments." He went on to observe that, "In fact, virtually every far-reaching social change in our history has come up in the private sector: the abolition of slavery, the reforms of populism, child labor laws, the vote for women, civil rights, and so on."[19]

Important social welfare initiatives have also originated in the voluntary sector. The War on Poverty—during which new social programs, such as Medicaid, Food Stamps, and the Job Corps were launched—can be traced to the Mobilization for Youth, a voluntary sector poverty program in New York City funded by the Ford Foundation. Two champions of community organization, the late Saul Alinsky and Cesar Chavez of the United Farm Workers Union, worked out of the privately run Industrial Areas Foundation in Chicago. More recently, services to battered women, patients with AIDS, and the homeless have been pioneered by voluntary sector organizations. Given public apathy toward these groups for so many years, the voluntary sector was the only source of service for these groups.

CONTEMPORARY NONPROFIT HUMAN SERVICE ORGANIZATIONS

The voluntary human service sector consists of a large constellation of organizations. In 1982, over 52,000 nonprofit organizations were active in providing individual and family services, job training, child care, residential care, and social services, and this figure excludes the over 13,000 health care and over 1000 legal services providers often grouped within social welfare.[20] The best depiction of the voluntary sector is not provided by statistics, however, but by a

description of the organizations that are instantly recognizable by most Americans (see Table 7.3).

The well-known voluntary sector organizations provide a wide range of service, and their sensitivity to community needs results in continuous demands for new programs. Inaugurating its second century in American social welfare, the United Way identified eight social problems as foci for its affiliates: *illiteracy* (programs to help the 23 million people who are functionally illiterate in the United States), *hunger and homelessness* (services to aid the 3 million homeless and 20 million Americans who go hungry at least two days each month), *AIDS* (initiatives to contend with a 60 percent increase in AIDS in 1987), *teenage pregnancy* (services to reduce the number of teenage girls who become pregnant [over 1 million] each year), *children in crisis* (efforts to improve the

TABLE 7.3. Nonprofit Human Service Organizations

Name	Budget ($ millions)	Affiliates	Services	Current Issues
American Foundation for the Blind	13.9	6 Regional Offices	Education, rehabilitation, and socialization of the blind; public education about vision impairment.	Enhance services to the multi-handicapped; develop special services for the aged blind and blind Native Americans.
American Red Cross	887.7	2,853 Chapters 277 Armed Forces stations 56 Regional blood centers	Disaster relief; blood donor program; water safety; first aid training.	AIDS education; human tissue banks for transplantation.
Arthritis Foundation	40.8	72 Chapters and divisions	Health and exercise programs for those with arthritis; biomedical research on the causes and relief of arthritis.	Establish a separate association for those with rheumatism; Pilot a special program for children.
Association for Retarded Citizens	4.9**	1,300	Research, education, and prevention of retardation and physical handicaps.	Bio-engineering projects to aid the physically handicapped.
Big Brothers/Big Sisters of America	2.0	468	Provide adult guidance for children from single-parent households.	Increase minority recruitment.

continued

TABLE 7.3. (cont.)

Name	Budget ($ millions)	Affiliates	Services	Current Issues
Boy Scouts of America	49.7	411 Councils	Leadership and citizenship training; drug and child-abuse awareness.	Enhance number of scouts and leaders; reduce costs of liability insurance.
Boys Club of America	187.0	1,100 Club units	Leadership education, socialization of poor youth.	Outreach to at-risk youth; delinquency prevention.
Campfire	3.9	292 Councils	Personal living skills; leadership development.	International reorganization; develop enterprise dept.; enhance revenue and membership.
Catholic Charities	636.8	120 +	Counseling; adoption; immigration; emergency support; housing.	Economic justice; family life; shelter; hunger; health care.
Child Welfare League of America	3.6	450 Member agencies	Abused children; adolescent pregnancy; child care; adoption services.	Developing child day care; adolescent pregnancy prevention; parenting effectiveness education.
Council of Jewish Federations	3,800.0	200 + in U.S., Canada, and Israel	Services to the families and the aged; community organization and planning; Jewish cultural development.	Make up for decrease in United Way funding; develop satellite transmission with programs in Israel.
Family Service America	356.0	290 Affiliates	Counseling and advocacy services to families.	Expand services in substance abuse and abuse in the family; internal organizational development.
Girl Scouts of the U.S.A.	23.9	335 Councils	Leadership, education, and socialization of girls.	Eliminate institutional racism; diversify funding; respond to council and community needs.
Goodwill Industries of America	463.0	177 in U.S. and Canada	Vocational rehabilitation for the disabled.	Compensate for cuts in govt. funds; focusing on hi-tech skills; responding to competition from retail firms.
National Council on Alcoholism	1.6	191	Prevention of alcoholism; public education policy analysis.	Include drugs other than alcohol in activities.
National Easter Seal Society	4.7	Approx. 200	Home health for the disabled; public education and advocacy for the disabled.	Computer application to assist the disabled. Design to accommodate disabilities.

TABLE 7.3. (cont.)

Name	Budget ($ millions)	Affiliates	Services	Current Issues
National Mental Health Association	32.0	600+	Client and public policy advocacy for the emotionally disturbed; direct client support services; public education.	Increasing mental health services as a national priority.
National Urban League	21.3	112	Advocating equality for minorities; public education; policy monitoring.	Improving behavior of adolescent males; mobilizing communities to fight crime.
Planned Parenthood Federation of America	274.4	183	Family planning; sexuality education in schools; abortion rights.	Expanding reproductive rights to underserved groups; respond to changes in health policy; review bio-ethical implications of new reproductive technology.
The Salvation Army	3.7**	1,097 Corps community centers	Homelessness, disaster relief; services to children and youth.	Balance evangelism and social service.
United Cerebral Palsy	200.0	196	Rehabilitation for those with cerebral palsy and other severe disabilities. Medical research on causes of cerebral palsy.	Increase public education efforts, fund raising, biomedical research.
USO	19.1	160 locations worldwide	Fleet and airport centers, family support; cultural and recreational services.	Making entertainment programs self-sufficient.
Visiting Nurses Association of America	700.0	Approx. 500	Home health services.	Decrease the cost of home health care to patients.
Volunteers of America	182.2	4,004 Programs in 200 communities	Shelter and food for the disabled; employment training; community corrections.	Literacy; child day care; at-risk youth.
Young Men's Christian Association	1,126.6	2,051	Personal and social development; child care; community development.	Obtaining liability insurance; retaining tax-exempt status.
Young Women's Christian Association	11.4**	Not Available	Develop potential of women; social and support services to women; advocates equality and justice.	Development of nonpartisan political training workshop.

* Source: annual reports of organizations. ** National office only.

plight of poor and minority children who suffer from high incidence of child abuse and neglect, suicide, and unstable homes), *alcoholism and drug abuse* (programs to counter the epidemic of substance abuse among teenagers and minorities), *aging population* (assure that the aged have an adequate supply of essential services), and *child care* (make provisions for the 20 million children who, in 1990, will come home to an empty house because their parents work.[21] Certainly, the extent to which the voluntary sector is able to respond to these and other worthwhile objectives depends on its ability to deploy new programs to address significant social changes.

THE DECLINING FISCAL CAPACITY OF THE VOLUNTARY SECTOR

During the early 1980s, the organizations comprising the voluntary sector appeared to make substantial headway in responding to increases in the demand for their services. Funding for nonprofit social service agencies increased comparably to revenue increases for nonprofit activity in education, religion, and the arts. From 1977 to 1984, total funds for voluntary sector activities increased from $114.2 billion to $253.5 billion, more than twofold.[22] Within the voluntary sector, the expenditures for social services increased from $11.4 billion in 1977 to $21.4 billion in 1984.[23] But these increases obscured deeper problems that have threatened the fiscal stability of nonprofit human service organizations.

Although contributions to social services increased in the early 1980s, social services obtained a smaller portion of all revenues contributed to the voluntary sector. In 1977, social services claimed 10 percent of voluntary sector contributions; in 1984, that had dropped to 8.6 percent.[24] In other words, social services received less in relation to other voluntary sector activities. More troubling is that nonprofit human service agencies faced competition from newer nonprofit organizations for those contributions to the voluntary sector. An example of this can be found in the united giving campaign directed at federal employees, the Combined Federal Campaign, the largest of such fundraising drives in the United States. Until recently, the United Way claimed about 90 percent of all campaign contributions not specifically designated for other purposes. But as a result of challenges brought by non-human service agencies as diverse as environmental groups and the National Rifle Association, nondesignated contributions are now apportioned among a larger number of organizations. Consequently, the United Way expected to get approximately 10 percent less than it had in the past from the Combined Federal Campaign.[25]

More discouraging to administrators of nonprofit human service organizations was the precipitous drop in federal governmental funds early in the 1980s. Federal funds to programs in which nonprofit agencies had been active (excluding Medicare and Medicaid) were reduced by about $26 billion each year (about 25 percent) between 1982 and 1984. Yet, increased fund-raising efforts to compensate for the loss of governmental funds recovered only 7 percent of the loss.[26] In 1977, government funds accounted for 53.5 percent of the funding for social services provided by nonprofits; in 1984, that amount dropped to 43.9 percent, a reduction of approximately one-fourth.[27]

Unfortunately, the prospect of individual contributors making up for the huge cuts in federal funding is not encouraging. Overall, individuals support the United Way in greater frequency than other nonreligious activities,[28] and the majority of United Way contributions, 63.3 percent, come from employees' workplace contributions.[29] Although soliciting higher contributions from employees would seem to be a plausible strategy for increasing voluntary revenues, the decline in wages for middle-income workers in the last several years has left them with less discretionary income to contribute to charitable causes. According to the

Economic Policy Institute, family income in 1985 was below that of 1973, when it peaked.[30] Not only do workers have less discretionary income to donate to charitable causes, but tax law now provides no incentives for many workers to make such contributions. The Tax Reform Act of 1986 prohibited individuals from claiming contributions to charitable causes as deductions if they did not itemize their income tax returns. Since much of the revenue for the voluntary sector comes from middle-income workers who are less likely to itemize their income tax returns, this tax reform threatened to cut into an important revenue source of nonprofit social service agencies. If the recent past provides little reason to expect increases in workers' giving, the future is no more encouraging. In a study of the American labor force at the turn of the century, the Hudson Institute predicted that future workers are more likely to be in lower-paying rather than middle- or higher-paying jobs.[31] Not surprisingly, advocates of the voluntary sector have recognized the limits in financial giving that these figures represent. Accordingly, the Independent Sector has asked individuals to contribute time to voluntary organizations if they are unable to contribute money. By 1991, Independent Sector hopes to have wide public exposure to the "fiver" concept; that is, individuals should contribute 5 percent of their income or five hours per week to nonprofit organizations.[32]

If individual contributions prove insufficient to mitigate cuts in government funds, the corporate sector becomes an important source of revenue. Business accounts for about one-fourth of contributions to the United Way,[33] a figure that had been slowly increasing since the Filer Commission encouraged greater corporate giving in the late 1970s. By the mid-1980s, major corporate donors were contributing up to 3 percent of pretax revenues to charity, slightly above the 2 percent contribution rate by all corporations. However, by 1986 the corporate sector was backing away from Independent Sector's goal of donating "at least 2 percent of pretax net income" to voluntary sector organizations.[34] The Conference Board reported that charitable contributions by major service and industrial companies actually declined about 2 percent in 1986.[35] Given this trend, the stock market crash of October 19, 1987, is particularly troubling. Corporations make charitable contributions from discretionary funds, the reserves of which are contingent on past economic performance and the prospects of future growth. Thus, the fact that the stock market lost a quarter of its value in one trading session is disturbing enough, but failure of the market to regain lost ground is critical because it means that business executives are unlikely to be optimistic about the future of the economy. With the prospect of a recession, corporate officers are not in a position to make commitments in the allocation of discretionary funds which may be needed in the event that the economic situation worsens. Without continuous improvement in the economy, the voluntary sector is not likely to find the business community willing to compensate for cuts in governmental funding.

As a result of diminishing prospects for raising funds from traditional sources, voluntary sector organizations have been forced to consider the entrepreneurial option—engaging in commercial activities to raise needed revenues. It is already standard practice for nonprofit service providers to charge fees for service and bill public and private insurance programs to recoup expenses. Thus, "vendorism" is a common practice of nonprofit social service agencies. But, "entrepreneurialism" is a newer and more significant development. While it may seem innocuous for financially hard-pressed nonprofit agencies to engage in commercial ventures, some small business operators have complained about the unfair competitive advantage enjoyed by nonprofits because of their tax exempt status. (The reaction by the business community to voluntary sector entrepreneurialism is considered in more detail in the discussion of privatization.) Many welfare professionals are also uncomfortable about commercial behavior by nonprofit organizations. Ralph Kramer, an authority on nonprofit social services, has stated the concern well:

> In competing with for-profit and other nonprofit organizations for governmental service contracts and for customers for their income producing subsidiaries, it is feared that voluntary agencies can lose their distinctive identity and become more like a commercial organization.[36]

Thus, the negative response of the business community and the ambivalence felt by many welfare professionals impose limits on the use of commercial methods to enhance the fiscal capacity of the voluntary sector.

From a broader perspective, it is difficult to be sanguine about the future of the voluntary sector in social welfare. As voluntary sector agencies become more dependent on the communities in which they are located, their success is tied to the affluence of those communities. Compared to those of wealthier communities, agencies in poor communities are unlikely to fare well. For example, the voluntary agencies of Jackson, Mississippi, which depend on government for 66 percent of revenues, while generating only 7 percent from fees, are less well positioned than those of Flint, Michigan, which depend on government for 33 percent of funding, but generate fees which account for 32 percent of revenues.[37] In a pattern all too familiar to many welfare professionals, voluntary agencies in the poorer areas of the United States—rural areas, Appalachia, inner cities, Indian reservations—will again be less able to care for their neighbors in need.

If statistics fail to capture the social significance of many events, the same holds true for recent developments in the voluntary sector. If the voluntary sector possesses a social significance that is larger than its economic predicament, its advocates should be able to find solace in continuing those peculiarly American activities with which it is associated. But even these

activities seem to be in jeopardy. Late in 1987, the Girl Scouts cookie drive in Fort Collins, Colorado—intended to fund summer camp—incited the outrage of many mothers when city officials instituted a sales tax on every box of cookies sold.[38] In another incident, community advocates fought back. When the Marriott Corporation objected to a student bake sale to fund a high school foreign exchange program because it competed with the company's food service contract, students pointed out that Marriott was a $5 billion company, then boycotted the food service until the company dropped its objection to the bake sale.[39] As these instances suggest, advocates of the voluntary sector may claim as their ultimate resource the allegiance of their neighbors.

NOTES

1. Peter Berger and Richard Neuhaus, *To Empower People: The Role of Mediating Structures in Public Policy* (Washington, D.C.: American Enterprise Institute, 1977).
2. Ralph Kramer, "The Future of Voluntary Organizations in Social Welfare," in *Philanthropy, Voluntary Action, and the Public Good* (Washington, D.C.: Independent Sector/United Way, 1986).
3. Neil Gilbert, *Capitalism and the Welfare State* (New Haven: Yale University Press, 1983), pp. 6–7; Neil Gilbert and Harry Specht, *Dimensions of Social Welfare Policy*, 2d ed. (Englewood Cliffs, N.J.: Prentice-Hall, 1987), pp. 46–47.
4. *Statistical Abstract of the United States*, 108th ed. (Washington, D.C.: U.S. Government Printing Office, 1988), p. 337.
5. Ibid.
6. Alan Abramson and Lester Salamon, *The Nonprofit Sector and the New Federal Budget* (Washington, D.C.: Urban Institute, 1986), p. xi; Waldemar Nielsen, *The Third Sector: Keystone of a Caring Society* (Washington, D.C.: Independent Sector, 1980).
7. Virginia Hodgkinson and Murray Weitzman, *Dimensions of the Independent Sector*

(Washington, D.C.: Independent Sector, 1986), p. 3.

8. Brian O'Connell, *State of the Sector: With Particular Attention to Its Independence* (Washington, D.C.: Independent Sector, 1987), p. 1.

9. *Americans Volunteer 1985* (Washington, D.C.: Independent Sector, 1986), p. 4.

10. *Charitable Behavior of Americans* (Washington, D.C.: Independent Sector, 1986), p. 1.

11. Brian O'Connell, *Origins, Dimensions and Impact of America's Voluntary Spirit* (Washington, D.C.: Independent Sector, 1984), p. 2.

12. Hodgkinson and Weitzman, *Dimensions of the Independent Sector*, p. 17.

13. W. Harrison Wellford and Janne Gallagher, *The Role of Nonprofit Human Service Organizations* (Washington, D.C.: National Assembly of Voluntary Health and Social Welfare Organizations, 1987), Chapter III, p. 15.

14. Ibid., p. 16.

15. Hodgkinson and Weitzman, *Dimensions of the Independent Sector*, p. 119.

16. Ibid., p. 21.

17. Ibid., pp. 27–29.

18. Gardner quoted in O'Connell, *Origins, Dimensions and Impact of America's Voluntary Spirit*, p. 6.

19. John W. Gardner, *Keynote Address* (Washington, D.C.: Independent Sector, 1978), p. 13.

20. Hodgkinson and Weitzman, *Dimensions of the Voluntary Sector*, p. 128.

21. *Centennial Report* (Alexandria, Va.: United Way of America, 1988), pp. 1–2.

22. Hodgkinson and Weitzman, *Dimensions*, pp. 117–18.

23. Ibid.

24. Ibid., p. 121.

25. Judith Havemann, "Federal Charity Drive Opened to More Groups," *Washington Post*, January 2, 1988.

26. Abramson and Salamon, *The Nonprofit Sector and the New Federal Budget*, pp. xvi, xvii.

27. Hodgkinson and Weitzman, *Dimensions*, pp. 119–21.

28. *The Charitable Behavior of Americans*, p. 21.

29. *Centennial Report*, p. 1.

30. "Family Incomes in Trouble," (Washington, D.C.: Economic Policy Institute, 1986), p. 1.

31. William Johnston et al., *Workforce 2000* (Washington, D.C.: U.S. Department of Labor, 1987), p. 31.

32. *Program Plan 1986–1990* (Washington, D.C.: Independent Sector, 1986), p. 26.

33. *Centennial Report*, p. 1.

34. *Program Plan 1986–1990*, p. 27.

35. Cindy Skrzycki, "Pace of Giving by U.S. Firms Slowed in '87," *Washington Post*, January 2, 1988.

36. Kramer, "The Future of Voluntary Organizations in Social Welfare," p. 504.

37. Hodgkinson and Weitzman, *Dimensions*, p. 140.

38. "Girl Scouts View Sales Tax on Cookies as Crummy," *San Diego Tribune*, December 17, 1987.

39. National Public Radio, November 20, 1987.

CHAPTER 8

The Corporate Sector

This chapter considers the role of the business community in American social welfare. Historically, business leaders have made important contributions to the health and welfare of employees by envisaging utopian work environments and pioneering the provision of benefits to employees. Business leaders were also instrumental in fashioning early governmental welfare policies. More recently, emphasis on the "social responsibility" of corporations has encouraged business leaders to assess the broader implications of corporate activities. Corporations also shape social welfare policy through influencing the political process and subsidizing policy institutes. Human service professionals have become more involved in the corporate sector with the creation of Employee Assistance Plans through which social workers engage in occupational social work.

The business community in the United States influences social welfare in several important ways. Benefit packages for employees, which are usually available to dependents, provide important health and welfare benefits to a large segment of the working population. Corporate philanthropy has sponsored important—and in some cases, controversial—social welfare initiatives. And policy institutes reflecting the priorities of the business community have made substantial changes in American "public philosophy." More recently, the corporate sector has begun to exploit the growing human service markets in long-term care, health maintenance, and corrections. These instances reflect the significant role that the corporate sector has played in American social welfare.

Among welfare theorists, corporate activities have tended to be underappreciated. Many progressive scholars attributed the cause of much social and economic dislocation to industrial capitalism, and therewith implicated its institutional representative, the corporation. Thus, the corporation was not a source of relief, but the perpetrator of social and economic hardship. As a result, liberal theorists concluded that the government was the only institution capable of regulating capitalism and compensating the victims of its caprices. Welfare state ideology, as it evolved, left little room for the corporation, viewing the corporation as the source of much suffering and generally unwilling to pay its share of the tax burden to remediate the problems it had spawned. As an example of this, Citizens for Tax Justice, a liberal advocacy group, reported that between 1981 and 1983

> 128 (or 51%) of the 250 major corporations [studied] paid no federal income taxes or less (i.e., they received rebates of taxes paid in earlier years or sold "excess" tax benefits) in at least one of the three years, while earning profits of $57.1 billion. [original emphasis][1]

While societal abuses committed by the business community have been well chronicled by advocacy groups—e.g., the disruption, then abandonment of Love Canal because of improper disposal of toxic waste; the exploitation of Mexican agricultural workers in the Southwest; and the extortion of huge sums from New York City housing officials by landlords who provide single-room occupancy for the homeless—the contribution of the corporate sector to the commonweal is less often recognized. Ironically, many welfare advocates who had leveled blanket indictments at the corporate sector during the 1960s found themselves furtively seeking grants from corporate foundations when government funds for new social programs dried up in the 1980s.

At this point, it would be fair to conclude that many welfare theorists are beginning to re-examine the role of the corporate sector in American social welfare. The concept of "the mixed welfare economy" has served to combine the corporate, proprietary sector with the governmental and voluntary sectors, as primary actors in social welfare.[2] And the issue of "privatization" has provoked a vigorous argument about the proper balance between the public and private (including corporate) welfare sectors.[3] Although Neil Gilbert's *Capitalism and the Welfare State* provides a timely review of the issues presented by "welfare capitalism,"[4] empirical investigations of for-profit human service corporations have only begun.[5] Thus, the role of the corporate sector in American social welfare has yet to be fixed.

HISTORY OF THE CORPORATE SECTOR

For most of the history of the United States, private institutions have been the basis of welfare provision. During the colonial era, the town overseer contracted out the poor to the resident who was willing to provide food and shelter at the lowest bid. Similarly, medical care for the poor was subsidized through purchase of physicians' services. Through the eighteenth and nineteenth centuries this practice contributed to the emergence of private institutions—hospitals and orphanages, among others—that served the needy.[6] Although many of these early welfare institutions were communal efforts and not developed as private businesses, others were precisely that. Thus, many early hospitals in the United States were owned and operated by physicians who became wealthy by providing health care to the community. By 1900, approximately 60 percent of hospitals were privately owned by physicians.[7]

With industrialization, however, the business community took a new interest in the health and welfare of employees. To be sure, certain captains of industry saw employee welfare as a concession to be made as a last resort—sometimes only after violent confrontation with organized workers. But, such was not always the case. Early in the industrial revolution, before government assumed a prominent role in societal affairs, altruistically minded businessmen saw little recourse but to use their business firms as an instrument for their social designs. In some cases, their experiments in worker welfare were nothing less than revolutionary. During the early 1820s, the utopian businessman, Robert Owen, transformed a bankrupt Scotch mill town, New Lanark, from a wretched backwater populated by paupers, into a "marvelously profitable" experiment in social engineering. Owen abolished child labor, provided habitable housing for workers, and implemented a system to recognize the efforts of individual employees. Soon, New Lanark attracted thousands of visitors who were as awed at the contrast between the squalor of other mill towns and the brilliance of New Lanark as they were at the substantial profit— eventually 60,000 pounds—Owen realized from the venture. A humanist, Owen believed that the solution to the problem of poverty lay not in the stringent and punitive English Poor Laws, but in "making the poor productive." An irrepressible idealist, Owen later transported his utopian vision to the United States where he attempted to establish a rural planned community in New Harmony, Indiana. Ultimately, this American experiment in local socialism failed.[8]

Business leaders in the United States began to acknowledge that industrial production on a grand scale required a healthy and educated work force. Locating such workers was not easy amid the poverty and ignorance that characterized much of the population of the period. To improve the dependability of labor, several large corporations built planned communities for workers. During the early 1880s, the Pullman Company, manufacturer of railroad sleeping cars, "constructed one of the most ambitiously planned communities in the United States—a company town complete with a hotel, markets, landscaped parks, factories, and residences for over 8,000 people."[9] Although some industries later built communities as a means to control and, in some cases, oppress workers—e.g., "the company store," operated by mining companies to keep miners forever in debt—many expressions of corporate interest in employee well-being clearly enhanced the welfare of the community.

In other instances, businessmen experimented with alternative forms of business ownership. Current "workplace democracy" and "employee ownership" programs can be traced to the Association for the Promotion of Profit Sharing, established in 1892. In 1890, Nelson Olsen Nelson, a founder of the Association, set aside a 250-acre tract in Illinois for workers in his company. Naming the village "Leclair" after a French pioneer of profit sharing, Nelson included in the town plan gardens, walkways, and a school, and encouraged employees to build residences in the community. Consistent with his philosophy, Nelson offered employees cash dividends as well as stock in the company; and by 1893, 400 of the 500 employees held stock, thus earning 8 to 10 percent added to their wages. Not content with an isolated experiment in industrial socialism, Nelson advanced his ideas in a quarterly journal that promoted profit sharing. Eventually, Nelson went so far as to convert his company into a wholly employee-owned cooperative, but overexpansion and irregular earnings led to his ouster in 1918.[10]

It is important to recognize that such experiments in the social function of the business firm were not solely the work of utopian crackpots, nor were they idiosyncratic to peculiar circumstances. Welfare capitalism, "industry's

attending to the social needs of workers through an assortment of medical and funeral benefits, as well as provisions for recreational, educational, housing, and social services," was a popular idea among some business leaders prior to World War I.[11] Indeed, concern about the optimal purpose and value of business in the national culture was a frequent subject of discussion among the elite of American commerce. Even a staunch capitalist such as John D. Rockefeller took a relatively progressive stance on the corporate role when, in 1918, he asked on behalf of the Chamber of Commerce of the United States:

> Shall we cling to the conception of industry as an institution, primarily of private interest, which enables certain individuals to accumulate wealth, too often irrespective of the well-being, the health and happiness of those engaged in its production? Or shall we adopt the modern viewpoint and *regard industry as being a form of social service*, quite as much as a revenue-producing process?.... The soundest industrial policy is that which has constantly in mind the welfare of employees as well as the making of profits, and which, when human considerations demand it, *subordinates profits to welfare*.[12]

As often ill-begotten fortunes accumulated in the hands of a few, some wealthy individuals felt compelled to return a portion of their largess to the commonweal. "In the latter part of the nineteenth century, men who had great fortunes from the massive industrial growth of the post-Civil War period developed a humanistic concern which was manifested in lavish contributions toward social betterment."[13] Andrew Carnegie—who in 1812 had hired "an army of 300 Pinkerton detectives" to put an end to the violent Haymarket strike[14]—wrote seven years later that massive wealth was a public trust to be put toward the public interest. Eventually, Carnegie donated about $350 million through foundations, most visibly for community libraries (often bearing his name) that began to dot communities across the country. For his part, John D. Rockefeller contributed about $530 million.[15]

Although largely based on the manifestation of guilt associated with the great fortunes won by a handful of individuals in the midst of cruel circumstances for many, philanthropic foundations also fostered enduring contributions to social welfare. The Commonwealth Fund proved instrumental in the execution of a series of child guidance experiments during the 1920s, which served as prototypes for today's juvenile service departments.[16] The Rockefeller Foundation took a leading role in providing health care to a southern black population that went neglected by state officials, thus helping "to combat hookworm and then stamp out pellagra."[17] The Russell Sage Foundation funded the publication of important works on the development of social welfare, including the classic, *Industrial Society and Social Welfare*, as well as a series of volumes which were precursors to the *Encyclopedia of Social Work*.[18]

The American business community was also involved in early insurance programs designed to assist injured workers. Although initial court decisions absolved employers of liability for injuries incurred by employees, a swell in jury-awarded settlements to disabled workers convinced corporations to establish insurance funds to pool their risk against employee suits. Eventually, companies realized that they would pay lower premiums through state-operated workers' compensation programs than they had through commercial insurance. Consequently, between 1911 and 1920, all 45 states had enacted workers' compensation laws.[19] Later, when the Depression overtaxed voluntary social welfare agencies, and when labor volatility resulting from high unemployment threatened political stability, it is not surprising that politicians, businessmen, and labor leaders drew on their workers' compensation experience in designing the New Deal. Instrumental in creating federal social

programs in the Roosevelt era was Gerald Swope, an executive with the General Electric Company. Having envisaged a "corporate welfare state," including "a national system of unemployment, retirement, life insurance, and disability programs and standards," Swope helped fashion the Social Security program from his position as chair of Roosevelt's Business Advisory Council.[20] Moreover, the Social Security program clearly bore the imprint of the business community. As conceived, only workers who had contributed to a trust fund would be able to draw benefits, assuring that no public funds would be required to operate the program.[21] What had essentially become known as the "social security concept" illustrated a public pension program that was modeled on programs of the private sector. As such, it "represented the acceptance of approaches to social welfare that private businessmen, not government bureaucrats, had created."[22]

The Social Security Act, the crown jewel of the New Deal, meant that the social and economic security of many Americans would be underwritten by the state. While benefits from programs mandated by the Social Security Act became a staple of the American welfare state, the business community continued to make independent decisions regarding the welfare of workers. Major corporations, such as General Electric, General Motors, and IBM, began offering "fringe" benefits as supplements to salaries, and these became important incentives to attract desirable employees. By standards of the time, the benefits offered by large corporations were quite generous, including annual vacations, health care, recreation, life insurance, and housing. Business historians Edward Berkowitz and Kim McQuaid have suggested that the conscientiousness with which some corporations cared for their employees was "almost as if these firms were consciously demonstrating that the true American welfare state lay within the large and progressive American corporation."[23] Indeed, the extent

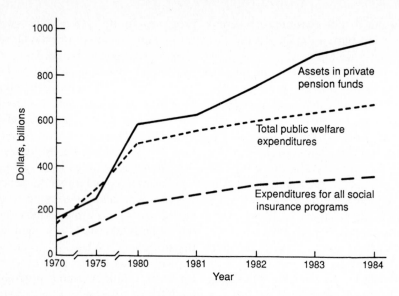

Figure 8.1. Assets in Private Pension Funds and Expenditures for Social Insurance and Public Welfare

Sources: *Statistical Abstract of the United States* (Washington, D.C.: U.S. Government Printing Office, 1986), p. 369; *Social Security Bulletin, Annual Statistical Supplement* (Washington, D.C.: U.S. Government Printing Office, 1986), p. 67.

to which the business community provided benefits for its workers eclipsed the federal welfare effort. As indicated in Figure 8.1, assets in private pension funds have exceeded expenditures for all social insurance programs and have, with the exception of a period in the mid-1970s, exceeded total public welfare expenditures.[24] In 1983, 43.4 percent of employees had private pension plans, and 61 percent were covered by group health insurance.[25]

CORPORATE SOCIAL RESPONSIBILITY

The corporation has also influenced American social welfare as a result of accusations that it has been insensitive to the needs of the poor, women, minorities, and consumers. During the 1960s, criticism of the corporation focused on the neglect of American business toward minorities and urban blight. A decade later, issues relating to affirmative action, environmental pollution, and consumer rip-offs were added to

the list. These problems led to a public relations crisis, as a leading business administration text noted.

> The corporation is being attacked and criticized on various fronts by a great number of political and citizens' organizations. Many young people accuse the corporation of failing to seek solutions to our varied social problems. Minority groups, and women, contend that many corporations have been guilty of discrimination in hiring and in pay scales.[26]

Melvin Anshen, Paul Garret Professor of Public Policy and Business Responsibility of Columbia University's Graduate School of Business, bemoaned that "profit-oriented private decisions are now often seen as antisocial."[27]

In order to improve their public image, many corporations established policies on social responsibility. Corporations that were reluctant to take the social implications of their operations seriously ran the risk of inviting the surveillance of public interest groups. As an example, the Council on Economic Priorities (CEP), founded in 1969, developed a reputation for investigating the social responsibility of American corporations. In 1986, CEP released *Rating America's Corporate Conscience*, a rating of 125 large corporations according to seven issues: charitable contributions, representation of women on boards of directors and among top corporate officers, representation of minorities on boards of directors and among top corporate officers, disclosure of social information, involvement in South Africa, conventional weapons-related contracting, and nuclear weapons-related contracting.[28] Social responsibility audits, such as this, provide a guide for consumers to select companies whose products they may prefer, and thereby create an incentive for companies to follow socially responsible practices.

Although the facade of public relations frequently glosses over the substantive abuses of business interests, specific corporate social responsibility policies have advanced social welfare. General Electric and IBM instituted strong policies on equal opportunity and affirmative action toward minorities and women during the late 1960s. Under the concept of "public interest director," Leon Sullivan assumed a position on the General Motors Board of Directors, from which he presented six principles governing ethical practices for American corporations doing business in South Africa.[29] According to the "Sullivan principles," American firms with affiliates in South Africa are engaged in ethical practices when they adhere to the following:

1. non-segregation of the races in all eating, comfort, and work facilities,
2. equal and fair employment practices for all employees,
3. equal pay for all employees doing equal or comparable work for the same period of time,
4. initiation of and development of training programs that will prepare, in substantial

numbers, blacks and other non-whites for supervisory, administrative, clerical and technical jobs,
5. increasing the number of blacks and non-whites in management and supervisory positions, and
6. improving the quality of employees' lives outside the work environment in such areas as housing, transportation, schooling, recreation and health facilities.[30]

In another instance, Control Data Corporation has actually sought out "major unmet social needs, designed means for serving them within the framework of a profit-oriented business enterprise, and brought the needs and the means for serving them together to create markets where none had existed before."[31] These and other initiatives demonstrate that the corporate sector has been willing to undertake significant programs to support troubled communities.[32]

Corporate practices have also been applied directly to social problems. In a venture reminiscent of Robert Owen, developer James Rouse established the Enterprise Foundation in 1981. While technically a foundation which supports charitable projects, what makes it different is that within the foundation is the Enterprise Development Company, a wholly owned taxpaying subsidiary. Profits from the Development Company, projected as $10 to $20 million by 1990, are transferred to the foundation to fund projects. By the late 1980s, this fiscally self-sufficient "charity corporation" had developed innovative projects for low-income housing in dozens of cities.[33]

Recognizing the tendency of community institutions in poor areas to become dependent on government or philanthropy for continuing operations, the Ford Foundation sought contributions from corporations for a program to apply business principles to social problems. By 1983, the Local Initiatives Support Corporation (LISC) had developed investment funds in 24 regions which supported 197 community development projects.[34] LISC projects provided jobs and commodities needed in disadvantaged communities, including a fish processing and freezing plant in Maine, a for-profit construction company in Chicago, and a revolving loan fund to construct low- and moderate-income housing in Philadelphia.[35]

In light of such ventures, some business leaders have become enthusiastic about the proactive response on the part of the corporation toward social problems. David Linowes, a corporate leader, foresaw a new role for business in public affairs.

> Mounting evidence proves that the private sector is uniquely well qualified to fulfill many of the social goals facing us more economically and expeditiously than government working alone.... I can visualize a wholesale expansion of existing incentives along with a spate of new reward strategies introduced to America's socio-economic system. Increasingly, I believe, this will help to change the attitude of businessmen regarding social involvement. I look forward to the day, in fact, when competition to engage in government-business programs will be every bit as spirited as competition for the consumer dollar is today.[36]

As chairman of the President's Commission on Privatization, Linowes worked to define ways in which the private sector could complement the responsibilities of government.[37]

CORPORATE INFLUENCE ON SOCIAL WELFARE POLICY

Corporate social responsibility notwithstanding, it would be naive to think that the corporate sector is above self-interest in its orientation toward socal welfare. The conservative political economist, Irving Kristol, stated candidly,

> corporate philanthrophy is not obligatory. It is desirable if and only if it serves a corporate purpose. It is expressly and candidly a self-serving

activity, and is only legitimate to the degree that it is ancillary to a larger corporate purpose. To put it bluntly: There is nothing noble or even moral about corporate philanthropy.[38]

Moreover, corporate influence in social welfare is not exerted simply through myriad corporations acting independently. Special interest organizations, such as the National Association of Manufacturers and the United States Chamber of Commerce, have routinely pressed for public policies that clearly reflected the priorities of the business community. In 1974 Congress passed campaign reform legislation that defined contribution limits to political action committees (PACs). Unfortunately, these attempts to control political influence actually contributed to the proliferation of PACs, particularly those financed by the corporate sector. In 1974, corporations had created 89 PACs, but by 1986 the number had grown to 1,902. That corporate PACs influence the political process conservatively is well known. Labor organizations, which tend to be liberal in inclination, fielded only 418 PACs in 1986, a poor showing compared to the number of corporate PACs. Consequently, corporate PACs favor Republican candidates for office, sometimes overwhelmingly. In 1982, for example, the U.S. Chamber of Commerce PAC endorsed only Republican candidates.[39]

Corporations exert an indirect influence on social policy by funding public interest organizations, nonprofits engaged in research, policy analysis, and public education. In the past, corporations have been an important source of support for liberal organizations, such as the Brookings Institution, that have advocated governmental policies to help the disadvantaged. More recently, argues conservative scholar Marvin Olasky, corporations have used their contributions to placate "specific vocal minorities."[40] But corporations also give a substantial portion to conservative public policy groups. In 1985, corporations contributed $4.3 billion to nonprofit organizations. In that year,

TABLE 8.1. Contributions to Organizations from the Largest American Corporations

Organizational Recipient	Number of Corporations Contributing	1985 Contributions
Urban League	24	$1,586,000
American Enterprise Institute	18	1,133,000
NAACP/NAACP Legal Defense and Education Fund	20	707,000
Urban Institute/Center for Community Change	10	567,000
Independent Sector/Council on Foundations	17	479,000
La Raza and other Hispanic groups	14	418,000
Brookings Institution	16	366,000
Heritage Foundation/Hoover Institution	11	347,000

Source: Marvin Olasky, *Patterns of Corporate Philanthropy* (Washington, D.C.: Capital Research Center, 1987), p. 2.

the largest corporate contributors were Exxon ($72,756,000), Chevron ($32,341,000), Atlantic Richfield ($31,846,000), AT&T ($30,974,000), and General Motors ($28,019,000).[41] Table 8.1 illustrates the diversity of contributions from the largest American corporations.[42]

Funding of PACs and public interest organizations, however, proved unreliable vehicles for influencing public policy. PACs subsidized the campaigns of individual candidates, of course, but did little to forge consensus around, or propose new directions for, public policy. Public interest organizations, on the other hand, represented a wide diversity of thought, and were largely independent of the ideological preferences of corporate donors. Subsequently, during the 1970s, the corporate sector turned to the policy institute as a method for influencing social policy. Also known as "think tanks," the policy institutes favored by the business community were the American Enterprise Institute for Public Policy Research (AEI) and the Heritage Foundation. Established as nonpartisan institutions for the purpose of enhancing the public's understanding of social policy, these policy institutes distanced themselves from the special interest connotation of earlier business advocacy groups. At the same time, conservative think tanks served as vehicles for the business community to take a less reactive stance regarding social policy. Conservative policy institutes, then, addressed the complaint voiced by Lawrence Fouraker and Graham Allison, Deans of Harvard's Graduate School of Business Administration: "Public policy suffers not simply from a lack of business confidence on issues of major national import, but from a lack of sophisticated and balanced contribution by *both* business and government in the process of policy development."[43]

The American Enterprise Institute (AEI)

Once noted for its slavish adherence to probusiness positions on social issues, AEI had developed, by the early 1980s, an appreciation for American "intellectual politics."[44] With a budget and staff comparable to that of a prestigious college, AEI was able to recruit an impressive number of notable people and scholars, and maintain projects in several domestic policy areas: economics, education, energy, government regulation, finance, taxation, health, jurisprudence, and public opinion. The significance of these activities for social welfare was stated by AEI's then-president, William J. Baroody, Jr.

The public philosophy that has guided American policy for decades is undergoing change. For more than four decades, the philosophy of Franklin Delano Roosevelt's New Deal prevailed, in essence calling upon government to do whatever individual men and women could not do for themselves.

Today we see growing signs of a new public philosophy, one that still seeks to meet fundamental human needs, but to meet them through a better balance between the public and private sectors of society.

The American Enterprise Institute has been at the forefront of this change. Many of today's policy initiatives are building on intellectual foundations partly laid down by the Institute.[45]

For such an ambitious mission, AEI empaneled a staff of influential and talented personnel. At the height of its influence, from the late 1970s through the mid-1980s, AEI maintained a stable of over thirty scholars and fellows *in residence* who prepared analyses on the various policy areas.[46] The Institute's senior fellows included the aforementioned Irving Kristol, Herbert Stein, an economist and chairman of the President's Council of Economic Advisors in the Nixon Administration, and Ben Wattenberg, a veteran public opinion analyst. The AEI "distinguished fellow" was Gerald R. Ford, thirty-eighth president of the United States. Michael Novak, Director of AEI's project on democratic capitalism, prepared analyses that focused on social welfare policy.

Instrumental in shaping the social priorities of the Reagan administration, AEI was to become the most important organization in the idea industry of the period. And AEI's budget ballooned accordingly—from $800,000 in 1970, to $5 million in 1978, to $11.7 million in 1982. Forty-three percent of the 1982 budget was derived from large corporate contributors, such as Bethlehem Steel, Exxon, J. C. Penney, and the Chase Manhattan Bank.[47] With a budget so heavily dependent on corporate funding, AEI required a lifeline to the business community, and the Board of Trustees served that function. Of the 24 members of the AEI Board of Trustees in 1984, 21 were chief executives of *Fortune* 500 firms.[48] AEI was also careful to select its staff from government service and to grant leaves to staff when their services were

desired by an administration. Two AEI scholars were former members of the President's Council of Economic Advisors. When Ronald Reagan assumed office, 18 AEI staff joined the new administration, claiming such important offices as Director of the Congressional Budget Office and the Director of the Office of Management and Budget.

This situation assured that no social policy proposal received serious consideration without first passing the review and comment of AEI. By the time a policy proposal had reached the legislative arena, the odds were high that the AEI imprint would be reinforced by testimony from one or more of the highly credentialed scholars in residence, the 77 adjunct scholars, or the 250 professors across the nation who were affiliated with AEI.[49] Influence was sometimes exerted in a subtle manner. In 1982, for example, AEI marked the completion of its project "to determine whether the private sector [could] play a larger role in dealing with a range of problems in our society and in delivering needed human services" by publishing *Meeting Human Needs: Toward a New Public Philosophy*. The first copy was delivered personally to President Reagan by AEI's President William Baroody.[50]

In domestic affairs, AEI established two projects which influenced social welfare policy. In launching the "mediating structures" project, AEI enlisted the services of Peter Berger, a sociologist, and Richard Neuhaus, a theologian. In the major publication of the project, *To Empower People*, Berger and Neuhaus stated that the fundamental social problem of American society was the growth of megastructures, such as big government, big business, big labor, and professional bureaucracies, and a corresponding diminution of the individual. The route to empowering people, then, was to revitalize "mediating structures," among them, the neighborhood, family, church, and voluntary association.[51] *To Empower People* proved a readable and lucid booklet that served AEI well, and the project's implicit critique of government programs became clearly evident in other studies of "mediating structures." For example, in *Federalizing Meals on Wheels*, Michael Balzano argued that the federal Older Americans Act was wrong because it allegedly reduced the voluntary impulses of church and community groups (mediating structures) by subsidizing nutritional programs for the elderly. "In most cases, common sense and the desire to help one's neighbor are all that are necessary." Balzano concluded sarcastically, "One does not need a master's degree in social work or gerontology to dish out chow at a nutrition center."[52]

Following the mediating structures project, AEI's project on democratic capitalism endeavored to elevate the role of the corporation in public life. This necessitated a bit of theoretical hanky-panky since the mediating structures project had portrayed big business as a megastructure and, therefore, inimical to the vitality of mediating structures, but the problem was disposed of deftly by Michael Novak, a philosopher of religion and director of the project. In *Toward a Theology of the Corporation*, Novak used no more than a footnote to transfer big business from its designation as a megastructure to that of a mediating structure, effectively characterizing big government as an institution of cultural and economic oppression against a corporate sector that had been the genius behind the American experience.[53]

Under the direction of Novak, the project on democratic capitalism intended to reform public philosophy by depicting the corporation as a promoter of cultural enlightenment rather than a perpetrator of inequality. "The social instrument invented by democratic capitalism to achieve social goals is the private corporation," he proselytized.

The corporation . . . is not merely an economic institution. It is also a moral and a political institution. It depends on and generates new political forms. . . . Beyond its economic effects, the corporation changes the ethos and the cultural forms of society.[54]

At the same time, Novak took careful aim at the public sector, explaining, "I advise intelligent, ambitious, and morally serious young Christians and Jews to awaken to the growing danger of statism. They will better serve their souls and serve the Kingdom of God all around by restoring the liberty and power of the private sector than by working for the state."[55]

The Heritage Foundation

In 1986 AEI faltered, and organizational problems led to the resignation of Baroody. With the weakening of AEI, the Heritage Foundation assumed leadership in defining a pro-business and antigovernmental outlook on social policy. Established in 1973 by a $250,000 grant from the Coors family,[56] the Heritage Foundation's 1983 budget of $10.6 million already approximated those of the liberal Brookings Institution and the American Enterprise Institute.[57] Espousing a militant conservative ideology, Heritage influenced social policy by proposing private alternatives to establishing governmental programs and by slanting its work to the religious right. By breaking new ground while building mass support for policy initiatives, Heritage complemented the less partisan analyses of AEI. Like AEI, Heritage sustained a group of conservative scholars— over 100—who prepared position statements. Also like AEI, Heritage placed some of its staff—26 full-time and 13 part-time—in government posts during the Reagan administration.[58]

Heritage social policy initiatives emphasize privatization that, in this case, means transferring activities from government to business. Implicit in this is an unqualified antagonism toward government intrusion in social affairs. Government programs are faulted for a breakdown in the mutual obligations between groups, the lack of attention to efficiencies and incentives in the way programs are operated and benefits awarded, the induced dependency of beneficiaries on programs, and the growth of the welfare industry and its special interest groups, particularly professional associations.[59]

This critique served as a basis for the aggressive stance taken by the Heritage Foundation in urban development, income security, and social welfare policies. With regard to urban development, Heritage proposed the Urban Enterprise Zone (UEZ) concept, which would enable economically disadvantaged communities to attract industry by reducing taxes, employee costs, and health and safety regulations.[60] The UEZ concept came to the attention of then Congressman Jack Kemp who convinced the Reagan administration to make it the centerpiece of its urban policy, thus replacing the Economic Development Administration and Urban Development Action Grant programs in which government had provided technical assistance and funds for urban development.[61] When UEZ legislation stalled in Congress, Heritage changed tactics and targeted states and localities directly. By late 1984, 30 states and cities had created over 300 UEZs.[62] As secretary of Housing and Urban Development in the Bush administration, Kemp is well placed to reintroduce the enterprise zone concept as a way to aid troubled communities.

In the area of income security, the Heritage Foundation—in conjunction with the conservative CATO Institute—prepared an oblique assault on the Social Security program, promoting a parallel system of Individual Retirement Accounts (IRAs). Under "The Family Security Plan," proposed by Peter Ferrara, former senior staff member of the White House Office of Policy Development, the initial IRA provisions of the 1981 Economic Recovery and Tax Act would be expanded to allow individuals "to deduct their annual contributions to ... IRAs from their Social Security payroll taxes."[63] While the idea of substituting IRA investments for Social Security contributions was blocked by liberal politicians, Heritage

was clearly banking on future support from the egoistic workers of the baby-boom generation. "If today's young workers could use their Social Security taxes to make ... investments through an IRA," hypothesized Ferrara, "then, assuming a 6 percent real return, most would receive three to six times the retirement benefits promised them under Social Security."[64] According to this calculus, the interaction of demographic and economic variables would lead to increasing numbers of young workers salting away funds for themselves because of high investment returns as well as the fear that Social Security would provide only minimal benefits on retirement. If correct, the result would be a sure-fire formula for eroding the popular and financial support for Social Security.

Regarding welfare policy, Heritage was instrumental in scouting Charles Murray, whose *Losing Ground* provided much of the rationale for the conservative assault on federal welfare programs. In 1982, a pamphlet Murray had written for Heritage, entitled "Safety Nets and the Truly Needy," came to the attention of the Manhattan Institute, a conservative New York think tank.[65] Traded by Heritage to Manhattan, Murray elaborated his allegation that government social programs of the War on Poverty had actually worsened the conditions of the poor. Murray's wrecking-ball thesis advocated no less than a "zero-transfer system" which consisted of "scrapping the entire federal welfare and income support structure for working-aged persons."[66] Remembering his earlier sponsor, Murray returned to Heritage on December 12, 1984, to promote his book to a standing-room-only audience for a symposium entitled, "What's Wrong with Welfare?"

Unlike the more restrained AEI, Heritage has been willing to lend its name to militant conservatives of the religious right, providing intellectual support to "the traditionalist movement." The most comprehensive and sympathetic treatment of the traditionalist movement is found in *Back to Basics*, by Burton Pines, vice president of Heritage. In this highly readable book, Pines applauds local conservative activists for their challenge to liberal values and chronicles the offensive launched against programs of the welfare state. "Profamily" traditionalists had disrupted the Carter administration's White House Conference on Families, a grass-roots mobilization that effectively precluded any progressive legislation that might have evolved out of the Conference. Traditionalists also enjoined proponents of the Domestic Violence Bill in protracted debate, holding up the legislation until a Republican-controlled Senate let it expire. Finally, traditionalists supported the Family Protection Act, a conservative proposal limiting contraception, abortion, children's rights, and sex education, and reducing federal support for programs aiding homosexuals and the divorced.[67] Although the Family Protection Act was not passed, it succeeded at diverting the attention of the public toward traditional values, which were portrayed positively, and away from liberal values, which were considered ruinous.

Pines noted the pivotal role of conservative think tanks in the traditionalist movement, and was quick to acknowledge his debt to AEI, an organization he described as focusing "primarily on long (sometimes very long) range and fundamental transformation of the climate of opinion." Bringing the conservative Hoover Institution of Stanford into the fold, Pines characterized their work as a crusade. "Together," he concluded, "Hoover, AEI and Heritage can today deploy formidable armies on the battlefield of ideas—forces which traditionalist movements previously lacked."[68]

THE FUTURE OF CORPORATE INVOLVEMENT IN SOCIAL WELFARE

Corporations will continue to influence social welfare policy through the remainder of the century, reflecting the preference of business leaders that the corporate sector assume a primary role in activities of both the voluntary and governmental sectors. John Filer, Chairman of Aetna Life and Casualty and Chairman of the 1975 Commission on Private Philanthropy and Public Needs, contended that "the future of corporate America depends critically on our ability to recognize promptly the changing role of the corporation, the changing expectations and demands of the public, and the changing constituencies which we serve."[69] Filer encouraged corporations to increase contributions to philanthropic causes, and from 1975 to 1984 corporate contributions to the voluntary sector increased from $1.2 billion to $3.8 billion.[70] But corporate giving is contingent on corporate performance, and there is little question that the generosity of chief executive officers was dampened suddenly when the Dow Jones Industrial Average plunged 508 points on October 19, 1987. "Everybody is just reeling," the director of planned giving for a major West Coast philanthropy said of the stock market crash, "People are not doing a lot of thinking about giving at this moment."[71]

The social responsibility of the corporate sector was questioned when a national campaign launched by Trans-Africa to pressure American corporations to cease doing business in South Africa brought negative publicity to firms that refused or were slow to divest. Fewer corporations were willing to adopt the Sullivan principles. During the last two reporting periods, the number of American corporations which had "signed" the Sullivan principles dropped by approximately one-half.[72] Further, the high proportion of employee costs attributed to fringe benefits drove many employers to demand concessions or "give-backs" from employees, thus drawing the wrath of unions. Still, holding corporations to some social standard served as a rationale for advancing social programs. A creative illustration of this appears in the "Decency Principles" proposed by Nancy Amidei, a social worker and syndicated columnist. Noting that the Sullivan principles addressed the responsibility of firms doing business in South Africa, Amidei wondered about the responsibility of firms doing business in the United States. Her standards for responsible business practices include:

1. *Equitable Wages* (high enough to escape poverty; comparability across lines of race, age, sex, and handicapping conditions);
2. *Employee Rights* (to equal opportunity, to organize for collective bargaining, to affordable child care, to safe working conditions, and to health coverage);
3. *Housing* (working for more affordable housing, helping relocated or migrant workers obtain affordable housing);
4. *Environmental* (responsible use of resources, sound handling of dangerous substances, conformance with environmental protection laws).

Amidei suggested that a corporation's adherence to the "Decency Principles" be a basis for decisions on such matters as providing tax abatements to attract new industry or awarding government contracts.[73]

Financed by the business community, conservative policy institutes persisted in efforts to roll back the welfare state. While the Heritage Foundation appeared unable to fashion "a conservative vision of welfare,"[74] AEI reasserted its influence by publishing *The New Consensus on Family and Welfare.* Under the direction of Michael Novak, a group of 20 scholars—including prominent liberal scholars from the Brookings Institution—presented a conservative platform for welfare reform. Suggesting that "existing welfare policy [was] toxic," the group's report judged that initiatives of the states, local jurisdictions, and the voluntary sector were preferable to federal social programs.[75] *The New Consensus* implied that poverty in America was inevitable and concluded that, "the nation's goal ... should not be to 'eliminate' poverty but to reduce it as much as possible by adapting quickly to its ever new forms and unforeseen necessities."[76]

While business leaders remained antagonistic toward governmental social policies, others adopted a more liberal stance, viewing public policy as an essential component of an internationally competitive economy. As early as 1980 the editors of *Business Week* noted that the nation's attention should be diverted away from social needs and toward economic revitalization:

> In the U.S. during the past 20 years, policy has emphasized improving the quality of life, particularly attempts to redistribute income to low-income groups and minorities and to create an egalitarian society. Now it is clear that the government cannot achieve such goals, no matter how admirable, without economic growth.[77]

"We have become so concerned with problems of redistributing wealth," echoed Reginald H. Jones, chairman of the General Electric Company, "that we've forgotten about creation of wealth."[78] This call for governmental intervention to aid the business community was reinforced by an increasingly rapid loss of economic advantage to the economies of Japan and Germany, both of which received substantial governmental assistance. Governmental aid to business, labeled "industrial policy," was endorsed by liberal economists, such as MIT's Lester Thurow, who proposed "the national equivalent of a corporate investment committee" to coordinate economic policy.[79] Subsequent industrialization would provide increased revenues for welfare programs but, more importantly, create jobs for the unemployed. In the final analysis, further improvement in the economic circumstances of the poor and the unemployed was politically feasible only under conditions of an expanding economy.

The accommodation of social needs to economic requirements—social welfare policy to corporate economic policy—was advocated by Robert Reich of the Kennedy School of Government at Harvard University. According to Reich, much of the American industrial malaise was attributable to our under-investment in human capital. However, human capital investments can be wasteful, leading to nonproductive dependency, if not coupled to the needs of industry. "Underlying many of the inadequacies of American social programs, in short, is the fact that they have not been directed in any explicit or coherent way toward the large task of adapting America's labor force."[80] The attachment of social needs to industrial productivity would fundamentally alter social welfare. "Government bureaucracies that now administer these programs to individuals will be supplanted, to a large extent, by companies that administer them to their employees," suggested Reich. "Companies, rather than state and local governments, will be the agents through which such assistance is provided."[81]

Significantly, industrial policy has attracted conservative adherents as well. Influential analyst, Kevin Phillips, has proposed a more business-directed version of industrial policy. In Phillips's "business-government partnership," labor and business would agree to work cooperatively with government so that the United States could regain its dominant role in the international economy. For Phillips, however, industrial policy offers less for social welfare:

> Political liberals must accept that there is little support for bringing back federal agencies based on New Deal models to run the U.S. economy, and that much of the new business–government cooperation will back economic development and nationalist (export, trade competition) agendas rather than abstractions like social justice or social welfare.[82]

The primacy of business interests in public policy is not accepted by many social welfare advocates. While "corporatism"[83] may be plausible for corporate executives, governmental officials, and labor unions, it offers little to the unemployed and welfare or working poor. In fact, some critics of industrial policy suggest that its very emergence signifies the inability of advanced capitalism to assure the provision of basic goods and services to the economically disadvantaged through the Welfare State.[84] If these critics are correct, industrial policy is an indication of the demise of welfare capitalism, rather than a blueprint for enhancing social welfare. Exactly how the relationship among business, labor, and government will be articulated in the future has much to do with the development of public policy. While the precise nature of such policy must be left to conjecture, the increasing sophistication of the corporate sector in shaping social policy suggests that social welfare policy of the future will show greater congruence with the priorities of American business.

Although many welfare advocates are distrustful of corporate involvement in social welfare, other social welfare professionals have found the corporate sector a desirable context in which to practice clinically. Since the 1970s, social workers began establishing Employee Assistance Programs (EAPs) which provided a range of services to workers, a population often neglected by traditional welfare programs.[85] By the late 1980s, occupational social welfare had become a popular specialization within social work, with graduate schools offering special curricula on the subject, a national conference inaugurated for specialists in the field, and a special issue of Social Work dedicated to it.[86] Although studies of EAPs are scarce,[87] there is evidence that occupational social work is likely to expand, particularly when located within the corporation. In a modest study of 23 "private-sector, management-sponsored" EAPs, Shulamith Straussner found that those located in-house demonstrated notable advantages over those contracted out. For example, EAPs located within the corporation cost one-third those of contracted-out services. In-house EAPs proved adaptable to management priorities, developing "short-term programs to deal with company reorganization

or retrenchment, special health concerns...
[and] other organizational needs." Significantly, union representatives approved in-house
EAPs twice as frequently as contracted-out
programs.[88] These findings suggest that EAPs
which are managed by employers are perceived
by management and unions to be superior to
services provided by an external agency. If
corporate executives and labor leaders develop
personnel policies consistent with these findings, welfare professionals will find the business community a hospitable setting in which
to practice. In that event, occupational social
work within the corporation may become as
prevalent an auspice of practice as the voluntary and governmental sectors.

NOTES

1. Robert McIntyre and Robert Folen, *Corporate
    Income Taxes in the Reagan Years* (Washing-
    ton, D.C.: Citizens for Tax Justice, 1984), p. 5.
2. Sheila Kamerman, "The New Mixed Econ-
    omy of Welfare," *Social Work* 28 (January–
    February 1983).
3. Paul Starr, "The Meaning of Privatization,"
    and Marc Bendick, "Privatizing the Delivery
    of Social Welfare Service," in *Working Paper 6*
    (Washington, D.C.: National Conference on
    Social Welfare, 1985); David Stoesz, "Privati-
    zation: Reforming the Welfare State," *Journal
    of Sociology and Social Welfare* (Summer
    1987); Mimi Abramovitz, "The Privatization
    of the Welfare State," *Social Work* 31, no. 4
    (July–August 1986), pp. 257–64.
4. Neil Gilbert, *Capitalism and the Welfare State*
    (New Haven: Yale University Press, 1983).
5. David Stoesz, "Corporate Welfare," *Social
    Work* 31, no. 4 (July–August 1986): 245–49;
    and "Corporate Health Care and Social Wel-
    fare," *Health and Social Work* (Summer 1986);
    and "The Gray Market," *Journal of Geronto-
    logical Social Work* (forthcoming, 1989).
6. Abramovitz, "The Privatization of the Welfare
    State," p. 257.
7. Theodore Marmor, Mark Schlesinger, and
    Richard Smithey, "A New Look at Nonprofits:
    Health Care Policy in a Competitive Age,"
    Yale Journal of Regulation 3, no. 2 (Spring
    1986), p. 322.
8. Robert Heilbroner, *The Worldly Philosophers*
    (New York: Simon and Schuster, 1967), pp.
    98–106.
9. Edward Berkowitz and Kim McQuaid, *Creat-
    ing the Welfare State* (New York: Praeger,
    1980), p. 4.
10. Ibid., pp. 5–10.
11. Gilbert, *Capitalism and the Welfare State*,
    p. 3.
12. Original emphasis, quoted in Norman Furniss
    and Timothy Tilton, *The Case for the Welfare
    State* (Bloomington, Ind.: Indiana University
    Press, 1977), p. 156.
13. Murray Levine and Adeline Levine, *A Social
    History of Helping Services* (New York: Ap-
    pleton-Century-Crofts, 1970), p. 237.
14. Harold Wilensky and Charles Lebeaux, *Indus-
    trial Society and Social Welfare* (New York:
    Free Press, 1965), p. 88.
15. James Leiby, *A History of Social Welfare and
    Social Work in the United States* (New York:
    Columbia University Press, 1978), p. 170.
16. Levine and Levine, *A Social History of Help-
    ing Services*, pp. 236–43.
17. James Jones, *Bad Blood* (New York: The Free
    Press, 1981), p. 34.
18. Wilensky and Lebeaux, *Industrial Society and
    Social Welfare*, p. 9; National Association of
    Social Workers, *Encyclopedia of Social Work*,
    18th ed. (Silver Spring, Md.: NASW, 1987),
    p. 781.
19. Berkowitz and McQuaid, *Creating the Welfare
    State*, pp. 33–36.
20. Ibid., p. 83.
21. Michael Boskin, "Social Security and the
    Economy," in Peter Duignan and Alvin Ra-
    bushka, eds., *The United States in the 1980s*
    (Stanford, Calif.: Hoover Institution, 1980),
    p. 182.
22. Berkowitz and McQuaid, *Creating the Welfare
    State*, p. 103.
23. Ibid., p. 136.
24. *Statistical Abstract of the United States* (Wash-
    ington, D.C.: U.S. Government Printing
    Office, 1986), p. 369; *Social Security Bulletin,
    Annual Statistical Supplement* (Washington,
    D.C.: U.S. Government Printing Office, 1986),
    p. 67.

25. *Statistical Abstract of the United States*, p. 421.

26. Michael Misshauk, *Management: Theory and Practice* (Boston: Little, Brown, 1979), p. 6.

27. Melvin Anshen, *Managing the Socially Responsible Corporation* (New York: Macmillan, 1974), p. 5.

28. Steven Lydenberg et al., *Rating America's Corporate Conscience* (Reading, Mass.: Addison-Wesley, 1986).

29. Theodore Purcell, "Management and the 'Ethical' Investors," in S. Prakash Sethi and Carl Swanson, eds., *Private Enterprise and Public Purpose* (New York: John Wiley, 1981), pp. 296–97.

30. *The [Sullivan] Statement of Principles: Fourth Amplification* (Philadelphia: International Council for Equality of Opportunity Principles, 1984).

31. James Worthy, "Managing the 'Social Markets' Business," in Lance Liebner and Corrine Schelling, eds., *Public-Private Partnership: New Opportunities for Meeting Social Needs* (Cambridge, Mass.: Ballinger, 1978), p. 226.

32. Melanie Lawrence, "Social Responsibility: How Companies Become Involved in Their Communities," *Personnel Journal* 61, no. 7 (July 1982); James Chrisman and Archie Carroll, "SMR Forum: Corporate Responsibility—Reconciling Economic and Social Goals," *Sloan Management Review* 25, no. 2 (Winter 1984).

33. Enterprise Foundation, *Annual Report 1983* (Columbia, Md.: Enterprise Foundation, 1983), p. 1.

34. Brian O'Conell, *Philanthropy in Action* (New York: The Foundation Center, 1987), p. 218.

35. Local Initiatives Support Corporation, *The Local Initiatives Support Corporation* (New York: LISC, 1980); "A Statement of Policy for Programs of the Local Initiatives Support Corporation" (New York: LISC, 1981).

36. David Linowes, *The Corporate Conscience* (New York: Hawthorn Books, 1974), p. 209.

37. *Privatization: Toward More Effective Government* (Washington, D.C.: U.S. Government Printing Office, 1988), pp. 2–3.

38. Irving Kristol, "Charity and Business Shouldn't Mix," *New York Times*, October 17, 1982.

39. Hedrick Smith, *The Power Game: How Washington Works* (New York: Random House, 1988), pp. 252–53, 260.

40. Marvin Olasky, *Patterns of Corporate Philanthropy* (Washington, D.C.: Capital Research Center, 1987), p. 2.

41. Ibid., p. 19.

42. Ibid., p. 11.

43. Lawrence Fouraker and Graham Allison, "Forward," in John Dunlop, ed., *Business and Public Policy* (Boston: Harvard University Press, 1980), p. ix.

44. Peter Steinfels, "Michael Novak and His Ultrasuper Democraticapitalism," *Commonweal*, February 15, 1983, p. 11.

45. William J. Baroody, Jr., "The President's Review," *AEI Annual Report 1981–82* (Washington, D.C.: American Enterprise Institute, 1982), p. 2.

46. Peter Stone, "Businesses Widen Role in Conservatives' 'War on Ideas,'" *Washington Post*, May 12, 1985.

47. Bernard Weinraub, "Institute Plays Key Role in Shaping Reagan Programs," *New York Times*, January 5, 1981.

48. David Stoesz, "Policy Gambit: Conservative Think Tanks Take on the Welfare State," *Journal of Sociology and Social Welfare* (forthcoming, 1989).

49. Stone, "Businesses Widen Role in Conservatives' 'War on Ideas.'"

50. American Enterprise Institute, *Annual Report 1981–82*, (Washington, D.C.: American Enterprise Institute, 1982).

51. Peter Berger and Richard Neuhaus, *To Empower People* (Washington, D.C.: American Enterprise Institute, 1977).

52. Michael Balzano, *Federalizing Meals on Wheels* (Washington, D.C.: American Enterprise Institute, 1979), p. 37.

53. Michael Novak, *Toward a Theology of the Corporation* (Washington, D.C.: American Enterprise Institute, 1981), p. 5.

54. Ibid., p. 50.

55. Ibid., p. 28.

56. Richard Reeves, "How New Ideas Shape Presidential politics," *New York Times Magazine*, July 15, 1984.

57. Heritage Foundation, *The Heritage Foundation Annual Report* (Washington, D.C.: Heritage Foundation, 1983).

58. Reeves, "How New Ideas Shape Presidential Politics."
59. Stuart Butler, Interview at the Heritage Foundation, Washington, D.C., October 4, 1984.
60. George Sternlieb, "Kemp-Garcia Act," in George Sternlieb and David Listokin, eds., *New Tools for Economic Development* (Piscataway, N.J.: Rutgers University Press, 1981).
61. Stuart Butler, "Enterprise Zones," in Sternlieb and Listokin, *New Tools for Economic Development*.
62. Gilbert Lewthwaite, "Heritage Foundation Delivers Right Message," *Baltimore Sun*, December 9, 1984.
63. Peter Ferrara, *Social Security Reform* (Washington, D.C.: Heritage Foundation, 1982), p. 51.
64. Peter Ferrara, *Rebuilding Social Security* (Washington, D.C.: Heritage Foundation, 1984), p. 7.
65. Chuck Lane, "The Manhattan Project," *The New Republic*, March 25, 1985.
66. Charles Murray, *Losing Ground* (New York: Basic Books, 1984), pp. 226, 227.
67. Burton Pines, *Back to Basics* (New York: William Morrow, 1982).
68. Ibid., p. 254.
69. John Filer, "Editorial Notes: Commission on Private Philanthropy and Public Needs," *Social Casework* (May 1976), p. 342.
70. Virginia Hodgkinson and Murray Weitzman, *Dimensions of the Independent Sector* (Washington, D.C.: Independent Sector, 1986), p. 53.
71. Donald Bauber, "Small Dent Expected in Charitable Giving as a Result of Crash," *San Diego Tribune*, November 1, 1987, p. I–1.
72. *Eleventh Report of the Signatory Companies to the Statement of Principles for South Africa* (Cambridge, Mass.: Arthur D. Little, November 5, 1987), p. 3.
73. Nancy Amidei, "How to End Poverty: Next Steps," *Food Monitor* (Winter 1988), p. 52.
74. Stuart Butler, "A Conservative Vision of Welfare," *Policy Review* (Spring 1987).
75. Michael Novak et al., *The New Consensus on Family and Welfare* (Washington, D.C.: American Enterprise Institute, 1987), pp. xiv, 101–119.
76. Ibid., p. 120.
77. "Government's Role in the Consensus," *Business Week*, June 30, 1980, p. 87.
78. "Expectations That Can No Longer Be Met," *Business Week*, June 30, 1980, p. 84.
79. Lester Thurow, *The Zero-Sum Society* (New York: Basic Books, 1980), p. 95.
80. Robert Reich, *The Next American Frontier* (New York: Times Books, 1983), p. 223.
81. Ibid., pp. 247–48.
82. Kevin Phillips, *Staying on Top: The Business Case for a National Industrial Policy* (New York: Random House, 1984), pp. 5–6.
83. Yeheskel Hasenfeld, "The Changing Context of Human Services Administration," *Social Work* 29, no. 4 (November–December 1984), p. 524.
84. James O'Connor, *The Fiscal Crisis of the State* (New York: St. Martin's Press, 1973); Ian Gough, *The Political Economy of the Welfare State* (London: Macmillan, 1979).
85. See S. Akabas, P. Kurzman, and N. Kolben, eds. *Labor and Industrial Settings: Sites for Social Work Practice* (New York: Council on Social Work Education, 1979); M. Ozawa, "Development of Social Services in Industry: Why and How?" *Social Work*, November 1980; D. Masi, *Human Services in Industry* (Lexington, Mass.: D. C. Heath, 1982).
86. "Social Work in Industrial Settings," *Social Work*, January–February 1988.
87. J. Decker, R. Starrett, and J. Redhorse, "Evaluating the Cost-Effectiveness of Employee Assistance Programs," *Social Work*, September–October 1986.
88. Shulamith Straussner, "Comparison of In-House and Contracted-Out Employee Assistance Programs," *Social Work*, January–February 1988, p. 53.

CHAPTER 9

Human Service Corporations

This chapter examines for-profit providers of human services. Proprietary human service firms are well established in several markets: nursing care, hospital management, health maintenance, child care, life/continuing care, and corrections. The emergence of human service corporations in American social welfare presents important issues for clients and professionals. The recent development of Employee Assistance Programs illustrates how human service professionals are adapting to practice opportunities in the corporate sector.

As the postindustrial service sector expands, continued demand for human services has drawn the corporate sector directly into social welfare in the United States. Corporate exploration of the growing human services market has proceeded rapidly while government welfare programs have been held in check. Heavily dependent on government support and the contributions of middle-income Americans who have experienced a continual erosion of their economic position, the voluntary sector has been unable to meet this demand. Relatively unfettered by government regulation and with easy access to capital from commercial sources, the corporate sector has made dramatic inroads into service areas previously reserved for governmental and voluntary sector organizations.

Interestingly, the incentives for corporate entry into human services were initially provided through government social programs. Between 1950 and 1979, government expenditures for social welfare increased from $23.5 billion to $430.6 billion, a factor of 18.[1] Per capita expenditures for welfare increased from $153 to $1,912 during these years, a 13-fold

increase.[2] In addition, health care allocations figured prominently in public welfare expenditures. In 1970, the government spent $27.8 billion on health care; by 1985 that figure had grown to $148.8 billion.[3] The potential profits for corporations entering the social welfare market were unmistakable.

Concomitantly, public policy decisions have encouraged proprietary firms to provide welfare services. This was the case when Medicaid and Medicare were enacted in 1965. By using a market approach to assure the availability of health care for the medically indigent and the elderly, Medicaid and Medicare avoided the costs of constructing a system of public sector facilities and, in so doing, contributed to the restructuring of American health care. What had essentially been a haphazard collection of mom-and-pop nursing homes and small private hospitals was transformed, in a short period, into a system of corporate franchises, complete with stocks traded on Wall Street. Incentives offered through Medicaid and Medicare to encourage the corporate sector to become involved in hospital care were replicated in the health maintenance industry almost a decade later. The Health Maintenance Organization Act of 1973 stimulated a sluggish health maintenance industry that has since grown at an explosive rate.

Initially dependent on government welfare programs, the corporate sector has developed a life of its own. Exploitation of the nursing home, hospital management, and health maintenance markets has led to corporate interest in other markets. By the 1980s, human service corporations had established prominence in child care, ambulatory health care, substance abuse and psychiatric care, home health care, and life and continuing care.[4] Increasingly, proprietary firms were able to obtain funds for facilities through commercial loans or sales of stock, and to meet ongoing costs by charging fees to individuals, companies, and nongovernmental third parties. Insofar as resources for human service corporations are not financed by the state, firms are free to function relatively independent of government intervention.

THE SCOPE OF HUMAN SERVICE CORPORATIONS

How big is the corporate sector in American social welfare? In 1985, two of the largest firms—Hospital Corporation of America and National Medical Enterprises—reported annual revenues greater than all contributions to the United Way of America.[5] Each of these corporations employed over 80,000 workers, easily more than the number of state and local workers for public welfare programs in any state in the union.[6] Some of the more salient features of the larger human service corporations are depicted in Table 9.1.

Human service corporations in the United States share several striking features. First, virtually all were incorporated after World War II, the benchmark of the post-industrial era, and the great majority of these were incorporated after 1960. All told, the overwhelming majority of these large firms have been in business for less than 25 years. Second, these corporations record rapid growth in revenues. Of the 66 human service corporations reporting annual revenues above $10 million, 14 had more than doubled their earnings, 17 had more than quadrupled their earnings, and 23 had actually increased their income by a factor greater than ten since 1980! This is particularly significant because the earnings escalated at a time not particularly favorable to the business community. Nevertheless, human service corporations seemed immune from the recession of the early 1980s and continued to thrive despite attempts by the Carter and Reagan administrations to contain costs for health and human service programs. Although most of the companies focus on health-related services, many diversify into other service areas and, in some instances, other types of corporations acquire human service firms in order to balance their operations. For example, when cigarette sales plummeted, GrandMet USA acquired soft drink and pet food subsidiaries, then diversified further by acquiring Children's World, the second largest franchise of child care centers, and Quality Care, a leading provider of home

TABLE 9.1. Prominent Human Service Corporations

Firm	Revenues ($mils)	Markets	Employees
Beverly Enterprises	$2,019.3	Long-term retirement facilities	116,000
Caremark	133.2	Home-health services	1,100
Charter Medical Corporation	666.2	Psychiatric services	13,400
Community Psychiatric Centers	231.4	Psychiatric services	4,514
Comprehensive Care Corporation	190.8	Chemical dependency	4,560
Health Care and Retirement Corporation of America	497.6	Nursing homes, retirement facilities	45,000
Hospital Corporation of America	4,930.7	Acute health care	89,000
Humana	2,600.6	Acute health, psychiatric care	45,300
Kinder-Care Learning Centers	41.5	Child day care	14,300
Maxicare Health Plans	880.9	Health maintenance	5,523

Source: *Standard and Poor's*, 1988.

health care. Overall, corporate activity in the new human service markets is characterized by rapid expansion and consolidation.

THE NEW HUMAN SERVICE MARKETS

Within social welfare, human service corporations have become prominent—if not dominant—in several areas: nursing homes, hospital management, health maintenance organizations (HMOs), child care, and home care. More recently, proprietary firms have established beach-heads in other markets, notably life/continuing care and corrections.

Nursing Homes

Among corporate initiatives in social welfare, expansion into the nursing home industry is unparalleled. Between 1965 and 1978, expenditures for nursing home care increased 16.9 percent *annually*.[7] By the early 1980s, nursing homes had become a $25 billion per year industry, and the number of nursing home beds exceeded those in acute care facilities for the first time.[8] At that time, 70 percent of nursing homes were under proprietary management. Market conditions such as these led to the following observation in *Forbes* magazine: "This is a guaranteed opportunity for someone. How the nursing home industry can exploit it is the real question."[9] Under favorable market conditions, nursing home corporations proliferated. David Vaughan, president of a real estate firm specializing in facilities for the elderly, noted:

> The overall affluence of the over fifty-five population makes investments in special care facilities an extremely attractive venture. The need of capital in meeting the housing needs of this segment of the U.S. population has been so great that we have been able to invest in these facilities with only limited competition.[10]

Guaranteed growth of the nursing home market led to the consolidation of proprietary firms and the emergence of an oligopoly. As early as 1981, the following three corporations held more than 10,000 nursing home beds: Beverly Enterprises held 38,488; ARA Services held 31,325; and National Medical Enterprises (NME) held 14,534.[11] Beverly Enterprises attained first ranking by its purchase, in 1979, of Progressive Medical Group, which was the eleventh largest chain of nursing homes. NME attained third ranking in 1979 by purchasing Hillhaven, then the third largest operation. ARA Services grew 26 percent in 1979, thereby attaining second ranking, by consolidating smaller operations in Indiana, Colorado, and California.[12] Undeterred by the filing of the first antitrust action in the nursing home industry, such acquisitions and mergers continued.[13] In 1984, using its Hillhaven subsidiary, NME acquired Flagg Industries, which held 12 facilities in Idaho, bringing its total holdings to 339 health care facilities with 42,000 beds. Not to be outdone, Beverly Enterprises acquired Beacon Hill America for $60 million, thereby retaining its top ranking. By the mid-1980s, Beverly Enterprises controlled 781 nursing homes with a total of 88,198 beds in 44 states and the District of Columbia.[14] Given this trend, one industry analyst hypothesized that "by 1990, the top thirty nursing homes will control all of the [nursing home] beds." Another industry expert believed that the industry would eventually fall into the hands of "five or six corporations."[15]

Hospital Management

The growth of the nursing home industry is matched by corporate involvement in hospital management. Between 1976 and 1982, the number of investor-owned or investor-managed hospitals increased from 533 to 1,040, accruing gross revenues of approximately $40 billion.[16] Richard Siegrist, Jr., a Wall Street analyst, concluded that the future for the industry looked bright, noting that revenues and bed ownership for the five largest companies had roughly tripled between 1976 and 1981. According to this analyst, in 1978, Humana doubled its size through an unfriendly takeover of American Medicorp (worth $450 million), gaining 39 hospitals and 7,838 beds. Meanwhile, Hospital Corporation of America (HCA) purchased Hospital Affiliates (worth $650 million), gaining 55 hospitals, 8,207 beds, and 102 hospital management contracts; General Care Corporation (worth $78 million), gained eight hospitals with 1,294 beds; and General Health Services (worth $96 million), gained six hospitals with 1,115 beds. At the same time, American Medical International (AMI) acquired Hyatt Medical Enterprises (worth $69 million), with eight hospitals, 907 beds, and 26 hospital management contracts, as well as Brookwood Health Services (worth $156 million), with nine hospitals, 1,271 beds, and five hospital contracts.[17]

AMI's strategy of purchasing financially troubled community hospitals proved so successful that the company reported a 29 percent increase in net income for 1983 as compared to 1982, accomplished a four-for-three stock split in February 1983, and declared a 21 percent dividend per share. Moreover, in 1984, AMI acquired Lifemark's 25 hospitals and three alcoholism treatment centers through a $1 billion stock transfer.[18] Despite such large-scale growth, AMI continued to rank second behind HCA, which owned 393 hospitals having 56,000 beds.[19]

Health Maintenance Organizations

Pioneered by the nonprofit Kaiser-Permanente in California, the concept of Health Maintenance Organizations (HMOs) was slow to attract the interest of the corporate sector. However, from 1973 to 1981, the Health Maintenance Organization Act of 1973 authorized funds for the establishment of facilities in a large number of favorable marketing areas. This funding, coupled with the growth in the nursing home and hospital management industries, reversed investor apathy. By 1983, 60 HMOs were operating on a proprietary basis.[20]

An early leader in the HMO industry was HealthAmerica, a for-profit HMO begun in 1980. Within a few years HealthAmerica enrolled almost 400,000 members in 17 locations across the nation, becoming the largest proprietary HMO (second in size only to nonprofit Kaiser-Permanente). Seeking capital for further expansion, HealthAmerica offered stock publicly in July 1983 and raised $20 million for 1.5 million shares. One month later, Phillip Bredesen, Chairman and President of HealthAmerica, reported that he anticipated "dramatic growth in the HMO segment of the health care business," and that "HealthAmerica [was] well-positioned with the people and systems that this growth [would] represent."[21]

HealthAmerica's growth did not go unnoticed by Fred Wasserman, founder of Maxicare, a proprietary HMO. Wasserman suspected that Bredesen had stretched his company too thin in an ambitious expansion into new market areas. In November 1986, HealthAmerica was purchased by Maxicare for $372 million. Coupled with its earlier acquisition of HealthCare USA for $66 million, the purchase of HealthAmerica enabled Maxicare to claim more than 2 million members nationwide and annual revenues approaching $2 billion. After the HealthAmerica takeover, Wasserman spoke optimistically about overtaking Kaiser-Permanente in pursuit of a health maintenance market[22] anticipated to consist of 30 million members and $25 billion in revenues by 1990.[23]

Child Care

As a human services market, child care is exploited effectively by proprietary firms. In an important study of child welfare services delivery, Catherine Born showed the influence of for-profit providers relative to that of providers in the voluntary and public sectors. She noted that:

... in the case of residential treatment, among all services purchased, 51 percent was obtained from for-profit firms, 26 percent from voluntary organizations, and 22 percent from other public agencies having contractual agreements with the welfare department. For contracted institutional services, 48 percent was provided by proprietary concerns, 14 percent by voluntary vendors, and 38 percent by other public agencies. The pattern was similar in the case of group home services where 58 percent was proprietarily contracted, 17 percent was obtained from the private, nonprofit sector, and 25 percent was purchased from other public agencies.[24]

The day care market—along with its largest provider, Kinder-Care—has expanded rapidly. Begun in 1969, Kinder-Care has demonstrated prodigious growth, claiming approximately 825 "learning centers" in 1983, representing $128 million in revenue. The net earnings for Kinder-Care in fiscal year 1983 represented a 68 percent increase over fiscal year 1982. The company executed a five-for-four stock split in November 1982 and a four-for-three stock split in May 1983. Also, during fiscal year 1983, the company entered the market of freestanding immediate medical care by purchasing First Medical Corporation and its 10 facilities for an undisclosed sum.[25] By the second quarter of 1984, Kinder-Care reported that more than 100 new learning centers and 20 new clinics were under construction.[26]

Home Care

Several companies in the home care market have replicated the success of corporations in the nursing home industry. Home Health Care of America, renamed Caremark, began in 1979. A leader in the field, the company has grown particularly quickly. Caremark generated net revenues of $1 million in 1980, $35.8 million in 1983, and $133.2 million in 1986. In 1983, Caremark increased the number of regional service centers from 10 to 31 and, despite the costs incurred by this expansion, net income for the

year increased 129 percent.[27] Growth of this magnitude is characteristic of the home care market, which is expected to quadruple its consumer expenditures to $10.2 billion by 1990.[28] Elsie Griffith, chief executive officer of the Visiting Nurse Service of New York and chair of the board of the National Association for Home Care, observed that home health care "is expanding at a phenomenal rate."[29]

Corrections

Among the more ambitious of human service corporations is the Correction Corporation of America (CCA), founded in 1983 by Tom Beasely, with the financial backing of Jack Massey, founder of the Hospital Corporation of America. CCA officials noted that many states were unable to contend with overcrowding of facilities and proposed contracting with state and local jurisdictions for the provision of correctional services. As CCA acknowledged in its 1986 annual report, court orders to upgrade facilities, coupled with governmental reluctance to finance improvements, provided strong incentives for jurisdictions to consider contracting out correctional services.

> Government response to ... [overcrowding] ... has been hampered by the administrative and budgetary problems traditionally plaguing public sector facilities. Most systems have suffered a lack of long-term leadership due to their ties to the political process, and many jurisdictions have placed a low priority on corrections funding. The outcome has been a proliferation of out-dated facilities with a lack of sufficient capacity to meet constitutional standards.[30]

By 1986, CCA operated nine correctional facilities, totaling 1,646 beds, and was negotiating with the Texas Department of Corrections " to build and manage two minimum security prisons which will provide an additional 1,000 beds."[31]

Most analysts expect that proprietary correctional facilities will grow in popularity as governmental agencies recognize the cost savings of contracting out correctional services. CCA's per diem charge in 1986 was $29.77, about twenty-five percent less than the cost of public facilities.[32] In the near future, Texas, Oklahoma, and Arkansas are to put 3,000 correctional "beds" out to bid, perhaps signifying the willingness of states to use proprietary firms on a large scale.[33] The most dramatic example of the prospective growth of for-profit corrections almost occurred in 1985, when CCA startled Tennessee state officials by offering to take over the state's entire prison system. Like thirty other states and the District of Columbia, Tennessee's system was characterized by too many prisoners in archaic facilities and was operating under court supervision. When CCA offered the state $250 million for a 99-year contract, state officials were hard pressed not to give it careful consideration. Ultimately, state officials balked at the idea, primarily because of conflict of interest between CCA and leaders of state government.[34]

Life and Continuing Care

The graying of the American population has led some corporations to construct special residential communities which include health care as a service. Life care—or continuing care—provides more affluent elders an opportunity to purchase a higher level of long-term care than is ordinarily found in nursing homes. Life care communities usually feature recreational, cultural, and other services in addition to health care. By the mid-1980s, 275 life care communities housed 100,000 elders.[35] Robert Ball, former Commissioner of Social Security, estimated that perhaps 15 million elders could afford this type of care.[36]

Despite well-publicized bankruptcies of several life care communities, the prospect of a market of this magnitude has attracted the interest of several corporations. Beverly Enterprises, the largest nursing home operation,

intends to build or acquire several such communities.[37] Subsequently, the Marriott Corporation announced plans to have 200 Lifecare Retirement Communities in operation by the year 2000.[38] Despite the recession of the early 1980s, the interest of brokerage houses in life care has remained high. Harold Margolin, a vice president of Merrill Lynch, stated that "the financial climate could impact on the growth of the continuing care segment of the health care industry, but only on the timing. It's going to be a very large industry."[39]

As corporate performance in the new human service markets demonstrates, substantial investments are being made in social welfare by the corporate sector. In fact, the number of human service corporations has almost doubled in the relatively short period between 1981 and 1985, as illustrated in Figure 9.1.

IMPLICATIONS FOR SOCIAL WORKERS

Despite the proliferation of human service corporations, social workers have been slow to adopt the corporate sector as a setting for practice. The number of welfare professionals practicing in the corporate sector is difficult to determine since the largest organization of social workers, the National Association of Social Workers, does not differentiate between private practice (which is proprietary but on a small scale) and the larger corporate providers. Based on data from a survey of California welfare professionals, Elizabeth Ortiz speculates that as few as 1.4 percent consider it primary employment, while 7.7 percent count it as secondary.[40] This level of participation does not correspond with the size of the for-profit sector in human services, suggesting that social work is underrepresented. Under circumstances when organizations under traditional auspices—the voluntary and governmental sectors—are limited in their capacity to provide services, it is probable that social workers will discover

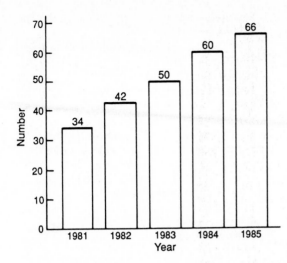

Figure 9.1. Human Service Corporations Reporting Annual Revenues Above $10 Million

Source: *Standard and Poor's*, 1986

that human service corporations are a suitable location for practice.

Social workers electing to work within the for-profit sector could find it advantageous for several reasons. Proprietary firms may provide access to capital needed for expansion of social services. A primary explanation for the rapid growth of human service corporations is their ability to tap commercial sources of capital. Through loans and the sale of stock, human service firms are able to quickly obtain funds necessary for expansion. This has given them an enormous advantage over their competitors of the voluntary sector, which often resort to arduous and painstaking fundraising campaigns, or the governmental sector, which must rely on even more protracted methods of bond sales or tax increases to raise funds. For human service corporations, the cost of commercially derived capital can be reduced by depreciating assets and writing off the interest against income during the first years of operation. This presents obvious advantages for human service administrators who are faced with diminishing revenues derived from charitable or governmental sources. Perhaps the best example of this advantage is the meteoric rise of long-term care corporations, which were almost nonexistent twenty years ago. By convincing commercial lenders and investors that long-term care was viable, for-profit firms eventually gained control over the industry.[41]

In some instances, the corporate sector offers opportunities in program innovation more readily than those possible under other auspices. Governmental programs must be mandated by a public authority, and this requires a consensus on how to deal with particular concerns. Voluntary sector agencies are ultimately managed by a board of directors which reflects the interests of the community in organizational policy. When human service issues are controversial, welfare professionals can encounter stiff opposition to needed programs. Some of this can be obviated by a corporate organizational form which is not so directly held to the status quo. An example of how a human service corporation offers opportunities not possible through traditional human service organizations is the ability of for-profit correctional companies to expand the scope of correctional facilities when government is reluctant to finance new construction and the voluntary sector is unable to raise the necessary capital.

In a related matter, the corporate sector offers greater organizational flexibility than that usually found in governmental agencies and a level of sophistication in managerial innovation not often found in the voluntary sector. To be sure, economic advantages enjoyed by the corporate sector make this possible, but the track record in organizational experimentation by the corporate sector is undeniable. In fact, examples of alternatives which could be of value to traditional welfare organizations are frequently derived from the corporate sector, as the popularity of *In Search of Excellence*[42] and *The Changemasters* attest.[43]

Of course, some human service professionals are skeptical about the assurance of social welfare through human service corporations. According to the critics of proprietary human service delivery, the corporate sector is the organizational manifestation of a capitalist economy which is at the root of much social injustice and human need. For these welfare advocates, professional practice within a corporate context is antithetical to what is "social" about social work. In fact, studies of organizational practices of human service corporations raise important questions about their suitability to promote social welfare. Human service corporations are less cost-effective than nonprofit and governmental agencies, engage in discriminatory selection of clients which penalizes the poor, and attract clients away from voluntary social service agencies. (These practices are considered in greater detail in the chapter on "privatization.") Despite the undesirable attributes of proprietary human service providers, they are likely to continue to play an active role in defining social welfare. The economy of the United States, after all, is capitalistic, and entrepreneurs are free to establish businesses in markets which they consider profitable. Unless government strictly regulates —or prohibits—the for-profit provision of human service, human service corporations are likely to continue to influence American social welfare in the future.

NOTES

1. Social Security Administration, *Social Security Bulletin* 46, no. 8 (August 1983), pp. 10–12.
2. Social Security Administration, *Social Security Bulletin* 44, no. 11 (November 1981), p. 8.
3. Bureau of the Census, *Statistical Abstract of the United States, 1984* (Washington, D.C.: U.S. Government Printing Office, 1984), p. 103.
4. Life/continuing care refers to residential communities for the elderly which have a complete range of health services available to residents. Such communities usually require residents to purchase residences and pay a monthly fee for a comprehensive range of service, including health care.
5. David Stoesz, "Human Service Corporations and the Welfare State," *Transaction/Society* (forthcoming, 1989).
6. Bureau of the Census, *Statistical Abstract of the United States, 1986* (Washington, D.C.: U.S. Government Printing Office, 1986).
7. U.S. Department of Commerce, *1982 U.S. Industrial Outlook for 200 Industries with Projections for 1986* (Washington, D.C.: U.S. Government Printing Office, 1982), p. 406.
8. J. Avorn, "Nursing Home Infections—The Context," *New England Journal of Medicine*, 305 (September 24, 1981), p. 759.
9. J. Blyskal, "Gray Gold," *Forbes*, November 23, 1981, p. 84.
10. D. Vaughan, "Health Care Syndications: Investment Tools of the '80s," *Financial Planner* (December 1981), p. 49.
11. Blyskal, "Gray Gold," p. 80.
12. V. DiPaolo, "Tight Money, Higher Interest Rates Slow Nursing Home Systems Growth," *Modern Health Care* (June 1980), p. 84.
13. National Senior Citizens' Law Center, "Federal Antitrust Activity" (Los Angeles: National Senior Citizens' Law Center, 1982), p. 2.
14. "NME Makes More Health Care Acquisitions," *Homecare News*, 3 (February 17, 1984), p. 4.
15. Quoted in W. Spicer, "The Boom in Building," *Contemporary Administrator* (February 1982), pp. 13–14.
16. B. Gray, "An Introduction to the New Health Care for Profit," in B. Gray, ed., *The New Health Care for Profit* (Washington, D.C.: National Academy Press, 1983), p. 2.
17. R. Siegrist, Jr. "Wall Street and the For-Profit Hospital Management Companies," in B. Gray, ed., *The New Health Care for Profit*, p. 36.
18. American Medical International, *1983 Annual Report* (Beverly Hills, Calif.: AMI, 1983).
19. "GAO Says Proprietary Hospital Chain Mergers Raise Medicare/Medicaid Costs" *Homecare News*, 3 (February 17, 1984), p. 6.
20. National Industry Council for HMO Development. *Ten Year Report 1971–1983* (Washington, D.C., 1983).
21. HealthAmerica, *Company Profile* (Nashville, Tenn.: HealthAmerica, 1983).
22. M. Abramowitz, "Maxicare HMO Soars with

Farsighted Founder," *Washington Post*, November 30, 1986.

23. National Industry Council, *Ten Year Report*, p. 22.

24. Catherine Born, "Proprietary Firms and Child Welfare Services: Patterns and Implications," *Child Welfare*, 62 (March–April 1983), p. 112.

25. Kinder-Care, *Annual Report 1983* (Montgomery, Ala.: Kinder-Care, 1983).

26. Kinder-Care, *Second Quarter Report* (Montgomery, Ala.: Kinder-Care, March 16, 1984).

27. "Home Health Care of America," *Standard and Poor's Stock Reports* (March 1984), p. 4165.

28. T. Woolk, "Home Care Is Where the Dollars Are," *Medical Marketing and Media* (November 1982), p. 84.

29. "Interview with Elsie Griffith," *American Journal of Nursing* (March 1984), p. 341.

30. "Digest of Earnings Reports," *The Wall Street Journal*, August 13, 1987.

31. Stephen Boland, "Prisons for Profit," unpublished manuscript, School of Social Work, San Diego State University, 1987, pp. 5–6.

32. Ibid., p. 8.

33. Eric Press, "A Person, Not a Number," *Newsweek*, June 29, 1987, p. 63.

34. D. Vise, "Private Company Asks for Control of Tennessee Prisons," *Washington Post*, September 22, 1985.

35. U.S. Senate Special Committee on Aging, *Discrimination Against the Poor and Disabled in Nursing Homes* (Washington, D.C., U.S. Government Printing Office, 1984), p. 8.

36. Ibid.

37. "Sun City—With an Add-On," *Forbes*, November 23, 1981, p. 84.

38. Paul Farhi, "Marriott Corp. Caters to America's Rapidly Aging Population," *Washington Post*, January 2, 1989.

39. "Merrill Lynch: Bullish on Health Care," *Contemporary Administrator* (February 1982), p. 16.

40. Elizabeth Ortiz, "For-Profit Social Services and Social Work Education: Rapid Change and Slow Response," *Journal of Independent Social Work* 2, no. 1 (Fall 1987), pp. 20–21.

41. D. Stoesz, "The Gray Market," *Journal of Gerontological Social Work* (forthcoming, 1989).

42. T. Peters and R. Waterman, Jr., *In Search of Excellence* (New York: Harper and Row, 1982).

43. R. Kanter, *The Changemasters* (New York, Simon and Schuster, 1983).

CHAPTER 10

Private Practice

This chapter considers private practice as an increasingly important form of human service delivery. A form of independent practice, private practice is influenced by policies of states in which it is regulated, by professional associations, and by insurance companies which pay clinicians for services. Private social work practice has been controversial within the social work profession. Despite this, private practice continues to be a popular form of practice.

Private practice has become an attractive vehicle for delivering clinical social service, and there is every indication that it will expand in the future. For some time, health and mental health services have been delivered by physicians and psychologists who work predominantly out of private offices. Recently, social workers have expressed interest in private practice, so that a large portion of students entering graduate programs in social work do so with the expressed intent of establishing a private practice. Professional schools of social work are specifically equipped to prepare graduate students for private practice. "MSW programs appear to offer more to the practitioner bound for private practice than to the social worker who would prefer to work in an agency setting," concluded researchers in a study of private and agency-based social workers.[1]

The current enthusiasm about private practice can be attributed to several factors. Private practitioners often enjoy a prestige and income that sets them apart from salaried professionals. A 1986–1987 survey of salaries of members of the National Association of Social Workers (NASW) revealed that the mean salary of private practitioners who were self-employed or in partnerships was above that of many practice settings.[2] In a subsequent survey of NASW members, researchers reported that the earnings of privately practicing social workers was significantly higher than those working in social service agencies: "Of those individuals in private practice, 65 percent have an annual income over $35,000, compared to 25.1 percent of those in agency practice."[3] It is not surprising that social workers, who are usually female and underpaid, would see private practice as a way to attain a measure of comparable worth. In fact, women are more likely to engage in private practice than work in traditional social service agencies; two-thirds of private practitioners are women.[4] Private practitioners also have a degree of independence and autonomy that is not available to professionals who are tied into the personnel policies of traditional agencies. In the study cited above, Srinika Jayaratne and her associates found that "whereas 55 percent of the private practitioners report a high level of congruence between their expectations and their activities, only 18.3 percent of the agency practitioners do so."[5] This is important for experienced professionals who find continued supervision unnecessary—or intrusive—and who require some flexibility in their work schedule to make it more compatible with other priorities. Finally, private practice allows professionals to specialize in activities at which they are best, instead of having to conform to organizational requirements of the private agency or governmental bureaucracy. Again, 66.5 percent of private practitioners reported that they were able to do those things at which they excelled, while only 22.9 percent of agency practitioners so responded.[6]

Subsequently, the image of private practice that emerges is often one of freedom and opportunity, sans rules and regulations. While private practice may involve comparatively fewer compliance requirements than does salaried employment, it is anything but unfettered practice. In actuality, private practice involves a number of policies with which practitioners must be familiar if they are to be successful. The policies which affect private practice are complex because they originate primarily from two sources: the professional community (a private entity) and government regulatory authority (a public entity). This is complicated by the provision of service through the marketplace of a capitalist economy which traditionally discriminates against groups—minorities, women, the aged, the handicapped—that do not participate fully in the labor market. These groups frequently lack the resources to purchase goods and services, such as those provided by private practitioners. For this reason, private practice is not easily reconciled with the traditional values of the human service professions which emphasize service to the community and the disadvantaged. Paradoxically, private practice has become a popular, yet controversial, method of social work practice.

THE SOCIOLOGY OF PROFESSIONS

In conventional usage, the term "private practice" is reserved for members of a professional community who are self-employed. Although persons providing technical services who do not belong to professional communities may be self-employed, they are not referred to as private practitioners. As a type of service delivery, private practice exists in several forms: solo practice, formal association, and group practice.[7]

Private practitioners enjoy status by virtue of their association with a profession. As special occupational groups, professions exhibit particular characteristics that, in the aggregate, serve to organize practitioners into a professional community. Historically, occupational groups have varied in the bases around which they have organized their activities. The classic professions—the military and the clergy—relied on custom, belief, and morality as bases for occupational specialization. Professions emerging after the Enlightenment, such as medicine, have striven to emphasize science as a base for specialization. Abraham Flexner, who was instrumental in elevating the status of physicians in the United States, stated as much in 1915, when he listed the criteria for the modern professions:

> Professions involve essentially intellectual operations with large individual responsibility; they derive their raw material from science and learning; this material they work up to a practical and definite end; they possess an educationally communicable technique; they tend to self-organization; they are becoming increasingly altruistic in motivation.[8]

With reference to social work, Ernest Greenwood identified five criteria for social work to be a profession. For social work to attain full professional status, it must generate (1) a systematic practice theory, (2) an authority which regulates the activities of professionals, (3) community sanction of professional objectives and practices, (4) an ethical code which informs practitioners and the community of the professionals' standards, and (5) a culture which is articulated and maintained by institutions of professional education and association.[9] Professions, of course, vary in the extent to which they demonstrate these essential elements; and, as a result, they hold different positions on the "professional hierarchy."[10] Thus, the attributes of professionalism represent a continuum, with any single community of experts falling somewhere between full professional and occupational status.

In addition to the conventional components of professionalism noted above, several theorists have added a variable which related to the form of service delivery. Noting the tendency for the "semi-professions"—nursing, teaching, and social work—to be salaried employees, Nina Toren introduced "the degree to which members of different professional groups are independent or salaried workers."[11] In other words, among the new professions, full professional status is positively associated with independent practice; and, conversely, semi-professional status is correlated with salaried employment.[12]

Among some observers, the concept of independent practice is inseparable from the concept of professionalism. Medical sociologist Eliot Freidson has gone so far as to state that the capacity of a profession to be "given the right to control its own work"[13] is fundamental to the very idea of professionalism. He argues that professions seek legislated independence in practice, initially through collaborating with societal elites, followed by convincing the public that professional services are indispensable, and then eventually gaining legislated monopoly. Freidson terms this condition "organized autonomy." Organized autonomy affords some professions the opportunity to practice independent of the institutional constraints affecting other occupations. With respect to the individual practitioner:

> ... the autonomy of his status and the individualism encouraged by the demands of his work make it difficult for the clinician to either submit to or participate in the regulatory process that attempts to assure high ethical and scientific standards of performance in the *aggregate* of practitioners. He wants to control the terms and content of his own work and is not inclined to want to lose that control to profession-wide systemic auspices.... To the consulting practitioner, his work and its results are seen almost as a form of private property.[14]

In an analysis of social work, Sidney Levenstein uses the concept "auspice" as roughly equivalent to the factors identified by Toren and Freidson which hierarchically order professions.

[auspice] ... differentiates between the private provision of a service and the provision of that service by an organization set up by the community at large, either through government or voluntary association, with accountability for, and control over, the service resting with the community at large. Such control and accountability are in contrast to the private control of the contractual relationship mutually exercised by a private practitioner and his client. This distinction is basic to any understanding of the private practice of any profession.[15]

In terms of the sociology of professionalism, private practice is one of several variables which differentiate professional communities. Within human services, private practice has become associated with the more affluent professions—medicine and psychology.

THE POLITICAL ECONOMY OF PRIVATE PRACTICE

The prevalence of private practice within a professional community is determined by the extent of its professional monopoly and its capacity to be reimbursed through vendorship. Professional monopoly refers to a privilege to practice which is reserved for particular groups, through enacted legislation. In the United States, the states are responsible for legislation which serves a regulatory function. In other words, states may reserve certain activities to professional groups because those activities are too important to be practiced by just anyone. The mechanism for assuring the public of safe, professional practice is the creation of a governmental authority which licenses professionals to practice within its jurisdiction. But, how can the state, which is the creation of the lay public in a democratic polity, effectively oversee a professional community which engages in activities that the public cannot practically appreciate? The solution to this problem has been to empanel a group of professionals, under state auspice, to regulate the activity of the professional community. "Professions historically are allowed to govern themselves, to control entrance into their ranks, to prescribe required training, and to set their own standards of practice somewhat free of the supervision and control of nonmembers."[16] Interestingly, licensing often regulates the use of a professional title, not necessarily any activity per se. For example, almost all states have licensed social workers, so that only duly licensed professionals may use the title "social worker." Unlicensed professionals may use methods typical of social workers, but they are in violation of the law only if they begin identifying themselves as "social workers."

Consequently, professional groups seek legislation that establishes, then strengthens, their professional monopoly. The exclusive right to practice enjoyed by professionals carries with it a social obligation to the public; namely, that professionals have the welfare of the community as their ultimate concern. Professional monopoly, then, is inseparable from the commonweal, and this is readily evident in the code of ethics of professions which specify the provision of care to the indigent. The NASW Code of Ethics specifies, for example, that "the social worker should regard as primary the service obligation of the social work profession." Moreover, "the social worker should promote the general welfare of society" through such activities as preventing discrimination, assuring access to services, respecting cultural diversity, and advocating social policies which promote social justice.[17] In sum, the justification for professional monopoly rests with the proposition that professions have as their ultimate concern the welfare of the society, and that their techniques should be used only by credentialed practitioners.

The development of private practice is only possible in a market economy. Under this condition, the clinician provides a service, the quality and cost of which are subject to the influences of supply and demand. According to Magali Larson, "Professions were and are means for earning an income on the basis of transacted services." Larson goes on to note that:

> ... in a society that has been reorganized around the centrality of the market, the professions could hardly escape the effects of this reorganization. The modern model of profession emerges as a consequence of the necessary response of professional producers to new opportunities for earning an income.[18]

As one of the "new opportunities for earning an income," private practice places the practitioner in the role of "clinical entrepreneur."[19] In this capacity, the practitioner is dependent on the market for his or her livelihood, with economic status being directly related to fees earned. Furthermore, to the extent that professions are able to develop a monopoly over their services—a characteristic of high status professions—they are assured a captive clientele whenever consumers are convinced that professional services are necessary. In an economic sense, this allows professionals the opportunity to increase fees beyond what they might be in a non-monopolistic *laissez-faire* market.[20]

Optimizing fees clearly is an important concern among private practitioners. Professional monopoly does not necessarily assure practitioners adequate reimbursement for services if their clientele cannot pay according to the prevailing fee structure. Many clients, regardless of their present economic circumstance, have insurance that pays for the cost of their care. As insurance is more widely used, vendorship (the collection of third-party payments) becomes an important issue within the professional community. Exactly which professional groups are eligible for reimbursement and for which practices is a matter determined by the insurance carrier. In some instances, state insurance authorities, which regulate practices of insurance companies, designate practitioners who can be reimbursed.

For a variety of reasons, then, it is in the interest of private practitioners to become vendors. Some companies will make payments directly to the practitioner, obviating the provider's need to collect first from the client, who is later reimbursed by the insurance company. In this instance, payment is not only more prompt, but the client may not be directly involved in the fee. Insurance companies ordinarily pay according to the "usual, customary, and reasonable" (UCR) fee of the professional community, an amount that may be above what the client is prepared (or able) to pay. Thus, the practitioner is often more likely to realize the value of the service rendered when insurance pays for the cost of care rather than when the client pays directly. Because of its significance in private practice, the UCR warrants further consideration.

The UCR is defined as the amount charged by the majority of practitioners within a geographic area. When, for example, most social workers charge $50 per fifty-minute session of clinical service, the UCR is $50. Because the UCR is the prevailing fee, it has normative features that are important for individual practitioners. Clinicians who charge less, perhaps in order to establish a practice or make service more accessible to the poor, may be subverting the UCR. Subsequently, the practitioner may be receiving fewer referrals from colleagues. As a result of this, many private practitioners employ a sliding-fee scale from which they bill clients who pay cash. Clients who are insured may be billed on an alternative fee scale, usually higher. Because the UCR represents the normative fee of the professional community, it changes with the billing practices of practitioners. While the UCR could logically be driven down if a large number of clinicians lower their fees in order to compete for a limited number of clients, this has not been the case. Instead, the UCR has increased steadily. In 1976, the average fee was $28, but a decade later more than half of the private practitioners were charging between $51 and $75 per hour.[21]

While fees increased, the number of social workers in private practice grew. But a finite client pool meant that too many clinicians were chasing too few clients, resulting in the proliferation of part-time private practice. In 1975, 22.6 percent of social workers identified private practice as a secondary source of employment, but 40.9 percent were to do so a decade later.[22]

Professional monopoly and vendorship contribute to private practice being a positive experience for many human service professionals who enjoy higher status and increased incomes. It follows that private practice can be made that much more lucrative by making the professional monopoly more restrictive and further exploiting vendorship. In fact, these are major objectives of professional associations which promote the interests of the professional community to the public. "The professional associations in social work today," concluded one study of private practice, "are indeed a major driving force behind the privatization of social work."[23] In social work, licensing and vendorship have been central and long-standing issues of the National Association of Social Workers. However, the ability of professional associations to enhance their status through leveraging the political economy is hampered somewhat by the role of the states in regulating professional activity. While there may be only one association representing social workers, there are 50 state authorities which can or do regulate social work practice.

PRIVATE PRACTICE IN SOCIAL WORK

The private practice of social work is a relatively recent phenomenon: the National Association of Social Workers (NASW) did not officially sanction this form of service delivery for its members until 1964. Prior to that, privately practicing social workers identified themselves as psychotherapists and lay analysts. Typically, they relied on referrals from physicians and psychiatrists,[24] and, after World War II, they began to establish "flourishing and lucrative" practices.[25] By the 1970s, private practice in social work was developing as an important form of service delivery. While the NASW Manpower Survey noted that less than 3 percent of its members engaged in private practice in the early 1970s, these were members reporting full-time commitments.[26] Of survey respondents, 22.6 percent identified private practice as secondary employment, usually ten or fewer hours per week.[27] But by 1985 the number of social workers in private practice increased substantially—10.9 percent reporting it as primary employment and 54.6 percent reporting private practice as secondary employment.[28] Nationwide, as many as 30,000 social workers engage in private practice to some degree.[29]

By the end of 1987, 45 states had licensed social workers,[30] with the majority of these requiring a master's degree in social work (MSW) for licensing. However, a social work license is not automatically awarded to those holding the MSW degree. Many states require candidates for licensure to have two years of post-MSW experience under the supervision of a Licensed Certified Social Worker (LCSW) and to have passed an examination. Beyond these common requirements, states vary greatly in their licensing practices. Maryland, for example, has a three-tier system: the LCSW for MSWs who have two years of post-MSW experience and who have passed an examination; the Licensed Graduate Social Worker (LGSW) for newly graduated MSWs; and the Social Work Associate (SWA) for those with baccalaureate degrees in social work. To further complicate matters, new licensing legislation often allows candidates who have practiced professionally to become licensed without meeting the requirements of new licensing legislation. This practice, called "grandfathering," is characteristic of new licensing legislation and, since social work licensing is a relatively recent development in many states, there are many

LCSWs who do not meet the technical requirements for a license. Moreover, some states exempt state employees from licensing requirements, so many "social workers" in public welfare do not meet the licensing requirements necessary for the title of social worker. As a result, many social workers are licensed but have not met the requirements with which their colleagues must comply. Consequently, states often establish additional requirements for professionals to be eligible for vendorship. Special registries for clinical social workers may be used to identify LCSWs who are eligible for third-party payments.

Professional associations also designate practitioners who have expertise in particular areas. In social work, the most common distinction is membership in the Academy of Certified Social Workers (ACSW). Requirements for the ACSW are two years of post-MSW experience under the supervision of an ACSW and passage of an examination. These are similar to the LCSW, but the two designations should not be confused. Because states have the legal authority to license professions, special distinctions established by professional associations are neither equivalent to, nor a substitute for, state licensure. Thus, it is common for experienced clinicians to list both LCSW and ACSW after their names as indications of professional competence. Recently, the NASW (which administers the ACSW) developed a "diplomate" which identifies those practitioners with skills above those required of the ACSW. Credentials, such as the ACSW, serve the function of distinguishing expertise among members of the professional community. Such credentials are determined by policies of the professional community and not by a public authority, as in the case of state licensure.[31]

The private practitioner who holds an LCSW and is eligible for third-party reimbursement stands to do well economically. For the agency-based social worker, private practice provides an important supplement to what is often a low salary. Assuming a modest fee of

$30 per hour, working ten hours per week, with four weeks off each year, and subtracting 30 percent for overhead, the private practitioner will net $10,080 per year. On the other hand, the clinician willing to take the plunge into private practice full-time may do very well. Assuming a fee of $50 per hour, working forty hours per week, with four weeks off each year, and subtracting 30 percent for overhead, the social worker will clear $67,200 per year. Many private practitioners will fall between these scenarios, varying the number of hours they work to suit their needs. Since private practitioners can generate more income while working fewer hours than agency-based social workers, they have more freedom in their work hours. In fact, flexibility in work hours is rated by private practitioners as a significant advantage of working in the setting, ranking second to "professional challenge."[32] In 1978, *Psychotherapy Finances*, a trade journal for private practitioners, reported that half of all social workers in private practice earned $20,000 or more;[33] within five years over half of social workers in private practice reported earnings above $35,000.[34] Given the earning potential of private practice, it is no wonder that social workers have found it attractive, particularly in light of reductions in funding for programs of the voluntary and governmental sectors.

ISSUES IN PRIVATE PRACTICE

Despite the popularity of private practice, it has provoked a great deal of controversy within the professional community. There are several aspects to this controversy, not the least of which is that many practitioners who have committed themselves to helping the disadvantaged through working with the voluntary and governmental sectors view the instant popularity of private practice as antithetical to everything that is "social" about social work. For professionals who have committed themselves to furthering social justice through careers in the voluntary and governmental sectors, private practice is often viewed with disdain. Donald Feldstein, head of the Federation of Jewish Philanthropies of New York, suggested that private social work practice is similar to private medical practice in that it presents "new opportunities for ripoffs by the privileged." Private practice, he maintained, replaced social decision making with market decision making. According to Feldstein, "Social decision making is preferable to marketing human services like soap . . . the private practice of social work is still against everything that is social about the term social work."[35] Another critic impugned the motives of social workers in private practice.

> Over 15 years ago, when I first had exposure to private practitioners, they were objects of envy, never of nonacceptance. Obviously this envy has continued. For we see more social workers developing private practices. But why all the sham? Let's be honest enough to say it's usually done for the money.[36]

Defenders of private practice emphasize the benefits of the method for practitioners and clients. Why should social workers not enjoy the same professional freedom and responsibility as other professions which use private practice extensively, i.e., law, medicine, and psychiatry? Moreover, "some clients prefer the opportunity to choose their own practitioner and a service they consider more personal and confidential."[37] Concern for the client's perceptions means that practitioners must be concerned about their image. This is evident in one privately practicing social worker's description of her office:

> It is decorated with comfortable chairs, built-in book cases, soft lighting, etc., and is arranged in such a way as to offer several different possibilities for seating. It is commensurate with most of the socio-cultural levels of my client group and provides him or her the opportunity for free expression without being overheard

... Dealing with only one socio-cultural client group allows me to provide physical surroundings which facilitate the client's identification with the worker.[38]

On the surface, then, private practice often provokes strong responses from welfare professionals who perceive private practitioners as avoiding efforts by the voluntary and governmental sectors to advance social equity. On the other hand, some believe that private practice offers an opportunity to enhance their status and to provide services to a middle class that the profession has neglected.

Beneath this surface issue, there are more substantial problems raised by private practice. Perhaps the most important of these is "preferential selection," the practice of selecting certain clients for service while rejecting others. In an era of specialization, professionals will refer clients with problems that are inappropriate for their practice to other providers. Preferential selection becomes an issue when private practitioners elect to serve less-troubled clients (who are able to pay the full cost of care) while referring multi-problem clients (who are unable to pay the practitioner's fee for service directly or indirectly through insurance) to agencies of the voluntary sector. Such "creaming" of the client population places an enormous burden on public agencies, which are left carrying a disproportionate share of the chronically disturbed and indigent clients. In effect, then, the public sector absorbs the losses that would be suffered by private practitioners if they served this population. Preferential selection has become so pronounced that researchers have facetiously identified it as a syndrome. According to Franklin Chu and Sharland Trotter, the commercialization of private practice contributes to the "YAVIS syndrome"—the tendency of clients of private practitioners to be *young, attractive, verbal, intelligent*, and *successful*. One might add "W" to the syndrome, since the clients also tend to be disproportionately white.[39] Consequently, clients of private practitioners are less likely to be poor, unemployed, old, and uneducated.

THE BUSINESS OF PRIVATE PRACTICE

Aside from preferential selection, another set of issues relates directly to the business nature of private practice. Because private practice *is* a business, economic considerations figure highly in a professional's activities. Robert Barker, an authority on private social work practice, explained how economic factors shaped a new practice he established with a colleague:

> We hired a good secretary, employed interior decorators to redo our offices and waiting room. We hired an investment counselor and established retirement accounts and insurance programs. Most of all we became more serious about getting our clients to meet their financial obligations.[40]

The market nature of private practice, coupled with economic entrepreneurship, presents the possibility of questionable accounting practices, such as the creation of "uncollectible accounts," the use of "deliberate misdiagnosis," and the practice of "signing off." These practices involve income derived from third-party sources, usually health insurance. As private practitioners become more dependent on insurance reimbursement, questionable accounting practices become important for the professional community at large.

Health insurance frequently covers outpatient psychiatric care at a UCR rate that is determined by the insurance companies. The UCR is what the therapist charges, and not necessarily what he or she expects to collect from cash-paying clients. The practice of charging fees higher than what is expected to be collected is termed holding an "uncollectible account," and is frequently used with third-party fee payment arrangements. This practice is encouraged because insurance coverage rarely covers all of the practitioner's fee, leaving a certain percent as a copayment by a client. For example, a social worker may have a UCR of $50 per session while the client may have insurance paying only 50 percent of the UCR, leaving the client responsible for the remaining $25. If the client is unable to pay $25 per session, but can afford $10, a clinician will bill the insurance company directly, using an assignment of benefits procedure, for $50. Meanwhile, the client pays an affordable $10 per session, as opposed to an implied obligatory contractual amount of $25. While the therapist may collect a total of $35 per session, and not the UCR of $50, it may be economical to prefer that amount over an extended period of treatment or possibly until the client can afford the full amount of the copayment. At question here is a professional practice which is contrary to the implied contractual relationship among the client, the clinician, and the third-party payer. Yet, it is in the interest of the clinician to establish this as a regular accounting procedure due to the dependence on income through fees and the fear that the insurance company may lower the practitioner's UCR if a significant number of billings are below the customary rate, usually 50 percent.

A second example is "deliberate misdiagnosis," an intentional error in client assessment on the part of clinicians. In a survey of clinical social workers, 70 percent of whom had engaged in private practice, Stuart Kirk and Herb Kutchins found that 87 percent of practitioners used a less stigmatizing, or "mercy," diagnosis frequently or occasionally to avoid labeling. On the other hand, clinicians frequently misdiagnose in order to collect insurance payments.

> Seventy-two percent of the respondents are aware of cases where more serious diagnoses are used to qualify for reimbursement. At least 25 percent of the respondents ... indicated that the practices occurred frequently. Since

reimbursement is rarely available for family problems, it is not surprising that 86 percent are aware of instances when diagnoses for individuals are used even though the primary problem is in the family. The majority of respondents said that this occurred frequently.[41]

Of course, such "overdiagnosis" is unethical since it places the economic benefit of the clinician over the service needs of the client. Still, overdiagnosis continues to be a prevalent practice. Kirk and Kutchins suggest that "reimbursement systems, which have become increasingly important for psychiatric treatment for the last decade, are undoubtedly a major factor in encouraging overdiagnosis."[42] The undesirable consequences of a reimbursement-driven diagnosis system are multiple. First, of course, is the possibility that clients will be done harm, particularly if confidentiality is breached and the diagnosis becomes known to others outside of the therapeutic relationship. Second, the prevalence of severe mental disorders is over-reported to public officials who may make errors in program planning as a result. Third, and perhaps most importantly, overdiagnosis violates the "professional's obligation to their profession to use their knowledge and skill in an ethical manner."[43] While individual digressions can be reported to professional and governmental bodies for investigation, a greater problem exists for practitioners as a whole. Widespread misdiagnosis violates the social contract between the professional community and the state, and thus threatens to "corrupt the helping professions."[44]

Finally, there is the practice of "signing off." Sign off has become important because some insurance covers services provided only by psychiatrists or psychologists. In other instances, insurance will reimburse at a higher rate when services are provided by a psychiatrist or psychologist than when rendered by a social worker. The sign off practice is one in which the psychiatrist or psychologist signs the insurance claim, even though services were provided by a social worker, in order to maximize reimbursement. In some instances, psychiatrists and psychologists may recruit social workers, paying them half of the fees charged to insurance companies and pocketing the difference. Signing off is a type of fee splitting and is "unethical because it allows practitioners to refer clients not to the professional most suitable for the client's needs, but to the person who pays the highest fee."[45]

In a community where many private practitioners compete for a limited number of clients, aggressive business practices are likely to exacerbate questions about the ultimate concern of practitioners—client's welfare or clinician's income. While the question is not ordinarily couched in such crude terms, the behavior of private practitioners may not be lost on the client population. Since clients usually seek services voluntarily, their impressions of practitioners are important; negative perceptions will eventually hurt practitioners as their clients seek services elsewhere. When unfavorable impressions emerge—as a result of the practices described above—practitioners would be prudent to determine corrective actions. While the ethical code of the professional community can be a source for such action, much remains at the discretion of the individual practitioner.

Private practice is literally *private*, and practitioners enjoy "substantial discretion in conducting their activities."[46] Economic and other considerations may encourage private practitioners to engage in unethical or questionable practices. In such instances other practitioners are obliged to report allegations of violations to the state licensing board or the professional association. Ultimately, it is in the interest of the professional community to address questionable practices of practitioners, and this includes the unethical business practices of private practitioners. When the media report that "routine falsification of insurance billings and other peculiarities of the mental health professions have caused acute anxiety among insurance companies . . . [who] now think they have little control over what they are paying for," more government regulation is probably not far behind.[47] In other instances, the consequences are acutely embarrassing for the professional community, as when a leading proponent of third-party reimbursement for social workers in Kentucky was found guilty of insurance fraud and ordered to return $37,000 to Blue Cross-Blue Shield.[48]

THE FUTURE OF PRIVATE PRACTICE

As support ebbs for traditional bases of social work practice—the voluntary agency and the governmental bureaucracy—many welfare professionals have turned to private practice as a way to secure their economic and professional objectives. Private practice allows program administrators a chance to maintain their direct service skills, educators the opportunity to continue contact with clients, and clinicians with parental responsibilities the freedom to conform practice to family needs. Importantly, private practice may prove an adjunct to agency activities. "By fostering part-time practice," noted researchers, "the profession can keep its main focus on agency services where there is a commitment to serve persons without regard to their ability to pay and where there can be a basis for social action and reform."[49]

Reconciling economic opportunity with social responsibility will continue to be an issue in private practice. In 1985, the *New York Times* reported that 82 percent of clinical social workers earn at least $20,000 per year through private practice, while 15 percent earn over $60,000.[50] These income prospects will continue to attract social workers who are willing to take the risk of going into business. From another perspective, however, the seduction of private practice is a result of larger social forces. Ellen Dunbar, Executive Director of the California Chapter of NASW, observed that "The major overriding trend that engulfs all others is that social work along with other service professions is becoming more commercial. . . . [and] more an integral part of the free enterprise system."[51] In fact, the commercialization of social work attracted wide attention as the profession became more immersed in private practice. "There is concern," reported *Newsweek* magazine, "that too many social workers are turning their backs on their traditional casework among the poor to practice therapy." Quoting a discussion at the NASW 1987 annual meeting, *Newsweek* wondered at the consequences of "an apparent middle-class therapy explosion at the expense of public welfare and grassroots service."[52] How social work will reconcile its commitment to social justice with the new opportunities presented by private practice remains a central question before the professional community.

NOTES

1. Srinika Jayaratne, Kristine Siefert, and Wayne Chess, "Private and Agency Practitioners: Some Data and Observations," *Social Service Review* (June 1988), p. 331.
2. *Salaries in Social Work* (Silver Spring, Md.: NASW, 1987), p. 7.
3. Srinika Jayaratne et al., "Private and Agency Practitioners: Some Data and Observations," pp. 327–28.
4. Ibid., p. 327.
5. Ibid., p. 329.
6. Ibid.
7. Eliot Freidson, *The Profession of Medicine* (New York: Dodd, Mead, 1970), pp. 92–96.
8. Quoted in R. Pumphrey and M. Pumphrey, *The Heritage of American Social Work* (New York: Columbia University Press, 1961), p. 393.
9. Ernest Greenwood, "Attributes of a Profession," *Social Work* 2 (1957), pp. 45–55.
10. Ibid., p. 54.
11. Nina Toren, *Social Work: The Case of the Semi-Profession* (Beverly Hills: Sage, 1972), pp. 38–39.
12. A. M. Carr-Saunders, "Metropolitan Conditions and Traditional Professional Relation-

ships," in R. M. Fisher, ed., *The Metropolis and Modern Life* (New York: Russell Sage, 1967), pp. 279–89.
13. Freidson, *The Profession of Medicine*, p. 71.
14. Ibid., p. 184.
15. Sidney Levenstein, *Private Practice in Social Casework* (New York: Columbia University Press, 1964), p. 4.
16. Stuart Kirk and Herb Kutchins, "Deliberate Misdiagnosis in Mental Health Practice," *Social Service Review* (June 1988), p. 235.
17. "Code of Ethics of the National Association of Social Workers," *Encyclopedia of Social Work, 18th Edition* (Silver Spring, Md.: NASW, 1987), pp. 952–56.
18. Magali Larson, *The Rise of Professionalism* (Berkeley: University of California Press, 1977), pp. 9–10.
19. Irving Piliavin, "Restructuring the Provision of Social Services," *Social Work* 13 (1968), pp. 34–41.
20. Larson, *The Rise of Professionalism*.
21. Srinika Jayaratne et al. "Private and Agency Practitioners: Some Data and Observations," p. 328.
22. *NASW Data Bank* (Silver Spring, Md.: NASW, 1985), p. 3.
23. Srinika Jayaratne et al. "Private and Agency Practitioners: Some Data and Observations," p. 334.
24. M. A. Golton, "Private Practice in Social Work," in *Encyclopedia of Social Work* (Silver Spring, Md.: NASW, 1973), p. 949.
25. Walter Trattner, *From Poor Law to Welfare State* (New York: Free Press, 1974), p. 250.
26. National Association of Social Workers, *Manpower Data Bank Frequency Distributions* (Silver Spring, Md.: NASW, 1973 and 1975).
27. Patricia Kelly and Paul Alexander, "Part-Time Private Practice: Practical and Ethical Considerations," *Social Work* 30, no. 3 (May–June 1985), p. 254.
28. *NASW Data Bank* (Silver Spring, Md.: NASW, 1985), p. 3.
29. Robert Barker, "Private and Proprietary Services," *Encyclopedia of Social Work*, 18th ed. (Silver Spring, Md.: NASW, 1987), p. 326.
30. "Licensure Act Passed," *NASW News* 32, no. 8 (September 1987), p. 10.
31. For details on state licensure and professional

certification, see Robert Barker, "Private and Proprietary Services."

32. Srinika Jayaratne et al. "Private and Agency Practitioners: Some Data and Observations," p. 333.

33. "Special Report," *Psychotherapy Finances*, 1978.

34. Srinika Jayaratne et al., "Private and Agency Practitioners: Some Data and Observations."

35. Donald Feldstein, "Debate on Private Practice," *Social Work* 22, no. 3 (1977), p. 3.

36. H. Feldman, "Debate on Private Practice," *Social Work* 22, no. 4 (1977), p. 4.

37. Patricia Kelley and Paul Alexander, "Part-Time Private Practice," p. 255.

38. N. T. Edwards, "The Survival of Structure and Function in Private Practice," *Journal of the Otto Rank Association* 13 (1979), pp. 12, 15.

39. Franklin Chu and Sharland Trotter, *The Madness Establishment* (New York: Grossman, 1974), p. 61.

40. Robert Barker, *The Business of Psychotherapy* (New York: Columbia University Press, 1982), p. xi.

41. Ibid., p. 230.

42. Ibid., p. 234.

43. Ibid., pp. 232, 234–35.

44. Ibid., p. 235.

45. Robert Barker, *Social Work in Private Practice* (Silver Spring, Md.: NASW, 1984), p. 113.

46. Kirk and Kutchins, p. 232.

47. Kathy Sawyer, "Insuring the Bureaucracy's Mental Health," *The Washington Post*, April 10, 1979, p. A8.

48. "'Signing Off' Fraud Charge Warns Kentucky Clinicians," *NASW News* 32, no. 6 (June 1987), p. 1.

49. Patricia Kelley and Paul Alexander, "Part-Time Private Practice," p. 254.

50. Daniel Goleman, "Social Workers Vault into a Leading Role in Psychotherapy," *New York Times*, April 3, 1985, C1.

51. Ellen Dunbar, "Future of Social Work," *NASW California News* 13, no. 18 (May 1987), p. 3.

52. David Gelman et al., "Growing Pains for the Shrinks," *Newsweek*, December 14, 1987, p. 71.

PART THREE
The Government Sector

CHAPTER 11

Social Insurance and Income Maintenance Programs

This chapter will explore major social insurance and income maintenance programs. Specifically, the chapter will examine federal Old Age, Survivors, Disability and Health Insurance (OASDHI), Unemployment Insurance (UI), and Workers' Compensation (WC). This chapter will then examine the major income maintenance programs, including Aid to Families with Dependent Children (AFDC), Supplemental Security Income (SSI), and General Assistance (GA).

The American social welfare state is a complex labyrinth of programs, policies, and services. Perhaps few people, including many policymakers, fully understand the complexity of the welfare system. One reason is that unlike many European countries which operate under a comprehensive and integrated welfare plan, the U.S. system of social welfare is a patchwork quilt. Because the U.S. has been historically ambivalent about providing public relief, most welfare legislation has resulted from compromises and adroit political maneuvering, rather than from a systematic plan. In short, the U.S. welfare state does not represent a coordinated, comprehensive, integrated, and nonredundant series of social welfare services; instead, it is a helter-skelter mix of programs and policies that defy a systematic understanding of the welfare state.

DEFINITION OF SOCIAL INSURANCE

Social insurance is a system whereby people are compelled—through payroll taxes—to insure themselves against the possibility of their own indigence resulting from the loss of a job, the death of the family breadwinner, or physical disability. Based on some of the principles used in private insurance, social insurance sets aside a sum of money that is held in trust by the government and earmarked to be used in the event of the death, disability, or unemployment of the worker. The major goal of social insurance is to maintain income by replacing lost earnings. It is a pay-as-you-go system where the workers and employers of today pay for those who have already retired. Although originally intended to replicate a private insurance fund, the Social Security program has broadened to encompass a series of programs that attempt to provide a socially adequate replacement income. Moreover, because the benefits for retired workers exceed their contributions to the system, Social Security has taken on some of the characteristics of an income redistribution scheme.

Substantial differences exist between social insurance and public assistance programs. For example, one difference is that beneficiaries of social insurance programs are required to make contributions to the program before claiming any benefits (Table 11.1). A second difference is that social insurance is universal; in other words, people receive benefits as legal entitlements regardless of their personal wealth. Because the benefit structure is linked to occupationally defined productive work, social insurance programs tend to be less stigmatized.

Public assistance programs, on the other hand, are generally financed out of general tax

TABLE 11.1. Benefit Payments and Number of Recipients in Major Social Insurance Programs, 1980 and 1986 (beneficiaries are in thousands and benefits in millions)

Programs	1980	1986
OASDHI		
Federal Cost	$152,110	$260,469
State or Local Cost	38,592	(NA)
Beneficiaries	35,585	37,708
Medicare		
Federal Cost	34,992	72,194
State or Local Cost	—	—
Beneficiaries	28,478	31,083
Unemployment Compensation		
Federal Cost	4,408	2,604
State or Local Cost	13,319	15,740
Beneficiaries	2,830	2,287
Workers' Compensation		
Federal Cost	2,668	3,067
State or Local Cost	10,789	19,197
Beneficiaries	(NA)	(NA)

Source: U.S. Bureau of the Census, *Statistical Abstracts, 1988*, Table Nos. 553, 557, 558. Washington, D.C.: U.S. Government Printing Office, 1988, pp. 335–38.

revenues, tend to not be occupationally linked, and are not based on a previous record of productive work. In addition, the recipients must be determined indigent through a means or income test. Public assistance recipients are often stigmatized as compared to social insurance beneficiaries.

Although some people complain about the costs of public assistance programs, social insurance schemes are financed at a level about four times higher than public welfare. For example, social insurance programs (OASDHI, Workers' Compensation, Medicare, and Unemployment Insurance, among others) cost $330.6 billion in 1983 compared to $85.8 billion for income maintenance programs (AFDC, SSI, Food Stamps, and others). Furthermore, social insurance programs accounted for 26 percent of the total GNP in 1983 while public assistance programs accounted for only 10 percent. Lastly, the average OASDHI beneficiary received $460.57 a month in 1984 compared to $221.87 for the SSI recipient. (The AFDC recipient received only $114.56).[1]

THE BACKGROUND OF SOCIAL INSURANCE

The first old age insurance program was introduced in Germany in 1889 by Chancellor Otto von Bismarck. Although originally intended as a way to curb the growing socialist trend in Germany, by the onset of World War I, nearly all European nations had old-age assistance programs of one sort or another. In 1920 the U.S. government began its own Federal Employees Retirement program. By 1931, seventeen states had enacted their own old age assistance programs, although often with stringent eligibility requirements. For example, in some cases where relatives were capable of supporting an elderly person, benefits were denied. Often the elderly who applied for assistance had to sign over all their assets to go to the state when they died. These state-administered welfare programs were restrictive and often punitive.[2] Nevertheless, the concept of governmental responsibility for welfare grew during the early part of the twentieth century and, by 1935, all states—with the exception of Georgia and South Carolina—had programs that provided financial assistance to widows and children.[3]

Spurred on by the Great Depression of the 1930s, and the growing rebellion inspired by a California physician named Francis Townsend (who advocated a flat $200 per month for each retired worker), Franklin Roosevelt championed a government assistance program that would cover both unemployed and retired workers.[4] The result of Roosevelt's efforts was the Social Security Act of 1935, through which the federal government established the basic framework for the modern social welfare state.

The current Act, as amended, now provides for: (1) OASDHI; (2) UI programs under joint federal and state partnership; (3) federal assistance to the aged, blind, and disabled under the SSI program; (4) public assistance to families with dependent children under the Aid to Families with Dependent Children program (AFDC); (5) federal health insurance for the aged (Medicare); and (6) federal and state health assistance for the poor (Medicaid). Although all of the above programs fit under the rubric of the Social Security Act of 1935, not all are social insurance programs (e.g., Medicaid, AFDC, and SSI). The following section will focus on the social insurance programs covered under the Social Security Act.

The insurance feature of Social Security emerged as the result of an intense debate: Progressives wanted Social Security funded out of general revenue taxes while the conservatives wanted it funded solely out of employee contributions. A compromise was reached that old-age insurance would be financed by employer and employee contributions of one percent on a base wage of $3,000, with a maximum cap for worker contributions set at $30 per year. At age 65 single workers would receive $22 per month, while married workers would get $36. In order to allow the trust fund to accumulate reserves, no benefits were paid out until 1940.

The Social Security Act of 1935 has re-peatedly been modified—almost always in the direction of increasing its coverage. The original Social Security Act of 1935 afforded retirement and survivor benefits to only about half of the labor force—farm and domestic workers, the self-employed, and state and local government employees were excluded. In 1950 farmers and self-employed persons were added, thereby bringing the coverage to over 90 percent of the labor force. Congress made survivors and dependents of insured workers eligible for benefits in 1939, and in 1956 disability insurance was added to include totally and permanently disabled workers. In 1965 Health Insurance for the Aged (Medicare)—a prepaid health insurance plan—was incorporated into the law. In later years the Act was amended to allow workers to retire as early as age 62, provided they agreed to accept only 80 percent of their benefits. In 1977 an automatic cost-of-living index was affixed to benefit payments. One major attempt to constrict the Social Security program was tried unsuccessfully by the Reagan administration when they urged that the minimum benefit of $122 per month be retained for present beneficiaries, but eliminated for future recipients. Other Reagan-inspired changes in Social Security included the elimination of payments for children 18 to 21 of deceased, disabled, and retired workers.

KEY SOCIAL INSURANCE PROGRAMS

OASDHI

OASDHI, or what most people refer to as Social Security, is currently the largest social program in the nation, covering approximately nine out of every 10 workers. About 38 million people received benefits from OASDHI in 1987, with a total yearly expenditure of around $210 billion. OASDHI is a completely federal program administered by the Social Security Administration, part of the Department of

Health and Human Services. It is also a stellar example of a program that has worked. For example, the poverty rate for the elderly in 1986 was about the same as for the general population, roughly 12.4 percent. As recently as 1969 the poverty rate for the elderly was double that of the general population, 25.3 percent and 12.1 percent, respectively.[5] According to Michael Harrington, without Social Security the poverty rate among the elderly in 1984 would have gone from 12.4 percent to 47.6 percent.[6] OASDHI operates in the following manner:

1. In 1987 OASDHI was financed by a compulsory employee/employer contribution (each paid half the tax) based on a tax rate of 7.15 percent of an employee's wages. (The full Social Security contribution was therefore 14.3 percent.) A wage cap of $43,800 (maximum taxable wages are set by Congress and increased in multiples of $300 if Social Security benefits have a cost-of-living increase) was in effect. The highest Social Security tax a worker could pay in 1987 was $3,131.70, with a joint tax of $6,263.40. A self-employed worker in 1987 paid 12.3 percent of annual earnings up to $43,800.

2. Based upon the age at retirement (retired workers aged 62 receive only 80% of their entitled benefits) and the amount earned during their working years, workers will receive a monthly benefit payment. Benefits are modest and an average worker received $478.62 per month in 1985.[7] The maximum benefit in 1987 for a retired worker at age 65 was $769 per month, and at age 62, $662.

3. In addition to retirement benefits, survivors benefits are payable to the dependents of an insured worker.

4. A lump sum benefit of $255 is payable upon the death of an insured worker.

5. Disability benefits are payable to an insured worker with a total and/or permanent disability.

6. Almost all people, whether they paid into Social Security or not, are eligible for Medicare benefits (Medicare will be treated in depth in a subsequent chapter).

7. Social Security beneficiaries are required to have completed at least forty quarters of work (10 years) before they are eligible to draw benefits.

Charles Prigmore and Charles Atherton maintain that the Social Security program is guided by several principles including: (1) The program should be financed by both employer and employee contributions, (2) benefits ought to be work connected and based on earnings, (3) coverage should be universal and participation mandatory, (4) benefits should not be dependent on need, and (5) benefits should move in the direction of social adequacy.[8]

Social Security, especially OASDHI, has been a heated topic for much of its relatively short history. Political conservatives and laissez-faire economists are troubled because social security basically socializes a portion of the national income. Other critics claim that Social Security will lead to moral and economic ruin, because it discourages savings and causes retired people to become dependent on a supposedly fragile governmental system. On the other hand, the Social Security system is popular with the elderly who rely on it for much of their income, and with their grown children, for whom it helps to provide peace of mind.

The criticism leveled at the Social Security system was particularly pointed during the 1980s. Adversaries argued that Social Security was depressing private savings (thereby providing less capital for investment), overpaying the elderly, slighting the younger workers (who could get a better return if they invested privately), and was leading the country to fiscal collapse. Despite these criticisms, the system has held up remarkably well, probably as a result of its vast public support.

A recent book by Merton and Joan Bernstein challenges the criticisms leveled at Social Security. The authors allege that contrary to discouraging private savings, Social Security actually stimulates financial planning for retirement and thus encourages savings. Moreover, the overpayment argument is countered by noting that only 2 percent of single people over 65 have total annual earnings exceeding $25,000, and that only 11 percent of all elderly—mainly married couples—have annual incomes over $30,000. Almost 61 percent of elderly people have incomes between $4000 and $15,000 per year. In addition, the median financial wealth of retired persons is only $1,500.[9] These statistics do not portray an aged population that has become wealthy by exploiting an overly generous Social Security system.

Although OASDHI has become an important component of economic security for many of the nation's elderly, problems exist which threaten its future viability. The original strategy of the Social Security Act of 1935 was to create a self-perpetuating insurance (reserve) fund, with benefits for the elderly being in proportion to their contribution. That scenario did not materialize. For example, in 1987 workers retiring at age 65 would receive a maximum Social Security benefit of $9228 per year. If those workers started contributing to the Social Security fund in 1940, and regularly contributed at the maximum level, their total contribution would be about $25,000. In under three years they will have received their entire contribution back in benefits. If they survive to age 72 (the average life expectancy for a male) they would have realized a benefit level of over $37,000 in excess of their contributions. That amount does not include any cost of living increases or Medicare benefits. This situation that has led some observers to doubt the long-term viability of Social Security.

By the middle 1970s Social Security began to show signs of being in trouble. Between 1975 and 1981, the Old Age and Survivors Fund saw a net decrease in funds with a deficit in the reserve of between $790 million and $4.9 billion a year, an imbalance between incoming and outgoing funds, that threatened to deplete the reserve by 1983. Moreover, the prospects for Social Security seemed bleak. While the current ratio of workers supporting beneficiaries (the dependency ratio) is three to one, by the end of the century (with the retirement of the baby boom generation) the ratio was expected to be two to one. The long-term costs of the program would have thus exceeded its projected revenues. The crisis in Social Security was fueled by demographic changes (a dropping birth rate plus an increase in life expectancy), more liberal benefits paid to retiring workers, high inflation, high unemployment, and the cost-of-living adjustments (COLA) passed by Congress.

Facing those short- and long-term problems, Congress moved quickly and passed P.L. 98-21—the Social Security Amendments of 1983. Among the newly legislated changes were a delay in the Cost-of-Living Adjustments (COLA) and a stabilizer placed on future COLAs; that is, if trust funds fall below a certain level, future benefits will be keyed to the Consumer Price Index (CPI) or the average wage increase, whichever is lower. Another change was that Social Security benefits became taxable if taxable income plus Social Security benefits exceeded $25,000 for an individual or $32,000 for a couple. A third change is that by 2027 the retirement age will be increased to 67 for those wanting to collect full benefits. Although people could still retire at age 62, they would receive only 70 percent of their benefits, down from the current 80 percent. And lastly, coverage was extended: new federal employees were covered for the first time, as well as members of Congress, the president and vice president, federal judges, and employees of nonprofit corporations.

Despite changes in the Social Security law, the question remains: "Is Social Security now financially sound?" Unfortunately, no unequiv-ocal answer is possible. Some analysts suggest that Social Security is on sound footing. These analysts point to the fact that the current re-serve stands at $60 billion, and by 2020 that amount is projected to peak at $9.6 trillion.[10] Proponents maintain that the finances of the system will be in close actuarial balance for the next 75 years, with no more than a 5 percent difference between incoming and outgoing revenues.[11]

Although the Social Security Amendments of 1983 provided a short-term solution, struc-tural problems continue to plague the system. For example, one problem is the "graying of America." Since 1900 the percentage of Ameri-cans 65 years and older has tripled, from 4.1 percent in 1900 to 11.9 percent in 1984. The actual number has increased nine times, from 3.1 million to 28 million. Demographic projec-tions suggest that by 2030 the number of per-sons over the age of 65 will increase to over 64 million. In other words, the percentage of elderly is expected to climb from the current rate of 12 percent to over 21 percent by 2030. Furthermore, the elderly are living longer. Between 1900 and 1984 the 75 to 84 year old group increased 11 times while the 85 and over group was 21 times larger.[12] These demographic trends suggest that the dependency ratio will significantly increase, as will the pressures on the Social Security system. Whether the Social Security system—as least as presently struc-tured—can support over 20 percent of the American population remains in doubt.

Another problem facing Social Security is the increasing tax burden. The combination of rising tax rates and maximum taxable earnings boosted the maximum Social Security tax by over 200 percent from 1966 to 1976, an in-crease from $277 to $895 per year. Between 1976 and 1986, Social Security taxes increased by another 200 percent, this time from $895 to $3003 per year. From 1937 to 1986 the maxi-mum Social Security tax was increased 100 times.[13] Social Security taxes now represent the second largest revenue producer for the federal government. The tax burden of Social Security rests on the shoulders of workers and employers and eventually results in a net de-crease in both consumption and production.

Projections about the future of Social Security are predicated on the belief that cer-tain economic and demographic factors will be in play for the next 50 years. Shifting economic and demographic changes could easily interrupt the most earnest predictions, and Social Secur-ity could again go into crisis. For example, a drop in the birth rate is likely in a severe reces-sion, and clearly, that drop would have pro-found consequences for the future of Social Security. Furthermore, stagnant industrial pro-ductivity, changing demographic trends, an oil crisis, and major changes in immigration pat-terns would have a significant impact on Social Security.

There is nothing inviolate, however, about the way Social Security is presently funded. An act of Congress could easily eliminate the in-surance feature of Social Security and replace it with general revenue taxation. Given the widespread dependence on Social Security, which was illustrated by the prompt action Congress took on the Social Security crisis in the early 1980s, it is unlikely that the public will allow Social Security to disintegrate.

Unemployment Insurance

The objective of Unemployment Insurance (UI) is to assure an uninterrupted—although irregular—flow of income to workers during involuntary periods of unemployment. The guidelines of the UI program require employers to contribute to a trust fund, which would then be activated in the event of the loss of an em-ployee's job. Federal regulations governing UI compel employers to contribute a payroll tax (usually between 1 and 4 percent of their total payroll) into a state administered unemploy-ment insurance fund that meets federal stan-dards.[14] The federal government also maintains a trust fund to bail out state trust funds that are depleted.

To be eligible for benefits a worker must be ready and willing to work, unemployed, registered for work with the state employment service, and have been working in covered work during a base eligibility period. Conversely, a worker who is fired for misconduct, quits a job without a legally acceptable reason, fails to register with the state employment service, refuses a job equal to or better than the one previously held, or goes on strike, is ineligible for unemployment benefits.

States cannot deny benefits to workers who refuse to be strikebreakers or who refuse to work for less than the prevailing rate. However, basic decisions concerning the amount of benefits, eligibility, and length of benefit time are determined by the states. In all states unemployment benefits are temporary (usually lasting only thirty-nine weeks). Benefits are not equal to previously earned income, and an average unemployed worker in 1986 received benefits totaling 36 percent of his or her previous wage. Normal state unemployment benefits range from $80 to $150 per week, and in 1983 the average benefit was $119 per week.[15] While UI benefits are time-limited, states can choose to increase the maximum benefit period.

The UI program is fraught with difficulties. For one, in recent years many of the states have tightened eligibility requirements, and the federal government has restricted that part of the program which provides additional weeks of unemployment insurance to the long-term unemployed. In addition, the UI program often fails to help states with severe unemployment problems. For example, unemployment rates are calculated based on a study conducted by the Department of Labor in which 60,000 households (individuals sixteen years or older are included in the survey) are interviewed each month. In this study part-time workers are counted as employed, and those who are discouraged and have dropped out of the labor force are not counted at all. Although the UI program includes mechanisms which allow states to receive heavier federal reimbursement when unemployment rates are especially high, many unemployed are not counted, thereby lowering the official state rate and not setting off the mechanism.[16] Furthermore, states with 'pockets of poverty' receive no additional help, because the overall state unemployment rate may not be high enough to set off the triggers. This problem is exacerbated by the rural crisis which has caused many bankrupt farmers to join the ranks of the unemployed.

Another problem with the UI program involves coverage. In 1967 the unemployment rate stood at 3.8 percent and 43 percent of all unemployed workers were covered under the UI program. By 1975, the unemployment rate soared to 8.5 percent and over 75 percent of the unemployed were covered. By 1985, the unemployment rate was at 7.2 percent but only 33 percent of the unemployed were covered under UI. In every year from 1980 to 1987 fewer of the unemployed have been covered under Unemployment Insurance. In other words, 1.9 million workers were not receiving unemployment benefits in 1976; by 1985 that number had increased to over 5.6 million.[17] Less than one out of every three unemployed workers were covered under UI in 1987.

Disaggregating the national data illustrates an even starker picture. In 1986 there were only three states in which more than half of the unemployed received benefits. In that same year, 11 states gave benefits to less than one in four unemployed people. This situation was exacerbated because in 17 of the 26 states in which fewer than 33 percent of unemployed persons were receiving benefits in 1986, there was no Aid to Families with Dependent Children–Unemployed Parent (AFDC-UP) program for two-parent families with an unemployed worker, and in 24 of those 26 states there was no general assistance program covering the poor who were neither elderly nor disabled[18] (see Table 11.2).

TABLE 11.2. Unemployment and Unemployment Insurance Coverage, 1979 and 1986

State	Unemployment Rate, 1986	Percent of Unemployed Receiving Unemployment Insurance, 1986	Percent of Unemployed Receiving Unemployment Insurance, 1979	Percentage Point Change 1979 to 1986
Alabama	9.8%	23.6%	37.1%	−13.5%
Alaska	10.8	65.7	79.7	−14.0
Arizona	6.9	23.0	25.4	− 2.4
Arkansas	8.7	29.7	41.8	−12.1
California	6.7	44.5	43.0	+ 1.5
Colorado	7.4	26.7	24.6	+ 2.1
Connecticut	3.8	37.6	39.5	− 2.0
Delaware	4.3	41.0	28.7	+12.3
Dist. of Col.	7.7	36.9	44.6	− 7.7
Florida	5.7	18.3	23.7	− 5.4
Georgia	5.9	25.1	32.4	− 7.3
Hawaii	4.8	37.3	40.1	− 2.8
Idaho	8.7	37.8	49.7	−11.9
Illinois	8.1	30.4	48.1	−17.7
Indiana	6.7	24.4	27.6	− 3.2
Iowa	7.0	29.5	37.7	− 8.2
Kansas	5.4	37.3	36.3	+ 1.0
Kentucky	9.3	24.5	44.5	−20.0
Louisiana	13.1	36.1	29.0	+ 7.1
Maine	5.3	41.4	44.0	− 2.6
Maryland	4.5	34.6	28.4	+ 6.2
Massachusetts	3.8	55.4	48.5	+ 6.9
Michigan	8.8	28.5	52.9	−24.4
Minnesota	5.3	38.3	39.2	− .09
Mississippi	11.7	23.4	34.0	−10.6
Missouri	6.1	34.0	51.7	−17.7
Montana	8.1	31.9	49.6	−17.7
Nebraska	5.0	32.4	30.6	+ 1.9
Nevada	6.0	36.7	41.0	− 4.3
New Hampshire	2.8	22.8	33.0	−10.2
New Jersey	5.0	44.2	62.7	−18.4
New Mexico	9.2	27.5	24.2	+ 3.3
New York	6.3	36.7	45.0	− 8.3
North Carolina	5.3	29.5	29.5	+ 0.0
North Dakota	6.3	36.4	51.9	−15.4
Ohio	8.1	28.1	40.0	−11.9
Oklahoma	8.2	27.6	32.0	− 4.4
Oregon	8.5	37.8	41.4	− 3.6
Pennsylvania	6.8	43.1	52.3	− 9.1
Rhode Island	4.0	62.4	71.1	− 8.7
South Carolina	6.2	28.3	35.3	− 7.0
South Dakota	4.7	21.0	30.4	− 9.5
Tennessee	8.0	24.7	45.3	−20.6
Texas	8.9	23.0	24.0	− 1.0
Utah	6.0	31.7	43.8	−12.1
Vermont	4.7	38.1	53.0	−14.9
Virginia	5.0	16.6	23.7	− 7.1
Washington	8.2	37.0	35.3	+ 1.8
West Virginia	11.8	27.1	48.8	−21.7
Wisconsin	7.0	35.3	52.2	−16.9
Wyoming	9.0	34.7	26.9	+ 7.8
Nation	7.0	32.7	42.1	− 9.4

Source: Adapted from Isaac Shapiro and Robert Greenstein, *Holes in the Safety Nets* (Washington, D.C.: Center on Budget and Policy Priorities, 1988), Tables A-12 and A-13, pp. 63–64.

Workers' Compensation

Workers' Compensation, another social insurance program, is based on state laws that require employers to compensate employees who are victims of industrial accidents or occupational diseases. These programs are designed to provide medical care, rehabilitation services, and disability and death benefits to occupationally injured workers or their survivors. The laws governing Workers' Compensation vary from state to state, with little consistency in either the benefit levels or the administration of the program. For example, some states require employers to carry insurance, other states provide an insurance fund, and still others have no law compelling employers to seek private insurance. Nevertheless, because of the potential for large claims, most employers transfer their responsibility by purchasing insurance from private companies that specialize in Workers' Compensation.

Workers' Compensation programs are problematic in several ways. For one, there is great variability among states in the way claims are handled. Workers are often encouraged to settle out of court for an attractive lump sum, even though that amount frequently does not equal their lost wages. Benefits are often uneven and limited to one-third of the worker's salary. Moreover, the price attached to the loss of a body part has been interpreted differently from state to state. Prigmore and Atherton note that in Hawaii the loss of a finger is valued at $5,175, more than the courts in the state of Wyoming allow for an eye.[19] In addition, long delays often exist between the time the injury is incurred and the period in which benefits are paid. Lastly, employers in some states may be exempt from the Workers' Compensation tax if they can demonstrate that they are covered by private insurance. Unfortunately, private insurance coverage may prove inadequate after a disability benefit is determined. Even though injured workers or their survivors received $4.5 billion in benefits and medical payments in 1975, Workers' Compensation may not provide adequate protection for many disabled American workers.[20]

ISSUES IN SOCIAL INSURANCE

The structure of social insurance is replete with both contradictions and difficulties. The scope of these problems is most visible in the largest social insurance program, OASDHI. While originally intended to supplement private pension funds, and to operate as a pay-as-you-go insurance scheme, in the last fifty years OASDHI has taken on many of the characteristics of a public welfare program. For example, workers receive high benefit levels even though their fiscal contributions to the system have not justified them. Virtually everyone who is presently retired is realizing benefits far exceeding what they historically contributed in Social Security taxes. The bill for those benefits is being paid by the young worker of today.

Given this scenario, an important question emerges: "Should social insurance be modified to more clearly achieve social assistance and income redistribution goals?" If the answer is yes, then benefits must be structured to reflect the current needs of retired workers rather than their past contributions. Furthermore, if Social Security is viewed as a public welfare program, then its regressive tax structure should be modified to reflect a more progressive framework. For example, Social Security is the single largest tax paid by a low income worker, yet that same worker receives the lowest benefit levels when he or she become eligible. In other words, the worker who is hurt most by the tax receives the least benefit.[21] Using that same line of reasoning, "If Social Security is a program designed for social assistance, then should everyone, regardless of income, be eligible?" And in particular, "Should wealthy persons be allowed to be beneficiaries?" The answer to these complex questions will obviously be rooted in the values of the reviewer.

Another issue in Social Security involves the comparison between public (compulsory) and private (voluntary) pension plans. Some critics argue that private pension plans are preferable to public schemes, because they are based on less dependence on the government and have the potential for yielding higher returns. Private pensions originated as a means to encourage employee loyalty and as a way to ease out aging workers. However, only about one-third of all workers and one-fourth of current employees are covered under private pension plans. Moreover, only a small fraction of these plans are indexed for inflation.

Critics of private pension plans argue that they are basically unreliable. Employees can switch jobs and lose pension rights, some companies may go bankrupt, other companies may attempt to raid pension funds (in a quasi-legal manner), still others may terminate benefits because they do not want to be bothered, and corrupt or incompetent managers can wreak havoc on well-endowed pension plans (pension reserves in the United States are currently worth over one trillion dollars). Despite the federal tax subsidies to private pension plans, which totaled over $64 billion in 1988, coverage under these plans has actually decreased since 1980. Supporters of Social Security argue that unlike the riskier private pension plans, Social Security benefits are portable and indexed for inflation, workers are immediately vested, and benefits are not contingent on the financial condition of the employer.[22]

Social insurance programs, especially OASDHI, have become a mainstay of the American social welfare state. Despite the original intention of its architects, Social Security has become a major source of financial support for America's elderly. Moreover, OASDHI is one of the few social welfare programs that has demonstrated the ability not only to hold the poverty rate constant for its target group, but actually to reduce it. In short, a large group of Americans have come to view Social Security as a right and, as such, to count on its benefits.

INCOME MAINTENANCE PROGRAMS

Much of the function of social welfare is grounded in the concept of "safety nets," a series of governmental programs (cash, medical, and other forms of assistance) designed to insure that citizens will receive basic services and not fall below a certain economic level. Whereas the existence of a single safety net is often assumed, in reality, there are 51 separate safety nets—one in each state and the District of Columbia. Although federal guidelines help determine the level of aid for the poor, in other ways individual states ultimately fashion their own safety net. Thus, one large national study found that the vast majority of states do not provide an adequate safety net to help the poor and jobless.[23] In any case, a major component of the safety net consists of programs designed to ensure that families and individuals receive the resources necessary for survival.

This section will cover income maintenance programs and, in particular, the Aid to Families with Dependent Children (AFDC) programs, Supplemental Security Income (SSI), and General Assistance (GA). Income maintenance programs are one of the most misunderstood and badly interpreted facets of the American welfare state. Unlike social insurance, income maintenance programs are based entirely on need rather than entitlement, and, as such, all income maintenance programs are means tested (see Table 11.3).

Aid to Families with Dependent Children

AFDC is perhaps the most controversial program in the American social welfare state. The ostensible purpose of AFDC is to maintain and strengthen family life by providing financial assistance and care to needy dependent children in their own homes or in the homes of responsible caretakers. Despite these modest goals, the AFDC program and its recipients have often been used as symbols in the ideological struggle between liberals and conservatives around the

TABLE 11.3. Major Cash and Noncash Benefit Programs for Persons with Limited Income, 1980 and 1986
(Recipients are in thousands and expenditures in millions)

Program	1980	1986
Aid to Families with Dependent Children (AFDC)		
Federal Cost	$ 6,964	$ 9,536
State Cost	6,055	8,221
Recipients	10,499	10,995
Total Cost	13,019	17,757
Supplemental Security Income (SSI)		
Federal Cost	6,365	10,307
State Cost (State Supplements)	2,070	2,513
Recipients	4,160	4,449
Total Cost	8,435	12,820
General Assistance (GA)		
Federal Cost	—	—
State or Local Cost	1,386	2,605
Recipients	910	1,332
Medicaid		
Federal Cost	14,550	24,995
State or Local Cost	11,231	19,730
Recipients	21,735	22,592
Total Cost	25,781	44,725
Food Stamps		
Federal Cost	9,195	12,528
State or Local Cost	381	938
Recipients	21,100	20,900
Total Cost	9,576	13,466
Women, Infants and Children (WIC)		
Federal Cost	2,110	2,669
State or Local Cost	—	—
Recipients	1,980	3,318
Total Cost	2,110	2,669
School Lunch Program		
Federal Cost	2,110	2,669
State or Local Cost	—	—
Recipients	27,011	24,253
Total Cost	2,110	2,669
Head Start		
Federal Cost	736	1,013
State or Local Cost	184	254
Recipients	376	448
Total Cost	920	1,267
*Housing Assistance		
Federal Cost	9,606	13,250
State or Local Cost	—	—
Recipients	2,998	4,034
Total Cost	9,606	13,250
Low-Income Energy Assistance		
Federal Cost	1,539	1,905
State or Local Cost	—	44
Recipients	9,700	6,700
Total Cost	1,539	1,949

continued

TABLE 11.3. (cont.)

Program	1980	1986
**Jobs and Training Programs		
Federal Cost	8,625	3,625
State or Local Cost	81	75
Recipients	2,486	2,089
Total Cost	8,706	3,700
Title XX		
Federal Cost	2,785	2,584
State or Local Cost	863	—
Recipients	7,000	NA
Total Cost	3,648	2,584

* Housing assistance includes Section 8, low-rent public housing, rural housing loans, rural rental housing loans, and interest reduction payments. **Jobs and training programs include employment and training services, summer youth employment program, Job Corps, senior community service employment program, and the work incentive program, among others. Source: U.S. Bureau of the Census, *Statistical Abstracts, 1987,* Table No. 557. Washington, D.C.: U.S. Government Printing Office, 1988, p. 337.

goals and future of the welfare state. This situation has caused AFDC recipients to be victimized in two ways: (1) by their own poverty, and (2) by ideologically motivated assaults against their character and motives.

AFDC is the largest public assistance program. The requirement for receiving AFDC is the deprivation of the parental care of one parent because of death, desertion, separation, or divorce. In 1985 AFDC served close to 3.7 million families (about 10.8 million individuals) at a cost of almost $15 billion.[24] Out of the 10.8 million recipients about 66 percent or 7.1 million were children.[25] The median benefit level of AFDC for a family of three was $359 per month in 1987.[26] The AFDC–Unemployed Parent (UP) program—designed to extend AFDC benefits to two-parent families where the primary wage earner is employed less than 100 hours per month—assisted 251,000 families (over 1 million recipients, including 615,000 children) in 1987.[27]

A Brief History of the AFDC Program

Originally called Aid to Dependent Children (ADC), the AFDC program was part of the Social Security Act of 1935, and was designed to provide support for children through dis-

pensing aid to their mothers. In 1950 the adult caretaker (usually the mother) was made eligible for ADC benefits.[28] Also in the 1950s medical services were made available for ADC recipients, paid in part by the federal government. In the late 1950s and early 1960s, some critics began to believe that ADC rules led to the desertion of fathers, since only families without an able-bodied father were eligible for relief. By 1961 a new component was added which allowed families to receive assistance in the event of a father's incapacity or unemployment. The new program, Aid to Families With Dependent Children–Unemployed Parent (AFDC-UP), was not made mandatory for the states, and until the welfare reform act of 1988, only 25 states and the District of Columbia had adopted it. In 1962 the name of the program was changed to AFDC to emphasize the family unit.

By 1962 the focus of the AFDC program shifted to rehabilitating the poor. Policies were enacted that mandated massive casework and treatment services. To increase the chances for success, the social service amendments of 1962 limited social workers' caseload size to a maximum of 60. By 1967 the service requirement was transformed into job assistance. Before 1967 all services provided to AFDC recipients were delivered by one worker who was responsible for financial as well as social services. Since 1972 federal policy has dictated that the AFDC program be divided into social services and income maintenance. The new policy separating social services from income maintenance required that one worker be assigned the AFDC paperwork, while the other worker (social worker) was responsible for social services.

Despite intensive social services, the number of AFDC recipients grew dramatically throughout the 1960s. The number of AFDC families tripled in the 10-year period from 1960 to 1970, from 3 million to 9.6 million.[29] While in 1950 the number of AFDC families accounted for 1.5 percent of the population, by 1970 that proportion had reached 4.7 percent. The growth in AFDC rolls also gave rise to a grass-roots protest organization started by a former chemistry professor, George A. Wiley. Under the leadership of Wiley, by 1967 the National Welfare Rights Organization (NWRO), a direct-action advocacy group of welfare recipients, had grown to encompass more than 100,000 dues-paying members representing some 350 local groups.[30] Although at its height the NWRO had a sizable constituency—and received a grant of $400,000 from the outgoing Johnson administration in 1968—its lasting effects remain unclear.

One of the more egregious chapters in AFDC history involved the man-in-the-house rule. This policy mandated that any woman who had an able-bodied man in the house was cut off from AFDC because, regardless of whether he was the father, it was thought to be his responsibility to support the family. This policy was manifested in "midnight raids," whereby social workers would make a late-night call to ascertain if a man was present. Even a piece of male clothing found on the premises could be used as an excuse for cutting off aid. In some states the man-in-the-house rule was extended to also include rules on dating. In 1968 the U.S. Supreme Court struck down

the rule in Alabama, and later reinforced its decision in a California case.[31]

During President Ronald Reagan's term in office, several changes were made in AFDC rules, including: (1) new AFDC rules made it unlikely that a family with a parent working at a low-paying job would receive a supplementary AFDC benefit;[32] (2) children in AFDC families not expected to graduate high school or vocational training programs by age 19 were no longer eligible for benefits (before 1981, over two-thirds of the states provided assistance to students living at home until they reached 21);[33] (3) pregnant women with no other children were made ineligible for AFDC benefits until their sixth month of pregnancy[34]—a policy which resulted in many expectant mothers being declared ineligible for Medicaid, and thus being denied early access to prenatal care; (4) the income of stepparents was counted in determining a child's eligibility;[35] (5) a limit was placed on how much child care costs a working AFDC mother could defer from her benefit check;[36] and (6) the efforts of states to collect child-support payments were improved.[37] During the early and middle 1980s, almost 450,000 families were removed from the welfare rolls because of these and other AFDC changes.[38]

The belief that welfare mothers ought to work is a constant theme in AFDC debates. While conservatives argue that work is the best antipoverty program, some liberals assert that child rearing is also a productive form of work. Moreover, liberal supporters contend that while it is socially acceptable for middle-class mothers to stay at home with young children, when poor mothers try to do the same thing they are often considered lazy and unmotivated. Despite this nagging debate, workfare programs have been a constant part of the welfare landscape since 1967, when new AFDC amendments were added that pressured recipient mothers into working. As part of those new rules, work requirements became mandatory for unemployed fathers, mothers, and certain teenagers.

AFDC recipients who were deemed employable and refused to work could be terminated.[39] A work incentive program (WIN) was developed to provide training and employment for all welfare mothers considered employable (recipients with pre-school age children were exempt). Day care was made available to facilitate the WIN program. As a further incentive, AFDC recipients were allowed to retain the first $30 of their monthly earnings in addition to having one-third of the remainder exempt from consideration for eligibility assistance. However, due to a lackluster federal commitment (in 1985 the total federal contribution to WIN was only $258 million), the performance of the program was disappointing. In addition, many states were reluctant to enact mandatory job requirements because they believed that it would ultimately cost more than simply maintaining families on AFDC.

In 1975 the AFDC rules were revised to allow states to track down biological parents and force them to pay child support. In 1984 this law was further strengthened by extending assistance to all families where the children need financial support. Under this new law states could: (1) withhold a parent's wages if support payments were thirty days overdue, (2) impose liens against the assets of a delinquent parent, and (3) intercept federal and state income tax refunds. Even with stringent enforcement laws, the track record for collecting child support payments was dismal. In 1986 the states attempted to collect child support in 16.3 percent of AFDC cases: 8.6 percent of AFDC payments were recouped through collections and only 6.6 percent of recipients were able to leave the rolls because of those collections.[40]

The twin themes of workfare and parental responsibility for child support formed the backbone of the new welfare reform bill passed in the fall of 1988. Touted by some supporters as "the most significant change in the welfare system since its inception over 50 years ago,"[41] the new welfare reform bill (costing $3.34 billion over a five-year period) contains several interesting components. For one, the bill attempts to change AFDC from an income support to a mandatory work and training program. The stated objective of the bill is to encourage self-sufficiency among welfare recipients. To carry out its goal, the bill requires women on welfare with children under age 3 (at state option, age 1) to participate in a work or training program. By 1990 each state is required to enroll at least 7 percent of its recipients in a state basic education program, job training, a work experience program, or a job search program. By 1993 that requirement will rise to 20 percent. As a further incentive, recipients who become employed will get 12 months of child care assistance and Medicaid benefits after they terminate AFDC.[42]

Adoption of the AFDC-UP program will become mandatory for all states, although they can decide to limit enrollment for two-parent families to six out of twelve calendar months in a year. Moreover, starting in 1994 one family member of an AFDC-UP household must participate at least 16 hours per week in a make-work job in return for benefits. In 1994, 40 percent of AFDC-UP recipients will be expected to be in a make-work program, and by 1997 that number will increase to 70 percent.

In addition, the new bill calls for mandatory child support payments to be automatically deducted from an absent parent's paycheck, even though they may not be in arrears. Lastly, the bill allows states to require a welfare recipient under age 18 to live with a parent or in a "supervised environment" in order to continue to receive benefits. Although the bill may not be as significant as some of its more enthusiastic supporters maintain, it does represent a shift in the direction of public welfare.

AFDC Funding and Eligibility Criteria

The funding and eligibility criteria for AFDC are complex. By 1985 states were given an option to select between two methods of federal reimbursement for AFDC. Under the first method the federal government paid five-sixths of the average monthly AFDC payment up to $18. For the amount of the average payment above $18 and up to $32, the federal government paid the "federal percentage" assigned to an individual state, a percentage set according to the per capita income (the income of a family divided by the number of family members) of the state. States assumed the entire costs of monthly benefits over $32 per person and, in addition, they paid 50 percent of the costs of program administration and 25 percent of the costs of client rehabilitation services.[43] The second option—which by 1984 all states had adopted—was also based on state per capita income and required the federal government to pay no less than 50 percent nor more than 65 percent of the total state expenditures for AFDC.[44] The federal share of administrative and social service expenditures remained the same.[45] Based upon these formulas states with a low per capita income received a higher federal contribution. On the average, states paid approximately 46 percent of their total AFDC program costs.

AFDC benefits are based on a family's countable income and needs as determined by state law. The concept of "total basic need" is a major criterion for eligibility. AFDC guidelines require that if a family's total basic need is greater than its countable income, the family is eligible for AFDC. Countable income and total basic need (the need standard) are determined almost exclusively by the states. Moreover, while the federal government requires each state to have a needs standard, it does not compel them to pay that amount to AFDC beneficiaries. Therefore, maximum payment schedules differ widely from state to state.[46]

SOME ASSUMPTIONS THAT UNDERLIE THE AFDC PROGRAM

American attitudes toward AFDC are marked by a complex web of indifference, compassion, and hostility. This ambivalence plays out in a series of harsh and often conflicting assumptions about AFDC and its recipients. Moreover, the struggle around AFDC is a symbolic one—it reflects the tension surrounding the ideology of wealth, opportunity, privilege, and the myth of the American dream.

The argument goes like this: If privilege in America is something that is earned by application and hard work, then people are poor because they lack the desire to elevate themselves out of poverty. In short, the poor have not applied themselves and thus are lazy. Moreover, the poor refuse to compete and sacrifice, a characteristic held in low regard by those who feel overwhelmed by the intense competition that marks capitalist society. On the other hand, all that separates the welfare recipient from the average citizen is a few paychecks—thus the compassion. While the tenets of capitalism imply that hard work guarantees success, the reality of people's lives often tells a different story. The tensions and contradictions that characterize contemporary life shade people's view toward both AFDC and the welfare state. The following assumptions, among others, underlie the AFDC program: (1) generous AFDC benefits create a disincentive to work (recipients must always get fewer benefits than the minimum wage provides); (2) welfare recipients need prodding to work because they lack internal motivation; (3) although economic opportunities are available, recipients must be forced to take them; (4) work is the best antipoverty program; (5) AFDC and other income maintenance programs must be highly stigmatized, because if they lost their stigma, people would use them too readily; and (6) all welfare mothers should work and thus poor children should not have the luxury to be raised by a full-time mother. Although middle- and upper-class children should ideally be brought up by a full-time mother, bringing up poor children is not an acceptable occupation. These assumptions about AFDC—many of which are remarkably similar to those that underlie the

Elizabethan Poor Laws—lead to numerous myths and fears, most of which are not borne out by the facts.

The Myths of AFDC

This section examines commonly held myths about AFDC, and attempts to discriminate between facts and fiction.

MYTH 1: The AFDC rolls are composed of many families containing an able-bodied father who refuses to work.

FACT: The truth is that 93 percent of AFDC families are headed by one parent, with only 7 percent of AFDC households being two-parent families. Ninety percent of AFDC kids live with their mother and 13 percent with their father. Sixty-six percent of AFDC recipients are children, with the remaining recipients being mothers (18.6 percent) and the aged (15.6 percent). Less than 1 percent of all welfare recipients are able-bodied males. Among the children who are AFDC recipients, almost 34 percent have parents not married to each other.[47] Forty-one percent of fathers of AFDC children cannot be found.[48]

MYTH 2: Most poor people are on AFDC.

FACT: Two-thirds of the poor (22.1 million of the 32.5 million poor people in 1985) received no money from AFDC. Furthermore, more than half of the poor

neither get food stamps nor Medicaid.[49]

MYTH 3: AFDC mothers have more children to collect greater benefits (see Table 11.4).

FACT: The average AFDC family has 1.9 children and nearly three-quarters of all recipients have just 1 or 2 children.[50] Almost 68 percent of AFDC families have only one child; only 8 percent have five or more children.[51] Moreover, having additional children to increase an AFDC benefit hardly seems worth the effort. For example, in Missouri in 1985 the difference in gross AFDC benefits for a family of two and a family of three was $55 per month. As the family size increases the benefit is lowered, i.e., the difference between a family of three and a family of four was $46 per month, and for a family of six and a family of seven the benefit difference was $38 per month.[52] This may explain why mothers on AFDC have only one-fourth the number of babies while they are recipients as non-welfare mothers.[53] Furthermore, some of the lowest benefit states have the highest out-of-wedlock birth rates.

MYTH 4: Once on welfare always on welfare.

FACT: In 1986 the Domestic Policy Council Low Income Opportunity Working Group reported to President Reagan that research indicates that the majority of recipients receive AFDC for

TABLE 11.4. Public Assistance: Number of Recipients, 1965–1984*

	AFDC			General Assistance		
	Families	Total Recipients	Children	Cases	Recipients	Emergency Assistance
1965	1,054	4,396	3,316	310	677	
1970	2,552	9,659	7,033	547	1,056	9.7
1975	3,568	11,404	8,106	692	977	34.1
1980	3,843	11,101	7,599	796	986	52.0
1984	3,668	10,694	7,080	1,080	1,324	27.5

* Number of recipients are in thousands. Source: *Social Security Bulletin*, December 1986, Vol. 49, No. 12, Table M-27, p. 48.

a relatively short period of time.[54] According to one study, turnover among welfare recipients is widespread[55] and, while occasional welfare receipt is common, persistent welfare is not.[56] Although 25 percent of all children at some time will be in a family that receives AFDC, only 4 percent of all recipient families derive at least half of their income from the program. Half of all recipients stay in the program for less than two years, and the average AFDC spell for two-parent families lasts less than six months.[57] According to the Department of Health and Human Services, 25 percent of all AFDC cases are closed within six months, one-third within the first year, and 75 percent of all AFDC cases are closed after three years. Only 7.3 percent of AFDC cases are on welfare for ten years or more.[58]

Another myth centers around the dependency created by welfare programs. According to Greg Duncan and Saul Hoffman, income packages of welfare families often contain more income from other sources than from welfare, with labor income being mixed with welfare income.[59] Moreover, roughly 25 percent of the U.S. population lived in families where some form of welfare was received between 1969 and 1978, but fewer than 44 percent of those families received income from welfare sources for at least eight of those 10 years.

MYTH 5: Welfare dependency is transmitted intergenerationally.

FACT: According to Duncan and Hoffman, only a minority of black and white women growing up in heavily dependent welfare households were themselves heavily dependent on welfare. There is no significant link for black women between the welfare dependence of parent and child. Only 19 percent of black women coming from heavily dependent welfare homes were observed to be heavily dependent on welfare themselves, while 39 percent received some welfare but not enough to total more than 25 percent of their income. The 19 percent of black women heavily dependent on welfare was the same percentage as black women heavily dependent on welfare who did not come from heavily dependent welfare households.[60]

Black men who came from heavily dependent welfare households showed no decrease in the average number of working hours; in other words, parental receipt of welfare had no significant effect on the work hours of black men. However, white men from heavily dependent welfare homes averaged fewer hours of work a week than did otherwise similar white men.

MYTH 6: Most welfare recipients are black.

FACT: Close to the same number of whites as blacks receive AFDC. In 1983 whites constituted 41.7 percent of all recipients, blacks 43.9 percent, and Hispanics 11.7 percent. The remaining 3 percent were composed of American Indians and other minorities.[61]

MYTH 7: Fraud and cheating are rampant among welfare recipients.

FACT: According to Elizabeth Huttman, a 1977 HEW study found that 51 percent of AFDC errors were made by welfare agencies or social workers.[62] The report noted that 5.3 percent of the 11.2 million AFDC recipients were ineligible, 13 percent were overpaid, and 4.9 percent were underpaid. According to HEW, fraud or misrepresentation occurred in less than four-tenths of one percent of the total national caseload.[63]

MYTH 8: AFDC benefits provide a disincentive to work.

FACT: There are only three states where

the AFDC cash benefit for a family of three reaches 75 percent of the poverty line. In 32 states AFDC benefits are below 50 percent of the poverty threshold. Seven states (Alabama, Kentucky, Louisiana, Mississippi, South Carolina, Tennessee, and Texas) provide a single parent with two children less than $200 per month in AFDC benefits; two of those states (Alabama and Mississippi) provide $120 or less. The maximum AFDC benefit level for a family of three ranges from a low of 15.6 percent of the poverty line in Alabama to a high of 83.7 percent in California. In a typical state, AFDC benefits for a three-person family equal $359 per month, or 47.5 percent of the poverty line.[64] Even with the inclusion of Food Stamps, in every state except Alaska, the combined benefits fall below the poverty line, and in half the states the combined benefit of food stamps and AFDC do not equal two-thirds of the poverty line.[65] Furthermore, most of the poor either work or desire a job, although their employment frequently does not allow them to overcome poverty. Compulsory experiments in workfare suggest that AFDC recipients believe they *ought* to work for their checks.[66]

MYTH 9: AFDC recipients are doing better than ever.

FACT: Unfortunately, the reverse is true —AFDC recipients are doing worse than ever. Specifically, benefit levels have not kept pace with inflation, having fallen 31.4 percent in the typical state from 1970 to 1987.

MYTH 10: Unmarried mothers constitute the bulk of welfare recipients.

FACT: According to Duncan and Hoffman, the most important causes for beginning welfare spells are (1) divorce or separation (45 percent), (2) an unmarried woman becoming a pregnant female household head (30 percent), and (3) a drop in earnings of the female head of the household (12 percent). Conversely, the predominant reasons for terminating welfare spells are (1) remarriage (35 percent), (2) an increase in the earnings of a female householder (21 percent), and (3) children leaving the parental home (11 percent).[67]

ISSUES IN AFDC

Despite the promise of the welfare reform bill of 1988, the system remains plagued by serious problems. Perhaps the most important problem that the new bill fails to address is the adequacy of AFDC benefit levels. The argument over AFDC benefit levels has three primary dimensions: (1) the adequacy of the poverty index as a determinant of poverty, (2) the adequacy of state established need levels, and (3) whether states meet their own formulated need levels. Since the adequacy of the poverty index has been addressed in an earlier chapter, the subsequent discussion will focus on the latter two questions.

The AFDC program is characterized by dramatically different state benefit levels. In 1987 the average monthly benefits for an AFDC family of three (one adult and two children) went from $120 a month in Mississippi to a high of $749 in Alaska. In 1987 the average three-person AFDC family received a benefit of $359 per month. AFDC benefits paid to recipients are largely determined by the need standards (a projection of the minimum income necessary for a family to survive) established by the states—standards which reflect wide fluctuations. For example, in 1987 Kentucky claimed that a family of three (one adult and two children) had a need standard of $197 per month. Louisiana, another southern state with a similar per capita income, claimed that for the same hypothetical family the need standard was $610 per month. Establishing a need standard, however, does not require the state to meet that standard. For example, in 1987 Illinois failed to match its own need standard of $689; instead, it provided AFDC recipients with only $342 per month, or less than 50 percent of its own established need standard. Despite Louisiana's need standard of $610 per month, the AFDC benefit level was only $190. On the other hand, Delaware was able to fully meet its meager need standard of $310 per month. Only 20 states met their own need standards in 1987 (see Table 11.5).

As was noted earlier, regardless of the states' need standards or their AFDC payment levels, there were only five states in 1987 in which AFDC benefits reached 75 percent of the poverty line; in 32 states the AFDC benefit levels were less than 50 percent of the poverty line. In the median state, the combined benefits of AFDC and Food Stamps (for a family of three with no other income) equal $559 per month, just 74 percent of the poverty line.

In 1987, the typical state provided a benefit level equal to only 47.5 percent of the poverty

TABLE 11.5. AFDC Benefits by State—Need Standards and Payments to AFDC Families with No Countable Income, 1987

	AFDC Family Composed of One Adult and Two Children			
State	Need Standard (Monthly)	Payments (Monthly)	Maximum Benefit Level as Percentage of Need Standard	Inflation-Adjusted Change in the Value of Need Standard (1970–87)
Alabama	$384	$118	30.7%	−28.5%
Alaska	749	749	100.0	−28.7
Arizona	621	293	47.2	+ 0.1
Arkansas	695	202	29.1	+59.6
California	633	633	100.0	−40.3
Colorado	421	346	82.2	−25.7
Connecticut	601	601	100.0	−27.3
Delaware	310	310	100.0	−56.7
Dist. of Col.	712	364	51.1	+ 6.4
Florida	775	264	34.1	+43.3
Georgia	366	263	71.9	−28.9
Hawaii	491	491	100.0	−25.3
Idaho	554	304	54.9	−21.1
Illinois	689	342	49.6	− 5.5
Indiana	320	288	90.0	−59.1
Iowa	497	381	76.7	−34.0
Kansas	409	409	100.0	−39.7
Kentucky	197	197	100.0	−68.1
Louisiana	610	190	31.1	+20.6
Maine	558	405	72.6	−31.1
Maryland	497	359	72.2	−32.2
Massachusetts	510	510	100.0	−35.1
Michigan	630	427	67.8	− 2.1
Minnesota	532	532	100.0	−28.9
Mississippi	368	120	32.6	−34.6
Missouri	312	282	90.4	−61.5
Montana	434	359	82.7	−28.4
Nebraska	350	350	100.0	−56.4
Nevada	285	285	100.0	−63.2
New Hampshire	486	486	100.0	−37.0

continued

TABLE 11.5. (cont.)

	AFDC Family Composed of One Adult and Two Children			
State	Need Standard (Monthly)	Payments (Monthly)	Maximum Benefit Level as Percentage of Need Standard	Inflation-Adjusted Change in the Value of Need Standard (1970–87)
New Jersey	424	424	100.0	−51.8
New Mexico	264	264	100.0	−46.5
New York	497	497	100.0	−39.3
North Carolina	518	259	50.0	+ 5.3
North Dakota	371	371	100.0	−45.3
Ohio	674	309	45.8	+10.7
Oklahoma	471	310	65.8	− 8.4
Oregon	412	412	100.0	−38.9
Pennsylvania	614	382	62.2	−18.0
Rhode Island	479	479	100.0	−28.9
South Carolina	388	200	51.5	−19.2
South Dakota	366	366	100.0	−53.4
Tennessee	353	159	45.0	−32.0
Texas	574	184	32.1	− 1.0
Utah	693	376	54.3	+ 2.2
Vermont	889	603	67.8	+ 4.4
Virginia	393	354	90.1	−43.9
Washington	835	492	58.9	+11.0
West Virginia	497	249	50.1	−19.5
Wisconsin	647	549	84.9	+ 3.7
Wyoming	360	360	100.0	−51.8

Source: Adapted from Isaac Shapiro and Robert Greenstein, *Holes in the Safety Nets* (Washington, D.C.: Center on Budget and Policy Priorities, 1988), p. 56.

line; in other words, the amount provided for a family of three totaled $12.10 per day (see Table 11.6). According to federal poverty guidelines, a family of three required over $24.25 a day for subsistence.

The inadequacy of AFDC benefits is illustrated in the case of Missouri, a state with close to the median level of AFDC payments. In 1987 a family of three in Missouri could have received a maximum AFDC benefit of $282 per month. Since the federal poverty guideline was $755.75 per month, Missouri AFDC recipients received benefits that only brought them to 37.3 percent of the federal poverty line. Even with the addition of Food Stamps (maximum of $223 per month), the maximum income for an AFDC family of three in Missouri was only $6,060 per year, about 67 percent of the federal poverty guideline of $9,069. Although Missouri

raised its need standard in 1976, the cost of many necessities increased by 100 percent from 1976 to 1987.

Unlike federal programs such as Social Security and SSI, in most states (with the exception of Alaska, California, Connecticut, and the District of Columbia) AFDC benefits are not automatically adjusted for inflation, and from 1970 to 1987 benefits actually decreased by 31.4 percent. Moreover, while the national median decrease was 31.4 percent, AFDC benefits in states such as Idaho, Illinois, Kentucky, Texas, New Jersey, and South Dakota, have fallen over 50 percent since 1970. For example, AFDC benefits in Illinois fell from 92 percent of the poverty line in 1970 to 45.2 percent of the poverty line in 1987. Only three states, California, Maine and Wisconsin, reported net increases in AFDC benefits since

TABLE 11.6. Percentage Changes in Maximum AFDC Benefits for a Three-Person Family, 50 States and the District of Columbia, 1970 and 1987

State	Maximum Monthly Benefit for a Three-Person Family, 1987	Maximum Benefits As Percent of Three-Person 1987 Poverty Line ($9,069)	Inflation-Adjusted Change in Four-Person Maximum Benefit (1970–1987)
Alabama	$118	15.6%	−37.8%
Alaska	749	79.3	−23.9
Arizona	293	38.8	−27.6
Arkansas	202	26.7	−18.5
California	633	83.7	+16.7
Colorado	346	45.8	−38.8
Connecticut	601	79.5	−27.3
Delaware	310	41.0	−33.5
Dist. of Col.	364	48.1	−36.5
Florida	264	34.9	−20.3
Georgia	263	34.8	−20.2
Hawaii	491	56.5	−25.3
Idaho	304	40.2	−51.3
Illinois	342	45.2	−53.1
Indiana	288	38.1	−21.0
Iowa	381	50.4	−37.6
Kansas	409	54.1	−34.0
Kentucky	197	26.1	−54.9
Louisiana	190	25.1	−26.5
Maine	405	53.6	+ 3.8
Maryland	359	47.5	−24.5
Massachusetts	510	67.5	−35.1
Michigan	427	56.5	−31.4
Minnesota	532	70.4	−28.9
Mississippi	120	15.9	−29.5
Missouri	282	37.3	−13.1
Montana	359	47.5	−35.0
Nebraska	350	46.3	−28.1
Nevada	285	37.7	−18.3
New Hampshire	486	64.3	−37.0
New Jersey	424	56.1	−51.8
New Mexico	264	34.9	−40.4
New York	497	65.7	−39.3
North Carolina	259	34.3	−38.7
North Dakota	371	49.1	−40.4
Ohio	309	40.9	−34.6
Oklahoma	310	41.0	−28.9
Oregon	412	54.5	−23.7
Pennsylvania	382	50.5	−49.0
Rhode Island	479	63.4	−28.9
South Carolina	200	26.5	−20.2
South Dakota	366	48.4	−53.4
Tennessee	159	21.0	−48.5
Texas	184	24.3	−57.7
Utah	376	49.7	−29.1
Vermont	603	79.8	−23.8
Virginia	354	46.8	−46.2
Washington	492	65.1	−34.7
West Virginia	249	32.9	−22.6
Wisconsin	549	72.6	+ 3.5
Wyoming	360	47.6	−41.2
Median State	359	47.5	−31.4

Source: Adapted from Isaac Shapiro and Robert Greenstein, *Holes in the Safety Nets* (Washington, D.C.: Center on Budget and Policy Priorities, 1988), p. 7.

1970. According to the Consumer Price Index inflation has resulted in a 30 percent increase in the cost of living since 1981. AFDC grants, however, have only risen 10 percent in that period. Inflation, if calculated in terms of the basic necessities of life (food, shelter, and clothing), has risen even faster. Hence, because the welfare reform bill of 1988 did not establish a minimum national benefit level, its impact on the AFDC system is limited.

Apart from inadequate benefit levels, the AFDC program also faces other problems. For example, AFDC clients complain that they are denied the same rights to privacy as non-recipients. The finances of AFDC beneficiaries are scrupulously examined, and many are asked highly personal questions as well as being offered unsolicited advice regarding parenting and other family matters. In addition, AFDC recipients often report being treated as second-class citizens by many welfare departments. Lastly, AFDC recipients are forced to negotiate benefits and eligibility criteria that are complex and constantly prone to change.[68]

The AFDC program has frequently been accused of encouraging the breakup of families. In the past, intact families in the 25 states without AFDC-UP programs had to rely on highly limited state or local general assistance programs. For the most part, children in these non-AFDC-UP states were ineligible for assistance unless the families dissolved, which, unfortunately, many were forced to do. Because the new welfare reform legislation allows states to limit aid under AFDC-UP to six months out of a twelve-month period, many of these intact families will continue to suffer. If all states adopted the AFDC-UP program for the full year, it is estimated that an additional 100,000 families would be eligible for assistance.[69]

Myths abound around the welfare state, and especially, the AFDC program. In a symbolic sense, the debate around AFDC seems to have little to do with the program itself. Instead, the ideological controversy centers around the symbolic values reflected in AFDC.

SUPPLEMENTAL SECURITY INCOME

When President Richard Nixon took office in 1972, he attempted to streamline the welfare system by proposing a Family Assistance Plan (FAP). In this plan Nixon proposed a guaranteed annual income which would replace AFDC, Old Age Assistance (OAA), Aid to the Blind (AB), and Aid to the Permanently and Totally Disabled (APTD). Although the overall plan was rejected by Congress, the OAA, AB, and APTD programs were federalized under a new program called Supplemental Security Income (SSI). Basically, the federal government took the operation of those programs out of the hands of the state governments. No longer would the state governments set eligibility levels, establish minimum payment levels, or administer the programs. In essence, SSI is a program designed to provide cash assistance to the elderly poor and the disabled poor.

In 1986 the SSI program served over 4 million people and cost the federal government about $10 billion. Unlike OASDHI, SSI is a means-tested federal public assistance program funded through general revenue taxes. The basic SSI payment level is set nationally and is adjusted annually for inflation. A portion of the elderly receive SSI in conjunction with Social Security, but only if their income is lower than the income standard set under the SSI program. Age is not an eligibility criterion for SSI, and children may receive benefits under the disabled or blind portion of the Act (in determining benefits the income of the parents is a factor). Among others, the following people are eligible for SSI: (1) the mentally retarded, (2) the aged who are at least 65 years old and have little or no income, (3) those considered legally blind, (4) adults (at least eighteen years old) who qualify as disabled because of a physical or mental impairment expected to last for at least twelve months, (5) visually impaired persons who do not meet the criteria for blindness may qualify, and (6) drug addicts and alcoholics who enter treatment.

To qualify for SSI, an applicant's resources must be limited. In 1987, SSI applicants were required to have resources valued at less than $1,700 for an individual and $2,550 for a couple (excluding a house, and a car valued at under $4,500). SSI benefits are not generous, although they are higher in many states than AFDC benefits. For an individual in 1987 the maximum SSI benefit was $340 per month ($4,080 a year), and for a couple it was $510 per month ($6,120 a year). The payment levels for SSI equal 74.8 percent of the poverty line for an elderly individual and 88.9 percent for an elderly couple (the poverty line established by the Census Bureau is lower for elderly households and individuals). One-third of SSI payments is deducted if the person lives in the home of someone who is contributing to his or her support.

One major concern regarding SSI involves the low level of income and the requirements for eligibility. In fact, 27 states supplement SSI payments with an additional grant, and some states opt to have the federal government administer that stipend. In 23 out of the 27 states where a supplement is provided, the maximum combined benefits for an elderly individual still do not exceed the poverty line. For elderly couples, the maximum combined benefits fall below the poverty line in 14 of those states. States may also choose to set their own requirements for supplementary SSI payments, thereby including only certain beneficiaries or limiting disabilities. Only California indexes SSI supplements for inflation. In the median state which provides SSI supplements, the value of those supplements has fallen by 47.5 percent since 1974, after adjusting for inflation.[70] Despite SSI supplements, the recipients have fared worse throughout the 1970s and 1980s.

Under the changeover to SSI, states were not allowed to pay recipients less than they had been previously granted. However, stringent eligibility requirements and complex red tape have kept many people off the SSI rolls. For example, the cases of recipients are reviewed

every three years (usually involving a medical review) and "continuing disability reviews" may be required. Some critics believe that the federal government has purposely made entrance and continued maintenance in SSI difficult in order to discourage participation.

GENERAL ASSISTANCE

Although not formally connected to SSI or AFDC, General Assistance (GA) often serves a similar clientele. GA is a state or local program designed for individuals (aged, blind, disabled, or dependent) and families who fall through the safety net, thereby not meeting the eligibility criteria of the major social welfare programs. In addition, GA may be used in some cases where AFDC or SSI recipients have benefits that are too low to cover an emergency.

No federal funds or federal standards apply to GA; it is totally financed and managed by state or local governments and is administered differently from state to state. Because of its discretionary characteristics—the variability of benefits provided, eligibility, and the fact that it is administered by states or localities— in many ways the GA program represents a holdover from the days of county welfare. In San Diego, for example, GA is given as a loan which must be repaid. Moreover, because the federal government has no role in GA, some states and communities have no program, while in other states, GA is administered only on an emergency basis. In general, GA programs tend to have narrow eligibility guidelines, are usually very restrictive, and provide a low level of assistance.

Of the 21 states that have a GA program, 13 provide assistance only to the elderly or disabled. In the eight states which provide unrestricted coverage, the maximum benefits for an individual range from 28 to 68 percent of the poverty line, with an average grant of 44 percent of the poverty line given in the median state.[71] The overall cost of GA is estimated at over $1.5 billion, and in 1986 over 1 million households were beneficiaries, with an average grant of $160 per month.

SUMMARY

Social insurance programs represent a major source of security for both America's elderly and its present group of workers. In the last 50 years, Americans have come to believe that regardless of the ebb and flow of economic life, Social Security embodies a firm social commitment to care for the elderly. Economic gains made by the elderly since the mid-1960s have proved that belief correct. Furthermore, because Social Security is linked to past contributions, beneficiaries experience little stigma.

Unfortunately, recipients of income maintenance programs do not fare as well. Income maintenance programs such as SSI or AFDC contain a great deal of stigma, and the character of recipients is often maligned because of their need. Moreover, the relative success of Social Security in arresting poverty among the elderly has not been replicated in income maintenance programs. In fact, the reverse is true—AFDC recipients have endured greater levels of poverty during the 1980s. If, as some economists claim, the 1980s were an "economic party," then someone forgot to invite the poor.

NOTES

1. Sumner A. Rosen, David Fanshel, and Mary E. Lutz, eds., *Face of the Nation 1987* (Silver Spring, Md.: NASW, 1987).
2. Frances Fox Piven and Richard A. Cloward, *Regulating the Poor: The Functions of Public Welfare* (New York: Vintage Books, 1971).
3. David P. Beverly and Edward A. McSweeney, *Social Welfare and Social Justice* (Englewood Cliffs, N.J.: Prentice-Hall, 1987).
4. Piven and Cloward, *Regulating the Poor*, p. 100.
5. Department of the Census, *Current Population Reports, 1981*, Series P-60, No. 125 (Washington, D.C.: U.S. Government Printing Office, 1981).
6. Michael Harrington, with the assistance of Robert Greenstein and Eleanor Holmes Norton. *Who Are the Poor?* (Washington, D.C.: Justice for All, 1987), p. 24.
7. Social Security Administration, *Social Security Bulletin* (Baltimore, Md.: Social Security Administration, April 1986).
8. Charles Prigmore and Charles Atherton, *Social Welfare Policy* (Lexington, Mass.: D.C. Heath, 1979).
9. Merton C. and Joan Broadshaug Bernstein, *Social Security: The System That Works* (New York: Basic Books, 1987).
10. Ibid.
11. Bernard Gavzer, "How Secure is Your Social Security?" *Parade*, October 18, 1987.
12. American Association of Retired Persons, "A Profile of Older Americans: 1985," (Washington, D.C.: American Association of Retired Persons, 1985).
13. Social Security Administration, *Social Security Bulletin, Annual Statistical Supplement, 1984–85* (Baltimore, Md.: Social Security Administration, April 1986).
14. Diane M. DiNitto and Thomas R. Dye, *Social Welfare: Politics and Public Policy* (Englewood Cliffs, N.J.: Prentice-Hall, 1987), p. 82.
15. Rosen et al., *Face of the Nation*, p. 56.
16. DiNitto and Dye, *Social Welfare*.
17. Center on Budget and Policy Studies, *Smaller Pieces of the Pie* (Washington, D.C.: Center on Budget and Policy Studies, 1985).
18. Isaac Shapiro and Robert Greenstein, *Holes in the Safety Nets* (Washington, D.C.: Center on Budget and Policy Priorities), pp. 22–23.
19. Prigmore and Atherton, *Social Welfare Policy*, pp. 66–67.
20. W. Joseph Heffernan, *Introduction to Social Welfare Policy* (Itasca, Ill.: F. E. Peacock, 1979), p. 138.
21. Ibid.
22. Bernstein and Bernstein, *Social Security: The System That Works*.
23. Shapiro and Greenstein, *Holes in the Safety Nets*.
24. Beverly and McSweeney, *Social Welfare and*

Social Justice.

25. Rosen et al., *The Face of the Nation.*
26. Shapiro and Greenstein, *Holes in the Safety Nets*, p. 7.
27. *Congressional Record*, Senate, vol. 133, no. 120 (Washington, D.C.: U.S. Government Printing Office, July 21, 1987), pp. S10400–404.
28. Heffernan, *Introduction to Social Welfare Policy.*
29. Social Security Administration, *Bulletin, Annual Statistical Supplement* (Baltimore, Md.: Social Security Administration, 1985), p. 48.
30. Piven and Cloward, *Regulating the Poor.*
31. Elizabeth D. Huttman, *Introduction to Social Policy* (New York: McGraw-Hill,1981), p. 168.
32. Children's Defense Fund, *A Children's Defense Budget* (Washington, D.C.: Children's Defense Fund, 1986), p. 145.
33. Ibid.
34. Ibid., p. 146.
35. DiNitto and Dye, *Social Welfare.*
36. Ibid.
37. Ibid.
38. *See* Children's Defense Fund.
39. Huttman, *Introduction to Social Policy.*
40. *Congressional Record*, 1987, p. 1796–1811.
41. Representative Thomas Downey, chairman of the House subcommittee on public assistance. Quoted in William J. Eaton, "Major Welfare Reform Compromise Reached," *Los Angeles Times*, September 27, 1988, p. 15.
42. American Public Welfare Association, *Conference Agreement on Welfare Reform*, Washington, D.C., September 28, 1988, pp. 1–3.
43. Heffernan, *Introduction to Social Welfare Policy.*
44. Department of Health and Human Services, *Characteristics of State Plans for Aid to Dependent Children Under the Social Security Act, Title IV-A*, Social Security Administration, Office of Family Assistance, Washington, D.C., 1985.
45. Heffernan, *Introduction to Social Welfare*

Policy.

46. Department of Health and Human Services, 1985.
47. Department of Health, Education, and Welfare, *Aid to Families with Dependent Children*, Social Security Administration, Office of Research and Statistics, Washington, D.C., 1979.
48. See Children's Defense Fund; and Department of Health, Education, and Welfare, *Welfare Myths and Facts*, Social and Rehabilitation Service, Washington, D.C., circa 1972.
49. Harrington, *Who Are the Poor?* p. 20.
50. See Children's Defense Fund.
51. Department of Health, Education and Welfare, 1979.
52. Lutheran Family and Children's Services of Missouri, "Public Assistance Information Sheet," St. Louis, Missouri, July 1985.
53. See Children's Defense Fund.
54. Harrington, *Who Are the Poor?* p. 20.
55. Greg J. Duncan, and Saul D. Hoffman, "Welfare Dynamics and Welfare Policy." Unpublished paper. Ann Arbor, Mich.: Institute for Social Research, 1985.
56. Ibid.
57. See Children's Defense Fund.
58. Rowel, *Fact Sheet*, St. Louis, Mo.: Rowel, February 28, 1986.
59. Duncan and Hoffman, "Welfare Dynamics and Welfare Policy."
60. Ibid.
61. See Children's Defense Fund.
62. Huttman, *Introduction to Social Policy*, p. 179.
63. Department of Health, Education and Welfare, 1972.
64. Greenstein and Shapiro, *Holes in the Safety Nets*, p. 8.
65. Center on Budget and Policy Priorities, 1985.
66. Harrington, *Who Are the Poor?* p. 21.
67. Duncan and Hoffman, "Welfare Dynamics."
68. Huttman, *Introduction to Social Policy.*
69. Children's Defense Fund, p. 143.
70. Shapiro and Greenstein, *Holes in the Safety Nets*, pp. 11–12.
71. Ibid., pp. 13–14.

CHAPTER 12

The American Health Care System

This chapter will examine the American health care system—specifically, the demographics of U.S. health care, the organization of medical services, key governmental health programs such as Medicare and Medicaid, and federal attempts at cutting health-care costs. In addition, this chapter will examine how medical services are organized in other countries, i.e., the Scandinavian countries and Britain. Lastly, this chapter will explore the crisis in medical care and review alternative health care proposals.

The landscape of American health care is marked by several contradictions. While the vast majority (85 percent) of Americans have easy access to a wide variety of medical services through employment-based insurance programs, Medicaid, or Medicare, some 35 million people are totally without coverage. What makes the situation even more dramatic is that in every major city there exists at least one major medical center with an annual budget of $100 to $200 million.[1]

The cost of providing health care has risen dramatically in the last 25 years. In 1960 total health-care expenditures came to $26 billion; by 1986 that amount had increased to $400 billion. Put another way, 5.3 percent of the total GNP in 1960 was devoted to medical care; by 1986 that had increased to 11 percent. In 1981 hospital care alone cost $118 billion. Medical care costs have also been rising faster than the general rate of inflation. From 1975 to 1979 health-care expenditures grew at a rate of 13 percent a year. During the 1980s that rate of growth has increased to 15 percent a year.[2] As Table 12.1 suggests, the growth in the health-care industry eclipses that of most other American business sectors.

When health-care expenditures are broken down, the largest portion (41 percent in 1985) goes to hospitals. The second largest expenditure is physicians' services, accounting for 20 percent of all expenditures and totaling $69 billion in 1985. Nursing home care, the fourth largest expenditure, accounted for 8 percent of total health-care costs (almost $29 billion).[3]

The huge increases in health care costs have put increasing pressure on the government to subsidize more of the medical care budget, as shown in Table 12.2. From 1950 to 1984 the percentage of health-care costs paid for by the government rose from 27.2 to 41.4 percent. In other words, 39 cents of every health care dollar is paid for by federal or local government funds.[4]

THE ORGANIZATION OF MEDICAL SERVICES

A brief explanation of the organization of medical services is useful before proceeding to a discussion of Medicare and Medicaid. The organization of U.S. medical services contains five major components: (1) physicians in solo practice; (2) group out-patient settings, including groups of physicians sharing facilities, group health plans and HMOs, physicians in industrial (Employee Assistance Plans) settings, or doctors operating under university auspices (over the past few decades physicians have increasingly worked in group practices or other organized settings, and in 1984 that accounted for about half of all patient-physician services);[5] (3) hospitals—private, nonprofit, or public; (4) public health services delivered on state, local, regional, national, or international levels, including health counseling, family planning, prenatal

TABLE 12.1. U.S. Gross National Product (GNP) and National Health Expenditures, Selected Years 1929–1986

| Year | GNP (in billions) | National Health Care Expenditures | | |
		Amount (in billions)	Percentage of GNP	Amount Per Capita
1929	$ 103.9	$ 3.6	3.5%	$ 29
1940	100.4	4.0	4.0	29
1950	288.3	12.7	4.4	80
1960	515.3	26.9	5.2	142
1965	705.1	41.9	5.9	205
1970	1,015.5	75.0	7.4	349
1975	1,598.4	132.7	8.3	590
1980	2,731.9	248.1	9.1	1,054
1982	3,166.0	323.6	10.2	1,348
1984	3,765.0	391.1	10.4	1,598
1986	4,206.1	458.2	10.9	1,837

Source: U.S. Department of Health and Human Services, *Health, United States–1987*, DHHS Pub. No. (PHS) 88-1232, Table 94 (Washington, D.C.: U.S. Government Printing Office, 1988), p. 149.

TABLE 12.2. Sources of Payments for Personal Health Care (Percentage), Selected Years 1929–1986

| Year | Direct Payment | Private Health Insurance | Philanthropy and Industry | Governmental | | |
				Total	Federal	State and Local
1929	88.4%	NA	2.6%	9.0%	2.7%	6.3%
1940	81.3	NA	2.6	16.1	4.1	12.0
1950	65.5	9.1%	2.9	22.4	10.4	12.0
1960	54.9	21.1	2.3	21.8	9.3	12.5
1965	51.6	24.2	2.2	22.0	10.1	11.9
1970	40.5	23.4	1.7	34.3	22.2	12.1
1975	32.5	26.7	1.3	39.5	26.8	12.7
1980	28.7	30.7	1.2	39.4	28.4	10.9
1982	27.8	31.4	1.2	39.6	29.3	10.3
1984	28.8	30.7	1.2	39.3	29.5	9.8
1986	28.7	30.4	1.2	39.6	30.2	9.4

Source: U.S. Department of Health and Human Services, *Health, United States–1987*, DHHS Pub. No. (PHS) 88-1232, Table 102 (Washington, D.C.: U.S. Government Printing Office, 1988), p. 158.

and postnatal care, school health services, disease prevention and control, immunization, referral agencies, Sexually Transmitted Diseases (STD) services, environmental sanitation, health education, and maintenance of indexes, i.e., births, deaths, communicable diseases; (5) sundry and corollary health services, including home health services, physical rehabilitation, group homes, nursing homes, and so forth.

THE MAJOR HEALTH PROGRAMS: MEDICAID AND MEDICARE

For the most part, before 1965 medical care was a responsibility of state and local governments and charity. In 1950 the federal government authorized states to use federal/state funds, under the Social Security Act of 1935, to provide medical care for the indigent. In 1957 the Kerr-Mills Act provided for a federal/state matching program to provide health care for the elderly and poor. However, the program was not mandatory, and many states opted not to participate. Intended as a compromise to ward off more far-reaching health policies, in 1965 President Lyndon Johnson signed into law the Medicaid and Medicare programs (Titles XVIII and XIX of the Social Security Act).[6] Replacing all previous programs, Medicaid became the largest public assistance program in the nation, serving 21.3 million people in 1984 with a budget of $23.7 billion.

Medicaid is a means-tested public assistance program. Eligible persons receive services from physicians who accept Medicaid patients (in many places a minority of the physicians) and other health-care providers. These health-care providers are then reimbursed by the federal government on a per patient basis.[7]

Medicaid is a federal/state program. States determine eligibility within the following federal guidelines: (1) all AFDC families must be covered, (2) first-time pregnant women must be covered if they would qualify for AFDC upon the birth of their child, (3) coverage must be extended to pregnant women in two-parent families if the breadwinner is unemployed, (4) children up to age 5 in poor families must be covered, and (5) most SSI recipients are automatically covered (see Table 12.3). Thirty-seven

states also extend coverage to the medically indigent—those people ineligible for public assistance, but who cannot obtain either medical care or pay a medical bill. Over half of the states extend coverage to families where the breadwinner is receiving unemployment compensation.

Because Medicaid is based on a federal-state mix (on average, states pay 44 percent of the costs), states also help set benefit levels. While all states are required to provide inpatient and outpatient hospital care, physicians' services, laboratory and X-ray services, skilled nursing home services for adults, home health care, family planning, rural health clinics, nurse and midwife services, and early periodic screening services for children, they also have the option of further extending Medicaid benefits (e.g., prescription drugs and dental care). In addition, states have broad administrative powers over Medicaid, including the determination of reimbursement rates. As such, individual states can discourage Medicaid participation by promulgating low reimbursement rates and low state-defined income standards, as shown in Table 12.4.

One area in which states have discretion is whether to extend Medicaid coverage to poor families and their children who are not on AFDC or AFDC-UP. Another option involves the coverage of two-parent families. Although

TABLE 12.3. Medicaid Recipients by Category, 1972–1984 (in thousands)

Year	Total	Age 65 or Older	Blindness	Total Disability	Families with Dependent Children		
					Adults	Children	Other
1972	17,606	3,318	108	1,625	3,137	7,841	1,576
1975	22,013	3,643	106	2,265	4,529	9,598	1,800
1977	22,831	3,636	92	2,710	4,785	9,651	1,959
1980	21,605	3,440	92	2,819	4,877	9,333	1,499
1982	21,603	3,240	84	2,806	5,356	9,563	1,434
1984	21,365	3,165	80	2,870	5,598	9,771	1,185

Source: *Social Security Bulletin, Annual Statistical Supplement, 1984–85* Baltimore, Md.: (Social Security Administration), 1986, pp. 219–222.

TABLE 12.4. Medicaid Eligibility for Families and State Adoption of Service Options, 1987

State	Eligibility Limit as Percentage of Three-Person Poverty Line	Cover Two-Parent Families?	Ribicoff Option?	SOBRA for Children and Pregnant Women?	Medically Needy Program for Families?	Number of Optional Services Covered out of 32 Total Options (1986)
Alabama	15.6%	no	no	no	no	14
Alaska	79.3	no	yes	no	no	16
Arizona	53.0	no	yes	yes	yes	na
Arkansas	34.1	no	yes	yes	yes	20
California	112.5	yes	yes	yes	yes	29
Colorado	55.7	no	no	no	no	16
Connecticut	82.7	yes	yes	yes	yes	25
Delaware	41.0	yes	no	yes	no	14
D. of Col.	64.2	yes	yes	yes	yes	25
Florida	47.5	yes	yes	yes	yes	17
Georgia	46.3	yes	yes	no	yes	13
Hawaii	56.5	yes	no	no	yes	13
Idaho	40.2	no	no	no	no	14
Illinois	60.6	yes	yes	no	yes	27
Indiana	38.1	no	no	no	no	28
Iowa	57.3	yes	yes	no	yes	22
Kansas	61.5	yes	yes	no	yes	22
Kentucky	35.3	yes	no	yes	yes	23
Louisiana	30.8	yes	no	no	yes	16
Maine	73.8	yes	yes	no	yes	25
Maryland	55.2	yes	yes	yes	yes	17
Massachusetts	87.1	yes	yes	yes	yes	30
Michigan	71.4	yes	yes	yes	yes	26
Minnesota	93.8	yes	yes	no	yes	29
Mississippi	48.7	no	yes	yes	no	10
Missouri	37.3	yes	yes	yes	no	13
Montana	54.0	yes	yes	no	yes	27
Nebraska	59.5	yes	yes	no	yes	23
Nevada	37.7	no	no	no	no	24
New Hampshire	64.3	no	no	no	yes	26
New Jersey	74.9	yes	yes	yes	yes	28
New Mexico	34.9	no	no	yes	no	16
New York	81.6	yes	yes	no	yes	26
N. Carolina	46.3	yes	yes	yes	yes	20
N. Dakota	57.6	no	yes	no	yes	24
Ohio	40.9	yes	yes	no	no	25
Oklahoma	62.3	yes	yes	yes	yes	16
Oregon	72.6	yes	no	yes	yes	25
Pennsylvania	56.2	yes	yes	yes	yes	16
Rhode Island	83.8	yes	yes	yes	yes	12
S. Carolina	51.3	yes	yes	yes	no	17
S. Dakota	48.4	no	no	no	no	16
Tennessee	46.7	no	yes	yes	yes	20
Texas	35.3	no	yes	no	yes	15
Utah	91.7	no	yes	no	yes	26

continued

TABLE 12.4. (cont.)

State	Eligibility Limit as Percentage of Three-Person Poverty Line	Cover Two-Parent Families?	Ribicoff Option?	SOBRA for Children and Pregnant Women?	Medically Needy Program for Families?	Number of Optional Services Covered out of 32 Total Options (1986)
Vermont	99.2	yes	yes	yes	yes	18
Virginia	47.4	no	no	no	yes	15
Washington	76.1	yes	no	yes	yes	23
W. Virginia	38.4	yes	no	yes	yes	18
Wisconsin	84.8	yes	yes	no	yes	26
Wyoming	47.6	no	no	no	no	9

Sources: U.S. Department of Health and Human Services, Health Care Financing Administration, *Medicaid Services State by State*, Washington, D.C., 1986; and Isaac Shapiro and Robert Greenstein, *Holes in the Safety Nets* (Washington, D.C.: Center on Budget and Policy Priorities, 1988), pp. 19, 62.

23 states did not have an AFDC-UP program in 1988, they were not necessarily precluded from offering Medicaid coverage to poor two-parent families with an unemployed bread-winner. Under federal law, states have the option of extending Medicaid coverage to two-parent families even though the state has no AFDC-UP program. In 1988, only five out of the 23 states (Florida, Georgia, Kentucky, Louisiana, and Oklahoma) without an AFDC-UP program have elected this option.[8] However, under federal law all states are required to provide Medicaid coverage to pregnant women and their children below the age of seven (born after September 30, 1983) who live in families with incomes below the state's Medicaid income limits, and who meet other Medicaid eligibility criteria.

Federal law provides several other categories under which states can provide Medicaid coverage to poor children and pregnant women not covered under AFDC or AFDC-UP. For example, under the Ribicoff option (named after Senator Abraham Ribicoff from Connecticut), states can extend Medicaid coverage to all children under 21 who live in families with incomes below the state's Medicaid income guidelines. Under this option—which 32 states had adopted by 1988—coverage is extended to both single- and two-parent families.[9]

Another alternative is the SOBRA (Sixth Omnibus Budget Reconciliation Act of 1986) option, under which states can extend Medicaid coverage to all pregnant women and young children who live in families with incomes less than or equal to 100 percent of the poverty line. This option extends coverage to both single- and two-parent families. By 1988, 38 states had adopted or had taken action to implement the SOBRA option. In addition, new legislation passed in 1987 allows states to provide Medicaid coverage to pregnant women and children (under one year old) who live in families with incomes less than 185 percent of the poverty guideline.[10]

Another Medicaid option involves the establishment of a Medically Needy component as a part of the state Medicaid program. Under this option, a family whose countable income is greater than the state's Medicaid income eligibility limits, but which has medical expenses so large that the remaining income is below the poverty line, is eligible for Medicaid. The Medically Needy option allows states to set Medicaid income limits that are up to one-third higher than the state's maximum benefit for

AFDC. This option is particularly important for families who were self-sufficient, but who now face a medical catastrophe that will deplete their economic resources. Families whose health insurance limits are exhausted, or who have no insurance, could also be eligible. By 1988, 36 states had adopted a Medically Needy program.[11]

Five important gaps exist in the Medicaid program, including: (1) the low eligibility limits set for Medicaid, (2) the choice by states whether to adopt Medicaid options, (3) gaps in coverage for the elderly and disabled, (4) Medicaid service options, and (5) the general ineligibility of single poor persons and childless couples who are neither elderly nor disabled. In a median state in 1987, the Medicaid income eligibility limit for a three-person family equaled 55.7 percent of the poverty line; in 10 states the income limits were less than 40 percent of the poverty line. Thus, because many poor people were "not poor enough," they were ineligible for Medicaid. In other words, at 56 percent of the poverty line, a three-person family in 1987 with an income of over $5,079 would be ineligible for Medicaid in the median state.[12]

Another problem is the variability of the states in adopting Medicaid options. Some states have elected few, if any, Medicaid options. In fact, six states in 1988 (Colorado, Idaho, Indiana, Nevada, South Dakota, and Wyoming) had adopted none of the major Medicaid options. States also have discretion regarding which low-income and disabled people are covered under Medicaid. For example, within their Medicaid program states can choose to cover all or only some SSI recipients, to establish a Medically Needy program for the elderly and disabled, and to adopt a SOBRA option which covers the non-SSI elderly and disabled whose incomes fall below the poverty line. Fourteen states in 1988 did not extend coverage to all of their SSI recipients, 16 states did not have a Medically Needy program that covered the elderly and disabled, and only four jurisdictions (the District of Columbia, Florida,

New Jersey, and Rhode Island) had adopted the SOBRA option which covered the elderly poor and disabled not on SSI.[13]

Another discretionary matter allowed to states involves which medical services to cover. Although the federal government requires that certain basic services be covered for all Medicaid recipients, the states have the power to determine whether none, some, or all of 32 other medical services (e.g., emergency hospital services, dentures, eyeglasses, and so forth) will be covered. In the median state in 1988, 21 out of the 32 optional Medicaid services were covered. However, 10 states covered less than half of the possible services, and seven states did not pay for emergency hospital services. In 10 states Medicaid did not pay for dental services; in 15 states it did not pay for dentures; and in six states it did not cover eyeglasses for poor children, the elderly, and the disabled.[14]

Although two-thirds of Medicaid beneficiaries are AFDC recipients, they consume only one-fourth of Medicaid expenditures. Nursing home residents comprise only 7 percent of Medicaid recipients, yet they account for over 40 percent of the program costs. Close to three-fifths of all nursing home expenditures are paid for by the federal government.

The increase in the number of nursing home residents parallels the creation of Medicaid. From 1965 (the year Medicaid was created) to 1970 the number of nursing home residents rose by 18 percent. From 1970 to 1975 that number rose another 17 percent; from 1975 to 1980, 14 percent; and about 12 percent from 1980 to 1985. Moreover, since four-fifths of nursing homes are for-profit, public subsidization of the nursing home industry occurred as a result of Medicaid.

Despite the available options and the scope of coverage, serious inadequacies exist in the Medicaid program. According to the Bureau of the Census, in 1985 only about two-fifths of the nation's poor were covered under Medicaid. In 1986 close to 22 million people received Medicaid, considerably less than the

32.5 million in poverty. Moreover, about 5 million children and six of every 10 women of childbearing age below the poverty line were ineligible.[15] Despite its inadequacies, however, the results of the Medicaid program are significant. In 1963 only 63 percent of pregnant women received prenatal care; by 1976 that number had increased to 76 percent. Between 1964 and 1975, the use of physician services by poor children increased by 74 percent. In part, the increased utilization of medical services resulted in a 49 percent drop in infant mortality between 1965 and 1980. For black infants, the drop in mortality was even more startling: mortality had dropped by only 5 percent in the 15 years before Medicaid, but by 49 percent in the 15 years after the program began (see Table 12.5). Moreover, ongoing preventive care has cut program costs for Medicaid-eligible children by 10 percent.[16]

Medicaid is one of the most important government health programs. In 1986 Medicaid payments represented 55 cents of every public health dollar spent on children; 26 cents out of every dollar (public or private) spent on hospitalization for children under six; 30 cents of every dollar spent on delivery services for pregnant teens; and 10 cents out of every dollar spent on ambulatory pediatric services.[17]

Despite its effectiveness, from 1982 to 1985, Medicaid was under constant attack from the Reagan administration, Congress, and various state governments. Cuts in federal funds and rule changes led many states to reduce eligibility and provide fewer services. For example, in 1984–85, roughly 800 Medicaid-related cost containment measures were adopted in the vast majority of states. These measures included limiting the number of hospital days and reimbursable visits to physicians, reducing or freezing Medicaid provider rates, imposing co-payments and deductibles, requiring pre-admission screening, mandating second opinions for elective surgery, and limiting capital spending.[18]

According to the Children's Defense Fund,

TABLE 12.5. State Infant Mortality Rates by Rank, 1985

Rank	State	Rates Per 100,000 Births
1	District of Columbia	20.8
2	Delaware	14.8
3	South Carolina	14.2
4	Mississippi	13.7
5	Georgia	12.7
6	Alabama	12.6
7	Wyoming	12.2
8	Louisiana	11.9
9	Maryland	11.9
10	North Carolina	11.8
11	Illinois	11.7
12	Arkansas	11.6
13	Virginia	11.5
14	Tennessee	11.4
15	Michigan	11.4
16	Florida	11.3
17	Kentucky	11.2
18	Pennsylvania	11.0
19	Indiana	10.9
20	Oklahoma	10.9
21	Alaska	10.8
22	New York	10.8
23	Washington	10.7
24	West Virginia	10.7
25	New Jersey	10.6
26	New Mexico	10.6
27	Idaho	10.4
28	Montana	10.3
29	Ohio	10.3
30	Missouri	10.2
31	Connecticut	10.0
32	Oregon	9.9
33	South Dakota	9.9
34	Texas	9.8
35	Arizona	9.7
36	Utah	9.6
37	Nebraska	9.6
38	Iowa	9.5
39	California	9.5
40	Colorado	9.4
41	New Hampshire	9.3
42	Kansas	9.3
43	Massachusetts	9.1
44	Wisconsin	9.1
45	Maine	9.1
46	Hawaii	8.8
47	Minnesota	8.8
48	Vermont	8.5
49	Nevada	8.5
50	Rhode Island	8.2
Median		10.6

Sources: National Center for Health Statistics, "Advance Report of Final Mortality Statistics," Washington, D.C. 1985.

because of increased poverty and reduced access to health care, neonatal mortality rates rose an unprecedented 9 percent from 1982 to 1984. Between 1982 and 1983 (the height of the Medicaid cuts), black neonatal mortality rates rose by 5 percent. Moreover, in 1983, for the fifth year in a row, there was no improvement in the percentage of pregnant women receiving early prenatal care. According to the Robert Wood Johnson Foundation, in 1986 Medicaid reached 19 percent fewer poor and near-poor families than it did in 1976.[19]

MEDICARE

Medicare, Public Law 89-79, was added to the Social Security Act and enacted on July 30, 1965. This program was designed to provide prepaid hospital insurance for the aged, as well as voluntary medical insurance. Medicare is composed of two parts: Hospital Insurance (HI), known as Part A; and Supplemental Medical Insurance (SMI), known as Part B.

HI is a compulsory hospital insurance plan for the aged, with the premiums coming out of a payroll tax (1.35 percent in 1985) which is part of the Social Security deductions. SMI, a voluntary supplemental medical insurance plan, pays doctor bills and additional medical expenses. The costs of SMI are paid by the beneficiary (in 1988, $24.80 a month); the remainder of the program costs are subsidized by general tax revenues. SMI is open to anyone on HI willing to pay the premium. The SMI premium is paid by the federal government if the beneficiary is on public assistance. Coverage under Medicare includes physicians' services in the home, hospital, or office. Medicare will also pay for all covered services in a participating skilled nursing facility.

In 1988, President Ronald Reagan signed into effect what is commonly called the "Catastrophic Insurance Act," the most sweeping reform of Medicare since the bill was enacted in 1965. The purpose of this legislation was to provide 33 million elderly and disabled Medicare beneficiaries with protection from catastrophic hospital, doctor, and outpatient drug costs. The system is self-financing through premiums imposed on the beneficiaries. In addition, the premium is income-related and thus falls most heavily on higher-income beneficiaries.

In terms of hospital insurance, the bill provides for unlimited hospital care after payment of an annual deductible—about $564 in 1989. Previously, 60 days of hospital care were provided for each spell of illness, with a deductible for each admission. If necessary, patients could stay for another 30 days, but they were required to pay $135 per day. A patient needing to stay longer could draw on a "lifetime reserve" of 60 days, but had to pay $270 for each day. Once the total of 150 days was reached, Medicare would pay nothing further for that admission. Patients were also expected to pay the deductible *each* time they entered the hospital. It is estimated that this new policy will affect over 1.2 million Medicare beneficiaries each year.

Beginning in 1990, Medicare beneficiaries will not have to pay more than $1,370 per year for Medicare services covered under Part B (doctor insurance and other services). This ceiling—which will gradually rise—will apply only to Medicare-approved charges, not to doctor charges in excess of Medicare-approved payment. Under former rules, the patient paid the first $75 a year of covered medical expenses, with Medicare paying 80 percent of approved charges for any additional service. The remaining 20 percent was paid by the patient as a form of copayment. Previously, there was no cap on the yearly out-of-pocket costs of the patient. Thus, if a medical bill was $60,000 for the year, the patient paid the $75 deductible plus 20 percent of the bill, or in other words, the copayment was $12,075. Under the new rules, the maximum out-of-pocket cost for the patient is $1,370. Over 2 million patients are expected to benefit from this new cap.

The new bill also covers charges for outpatient drugs. Beginning in 1991, Medicare will pay 50 percent of the costs of a recipient's outpatient drugs in excess of $600 per year (an amount that will increase each year). By 1992, Medicare will cover 60 percent of those costs; and by 1993, the share paid by Medicare will increase to 80 percent. About 5 million patients a year are expected to be helped by this provision. In the past, there was no Medicare outpatient drug benefit.

The new law also increases the Medicare benefits for skilled nursing care from 100 days to 150 days a year. The patient pays 20 percent of the daily cost of nursing home care for the first eight days (an estimated $20.50 per day), and subsequent days are free. This benefit is not designed for long-term care, but for short recuperative stays in nursing homes. (Medicare does not provide benefits for long-term maintenance stays in nursing homes.) In addition, the new bill removes the 210-day limit on hospice care.

In 1990, Medicare will pay for up to 80 days a year of respite care. In short, this bill provides funds for outside aides to temporarily care for a homebound long-term Medicare beneficiary, thereby relieving family members who are providing the primary care. This benefit will be available to people for one year after they reach the Part B catastrophic limit or the outpatient drug catastrophic limit. Also beginning in 1990, Medicare recipients can receive benefits for up to 38 consecutive days of home health care.

This new catastrophic health insurance bill also affects Medicaid. The law allows the noninstitutionalized spouse of a nursing home resident applying for Medicaid to retain a sufficient portion of their combined income to avoid becoming destitute. The at-home spouse can retain a portion of their monthly income equaling at least 122 percent of the two-person poverty line ($786 per month in 1988). By 1992 that amount will rise to 150 percent of the poverty line. A second provision exempts $12,000 or half of the couple's combined liquid assets, whichever is higher, from being assessed to pay the nursing home costs of the other spouse. The amount that can be retained cannot exceed $60,000, and the noninstitutionalized spouse will retain the house and the car.

Lastly, the law requires states to provide pregnancy-related services to women with incomes below 75 percent of the poverty line, and full Medicaid benefits are also to be given to poor children under one year old. By 1990 that cutoff will rise to 100 percent of the poverty line.

The new Medicare benefits are financed by two premiums. The first premium is applicable to all Medicare enrollees and was $4 per month in 1989, rising to $10.20 by 1993. (This amount was paid in addition to the regular 1988 premium of $24.80 per month.) The second, income-related premium, is paid each year in conjunction with federal income taxes by the 40 percent of Medicare enrollees with the highest incomes. Although the premium is income-related, in 1989 it was capped at $800 per year, going up to $1,050 by 1993. Even if enrollees choose to forgo the catastrophic benefits, everyone eligible for Medicare hospital benefits is required to pay the supplemental premium if their incomes are high enough to meet the taxation threshold.[20]

Despite the catastrophic health insurance bill, the gaps in Medicare are extensive. For example, Medicare does not pay for long-term custodial nursing home care, most dental care, private duty nurses, eyeglasses, eye exams, most prescription drugs, routine physical exams, and hearing tests and devices.

CUTTING FEDERAL HEALTH-CARE COSTS: THE DIAGNOSTIC RELATED GROUPS (DRGs)

In 1986 Medicare served 30 million people and cost over $57 billion, a huge increase from the $3.2 billion the program cost in 1965. The scope and costs of the program have grown enormously since its inception: in 1967 Medicare accounted for 2 percent of the federal budget; by 1987 it consumed 7 percent of federal outlays. In addition, hospital care in 1981 accounted for 46.3 percent of personal health care expenditures, with the federal government subsidizing 75 percent of those costs. From 1966 to 1981 the federal contribution to hospital care rose from 13 to 41 percent.[21] This fiscal burden led the federal government to seek alternative ways to decrease hospital costs, including the Diagnostic Related Group system (DRG).

In 1983 Congress enacted the DRG form of medical payment. Although earlier Medicare rules restricted fees hospitals could charge, it generally reimbursed them for the entire bill. The style of reimbursement was called retrospective (after the fact) payment. DRGs, on the other hand, are a form of prospective (before the fact) payment; the federal government specifies in advance what it will pay for the treatment of 468 classified illness- or diagnosis-related groups.

The DRG, a system developed by health researchers at the Yale–New Haven Hospital, is designed to enforce economy by defining expected lengths of hospital stays. The system provides a treatment and diagnostic classification scheme, using the patient's medical diagnosis, prescribed treatment, and age as a means for categorizing and defining hospital services. In other words, the DRG system determines the length of a typical patient's hospital stay and reimburses hospitals only for that period of time.

Exceptions to the DRG classification system are made for long hospital stays, certain kinds of hospital facilities (i.e., psychiatric and rehabilitation units), hospitals which are the only facility in a community, and hospitals that serve large numbers of poor people. The DRG classification applies only to the HI part of Medicare.

Additional costs beyond the DRG allotment must be borne by the hospital. Conversely, if a patient requires less hospitalization than the maximum DRG allocation, the difference is kept by the hospital. Hospitals may not charge the patient more than the DRG allotment. Hence, patients not yet ready for discharge, and who may not have appropriate aftercare services available, may be discharged —a situation which can result in patient dumping.

Proponents of the DRG system argue that hospital costs must be curbed, and that no painless way exists to accomplish that goal. Moreover, supporters contend that DRGs require physicians to be designated as the primary professional responsible for cost containment. Because of that role, physicians are forced to relinquish some of the financial incentives for unnecessary hospital admissions, lengths of stay, the overuse of medical tests, ancillary services, surgery, and so forth. Physicians, often removed from the economics of cost containment, are forced to acknowledge that "maximum efficiency leads to maximum reimbursement in the DRG system."[22]

Critics maintain that to enforce the economies required by DRGs, patient care suffers. Erring on the side of cost containment, necessary medical tests and ancillary services are often curtailed. Moreover, DRGs resurrect the dominance of the medical model since they emphasize the physiological causes of disease at the expense of the psychological correlates of health and illness.

Social workers operating in a medical setting may experience more stress as they realize that the urgency of discharge planning overrides the psychosocial needs of clients. Patients requiring additional recuperative time must either be referred to relatives, re-diagnosed, transferred to nursing homes, or simply discharged early. Lastly, some observers argue that DRGs fail to take into account regional differences in medical costs. In sum, critics argue that instead of making hospitals more efficient, DRGs only cause more problems for patients and, in the end, increase medical costs. Regardless of the arguments, both sides agree that DRGs are revolutionizing the American hospital system.

OTHER GOVERNMENTAL HEALTH SERVICES

Other government-sponsored health services include the Veterans Administration Hospitals (the largest network of hospitals in America); Community and Migrant Health Centers; services provided under Title V, Maternal and Child Health Block Grant; and the Title X, Family Planning Program, to name a few. The federal government has also supported the development of health maintenance organizations (HMOs).

HMOs have experienced rapid growth as enrollments quadrupled between 1975 and 1985, reaching a total membership of about 15 million members (one-fourth of whom are in the largest HMO, Kaiser-Permanente).[23] The 343 HMOs that currently exist take several forms; some are small membership-supported health facilities that hire their own medical personnel and provide clinic services. Other HMOs are large investor-owned corporations. For example, by 1984 seven of the 14 largest HMOs were investor-owned and accounted for half of all new members. Moreover, stock prices of major investor-owned HMOs rose by two to five times between 1983 and 1985.[24]

 HMOs typically provide comprehensive health care, often prevention oriented, for enrolled members. The members usually pay a fixed fee and are then entitled to free physician and hospital care. In 1973 Congress passed the Health Maintenance Organization Act which offered federal assistance to groups who wished to start an HMO. The federal government is also currently allowing the elderly to use their Medicare benefits to join HMOs.

Advocates of HMOs maintain that the concept encourages more efficient and less expensive medical care, and stresses prevention over treatment. Because doctors employed by HMOs have little incentive to "overtreat" patients and recommend unnecessary medical care, the system is expected to be more efficient. The economic rationalization of the system has in some cases occurred by requiring patients to see nurses or physician assistants rather than doctors.

Critics maintain that research studies show no evidence that HMOs provide better quality services than traditional medical settings.[25] Furthermore, these critics have pointed out that the presumed administrative advantages in HMOs can also lead to greater bureaucratization and impersonality. Lastly, some opponents maintain that the lower cost of HMOs is attributable to two factors: the capitation method of reimbursement has removed the financial incentive for physicians to overuse services, and HMOs generally enroll young, healthy, employed, middle-class individuals whose use of hospital facilities is less than that of the general public. Because they are usually linked to employment, HMOs have generally avoided the high users—the disabled and the elderly.[26] Despite these criticisms, HMOs are expected to grow in numbers and strength.

A COMPARATIVE ANALYSIS: HEALTH CARE IN SCANDINAVIA AND BRITAIN

Often intoxicated by nationalist rhetoric, Americans sometimes overlook what is happening in other parts of the world. The following section will briefly explore the medical systems of two Scandinavian countries (Norway and Sweden) and Great Britain.

The Norwegian and Swedish Health Care Systems

Although Americans often think of Norway and Sweden as socialist countries, between 90 and 95 percent of their industries are privately owned; there is complete freedom of the press;

and the populations of both countries seem to enjoy a material standard of life similar to that of the United States. The social, political, and economic systems of Sweden and Norway fit more into the concept of welfare capitalism than into a rigid socialist definition. Moreover, the stereotype of Scandinavian homogeneity must be reconsidered in the light of the increased numbers of resident foreign workers, many of whom are Pakistani, Greek, Yugoslavian, and Turkish.

The Norwegian Gross National Product (GNP) portion devoted to health care is considerably lower than in the United States, about 6 to 7 percent. Eighty percent of economic support for the Norwegian health system comes from social insurance and government revenues. Hospital and medical care is extended to the entire population; the Norwegian hospital patient pays nothing except for special amenities such as a private hospital room, for which charges are low. Outpatient physician visits and drugs require 20 percent copayment on the first three visits; subsequent treatment of chronic illness is free. (The copayment fee is waived for pensioners and the poor.) Dental services are publicly financed for school children of all income levels, although adults must pay privately.[27]

The supply of physicians is about the same as in the United States, with a ratio of about one physician to 650 people. However, there is a greater proportion of general practitioners than in the United States. Nurses are found in the same number as in the United States, but their jobs and responsibilities are defined more broadly. Almost all normal maternity cases are delivered in hospitals by nurse-midwives. Nurses, moreover, perform all but the most complex anesthesia procedures. The primary line of care is provided by the general practitioner and, compared to the American system, their role in patient care is greater. Moreover, the general practitioner has few ties to the hospital.[28]

Norwegian hospitals are generally owned and operated by local units of government. A patient requiring specialist care is referred to the hospital where practically all service is provided by full-time salaried specialists. The salaries and prestige of specialists are relatively high, although they can spend a small percentage of their time in private practice. All hospitals have outpatient departments where specialists see patients referred by general practitioners.

Preventive health services are similar to those in the United States, except for their breadth. Public health clinics, specifically designed for promoting child health, serve about 90 percent of infants, regardless of the socioeconomic status of their parents.[29]

The quality of medical services is monitored by the government through their control of medical schools and training institutions. Qualifications for specialists are determined by the Norwegian Medical Association, a nongovernmental entity. Because medical education is financed almost entirely by the government, student tuition costs are low.[30]

The Norwegian health care system incorporates a stronger government role than in the United States. Health planning is the responsibility of the government, and health care resources are distributed more equitably. In recent years, the development of hospitals and medical services has been influenced by an emphasis on regionalization. Cost containment measures have focused on strengthening the role of the general practitioner in providing ambulatory care. The Norwegian health system, like many of its European counterparts, has chosen to focus on providing broad health coverage rather than specialized care.

Although similar to the Norwegian system, Swedish health care contains subtle differences. The Swedish system of health care is a mix between direct governmental ownership and provision of medical services (most medical facilities in Sweden are owned by the government), and reimbursement of costs through an employer-employee state supplemental-insurance system. Grounded in a belief in medical planning, Sweden has a National Board of Health and Welfare which determines the number of training positions for each medical specialty as well as for general practice.[31]

The national health insurance plan is financed by compulsory contributions from employees, employers, and the national government. Although this insurance pays for only a small part of the national costs for hospitalization, it covers ambulatory care and compensation for lost earnings during illness. The National Board of Health and Welfare plans at the national level and has ultimate responsibility for the Swedish health-care system. This power extends to both public and private facilities, and regulates the work of doctors, nurses, and midwives. In large measure, health policy is determined at the county and municipal level.[32]

Swedish health services are comprehensive and inexpensive. Health care services under national insurance include hospitalization (costing the patient $5.00 per day), dental care, and physician visits (in 1983, $6.50 per visit). Most maternal and child health care is provided free. The maximum cost of medication for a patient was about $10 in 1983, and the combined maximum cost to patients for doctors and drugs was $100 per calendar year. Swedish patients pay only 1 percent of their out-of-pocket hospital costs, while U.S. consumers pay 33 percent of personal medical costs.[33]

Overall, the Swedish system of health care is more concerned with access than technological developments. For example, until recently only four Swedish hospitals performed kidney transplants, and heart transplants were not permitted. On the other hand, 99 percent of all pregnant women receive complete prenatal and infant care, in part explaining the low infant mortality rate. (In Massachusetts, one of the more progressive American states, 81 percent of white and only 66 percent of black women received prenatal care.)[34]

Health in Sweden is defined broadly. Strict rules, replete with mandatory jail sentences, are encountered by drivers who drink. Mandatory seat belt laws were enacted as early as the mid-1970s. Moreover, worker health and safety committees have the power to stop factory production if they believe a dangerous condition exists.[35]

The British Health Service

The British health care system differs from the Swedish, Norwegian, and American systems in several fundamental ways. The British National Health Service (NHS) evolved from a report written by Sir William Beveridge in 1942. The Beveridge Report maintained that a "comprehensive system of health care was essential to any scheme for improving living standards."[36] The NHS began on July 5, 1948 and, in the words of the Act, the aim was to promote ". . . the establishment. . .of a comprehensive health service designed to secure improvement in the physical and mental health of the people . . . and the prevention, diagnosis and treatment of illness."[37] The principle of freedom of choice was upheld, in that people could use the NHS or seek outside doctors. Doctors were guaranteed there would be no interference in their clinical judgment and were free to take private patients while participating in the service. The essential goal of the Act was to make free medical services available to anyone in need.

The NHS Act developed a tripartite system: (1) hospital service with specialists, (2) general medical doctors, dentists, and eye doctors were maintained on a contractual basis, and (3) prevention and support systems were provided by local health departments.

The backbone of the NHS is the general practitioner (GP). GPs are paid by the NHS based on an annual capitation fee for each registered patient; in 1981 the average list was 2200 patients. The role of the GP is to provide primary medical care; they are forbidden to restrict their practice to any special client group. Individuals can register with any GP provided they are willing to accept them. GPs see almost 75 percent of their registered patients at least once a year and, since mobility is low in Britain, many people retain the same GP for a considerable length of time.[38]

The GP has considerable professional latitude and equips his or her own office, hires staff, and may choose to work singly, in pairs, in groups, or in government health centers. Close to 50 percent of all GPs practice in groups of three or more. Health centers, part of the original Health Service Act, mushroomed in the late 1960s and 1970s, and by 1975, there were 600 nationally. Sweeping changes in 1967 gave the GP increased benefits, including a higher capitation rate if they have a patient load between 2500 and 3500. In addition, extra remuneration was provided for each person on their list over 65, for night calls, for transients, for maternity care, for family planning services, and for certain preventive measures. GPs also receive partial reimbursement for secretaries, receptionists, and nurses, as well as for the rental costs of their premises. Extra payments are also provided for seniority, postgraduate education, vocational training, for working in groups of three or more, and for practicing in underdoctored areas. In 1982 the average salary for a GP was $32,500 per year, almost double that of the early 1970s.[39]

The second tier of the British health care system is the physician specialist. Most patient referrals to specialists—except for accidents and emergency care—occur through GPs. Although employed by the government and under contract to a public hospital, physician specialists are allowed a small private practice. Patients in the community are served by GPs; in the hospital they are under the care of specialists. As in the U.S. system, physician specialists are accorded greater prestige and remuneration. In 1982 physician specialists earned between $30,000 and $38,000 per year, with approximately 60 percent of them receiving

extra remuneration in the form of a merit award.[40]

The NHS was reorganized in 1974, and at its head is the Secretary of State for Social Services, the person ultimately responsible to the Parliament. The secretary is aided by junior ministers and civil servants in the Department of Health and Social Security (DHSS), a planning and administrative body.[41] DHSS in turn delegates many of the detailed responsibilities to the next level of administration—the Regional Health Authorities (RHAs).[43] The primary task of the RHAs is to distribute the region's health resources in accordance with national and regional policies. For example, RHAs are responsible for planning hospital and consulting services, appointing hospital staff, and distributing clinical work throughout the regional hospitals.[43] The fourteen RHAs delegate activities—retaining primarily planning and supervisory work—by placing the day-to-day activities in the hands of the 192 district health authorities. The district health authorities have the responsibility to study area health needs and coordinate duties, and provide community health services such as maternal health clinics, district general hospitals, family planning, and various child health programs.[44] Lastly, the 1974 reorganization called for the creation of district level community health councils (CHCs), designed to provide citizen participation in a health care system characterized by professionalized central planning.[45]

The vast majority of funding—over 80 percent—for the NHS comes from progressive general taxation, with less than 10 percent coming from the more regressive form of social security payments. Payments for services such as dental care and prescriptions account for less than 5 percent of the program's funding.[46]

Health services under the NHS are relatively comprehensive, with hospital and primary medical care being free. Charges exist for primary dental and ophthalmic treatment (e.g., in 1982 a course of dental treatment cost about

$16.50; dentures cost between $27 and $98). In 1982, the cost of prescription drugs was capped at $1.70 per item; however, exemptions exist for children, low-income people, expectant and newly delivered mothers, and pensioners.[47] In addition, the government subsidizes medical education so that the direct cost to the student is low.[48]

Much of the American-based reporting on the NHS has tended to emphasize its flaws. While GPs sometimes express dissatisfaction with the system, the public continues to use it in large numbers. In 1973, only 2 percent of British medical expenditures were in private medicine. Even though private health insurance coverage and the development of private hospitals has expanded, in 1981 only 6 percent of the population was covered by private insurance, and only 1.9 percent of acute illness beds were pay beds. Although the number of people using the private sector for hospital care is increasing, less than 5 percent of medical care is delivered privately.[49]

The NHS is plagued with problems despite its high utilization. Critics argue that despite government efforts, in parts of Britain there are serious shortages of doctors. Furthermore, expenditures and resources under the NHS seem to be slanted toward hospitalization rather than primary, first-level care. Consumers complain of long waits in GP offices, and long waits exist for elective surgery (sometimes over a year). There is believed to be little wait for urgent surgery.

The long tenure of Margaret Thatcher's conservative government has had a devastating effect upon the NHS. Chronic underfunding and attempts to privatize the system have cast doubts on the long-term viability of the NHS. Lured by the prospects of lucrative research grants and high salaries, many doctors have emigrated to the United States or Canada. Moreover, some critics charge that the inequality in the British health system has resulted in higher disease and mortality rates for lower socioeconomic groups. However, for a system that cost $500 per person in 1980 (compared to the U.S. cost of almost $1100 per person in that same year),[50] the NHS appears to be serving the majority of the British population at least as well, and in some ways better, than the American health system.

It is difficult to compare the quality of the Norwegian, Swedish, and British health care systems with that of the United States. For affluent or middle-class Americans with good health insurance, the U.S. system of health care may well provide the best medical care in the world. And for complex medical procedures that involve sophisticated medical equipment, the American system is probably unequaled. Moreover, unlike the European systems, the waiting period for surgery, tests, and other procedures is relatively short. Lastly, American physicians are probably some of the best trained in the world. However, the American emphasis on expensive technology is not without a price. Medical care which emphasizes

TABLE 12.6. 1982 Per Capita Expenditure on Medical Care (In US$ at 1982 Exchange Rates)

Australia	$828	Greece	$187	Norway	$ 930
Austria	644	Iceland	865	Portugal	132
Belgium	544	Ireland	486	Spain	302
Canada	989	Italy	441	Sweden	1168
Denmark	746	Japan	602	Switzerland	1158
Finland	692	Luxembourg	601	U.K.	508
France	931	Netherlands	836	U.S.	1388
Germany	874	New Zealand	440		

Source: OECD, *Measuring Health Care, 1960–1983* (Paris: Organization for Economic Cooperation and Development, 1985), p. 12.

specific diseases rather than preventive medicine usually results in good care, but for fewer people. On the other hand, the European systems which emphasize personal and primary care, accessibility, local control, and free or relatively inexpensive out-of-pocket expenses for consumers, often reach more people. Moreover, these European systems appear to more equitably distribute health resources than the American system. The examination of health care in other industrialized nations raises important questions for American medicine. What is society's responsibility for providing health care for all its members? How much technological medicine can a society afford? How should medical resources be allocated? What, if any, limitations on personal freedom are permissible in the name of health promotion and disease prevention? These questions and others urgently require answers.

THE CRISIS IN MEDICAL CARE

Any analysis of the American health-care system must examine whether it works. The following section will explore some parameters of that question. Specifically, the section will explore two dimensions of the question: how the American medical system fares in relationship to other health-care systems, and its internal effectiveness.

In 1982 the United States registered the highest per capita medical care expenditures in the world, as illustrated by Tables 12.6 and 12.7. In that same year, the U.S. spent 10.6 percent of its Gross Domestic Product (GDP) —again, the highest in the world—on health care.

Yet, of all the major industrialized nations, the U.S. has the least social protection against hospital care costs—in other words, the U.S. has the smallest percentage of its population (40 percent compared to most countries which cover 100 percent) eligible for publicly subsidized hospital care (see Table 12.8). Furthermore, the United States provides the least social protection for ambulatory medical care, and the government covers only 25 percent of the population for outpatient physician visits compared to between 90 and 100 percent for most other nations. Lastly, social protection for the cost of medical goods (pharmaceuticals) is provided to only 10 percent of the U.S. population, again a low figure when compared to about 90 to 100 percent for other industrialized nations.

Accounting for the enormous costs of U.S. health care is problematic. For example, in 1981 only 17 percent of the U.S. population was admitted to a hospital (the costliest of health-care services). This percentage was in the mid-range of European hospital admission rates—a range that went from 6.2 percent in Italy to 21.4 percent in Finland. Furthermore, in 1981 the average length of stay in a U.S. hospital was only 9.9 days, one of the lowest figures in the industrialized world. On the average, Americans consulted doctors 4.6 times a year, less than the average for consumers in many other industrialized nations. Lastly, Americans used about 4.3 drugs a year in 1977, one of the

TABLE 12.7. 1983 Share of National Expenditures on Health Costs (Percentage measured in gross domestic product)

Australia	7.5%	France	9.3%	Netherlands	8.8
Austria	7.3	Germany	8.2	Norway	6.9
Belgium	6.5	Greece	4.7	Sweden	9.6
Denmark	6.6	Italy	7.4	U.K.	6.2
Finland	6.6	Japan	6.7	U.S.	10.8

Source: OECD, *Measuring Health Care, 1960–1983* (Paris: Organization for Economic Cooperation and Development, 1985), p. 12.

TABLE 12.8. Social Protection Against Hospital Care Costs, 1983 (Percent of population eligible for hospital care under a public scheme)

Australia	100%	Greece	98%	Norway	100
Austria	99	Iceland	100	Portugal	100
Belgium	98	Ireland	100	Spain	87
Canada	100	Italy	100	Sweden	100
Denmark	100	Japan	100	Switzerland	97
Finland	100	Luxembourg	100	U.K.	100
France	100	Netherlands	88	U.S.	40
Germany	95	New Zealand	100		

Source: OECD, *Measuring Health Care, 1960–1983* (Paris: Organization for Economic Cooperation and Development, 1985), p. 68.

lowest rates of pharmaceutical consumption among the industrialized nations.

Despite the huge amount spent on health care, the net benefit appears questionable. Life expectancy for U.S. females in 1980 was 76.7 years, over 1 year longer than for the United Kingdom, but less than in 14 other countries.

For males the life expectancy in 1980 was 69.6 years, less than in 17 other nations, including the United Kingdom. Infant mortality rates tell an even more striking story (see Table 12.9). In 1985 the U.S. infant mortality rate equaled 10.6 per thousand births, a figure that compares unfavorably against 19 other nations.

For much of the upper-middle and upper classes, often protected by good medical insurance policies, the health-care system appears adequate. However, for the rest of society the appropriateness of American health care remains in doubt. Of the 37 million people currently without health coverage (more than 17 percent of the non-elderly population), 36 percent are children under age 18. Although 85 percent of health insurance coverage occurs through the workplace, more than 30 percent of employers who pay more than half of their work force the minimum wage do not provide health insurance. Three-quarters of the 37 million noncovered persons are spouses or children of workers, and one in four workers earning less than poverty-level income has no health insurance.[51]

In 1988, Governor Michael Dukakis signed the Massachusetts Health Security Act into law. The Act requires Massachusetts employers to pay a minimum amount toward each employee's health insurance. By 1992, everyone in Massachusetts will be able to purchase health coverage. Premiums will be adjusted to the purchaser's income and will be subsidized by the state and employers. The self-employed, workers in large and small businesses, the unemployed, students, mothers, children, and the disabled will be matched to an insurance offering. Employers with six or more employees will be required to pay $1,680 per employee for health insurance provided either by the employer or through the state. Employers and hospitals will pay a smaller tax which will help subsidize the unemployed. The law does not compel anyone to accept or pay for health insurance, and Massachusetts will have a special hospital fund for the uninsured.

Although this bill encourages accessibility to medical care, it does not rectify the fragmentation of the American health care system. Employers will be able to maintain their current health benefits program, while individuals will be able to choose whether to be covered. Private insurance companies will continue to make profits while they underwrite the new law for the state. Even though this bill encourages health maintenance organizations and discourages an oversupply of hospital beds, the Act essentially allows for business as usual. Hospitals will benefit from this legislation by receiv-

TABLE 12.9. Life Expectancy at Birth (1980) and Infant Mortality—Percent of Live Births (1983)

	Life Expectancy at Birth (1980)		Infant Mortality (% of live births—1983)
	Females	Males	
Australia	78.0	70.9	0.96
Austria	76.1	69.0	1.19
Belgium	75.5	69.8	1.12
Canada	79.0	71.0	0.85
Denmark	77.6	71.4	0.77
Finland	77.6	69.2	0.62
France	78.3	70.1	0.89
Germany	76.5	69.7	1.03
Greece	77.8	73.2	1.46
Iceland	80.5	73.6	0.61
Ireland	75.0	69.5	0.98
Italy	77.4	70.4	1.24
Japan	79.2	73.7	0.62
Luxembourg	75.1	68.0	1.12
Netherlands	79.2	72.5	0.84
New Zealand	76.4	69.7	1.25
Norway	79.0	72.2	0.79
Portugal	75.0	67.0	1.90
Spain	78.0	71.5	0.96
Sweden	78.9	72.6	0.68
Switzerland	79.1	72.4	0.80
Turkey	62.3	58.3	(11.0 in 1980)
United Kingdom	75.9	70.2	1.02
United States	76.7	69.6	1.09

Source: OECD, *Measuring Health Care, 1960–1983* (Paris: Organization for Economic Cooperation and Development, 1985), p. 131.

ing hundreds of millions of dollars for bad debts and for indigent care over the next four years. Moreover, Massachusetts will reimburse hospitals for up to $70 million a year if Medicare payments fail to keep pace with inflation. Despite its drawbacks, everyone will be potentially covered, and the law may well eliminate a major portion of medical indigence in Massachusetts.[52]

Despite the promising situation in Massachusetts, the economics of health insurance are particularly problematic for the poor. On the average, purchasing health insurance from an employment-based program costs about $3,500 per year, more than half the yearly income of a minimum wage worker. Almost one in five employers in 1980 contributed nothing toward coverage of dependents and, from 1980 to 1983, the proportion of employees required to

pay part of the premiums for family coverage rose from 40 to 50 percent. These high costs explain why 60 percent of poor working adults have some private insurance coverage, compared to only 50 percent of children from poor working families. The health insurance situation is exacerbated by high copayments, the absence of coverage for routine medical costs, and the lack of dental and vision care.[53]

Evidence suggests that the overall benefits of increased health-care spending are spurious. For example, although there is an adequate number of health-care facilities, they are maldistributed among and within the fifty states. Some urban areas have surpluses of medical facilities, while rural areas cannot attract a physician. Despite increases in health-care spending, the number of children immunized against diseases, i.e., diphtheria, polio, whooping cough, measles, etc., has actually declined over the past ten years. Preventable illnesses and deaths caused by smoking, alcohol, industrial accidents, and industrial and environmental pollution receive inadequate attention by the organized medical community. Moreover, arguably the largest single public health risk, nuclear war, is rarely addressed by the mainstream medical establishment.

Although the poor see doctors at close to the same rates as the nonpoor, their health appears to be worse. For example, while overall infant death rates have declined sharply over the last thirty years, the black infant death rate is still twice that of whites. Moreover, the risk of death from all causes (except suicide) is higher for blacks than whites. In 1984, black men lived on the average almost six years less than their white counterparts, 65.5 compared to 71.8 years. Lastly, deaths related to socioeconomic factors, i.e., homicide and cirrhosis of the liver, have risen sharply for blacks in the last twenty years.[54] Medical costs have risen considerably faster in recent years than family income, and from 1980 to 1985 the consumer price index for medical care rose by 50 percent. During that same period many unemployed or laid-off workers lost their health protection.[55]

Inadequate care for those relying on the American health-care system is exacerbated by the gaps in medical coverage even for those who are insured. Private health-care gaps may include limits placed on length of hospital stays, dollar limits on payments to hospitals and physicians, exclusion of certain laboratory tests, refusal to cover office visits and routine health care, declaring individuals ineligible who are found to be in poor health when applying for coverage, and refusing to cover preexisting conditions. One of the most dramatic gaps is the frequent failure of private insurance to cover catastrophic medical costs—those costs which could reduce a middle-class family to the status of "medically indigent" within only a few months.

The problems of the health-care system were aggravated by fiscal cutbacks enacted during the Reagan administration. Despite campaign promises that Medicare would not be cut, the DRG system has made the program more unfriendly to the elderly. In addition, Medicare premiums were raised, and out-of-pocket costs for the first hospital day soared from $180 in 1980 to $492 in 1986. Not included in Reagan's "safety net," Medicaid has been a major focus of attack for conservatives who have maintained that Medicaid is a poorly managed social program that fails to provide cost-effective services to the most needy. These attitudes have resulted in federal cuts in Medicaid for fiscal years 1982 through 1984 and, as a consequence of these cuts and other budgetary pressures, over 40 states pared down their Medicaid programs.

In addition to reductions in Medicaid, Reagan also cut the budget of the Community Health Centers, a group of public clinics operating in medically underserved areas. The Children's Defense Fund estimated that after the 1981 budget cuts, some 200 centers cut back operations and 725,000 people lost access to medical services. Although some funding was restored in 1983, present levels (after adjusting for inflation) remain below 1981 levels. Other programs affected include maternal and child health services, where 44 states made cuts after the 1981 federal budget reductions.

Acquired Immune Deficiency Syndrome (AIDS)

If there is a crisis in public health, it is undoubtedly exacerbated by the present AIDS situation. Some medical experts predict that in the next five years between one and four million people will die of AIDS.[56] The number of AIDS cases has grown exponentially since 1981, and more than half of the victims in the reported 32,000 cases have died.[57] Furthermore, 50,000 to 125,000 people in the United States show signs of infection, and over 1.5

million people may be asymptomatic carriers.[58] The Centers for Disease Control (CDC) predict that 270,000 AIDS cases will have been diagnosed in the United States by 1991.[59]

The effects of AIDS have had a differential impact on various groups. Ninety-three percent of American AIDS cases have occurred in males, with 89 percent of all adult cases occurring in people aged 24–49. According to the CDC, 90 percent of all AIDS cases fall into three high-risk groups: homosexual or bisexual males (65 percent), intravenous (IV) drug users (17 percent), and homosexual males who are also IV drug users (8 percent). In addition, over 400 pediatric AIDS cases have been reported, and some estimates state that 92 percent of the nation's hemophiliacs may be infected with the HIV virus as well as 9.5 percent of their spouses.[60]

The federal government responded to the AIDS crisis by proposing a federal budget for 1988 which included $519 million for biomedical research, $100 million for general education, $55 million for the education of intravenous drug users, $92 million for testing and counseling, and $24 million to maintain the safety of the blood supply. Nevertheless, the federal government continues to use a traditional approach to epidemics: research, educate, find a vaccine, and leave the treatment to the states and communities affected.[61]

The cost of the AIDS epidemic is far greater than the resources presently allocated. The average cost of acute hospital care for an AIDS victim is $147,000,[62] and many epidemiologists believe the percentage of cases attributed to intravenous drug abuse is likely to increase dramatically in the next few years. Moreover, they believe that the greatest threat to spreading the epidemic to the heterosexual population occurs through the infection of the sexual partners of IV drug users.[63]

Intravenous drug users in many parts of the United States tend to be disproportionately black, Hispanic, and poor. Furthermore, many homosexual men are also inclined to be in the lower economic bracket because of discrimination. Therefore, those people at the greatest risk from AIDS are often the ones least able to afford treatment and care. Many of these AIDS victims will gravitate toward the public health system—specifically, Medicaid—thereby straining a system that is already close to its breaking point. With acute hospital care at $147,000 per patient, even if only 100,000 of the projected 270,000 AIDS cases occur among the poor, the amount required for care would be staggering.

The AIDS crisis affects the entire health care system. As AIDS finds its way into the heterosexual population, the cost of private health insurance is likely to rise. Moreover, insurance companies may require HIV tests for all potential applicants. It is likely that hospitals will be strained as they attempt to meet the enormous care needs of AIDS victims—victims who may live two years or longer with proper care. In view of a potential torrent of AIDS cases, society may be forced to make decisions as to the resources it will allocate to the humane care of the terminally ill patient. The AIDS epidemic has the potential to shape a profound public debate around health care and public priorities.

The American medical system is in an acute state of crisis. An increasing reliance on technology has swelled health care expenditures, often at the expense of providing basic health services. For example, from 1979 to 1982 the number of CAT scans increased from 194,000 to 600,000,[64] while at the same time low birthweight and infant prematurity were on the rise. Expectations around cost containment measures have, for the most part, not been realized. Moreover, in 1986 health care administrative costs in the U.S. accounted for $77 billion or 22 percent of total health care expenditures. This figure compares unfavorably with 6 percent in the United Kingdom and 8 percent in Canada.[65] The crisis in health care has led some observers to propose alternative schemes for American medicine.

Alternative Proposals: National Health Insurance and a National Health Service

National health insurance (NHI) schemes date back to the turn of the century. According to Paul Starr, while the United States was on the brink of establishing national health insurance a number of times during the twentieth century, factors unique to the political and social institutions of America prevented its adoption.[66] In the 1930s, NHI plans began to proliferate as part of Roosevelt's New Deal, but the idea was abandoned because of the strident opposition of the American Medical Association (AMA) —originally a supporter of NHI—and the fear that its inclusion would jeopardize passage of the Social Security Act. President Harry Truman took up the NHI banner in the days following World War II, but by that time, most middle-class and unionized workers were covered by private insurance plans. Again the AMA set its powerful political lobbying machine into motion, this time equating national health insurance with socialized medicine and with Communism, a tactic that proved successful in the "red hysteria" of the late 1940s and early 1950s. NHI bills were introduced into Congress every year between 1935 and 1965, and every year they failed.

The United States is one of the few industrialized countries in the world which does not have a comprehensive plan for national health insurance or socialized medicine. Moreover, the United States is one of the few industrialized countries where medical expenses can cause poverty. One 1980 study showed that: (1) about 85 percent of all people have medical coverage (private insurance or public programs); (2) only 29 percent of the population have coverage that protects them from catastrophic or major medical expenses; (3) only 40 percent of the population is covered for outpatient doctor costs, and only 44 percent for nursing home care; (4) less than 20 percent of the population is covered for prescription drugs.[67]

Although several national health insurance plans have been advanced, the most comprehensive one was proposed by Senator Edward Kennedy (and a number of successive co-authors). The Kennedy plan, supported by large segments of organized labor, included the following provisions: (1) A National Health Board would be appointed by the president to develop policy guidelines, manage the program, and to plan and then direct the yearly federal health budget; (2) a national health insurance corporation would be developed to collect tax premiums from workers and disperse them to private insurance companies, which would then process all claims; (3) every American would have compulsory health insurance coverage—workers would be insured through their employers, the poor through a special federal insurance fund; (4) NHI would be largely funded by an employers' tax (employers would pay 65 percent of the costs) and by worker contributions (35 percent)—if required, additional money would be provided by special federal and state appropriations; (5) benefits would be comprehensive and include inpatient and outpatient hospital care, all physicians' costs, laboratory and X-ray costs, nursing home care, and prescription drugs; and (6) cost containment would occur through federal regulation of physician and hospital fees. The annual budget for NHI, including maximum hospital and physician fees, would be approved by Congress yearly.[68]

Based on its broad coverage, the Kennedy plan would have eliminated the need for Medicare and Medicaid. Although this plan required a copayment of 25 percent, no individual or family would have had to pay more than $1,000 in any year.[69] Realizing that the enactment of NHI legislation was unlikely, Kennedy eventually embraced HMOs.[70]

Critics of NHI argue that it would modify payment mechanisms rather than encourage major changes in the health-care system. They argue that the nature of private medical practice would remain intact, as would the organization of hospitals and other health institutions. Although NHI schemes would equalize the ability of patients to pay, they would not improve the accessibility or quality of services. Furthermore, most NHI proposals call for coinsurance (copayments), a sum that many poor people would find non-affordable.[71] Contrary to the position of some opponents, NHI plans are not socialized medicine: hospitals would remain private, doctors would continue to be private practitioners, and most plans preserve a major role for private insurance companies. In the end, the bulk of the profitability of the health-care industry would remain in the hands of those who prosper from the current arrangement, although coverage would be provided to the entire population.

The second proposal represents a radical departure from NHI. Since the middle 1970s, left-wing health planners have worked with certain members of Congress to draft proposals for a National Health Service. Proposed by Congressman Ronald Dellums (a social worker) in the late 1970s, the National Health Service (NHS) would establish health care as a right of citizenship. Similar to the British model, the NHS would provide free (no fee at the point of entry and no indirect payments from third-party vendors) and comprehensive health care, including diagnostic, therapeutic, preventive, rehabilitative, environmental, and occupational health services. Also included would be free dental and eye care, emergency and routine transportation to medical facilities, child care, homemaking, social work, and counseling. To improve the maldistribution of medical services, the NHS would provide free medical education in return for required periods of service in medically underserved areas. In addition, poor communities would receive extra resources for funding, personnel, and equipment needs.[72]

The NHS would designate elected boards (two-thirds consumers and one-third health care workers) at four tiers: community, district, region, and nation. The budget of each service area would be determined by a survey of local health needs. Certain health services would be offered at neighborhood health centers, including primary care, preventive medicine, and occupational health. The district level would provide hospital and specialist care for a specified number of communities. The regional unit would be served by a training institution and a specialty-oriented teaching hospital. The elected members of the regional board would be responsible for the recruitment and selection of medical students and other health care personnel, the licensing and assignment of graduates, and the purchase of equipment and drugs for the region, districts, and communities.[73]

Elected representatives from the national board would be responsible for national planning and budgeting. To accomplish this task, the board would appoint six commissions: (1) quality (including certification of facilities and personnel, and research priorities); (2) planning and education for health-care personnel; (3) occupational safety and health; (4) pharmaceutical and medical supplies; (5) health rights; and (6) financial planning.

NHS financing would come from progressive taxation on individual and corporate income, supplemented by a gifts and estate tax. The goal of the NHS would be the elimination of private profit in the health-care system, and a national commission would be responsible for establishing a formulary of drugs, equipment and supplies, with regional branches purchasing these goods in their inexpensive generic form. Although private insurance companies would have no role in the NHS, the Dellums bill is vague on the abolition of private medical practice. While a national storehouse would be created for medical supplies, the bill would not nationalize industries that manufacture medical products, nor would the NHS provide for its own construction, transportation, utilities or maintenance needs.[74]

Proponents argue that the nationalization of health care would allow coordination of health services and reduce profiteering by professionals and corporations. Moreover, these planners believe that the experiences in other countries show that strict budgeting, nationalization, and the elimination of the profit motive arrests the escalation of health costs and, in the end, may prove less expensive than the present system. The National Health Service, often referred to as socialized medicine, appears to be the most unlikely health-care proposal to be realized. However, the reality of the present does not always dictate the future. As was illustrated in the Depression-era programs of the 1930s, America can make abrupt changes in a short period of time, and naysayers who predict more of the same are wrong as often as they are right.

Left unchecked and convulsed by wildly escalating costs, health care in America may someday be out of reach for the majority of citizens. Moreover, the increasing share of the GNP and the federal budget currently allocated to health care may soon reach a saturation point, making it non-affordable for all but the most well-off. Some critics suggest this situation may lead to a system of health rationing, whereby each person is given a certain amount of redeemable health coupons that must last throughout their lives.[75] Although the likely outcome of the American health care crisis is unknown, what is known is that left solely to the caprice of the marketplace the situation will undoubtedly worsen.

NOTES

1. Irving J. Lewis and Cecil G. Sheps, *The Sick Citadel* (Boston: Oelgeschlager, Gunn, and Hain, 1983).
2. Victor W. Sidel and Ruth Sidel, *A Healthy State* (New York: Pantheon, 1983).
3. U.S. Public Health Service, *Health—United States, 1985* (Washington, D.C.: U.S. Government Printing Office, 1985), pp. 146–47.
4. Ibid.
5. Sumner A. Rosen, David Fanshel, and Mary E. Lutz, eds., *Face of the Nation 1987* (Silver Spring, Md.: NASW, 1987), p. 75.
6. For a good historical analysis of the Medicare program, see Theodore R. Marmor, *The Politics of Medicare* (Chicago: Aldine, 1973).
7. Arizona has developed its own state medical program and is therefore not represented in much of the discussion of Medicaid. In addition, it also has its own Medically Needy program.
8. Isaac Shapiro and Robert Greenstein, *Holes in the Safety Nets* (Washington, D.C.: Center on Budget and Policy Priorities, 1988), p. 15.
9. Ibid., p. 16.
10. Ibid.
11. Ibid., p. 17.
12. Ibid., p. 19.
13. Ibid.
14. Ibid.
15. Rosen et al., *Face of the Nation*, p. 75.
16. Children's Defense Fund, *A Children's Defense Budget* (Washington, D.C.: Children's Defense Fund, 1986), p. 109.
17. Ibid., p. 107.
18. Rosen et al., *Face of the Nation*, p. 76.
19. Children's Defense Fund, pp. 110–18.
20. Spencer Rich, "Provisions of 'Catastrophic' Insurance Act," *Washington Post*, July 1, 1988, p. A21.
21. Quoted in Marie A. Caputi and William A. Heiss, "The DRG Revolution," *Health and Social Work* 3, no. 6 (June 1984), p. 5.
22. Ibid., p. 9.
23. Rosen et al., *Face of the Nation*, p. 75.
24. Ibid.
25. Howard Waitzkin, *The Second Sickness: Contradictions of Capitalist Health Care* (New York: The Free Press, 1983), p. 220.
26. Thomas H. Ainsworth, *Live or Die* (New York: Macmillan, 1983), p. 89.
27. Milton I. Roemer, *Systems of Health Care* (New York: Springer Publishing Company, 1977), p. 10.
28. Ibid., p. 11.
29. Ibid., p. 12.
30. Ibid., p. 13.
31. Sidel and Sidel, *A Healthy State*, p. 129.
32. Ibid.
33. Ibid., p. 132.
34. Ibid., p. 139.
35. Ibid., pp. 139–40.

36. Ruth Levitt, *The Reorganised National Health Service* (London: Croom Helm, 1979), p. 15.
37. Quoted in Levitt, p. 17.
38. Sidel and Sidel, *A Healthy State*, p. 144.
39. Ibid., pp. 144, 157–59.
40. Ibid., p. 172.
41. Levitt, *The Reorganised National Health Service*, p. 27.
42. Ibid.
43. Sidel and Sidel, *A Healthy State*, pp. 161–62.
44. Ibid.
45. Ibid., p. 163.
46. Ibid., p. 164.
47. Organisation for Economic Co-Operation and Development (OECD), *Measuring Health Care, 1960–1983* (Paris: OECD, 1985), p. 67.
48. Sidel and Sidel, *A Healthy State*, p. 172.
49. Ibid., pp. 145, 171–74.
50. Ibid., p. 174.
51. Children's Defense Fund, p. 105.
52. Bruce Spitz and Stephen Crane, "Massachusetts Has You Covered," *Los Angeles Times*, August 30, 1988, p. II–7.
53. Ibid., pp. 105–6.
54. United States Bureau of the Census, *Statistical Abstract of the United States* (Washington, D.C.: U.S. Government Printing Office, 1984), p. 78.
55. Center for Budget and Policy Priorities, *A Smaller Piece of the Pie* (Washington, D.C., 1985).
56. The figure of 4 million was suggested by Dr. William B. Walsh, a member of the presidential commission on AIDS. Quoted in the *St. Louis Dispatch*, September 11, 1987, p. 9A.
57. D. Ostrow and T. Gayle, "Psychosocial and Ethical Issues of AIDS Health Care Programs," *Quarterly Review Bulletin* (August 1986), p. 284.
58. J. Hamilton, "AIDS and Business," *Business Week*, March 23, 1987, p. 126.
59. Quoted in V. Wilson, "AIDS ... Education Can Prevent It!" *The Horizon*, September 1987, p. 4.
60. Staff Report, "Surveillance of Hemophilia-Associated Acquired Immunodeficiency Syndrome," *Journal of the American Medical Association* 265, no. 23 (December 19, 1986), p. 3205.
61. Ann H. Ash, "Long-Term Care Policy in Missouri for the Care of AIDS Victims." Unpublished paper, 1987, School of Social Work, University of Missouri–Columbia, pp. 4–5.
62. A Scitovsky and D. Rice, "Estimates of the Direct and Indirect Costs of Acquired Immunodeficiency Syndrome in the United States, 1985, 1986 and 1991," *Public Health Reports*, 102, no. 1 (January–February 1987), p. 5.
63. Le Ann Vogt, "AIDS in the Correctional System." Unpublished paper, 1987, School of Social Work, University of Missouri–Columbia, pp. 8–9.
64. Rosen et al., *Face of the Nation*, p. 76.
65. Ibid.
66. Paul Starr, *The Social Transformation of American Medicine* (New York: Basic Books, 1984).
67. Quoted in Diane M. DiNitto and Thomas R. Dye, *Social Welfare: Politics and Public Policy* (Englewood Cliffs, N.J.: Prentice-Hall, 1987), p. 226. See also *Health Policy: The Legislative Agenda* (Washington, D.C.: Congressional Quarterly, 1980), p. 11.
68. Ibid.
69. Starr, *The Social Transformation of American Medicine*, p. 404.
70. Ainsworth, *Live or Die*, p. 92.
71. Waitzkin, *The Second Sickness*, p. 218.
72. Ronald V. Dellums et al., *Health Services Act* (H.R. 2969) (Washington, D.C.: U.S. Government Printing Office, 1979). For a good summary of the Act, see Waitzkin, *The Second Sickness*, pp. 222–26.
73. Dellums, *Health Services Act*.
74. Ibid.
75. See, for example, David Mechanic, *Future Issues in Health Care* (New York: Free Press, 1979).

CHAPTER 13

Mental Health Policy

This chapter reviews the provision of mental health services to the seriously mentally impaired. Prior to the community mental health movement, states were solely responsible for care of the mentally disturbed. The movement to improve mental health services through federal assistance to states stalled, leaving many with serious mental illness without care. Lack of adequate care was compounded by a series of legal decisions reinforcing the civil rights of mental patients while requiring states to provide adequate services. As a result of these developments, many former mental patients are now living on the streets or in squalid single-room-occupancy hotels. Plausible solutions to this problem conclude the chapter.

Throughout American social welfare, states have played a prominent role in mental health services. During the nineteenth century, social problems attributable to immigration, urbanization, and industrialization overwhelmed the local poorhouses established during the Colonial era. In the United States, Dorothea Dix championed humane treatment of the mentally disturbed and, by the 1840s, she was instrumental in convincing many states to construct special institutions to provide asylum to the emotionally deranged. In fact, Dix's leadership was so persuasive that Congress passed legislation authorizing federal aid to states for mental institutions. However, because President Franklin Pierce thought that the federal government should not interfere with the responsibility of the states to assure social welfare, he vetoed the legislation in 1854.[1] It would not be until more than a century later that the federal government would assume a central role in mental health policy through the Community Mental Health Centers Act.

Consequently, mental health policy in the United States was articulated through the various states that operated their own mental hospitals. Originally, state mental hospitals were intended to be self-sufficient communities offering good air, clean water, nutritious food, and healthful activities, consistent with the dictates of "moral treatment." Considering the quality of life experienced by many Americans at that time, such refuge was sorely needed. Conditions of rural nineteenth-century America were no less dire than the conditions of urban America already described in the earlier discussion of the history of social welfare. A sample of newspaper clippings from an immigrant community in Wisconsin, circa 1890, reveals social conditions that were truly despairing.

> The naked body of the wife of Fritz Armbruster, a woman who had worked in Best's Butcher Shop, was found frozen by the roadside near Albion, 6 miles from Black River Falls. She and her husband had separated, he living in town, she living alone in the house. Although no one had noticed that she had been suffering from any physical or mental disorder, 2 years ago, the loss of a child is said to have affected her very deeply and may have led to her becoming partially demented. The probability is that she rose in a fit of delirium and wandered away. . . .
>
> Mr. Axel, a farmer living about 6 miles east of Kiel, Manitowoc County, cut his wife's throat a few days ago so that she might not recover and then killed himself. There were various rumors as to the cause of the tragedy such as domestic infelicity etc., but a few who

had dealings with Axel of late attributed the act to an aberration of mind....

Milo L. Nichols, sent to the insane hospital a year or two ago after committing arson on Mrs. Nichols' farm is now at large ... and was seen near the old place early last week ... He has proven himself a revengeful firebug.[2]

In response to these psychological casualties, the state hospital offered haven for the disturbed as well as protection for the community.

Admitted July 19, 1893. Town of Black River Falls. Norwegian. Married. Age 29. Seven children. Youngest 8 months. Housewife. Poor. First symptoms were manifested...when patient became afraid of everything and particularly of mediums. She is also deranged in religion and thinks everyone is disposed to persecute her and to injure her husband....

Admitted January 20th, 1896. Town of Garfield. Age 52. Norwegian. Married. Two children, youngest 19 yrs old. Farmer. Poor. Illness began 10 months ago. Cause said to be his unfortunate pecuniary condition. Deluded on the subject of religion. Is afraid of injury being done to him. Relations say he has tried to hang himself...September 29, 1896: Discharged ... improved ... Readmitted May 4, 1898: Delusion that he and his family are to be hanged or destroyed.[3]

An adverse social climate, coupled with the absence of welfare programs that buffered people from poverty, joblessness, inadequate housing, and illness, served to swell the population of state hospitals. By the 1920s the state hospital was an asylum in name only, and much of the care consisted of warehousing patients. In this milieu, some of the scientifically minded reformers of the Progressive era found eugenics a straightforward explanation and a surgically precise solution to the inundation of state institutions by "mental defectives." Proponents of the eugenics movement who believed that the human race could be improved by selective breeding argued that mental patients often suffered from hereditary deficiencies, and that

generational patterns of mental impairment should be eliminated by sterilization. Since adherents of eugenics were less concerned about the civil rights of individual mental patients than they were about the future of civilization, the fact that some patients might object was merely an inconvenience. In such instances, eugenicists obtained court permission to sterilize patients involuntarily. Many patients, of course, lacked either the mental capacity to comprehend sterilization or the advocacy of civil libertarians and had no idea that the surgical procedures to which they were subjected terminated their reproductive rights. By the 1930s 30 states had passed laws authorizing involuntary sterilization, and by 1935, 20,000 patients had been sterilized, almost half of them in California. Involuntary sterilization of the feebleminded generated great controversy, eventually culminating in a Supreme Court decision, written by Oliver Wendell Holmes, which validated the practice. Tragically, the case on which the decision was based involved a young woman in Virginia who was sterilized, only to be judged psychologically normal years later.[4]

MENTAL HEALTH REFORM

More humane efforts to reform state institutions invariably involved the National Association for Mental Health (NAMH). Begun early in the century as an extension of the work of Clifford Beers, who had himself recovered after being hospitalized for mental illness, NAMH become critical of custodial institutions operated by state governments. The issue of mental health attracted wide public attention during the Second World War, when approximately one in four draftees were rejected for military service due to psychiatric and neurological problems.[5] In response to the public outcry about mental health problems, immediately after the war Congress passed the Mental Health Act, which established the National

Institute of Mental Health (NIMH). Accompanying the Mental Health Act of 1946 was an appropriation for an exhaustive examination of the mental health needs of the nation. In 1961, NIMH released *Action for Mental Health*, which called for an ambitious national effort to modernize the U.S. system of psychiatric care.[6]

As David Mechanic observed, *Action for Mental Health* was a utopian vision of mental health care, the idealism of which conformed perfectly with a set of extraordinarily propitious circumstances. First, the postwar economy was booming and, with cutbacks in military expenditures, a surplus existed that could be tapped for domestic programs. Second, a new generation of drugs—psychotropic medication—showed promise for stabilizing severely psychotic patients who had before been unmanageable. Third, a literature emerged that was critical of the "total institution" of the state hospital, implying that noninstitutional—and presumably community—care was better. Finally, because of his experience with mental retardation as a family problem, President John Kennedy was supportive of programs that promised to improve mental health care.[7] These political and social circumstances did not go unnoticed by Dr. Robert H. Felix, a physician who had grown up with the Menninger family in Kansas and had developed a sharp critique of the state mental hospital as an institution for care of the emotionally disturbed. Felix was later to become director of NIMH. A primary architect of the community mental health movement, Felix was able to draw on his depth of experience in the Mental Hygiene Division of the U.S. Public Health Service as well as the breadth of professional and political contacts that three decades of public service afforded.[8] Felix's objective was as simple as it was radical. He intended to pick up the banner last advanced by Dorothea Dix and reassert the role of the federal government in the nation's mental health policy. Through the community mental health movement, Felix would use federal legislation to reform the archaic state mental hospitals. The legislation which enabled NIMH to reform mental health care was the Community Mental Health Centers Acts of 1963 and 1965.

THE COMMUNITY MENTAL HEALTH CENTERS ACT

Under the unusually advantageous circumstances of the postwar era, the Community Mental Health Centers (CMHC) Act was passed by Congress and signed by President Kennedy on October 31, 1963. The enactment of CMHC legislation was not, however, without obstacles. To allay the American Medical Association's (AMA) fears that the Act represented socialized medicine, the CMHC Act of 1963 appropriated funds only for construction purposes. It was not until 1965, when the AMA was reeling from governmental proposals to institute federal health care programs for the aged and the poor, that funds were authorized for staffing CMHCs. Advocates of the CMHC Acts of 1963 and 1965 maintained that a constant target of the legislation was "to eliminate, within the next generation, the state mental hospital, as it then existed."

> The strategy of the mental health leadership and their allies was to "demonopolize" the state role in the provision of mental health services and attempt to establish a triad of federal, state, and local support for mental health services. At this time, federal bureaucrats planned to blanket the whole country with comprehensive community mental health services. Their intention was not to federalize the total program through its financing, but to obtain a degree of control through the resulting federal regulations and standards.[9]

The philosophical basis for transferring mental health to the community was borrowed from public health which had developed the concept of "prevention." In adopting this formulation, proponents of community mental health presumed that services provided in the community would be superior to the warehousing of patients in state institutions. Prevention, according to the public health model, was of three types. *Primary prevention* efforts were designed to eliminate the very origin of mental health problems. Certain psychiatric disturbances seemed to be caused by stress—depression and anxiety disorders—which could be reduced by eliminating the source of stress. *Secondary prevention* consisted of early detection and intervention to keep incipient problems from becoming more debilitating. For example, screening school children for attention deficit disorders and providing corrective treatment could enhance a child's educational career and, thereby, enhance development throughout adolescence. *Tertiary prevention* consisted of "limiting the disability associated with a particular disorder, after the disorder had run its course." Typically, tertiary prevention activities sought to stabilize, maintain, and—when possible—rehabilitate those with relatively severe impairments.[10] It was clear to the community mental health activists that the state hospital addressed only tertiary prevention (and then poorly), while community mental health offered the prospect of incorporating primary and secondary intervention with a more adequate effort at tertiary prevention. The structure through which prevention would be operationalized was the community mental health center (CMHC).

According to the CMHC Acts, the United States was to be divided into catchment areas, each with a population of from 75,000 to 200,000 persons.[11] Eventually, NIMH planned a CMHC for each catchment area, some 2,000 in all.[12] Programmatically, each CMHC was to provide all essential psychiatric services to the catchment area: inpatient hospitalization, partial hospitalization, outpatient services, 24-hour emergency services, and consultation and education for other service providers in the community. Soon after passage of the CMHC Act, child mental health as well as drug-abuse

and alcoholism services were added to the array of services provided. To assure that patients were not lost between programs within the CMHC network, a "case manager" role was defined, whereby every case was assigned to one professional who monitored the patient's progress throughout treatment. Financially, NIMH provided funding to disadvantaged catchment areas through matching grants over an eight-year cycle. At the end of the cycle the catchment area was supposed to assume financial responsibility for the CMHC.[13] With this framework, mental health reformers believed that the CMHC was an effective alternative to the state hospital.

DEINSTITUTIONALIZATION

Enthusiasm for community mental health reform ebbed when a series of circumstances, beyond the control of the CMHC architects, began to subvert the movement. Despite promising growth in the number of CMHCs during the Johnson presidency, the Nixon administration did not look favorably on CMHCs and impounded funds appropriated for mental health programs. Although funds were later released, the Nixon administration had clearly stated its disapproval of governmental mental health initiatives. Subsequent legislation to restore momentum to the flagging CMHC movement was crushed by a veto from President Ford. By the time a more sympathetic Carter administration had assumed office, economic problems were so serious that additional appropriations for mental health were constrained.[14] Still, at the end of the Carter administration, 691 CMHCs continued to receive federal assistance. With the Omnibus Budget and Reconciliation Act of 1981, however, the Reagan administration collapsed all mental health funding into a block grant available to states for any mental health services they deemed fundable. As a result, the designation of CMHCs in direct receipt of federal funds ceased in 1981.[15]

In the meantime, many states planned to shift responsibility for the mentally ill to the CMHCs. In fact, the community mental health movement had proved a timely blessing for officials in states where the maintenance of archaic state hospitals was an increasing economic burden. As states discharged patients from state institutions, immediate savings were realized; moreover, "the continuing fall in the numbers of patients to be housed provided state governments with plausible reasons for abandoning expensive schemes of capital investment designed to extend and (or) renovate their existing state hospital systems."[16] Subsequently, 14 state hospitals were closed between 1970 and 1973. The prospect of substantial cost savings through the "deinstitutionalization" of patients received wide support. As governor of California, Ronald Reagan proposed closing all state hospitals by 1980.[17] Unfortunately, the transfer of patients from state institutions to those in the community was not well planned. Through the middle 1970s, the deinstitutionalization movement was characterized by "severe fragmentation of effort and distribution of activity broadly throughout government with little effective coordination at the state or national level."[18] For purely economic reasons, then, state officials were strongly encouraged to facilitate deinstitutionalization, regardless of whether or not alternative forms of care were available for those discharged from state hospitals.

Deinstitutionalization was further confounded by a series of judicial decisions in the middle 1970s which enhanced the civil rights of mental patients while at the same time requiring states to provide them with treatment. In *Wyatt v. Stickney* Alabama District Court Judge Frank Johnson ruled that the state of Alabama was obliged to provide treatment to patients in state hospitals and ordered Governor Wallace and the state to appropriate millions of dollars for that purpose—a judgment with which the state subsequently failed to comply. Shortly thereafter, in *Donaldson v. O'Connor*, the

Supreme Court determined that "the state could not continue to confine a mentally ill person who was not dangerous to himself or others, who was not being treated, and who could survive outside the hospital." Finally, in *Halderman v. Pennhurst*, the Third District Court established that institutionalized patients deserved treatment in the "least restrictive alternative."

As a group, these rulings had a profound effect on institutional care for the mentally impaired. Only persons dangerous to themselves or others could be hospitalized involuntarily. Of those hospitalized, involuntarily or otherwise, states were obliged to provide adequate treatment in a manner that was least restrictive to the patient. These decisions promised to be enormously costly to state officials who were trying to curb mental health expenditures. To comply with the court decisions, states would have to pump millions of dollars into the renovation of institutions that had been slated for closure. The solution, in many instances, was to use a narrow interpretation of *Donaldson* to keep the emotionally disturbed out of state institutions. Judicial decisions, coupled with the fiscal concerns of state officials, provided a convoluted logic which served as the justification for emptying state hospitals of seriously disturbed patients, then requiring the manifestation of life-threatening behavior for rehospitalization. If people were not hospitalized in the first place, the states bore no obligation to provide the adequate—but expensive—treatment in compliance with *Wyatt v. Stickney*. The criteria for hospitalization specified the most serious self-destructive behaviors; but, once admitted, patients were stabilized as quickly as possible, then discharged. As a result, those in greatest need of mental health services, the seriously mentally ill, were often denied the intensive care they needed. The consequences for the mentally ill were profound. In his interpretation of the legal decisions influencing mental health services, Alan Stone, psychiatrist and professor in the Harvard

University School of Law, observed that the true symbol of the Supreme Court *Donaldson* decision was the bag lady.[19]

THE REVOLVING DOOR

The shortfall of the community mental health movement, state transfers of patients from mental hospitals, judicial decisions assuring patients of their civil rights, and the deinstitutionalization movement in mental health, all combined to leave tens of thousands of former mental patients adrift. By the late 1970s, some 40,000 poor, chronic mental patients had been "dumped" in New York City, alone. The 7,000 in the Upper West Side represented "the greatest concentration of deinstitutionalized mental patients in the United States."[20] Reporting in *Scientific American*, two mental health researchers described their experiences with deinstitutionalized patients.

> Time and time again we see patients who were released from state hospitals after months or years of custodial care; who then survive precariously on welfare payments for a few months on the fringe of the community, perhaps attending a clinic to receive medication or intermittent counseling; who voluntarily returned to a hospital or were recommitted ... who were maintained in the hospital on an antipsychotic medication and seemed to improve; who were released again to an isolated "community" life and who, having again become unbearably despondent, disorganized or violent, either present themselves at the emergency room or are brought to it by a police officer. Then the cycle begins anew.[21]

High incidence of readmissions of psychiatric patients, the "revolving door," has become an increasing problem in mental health. In 1970 the ratio of readmissions per resident of a mental hospital was 1.4; in 1974 the ratio was 1.74; but, by 1981 it had reached 2.83, double that of a decade earlier.[22] Through the mid-1980s, the ratio of admissions per resident continued to edge up, so that by 1986 it stood at 2.98.[23]

Coherent mental health policy ceased to exist in the United States by the 1980s. State hospitals had been divested of much of their responsibility for patients with serious psychiatric problems, but a complete system of CMHCs was not in place to care for many of those who had been deinstitutionalized. As state hospitals converted from long-term custodial care to short-term patient stabilization, psychotropic medication came to be a routine form of treatment. But the psychopharmacological revolution, though consistent with the relatively orderly movement toward deinstitutionalization in the late 1960s, seemed incongruent with the psychiatric chaos of two decades later. Shown to stabilize psychotic patients until environment and interpersonal treatment methods could be employed, the prescription of major tranquilizers—Prolixin, Haldol, Stelazine, to name a few—seemed clinically indicated within the controlled environment of the hospital. In a community setting, however, psychotropic medication became problematic. Once stabilized on major tranquilizers, patients frequently found the side effects of the medication—dry mouth, nervousness, torpor, lactation in women, impotence in men—unacceptable and stopped taking the medication. But, without medication, such patients frequently decompensated and, without the regular supervision of psychiatric personnel, patients disappeared into inner-city ghettos or rural backwaters, further populating a growing homeless population. Definitive data on the psychological condition of the homeless are difficult to generate; however, a study of the homeless in Fresno, California, revealed that "34 percent were rated severely impaired and urgently in need of [psychiatric] treatment. An additional 33 percent were rated moderately impaired so that treatment would be of substantial benefit."[24]

CMHCS UNDER SIEGE

The diversion of patients from state mental hospitals eventually posed an enormous burden on CMHCs. Since the seriously mentally ill were often unable to get care from hospitals, the CMHCs provided the only service these people received. A Philadelphia CMHC reported that 44 percent of its patients were chronically disturbed and these patients consumed 70 percent of mental health services provided.[25] As a result, CMHCs had to restructure their activities, focusing on immediate care for the seriously disturbed and cutting back on "indirect" services, such as prevention and evaluation (Table 13.1). A study of 94 CMHCs showed that increasing demand for direct services to the seriously mentally disturbed began to skew mental health service delivery.[26]

Rather than being a mental health agency which provided a comprehensive range of services to all persons in a catchment area, the CMHC rapidly became an outpost for the ser-

TABLE 13.1. Percent of CMHCs Reporting Changes in Services

Service	Percent
Community residential services	+75
Services for young chronic adults	+72
Day treatment/partial care services	+68
Case management	+63
Outpatient services	+49
Consultation and education	−57
Prevention	−48
Evaluation	−36

Source: Judith Larsen, "Community Mental Health Services in Transition," *Community Mental Health Journal* (Winter 1987), pp. 19, 20.

iously mentally disturbed, a population that it was not intended to serve, at least exclusively.

While client demand escalated, CMHCs faced significant cuts in federal funding. As Table 13.2 illustrates, the Reagan years, beginning in 1980, led to dramatic shifts in the sources of mental health funding.[27] As funding from the federal government evaporated, CMHCs became more dependent on the states which

TABLE 13.2. CMHC Revenue Sources in Percent

Sources	1976	1980	1984
GOVERNMENT			
Federal	24	17	2
State	30	39	50
Local	6	11	8
(Subtotal)	(60%)	(67%)	(60%)
ENTITLEMENT PROGRAMS			
Medicare	1	2	5
Medicaid	9	14	16
Title XX	—	5	1
(Subtotal)	(10%)	(21%)	(22%)
NON-GOVERNMENT			
Client fees	3	4	8
Insurance	4	3	3
Other services	22	3	5
All other	1	2	1
(Subtotal)	(30%)	(12%)	(18%)
			(100%)
(Total)	(100%)	(100%)	(100%)

Source: Judith Larsen, "Community Mental Health Services in Transition," *Community Mental Health Journal* (Winter 1987), p. 23.

TABLE 13.3. Types of Staffing Changes

Clinical Staff	Percent of Centers Reporting Change		
	1982	1983	1984
Layoff, hiring freeze, attrition	25	16	8
Reorganize clinical assignments	12	11	6
Reassign staff	17	7	15
Add staff to fill vacancies	18	2	8
Add staff to new programs	11	2	0

Source: Judith Larsen, "Community Mental Health Services in Transition," *Community Mental Health Journal* (Winter 1987), p. 22.

had historically defined mental health care in the United States. CMHCs were able to compensate for federal reductions to some extent by obtaining more funding from government assistance programs. Significantly, nongovernmental sources, such as client fees and private insurance, continued to account for a relatively minor portion of CMHC operating expenses.

Precisely how this reduction in federal assistance affected the CMHC effort varied, of course, with individual programs. CMHCs in wealthier states, for example, were better able to weather the fiscal turmoil than were those in poorer states. Generally, however, CMHCs had to reduce staffing and programming, as Table 13.3 shows.[28]

By the mid-1980s, CMHCs seemed to have made the necessary organizational adjustments to funding changes, but these were at the expense of staffing and programming needs that were increasing. CMHCs were able to hire some new staff to make up for earlier reductions, but programming had stagnated completely. Eventually, the morale of CMHC staff suffered as mental health professionals could no longer see any relief from their inability to provide even minimal care to the seriously mentally ill. In San Diego, for example, county officials decided to target scarce resources for only the most seriously disturbed, drawing this editorial response from a CMHC staff member.

In the future . . . the community mental health clinics will provide little or no "talking" therapy

to their thousands of clients. Instead, most patients will find their treatment limited to a 15-minute visit with a psychiatrist and a prescription for expensive psychotropic medications—bought, incidentally, at taxpayer expense.[29]

ALCOHOLISM AND SUBSTANCE ABUSE

Mental health services are often associated with alcoholism and drug abuse. Human service professionals in direct services are familiar with clients who chose to anaesthetize themselves from stress with alcohol and other substances. Individual psychological problems are compounded by retreat to such substances, of course, not only affecting families of substance abusers, but also becoming more severe when addiction is manifested. The interaction of emotional difficulties, alcoholism, and substance abuse is reflected in social welfare policy and has been institutionalized in the Alcohol, Drug Abuse, and Mental Health Administration (ADAMHA) of the Department of Health and Human Services. ADAMHA oversees the federal Alcohol, Drug Abuse, and Mental Health block grant which consolidated several separate, or "categorical" programs established earlier, such as the CMHC Act. A block grant enables states to apportion funds according to priorities that they deem important. As a result, some states may invest more in mental health services, other states may prefer to fund drug abuse programs, while still others favor alcoholism programs. While the block grant method of funding offers the advantage of providing states with the flexibility of tailoring programs to their needs, it also raises the risk of defunding programs that are not topical. For example, the recent concern about cocaine use may well lead to increased funding for substance abuse programs which could be at the expense of alcohol and mental health programs unless there is additional money budgeted for the ADAMHA block grant. Because increased funding is unlikely, new cocaine treatment programs will probably be developed at the expense of long-standing alcoholism and mental health programs. Thus, mental health, alcoholism, and substance abuse services are interrelated at levels of both treatment and policy.

With the exception of a small decrease after 1980, Americans have steadily increased their consumption of alcohol since the end of World War II. By the mid-1980s, the average American drank a little more than 2.5 gallons of alcoholic beverage a year. However, that amount was not evenly distributed throughout the population. One-third of the population abstains from alcohol consumption; one-third considers its consumption as light; and, the remaining third are considered moderate to heavy drinkers. Approximately 18 million adults in the United States have problems attributable to alcohol use.[30]

These problems are directly related to serious social problems. Forty-eight percent of all convicted offenders used alcohol just prior to committing a crime, and 64 percent of public order offenses are alcohol related.[31] As illustrated in Table 13.4, almost 100,000 deaths are related to alcohol consumption each year.[32] In 1980, the most recent year for which data were available, the cost of alcohol abuse was estimated at $89.5 billion, over half of which was accounted for by lost employment and productivity.[33]

In contrast with alcohol abuse, the prevalence of drug abuse is more difficult to ascertain, since the use of controlled substances—the focus of drug abuse—is illegal. It now appears that drug abuse has begun to decline after peaking during the period 1979 to 1980. Still, by the late 1980s as many as 30 million Americans used drugs illegally. "During each of the last few years," reported one analyst, "police made about 750,000 arrests for violations of the drug laws."[34] While drug abuse stabilized, use of cocaine—or its popular derivative "crack"—mushroomed. The spread of cocaine among residents of poor urban communities as well as professionals in middle-income communities had become epidemic by the late 1980s. Between 1976 and 1985, the number of emergency room episodes attributed to cocaine use rose by a factor of ten, to almost 10,000.[35] The cocaine epidemic proved to be extremely costly to governmental agencies that bore the primary responsibility for interdiction of controlled substances as well as the incarceration and treatment of substance abusers. One analyst placed these costs at about $10 billion per year,

TABLE 13.4. Estimated Number of Deaths Attributable to Alcohol, 1980

Cause of Death	Number Attributable to Alcohol
Alcohol as the main cause	19,587
Alcohol as a contributing cause	19,048
Accidents	37,849
Violence	21,144
Total	97,528

Source: *Alcohol and Health: Sixth Special Report to the U.S. Congress* (Washington, D.C.: Department of Health and Human Services, 1987), p. 6.

although this does not include the costs associated with loss of employment or productivity.[36] But the rise in cocaine use became of urgent concern to public health officials when it was discovered that as many as 25 percent of persons having contracted Acquired Immune Deficiency Syndrome (AIDS) were intravenous (IV) drug users.[37] This posed a haunting specter to public health officials—IV drug users were no longer tortured souls in the slow process of self-destruction, but had become transmitters of an epidemic that promised to be as costly as it was deadly.

In response to the pervasive use of alcohol and drugs, treatment facilities expanded rapidly. From 1978 to 1984, the number of hospital units treating alcohol and drug abusers increased 78 percent (from 465 to 829) and the number of beds in these facilities increased 62 percent (from 16,005 to 25,981). However, inpatient facilities provided only a fraction of treatment services to substance abusers. Of the 540,411 persons in treatment for alcohol and drug abuse in 1984, 8 percent were in an inpatient facility, while 10 percent were in residential facilities, *but* 82 percent were under outpatient care.[38] Despite the expansion of treatment facilities, federal substance abuse policy moved away from a focus on treatment, emphasizing interdiction and incarceration instead. The Drug-Free America Act of 1986, for example, authorized $1.7 billion to reduce substance abuse, yet only 25 percent was allocated for treatment. Most of the funds appropriated in the act were earmarked for interdiction. Experts were not optimistic that emphasizing law enforcement would solve the nation's drug problem. "It would be naive to assume that this well-meant legislative effort will be an end to our drug dilemma," concluded the late Sidney Cohen, former Director of the Division of Narcotic Addiction and Drug Abuse of the National Institute of Mental Health:

We have not yet come to understand the resolute, determined, amoral nature of the major traffickers or their enormous power. Perhaps we do not even recognize that, for tens of hundreds of thousands of field workers, collecting coca leaves or opium gum is a matter of survival.

At the other end of the pipeline is the swarm of sellers who could not possibly earn a fraction of their current income from legitimate pursuits. If they are arrested, they are out after a short detention. If not, many are waiting to take their place.[39]

Within two years of passage of the Drug-Free America Act, Congress proposed more serious measures relating to interdiction: a federal death penalty for those convicted of homicide in a crime involving drug trafficking, and use of the military to intercept drugs coming into the United States. In terms of reducing the domestic demand for drugs, "demand reduction," extensive testing of employees in the workplace was proposed. When these proposals seemed of doubtful utility because of constitutional questions or program costs, some analysts proposed simply legalizing many controlled substances.[40]

High incidence of alcohol and drug abuse posed another policy problem for practitioners and program administrators—should abusers be restrained from using substances when they threaten the health of others? Concern about Fetal Alcohol Syndrome raised the prospect of incarcerating pregnant women who were alcoholic and demonstrated an inability to control drinking. The possibility of compulsory treatment for drug abusers became an unavoidable issue when drug abuse was associated with physiological damage to infants as well as the transmission of AIDS.[41] But compulsory treatment ran contrary to individual liberties guaranteed by the Constitution since it was possible only through some commitment procedure. Proponents of compulsory treatment and preventive commitment argued that it was the only way to protect future victims against the uncontrolled and hazardous behavior of addicts. Critics, on the other hand, contended that effective public education and treatment would make such draconian measures unnecessary.

This dilemma has serious implications for clients of substance abuse programs, as it does for practitioners. Compulsory treatment is likely to deter some people from seeking care for problems that they might have sought voluntarily, though perhaps at a later date. Compulsory treatment also places the practitioner in a role of social control agent, a role not conducive with building a client's trust. Unfortunately, the current focus on interdiction of controlled substances is likely to exacerbate these problems, since such policy decisions tend to be at the expense of treatment programs. As money is drawn from education and treatment programs, the substance abuse problem becomes more serious. Discredited education and treatment programs eventually give rise to calls for more severe methods of intervention, such as compulsory treatment. Compulsory treatment, in turn, drives the problem underground, further exacerbating the very problem it is intended to remedy. Without adequate investments in education and treatment, the future of substance abuse policy appears likely to be plagued by a series of such negatively reinforcing decisions.

THE FUTURE OF MENTAL HEALTH POLICY

By the late 1980s, governmental mental health policy was in disarray. Deinstitutionalization had contributed to the homelessness problem, with as many as 50 percent of the homeless being former patients in mental hospitals.[42] When winter threatened the safety of some homeless in New York City, a team of mental health workers was authorized to pick up those who posed a danger to themselves and commit them to Bellevue Hospital for a three-week observation period, a policy referred to as "preventive commitment." The first person picked up was Joyce Brown, who "was dirty, malodorous and abusive to passersby and defecated on herself."[43] To the chagrin of Mayor Ed Koch, Brown had been stabilized in Bellevue when attorneys from the American Civil Liberties Union challenged her involuntary commitment. The prospect that pending litigation might cancel the program led one supporter to observe that, "for the severely mentally ill, liberty is not just an empty word but a cruel hoax."[44]

Despite initial setbacks in preventive commitment, 26 states and the District of Columbia have laws authorizing the practice. The high number of treatment dropouts from outpatient therapy and the revolving door of hospitalization served to encourage local authorities to find some method for assuring that the seriously mentally ill would not deteriorate due to lack of intervention by mental health professionals. Preventive commitment

> provides for commitment of individuals who do not meet the statutory standard for involuntary hospitalization but who, it is asserted, are mentally ill, are unable to voluntarily seek or comply with treatment, and who need treatment in order to prevent deterioration that would predictably result in dangerousness to self or others or grave disability.[45]

A seemingly humane policy, preventive commitment presents serious problems when there are inadequate mental health services to see that it is used properly. Without adequate staff resources, preventive commitment can become a form of social control—as opposed to therapy —where treatment "consists of mandatory medication and little else."[46] One authority on preventive commitment speculated that mental health professionals will have little choice but to use "forced medication" as "the treatment of choice" for those in preventive commitment, and "actually track down noncompliant patients at their place of residence or elsewhere and administer medication as part of a mobile outreach team."[47]

For those concerned for the civil rights of the mentally impaired, such an eventuality is nothing less than ghoulish, an exercise in tyranny on the part of the state in the name of social welfare.[48] Even under conditions of adequate staffing, preventive commitment remains problematic. The side effects of psychoactive medication are so pronounced for many patients that they simply refuse to take it, even under duress. Among the contraindications of psychoactive medication is tardive dyskinesia, permanent damage of the central nervous system as a consequence of long-term use of medications such as Prolixin and Stelazine. Because tardive dyskinesia is irreversible and is manifested by obvious symptoms—"protrusion of tongue, puffing of cheeks, puckering of mouth, chewing movements"[49]—the disorder raised a haunting specter: in an attempt to control psychological disturbances, psychiatry had created a host of physiological aberrations. Because tardive dyskinesia appeared after long-term use, and sometimes after medication was discontinued, the number of mental patients with the disorder only promised to grow. In fact, one observer prophesied that the mental health problem "of the next decade is tardive dyskinesia."[50] Unfortunately, the critics of preventive commitment who cite the danger of tardive dyskinesia have no alternative for care of the seriously mentally ill which is economically or politically plausible. As a result, preventive commitment is likely to be a feature—however troublesome—of future mental health policy.

A more comprehensive approach to future mental health policy involves the integration of services and payment through a capitation method, that is being developed in Philadelphia and California. Under a capitation method of payment, agencies are awarded a predetermined amount per client with which they must provide a range of services. Agencies are funded the capitation amount regardless of the actual cost of serving an individual client. Such an arrangement has the advantage of being easy to administer, and it builds into the reimbursement scheme certain incentives that do not exist in other arrangements. Under a capitation reimbursement method, for example, agencies are encouraged to cut down on expensive services, such as hospitalization, since a surplus can be realized when the actual cost of care is below the capitation amount. In addition, agencies are penalized for neglecting to serve clients, since every capitated client represents a resource base for the agency.

An example of how a capitation method of payment could be used in mental health service delivery is the Integrated Service System (ISS) concept being developed in California and modeled after an innovative program deployed by Wisconsin. Under the California version, an ISS would be a nonprofit agency which would serve adults who were identified as suffering from serious mental illness. Each ISS would be assigned 150 clients who would become "members" of the ISS. In each ISS a staff of approximately 10 human service professionals would provide core mental health services to its members: 24-hour crisis intervention, supported independent living, vocational assessment, socialization and recreation activities, transportation, legal assistance, money management, and consultation with landlords and employers. Funding for the ISS would be derived from pooling the existing categorical programs that are available to, but poorly used by, the seriously mentally ill: Food Stamps, Supplemental Security Income, Title XX, Medicaid, among others. Based on initial calculations, these categorical funds would generate a pool that, when divided according to the client population, would provide the ISS with a capitation of $28,000 per member, or approximately $3 million for all services.[51]

Under the capitation method, the ISS is encouraged to provide comprehensive services to clients, but to do so in the most thrifty manner possible. Since the ISS must pay the cost of hospitalization of its members, there are strong incentives to offer other services instead. However, since the ISS is not reimbursed for clients who are not active "members," there are strong incentives to make certain that members remain in the ISS and do not leave the program. The capitation method has immediate implications for mental health program administration, as well. If the ISS were to provide the range of mandated services for $23,000 per member, or $5,000 less than the capitation, program administrators would have $750,000 in surplus with which they would be free to experiment with improving staffing or expanding mental health programming. Thus, capitation could generate surpluses that could enhance services to the seriously mentally ill.

The idea of integrating services through an arrangement such as the ISS is likely to become an important source of innovation in future mental health policy. Such an eventuality has significant implications for human service professionals who may miss an important opportunity to shape mental health programs unless they are willing to sharpen their administrative skills. The capitation of mental health services, as might be suspected, places a premium on fiscal analysis, cost-accounting, and strategic planning skills. In a policy environment where capitation is an increasingly prevalent method of assuring access to service while containing program costs, mental health administrators who are not knowledgeable about fiscal management are apt to lose program control to professionals from business and public administration. Unfortunately, there is a precedent for such a loss of program control. When Medicare and Medicaid subsidized long-term care for the elderly, human service professionals were slow to take advantage of administrative opportunities in the emerging nursing home industry. Eventually, long-term care came under the control of business executives who were not particularly sensitive to the psychological and social problems of patients in nursing homes. Outside the nursing home industry, human service professionals have had to lobby aggressively for the inclusion of advocacy services for the hospitalized elderly, a struggle

that continues today. The prospect of a similar development in mental health policy is as troubling as it is plausible. Social workers have been reluctant to become managers in human service corporations,[52] yet case management services for the seriously mentally ill "have enjoyed a rapid increase in prominence within the mental health system."[53] Unless mental health professionals increase their understanding of innovative administrative practices, such as capitation, they may find themselves working under the direction of business executives, or outside mental health services altogether. Such a development is unlikely to be in the best interests of the seriously emotionally disturbed.

NOTES

1. Jean Quam, "Dorothea Dix," *Encyclopedia of Social Work*, 18th ed. (Silver Spring, Md.: NASW, 1987), p. 921.

2. Michael Lesy, *Wisconsin Death Trip* (New York: Pantheon, 1973), Chapter 1.

3. Ibid.

4. Stephen Gould, "Carrie Buck's Daughter," *Natural History* (July 1984).

5. Walter Trattner, *From Poor Law to Welfare State* (New York: Free Press, 1974), p. 175.

6. Joint Commission on Mental Illness and Health, *Action for Mental Health* (New York: Basic Books, 1961).

7. David Mechanic, *Mental Health and Social Policy* (Englewood Cliffs, N.J.: Prentice-Hall, 1969), pp. 59–60.

8. Henry Foley, *Community Mental Health Legislation* (Lexington, Mass.: D. C. Heath, 1975), pp. 13–14.

9. Ibid., pp. 39, 40.

10. Bernard Bloom, *Community Mental Health* (Monterey, Calif.: Brooks/Cole, 1977), pp. 74–75.

11. National Institute of Mental Health, *Community Mental Health Center Program Operating Handbook* (Washington, D.C.: U.S. Department of Health, Education, and Welfare, 1971), pp. 2–6.

12. Foley, *Community Mental Health Legislation*, p. 126.

13. The description of CMHCs is derived from the *Community Mental Health Centers Policy and Standards Manual*; see *Community Mental Health Center Program Operating Handbook*.

14. Bloom, *Community Mental Health*, pp. 46–56.

15. *Statistical Abstract of the United States, 108th Edition* (Washington, D.C.: U.S. Government Printing Office, 1987), p. 104.

16. Andrew Scull, *Decarceration* (Englewood Cliffs, N.J.: Prentice-Hall, 1977), p. 71.

17. Ibid., p. 69.

18. Donald Stedman, "Politics, Political Structures, and Advocacy Activities," in James Paul, Donald Stedman, and G. Ronald Neufeld, eds., *Deinstitutionalization* (Syracuse, N.Y.: Syracuse University Press, 1977), p. 57.

19. Alan Stone, *Law, Psychiatry, and Morality* (Washington, D.C.: American Psychiatry Press, 1984), pp. 116, 117.

20. Peter Koenig, "The Problem That Can't Be Tranquilized," *New York Times Magazine*, May 21, 1978, p. 15.

21. Ellen Bassuk and Samuel Gerson, "Deinstitutionalization and Mental Health Services," *Scientific American* 238, no. 2 (February 1978), p. 18.

22. Steven Segal, "Deinstitutionalization," *Encyclopedia of Social Work, 18th ed.* (Silver Spring, Md.: NASW, 1987), p. 378.

23. Per conversation with Joanne Atay on September 22, 1988. Source: Division of Biometry and Applied Sciences, *Additions and Resident Patients at End of Year, State and County Mental Hospitals, by Diagnosis and State* (Rockville, Md.: National Institute of Mental Health, 1988).

24. Joseph Sacks, John Phillips, and Gordon Cappelletty, "Characteristics of the Homeless Mentally Disordered Population in Fresno County," *Community Mental Health Journal* (Summer 1987), p. 114.

25. A. Anthony Arce and Michael Vergare, "Homelessness, the Chronic Mentally Ill and Community Mental Health Centers," *Community Mental Health Journal* (Winter 1987), p. 9.

26. Judith Larsen, "Community Mental Health Services in Transition," *Community Mental Health Journal* (Winter 1987), pp. 19, 20.

27. Ibid., p. 23.

28. Ibid., p. 22.

29. Donald Woolson, "Policy Makes Short Shrift of Mentally Ill," *Los Angeles Times*, November 2, 1986.

30. *Alcohol and Health: Sixth Special Report to the U.S. Congress* (Washington, D.C.: Department of Health and Human Services, 1987), pp. 2, 12.

31. Ibid., p. 13.

32. Ibid., p. 6.

33. Ibid., p. 21.

34. Ethan Nadelmann, "The Case for Legalization," *The Public Interest* (Summer 1988), p. 14.

35. C. Schuster, "Initiatives at the National Institute on Drug Abuse," *Problems of Drug Dependence 1987* (Rockville, Md.: Department of Health and Human Services, 1987), pp. 1–2.

36. Nadelmann. "The Case for Legalization," pp. 14–16.

37. Carl Leukefeld and Frank Tims, "An Introduction to Compulsory Treatment for Drug Abuse: Clinical Practice and Research," *Compulsory Treatment of Drug Abuse: Research and Clinical Practice* (Rockville, Md.: Department of Health and Human Services, 1988), p. 2.

38. *Alcohol and Health*, pp. 120–21.

39. Sidney Cohen, "The Drug-Free America Act of 1986," *Drug Abuse and Alcoholism Newsletter* (San Diego: Vista Hill Foundation, 1987), pp. 1–3.

40. Nadelmann, "The Case for Legalization."

41. *Compulsory Treatment of Drug Abuse*.

42. Community for Creative Non-violence, *Homelessness in America* (Washington, D.C.: CCNV, 1987).

43. Josh Barbanel, "Homeless Woman to be Released after Being Forcibly Hospitalized," *New York Times*, January 19, 1988.

44. Charles Krauthammer, "How to Save the Homeless Mentally Ill," *The New Republic*, February 8, 1988, p. 23.

45. "Developments in Mental Disability Law: 1986," *Clearinghouse Review*, 20 (January 1987), p. 1148, quoted in Ruta Wilk, "Involuntary Outpatient Commitment of the Mentally Ill," *Social Work* (March–April 1988), p. 133.

46. Ibid., p. 133.

47. Ibid., p. 136.

48. See, for example, Thomas Szasz, *The Myth of Mental Illness* (New York: Harper and Row, 1961); David Ingleby, ed., *Critical Psychiatry: The Politics of Mental Health* (New York: Pantheon, 1980).

49. *Physician's Desk Reference* (Oradell, N.J.: Medical Economics Company, 1986), p. 2014.

50. Harris Chaiklin, "The New Homeless and Service Planning on a Professional Campus," Chancellor's Colloquium (Baltimore, Md.: University of Maryland, December 4, 1985), p. 10.

51. Task Force for the Seriously Mentally Ill, Lieutenant Governor Leo McCarthy, Chairman, *An Integrated Service for People with Serious Mental Illness* (Sacramento, Calif.: 1987).

52. David Stoesz, "Human Service Corporations: New Opportunities for Administration in Social Work," *Administration in Social Work* (forthcoming).

53. Charles Rapp and Ronna Chamberlain, "Case Management Services for the Chronically Mentally Ill," *Social Work* (September–October 1985), p. 417.

CHAPTER 14

Child Welfare Policy

This chapter examines the evolution of child welfare policy in the United States. Child protective services, foster care, and adoption have been the focus of child welfare policy since the 1960s. More recent child welfare issues include child day care, teenage pregnancy, and maternal and infant health care. The erosion of basic welfare programs that support American families increases the likelihood that the circumstances of children will worsen and that demands for child welfare will increase in the future.

In American social welfare, the condition of children is inextricably linked to the status of families. Because the United States has failed to establish a family policy that assures basic income, employment, and social service supports to parents, they frequently have difficulty in caring for their children. As families are less able to care for children, the demand for child welfare services escalates. In recent years, there have been increases in the proportion of children living in poverty, the proportion of children in single-parent households, the percentage of mothers in the work force, and the birthrate of women in minority groups. While an increase in a broad range of family and child welfare policies might be expected as a result of these trends, the societal response has been extremely varied. As Jeanne Giovannoni notes, "at best we have a hodgepodge of funding and regulatory mechanisms, and we rely predominantly on market mechanisms dictating both the amount and variety of care available."[1] A classification of child welfare services has been completed by the Child Welfare League of America which identified nine diverse components: services in the home, day care,

homemaker service, foster care, adoption, group home care, institutional care, protective services, and services to un-married parents.[2] Of these, protective services, foster care, and adoption are most frequently identified as being exclusively child welfare in nature and, therefore, are the focus here.

Child welfare services are often controversial because they sanction the intervention of human service professionals into family affairs that are often assumed to be private matters relating to parental rights. This dilemma places an extraordinary demand on child welfare professionals who are mandated to protect the best interests of the child while not intruding into the privacy of the family. Recently, this conundrum has been more pronounced as advocates for child welfare services demand more programs while traditionalist groups attempt to cut programs which they perceive as designed to subvert the family. Ironically, much of this argument could be defused if the United States adopted a family policy which assisted parents in caring for children more adequately, thus reducing the need for the more intrusive child welfare interventions. For the moment, this is unlikely, and child welfare policy remains among the more controversial in American social welfare.

HISTORY OF CHILD WELFARE POLICY

Although many states had established orphanages during the eighteenth century, current child welfare policy has its origins in the

1870s.[3] The large number of child paupers led Charles Loring Brace, founder of New York's Children's Aid Society, to remove thousands of children from deleterious urban conditions in New York City to farm families in the midwest. Eventually, criticism of Brace's methods, which were divisive of family and community, contributed to more preventive approaches to children's problems.

By the beginning of the twentieth century, most large cities had children's aid societies which practiced the "boarding out" of children (the payment of a fee for child rearing) to a sponsor in the community.[4] The "boarding out" of children until adoption (or, in the case of children with handicaps, those who were unlikely to be adopted) was the beginning of foster care and adoption programs in the United States.

Protective services for children began with one of the more unusual incidents in American social welfare. In 1874, a New York church worker, Etta Wheeler, discovered that a nine-year-old child, Mary Ellen, was being tied to a bed, whipped, and stabbed with scissors. On investigating what could be done for Mary Ellen, Wheeler found that no laws or ordinances existed which could justify intervening on behalf of the indentured child. Using her imagination, Wheeler enlisted the aid of the Society for the Prevention of Cruelty to Animals. Under a writ of habeas corpus, Mary Ellen—protected as an animal rather than a child—was removed from her persecutors and placed in a new home. The following year the New York Society for the Prevention of Cruelty to Children was established.[5] By 1922, 57 societies for the prevention of cruelty to children had been established to protect abused youngsters.[6]

Child welfare proved an effective rallying issue for Progressives who advocated for intervention on the part of the federal government. In 1909, James E. West, a friend of President Theodore Roosevelt and later head of the Boy Scouts of America, convinced Jane Addams and other welfare leaders to attend a two-day meeting on child welfare. This first White House Conference on Children focused attention on the plight of destitute families, agency problems with "boarding out," and the importance of home care. The Conference proved so successful that it was repeated every ten years—with the exception of 1981 when the Conference was canceled by the Reagan administration. Still, the White House Conference on Children served as a model for legitimating and attracting attention to social welfare needs. One significant product of the White House Conference on Children was the call to establish a federal agency to "collect and exchange ideas and information on child welfare." With an initial appropriation of $25,640, the U.S. Children's Bureau was established in 1912 under the Department of Commerce and Labor.[7] Instrumental in the early years of the Bureau were Lillian Wald of New York's Henry Street Settlement House, and Florence Kelley, an alumna of Henry Street Settlement and Hull House. Julia Lathrop, a former resident of Hull House, was the Bureau's first director.[8]

Because of the economic circumstances of poor families, child labor emerged as a primary concern of early child welfare advocates. The absence of public relief meant that families were compelled to work at whatever employment might be available, however wearing and demeaning. Children worked full shifts in coal mines and textile mills; women labored in sweatshops. Neither were protected from dangerous or unhygienic working conditions. Under the guidance of Florence Kelley, the National Consumer League fought for children and women using a dual strategy. First, the League advocated for reform in working conditions of women through regulating sweatshops and factories, and by ending the exploitation of children through prohibiting child labor. Second, the grinding poverty of many families could be ameliorated by a family subsidy which would make such deplorable work less necessary. For Kelley, the family subsidy was a preventive measure with which she was quite familiar; she had successfully lobbied for passage of the Funds for Parents Act in 1911 in Illinois. This act was a precursor to the Aid to Dependent Children program, part of the original Social Security Act of 1935.[9]

Before the Depression, welfare advocates could boast of a series of unprecedented initiatives designed to improve the conditions of America's poor families. The Children's Bureau Act of 1912 established a national agency to collect information on children. The Child Labor Act of 1916 prohibited the interstate transportation of goods manufactured by children. The Maternity and Infancy Act of 1921 assisted states in establishing programs that dramatically reduced the nation's infant and maternal mortality rate. Yet, these successes, however hard won, were constantly at risk of being subverted. The Supreme Court ruled the Child Labor Act unconstitutional in 1918, and the Maternity and Infancy Act was terminated in 1929 when Herbert Hoover and Congress refused further appropriations.[10] Child and family welfare initiatives remained dormant until the Social Security Act of 1935 ushered in a complete set of welfare policies.

The Social Security Act addressed child welfare in two provisions of the Act. Title IV introduced the Aid to Dependent Children program which provided public relief to needy children through cash grants to their families. Title V reestablished Maternal and Child Welfare services (which had expired in 1929) and expanded the mandate of the Children's Bureau, whose goal was to oversee a new set of child welfare services "for the protection and care of homeless, dependent, and neglected children, and children in danger of becoming delinquent."[11] Significantly, both family relief and child welfare services were to be administered by the states through public welfare departments. As result, by 1935 the provision of child welfare services shifted largely from the private, voluntary sector to the public, governmental sector.

PROTECTIVE SERVICES FOR CHILDREN

Through the Social Security Act, states proceeded to develop services to children independent of one another and within the relatively loose specifications of the act. Free of a centralized authority that would assure standardized care throughout the United States, child welfare services varied greatly from state to state and even within states. In the two decades following the passage of the Social Security Act, child welfare services had become established within American social welfare, but with a high degree of fragmentation.

By the 1960s, the status quo in child welfare was upset by reports of increasing incidents of child abuse and neglect. A pediatrician, C. Henry Kempe, identified non-accidental injuries to children as the "battered child syndrome." As more states began to address the problem, child welfare advocates built a compelling case for a national standard for child protective services. This lobbying led to the passage of the Child Abuse Prevention and Treatment Act of 1974, establishing the National Center for Child Abuse and Neglect within the Department of Health and Human Services, as well as a model statute for state child protective programs. All 50 states eventually enacted the model statute which specified among its provisions:

1. a standard definition of child abuse and neglect;
2. methods for reporting and investigating abuse and neglect;
3. immunity for those reporting suspected injuries to children; and
4. prevention and public education efforts to reduce incidents of abuse and neglect.

As a result of these national standards, the National Center for Child Abuse and Neglect was able to report—for the first time—trends in the need for protective services for children.

Alarmingly, the data collected by the National Center revealed a dramatic increase in reports of child abuse, which more than doubled between 1976 and 1986 when reports of child abuse numbered 2 million.[12] Most troubling about this trend was that reports of child abuse continued to climb through the mid-1980s, while at the same time expenditures for child protective services were decreasing.[13]

Increases in child abuse reports and decreases in expenditures led to a crisis in child welfare services. The magnitude of this crisis has been mapped by Douglas Besharov, an authority on child welfare policy.

Of the 1,000 children who die under circumstances suggestive of parental maltreatment each year, between 30 and 50 percent were previously reported to child protective agencies. Many thousands of other children suffer serious injuries after their plight becomes known to authorities.... Each year, about 50,000 children with *observable injuries severe enough to require hospitalization are not reported* (original emphasis).[14]

Stories of child abuse fatalities began to appear with greater frequency in the media. Shortly before Thanksgiving of 1987, the report of the beating death of a six-year-old girl under the care of a middle-class couple in Greenwich Village became a feature story in *Newsweek*.[15] Unfortunately, incidents of child abuse were too often associated with child welfare programs mandated to protect children. In Kansas City, 25 percent of children in foster care were found to have been abused.[16] During the spring of 1988, National Public Radio broadcast a report of two Illinois state "social workers" who had been dismissed for failure to make home visits and falsification of records which were associated with the deaths of two children who had been reported as victims of child abuse.[17] In Baltimore, a group of current and former foster children won a decision in the Fourth District Court of Appeals—*Ruth Massinga v. L.J. et al.*—charging that 20 administrators and caseworkers of the Baltimore City Department of Social Services failed "to adequately monitor and protect children in foster care."[18] Such litigation placed child welfare personnel in a double bind: being faced with increasing demands for services, yet not having adequate staff resources to respond effectively. "If you take children out of the home, you're snatching them. If you leave them in the home [and they're abused], you didn't protect them," complained Jim Bell of the Massachusetts Department of Social Services. "We try to deal the best we can in that environment and protect the [case]workers. We don't want them hanging out there all alone."[19]

The rapid deterioration of child welfare services led children's advocates to call for more funding of social services. But proposals for increased support for child welfare services did not go unchallenged. Ambiguity in the definition of what constituted child abuse and neglect had contributed to incidents in which child welfare workers appeared to disregard parental rights in their eagerness to protect children. Perhaps the most notorious instance of such overzealousness occurred during the summer of 1984, when social workers from the Vermont state social and rehabilitation services department and the state police rounded up 112 children from "a radical Christian sect" and detained them for three days to detect indications of abuse. When the American Civil Liberties Union threatened to sue the state on behalf of the religious community, state officials reconsidered, and the children were returned to their parents.[20] Similar, but less newsworthy incidents enraged parents who, feeling unjustly accused, formed VOCAL (Victims of Child Abuse Laws) as an attempt to restore traditional parental rights in the face of what they perceive to be the intrusiveness of the state. The 3000 members of VOCAL have taken their complaint into the public arena, and, in Arizona, VOCAL held up a $5.4 million appropriation to improve child protective services.[21]

The critique of child welfare professionals has not been limited to fundamentalists. In *The War Over the Family*, Bridgette Berger, a sociology professor at Wellesley College, and Peter Berger, a sociology professor at Boston University, argued vociferously that middle-class social workers use the public social services as a method to evangelize among lower-class clients, thereby manipulating the concept of children's rights as a way to undermine the family for the purpose of establishing professional hegemony in family affairs. Consequently, the Bergers suggest that, in questions of parental versus child rights, it is preferable to "trust parents over against experts."[22] While the Bergers' analysis undoubtedly adds credence to groups such as VOCAL, it does little to advance solutions to the urgent problem of child abuse. Apart from reducing a complex social issue to a question of rights, the Bergers leave an important question unanswered: If public welfare workers are faulted for being so far removed from the experiences of their poor and troubled clients, how much more distant are professors from prestigious, private colleges?

FOSTER CARE FOR CHILDREN

When parents are unable to care for their children, foster care is often used to provide alternative care. As an extension of the practice of "boarding out," most foster care in the United States is at no cost to parents, and children are placed in homes of other families. There is an important relationship between child protective services and foster care in American social welfare. Foster care is a primary service for victims of child abuse; over half of children in foster care were placed there by child protective service workers. The second most prevalent reason for child foster care is the "condition or absence of the parent," ac-

counting for about 20 percent of foster care placements.[23]

As in the case of protective services, foster care for children was not coordinated under provisions of the Social Security Act. States adopted separate policies and, unfortunately, took few measures to monitor children in foster care. During the early 1960s, a series of studies began to document a disturbing development. Rather than being a temporary arrangement for child care, foster care had become a long-term experience for many youngsters—70 percent of children had been in foster care for more than one year.[24] Not only had states planned poorly for the reunification of children with their original families, but in many instances, child welfare agencies had lost track of children altogether.

In response to this situation, several demonstration projects were begun that offered intensive services to families in order to prevent placement of children in foster care, and to effectively reunite children with their biological parents. The demonstrations seemed to be cost-effective. In Virginia, 14 pre-foster care placement service projects concluded that family function improved in 69 percent of families receiving intensive support services. Moreover, the cost of support services was $1,214 per child, substantially less than the cost of foster care ($11,173) or residential care ($22,025) for the average length of time (4.6 years) a child was in these more intensive forms of treatments.[25] As a result of these field experiments, "permanency planning" became a central feature of the Adoption Assistance and Child Welfare Act of 1980.

Permanency planning is "the systematic process of carrying out, within a brief time-limited period, a set of goal-directed activities designed to help children live in families that offer continuity of relationships with nurturing parents or caretakers and the opportunity to establish lifetime relationships."[26] The Child Welfare Act was an ambitious effort, and one expert heralded it as making it "possible to

implement at state and local levels a comprehensive service delivery system for children."[27]
As a result of permanency planning, the number of children in foster care plummeted. In
1977, 500,000 children were in foster care; by
1983 the number had dropped to 251,000. Welfare workers swiftly removed children from
foster care and reunited them with their biological families under the rationale that community support services would assist parents.
Tragically, biological parents received few of
these support services, and the inability of
parents to care for their children contributed to
the need for child protective services. In the
absence of intensive support services, permanency planning for many children meant a
revolving door—placement in foster care, reunification with the biological parent(s), and a
return to foster care. In 1982, 43 percent of
children had been in multiple placements, but
by 1983, 53.1 percent had been in more than
one placement. Of this number, 20.1 percent
had been placed twice, 24.2 percent three to
five times and 8.8 percent six or more times.[28]
The National Association of Social Workers
newsletter reported the instance of a four-year-
old New York boy who was placed in 37 different homes in two months, and another who
had been placed in 17 homes in 25 days.[29]

In large measure, the permanency planning movement faltered due to lack of support
services to families. Not long after passage of
the Adoption Assistance and Child Welfare
Act of 1980, Ronald Rooney observed pro-
phetically that "if the promise of permanency
planning is to be realized, those who allocate
funds must provide money for a continuum of
services that are delivered from the point of
entry into foster care and include programs
designed to prevent the removal of children
from their homes."[30] Yet, in 1981 an important
source of family support services, Title XX,
was cut 21 percent. For 1986 the Title XX appropriation, $2.7 billion, was $200 million *less*
than the amount funded in 1981, *despite a 58
percent increase in reports of child abuse and*

neglect since that time.[31] A decade after the
early permanency planning demonstration projects, Theodore Stein feared that the movement was being subverted by budget cuts and a
reliance on crisis services in child welfare.[32]

To compound the problems faced by
foster care workers, quality foster care placements became scarce. A declining standard of
living forced many women into the job market,
restricting the pool of families with a parent at
home to supervise children[33]—a requisite for
desirable foster care. Soon the shortage of
foster homes became critical. The director of
the Illinois Department of Children and Family
Services pleaded for 1000 new foster parents to
prevent collapse of the state's foster care program.[34] In an investigation into the death of
one foster care child, a Virginia grand jury
cited "the acute shortage of suitable shelter for
the 6000 neglected, abused, and disabled children" in the state as a factor contributing to the
child's death.[35] Thus, by the late 1980s, permanency planning was beset with multiple problems, leaving foster care as an unreliable way
to serve many of the most troubled children in
the United States. In 1986 the National Committee for Prevention of Child Abuse reported
that child deaths had increased dramatically
due to "the current overload of state child
welfare systems."

> In the twenty-four states for which data were
> available, the number of confirmed or sus-
> pected child deaths increased 26.7 percent over
> 1985, from 386 to 489, whereas deaths in those
> same states had declined by 2 percent between
> 1984 and 1985.[36]

ADOPTION

From the standpoint of permanency planning,
adoption has become an important child welfare
service. In the early 1980s, the Children's
Bureau noted that 50,000 "hard to adopt"
children were waiting for homes. Many of
these children were of minority origin, handi-

capped, older, and had been in foster care for several years.[37] Because such children posed a financial burden for adopting parents, the Adoption Assistance and Child Welfare Act of 1980 provided subsidies to adoptive parents. In 1983, 6320 children were being subsidized each month at a cost of $12 million.[38] Providing incentives for parents to adopt hard-to-adopt children clearly supported the concept of permanency planning: "90 percent of subsidized adoptions involve foster parents whom the subsidy has enabled to adopt children with whom they had formed a relationship . . . and most of these are minorities or have special needs."[39] Moreover, subsidized adoption proved cost effective, costing 37 percent less than foster care.

Still, adoption is not without controversy. Because children come from a variety of racial and cultural groups, the issue of transcultural adoption is raised. Should consideration be given to maintaining the cultural identity of children placed for adoption by finding them homes in their "native" culture? This question is at the heart of the Indian Child Welfare Act of 1978. Native Americans were disturbed that "25 to 35 percent of all American Indian children [were] separated from their families and placed in foster homes, adoptive homes, or institutions."[40] However, the fact that 85 percent of such placements were in non-Indian families "without access to their tribal homes and relationships" raised the specter of cultural genocide.[41] To reinforce the cultural identity of Native American children, the Indian Child Welfare Act established:

> Minimal Federal standards for the removal of Indian children from their families and the placement of such children in foster or adoptive homes which will reflect the unique values of Indian culture, and [by providing] for assistance to Indian tribes in the operation of child and family service programs.[42]

Importantly, the Indian Child Welfare Act established tribes, rather than state courts, as the governing bodies for Indian foster children.

While provisions to retain the cultural identity of children are unquestionably valid for a pluralistic society, the circumstances of many racial and cultural minorities leave the implementation of such policies in doubt. Without basic health, education, and employment supports, minority families are likely to have difficulty in considering the adoption of children. For example, the number of black children available for adoption far outstrips the number of black families recruited to adopt children *despite the fact that "black families adopt at a rate 4.5 times greater than white or Hispanic families."*[43]

Changes in family composition further cloud the picture. The pool of adoptive families has diminished with the increase in the number of female-headed households. The combination of low wages for women and a shortage of marriageable men mean that mothers are encouraged to maintain small families, not expand them through adoption. Esther Wattenberg of the University of Minnesota Center for Urban and Regional Affairs suspected that:

> . . . the remainder of the 1980s and the decade beyond will be dominated by a sorting out of "the best interests of the child" in the extraordinary complex family relationships that develop out of extending family boundaries to stepparents, several sets of grandparents, and an assortment of new siblings from remarried families that join and unjoin family compositions.[44]

This high degree of family reorganization is likely to affect minority families, leaving child welfare workers with a small pool of traditionally structured families as foster or adoptive parents. To the extent that family reorganization becomes pronounced among minority populations, minority families will be less able to adopt children. At the same time, the comparative economic advantage enjoyed by white families, coupled with the low fertility rate of white women, means they will continue to adopt, and those adopted will often be minority children. As a result, the issue of transcultural adoption is likely to trouble child welfare professionals in the future.

EMERGING ISSUES IN CHILD WELFARE

Changes in the economic and social circumstances of American families have broadened the scope of issues that have defined child welfare policy of the past. Of these changes, three are likely to shape child welfare of the future: day care, maternal and child health, and teenage pregnancy. Day care for children has risen in importance as more parents with children work. The need for child day care is felt by both middle-income families, where both parents work in order to meet the income requirements of a middle-class life style, as well as low-income families, where a parent is encouraged, or required, to participate in a workfare program. The child care available for these families is often unreliable, expensive, and of questionable quality. Furthermore, available child care does not often conform to the work schedule of parents. A study of New York City families found that half had to patch together day care from multiple providers. Low wages fail to attract more-skilled providers to the field, leading the Children's Defense Fund to observe ruefully that "despite their higher levels of education, child care providers are paid less than animal caretakers, bartenders, or parking lot and amusement park attendants."[45]

The primary policies assisting parents with child care are the Federal Dependent Care Tax Credit and Title XX, neither of which has expanded child care for low-income families. The child care tax credit allows families to deduct up to 30 percent of $2,400 spent on child day care for a given year. Unfortunately, this policy requires poor families to pay the out-of-pocket expenses before they receive a partial rebate at a later date. Few poor families can afford this. Under Title XX, states were able to purchase day care for poor families, but few appropriated significant funds for that purpose.

The crisis in child day care received nationwide attention in 1986 when two Miami children, unsupervised because their mother had to work and could not locate child care, climbed into a clothes dryer in which they "tumbled and burned to death."[46] This incident was cited in the introductory remarks of the proposed $375 million Child Care Services Improvement Act. An indicator of the severity of the day care crisis is that the legislation was sponsored by Orrin Hatch, a conservative senator noted for his prior opposition to social welfare legislation.[47]

Maternal and child health has emerged as an issue among child welfare advocates as younger, poor women give birth to low birth weight babies for which they have received inadequate prenatal care. Low birth weight is a concern because such infants evidence higher incidence of developmental disabilities, some of which are permanent, and eventually require institutional care. The relationship between low birth weight and developmental disabilities, long recognized by public health officials, resurfaced in *Hunger in America*, a 1985 report by the Physician Task Force on Hunger in America funded through the Harvard University School of Public Health. In this report, researchers noted that "low birth-weight is the eighth leading cause of death in the United States." Efforts to sustain premature and low birth weight infants are expensive and, even when successful, the consequence is often "long-term growth and developmental problems." Infants born small and premature suffer 25 percent more major neurological problems and 117 percent more minor neurological problems compared to normal infants.[48] Despite such documentation, the incidence of low birth weight among infants in the United States is relatively high as indicated in Table 14.1. But, the percent of low birth weight infants born to nonwhite teenagers is alarming, ranging from a

TABLE 14.1. **Percent of Births That Were Low Birth Weight, Total, 1984**

Rank	State Name	Rate
1	North Dakota	4.8
2	Alaska	4.8
3	Iowa	4.9
4	Minnesota	4.9
5	New Hampshire	5.0
6	South Dakota	5.1
7	Washington	5.1
8	Idaho	5.1
9	Wisconsin	5.1
10	Oregon	5.2
11	Nebraska	5.4
12	Maine	5.5
13	Utah	5.6
14	Montana	5.8
15	California	5.9
16	Massachusetts	5.9
17	Rhode Island	6.0
18	Kansas	6.1
19	Vermont	6.1
20	Arizona	6.1
21	Indiana	6.3
22	Oklahoma	6.3
23	Ohio	6.4
24	Connecticut	6.6
25	Pennsylvania	6.6
26	Missouri	6.7
27	Nevada	6.7
28	Texas	6.8
29	West Virginia	6.9
30	Kentucky	6.9
31	Michigan	7.0
32	New Jersey	7.0
33	New York	7.0
34	Wyoming	7.1
35	Illinois	7.1
36	Virginia	7.2
37	Hawaii	7.2
38	Delaware	7.4
39	Florida	7.4
40	Maryland	7.4
41	Arkansas	7.5
42	New Mexico	7.6
43	Colorado	7.6
44	North Carolina	7.8
45	Alabama	7.9
46	Tennessee	7.9
47	Georgia	8.3
48	Louisiana	8.5
49	Mississippi	8.7
50	South Carolina	8.8
51	District of Columbia	12.5
Median	United States	6.7

Source: Children's Defense Fund, *The Health of America's Children* (Washington, D.C.: Children's Defense Fund, 1987), p. 50. Reprinted with permission.

low of 15.3 percent in Hawaii to a high of 32.9 percent in Mississippi.[49] Given the relatively high number of teen pregnancies in the nonwhite population, these figures show a disturbing reality: a substantial number of nonwhite infants in the United States are born with serious neurological deficits.

Of social programs to aid low-income families, the primary federal program to enhance prenatal care is WIC, the special supplemental food program for women, infants, and children. Under WIC, poor women who are pregnant and those who are breast-feeding youngsters are eligible for food coupons through which they may obtain especially nutritious foods. While the WIC program would seem a logical method for addressing the low birth weight problem of infants born to poor women, participation in the WIC program is not at desirable levels. Nationwide, only 40.4 percent of the population financially eligible to participate in WIC did so in 1986. *In forty-four states, fewer than half of eligible women and children were served through WIC.*[50]

The consequences of poor prenatal care are devastating. In 1986, twice as many black infants died compared to whites, a disparity that has widened since 1940.[51] This difference is depicted in Figure 14.1. By 1990 the first-year cost of extensive medical care for low birth-weight infants will rise to $2.1 billion, most of which could have been averted had the nation promoted maternal and child health more aggressively.[52]

Problems relating to maternal and infant health are exacerbated by a sharp rise in the numbers of adolescent females having children. Out-of-wedlock births became an important family issue in the 1980s when the incidence of unwed motherhood increased rapidly, so that by 1983 half of all nonwhite births were outside of marriage.[53] Most troubling about this development was that the percentage of unmarried teenage mothers was rising so rapidly that, by 1984, it was triple what it had been 25 years before.[54] By the mid-1980s, over half of all

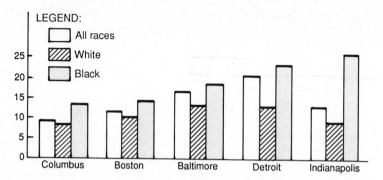

Figure 14.1. Infant Mortality Rates by Race, Selected* Cities with 500,000+ Population, 1984. Source: Children's Defense Fund, *The Health of America's Children* (Washington, D.C.: Children's Defense Fund, 1987), p. 12. Reprinted with permission.

teenage births were outside of marriage.[55] This increase in very young women having children on their own poses a serious problem for public policy for two basic reasons. First, teenage mothers are more likely to drop out of school and fail to gain those skills that would make them self-sufficient. As Figure 14.2 illustrates, adolescent mothers, particularly those who are black or Hispanic, are apt to have less of a command of basic skills. Poor skill development poses a critical problem when these skills are parenting skills. Second, teenage mothers are more likely to have to depend on welfare for assistance, the benefits of which are at levels that are lower than the actual cost of raising children. This combination of poor skill development and dependence on public welfare programs presents the specter of poor children bearing more poor children in an endless cycle of hopelessness. The consequences are particularly tragic for poor children who have little prospect of escaping the poverty trap. Reductions in the numbers of working males who are marriageable means that these children have little hope that their mother's marriage will pull them out of poverty, although this is the most prevalent way for mothers to become independent of public welfare.[56] The loss of earning power through the Aid to Families with Dependent Children program means that

public assistance will not provide an adequate economic base for poor children.[57] Moreover, the interaction of these factors has devastating implications for black children—30 percent of all black children are "persistently poor". Approximately 90 percent of children who are poor for 10 years or more of their childhood are black.[58] Unfortunately, the prevalence of teenage motherhood is likely to worsen the life opportunities of poor children, particularly those who are minorities.

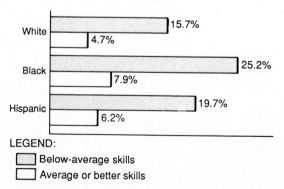

LEGEND:
Below-average skills
Average or better skills

Figure 14.2. Parenthood by Basic Skills Levels, 16–19-Year-old Women, 1981. Source: *A Children's Defense Budget* (Washington, D.C.: Children's Defense Fund, 1988), p. 172. Reprinted with permission.

THE FUTURE OF CHILD WELFARE

After a half-century of federal legislation, child welfare advocates could not be sanguine about the care provided to American youngsters. The prospect of using the family as the primary institution for child welfare has diminished because of the absence of economic and social supports to keep the family intact. Without a coherent family policy, families have been less able to care for children, and child welfare services—such as protective services, foster care, and adoption—have been deployed to ameliorate the most serious problems experienced by children. By the 1980s, however, even these programs became subject to budget rescissions, further exposing youngsters to economic and social insecurity as well as physical danger.

At the same time, child welfare advocates found that the plight of troubled children might prove to be a compelling justification for expanding social welfare programs. In promoting its welfare reform proposal, the American Public Welfare Association highlighted (in their publication of that title) that *One Child in Four* was poor in the United States.[59] Perhaps the most effective group among child welfare advocates, the Children's Defense Fund brought the nation's attention to a new set of child welfare problems—teen pregnancy, homeless and runaway youth, malnutrition among mothers and infants, and unemployment and school absence among adolescents. Although publicizing such problems may well lead to more child welfare services, the extent to which they will contribute to a comprehensive family policy—thus making rehabilitative child welfare services less necessary—remains to be seen.

NOTES

1. Jeanne Giovannoni, "Children," *Encyclopedia of Social Work*, 18th ed. (Silver Spring, Md.: NASW, 1987), p. 247.

2. Alfred Kadushin, "Child Welfare Services," *Encyclopedia of Social Work*, 18th ed. (Silver Spring, Md.: NASW, 1987), p. 268.

3. Walter Trattner, *From Poor Law to Welfare State* (New York: Free Press, 1974), p. 100.

4. Ibid., pp. 106–7.

5. Diana DiNitto and Thomas Dye, *Social Welfare* (Englewood Cliffs, N.J.: Prentice-Hall, 1987), p. 153.

6. Kathleen Faller, "Protective Services for Children," *Encyclopedia of Social Work*, 18th ed. (Silver Spring, Md.: NASW, 1987), p. 386.

7. Trattner, *From Poor Law to Welfare State*, pp. 181, 183.

8. James Leiby, *A History of Social Welfare and Social Work in the United States* (New York: Columbia University Press, 1978), pp. 148–49.

9. June Axinn and Herman Levin, *Social Welfare* (New York: Harper and Row, 1982), p. 159.

10. Trattner, *From Poor Law to Welfare State*, p. 186.

11. Axinn and Levin, *Social Welfare*, pp. 224–28.

12. Barbara Kantrowitz et al., "How to Protect Abused Children," *Newsweek*, November 23, 1987, p. 68.

13. Faller, "Protective Services for Children," pp. 387, 389.

14. Douglas Besharov, "Contending with Overblown Expectations," *Public Welfare* (Winter 1987), pp. 7, 8.

15. Kantrowitz et al., "How to Protect Abused Children," p. 68.

16. "Foster Care: Duty vs. Legal Vulnerability," *NASW News* (July 1988), p. 3.

17. "Social Workers' Neglect," *All Things Considered* (Washington, D.C.: National Public Radio, April 15, 1988). *NASW News* later reported that the employees cited in this broadcast were not professional social workers but employees of the state: (see n. 16 above).

18. "High Court Review Urged on Foster Care Liability," *NASW News* (July 1988), p. 3.

19. Ibid.

20. Fox Butterfield, "Sect Members Assert They Are Misunderstood," *New York Times*, June 24, 1984.

21. Besharov, "Contending with Overblown Expectations," p. 8.

22. Bridgite Berger and Peter Berger, *The War*

Over the Family (Garden City, N.Y.: Anchor, 1983), p. 213.

23. Theodore Stein, "Foster Care for Children," *Encyclopedia of Social Work,* 18th ed. (Silver Spring, Md.: NASW, 1987), pp. 641–42.

24. Ibid., p. 643.

25. *A Children's Defense Budget* (Washington, D.C.: Children's Defense Fund, 1988), p. 179.

26. A. N. Maluccio and E. Fein, "Permanency Planning: A Redefinition," *Child Welfare* (May–June 1983), p. 197.

27. Duncan Lindsey, "Achievements for Children in Foster Care," *Social Work* (November 1982), p. 495.

28. Stein, "Foster Care for Children," p. 641.

29. *NASW News*, p. 3.

30. Ronald Rooney, "Permanency Planning: Boon for All Children?" *Social Work* (March 1982), p. 157.

31. Children's Defense Fund, p. 54.

32. Stein, "Foster Care for Children," p. 649.

33. Esther Wattenberg, "The Fate of Baby Boomers and Their Children," *Social Work* (January–February 1986).

34. Kantrowitz et al., "How to Protect Abused Children," p. 71.

35. Mary Jordan, "Foster Parent Scarcity Causing Crisis in Care," *Washington Post*, July 20, 1986.

36. Children's Defense Fund, p. 55.

37. Elizabeth Cole, "Adoption," *Encyclopedia of Social Work*, 18th ed. (Silver Spring, Md.: NASW, 1987), p. 70.

38. Committee on Ways and Means, U.S. House of Representatives, *Background Material and Data on Programs within the Jurisdiction of the Committee on Ways and Means* (Washington, D.C.: U.S. Government Printing Office, 1985), p. 494.

39. Cole, "Adoption," p. 71.

40. Ronald Fischler, "Protecting American Indian Children," *Social Work* (September 1980),
p. 341.

41. Evelyn Lance Blanchard and Russel Lawrence Barsh, "What Is Best for Tribal Children?" *Social Work* (September 1980), p. 350.

42. Fischler, "Protecting American Indian Children," p. 341.

43. Cole, "Adoption," p. 70.

44. Wattenberg, "The Fate of Baby Boomers and Their Children," p. 24.

45. Children's Defense Fund, p. 207.

46. Ibid., p. 214.

47. Ibid., p. 32; National Association of Social Workers, "1986 Voting Record" (Silver Spring, Md.: NASW, 1987).

48. Physician Task Force on Hunger in America, *Hunger in America* (Boston: Harvard University Press, 1985), p. 65.

49. Children's Defense Fund, *The Health of America's Children* (Washington, D.C.: Children's Defense Fund, 1987), p. 72.

50. Ibid., p. 84.

51. Ibid., p. 195.

52. Ibid., p. 25.

53. Michael Novak et al., *The New Consensus on Family and Welfare* (Washington, D.C.: American Enterprise Institute, 1987), p. 135.

54. Lisbeth Schorr, *Within Our Reach* (New York: Anchor Press, 1988), p. 13.

55. Novak et al., *The New Consensus on Family and Welfare*, p. 48.

56. William Julius Wilson, "American Social Policy and the Ghetto Underclass," *Dissent* (Winter 1988).

57. David Ellwood, *Poor Support: Poverty and the American Family* (New York: Basic Books, 1988), p. 58.

58. Committee on Ways and Means, U.S. House of Representatives, *Children in Poverty* (Washington, D.C.: U.S. Government Printing Office, 1985), p. 44.

59. *One Child in Four* (Washington, D.C.: American Public Welfare Association, 1987).

CHAPTER 15

The Crisis in Housing

Problems associated with housing have recently entered the news by way of a national focus on homelessness. Although homelessness is undoubtedly a profound social problem, finding and maintaining adequate and affordable housing is also problematic for the working poor as well as for a large portion of the middle class. This chapter will examine the crisis in housing, with particular emphasis on problems related to low-income housing, issues in housing policy, homelessness, and proposals for housing reform.

The United States had no national housing policy prior to the Housing Act of 1937. The objective of the Act was to "... provide financial assistance to the states and political subdivisions thereof for the elimination of unsafe and unsanitary housing conditions, for the eradication of slums, for the provision of decent, safe and sanitary dwellings for families of low income, and for the reduction of unemployment and the stimulation of business activity, to create a United States Housing Authority and for other purposes."[1] Amending the 1937 Act, the Housing Act of 1949 called for federal money for slum clearance and urban redevelopment, and the creation of a public authority charged with building and administering 135,000 low-income housing units annually for six years. In addition, the Housing Act included the goal of providing a decent home and a suitable living environment for every American family.[2] Specifically, the bill required each locality to develop a plan for urban redevelopment, which contained provisions for "predominantly residential dwellings." This wording was construed by localities to mean that only one-half of new construction was to be devoted to low-income housing. Inadvertently, the federal government created a policy that encouraged urban redevelopment at the expense of existing low-income housing.

In 1954 the Housing Act of 1949 was amended again. The term urban development was changed to urban renewal and, as such, localities were required to submit a plan for the removal of urban blight and overall community development. The new Act removed the requirement that new federally subsidized urban construction be "predominantly residential," and thus cleared the way for massive slum clearance projects, the ability of the locality to lease or sell land more freely, and the ability to avoid public housing. Urban renewal, the eradication of slums through condemnation and bulldozing, led to charges that cities were insensitive to the needs of long-term residents. Through renewal projects, the localities were attempting to revitalize the inner cities by attracting middle- and upper-income families at the expense of displaced poor families. Indeed, from 1949 to 1963, urban renewal projects removed about 243,000 housing units and replaced them with only 68,000 units, of which 20,000 units were for low-income families.[3]

The Demonstration Cities and Metropolitan Development Act (Model Cities) was passed in 1966. This aggressive program was part of President Lyndon Johnson's War on Poverty and, in large part, focused on issues of deteriorated housing and blighted neighborhoods. The Model Cities legislation promised "... to concentrate public and private resources in a comprehensive five-year attack on social, economic, and physical problems of slum and blighted neighborhoods."[4] In 1974

243

the Model Cities and virtually all neighborhood development acts were superseded by the Housing and Community Development Act of 1974.

By the early 1970s the thrust of federal policy began to shift toward experimentation with general revenue sharing, a system that initially provided a more generous distribution of funds and, perhaps more importantly, a strategy that shifted major responsibility for the allocation of funds from the federal government to the local government. However, since these funds were now heavily controlled by local forces, they were also more vulnerable to the ebb and flow of local politics and the power of interest groups. Low-income groups, who formerly had many of their interests protected by the federal government, often became less conspicuous in the interplay of local political maneuvering.

The Housing and Community Development Act of 1974 was a wide-ranging bill that included provisions for urban renewal, neighborhood development, Model Cities, water and sewer projects, neighborhood and facility grants, public facilities and rehabilitation loans, and urban beautification and historic preservation grants.[5] Although spending priorities were determined at the national level, communities were required to submit a master plan, including specific reference to their low-income housing needs. The amount allocated for the fiscal years of 1978–80 was almost $11 billion, with more than 1800 communities receiving entitlement grants in the first two years of the program.[6]

Two other interesting pieces of legislation emerged in the 1970s: the Home Mortgage Disclosure Act (HMDA) and the Community Reinvestment Act (CRA). The Home Mortgage Disclosure Act was concerned with the problem of mortgage redlining. Housing observers argued that a major cause of community deterioration was a result of a "lending strike" (redlining) by financial institutions. Redlining is defined as "an outright refusal of an insurance

company, bank, or other financial institution to provide its services solely on the basis of the location of the property in question. The term is derived from the practice of marking on a map in red the area which is to be avoided by those responsible for the distribution of the services of that institution."[7] Through this policy, families seeking to purchase housing in a redlined neighborhood might be denied a mortgage loan, insurance, or other necessary services. In 1976 President Gerald Ford signed the Home Mortgage Disclosure Act, a law which required virtually every bank or savings and loan association to publicly disclose annually where it made its loans. Although useful for community groups trying to pressure local banks for greater neighborhood involvement, in cities without active community organizations the law was useless.

In 1977 Congress further recognized the problem of mortgage redlining and enacted the Community Reinvestment Act. Significantly broader than the HMDA, the CRA established the principle that each bank and savings institution had an obligation to make loans in every neighborhood in its service area. Virtually all lending institutions were covered under the CRA, and the law required a yearly evaluation by the federal government of the performance of each lending institution. Primary enforcement involved the control by federal regulatory agencies over new charters, bank growth and mergers, relocations, and acquisitions.

All told, the Department of Housing and Urban Development (HUD) manages over 50 separate housing programs. In 1981 the largest HUD programs included: (1) Public Housing (over 1.2 million subsidized units), (2) Section 8 (subsidized rental payments for over 1.3 million units), (3) Section 236 (rental housing assistance for 537,000 units), (4) Section 235 (home ownership assistance for low-income families, over 240,000 subsidized units), (5) Section 202 (housing for the elderly and handicapped, over 100,000 units), and (6) rent supplements (almost 158,000 units).

Apart from HUD, the Department of Agriculture, through the Farmers Home Administration (FmHA), also provides housing assistance to rural residents. In 1981 the major programs of FmHA included: (1) Section 515 (210,000 units of rental housing), (2) Section 504 (1.6 million home-ownership loans), (3) Section 504 (over 39,000 repair grants for low-income people), (4) rural rental assistance (over 1,500 units with Section 515), and (5) Section 514 (almost 1,400 farm labor housing loans). Overall, HUD subsidized about 3.5 million units in 1981, and the FmHA over 1.1 million.

ISSUES IN HOUSING POLICY

Some observers consider the housing situation in the United States to be in a state of crisis.[8] At best, housing in the U.S. is beset with almost insurmountable problems. On first examination, however, the American housing situation has a patina of success. Throughout the 1970s home ownership showed strong gains, as shown in Table 15.1.

From 1974 to 1984, close to 17 million housing units were started, a number far greater than the 11.6 million units completed between 1960 and 1970. In 1940, 43.6 percent of all dwelling units were owner occupied; by 1976 that proportion soared to 64.7 percent—the greatest absolute expansion of home ownership in the nation's history. Moreover, this phenomenon encompassed all sectors of the American population. For example, 23.6 percent of black and minority occupied units were owner occupied in 1940; by 1987 that rate had increased to 43.3 percent,[9] as shown in Table 15.2.

The quality of the housing stock also increased dramatically in the post-World War II period. For example, over 45 percent of U.S. housing units lacked some or all plumbing facilities in 1940. By 1976, that percentage declined to 3.4. Furthermore, 17.8 percent of all housing units were considered dilapidated or in need of major repairs in 1940; by 1970 that percentage was reduced to 4.6.[10]

Overall, the size and comfort of new owner-occupied homes are a positive development. More than half of the units built in 1977 contained a floor plan greater than 1600 feet, two or more bathrooms, and central air-conditioning. Apart from significant regional variations, on the average, almost 16 percent of the total U.S.

TABLE 15.1 Housing Stock, 1960–1987 (in thousands)

Category	1960	1970	1980	1987
Owner-occupied	32,797	39,886	51,795	58,164
Renter-occupied	20,227	23,560	28,595	32,724
Total	56,584	67,699	86,693	90,888

Source: U.S. Bureau of the Census, *Statistical Abstract of the United States, 1989* (Washington, D.C.: U.S. Government Printing Office, 1989), p. 719.

TABLE 15.2 Home Ownership by Race, 1960–1987

Race	1960	1970	1980	1987
White	64.4	65.4	67.8	67.4
Black	38.4	42.1	44.2	43.3

Source: U.S. Bureau of the Census, *Statistical Abstract of the United States, 1989* (Washington, D.C.: U.S. Government Printing Office, 1989), p. 720.

housing stock was constructed post-1970. In the South and West, one out of every five units was constructed between 1970 and 1976. Seven out of ten new housing starts were for single-family housing, underscoring the dramatic shift in home ownership.[11] These statistics can easily lead to the conclusion that the majority of Americans are purchasing good quality, large, and relatively new homes.

The true housing situation emerges only when the veneer of success is rubbed off. Beginning in the 1970s, structural problems have surfaced which call into question the ability of the system to adequately house the population. In the 1970s, and, especially, in the 1980s, many people were forced to spend a higher percentage of their income on housing than they could reasonably afford. Furthermore, a number of people were so financially overextended that they were vulnerable to mortgage default, eviction, or lacked the cash necessary for purchasing other necessities.

Between 1970 and 1980, median income for homeowners rose 104 percent (from $9,700 to $19,800), while median home value tripled (from $17,100 to $51,300). By 1984, the median price of a home was $73,000 compared with $32,000 in 1974. This median price, however, varied widely by city and region, with Los Angeles, New York, and San Francisco registering some of the highest home values.

Among mortgage payers, nearly one-third pay 25 percent or more of their income for housing; 21 percent pay 35 percent or over. On the average, the Consumer Price Index (CPI) for all items rose from 116 in 1970 to 269 in 1981. In that same period, the shelter index (rent, home purchase, mortgage interest rates, property taxes, and maintenance) rose from 123 to 308.[12] Chester Hartman provides an example.

> In 1975, the average-priced new single-family home cost $44,600, and the contract interest rate for a conventional first mortgage averaged 8.75 percent. With an 80 percent mortgage and housing costs at 25 percent of income, a family in 1975 would have needed a down payment of $8,920—65 percent of the median family income that year—and, on a thirty-year mortgage, would have had a monthly mortgage payment of $280.69, which in turn required a minimum annual income of $13,473—2 percent below the nation's median family income that year.
>
> In 1981, the average-priced new single-family home cost $94,100, and the contract interest rate for a conventional first mortgage averaged 14.1 percent. With an 80 percent mortgage and housing costs at 25 percent of income, a family in 1981 would have needed a down payment of $18,820—84 percent of median family income that year—and, on a thirty-year mortgage, would have had a monthly mortgage payment of $897.93, which in turn required a minimum annual income of $43,101—nearly double the nation's median family income that year.[13]

In the past, the high price of new homes was moderated by consumers' ability to purchase existing stock. However, because of low levels of new construction, high rates of new household formation, and increased investment and speculation, the median price of a used home is now only slightly lower than a new one.

Other factors, such as mortgage instruments, also impact upon homeowners. A variety of inflation-sensitive mortgage instruments have been introduced in the past several years, including variable or adjustable rate mortgages (ARM). These ARM mortgages usually include an initially lower interest rate, sometimes two or more percentage points below fixed rates. Although the loan is often capped, it may fluctuate five or more percentage points above the initial loan rate. Therefore, while a family using an ARM-based home loan may originate a mortgage at 7 percent, by the fifth year the interest rate may have climbed to 13 percent, thus causing a considerable increase in their mortgage payments. While this system helps protect lending institutions against inflation, it provides for a more tenuous home ownership status, because the homeowner no longer has the security of predictable fixed payments for the life of the mortgage.

The increase in the cost of housing has led to other alternatives, including "equity participation," whereby the lender shares in any future profits made from selling a mortgaged house. A more commonly used alternative is often called "Contract for Deed." In this financing scheme, the buyer sells the house, but instead of the seller receiving a bank loan, the buyer finances the sale. For example, a house is sold for $50,000, with the buyer required to put down a substantial down payment of 15 percent. The buyer is then required to pay the seller a monthly payment for the remainder of the purchase price, plus a defined interest rate. In essence, the buyer takes out a "note" or loan with the seller, usually for a given period of time, often one to five years. After the specified maturation period for the loan, the buyer is required to pay the seller for the balance of the house. Normally, the buyer will then originate a bank mortgage. Although initially it appears that the major risk is assumed by the seller, in many states, if the buyer is more than thirty days overdue on payments, the house reverts back to the seller, with the initial down payment being lost. Moreover, if after the predetermined time the buyer cannot arrange financing, the home is repossessed by the seller. The buyer is therefore highly vulnerable to economic distress, as well as increased rates of defaults and foreclosures.

The high price of housing, the fiscal overextension required to enter the housing market, the continued availability of attractive yet risky financing, and large rises in property taxes and utility rates, have led to an increase in mortgage delinquency rates and foreclosures. In the third quarter of 1981, 5.33 percent of all mortgage loans were 30 or more days overdue (in the Midwest that rate was 7.78 percent), the highest rate since the data were first recorded in 1953. In February 1983, 2.36 percent of

mortgages held by savings and loan institutions were at least 60 days overdue, a substantial increase over the .83 percent recorded in December 1981.[14]

Poverty and Housing

If the housing situation has become difficult for the middle class, it has reached crisis proportions for the poor with many poor families finding it all but impossible to find affordable housing, much less decent affordable housing. Structural and long-term unemployment, falling income levels among the poor and near-poor, and continued cutbacks in federal programs have contributed to a crisis in housing. Although some of the poor have been able to find affordable housing that is not federally subsidized, they constitute only a modest fraction of poor households. According to the Low Income Housing Information Service, in 1985 the number of *all* rental units available nationwide (both subsidized and unsubsidized) that was affordable for very low income renter households (i.e., rent that does not exceed 30 percent of income—a standard developed by the U.S. Department of Housing and Urban Development), equaled only about half the number of very low-income households.[15] (See Table 15.3.) A 1983 Congressional Research Service report found that over 60 percent of very low income households (those with 50 percent or less of the median national income) had serious housing problems. This group lived in housing that was either debilitated, overcrowded, or more expensive than their resources allowed. Moreover, some 2.8 million households in this group had "worst case" housing problems: they lived in housing which was physically inadequate and consumed more than 30 percent of their incomes.[16]

For the most part, the housing problems faced by the poor encompass four major issues: (1) the escalation of rents, (2) the rise in utility rates, (3) the decreasing availability of moderate- and low-priced housing, and (4)

TABLE 15.3. Changes in Median Rents and Median Rent/Income Ratios, 1978–1980

Income	Median Rent			Median Rent/Income Ratio		
	1980	1979	1978	1980	1979	1978
$3,000 or less	$179	$147	$130	+72%	+60%	+60%
$3,000–6,999	187	172	165	47	44	42
$7,000–9,999	222	205	193	32	31	29
$10,000–14,999	249	232	214	25	24	22
$15,000–19,999	274	252	233	20	18	17
$20,000–24,999	296	277	256	17	16	14
$25,000–34,999	327	303	284	14	13	13
$35,000–49,999	362	337	326	12	11	11
$50,000–74,999	393	401	347	−9	−10	−8
$75,000 +	423	359	283	−7	−6	−5
All Renters	241	217	200	27	26	25

Source: "The Low-Income Housing Crisis," Cushing N. Dolbeare, from *America's Housing Crisis*, Chester W. Hartman. Institute for Policy Studies, 1983, p. 32. Reprinted with permission.

the insufficient and declining support from the federal government. Median renter income rose 66 percent between 1970 and 1980 (from $6,400 to $10,600), while in that same period median monthly rents increased by 123 percent (from $108 to $241). In 1983, gross rents accounted for 29 percent of family income compared to 22 percent in 1973. Although median monthly rents increased for all groups by 21 percent from 1978 to 1980, for the lowest income group they rose by 38 percent. Furthermore, although the proportion of income required for housing grew for all groups, only those with yearly incomes below $15,000 paid at least 25 percent of their income for rent.[17]

In 1983 the Annual Housing Survey (the last year it was published) of the Bureau of the Census found that 55 percent of all renters with incomes below $7,000 a year were spending more than 60 percent of their incomes for rent and utilities. The General Accounting Office found that from 1975 to 1983, the number of low-income households paying more than 50 percent of their income on rent and utilities rose 70 percent, from 3.7 million to 6.3 million.[18] These figures suggest that the housing crisis for the poor is rapidly worsening.

The housing crisis is exacerbated by prop-erty taxes—the heart of local revenue gathering. The escalating costs of providing services has resulted in significant increases in property taxes for homeowners. Apart from homeowners, renters are affected by property taxes since they are generally passed along by landlords in the form of higher rents. The most common form of property tax relief occurs through a "circuit breaker" program. A typical circuit breaker program takes effect when taxes exceed a specified proportion of household income and, in most programs, low-income households are sent a yearly benefit check in which all or a part of the property tax is refunded. Circuit breaker programs for low-income renters operate in a similar manner. Typically, a portion of the rent paid by a low-income household (usually 15–25 percent) is considered to represent the property tax passed on by the landlord, and is thus refunded by the state government. Although circuit breaker programs can provide significant relief, they are often restricted only to the elderly or disabled. While 31 states have circuit breaker programs, 21 of those states restrict eligibility to elderly, disabled, or elderly disabled households. Twenty-five of those 31 states cover both renters and homeowners; 6 states restrict eligibility to homeowners. On the other hand, 10 states have broad circuit breaker programs which cover low-income families (both renters and homeowners) who are neither elderly nor disabled.

Escalating rents are also compounded by escalating utility rates. In many parts of the U.S., especially the Northeast and the Midwest, the average family pays thousands of dollars a year in utility bills. According to the National Consumer Law Center, in 1984 families in 21 states had average annual heating bills that exceeded $1,000. In 1986, the average low-income household eligible for energy assistance spent over 15 percent of its income on utility bills, nearly four times the average (3.9 percent) spent by all other U.S. households. Moreover, the cost of home heating oil increased by almost 450 percent from 1972 to 1984, while the cost of heating with natural gas increased fivefold and residential electric rates threefold. Increases in home energy bills have disproportionately affected the poor, and, in some cases, have resulted in massive utility shutoffs. For example, it is estimated that in 1984 over 1.4 million households had their natural gas shut off because of delinquent payments.[19]

In order to counter the effects of the federal deregulation of oil prices and the large OPEC oil increases, the Carter Administration instituted the Low Income Home Energy Assistance Program (LIHEAP), a program whose original intent was to offset the portion cf income paid by low-income consumers for utility bills, especially for home heating. Originally funded at $2.6 billion, the budget cuts of the Reagan years reduced the funding level to $1.5 billion in 1988. In that same year, the LIHEAP covered less than one-fifth of the heating and cooling bills of low-income households eligible for assistance.[20]

Another problem facing the poor is a decline in low and moderate income housing stock. Several factors since the 1970s have converged to deplete the stock of low-income

housing. According to Sternlieb and Hughes, there is evidence that "a new town may be evolving in town."[21] This new town, or "gentrified" neighborhood, is a major component of the urban renaissance. Attracted by unique houses amenable to restoration, good transportation facilities, and a close proximity to employment and artistic, cultural, and social opportunities—young, professional, white-collar workers have begun to resettle the poor, aging, and heavily minority sections of central cities (in the process called "gentrification").

Although the renovation of central city areas, such as New York's Soho district, often make a neighborhood more attractive (and potentially a tourist attraction), the effect on the indigenous—and often poor—population is often devastating. As homes become renovated, the prices of surrounding homes may increase. Although low-income home-owners may be able to command a high resale for their homes, they may find few other suitable places they can move to. Furthermore, as neighborhoods become affluent, property taxes are likely to increase, thus creating a burden on the low-income homeowner. Previously affordable rental housing may undergo huge rent increases as the neighborhood becomes more desirable, thereby driving out older and poorer tenants as well as obviating the possibility of new low-income residents. Although gentrification has been selective—the main demographic movement continues to be suburban—it has had a striking impact on some neighborhoods.

The conversion of apartment buildings into condominiums represents another threat to the poor. As a consequence of tax breaks and income shelters, previously affordable rental housing is rapidly being turned into condominiums. Initiated by either tenants or developers, these condominiums represent a serious depletion of good quality rental stock. Because apartments in these conversions may cost $50,000 or more, low-income tenants can rarely afford the benefits of condominium living, and although renters are often offered a separation fee when a building is converted into a condominium, this amount is usually nominal and may not even cover the costs of moving, much less make up for the difference between the current rent and an alternative rent.

The renovation of downtown areas in central cities is another problem for the poor. The development of new office buildings, large apartment complexes, shopping areas, and parking lots often replaces the low-income housing bordering on downtown areas. Traditionally affordable (and often rundown) apartment buildings, cheap hotels, rooming houses, and bed-and-boards are razed as glittering new edifices of downtown redevelopment are erected. Displaced people, often longtime residents, are forced to find housing in more expensive neighborhoods, double up with family or friends or, in many cases, become part of the estimated 300,000 to 3 million homeless people who walk the streets of American cities. According to HUD, demolition, arson, abandonment, condominium conversion, or conversion to nonresidential use has removed some 2.8 million rental units between 1970 and 1977. The federal government estimates that 2.8 million families are displaced by private or governmental action each year.[22]

The search for decent, low-income hous-ing is hindered by the decrease in housing starts which, having peaked at over 2 million in 1973, has since stayed at lower levels.[23] In addition, construction starts for multifamily housing—the units low-income families are most likely to afford—fell from 456,000 in 1978 to 283,000 in 1983[24] (see Table 15.4).

Discrimination in housing is another barrier facing the poor. Although it is illegal, racially based housing discrimination is still prevalent. And, despite isolated legislation by some cities and states, no federal law exists to ban discrimination in housing against families with children. According to a 1980 study, 26 percent of housing units totally barred families; another 50 percent instituted restrictions based on the number, age, or gender of children.[25]

The Federal Government and Housing

Federally funded programs represent the major form of housing assistance for the poor. Overall, there are two primary forms of federal housing assistance: publicly owned housing and rental subsidies for low-income families living in private housing. Residents in both of these categories generally pay 30 percent of their incomes in rent. Unlike income maintenance programs such as SSI and AFDC, housing programs are not entitlement programs,

TABLE 15.4. New Housing Units Started, Selected Years 1960–1986

Year	Total (in thousands)	Percentage Change from Previous Year	Privately Owned	Publicly Owned
1960	1,296	−16.6	1,252	44
1965	1,510	−3.3	1,473	37
1970	1,469	−2.1	1,434	35
1975	1,171	−13.4	1,160	11
1979	1,760	−13.6	1,745	15
1980	1,313	−25.4	1,292	20
1982	1,072	−2.6	1,062	10
1983	1,712	59.7	1,703	9
1984	1,756	2.6	1,750	6
1985	1,745	−0.6	1,742	3

Source: U.S. Bureau of the Census, *Statistical Abstracts of the U.S., 1987*, Table No. 1270 (Washington, D.C.: U.S. Government Printing Office, 1988), p. 704.

and therefore benefits are not automatically provided to all eligible applicants. In essence, the federal government allocates a fixed amount of money toward low-income housing, and since funding levels are usually low, only a portion of eligible applicants actually receive assistance. This situation has resulted in long waiting lists for subsidized housing which, on the average, totals twenty months in a cross-section of cities. According to the Council of Large Public Housing Authorities, in late 1982 the average wait for families on public housing lists was 29 months.[26]

In 1987 there were about 4 million federally subsidized housing units in the U.S. In contrast to these 4 million units, there are approximately 20 million households with incomes below 50 percent of median and more than 30 million families with incomes below 80 percent of median.[27] It is not surprising, then, that even before the major budget reductions of the 1980s, less than 25 percent of households below the poverty line lived in federally subsidized housing. Furthermore, the total of 4 million units stands in stark contrast to the estimated need of about 16 million subsidized units.

The crisis becomes even more evident when the shortage of low-income housing is broken down on a state-by-state basis, as shown in Table 15.5. In no state in 1985 did the level of housing assistance come close to meeting the number of low-income households that were eligible. Only two states (Alaska and Rhode Island) in 1985 provided housing assistance that exceeded half of the number of eligible very low-income renters. In eight states (Arizona, California, Colorado, Florida, Idaho, Oregon, Utah, and Wyoming), the number of households in subsidized rentals did not equal one-quarter of the eligible very low-income households.

TABLE 15.5. Low-income Housing Assistance

State	Number of Renter Households Assisted	Number of Very Low Income Renter Households 1983	*Maximum Percentage of Very Low Income Renter Households Assisted
Alabama	75,469	224,320	33.6%
Alaska	9,224	16,980	54.3
Arizona	34,638	139,320	24.9
Arkansas	38,709	130,840	29.6
California	336,310	1,546,110	21.5
Colorado	39,305	159,850	24.8
Connecticut	64,225	154,030	41.7
Delaware	10,422	29,060	35.9
Dist. of Col.	28,131	69,330	40.6
Florida	134,471	587,050	22.9
Georgia	115,297	337,760	34.1
Hawaii	16,175	53,160	30.4
Idaho	9,072	40,630	22.3
Illinois	164,448	646,150	26.1
Indiana	79,052	214,860	36.8
Iowa	31,076	115,350	26.9
Kansas	26,702	103,130	25.9
Kentucky	68,314	192,420	35.5
Louisiana	69,307	261,240	26.5
Maine	21,473	54,720	39.2
Maryland	81,215	210,330	38.6

continued

TABLE 15.5. (cont.)

State	Number of Renter Households Assisted	Number of Very Low Income Renter Households 1983	*Maximum Percentage of Very Low Income Renter Households Assisted
Massachusetts	144,490	347,830	41.7
Michigan	123,958	409,380	30.3
Minnesota	77,519	169,070	45.9
Mississippi	40,148	143,000	28.1
Missouri	73,636	237,110	31.1
Montana	14,346	38,290	37.5
Nebraska	22,715	67,950	33.4
Nevada	15,016	47,620	31.5
New Hampshire	16,042	40,530	39.6
New Jersey	139,169	403,040	34.5
New Mexico	21,749	69,530	31.1
New York	454,852	1,484,980	30.6
North Carolina	97,754	305,840	32.0
North Dakota	12,311	27,840	44.2
Ohio	190,309	537,230	35.4
Oklahoma	55,721	153,030	36.4
Oregon	34,491	154,350	22.3
Pennsylvania	189,449	564,120	33.6
Rhode Island	32,398	63,370	51.1
South Carolina	45,692	156,080	29.3
South Dakota	16,827	35,230	47.8
Tennessee	91,364	259,260	35.2
Texas	196,290	766,090	25.6
Utah	10,039	57,390	17.5
Vermont	7,077	26,220	27.0
Virginia	79,566	262,530	30.3
Washington	57,265	224,990	25.5
West Virginia	26,844	86,230	31.1
Wisconsin	67,385	193,200	34.9
Wyoming	3,915	16,620	23.6
Total	**3,816,172**	**12,652,690**	**30.2**

* This is a maximum because not all households receiving assistance have "very low incomes." The number of "very low income" households in 1983 was compared to the number of assisted units in 1985 because both sets of data are the latest available on a state-by-state basis. (Source: Isaac Shapiro and Robert Greenstein, *Holes in the Safety Net* (Washington, D.C.: Center on Budget and Policy Priorities, 1988), p. 68.

Nevertheless, federal housing programs have made a substantial difference for the poor. In 1980 almost 60 percent of federally subsidized rentals went to families: 23.7 percent to married couples and 34.5 percent to female-headed households. Myths not-withstanding, over one-third of tenants in subsidized housing are over age 65, almost three-fifths of the households are white, about two-fifths of sub-sidized tenants have at least one member who works part-time, and almost half have incomes below the poverty level, with over three-fifths having incomes below 125 percent of the poverty level. The median income in 1980 for subsidized households was $4,978 per year.[28]

While the federal government has demonstrated a commitment to home ownership for the middle and upper classes (i.e., mortgage interest deductions and various other housing-related tax breaks), it has not shown a corresponding commitment to low-income housing. For example, housing-related tax deductions for the middle and upper classes were valued at $44 billion in 1987—more than three times the total cost of low-income housing assistance.

The bulk of housing-related tax deductions benefits the top 25 percent of the income bracket. Seventy percent of the homeowner deductions go to taxpayers with incomes above $30,000 per year. The top 2 percent of the population receive more housing-related tax subsidies than the bottom 20 percent get in direct aid.[29] Moreover, low-income housing assistance has never even totaled 1 percent of federal outlays in any given year. Dolbeare sums up the issue: "Benefits from federal programs are so skewed that *the total of all the assisted housing payments ever made under all HUD assisted housing programs, from the inception of public housing in 1937 through 1980, was less than the costs to the federal government of housing-related tax expenditures in 1980 alone* [original emphasis]."[30]

Dolbeare goes on to state that in 1980:

1. Over 14 percent ($4.2 billion) of all direct and indirect housing subsidies went to households with annual incomes below $5,000. Only one in eight households received housing assistance, and the average recipient realized $132 in monthly benefits.
2. Four percent ($1.2 billion) of all direct and indirect housing subsidies went to households with annual incomes between $5,000 and $10,000. Less than one household in ten received these benefits, and the average monthly amount was $60 per recipient.
3. Over 50 percent ($16.7 billion) of all direct and indirect housing subsidies went to households with annual incomes of between $20,000 and $50,000. Two-fifths of all households in this group

received benefits. Each recipient in this group received benefits which totaled $67 a month.
4. Over 25 percent ($7.5 billion) of all direct and indirect housing subsidies went to households with annual incomes above $50,000. More than four-fifths of these households received tax benefits. The average monthly benefit per recipient was $309.[31]

Despite the housing crisis, the federal government slashed low-income housing assistance by 60 percent between 1981 ($31 billion) and 1985 ($10 billion). Federal funding for FmHA low-income home loans and rental assistance was reduced by 50 percent, and in addition, HUD cancelled several proposed housing developments and, in many cases, did not reappropriate the money to other projects. Through its Public Housing Homeownership Demonstration project, HUD attempted to sell 2,000 public housing units to tenants, thereby eliminating them from the long-term rental stock.

Prior to 1981, low-income families could not be charged more than 25 percent of their income for rent and utilities. However, Congress passed a law in 1981 that forced recipients to pay 30 percent of their income in order to qualify for a subsidy. Low-income families are now paying more than $500 million a year for subsidized housing; in five years the federal government will have wrested nearly $6 billion from the poor.

Under the Reagan administration, HUD shifted its focus from long-term to short-term policy measures, a move which de-emphasized new construction or renovation of publicly owned rental stock. Instead of acquiring new housing units, HUD emphasized the subsidization of tenants through a voucher system (Section 8), thus allowing low-income tenants to occupy existing and privately owned housing. In short, the Section 8 program gives low-income families a cash subsidy, thus allowing them to rent privately owned existing housing stock. Ideally, the program was expected to allow low-income people to secure better housing than existed in the public sector, reduce the ghetto effect common in public housing, integrate neighborhoods, and ultimately be cost effective. However, studies show that even with subsidies, the quality of housing available for the poor is often substandard. In 1979 a General Accounting Office survey found that 42 percent of Section 8 housing surveyed contained one or more conditions violating federal housing standards or endangering the life, health, safety, or welfare of the occupants.[32] The cost/income squeeze in housing has proved to be highly problematic for both middle- and lower-income groups. Because of high housing costs, many middle-class families are compelled to become two-wage-earner families. Moreover, in some cases the second wage is used entirely to pay for the costs of home ownership. This situation is exacerbated for the poor, where two wage earners making the minimum wage or slightly above may have an insufficient combined income to cover the cost of adequate housing. This housing crisis generates serious problems, including homelessness.

HOMELESSNESS

The problem of homelessness has recently found its way into the American conscience. Although a long-standing problem in most large urban areas, homelessness has been on the rise, propelled onto center stage by media-generated images of "bag ladies," the mentally ill, chronic alcoholics, "street people," and uprooted families. Although interesting copy, popular stereotypes obscure the extent of homelessness and the true nature of the problem.

The actual number of homeless persons in the United States has become a matter of considerable public debate, with official HUD estimates ranging from 250,000 to 350,000—a number well below the generally accepted figure of 2 to 3 million.[33] Debates about the size of the homeless population also occur at the local level. For example, a mayoral task force estimated that there were from 800 to 1000 homeless people in the city of St. Louis in 1985. A survey by the Missouri Task Force on Survival placed the number of homeless in St. Louis between 8,000 and 10,000.[34] In any case, determining the number of homeless people a research question: fearful that an irate public will demand more services if the actual extent of homelessness is acknowledged, financially strapped federal, state, and local authorities often try to downplay the problem.

Although the exact number of homeless people is unknown, the population appears to be rapidly growing. A report released in 1987 by the U.S. Conference of Mayors assessed the extent of hunger, homelessness, and poverty in 26 American cities. Results showed that in all but one city the demand for emergency shelter increased by an average of 21 percent. As a consequence of this increase, almost two-thirds of the cities reported that resource limitations forced shelters to turn people away.[35] An earlier survey of emergency shelters in 83 cities done by the U.S. Conference of Mayors found that the number of homeless persons served by shelters increased by 71 percent from 1982 to 1983.[36] These data are corroborated by a study which estimated that the number of homeless in Missouri had doubled from 1980 to 1982.[37]

While it was once believed that the average homeless person was a skid row drunk, it is now apparent that a wide range of people are without permanent shelter. The homeless include retired people on small fixed incomes, many of whom lost their cheap single room occupancy (SRO) hotel rooms to gentrification; runaway teenagers; school dropouts; drug addicts; disabled and mentally ill people lost in a maze of outpatient services; unemployed people who have worn out their welcome with family or friends; young mothers on welfare who remain on long waiting lists for public housing;

TABLE 15.6. Primary Reason for Seeking Shelter by Ethnic Group, St. Louis Homeless Reception Center (May 1986–April 1987)

Primary Reason	Percent	Ethnic Composition				Total
		Black	White	Hispanic	Other	
Stranded/Relocating	12.21	134	167	9	4	314
Family Disturbance	8.44	143	69	1	4	217
Income Loss	1.87	29	19	0	0	48
Loss of Residence	19.60	417	72	2	13	504
Multi Family Occupancy	42.92	953	131	9	11	1104
Substandard Housing	3.30	80	5	0	0	85
Deinstitutionalization	2.33	32	26	0	2	60
Mental Illness	1.56	25	14	0	1	40
Other	5.21	101	31	0	2	134
Shelter time up	1.44	26	7	0	3	37
Missing Data	1.09	4	5	0	19	28
Totals	**100.00**	**1946**	**564**	**21**	**59**	**2572**

Source: Copyright 1987, National Association of Social Workers, Inc. Reprinted with permission, from Conference on Minority Issues, June 5, 1987, p. 9.

families who lost their overcrowded quarters; and "street people." About one-third of the homeless are mentally disabled, many of whom have been deinstitutionalized during the past 15 years.[38] The homeless also include infants who have never had a permanent bed or a bath in a real bathtub.

A 1987 report by the U.S. Conference of Mayors found that in all but one of the 26 cities surveyed, there was an increase in the number of homeless families with children.[39] In 1987 an interesting study of the homeless seeking shelter in St. Louis was done by Larry Kreuger, John Stretch, and Alice Johnson, using data collected by the Salvation Army Emergency Lodge and Reception Center. The study, summarized in Tables 15.6, 15.7, and 15.8, found that in the 2574 service cases (6541 nonduplicated individuals) studied from May 1986 to April 1987, there was a complex web of causality which produced or exacerbated homelessness in families, especially black families. The authors maintain that the major causes for homelessness in St. Louis include: (1) diminishing kinship support systems which have become inadequate to maintain families in multiple-family occu-

pancies, (2) a persistent shortage of low-cost housing, (3) an increased loss of tenancy, (4) an institutionalized system of income instability, (5) severe family disturbances (e.g., child abuse and domestic violence), (6) increased geographic mobility, and (7) a policy of deinstitutionalization unaccompanied by provision of necessary services.[40]

The Kreuger et al. study found that 76 percent of the people requesting emergency

TABLE 15.7. Age Distribution for Homeless Children St. Louis Homeless Reception Center (May 1986–April 1987)

Age Category	Count	Percent
0–3 yrs	1368	35.31%
4–6 yrs	910	23.49%
7–9 yrs	684	17.66%
10–12 yrs	503	12.98%
13–15 yrs	272	7.02%
16–18 yrs	137	3.54%
Total	**3874**	**100.00%**

Source: Copyright 1987, National Association of Social Workers, Inc. Reprinted with permission, from Conference on Minority Issues, June 5, 1987, p. 16.

TABLE 15.8.   Family Composition by Ethnic Group, St. Louis Homeless Reception Center (May 1986–March 1987)

Family Composition	Ethnic Composition				Total	Percent
	Black	White	Hispanic	Other		
Single Female without children	327	209	6	6	548	20.98%
Single Male without children	109	105	10	4	228	8.75%
Female with children	1433	162	4	26	1625	53.48%
Male with children	18	6	0	0	24	0.93%
Couple without children	8	20	0	1	29	1.10%
Couple with children	37	36	1	2	76	3.01%
Extended Family	13	7	0	0	20	0.81%
Other	1	1	0	1	3	0.13%
Missing Data	0	0	0	19	19	0.81%
Total	**1946**	**546**	**21**	**59**	**2572**	**100.00%**

Source: Copyright 1987, National Association of Social Workers, Inc. Reprinted with permission, from Conference on Minority Issues, June 5, 1987, p. 20.

assistance were black; 21 percent were white; and the remainder were from Hispanic or other minority groups. Although recording a higher number of minorities than other studies—for example, one study found that 47 percent of the homeless in Providence, Rhode Island, were nonwhite[41]—it appears that minorities are at a greater risk for homelessness. According to the St. Louis study, for blacks the major factor influencing a call for assistance in finding shelter was the elimination of a multi-family (several families occupying one domicile) occupancy.

The Kreuger et al. study also found that over 76 percent of homeless children (2962 children) were under the age of 10. According to Ellen Bassuk, children living in Boston shelters experienced profound effects of homelessness, including the following: 47 percent of the children showed at least one developmental lag on the Denver Developmental Screening Test; one-third had difficulty with language skills, fine and gross motor coordination, and with social and personal development; almost half of the school-age children were depressed and anxious, with one-third showing signs of clinical

depression; 43 percent had failed a grade, 24 percent were in special education classes, and nearly half were failing or doing below-average work in school.[42] Many of Bassuk's findings are corroborated by a study done by the Health Care for the Homeless Coalition of Greater St. Louis. Reporting for the period of August 1985 to March 1987, the coalition found that among the 360 homeless children given an on-site physical examination in a shelter, over 32 percent suffered from upper respiratory infections, 25 percent had incomplete immunizations, more than 14 percent suffered from infestation and skin disorders, and almost 9 percent had poor dentition.[43]

Bassuk also reports that 85 percent of homeless families in Massachusetts shelters are comprised of single mothers and their children. Although the majority of these families are receiving AFDC, the benefits are not high enough for them to secure a permanent domicile.[44] While not finding as high a number, Kreuger et al. found that over 63 percent of the potentially homeless population in St. Louis was composed of single female-headed households (most of them black) with children.

Causes for Homelessness

Although homelessness represents a single problem—people without homes—its complex etiology is illustrated by examining the homeless population. For example, some regard homelessness as a life choice, a freedom to roam without being tied down to a place. For others, particularly the mentally ill and chronic alcoholics, homelessness embodies the deterioration of an already overburdened public mental health system. The breakdown of the public health system is compounded by an influx of previously healthy people who, when forced into economic deprivation and homelessness, develop symptoms of mental disturbance. For other people, homelessness occurs because of cuts in federally subsidized housing stock and the cost-income squeeze of the housing market. Finally, a large group of people experience homelessness as a result of the inability of AFDC benefits to keep pace with the cost of living, especially in the area of housing and utilities. Despite the variety of causes, almost all forms of homelessness are connected by one factor—poverty. In that sense, homelessness—the inability to afford housing—is simply another symptom of poverty.

Proposals for Ending Homelessness

On July 22, 1987, President Ronald Reagan signed into law the Stewart B. McKinney Homeless Assistance Act. Although a step in the right direction, most observers believe that the 1987 allocation of $32 million was far too little to seriously impact the problem. Several broader proposals have emerged, however, for ameliorating the problem of homelessness. Chester Hartman suggests a nine-pronged solution, including: (1) a massive increase in the number of new and rehabilitated units offered to lower-income households; (2) lowering the required rent/income ratio in government housing from 30 to 25 percent; (3) arresting the depletion of low-income housing occurring through neglect, abandonment, conversion,

and sale; (4) preservation of the SRO hotels; (5) establishment of a national "right to shelter"; (6) local governments making available properties that could be used as shelters and secondstage housing; (7) creating legislation that would give tenants reasonable protection from eviction; (8) providing homeowners facing foreclosure with governmental assistance; and (9) the provision of suitable residential alternatives for mentally ill people.[45]

A proposal by Kim Hopper and Maria Foscarinis includes: (1) providing outreach to homeless persons eligible for Food Stamps and SSI benefits, (2) allowing homeless people to use Food Stamps to purchase prepared meals, (3) providing health and maternal benefits to homeless people, (4) ending permanent address requirements for receipt of welfare benefits, and (5) increasing Section 8 and public housing units.[46]

On the whole, Americans paid little attention to poverty for much of the 1970s and 1980s. Only when the despair turned public—when private despair turned into public homelessness—were people shocked into responding to the problems of poverty and homelessness. Perhaps it was the realization that America was beginning to resemble the impoverished Third World. Pictures of New Delhi were becoming the pictures of New York, Chicago, and Los Angeles. Whatever the reason, at least for the moment, homelessness appears to have captured the attention of the public.

HOUSING REFORM

The housing crisis faced by low-income people has led to a myriad of remediative proposals. Some conservative critics argue that low-income housing assistance should be abolished, thus allowing the law of supply and demand to regulate rents, and, ultimately, to drive down prices. Free market philosophy suggests that as rents increase, demand slackens, and, eventually, rents will drop to levels that encourage consumer activity. Other critics contend that government intervention in housing should occur through the supply side—in other words, the government should stimulate production in rental housing by offering financial incentives (e.g., tax breaks) to builders, entrepreneurs, and investors. If rental housing is made more profitable, more units will be built, and the increase in the housing stock would lower prices.

Some liberal critics argue that because housing is a necessity, and its demand is relatively inelastic, marketplace laws should not be allowed to dominate. The National Low Income Housing Coalition developed an eight-point housing program, including: (1) an income-based housing payment entitlement program, (2) expanded production and preservation programs for needs not met by housing payments, (3) guaranteed fair access to housing, (4) progressive and redistributive tax and spending policies, (5) greater reliance on community-based non-profit organizations, (6) retention of the existing housing stock, (7) less expensive and more accessible housing credit, and (8) a reduction in displaced residents caused by private or governmental action.[47]

Other observers argue that there is a need to impose federal credit and price controls to dampen speculation and encourage socially useful investment.[48] Still others argue that housing should be "decommodified"[49] through social rather than profit-oriented ownership and production. This sweeping policy would include public financing, land-use and cost controls, socially determined allocation of resources, local control of neighborhoods, and guarantees of housing choice.[50]

The housing problem is grounded in issues of availability and affordability. At its roots, it is a structural crisis situated in the failure of incomes to keep up with housing costs (a phenomenon accelerated in the bi-coastal regions of the United States), in an overdependence on credit to build and buy houses, and in the workings of a profit-making system that drives housing ownership, development, and management. Manifested in speculation, the profit motive has driven up the price of rental and residential property faster than income growth. As a profit is made by each succeeding link in the housing chain (real estate developers, lenders, builders, materials producers, investors, speculators, landlords, and homeowners), renters and homeowners are compelled to pay the costs. In that sense, the cost of every rental unit or home reflects the speculative gains made by past and present actors who directly and indirectly came into contact with that property.

The difficulty in securing decent low- and moderate-income housing is a serious problem facing modern society. The poor have a difficult time finding good quality housing, while the middle class, caught in the classic cost and income squeeze, are having an increasingly difficult time both in buying and holding onto their homes. This "affordability squeeze" affects both owners and renters and will likely result in increased mortgage foreclosures; elevated rates of property tax and delinquency defaults; more evictions and homelessness; overcrowding and doubling up of families; decreases in the consumption of other necessities; deteriorating neighborhoods; increased business failures; higher rates of unemployment in the building trades; and the collapse of some financial institutions—especially, some already shaky savings and loan associations.

Past and present government programs have only minimally ameliorated the housing crisis. Current housing programs are seriously underfunded, fragmentary, and without clear and focused goals. Because the federal government has often been viewed as an arbiter of the last resort, some critics contend that the government has the responsibility to insure that adequate housing becomes a right rather than a privilege, and that healthy, sound, and safe neighborhoods become a reality.

NOTES

1. Quoted in Charles S. Prigmore and Charles R. Atherton, *Social Welfare Policy: Analysis and Formulation* (Lexington, Mass.: D. C. Heath and Company, 1979), pp. 146–47.

2. Robert Morris, *Social Policy of the American Welfare State*, 2nd ed. (New York: Longman, 1985), p. 131.

3. Ibid., p. 132.

4. Barbara Habenstreit, *The Making of America* (New York: Julian Messner, 1971), p. 46.

5. Richard Geruson and Dennis McGrath, *Cities and Urbanization* (New York: Praeger, 1977), pp. 6–7.

6. Ibid., p. 40.

7. National Training and Information Center. *Insurance Redlining: Profits v. Policyholders* (Chicago: NTIC, 1973), p. 1.

8. See for example, Chester Hartman, ed., *America's Housing Crisis* (Boston: Routledge & Kegan Paul, 1983).

9. George Sternlieb and James W. Hughes, "Housing in the United States: An Overview," in George Sternlieb, James W. Hughes, Robert W. Burchell, Stephen C. Casey, Robert W. Lake, and David Listokin, *America's Housing* (New Brunswick, N.J.: Rutgers University, Center for Urban Policy Research, 1980), pp. 5–7; and Sumner M. Rosen, David Fanshel, and Mary E. Lutz, eds., *Face of the Nation, 1987* (Silver Spring, Md.: NASW, 1987), p. 68.

10. Ibid.

11. Ibid.

12. Hartman, *America's Housing Crisis*, p. 18.

13. Ibid., pp. 18–19.

14. Ibid., pp. 19–20.

15. Low Income Housing Information Service, "Rental Crisis Housing Index," Washington, D.C., 1986, p. 7.

16. Children's Defense Fund, *A Children's Defense Budget* (Washington, D.C.: Children's Defense Fund, 1986), pp. 194–95.

17. Cushing N. Dolbeare, "The Low-Income Housing Crisis," in Chester Hartman, *America's Housing Crisis*, pp. 31–33.

18. Center on Budget and Policy Priorities, *Smaller Slices of the Pie* (Washington, D.C.: Center on Budget and Policy Priorities, November 1985), p. 33.

19. Ibid.

20. Isaac Shapiro and Robert Greenstein, *Holes in the Safety Net* (Washington, D.C.: Center on Budget and Policy Priorities, 1988), p. 33.

21. George Sternlieb and James W. Hughes, "Back to the Central City: Myths and Realities." In Sternlieb et al., *America's Housing*, p. 173.

22. Children's Defense Fund, p. 196.

23. Rosen et al., *Face of the Nation*, p. 68.

24. Children's Defense Fund, p. 196.

25. Ibid.

26. Quoted in Dolbeare, "The Low-Income Housing Crisis," p. 200.

27. Ibid., pp. 36–37.

28. U.S. Bureau of the Census, "Characteristics of Households and Persons Receiving Noncash Benefits, 1979." Preliminary data from *Current Population Survey*, Table 5 (Washington, D.C.: U.S. Government Printing Office, March 1980); and *Current Population Reports*, Series P-23, No. 110 (Washington, D.C.: U.S. Government Printing Office, 1981).

29. Dolbeare, "The Low-Income Housing Crisis," p. 53.

30. Ibid., p. 69.

31. Ibid., pp. 69–70.

32. Ibid., p. 203.

33. Chester Hartman, "The Housing Part of the Homelessness Problem," in the Boston Foundation, *Homelessness: Critical Issues for Policy and Practice* (Boston: Boston Foundation, 1987), p. 16.

34. Larry W. Kreuger, John J. Stretch, and Alice K. Johnson, "Differentials Among Black and White Homeless Seeking Shelter: Inequality and Injustice Among Traumatized Families." Paper presented at Conference on Minority Issues, National Association of Social Workers, Washington, D.C., June 5, 1987, p. 1.

35. CHAMP, "Mayors' Report of Homelessness in Cities," *Notes from CHAMP*, February 1988, p. 7.

36. Center on Budget and Policy Priorities, *A Smaller Piece of the Pie*, p. 6.

37. Task Force on Survival, "Homeless in Missouri," Missouri Association for Social Welfare, Jefferson City, Missouri, December

1985, p. 8.

38. Louisa Stark, "Blame the System, Not the Victims," in Boston Foundation, *Homelessness*, p. 10.

39. CHAMP, *Notes*, p. 5.

40. Kreuger et al., "Differentials Among Black and White Homeless Seeking Shelter," p. 6.

41. CHAMP, *Notes*, p. 5.

42. Ellen Bassuk, "Homeless Families: Single Mothers and Their Families in Boston Shelters," in Ellen Bassuk, ed., *The Mental Health Needs of Homeless Persons* (San Francisco: Jossey-Bass, 1987).

43. Health Care for the Homeless Coalition of Greater St. Louis, "Progress Report," St. Louis, Missouri, 1987.

44. Bassuk, "Homeless Families," p. 18.

45. Chester Hartman, "The Housing Part of the Homelessness Problem," in Boston Foundation, *Homelessness*, pp. 17–19.

46. Kim Hopper and Maria Foscarinis, "Model Legislation: The Homeless Persons' Survival Act of 1986," in Boston Foundation, *Homelessness*, pp. 59–61.

47. Dolbeare, "The Low-Income Housing Crisis," pp. 50–51.

48. Michael E. Stone, "Housing and the Economic Crisis: An Analysis and Emergency Program," in Chester Hartman, *America's Housing Crisis*, pp. 136–37.

49. Decommodification is the term used by Claus Offe, *Contradictions of the Welfare State* (Cambridge, Mass.: The MIT Press, 1984). Offe defines decommodification as the transformation of a need or resource that was previously satisfied in the marketplace into a non-market commodity. For example, socialized medicine takes health care from the private marketplace and makes it an entitlement.

50. Emily Paradise Achtenberg and Peter Marcuse, "Toward the Decommodification of Housing: A Political Analysis and a Progressive Program," in Chester Hartman, *America's Housing Crisis*, pp. 220–26.

CHAPTER 16

Food Policy and Politics

This chapter will examine the federal response to hunger and the subsequent attempts to distribute foodstuffs to the poor. As part of that examination, this chapter will explore Food Stamps, WIC and other food programs, U.S. farm policy and the farm crisis, and overall problems of food production and distribution.

GOVERNMENTAL FOOD PROGRAMS

The politics of food—the way food is distributed in American society—is a complex phenomenon. Like all resources in capitalist society, food is a commodity that is bought and sold. In a pure market sense, those people who cannot afford to purchase food are unable to consume it. Left to the caprice of the marketplace many poor people would face malnutrition or starvation. This problem is particularly acute in an urban society where many people lack the necessary gardening skills and have little access to land. Providing the poor access to food is a redistributive function of the welfare state. The obligation of the government to provide food to the poor is similar to that of providing economic opportunity: when both are unavailable in adequate quantities, it is the responsibility of the welfare state to respond.

The federal government's response to hunger and malnutrition has consisted of several major programs: (1) Food Stamps, (2) the Commodity Distribution program, (3) the National School Lunch and Breakfast programs, (4) the Special Milk program, (5) Special Supplemental Nutrition Program for Women, Infants and Children (WIC) pro-

gram, (6) Child Care Food, (7) Summer Food program, (8) and the Meals on Wheels and Congregate Dining programs.

A Short History of Food Stamps and a Description of the Program

In 1933 Congress established the Federal Surplus Relief Corporation, an agency designed to distribute surplus commodity foods, as well as coal, mattresses, and blankets. In 1939 Congress established the Food Stamp program. By 1943, however, the Food Stamp program was terminated and a commodity food distribution program was reestablished. A pilot Food Stamp program was begun during the presidency of John F. Kennedy, and in 1964, the current Food Stamp Act (FS) was passed.

Although Food Stamps is a federal program administered by the United States Department of Agriculture, state and local welfare agencies qualify applicants and provide them with stamps. Recipients are given an allotment of stamps based upon family size and income, with eligibility requirements and benefits determined at the federal level. Food Stamp eligibility is based upon a means test. Recipients originally had to pay a set price (depending on family size and income) for their stamps, with the amount to be paid always less than the face value of the stamps. Therefore, some people were able to purchase $75 worth of stamps for $35. The difference between the amount paid and the face value of the stamps was called a "bonus." This system proved unwieldy, because many poor people could not even afford to purchase the stamps. In 1977 purchase requirements were dropped and, not surprisingly, national participation rates rose by 30 percent.

Several major changes in the FS program were enacted during the Reagan administration: (1) Income deductions were tightened so that only people on or near the poverty level could qualify for FS, (2) family income was calculated partly on past income rather than solely on current income, (3) programs were more closely monitored to reduce fraud and error, (4) benefits were cut by 1 percent, and (5) adjustments for inflation were delayed. Table 16.1 gives data for the state of Missouri as of October 1987.

Food Stamps: Who Is on the Program and What Does It Cost?

In 1985, 19.8 million people a month were on Food Stamps—close to 10 percent of all U.S. families. Of those households, about 58 percent were white, 33 percent black, and 9 percent Hispanic.[1] Forty-one percent of all FS recipients live in the South, 23 percent in the north-central area, 20 percent in the Northeast, and the remaining 16 percent in the West.[2] Forty-three percent of FS recipients have annual incomes of under $5,000, while 31 percent have incomes between $5,000 and $10,000. Only 26 percent of the recipients have annual incomes over $10,000.[3]

AFDC families are automatically eligible for FS. Eligibility is determined by gross income, which cannot exceed 130 percent of the federal poverty line, and by net income (after subtracting taxes, work expenses, and part of rent and utility bills), which must fall below the poverty line. Total assets cannot generally exceed $1,500 dollars.

FS program costs tend to be relatively high because of heavy utilization. In 1965 the FS program cost $32 million; by 1970 the costs had risen to $473 million, and by 1980 FS expenditures had jumped to $9 billion. In 1986 the cost of running the FS program stood at $11.7 billion.

Special Supplemental Nutrition Program for Women, Infants, and Children (WIC)

The WIC program was created by Public Law 92-433, and enacted on September 26, 1972. The program originally began as a two-year pilot program to provide nutritional counseling and supplemental foods to pregnant and breast-feeding women, infants, and young children at a nutritional risk. The goal of the program was to address areas of child development which were most affected by poor health and inadequate nutrition, including impaired learning.[4]

WIC is administered through the Food and Nutrition Service of the USDA, in conjunction with 1500 local agencies (mainly health departments). Each state receives cash grants and is responsible for developing, implementing, and monitoring its WIC program.[5] Eligibility is limited to low-income pregnant women, mothers who breast-feed their infants, and children up to age five. Qualified beneficiaries are given about $28 dollars a month in coupons to buy nutritious foods. About $1.5 billion was spent in 1986 and the program served roughly 3.2 million women and children.

Other Food Programs

Although FS is the largest food program in the United States, it is by no means the only program. In 1946 the National School Lunch Act was passed, which provides school-age children with hot lunches at reduced rates, or free if parents are unable to pay. The federal government, through the Food and Nutrition Service of the USDA, provides cash assistance and food commodities to state departments of education. Federal expenditures for the program were $3 billion in 1986 and 3.7 billion lunches were served to 22.9 million children. Free lunches are provided to school-age children whose family incomes are at or below 130 percent of the federal poverty level.

After research studies found a positive correlation between poor school performance and the failure of school-age children to have a nutritious breakfast, the federal government instituted the School Breakfast program that has the same eligibility standards as the School Lunch program, i.e., parents must be at or below 130 percent of the federal poverty line. Smaller than the School Lunch program, the breakfast program serves only about 15 percent of those served by the School Lunch program,[6] in 1983, 553 million breakfasts were served to 3.4 million children. The cost of the program in 1986 was about $410 million.

Although some of the low-income elderly receive Food Stamps, they can also be served by Meals on Wheels and the Congregate Meal Dining program. Meals on Wheels was begun in 1972 and was designed to improve nutrition for the elderly. Various community agencies arrange the daily delivery of meals to elderly persons living at home, and aged persons who receive FS can use them to purchase the meals (for others a donation is requested). The Congregate Meal Dining program provides meals at such places as Senior Citizen Centers.

Other federal food programs include the emergency food and shelter program, which provides funds to local agencies through a national board of charitable organizations. This national charitable board, in part consisting of the United Way, the Salvation Army, and Catholic Charities, distributes funds ($70 million in 1986) to local charities, soup kitchens, shelters, and other organizations that deal with hunger and homelessness.[7] The federal government also provides funding ($50 million in 1986) to help subsidize emergency food agencies and to help pay for the storage and distribution of federal surplus food commodities.[8]

Have the Food Programs Worked?

Evidence on the effectiveness of federal food policies is inconclusive. For example, the American Dietary Association found little hard evidence that the WIC program was effective.[9] A report by the General Accounting Office (GAO) to the Committee on Agricul-

ture, Nutrition, and Forestry, stated that "no group of studies provided the kind of evidence to refute or confirm the claims that WIC is effective."[10] The GAO report did affirm that the WIC program was responsible for decreasing the proportion of low-birth-weight babies of eligible mothers by 16 to 20 percent.[11] Moreover, WIC's effects on mean birth weights also appears to be positive. The report tentatively concluded that black and teenage mothers who participated in WIC had better birth outcomes than comparable women. According to Michael Harrington et al., studies by the USDA and others show that WIC has: (1) improved the diets of low-income women, infants, and children, (2) increased the proportion of low-income pregnant women who utilize prenatal care, and (3) reduced anemia among WIC recipients. Harrington also maintains that research conducted at the Harvard School of Public Health demonstrated that every $1 spent on the prenatal portion of WIC saved $3 in short-term hospital costs.[12]

Despite the severe budget cuts during the Reagan administration, WIC is one of the few programs that avoided major cuts between 1980 and 1987. However, given its level of funding, WIC reaches only a minority of eligible women and children, and in 1987, only 45 percent of all women and children eligible for WIC were served. More than 100 counties have no WIC program, and many counties turn away people or have long waiting lists.[13] While states may provide additional funds for WIC, in early 1988 only 11 states or jurisdictions (District of Columbia, Illinois, Indiana, Massachusetts, Michigan, Minnesota, New York, Pennsylvania, Texas, Washington, and Wisconsin) supplemented the program, and in two of those states (Michigan and Washington), the additional funds were used solely to cover administrative costs.[14]

Because of red tape and inadequate outreach services, the Food Stamp program fails to reach millions of people—one-third of those eligible (12 to 15 million people) presently receive no assistance. In addition, the gap between those served and those in need has widened. Only 59 percent of eligible people received FS in an average month in 1985, compared to 68 percent in 1980.[15] Although the causes for nonparticipation are complex, one University of Michigan study found that more than half of all eligible persons who fail to participate either mistakenly believe they are ineligible or don't know of their eligibility.[16] Modest government efforts to alleviate this problem were ended in 1981 when Congress terminated federal funding for outreach efforts.

Harrington maintains that USDA surveys indicate that FS has been effective in improving the nutrition of millions of Americans.[17] However, the 1985 Physicians' Task Force on Hunger identified 150 "hunger counties"—counties in which substantial numbers of poor people are undernourished and not receiving Food Stamps. The Task Force report recommended: (1) giving recipients cash or credit cards to reduce the stigma associated with coupons, (2) improving outreach efforts to nonparticipants, and (3) simplifying the process for obtaining Food Stamps.

Food Stamp benefits are not overly generous, with the average 1987 benefit being about 49 cents per meal per person. The maximum benefit—only available to persons who have no income after necessities—is 73 cents per person per meal. Studies by the USDA reveal that most families whose food expenditures equal the maximum FS benefit lack adequate diets, and only one-tenth of those families receive adequate nutrition.[18] Moreover, a 1982 study issued by the USDA found that only 50 percent of the eligible elderly were receiving FS, a situation apparently more acute in rural areas.

The budget cuts of the early and middle 1980s compounded an already difficult situation by reducing the FS budget by $6.8 billion from 1982 to 1985, including a $1.9 billion cut in 1985 alone. Approximately two-thirds of those cuts were achieved by cutting benefits for poverty-level households, thereby eliminating several hundred thousand people and reducing benefits for close to 20 million.[19]

Other large reductions were made in child nutrition programs, including the School Lunch and School Breakfast programs. In 1981 child nutrition programs were cut by 28 percent, an amount exacerbated by the major cuts made in 1980. As a result, about 2 million fewer children ate free or subsidized school lunches in 1988 than before the cuts were made. Moreover, roughly one-third of the decline in school lunch participation occurred among low-income children. School lunch charges to parents of children from moderate income ($14,000–$20,000 a year for a family of four) families have quadrupled since 1980, and as a consequence of the budget cuts, a middle-income family with two children in school paid over $100 more in 1988.

THE FARM CRISIS

Because most USDA food programs function as an indirect income support for farmers, the relationship between food prices, governmental supports, and food subsidization forms a complex fabric interweaving both consumers and producers. In many places in rural America a farming crisis has reached epidemic proportions rivaling the 1930s.[20] Agricultural members of the American Bankers Association estimated that 3.8 percent of all farmers had filed for bankruptcy in 1985 alone.[21] A USDA (1985) study of 1.7 million farms indicated that 214,000 were in serious financial difficulty, with 38,000 classified as technically insolvent.[22] Former Secretary of Agriculture Bob Bergland identified 700,000 U.S. farms as being family or commercial farms and noted that 220,000 of them would not financially survive.[23] On November 10, 1988, just two days after the presidential election, the FmHA sent out 85,000 notices to farmers advising them of their options and the need for debt restructuring. In short, the in-

TABLE 16.1. State of Missouri Food Stamp Program, October 1987.

Number of Persons in Household	Limit AFDC/SSI Monthly Income	Limit Maximum Gross Income	Limit Maximum Net Monthly Income	Allotment Maximum Coupon
1	*	$596	$459	$ 87
2	*	802	617	159
3	$775	1008	756	228
4	963	1214	934	290
5	1143	1420	1092	344
6	1373	1625	1250	413
7	1520	1831	1409	457
8	1736	2037	1567	522
9	1953	2243	1726	587
10	2170	2449	1885	652
11	2386	2655	2044	717
12	2603	2861	2203	782
13	2820	3067	2362	847
14	3036	3273	2521	912
15	3253	3479	2680	977
16	3470	3685	2839	1042
17	3686	3891	2998	1107
18	3903	4097	3157	1172
19	4120	4303	3316	1237
20	4336	4509	3475	1302
For Each Additional Member Add		+206	+159	+65

* Categorically eligible one and two-person households are always entitled to at least $10 in benefits.

ability of many farmers to restructure debt will result in substantial foreclosures now and in the future.

A good indicator of the rural crisis is farm indebtedness. Low crop prices have created a national farm debt of $215 billion (growing by $58 million a day).[24] Financially strapped farmers owe about $50 billion in farm debts which they cannot repay—debts which account for roughly 23 percent of the total farm debt in the agricultural sector.[25] A 1985 USDA report indicated that about 18 percent (386,000) of U.S. farms have less than 60 percent equity in their farm businesses, with these farms accounting for 56 percent of all farm debt. The USDA estimates that if current economic conditions continue, 2.8 percent of family farms will become insolvent yearly. Moreover, according to Bruce Bullock, USDA data reveal that as much

as 24 percent of existing farm debt could not be repaid at a zero interest rate or even if farm product prices increased by 50 percent.[26] These economic statistics translate into the fact that over 2,000 farms closed weekly in 1986.[27]

Causes for the Farm Crisis

The causes for the farm crisis are complex. Historically, American agriculture has never been a stable enterprise. Since the nineteenth century, farmers have ridden an economic roller coaster of good and bad times, with much of this instability due to variables outside their control, i.e, weather, international trade and monetary policy, and government farming policies.

American agriculture was heavily influenced by large-scale operations from the early days of European colonization. Early agriculture was characterized by the slave plantations of the South, the Spanish haciendas of the Southwest, and the large wheat and cattle farms of the West. Much of the agricultural production was in the hands of wealthy individuals or foreign investors.

By the mid-1800s, federal government policies began to encourage the growth of small family farms. The development of small-scale agriculture was aided by the defeat of slavery, the institution of the Homestead Acts, and the general movement westward. Despite the new agricultural opportunities, farmers found themselves caught in the classic cost-price squeeze. High prices for seeds, credit, and transportation often exceeded the crop prices offered by the large grain monopolies. This situation resulted in a series of rural depressions in the late nineteenth and early twentieth centuries.[28]

Angry farmers responded to these injustices by demanding protection from the railroads, banks, and grain monopolies. Through political organizing they created the Farmers Alliance, the Populist Party, the Greenback Party and the Non-Partisan League.[29] Although the World War I period brought some relief, it was quickly followed by a major farming disaster almost a decade before the Great Depression of the 1930s.

Coupled with severe droughts, the Depression of the 1930s seriously crippled rural America. Outraged by years of poor farming and inadequate or nonexistent governmental policies, farmers began to engage in direct action. In the plains states, farmers barricaded highways to stop foreclosures, insisted that local lenders exercise leniency, called farm strikes and, in some cases, rioted.[30] Legislatures in farm states tried to curb the insurgency by enacting moratoriums on foreclosures, while the federal government moved to set prices at parity levels (the ratio between farm prices and input/output costs).[31]

In the 1930s Congress passed the Parity Farm Program, an innovative piece of legislation which contained three central features:

1. The Commodity Credit Corporation (CCC) was established to set a minimum floor under farm prices. The CCC was designed to make loans to farmers whenever the prices offered by the grain companies were less than the cost of production. Crops were to be used as collateral, and whenever prices became normal, farmers were to repay the loans with interest.

2. Farm production was managed in order to maintain a balance between supply and demand and thus prevent surpluses. Managing supply and demand would also reduce the government's responsibility for storing and purchasing surpluses.

3. A national grain reserve was created to stabilize consumer prices in the event of droughts or natural disasters.[32]

In 1942 Congress established the price support levels at 90 percent of parity. From 1942 to 1953, the average prices paid to farmers were at 90 to 100 percent of parity, thereby raising market prices, insuring a secure income for farmers, reducing the need for excessive debt, and encouraging stabilization in the price of grain.

By the end of World War II, powerful corporations, academics, "free-traders," and others began waging war on the Farm Parity Program. Soil conservation, supply management, and parity were characterized as socialistic programs which interfered with a free market economy. Grain companies called for lower prices in order to sell abroad, arguing that expanded exports and food-aid programs would compensate for lower commodity prices. Industrialists maintained that lower food prices would translate into cheaper labor costs, and agribusiness corporations believed that lowered commodity prices would result in more production, thereby increasing the use of their products. The small farmer lost to this corporate coalition, and in 1953 President Eisenhower and his Secretary of Agriculture, Ezra Taft Benson, helped defeat the Farm Parity Program.

At least for the farmer, the optimism of the corporate sector proved ill-founded. The purchasing power of net farm income decreased even as exports rose. Held constant in 1967 dollars, the purchasing power of net farm income dropped from an annual average of $25 billion during 1942–52 (the years of farm parity) to an average of $13.3 billion from 1953–72. In 1952 net farm income was greater than total farm debt; by 1983 net farm income was less than farm interest payments.[33]

The rural crisis does not affect all classes of farmers equally. For example, in 1984 almost one-sixth of all U.S. farming households suffered net income losses while a ninth had total incomes of over $60,000.[34] Farmers with middle-sized operations (80- to 500-acre range) were being forced to abandon farming, while large farms appeared to be growing, as were the number of small farms. This economic stratification is further illustrated by the fact that in 1984 more than two-fifths of all U.S. farms had total annual sales of less than $10,000, accounting for only 2 percent of all farm sales. These farms experienced an overall net loss of income, and farm households with sales of less than $100,000 per year earned most of their income from nonfarm employment. On the other hand, farm households with sales exceeding $500,000 a year earned an average income of $219,000 in 1984. Three-fifths of the total income of farming families (a figure that is growing) in 1984 came from nonfarm employment.[35]

Unfortunately, statistics do not tell the human side of the farm crisis. An article in the Sioux Falls, South Dakota, *Argus Leader*, tells a different story:

Out in the fields, in the countryside beyond the small-town street lights, the harvest continues.

But it's not corn being plucked from the snow cover. It's men and women, farmers and farm wives.

A gunshot explodes in rural Pipestone; a farmer is dead.

Four graves are dug in Hills, Iowa, after a distraught farmer kills a banker, a neighbor, his wife and himself.

And the tears falling on the kitchen table in southwest Aurora County are only ripples in a growing sea of agricultural anguish.[36]

Family farming symbolizes many of America's cherished traditional values—hard work, independence, strong families, close-knit communities, and democratic institutions. Farming for many rural families is not a vocation but a way of life. The connection to the land, often a legacy from parents or grandparents, creates a commitment to place, family heritage, and a dedication to environmental preservation.[37] Consequently, the psychological connection to farming means that many farmers see themselves as farmer-caretakers, and without that identity, the sense of "self" becomes emptied. Financial failure may therefore leave farmers with a sense of personal failure as well as with shame and disgrace for having failed both their families and their legacies. This situation can result in emotional disturbances ranging from stress and depression to self-destructive or aggressive behavior.[38] Reverend Paul Tidemann, a Lutheran minister who studied the farm crisis, reported that, "The loss of a farm . . . is not the same as a loss of a job. It signals the loss of personal and family connection to the land. It prompts a sense of betrayal, in many cases, of generations of farmers, past, present, and future."[39]

Many experts attribute the farm crisis to several factors, including (1) excessive debt, (2) high interest rates, (3) poor advice from the federal government, (4) the machinations of grain traders, agribusiness, and commodity trading, (5) the slowing down of foreign export markets, (6) the strong dollar of the early and middle 1980s, (7) falling farmland prices and lower inflation, (8) the effect of the free-trade ideology, and (9) U.S. foreign policy initiatives that affect agriculture. According to Bullock, "The agricultural sector financed its trip to the current situation on borrowed capital. Unfortunately, for a large part of the agricultural debt expansion over the past 10 years, the capacity to repay from farm earnings never existed."[40]

The almost frantic borrowing of large amounts of capital by farmers was based on several factors. For one, in the early and middle 1970s, USDA and farm extension experts advised farmers to plant "fencerow to fencerow" in order to take advantage of export markets and the high rate of inflation. Moreover, these experts were advising farmers that either they would have to "get big or get out." Heeding this advice, and developing a high production mentality, farmers were forced to raise their input costs by upgrading their farming operation through buying or renting more land, purchasing modern equipment, and relying more heavily on chemical means for increasing production.

The capital for this expansion was raised by borrowing money on the "paper value" of inflated farmland. Although farmers kept losing money on their crops and livestock, eager private, cooperative, and government lenders offered loans based on their belief that farmland prices would continue to rise. The increase in production and the softening of foreign markets (sometimes based on foreign policy, e.g., President Carter's ban of grain exports to the Soviet Union) created huge surpluses. The slowing down of inflation, coupled with the high interest rates of the Reagan administration, began to force down land prices. For example, the USDA estimated that the price of farmland fell by more than 30 percent in 1984; in ten midwestern states land values fell between 40 and 59 percent.[41] As a result, vulnerable farmers were forced into bankruptcy, and as their land and machinery went to auc-

tion, values were forced down for all farmers. A downward spiral of falling values led to insolvency for farmers and bankers nationally. In the end, farmers who went into substantial debt for capital and operating loans (using their inflated land as collateral) found themselves with high debt-asset ratios. This situation, coupled with the strong dollar of the mid-1980s (making food and other American exports expensive), and the adverse weather in many parts of the farmbelt, caused farmers to become unable to repay their debts.

Some critics maintain that traders and the grain monopolies lay at the heart of the problem. For example, while farm exports increased by 143 percent from 1973–1983, net farm income dropped by 40 percent.[42] On the other hand, grain traders profited from the renewed price instability, allowing them to reap enormous profits through speculation, and therefore, to increase their control over agricultural, transportation, and food processing industries.[43] The ideological tool used by these large multinational corporations was the concept of free trade. While the tenets of free trade suggest that markets will regulate price and demand, in reality, free trade worked to the advantage of powerful multinational corporations. Moreover, the ideology of free trade was problematic because it encouraged high-volume production at lower profit margins, thereby making it difficult to use sound soil, water, and conservation practices.[44]

The U.S. commodities trade is dominated by a few large corporations such as Cargill, Louis Dreyfus, Bunge and Born, Mutsui/Cook, and Andre/Garnac. These corporations handle 96 percent of all U.S. wheat exports, 95 percent of corn and 80 percent of oats and sorghum. According to critics, these corporations lobbied for lower price supports, further exposing farmers to a predatory marketplace stacked against them. When farm debt rose, multinationals argued that the solution lay in increased exports, a move that required cutting price support levels even further. Thus, instead of ushering in prosperity, the export expansionists brought the farming community a 1930s style depression.[45]

The effects of the farm crisis extend beyond the farming community. As farmers go bankrupt, other agriculturally linked systems experience the ripples. Agricultural and rural banks—often overextended—feel the economic stress of bankrupt farmers, and many have gone under. Agricultural implement and feed dealers have been severely affected by the inability of farmers to purchase their goods or repay their debt. Rural churches report declines in membership and paltry collections as farm families are forced to move away or decline to attend because of their inability to contribute. Counties face eroded tax bases as land values deteriorate and out-migration occurs. Most observers agree that the farm crisis has profound consequences for the entire farm-to-market chain as well as the whole fabric of rural life.

The farm crisis also has secondary economic effects. For example, almost 21 percent of the work force is linked to agriculture, including 55,000 jobs in steel mills. When a farm is sold and equipment auctioned off, an oversupply of used machinery occurs, thereby creating a disincentive for the purchase of new machinery. Every liquidated farm means the loss of five to seven jobs; every three bankrupt farms destroys another rural business.[46] On the other hand, each dollar earned by a farmer creates an additional five dollars in goods and services.[47]

U.S. Farm Policy

In recent years, the federal government has made several attempts to reduce the agricultural surplus resulting from overproduction. One such attempt occurred in 1983 under the auspices of the Payment-in-Kind (PIK) program. To encourage farmers to participate in this set-aside program, the Secretary of Agriculture offered to compensate them by offering a partial payment in the form of grain stored in government stockpiles. The intent of the PIK program was to avoid cash payments to farmers while at the same time reducing the cost of maintaining a large government inventory of grain. A major drought occurred simultaneously with the PIK program which, in effect, raised market prices by reducing production. Without the effects of the drought the release of government grain stocks under the PIK program would have further depressed market prices. In any event, the PIK program was developed only as a short-term measure.[48]

After years of debate among farm, agribusiness, corporate, and commodity groups, President Reagan signed into effect the Food and Security Act of 1985. This legislation is distinctive in three ways: (1) it is the most complicated farm bill ever passed, (2) it costs the federal government more than previous farm bills, and (3) the price supports, at least in terms of parity, are lower than in previous bills.[49] The 1985 farm bill operates in the following manner. A target price is set by Congress and the Secretary of Agriculture, and if prices fall below that level, participating farmers receive a deficiency payment from the government. This system is directly connected to the loan rates set by the Commodity Credit Corporation (CCC). For example, in 1986 the CCC loan rate for a bushel of corn was only $1.92 while the target price was $3.03. Because the market price is roughly the CCC loan rate, the federal government made up the deficiency of $1.10 per bushel of corn. On 7 billion bushels of corn, this requires almost $8 billion in subsidies. Despite this, the 1986 target price of $3.03 per bushel of corn was, according to USDA estimates, 17 cents less a bushel than it actually costs to raise corn.[50] This means that farmers are losing money on every bushel harvested, forcing them to borrow money to cover their losses. Grain corporations and foreign buyers are thus allowed to purchase grain at prices over $1.00 below the cost of production. Hence, federal policy subsidizes the grain corporations at the expense of farmers, taxpayers, and the general public.

An alternative proposal to the 1985 farm bill has been HR-1425 and S-658, the Farm Act of 1987. Sponsored by Tom Harkin (D-Iowa) and Richard Gephardt (D-Missouri), this bill would establish price supports at 70 percent of the government calculated parity price for each commodity. In each year of the program the parity price would be increased by 1 percent until, in the eleventh year, 80 percent of parity is reached. In addition to price increases, there would be mandatory production controls (subject to approval by a farmer referendum) limiting agricultural commodity production to meet domestic consumption demands, export, humanitarian, and strategic reserve needs. Excess production by a farmer would be stored and applied toward the following year's quota. In addition, components of the bill would discourage the sale of farmland to other than working farm families.[51] Although the bill would not result in 100 percent of parity, it might allow at least some farmers to survive.

If enacted, proponents claim the bill would increase net farm income by $21 billion a year, cut government spending by $14.4 billion, eliminate costly subsidy payments and the need for government purchase of surplus commodities, and increase export earnings (despite slightly lower export volume). The effect of higher food prices would be offset by allocating an additional $1 billion for Food Stamps, and by expanding eligibility. In addition, the bill would discourage the dumping of heavily subsidized commodities into underdeveloped nations, thereby aiding their agricultural producers. Lastly, the bill would prohibit the importation of food which has been grown with pesticides banned for use by U.S. producers, disallow imported food containing chemicals that exceed the levels tolerated in U.S. food production, and require the labeling of food containing imported substances. Some supporters argue that this bill would raise inflation by less than .25 percent.[52]

The domestic crisis in food is reflected in international markets. The great volume of American farm goods sent abroad is sharply decreasing yearly. Without vast foreign markets for American food, and with an overproduction of farm goods domestically, the American farmer has nowhere to turn. Paradoxically, a primary factor that helped make America a great industrial nation—cheap food—threatens the existence of American rurality. In short, without major structural reforms such as higher farm price supports, increased food prices, and debt relief, it can be expected that a greater number of family farms will fail each year.

Rural Poverty

The problems in food production have helped to contribute to an overall rural crisis. Contrary to some misconceptions, the population of nonmetropolitan counties grew by 16 percent from 1970 to 1980, and it is estimated that close to 25 percent of the U.S. population now lives in nonmetropolitan counties. Moreover, for the first time in 160 years the growth in rural and small town communities has been greater than in metropolitan areas. Nevertheless, this rural growth has been variable, with most of it occurring in the nonmetropolitan counties of Southern Appalachia, the upper Great Lakes, Northern New England, the Nevada-Utah-Colorado basin, the Ozarks, the Gulf Coast, East Texas, and the Texas Hill Country. Other areas, especially the Corn Belt, the Southern Coastal Plains, and the Great Plains states have experienced depopulation.[53]

Despite this population growth, rural income is only 78 percent of urban income, and 40 percent of the 32.5 million poor people in the United States live in nonmetropolitan areas. Members of rural communities, especially minorities, are among the most impoverished. Most of the 85 counties in which up to 50 percent of the population are below the poverty line are located in Appalachia, the Ozarks, areas of the Southern Coastal Plain, the Southwest, and the Northern Plains. At least 40 percent of the population in many of these counties is either black, American Indian, or Hispanic.[54] In addition, rural people are often overrepresented in state hospitals, public homes for the aged, state schools for children, and other agencies normally viewed as institutions of the last resort.

Contemporary rural life has been shaped by several socioeconomic factors, including the absence of economic opportunity and social mobility. In particular, the lack of good-paying jobs has resulted in a migration of rural families to urban areas, particularly in families where the primary breadwinner possesses skills and education. For the younger worker, the lure of better paying jobs in urban areas is a powerful enticement. The college graduate from a rural area may find it almost impossible to return home given the dearth of economic opportunities that characterize many nonurban areas. In essence, the lure of economic opportunities creates a "bright flight" from rural to urban areas. As the pool of skilled and intellectual workers in rural areas begins to evaporate, few industries are attracted to the area and, in general, the economic conditions further deteriorate. Moreover, as rural counties begin to experience the same social and economic desperation as impoverished urban areas, similar manifestations of poverty begin to appear. Drug use, alcoholism, theft, high dropout rates, teenage pregnancies, and other social problems begin to become more commonplace in the rural landscape. The increased need for mental health and economic development services creates a fertile area for rural social work activities.

The production, distribution, and consumption of food has traditionally been a political issue. The federal government must respond to the needs of diverse groups that have an interest in food—farmers, consumers, the poor or their advocates, food distributors, grain traders, Third World countries that depend on America for food, and wealthier nations that purchase U.S. food (and occasionally compete for foreign food markets).

The federal government has responded to these interests by creating a patchwork quilt of policies and programs. Primary among them is Food Stamps, an ingenious approach that helps keep food affordable for low-income consumers, helps stabilize farm prices, slows down agricultural surpluses by subsidizing consumption, and allows food merchants and distributors to increase profits by insuring a volume of subsidized consumers. The food situation in America, at least for farmers and the poor, can best be described as a crisis. Ironically, many farmers now profit from Food Stamps not because it helps control the surplus of farm goods, but because it provides them benefits as recipients. It is truly a tragedy when the producers of food are unable to purchase what they grow.

NOTES

1. Diane DiNitto and Thomas R. Dye, *Social Welfare: Politics and Public Policy* (Englewood Cliffs, N.J.: Prentice-Hall, 1987), p. 172.
2. Ibid.
3. Ibid.
4. Illa Tennison, "WIC Policy Analysis." Unpublished paper, 1987, School of Social Work, University of Missouri–Columbia, p. 5.
5. Ibid.
6. Children's Defense Fund, *A Children's Defense Budget* (Washington, D.C.: Children's Defense Fund, 1986), p. 185.
7. Children's Defense Fund, p. 189.
8. Ibid.
9. Tennison, "WIC Policy Analysis," p. 12.
10. Ibid.
11. Ibid., p. 13.
12. Michael Harrington, with the assistance of Robert Greenstein and Eleanor Holmes Norton, *Who Are the Poor?* (Washington, D.C.: Justice for All National Office, 1987), p. 26.
13. Children's Defense Budget, p. 186.
14. Isaac Shapiro and Robert Greenstein, *Holes in the Safety Nets* (Washington, D.C.: Center on

Budget and Policy Priorities, 1988), pp. 33–34.

15. Children's Defense Budget, p. 183.

16. Ibid.

17. Harrington, *Who Are the Poor?* p. 26.

18. Ibid.

19. Children's Defense Fund, p. 182.

20. M. Drabenstott and M. Duncan, "Another Troubled Year for U.S. Agriculture," *Journal of the American Society of Farm Managers and Rural Appraisers* 1, no. 49 (1985), pp. 58–66.

21. Cited in Joanne Mermelstein, "Criteria of Rural Mental Health Directors in Adopting Farm Crisis Programming Innovation." Unpublished Ph.D. dissertation, Public Policy Analysis and Administration, St. Louis University, 1986, p. 3.

22. Ibid.

23. Ibid., pp. 3–4.

24. John M. Herrick, "Farmers' Revolt! Contemporary Farmers' Protests in Historical Perspective: Implications for Social Work Practice," *Human Services in the Rural Environment* 10, no. 1 (April 1986), p. 9.

25. J. Bruce Bullock, "The Farm Credit Situation: Implications for Agricultural Policy," *Human Services in the Rural Environment* 10, no. 1 (April 1986), p. 20.

26. Ibid., p. 12.

27. Steve Little, "Parity: Survival of the Family Farm." Unpublished paper, 1986, School of Social Work, University of Missouri–Columbia, p. 3.

28. G. Kaye Kellogg, "The Crisis of the Family Farm in America Today." Unpublished paper, 1987, School of Social Work, University of Missouri–Columbia, p. 3.

29. Howard Jacob Karger, *The Sentinels of Order: A Case Study of the Minneapolis Settlement House Movement, 1915–1950* (Lanham, Md.: University Press of America, 1987).

30. Everett E. Luoma, *The Farmer Takes a Holiday: The Story of the National Farmer's Holiday Association and the Farmers' Strike of 1932–33* (New York: Exposition Press, 1967).

31. United States Department of Agriculture, "History of Agricultural Price Support and Adjustment Programs, 1933–84," *Bulletin No. 485*, Economic Research Service, Washington, D.C., 1984, pp. 8–9.

32. Kellogg, "The Crisis of the Family Farm," p. 4.

33. Little, "Parity," pp. 8–9.

34. Mary Ahearn, "Financial Well-Being of Farm Operators and Their Households," United States Department of Agriculture, Economic Research Service, *Report No. 563*, Washington, D.C., September 1986, p. iii.

35. Ibid.

36. Steve Young, *Argus Leader*, December 25, 1985. Quoted in "Editorial," by Joanne Mermelstein and Paul Sundet, Guest Editors, *Human Services in the Rural Environment*, 10, no. 1 (April 1986), p. 2.

37. Mermelstein, "Criteria of Rural Mental Health Directors," pp. 5–6.

38. Ibid., p. 7.

39. Quoted in Herrick, "Farmer Revolt," p. 9.

40. Bullock, "The Farm Credit Situation," p. 12.

41. Mermelstein, "Criteria of Rural Mental Health Directors," pp. 2–3.

42. Little, "Parity," p. 9.

43. Ibid.

44. United States Department of Agriculture, "Economic Indicators of the Farm Sector," *Farm Sector Review, ERS, ECIFS* 4-3, Washington, D.C., 1984, pp. 4, 16.

45. Little, "Parity," pp. 10–11.

46. Doug Wertish, "The Effects of Losing 10 Percent of the Faribault Area Farmers." Faribault, Minn.: Faribault Area Vo-Tech Institute, 1985.

47. Kellogg, "The Crisis of the Family Farm," p. 9.

48. Little, "Parity," p. 12.

49. Ibid.

50. Kellogg, "The Crisis of the Family Farm," pp. 9–10.

51. League of Rural Voters, "The Family Farm Act of 1987 (Harkin-Gephardt Bill)," Washington, D.C., February 26, 1987.

52. Ibid.

53. Emilia E. Martinez-Brawley, "Rural Social Work," *Encyclopedia of Social Work*, 18th ed. (Silver Spring, Md.: NASW, 1987), p. 522.

54. Ibid., p. 523.

CHAPTER 17

Employment Policies

This chapter examines the relationship between employment policy and social welfare. The absence of adequate employment contributes to a variety of psychological and physiological problems; therefore, a range of social programs has been deployed to aid Americans who are unemployed or underemployed. The history of employment policy in the United States shows a gradual expansion of programs until the policies of the Reagan administration reduced them sharply. Employment policy has become more important for social welfare, as the popularity of workfare programs demonstrates. At the same time, however, the lack of employment opportunity contributes to a growing American underclass.

In a market economy most people are expected to meet their needs by participation in the labor market. Work provides them income with which to purchase goods and services, as well as benefits which provide some security against the cost of health care and retirement. The labor market in capitalist economies, however, is not well synchronized with productivity, thus resulting in the failure of employment as a method to provide the basic needs of people. As a consequence, many people who could work must depend on social welfare programs for economic support. A little over half–56 percent–of the poor people in the United States are adults of working age.[1]

The failure of the labor market to meet the economic needs of the population has been the source of important distinctions in employment policy. One set of distinctions focuses on the experiences of workers. People over 16 looking for work are counted by the Department of Labor as *unemployed*. But the unemployment rate does not assess the adequacy of employment. For example, part-time workers who wish to work full-time are counted as employed and workers holding jobs below their skill levels are not identified, even though such workers are *underemployed*. Finally, some workers simply give up and stop looking for work, relying on other methods to support themselves. Such *discouraged workers* do not appear in the unemployment rate because they are not actively looking for work.

A second set of distinctions relates to economic performance. In a robust economy, businesses start up and close down in significant numbers, leaving workers temporarily out of work until they find other jobs. Such *frictional unemployment* is considered unavoidable and the cost of a constantly changing economy. *Structural unemployment* "refers to deeper and longer-lasting maladjustments in the labor market," such as the changes in the technical skills required for new forms of production.[2] Because of swings in economic performance, unemployment may be *cyclical* as when recessions pitch the rate upward. And because certain groups of workers in certain regions have persistent difficulty finding work because of the absence of jobs, unemployment is sometimes *chronic*. Michael Sherraden has examined how these components vary in the composition of the unemployment rate, concluding that structural and frictional factors account for about one-third, the cyclical factor for about one-fourth, and chronic unemployment for about one-half.[3]

These distinctions are important because social welfare is often connected directly to the employment experience of Americans. When people are out of work, they frequently rely on welfare benefits to tide them over. Thus, welfare programs are often designed to complement the labor market. This has led some observers to refer to welfare as a "social wage," or, in other words, the amount paid workers by the government through welfare programs when they are not able to participate in the labor market. Logically, much of welfare could be eliminated if well-paying jobs were plentiful, but such has not been the case in the United States. An unemployment rate of 7 percent has been tacitly accepted by policymakers, meaning that between 7.5 and 8 million workers at any given time are not employed.[4] Yet, in 1978, Congress enacted the Humphrey-Hawkins Full Employment Act which set an unemployment rate of 3 percent—equivalent to frictional unemployment—as a national goal. Since then, many government programs to aid the unemployed, underemployed, and discouraged workers have been reduced or eliminated, leaving many Americans dependent on welfare programs for support.

Moreover, absence of employment opportunity contributes to other social dysfunctions. Research by Dr. M. Harvey Brenner shows that a seemingly small increase in the unemployment rate is associated with an increase in several social problems. For example, during the 1973–74 recession the unemployment rate increased by 14.3 percent and was associated with the problems shown in Table 17.1. Brenner calculated that the combination of the 1973–74 increase in the unemployment rate, the decrease in real per capita income, and an increase in the business failure rate was related to "an overall increase of more than 165,000 deaths [from cardiovascular disease] over a ten-year period (the greatest proportion of which occurs within three years)." Overall, the total economic, social, and health care costs of this seemingly slight increase in unemployment totaled $24 billion.[5]

HISTORY OF EMPLOYMENT POLICY

The most significant developments in American employment policy occurred during the New Deal. Faced with an unemployment rate of 25 percent and increasing militancy among the unemployed, President Roosevelt initiated the Federal Emergency Relief Administration (FERA) and recruited as its head Harry Hopkins, a social worker who had administered a work relief program for Roosevelt when he had been Governor of New York. Hopkins quickly conceived a series of work relief programs to get the unemployed back to work. The result was an alphabet soup of programs: the Civilian Conservation Corps (CCC), the

TABLE 17.1. Consequences of Increases in Unemployment

Pathological Indicator	% Increase due to Rise in Unemployment	Increase in Incidence of Pathology
Total mortality	2.3	45,936
Cardiovascular mortality	2.8	28,510
Cirrhosis mortality	1.4	430
Suicide	1.0	270
Population in mental hospitals	6.0	8,416
Total arrests	6.0	577,477
Arrests for fraud and embezzlement	4.8	11,552
Assaults reported to police	1.1	7,035
Homicide	1.7	403

Source: Reprinted from M. Harvey Brenner, *Estimating the Effects of Economic Change on National Health and Social Well-Being* (Washington, D.C.: U.S. Government Printing Office, 1984), p. 2.

Civil Works Administration (CWA), the Public Works Administration (PWA), and the Works Progress Administration (WPA). The flurry of work relief programs served to defuse a volatile labor problem, but—short of some conspicuous public construction projects—did little to remedy the social and economic consequences of the Depression. "The sums expended on public works and relief were never enough (even allowing for a generous 'multiplier' effect) to support more than a fraction of the vast numbers of jobless and destitute at anything but a minimum level," concluded a scholar on the fiftieth anniversary of the New Deal.[6] The unemployment problem precipitated by the Depression was not to be fully resolved until the entry of the United States into World War II, when the armed services recruited young men for the war effort.

The legacy of the New Deal for employment policy appears in three programs: the United States Employment Service (USES), which was established under the Wagner-Peyser Act of 1933; the Unemployment Compensation provision of the Social Security Act of 1935; and the Fair Labor Standards Act of 1938 which established the minimum wage. The USES consists of 2,400 offices nationwide where employers can list job openings. Funded by federal unemployment insurance taxes, the USES offices are operated by state agencies and provide services at no charge to either employers or prospective employees.[7] Although the USES claims to place about 5 million people a year, it is hampered by two problems. First, other welfare programs, such as Unemployment Compensation and Food Stamps, require workers to file with the local USES in order to obtain benefits, resulting in unnecessary paperwork for the USES. Second, a system of private employment agencies, such as Manpower Temporary Services and Kelly (Girl) Services, provides private sector employers with a method for selecting more desirable workers. As a result of this "creaming" of the labor pool, the USES is left with a dispropor-

tionate number of less-skilled and lower-wage job seekers.

As an insurance program, unemployment compensation provides benefits to workers whose employers have contributed to a fund for a minimum number of work quarters. Workers wishing to receive benefits must (1) demonstrate that they were unemployed through no fault of their own, (2) appear in person at a state employment office to register for work, and (3) demonstrate continued effort to locate employment. Because the unemployment compensation fund is derived from compulsory contributions of employers, and because the amount that employers pay varies according to their history of laying off workers, it is in the interest of employers to challenge claims by former workers seeking benefits, since fewer claims will decrease their contribution rate. In other instances, the Unemployment Compensation obligations of employers are folded into operating costs. This is common practice among defense contractors and within the construction industry where relatively high-wage workers are able to draw unemployment compensation between contracts or during the off-season. When the unemployment rate exceeds the national rate, localities are automatically eligible for a 15-week extension of the normal benefit period. Altogether, Unemployment Compensation covers 97 percent of employed workers.[8] Yet, Unemployment Compensation does not adequately address the needs of those at the margin of the labor force. In 1982, for example, Unemployment Compensation covered only 42 percent of workers who were unemployed.[9]

The minimum wage, $3.35 per hour in 1986, covers about 90 percent of all nonsupervisory workers. Despite its extensive coverage, the minimum wage has been criticized by both conservatives and liberals. Looking at the persistently high unemployment rate among younger workers—about 35 percent of black teenagers[10]—some conservatives have argued that the minimum wage is a deterrent for employers to hire unproven workers. Lowering (or eliminating) the minimum wage would encourage employers to make more jobs available to the disadvantaged. On the other hand, liberals have contended that the minimum wage is far from adequate. At its present level, a worker employed forty hours per week would earn approximately $7,000 per year, far below the 1985 poverty line of $10,650 for a family of four. The controversy surrounding the minimum wage is compounded by the fact that a portion of the service industry—notably convenience stores and fast food franchises—have taken advantage of the large number of younger workers who are available, and have hired them on a part-time basis for limited periods of time in order to avoid the expenses of paying benefits associated with full-time employment. In this instance, an industry has clearly profited from the use—or abuse—of young workers who rely on the minimum wage.[11]

JOB TRAINING PROGRAMS

The failure of the labor market to provide adequate employment opportunity to large numbers of workers led to a series of governmental efforts to better prepare the un- and underemployed. The first of these was the Manpower Development and Training Act (MDTA) of 1962. Intended as a program to assist workers displaced by technological and economic change, MDTA was also expected to serve the disadvantaged when the Office of Economic Opportunity was established in 1964. As one of the primary weapons for the newly declared War on Poverty, the MDTA grew rapidly, from $93 million in 1964 to $358 million in 1973. In 1973, 119,600 people were enrolled in MDTA. Still, the program was only one of several War on Poverty job programs to aid the disadvantaged, including the Neighborhood Youth Corps (for high school students), the Job Corps (for young adults), and the Work Incentive Program (for AFDC recipients).[12]

By the mid-1970s the proliferation and cost of job-training programs prompted the Nixon administration and Congress to consolidate MDTA and other job training programs under the Comprehensive Employment and Training Act (CETA) of 1973. In addition to consolidating federal job-training programs, CETA also decentralized program responsibilities for local governments. By 1978, CETA was budgeted at $11.2 billion and enrolled 3.9 million persons[13] (by comparison, the unemployed numbered 6.2 million in 1978).[14] Yet, the nation's most ambitious program for contending with joblessness soon became the center of controversy. The recession of 1974–75 placed financial hardship on local government, and budget limiting acts, such as California's Proposition 13 (1978), capped the fiscal capacity of local government. Consequently, strong incentives were created for local governments to use the CETA program to fill civil service positions left vacant because of retrenchment by local government. Because many of these jobs required work experience, CETA became a conduit whereby local government subsidized its personnel budget—often hiring relatively skilled persons and neglecting the chronically unemployed. This inflamed white collar labor organizations which saw civil service rosters being decimated while state and municipal employees were replaced by CETA workers. Moreover, Ronald Reagan, governor of California during the Proposition 13 revolt, was irate that the federal government would subsidize local governments for activities which their taxpayers had determined as excessive. As president, Reagan would move quickly to clip the CETA program. Finally, many critics—both conservatives and liberals—charged that the chronically unemployed were often given dead-end, make-work jobs that failed to integrate them fully into the private sector.

Superseding CETA, the Job Training and Partnership Act (JTPA) of 1982 attempted to focus training on the hard-core unemployed in order to make them economically self-sufficient through private sector employment. Approximately 600 Private Industry Councils were created locally to synchronize training and job opportunities. Initially, the Reagan administration allocated $2.8 billion for the first year of JTPA, approximately three-quarters of what had been spent on CETA in 1980.[15] But appropriations were reduced in later years even though the unemployment rate rose above 7 percent. In 1988 appropriations for JTPA were approximately $1.8 billion.[16] The relationship between funding of JTPA and the unemployment rate is depicted in Figure 17.1.

DUAL LABOR MARKETS

Despite large enrollments in government employment programs and the substantial expenditures of public funds, the difficulty in elevating people out of poverty through job training programs led several scholars to examine the nature of the work that participants are expected to find. Labor market analysts, such as Peter Doeringer, Michael Piore, and David Gordon, found that "a group of low-wage, and often marginal, enterprises and a set of casual, unstructured job opportunities where workers with employment disadvantages tend to find

work" characterized job seekers and employers participating in job training programs.[17] These researchers reasoned that the segmentation of the labor market—into better jobs versus disadvantaged jobs—explained much of the problem of government employment programs.

According to Piore, the labor market can be divided into two segments—a primary labor market and a secondary labor market. Hence, a theory of "dual labor markets":

> ... the primary market offers jobs which possess several of the following traits: high wages, good working conditions, employment stability and job security, equity and due process in the administration of work rules, and chances for advancement. The other, secondary sector, has jobs which, relative to those in the primary sector, are decidedly less attractive. They tend to involve low wages, poor working conditions, considerable variability in employment, harsh and often arbitrary discipline, and little opportunity to advance. The poor are confined to the secondary labor market.[18]

Piore noted that to the extent that employment is expected to solve the poverty problem, the trick is to see that the poor "gain access to primary employment."[19]

The magnitude of the secondary labor

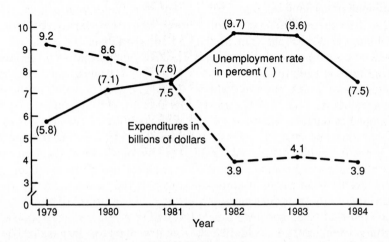

Figure 17.1. Federal Expenditures for Employment Services and the Unemployment Rate

market has been explored by researchers who calculated that 36.2 percent of workers in 1970 fell into the secondary labor market, a modest increase over the number in 1950, 35 percent.[20] By the 1980s, however, two factors increased the proportion of workers in the secondary labor market. First, membership in labor unions— the best security for nonprofessional workers —fell from 30.8 percent of nonagricultural workers in 1970 to 25.2 percent in 1980, leaving millions of workers vulnerable to employment insecurity typical of the secondary labor market.[21] Second, a higher proportion of new jobs created were in the service sector of the economy, which largely consists of secondary labor market jobs. Between 1979 and 1985, 44 percent of new jobs paid less than $7,400 per year.[22]

For workers in the secondary labor market, social welfare is an important source of support, whether in the form of income payments, such as AFDC, or in-kind benefits, such as Medicaid and Food Stamps. Yet, the relationship between public assistance and the secondary labor market is a poor fit. With the exception of Alaska, none of the states provide benefits above the poverty level, even when the cash equivalent of Food Stamps is added to the AFDC benefit.[23] Consequently, most families have strong incentives to work in order to supplement meager welfare benefits. The relatively punitive treatment of earnings under AFDC encourages families to under-report income from work.[24] Piore concluded that "The public assistance system discourages full-time work . . . and forces those on welfare into jobs that are either part-time or which pay cash which will not be reported to the social worker or can be quickly dropped or delayed when the social worker discovers them or seems in danger of doing so."[25] Not surprisingly, public assistance is fraught with inaccurate payments because clients conceal income from irregular employment that they are, for all practical purposes, obliged to seek in order to compensate for inadequate welfare benefits. The circularity of the dilemma is as frustrating for administrators

of public assistance programs as it is for public assistance beneficiaries, especially those with children, who often resort to deception for purposes of survival.

WORKFARE

The question of assisting workers from the secondary labor market to become economically self-sufficient was investigated by the Manpower Development Research Corporation (MDRC) in a series of five-year experiments. At 21 sites nationwide, over 6500 hard-core unemployed subjects were provided with special benefits and training. According to the summary of MDRC,

> . . . the guiding principle of the supported work experiment is that by participating in the program, a significant number of people who were severely handicapped for employment may be able to join the labor force and do productive work, cease engaging in socially destructive or dependent behavior, and become self-supporting members of society.

The goals of the supported work experiment were ambitious considering the four groups MDRC elected to train: women who had been on AFDC for several years, ex-addicts, ex-offenders, and young high school dropouts who were often delinquents. Including the cost of antisocial behavior with that of job training, MDRC figured that an investment of $5,000 to $8,000 per trainee was justifiable.[26] In *The Underclass*, Ken Auletta followed one group of trainees through the supported work program, confirming the mixed results reported by MDRC: "after five years, the MDRC found that for only two of the four target groups— ex-addicts and mothers receiving AFDC payments—'the benefits exceed the costs.'" All told, only one-third of all the trainees who enrolled in the year-long supported work experiment went on to "unsubsidized jobs or returned to public school."[27]

Still, the relative success of the AFDC group proved noteworthy, especially in light of attempts by the Reagan administration to reform welfare by emphasizing work in exchange for benefits ("workfare"). Under the Omnibus Budget Reconciliation Act (OBRA) of 1981, which reordered many social welfare programs, states were free "to design their own work-related programs for AFDC applicants and recipients."[28] Almost overnight, the supported work experiments—a marginal success at best —became the basis for welfare reform; and, once again, MDRC was instrumental in designing a training program for welfare beneficiaries.

During the early 1980s, MDRC conducted a series of "work/welfare" demonstrations in 11 states, which evaluated several strategies to enhance the employability of AFDC recipients under the Community Work Experience Program (CWEP). As reported by Judith Gueron, president of MDRC, interim findings of CWEP were generally positive. Of five states reporting, MDRC found that, while jobs were often entry-level and did not provide much skill development, neither were they make-work jobs. Moreover, "a high proportion of participants interviewed were satisfied with their work sites, felt positive about coming to work, believed that they were making a useful contribution, and felt that they were treated as part of the regular work force."[29] Gueron could be no more sanguine about the CWEP demonstrations at the conclusion of the experiments. Generally, program costs were more than offset by the economic benefits of the employment-related activities expected for AFDC recipients. Unfortunately, the gains won by program participants were usually insufficient to make them financially independent of welfare. Furthermore, the CWEP experiment suggested that even these modest gains were predicated on "an accessible pool of regular jobs," a condition that did not exist in West Virginia which reported no fiscal savings from CWEP.

MDRC later reinterpreted data from five workfare experiments to determine if some groups of welfare recipients benefited more than others from variously designed programs. Workfare participants were classified into three groups in relation to their earnings in the year prior to going on AFDC and the length of time they had been on AFDC, resulting in a three-tier ladder of dependency. According to performance in workfare programs, the top tier— those with earnings of more than $3,000 and who had never been on AFDC—showed the *least* program savings, primarily because this group was able to leave AFDC without having to rely on the workfare program. Of the other two groups, the most welfare dependent—those with no earnings and who had been on AFDC more than two years—"attained below-average earnings" in comparison to the other two groups. Yet, because the most dependent group represented such high program costs, their participation in workfare resulted in greater program savings. Nevertheless, the report suggested that workfare administrators were likely to realize increased earnings of workfare participants by focusing on the second tier, the mid-dependency group. The conclusions from this MDRC study suggested that workfare programs could claim greater *earnings* of AFDC recipients by focusing on the middle tier of workfare participants, but yield greater welfare program *savings* by focusing on the lowest tier.[30] These conclusions are important since they point to different directions for workfare programs. If welfare officials are under pressure to report lower program costs, they should ration workfare resources and reserve them for the most welfare-dependent. On the other hand, if the objective of workfare is to boost recipients off AFDC, workfare should be reserved for the mid-dependent group. Because workfare programs are unlikely to be funded generously, there will be strong incentives for workfare administrators to conserve resources by focusing on the most dependent; yet, this strategy may be self-defeating since it is least likely to increase the earning of workfare participants sufficiently to get them off AFDC. Thus, workfare may prove to be a method for containing AFDC program costs, but ineffective at helping those on AFDC become economically self-sufficient.

On the eve of several welfare reform proposals put before the 100th Congress, Gueron summarized MDRC's conclusions on CWEP: "the results do not point to a uniform program structure that merits national replication … while it is worthwhile to operate these programs, they will not move substantial numbers of people out of poverty."[31] Subsequently, the *Washington Post* editorialized to federal policymakers that, based on an MDRC demonstration in Chicago, the work program "was *not* successful in speeding people off the [welfare] rolls."[32] Cautious statements such as these were reinforced by David Ellwood, Professor of Public Policy at Harvard's John F. Kennedy School of Government. "Most work-welfare programs look like decent investments, but no carefully evaluated work-welfare programs have done more than put a tiny dent in the welfare caseloads, even though they have been received with enthusiasm," Ellwood concluded. "So these work-welfare programs alone are not likely to solve the welfare 'problem,' in spite of the grand claims by some proponents."[33] Despite these reservations, Congress seems intent on including workfare in welfare reform legislation. While a work requirement may satisfy adherents of the work ethic, the realities of the hard-core unemployed and the secondary labor market make it highly unlikely that a workfare program—even a relatively generously funded one—will reduce the number of dependents or the costs of welfare programs.

THE UNDERCLASS

A decade of MDRC sponsored work experiments served to reinforce a suspicion among social policy analysts that an underclass was emerging in the United States. Estimated at 9 million, this population was characterized by socioeconomic immobility and self-destructive behavior.[34] In *The Black Underclass*, Douglas Glasgow attributed the underclass to "structural factors found in market dynamics and institutional practices, as well as the legacy of racism, [that] produce and then reinforce the cycle of poverty and, in turn, work as a downward pull toward underclass status."[35] Auletta identified four groups that comprise the underclass: the "passive poor," usually those dependent on welfare; hostile "street predators," often dropouts and addicts; "hustlers," or opportunists who do not commit violent crimes; and, "traumatized" alcoholics, shopping bag ladies, and casualties of deinstitutionalization.[36] These groups share characteristics that, according to Robert Reischauer of the Brookings Institution, differentiate them from "lower class" status with its connotation of merely being further down on the socioeconomic ladder. The underclass suffers from persistently low income, weak connection to the labor force, poor education and skills, and "a sense of alienation from mainstream society which manifests itself in dysfunctional behavior that imposes costs on society or on future generations."[37]

The seriousness of the underclass phenomenon was underscored in research conducted by David Ellwood and Mary Jo Bane. In an examination of the Michigan Panel Study of Income Dynamics, Bane and Ellwood discovered that, although most people are in poverty for short periods of time, a significant number have protracted spells in poverty. Table 17.2 shows the experiences of people in poverty for varying lengths of time. Significantly, 18 percent of poverty is long-term, and almost 60 percent of people who are poor at any given time are experiencing a long-term spell of poverty. When the costs of this poverty are borne by minority families who are disproportionately poor, the consequences are disastrous. Since 1970, poor urban families have been more likely to have poor neighbors, evidence of a continuing deterioration of the socio-eco-

TABLE 17.2. Spells of Poverty for Non-Elderly Persons by Percentage

Spell Length in Years	Persons Beginning a Spell at Any Time during Survey	Persons Observed Poor at Any Point in Time during Survey
1	41.1	9.7
2–3	27.7	15.5
4–7	13.2	15.8
8+	18.0	59.1
Total	100.0	100.0
Average (years)	4.2	11.0

Source: Reprinted from Committee on Ways and Means, U.S. House of Representatives, *Children in Poverty* (Washington, D.C.: U.S. Government Printing Office, May 22, 1985), p. 46.

nomic condition of poor communities which makes it increasingly difficult to alleviate the pathology due to "ghetto culture."[38]

Of the few proposals advanced to reduce the underclass, most emphasize employment. New Deal-type job programs were proposed in articles that received wide circulation, such as Nicholas Lemann's "The Origins of the Underclass," in the *Atlantic Monthly*,[39] and Mickey Kaus's "The Work-Ethic State," in *The New Republic*.[40] According to William Julius Wilson, increasing job opportunities for employable members of the underclass would have several related payoffs. For example, much welfare dependency among female heads of households can be attributed to the fact that large numbers of young men in poor neighborhoods are not good candidates for marriage because of poor education, engagement in illicit activities, and unemployment. According to Wilson, employment programs that would make young men more marriageable would not only reduce the social costs of their current status but also those of women with children who are dependent on welfare.[41]

Experience with employment training programs over the past two decades suggests that the proposition introduced at the beginning of this chapter—a substantial portion of the welfare problem could be solved if people on welfare found adequate employment—is not likely to be achieved solely through workfare. Al-

though workfare programs may enhance the self-worth of welfare beneficiaries, make for good public relations, and assuage irate taxpayers, these programs—whether coercive or voluntary—have achieved only marginal results in terms of their ability to get welfare beneficiaries into jobs that would make them self-sufficient. Given the experience of the MDRC demonstrations, a more effective strategy would be a national labor policy directed at the secondary labor market. Such a policy would include a supplement to the minimum wage or the development of a benefit package to complement the minimum wage. In addition, tight labor market policies or the certification of completion of tough government training programs would make the disadvantaged more desirable workers to employers. Without a national labor market strategy that addresses the secondary labor market—and therefore the plight of the unemployed, the underemployed, and discouraged workers— workfare is likely to be punitive and the underclass is likely to grow.

NOTES

1. Michael Novak et al., *The New Consensus on Family and Welfare* (Washington, D.C.: American Enterprise Institute, 1987), p. 58.
2. Michael Sherraden, "Chronic Unemployment:

A Social Work Perspective," *Social Work* (September–October 1985), p. 403.

3. Ibid., pp. 404–6.

4. As Sherraden notes, the common understanding that an unemployment rate of 7 percent is "normal" is not supported by economists who calculate that structural and frictional unemployment can be reduced to 3 percent under propitious social policies.

5. M. Harvey Brenner, *Estimating the Effects of Economic Change on National Health and Social Well-Being* (Washington, D.C.: U.S. Government Printing Office, 1984), pp. 2–4.

6. Bradford Lee, "The Welfare State Reconsidered," *Wilson Quarterly* 6 (Spring 1982), pp. 69–70.

7. Diana M. DiNitto and Thomas Dye, *Social Welfare: Politics and Public Policy*, 2nd ed. (Englewood Cliffs, N.J.: Prentice-Hall, 1987), p. 200.

8. Committee on Ways and Means, U.S. House of Representatives, *Background Material and Data on Programs within the Jurisdiction of the Committee on Ways and Means* (Washington, D.C.: U.S. Government Printing Office, 1985), p. 279.

9. Children's Defense Fund, *A Children's Defense Budget* (Washington, D.C.: Children's Defense Fund, 1985), p. 180.

10. Michael Novak, *The New Consensus on Family and Welfare*, p. 32.

11. Amitai Etzioni, "The Fast-Food Factories: McJobs Are Bad for Kids," *The Washington Post*, August 24, 1986.

12. Sar A. Levitan and Joyce Zickler, *The Quest for a Federal Manpower Partnership* (Cambridge, Mass.: Harvard University Press, 1974), pp. 1–6.

13. Lawrence Mead, *Beyond Entitlement* (New York: Free Press, 1986), p. 27.

14. U.S. Bureau of the Census, *Statistical Abstract of the United States 1982–83* (Washington, D.C.: U.S. Government Printing Office, 1983), p. 391.

15. David Rosenbaum, "Federal Job Program Aids the More Able, According to Critics," *New York Times*, July 22, 1984.

16. Committee on Ways and Means, U.S. House of Representatives, *Background Material and Data on Programs within the Jurisdiction of the*

17. Peter B. Doeringer and Michael Piore, *Internal Labor Markets and Manpower Analysis* (Armonk, N.Y.: M. E. Sharpe, 1985), p. 163.

18. Michael Piore, "The Dual Labor Market," in David Gordon, ed., *Problems in Political Economy* (Lexington, Mass.: D. C. Heath, 1977), p. 94.

19. Ibid.

20. David Gordon, Richard Edwards, and Michael Reich, *Segmented Work, Divided Workers* (New York: Cambridge University Press, 1982), p. 211.

21. U.S. Bureau of the Census, *Statistical Abstract of the United States 1982–83*, p. 409.

22. Michael Harrington, *Who Are the Poor?* (Washington, D.C.: Justice for All, 1987), p. 10.

23. *To Form a More Perfect Union* (Washington, D.C.: National Conference on Social Welfare, 1985).

24. Committee on Ways and Means, U.S. House of Representatives, *Background Material and Data on Programs within the Jurisdiction of the Committee on Ways and Means*, p. 330.

25. Michael Piore, "The Dual Labor Market," p. 95.

26. Board of Directors, Manpower Demonstration Research Corporation, *Summary and Findings of the National Supported Work Demonstration* (Cambridge, Mass.: Ballinger Publishing Co., 1980), pp. 1–2.

27. Ken Auletta, *The Underclass* (New York: Random House, 1982), pp. 221, 222.

28. Judith Gueron, "Working for People on Welfare," *Public Welfare* 44, no. 1 (Winter 1986), p. 7.

29. Ibid., p. 10.

30. Daniel Friedlander, *Subgroup Impacts and Performance Indicators for Selected Welfare Employment Programs* (New York: MDRC, 1988), pp. 7–15.

31. Judith Gueron, "Reforming Welfare with Work," *Public Welfare* 45, no. 4 (Fall 1987), p. 23.

32. "Warning on Welfare Reform," *Washington Post*, January 19, 1988, p. A–14.

33. David Ellwood, *Poor Support: Poverty in the*

American Family (New York: Basic Books, 1988), p. 153.

34. William Kornblum, "Lumping the Poor," *Dissent* (Summer 1984), p. 296.

35. Douglas Glasgow, *The Black Underclass* (New York: Vintage, 1981), p. 4.

36. Ken Auletta, *The Underclass*, p. xvi.

37. Robert Reischauer, "America's Underclass," *Public Welfare* 45, no. 4, (Fall 1987), p. 28.

38. Christopher Jencks, "Deadly Neighborhoods,"

The New Republic, June 13, 1988, p. 30.

39. Nicholas Lemann, "The Origins of the Underclass," *Atlantic Monthly*, June 1986 and July 1986.

40. Mickey Kaus, "The Work-Ethic State," *The New Republic*, July 7, 1986.

41. William Julius Wilson, "American Social Policy and the Ghetto Underclass," *Dissent*, Winter 1988.

PART FOUR

The Future of American Social Welfare

CHAPTER 18

The Fragmentation of Welfare State Ideology

Since the late 1970s, conservatives have raised fundamental questions about the most desirable way to provide social welfare in the United States. The election of Ronald Reagan to the presidency and the subsequent changes in public welfare programs led many liberals to reconsider the philosophical basis of social welfare. As a result of this shift in public philosophy, the liberal rationale for public policy—that government should be the insurer of opportunity and security through social programs—began to dissolve. Subsequently, a variety of issues have appeared which have particular significance for the future of American social welfare. Among these issues are *welfare reform* —how to make public assistance a more productive program; *privatization*—the extent to which the private sector, as opposed to government, should provide welfare; *social service delivery*—how technology and unions are changing the settings in which welfare professionals practice; and *political action*—how social welfare professionals can exert more influence in making social welfare policy. Each of these is addressed in greater detail in the following chapters. Important decisions about the shape of welfare for the next century will depend on how these issues are resolved, and how they are resolved will depend, in turn, on the future of welfare state ideology.

The American welfare state is in a period of fundamental transformation. Since the late 1970s, several factors have converged to challenge the liberal premise behind social welfare, that major government social programs are the most desirable way to protect vulnerable populations from social and economic insecurity. The mobilization of the evangelical right helped to effectively curtail the liberal momentum in expanding social programs. Stung by electoral reversals, politicians of the Democratic party adopted more cautious positions regarding social programs. An unprecedented federal budget deficit made expenditures for new social programs implausible, and even led to consideration of trimming existing programs. Finally, the October 1987 stock market crash cast a pall of uncertainty about the economy, leaving many policy analysts with a sense that prudent action consisted of waiting out an impending recession.

The consequences of this crisis for social welfare professionals proved disturbing. For example, draconian proposals for arresting health care costs have included plans for rationing federally subsidized health care, despite the tens of millions of Americans who remain without health insurance. Major cutbacks in housing and mental health programs have occurred, despite the millions of Americans who remain homeless. In order to save money, public welfare services may be further reduced by downgrading civil service positions, thus making governmental programs an even less desirable setting for professional practice. Besieged by criticism from conservatives, portrayed as a fiscal albatross around the neck of a shaky economy, and justified by an ideology that is at variance with the dominant market values of capitalism, the American welfare state appears to be perched at a precipice. The deep cuts executed on welfare programs during the early

1980s, a diminution of public acceptance of governmental welfare expenditures, and the restrictions imposed by the Gramm-Rudman-Hollings deficit reduction act, all point to a continuation of the crisis.

IDEOLOGY AND THE WELFARE STATE

For human service professionals accustomed to an American welfare state that had expanded continuously for half a century, conservative attacks on social welfare were felt keenly. Many welfare professionals had built their careers around a vision of an American welfare state that was European in origin.[1] Social workers in the United States tended to adhere to a liberal philosophy toward welfare which assumed that a system of national programs would be deployed as a greater portion of the citizenry demanded a variety of services and benefits through governmental social programs. The implicit vision behind the expansion of the government-driven welfare state was the European model, especially the Scandinavian variant in which health care, housing, income benefits, and employment opportunities were available more equitably throughout the population than any region in the world.[2] It was this example that led the English social scientist, Richard Titmuss, to hope that the welfare state, as an instrument of government, would eventually lead to a "welfare world."[3] Ultimately, governmental programs, which were the basis of the welfare state, were treated by most welfare philosophers as synonymous with social welfare.

This convention was followed in the United States, as well. For American welfare philosophers, government programs designed to ameliorate the caprices of capitalism were both desirable and inevitable. In their classic *Industrial Society and Social Welfare*, Harold Wilensky and Charles Lebeaux suggested that "under continuing industrialization all institutions will be oriented toward and evaluated in terms of social welfare aims. The 'welfare state' will become the 'welfare society,' and both will be more reality than epithet."[4] Accordingly, from the New Deal through the War on Poverty, the notion that government should be the primary institution for promoting social welfare was to become a persistent theme among American welfare philosophers.[5]

These explanations of the emergence of social welfare in American society were experienced by welfare professionals who took jobs with governmental agencies or with voluntary sector agencies which were heavily dependent on governmental contracts. In fact, the combination of a government bureaucracy and casework agency became so prevalent that Wilensky and Lebeaux concluded, "virtually all welfare service is dispensed through social agencies . . . and virtually all social workers operate through such agencies."[6] For most social welfare professionals, the welfare state was not a philosophical abstraction; it was the basis of livelihood.

Yet, the promise of the American welfare state to eventually expand to provide the degree of protection typical of the European model was compromised by the ambivalence of many Americans toward centralized government. "The emphasis consistently has been on the local, the pluralistic, the voluntary, and the business-like over the national, the universal, the legally entitled, and the governmental," observed policy analyst Marc Bendick.

> Given such a consistent pattern of anti-government bias in the American response style, it is unfortunate that much of American social policy has looked to Europe for models of both specific programs and general approaches. Reflecting political, social, economic, and intellectual circumstances very different from those in the United States, most European nations have evolved an approach to social welfare services that is strongly state-centered . . . When presented explicitly to the American public, the European welfare state approach has won few adherents outside of academic circles.[7]

Given the pluralism of American society, it was perhaps inevitable that questions about a dominant role of government in social welfare would emerge.

This intrinsic problem of the American welfare state—distrust of centralized government—was exacerbated by the desertion of New Deal allies. Staunch defenders of social programs—Democratic politicians such as George McGovern, Hubert Humphrey, and Daniel Patrick Moynihan—have either retired, died, or changed their ideological allegiance. Even liberal holdouts have had second thoughts about the traditional formulations of American social welfare. Speaking to the Women's National Democratic Club, Senator Edward Kennedy—"the last of the liberal lions"— questioned the basis of American social policy.

> We now stand between two Americas, the one we have known and the one toward which we are heading. The New Deal will live in American history forever as a supreme example of government responsiveness to the times. But it is no answer to the problems of today.[8]

All but confirming that the New Deal was dead, Harvard University academician Michael Sandel stated that as early as "the 1970s the New Deal agenda had become obsolete."[9] During the 1980s public ambivalence about social programs was exploited by the Reagan administration, placing liberals on the defensive. Having conceded the middle ground in the public policy debate, liberals were in a poor position to press for additional programs that would benefit vulnerable populations which remained unprotected by the "reluctant" American welfare state.[10] Cuts in social welfare programs executed by the Reagan administration were met with ineffectual response, and the prospect of increasing welfare—even among leaders of the Democratic party, the traditional defenders of the welfare state—was jettisoned.

Meanwhile, the conservative critique of the welfare state gained plausibility, if only because it was repeated so frequently. Conservatives maintained that high taxation and the government regulation of business caused disincentives for investment, while individual claims on social insurance and public welfare grants discouraged work. Together, critics of social policies alleged, these factors led to a decline in economic growth and an increase in the expectations of beneficiaries of welfare programs. For conservatives, the only way to correct the irrationality of government social programs was to smash them completely. Charles Murray, in his much-celebrated *Losing Ground*, suggested that

> the proposed program, our final and most ambitious thought experiment, consists of scrapping the entire federal welfare and income support structure for working-aged persons, including AFDC, Medicaid, Food Stamps, Unemployment Insurance, Worker's Compensation, subsidized housing, disability insurance, and the rest. It would leave the working-aged person with no recourse whatsoever except the job market, family members, friends, and public or private locally funded services. It is the Alexandrian solution: cut the knot, for there is no way to untie it.[11]

VOICES FROM THE LEFT

Against the conservative tide, the left was also having to adjust its position. Despite their general disenchantment with social welfare—its failure to strike at the root cause of social injustice, capitalism—many leftists were unprepared for the conservative assault on the welfare state that occurred during the 1980s. Writing the introduction to *Beyond the Welfare State*, on the eve of the 1980 presidential election, Irving Howe made a glaring error when he predicted that "the over-heated reaction against the welfare state [would] prove to be a last gasp of the American right."[12] Noted scholars Frances Fox Piven and Richard Cloward suddenly revised their previously harsh criticism of welfare:

Relief recipients benefit enormously from some of these programs, especially those providing subsidies for food, fuel, and medical care, so that their condition has not worsened on the whole. Public relief, once the sole form of state intervention to ameliorate destitution, has thus come to be embedded in a general structure of income support programs for a wide range of constituencies, from the aged to the disabled to the unemployed. The changes in American society that gave rise to this development lead us to the conclusion that the cyclical pattern of providing subsistence resources by the state has been replaced by a variety of permanent income-maintenance entitlements.[13]

Led by Michael Harrington—whose book, *The Other America*, helped inspire the War on Poverty—many leftists stuck to the traditional progressive agenda for reform: national economic planning, a progressive tax structure, universal entitlement for basic health and welfare services, and reductions in defense spending. A more conservative climate brought other leftists toward a pragmatic middle ground. Recognizing the obstacles to a broad reform effort, Robert Morris, a champion of liberal social policy, suggested prioritizing objectives, building consensus around selected goals (e.g., national health insurance and a national employment program), and leaving other goals as optional.[14]

Robert Kuttner, a prominent liberal economist, insisted that an economics of equality could be the basis for universalistic social programs, yet conceded that the political, economic, and ideological direction of the nation made a replication of the European model of the welfare state unlikely.[15] Seven years of Reaganomics were to take a toll on Kuttner's progressive orientation to social policy. In a review of welfare reform proposals, Kuttner eventually backed a modest $2 billion to $3 billion incremental restructuring of welfare, noting that "most liberals and conservatives now agree that the welfare system encourages

dependency, promotes the breakup of families, legitimizes a culture of illegitimacy, and offers too few opportunities to escape from poverty."[16]

Of course, it is conceivable that the left would take its case directly to the people, in the tradition of social movements of the past, and seek more governmental commitment to social programs. However, the ability of the left to inject itself into American social life with the same success it enjoyed in the 1960s is unlikely. As Russell Jacoby has pointed out, many radical-progressive-left intellectuals have abandoned the public arena for an academic life where they communicate more with each other rather than with the public.[17] Tied to the university, leftist intellectuals have little recourse but to rely on public officials to serve as conduits for their ideas, but, as many of the most likely candidates for this function—Democratic politicians—have abandoned the New Deal, the plausibility of this option seems doubtful.

CONCEPTIONS OF SOCIAL WELFARE

The ideological shifts between liberals and conservatives, the left and the right, Democrats and Republicans, reflect the tenuous relationship between the welfare state and the American economy. On the one hand, the welfare state stresses dependence and interconnectedness; on the other hand, the market economy emphasizes self-reliance and individualism. Wilensky and Lebeaux summarize this conflict when they describe the American welfare state as "a constantly moving compromise between the values of security and humanitarianism on the one hand, and individual initiative and self-reliance in the competitive order on the other."[18] Through much of the history of American social welfare, these oppositional values have been melded through policies that stress self-support conditioned by the provision of benefits at a minimal level. However, the characteristics of advanced capitalism within a global economic context have raised new questions about the optimal relationship between welfare and the economy. Recently, stiff economic competition from Japan, the European economic community, and even some third-world nations has led Claus Offe to observe that "rather than being a separate and autonomous source of well-being which provides incomes and services as a citizen right . . . [the welfare state] . . . is itself heavily dependent upon the prosperity and continued profitability of the economy."[19]

Clearly, the ideal relationship between welfare and the society changes with time. In the United States, transitions in social welfare can be described by identifying three conceptual bases: the residual, the institutional, and the functional. According to the *residual* conception of social welfare, the family and the market are the primary sources of assistance for those in need. Of course, these sometimes fail, in which case the social "safety net" of government welfare programs may be deployed. Although the residual conception of welfare accounts for governmental social programs, it is important to recognize that these attend "primarily to emergency functions, and [are] expected to withdraw when the regular social structure—the family and the economic system—is again working properly."[20] While this marginal role for government in social welfare is plausible, it has a connotation of providing limited benefits in a stigmatizing manner. The residual rationale for welfare is primarily responsible for the negative image of welfare in American culture.

The residual conception was dominant prior to the Depression when welfare consisted largely of activities of private, nonprofit agencies which tended to be restrictive in both the volume of benefits and the eligibility criteria for benefits. At that time government involvement in social welfare was brief, as evident in the Freedmen's Bureau. Other examples of

residual welfare include federal disaster assistance and the temporary extension of unemployment insurance benefits when the unemployment rate is particularly high in a community. As a limited justification for government welfare, the residual conception is often favored by conservatives who prefer the "private sector"—the market and voluntary agencies—to be the first line of defense against need. Of course, the residual conception can also be used as a rationale to reduce governmental welfare initiatives. Those who prefer a limited role of government in social affairs frequently appeal to the philanthropic impulses of the private sector, while calling for a limited scope of government social programs.

In contrast, the *institutional* conception assumes that welfare is "a proper, legitimate function of modern industrial society in helping individuals achieve self-fulfillment."[21] In assuming that modern society is complex, and that the dislocation of large numbers of people is costly, the institutional conception leaves government as the logical institution to assure that society functions smoothly and humanely. In this sense, it is as unthinkable to limit social programs to temporary measures as it would be to limit public education to emergencies. According to the institutional conception, social welfare programs are investments in human capital that any industrial society must make if it is to maintain a healthy, educated, contented work force. Further, the institutional conception is equated with fairness and equality when it is used to provide services, benefits, and opportunities to populations victimized by discrimination.

Since the Depression, proponents of the institutional conception of welfare have enacted an impressive list of government social programs which, as a whole, constitute the American welfare state: the Social Security Act (1935), the Housing Act (1937), the G.I. Bill (1944), the Community Mental Health Centers Act (1963), the Civil Rights Act (1964), the Food Stamp Act (1964), the Economic Opportunity

Act (1964), the Elementary and Secondary Education Act (1965), the Older Americans Act (1965), Medicare and Medicaid (1965), Supplemental Security Income (1974), and Title XX of the Social Security Act (1975). By most accounts the governmental welfare state began to ebb in the mid-1970s, when skyrocketing inflation made the addition of new social programs impolitic. The passage of the Full Employment and Balanced Growth Act of 1978 (originally known as the Humphrey-Hawkins bill), probably marked the last of major liberal social legislation. Despite provisions of this act specifying that the unemployment rate was not to go beyond a minimal level of about 3 percent, the Full Employment Act proved unable to counter unemployment levels that pushed 10 percent in the early 1980s.

The institutional conception of welfare is advanced by liberals who view government welfare initiatives as essential to ameliorating the disadvantages imposed on some groups by a persistently unjust economic system. In making the case for continual governmental action, liberals are supported by the constituencies which are dependent on social programs. In fact, it is not difficult to see the direct relationship between certain social programs and the interest groups that these social programs serve—for example, the G.I. Bill and the Veterans of Foreign Wars; the Civil Rights Act and the National Association for the Advancement of Colored People; and the Social Security Act and the American Association of Retired Persons. The strong constituency base of these social programs assured their institutional permanence in the national culture; however, it also made them vulnerable to accusations that the large volume of resources commanded by them were at the expense of other social needs.

The *functional* conception of welfare assumes that expenditures for social programs should be consistent with needs of the larger society, particularly economic productivity.[22] In this regard, the functional conception represents a divergence from traditional conservatives, who pursue a restrictive approach to welfare provision (evident in the residual conception) as well as from traditional liberals, who prefer open-ended welfare programs (associated with the institutional conception). Functional welfare reinforces social institutions and insists that beneficiaries participate in them in an appropriate manner.[23] Following the norm of reciprocity, the larger society is due compliant behavior on the part of beneficiaries of welfare programs that are funded by the public. For example, mothers on AFDC can be expected to enroll in educational programs or engage in job-finding activities in exchange for benefits—or they risk being dropped from public assistance. The reciprocity in social relations that is implicit in functional welfare shows the inherent conservatism of the concept. On the other hand, "functional" welfare initiatives that promise to enhance productivity are probably more consonant with the political constraints imposed by conservatism and the economic constraints imposed by the budget deficit and thereby stand a better chance of being enacted than those justified by other conceptions. By functional criteria, policies associated with the residual conception are too inhumane, while those associated with the institutional conception are too wasteful, considering the imperatives of the times.

By bringing welfare closer to the economic requirements of the society, the functional conception is attractive to those concerned about the competitiveness of America in the global economy. Functional welfare promises investments in human capital which can benefit the society as a whole, not just special interests. Further, functional welfare can be a basis for seeking additional benefits for groups that have not been adequately served by current social programs. For example, governmental initiatives to provide child care for working mothers and employment and educational benefits for mothers on AFDC are justifiable human resource expenditures, because they contribute to the economic performance of the society by encouraging workers to enter the labor market and by reducing the demand for costly public welfare programs. Under the functional conception, welfare benefits are carefully targeted and monitored in relation to the contribution they make to the national culture.

The functional conception of welfare appears to be emerging as a successor to the institutional conception as a basis for organizing thinking about social welfare. An influential group of post-New Deal liberals—or neoliberals—have recognized that functional welfare offers a way to escape the accusation that proponents of social programs are irresponsible spenders of public funds, while providing a way to provide additional benefits to select populations in need. Robert Reich, an advocate for prudent investments in human capital, has criticized the traditional liberal position that the needy were "entitled" to a wide range of benefits through unconditional government social programs. Reich maintains that "the language of entitlement suggested that the claimants owed nothing to the majority in return; because claimants had a presumptive right to what they were demanding, obligations all flowed in one direction, to 'them' from the rest of us."[24] According to Reich and other neoliberals, the unconditional entitlements of institutional welfare programs met with a strong backlash when the public objected to higher taxes which additional social benefits would entail. The functional conception is also popular among neoconservatives, conservatives who do not reject outright the need for social welfare but who believe social programs should conform more to traditional American values. The Free Congress Research and Education Foundation, for example, has coined the phrase "cultural conservatism" to describe the use of public policy to reinforce traditional norms. Regarding social welfare, cultural conservatives are not "anti-welfare" and acknowledge the

need for social programs. "We accept the obligation to the less fortunate that welfare represents," explained authors of the Foundation's manifesto on cultural conservatism:

> We accept it because it is one of the West's longest-standing traditions; help for the poor, the sick, the crippled, the widowed and the orphaned is mandated in the Old Testament, our culture's oldest code. We also accept the obligation on functional grounds. To the degree we can help others become productive, contributing members of society, we help society as a whole.[25]

In coupling social welfare to economic productivity, the functional conception would, in the long run, be somewhat more generous than what traditional conservatives would desire, but less so than that preferred by traditional liberals.

THE FUTURE OF AMERICAN SOCIAL WELFARE

The future of social welfare in the United States depends on how public philosophy redefines the structure of social welfare. Ideology shapes public philosophy, in effect defining what becomes the field of desirable options, some of which will become public policy. Because the United States has such a large private or nongovernmental sector, those options not placed on the public agenda and enacted through legislation will become optional in the sense that they will be left to the discretion of the voluntary or corporate sectors. In other words, leaving social issues to the private sector does not assure that they will be addressed, since the voluntary and corporate sectors have the freedom to address certain issues as well as to ignore others.

In a general sense, the conceptions of welfare around which future decisions are made reinforce the role of the major institutional sectors in American social welfare. For example, reliance on the residual conception of social welfare elevates the importance of the voluntary sector, while diminishing the role of the governmental sector. The institutional conception tends to favor governmental provision of a range of social and economic benefits, at the same time treating the voluntary sector as an auxiliary of government programs. In emphasizing productivity, the functional conception reinforces the corporate sector and the voluntary sector. Because the corporate sector is a primary source of employment, it becomes central to policies that promote productivity. And, because the functional conception is associated with traditional social norms, it reinforces the role of the voluntary sector. To the extent that one of the three concepts of social welfare—residual, institutional, functional—sways public philosophy, different sectors of American social welfare (i.e., voluntary, governmental, and corporate) stand to benefit. The interplay of ideology and structure, then, determines the future of social welfare in the United States.

As we approach the end of the twentieth century, three scenarios for American social welfare seem plausible.

The Mixed Welfare Economy

According to this scenario, the governmental, voluntary, and corporate sectors coexist, under a variety of justifications—residual, institutional, and functional. Through some natural social process, each sector assumes a role in serving a particular population. This differentiation requires a minimal degree of organizational accommodation, but the principal parties in the welfare industry remain viable and essential, complementing each other. The voluntary, governmental, and corporate sectors illustrate the pluralistic nature of American social welfare.

The mixed welfare economy model is valid so long as there is some parity among parties involved in the "mix." This presumed balance is open to question. While the governmental sector is likely to continue to reserve a central role for itself in public welfare policy, the role of the voluntary sector is diminishing, while the role of the corporate sector has become more influential. Through preferential selection, the corporate sector has elected to care for more profitable clients, leaving more costly social problems to the other sectors. Because of governmental reductions in welfare efforts, critical problems have emerged, such as homelessness, which have been left to the charitable impulses of the voluntary sector. If the voluntary sector is to shoulder a fair share of the welfare burden, additional resources must be found for nonprofit initiatives.

The Corporate Welfare State

Following this scenario, the corporate sector expands beyond its control of the long-term care, health maintenance, child welfare, and hospital management industries to exploit markets in corrections, education, and social services. The administrative sophistication, quick access to capital, marketing ability, and manipulation of public policy make the larger human service corporations much more effective competitors than agencies of the beleaguered voluntary sector. To the extent that the corporate sector monopolizes portions of the welfare market that are subsidized by government, it is in a powerful position to determine the costs of service, especially if the governmental sector is unwilling to avoid the corporate sector and absorb the cost of deploying a public system of service delivery. The influence of the corporate sector on public policy is likely to become more profound as human service corporations gain a greater share of social welfare. Eventually, the interdependence of government and the corporate sector could lead to an interchange of personnel and the establishment of accords on social welfare policy typical of a human services–industrial complex. The larger role played by the corporation in public policy has been labeled "corporatism." As Yeheskel Hasenfeld has noted, under a social policy that has been redesigned to more closely reflect corporate interests, "the social contract between the welfare state and its citizens is redefined." Essentially, "government plays an active role in stimulating industrial expansion, with labor and business cooperating with each other in the trade-offs between welfare state benefits and control over production costs."[26]

The primary limits to the corporate welfare state will be imposed by the saturation of the human service markets, the competition of voluntary sector providers, and the regulatory authority of government. If the corporate sector reaches the limits of new markets and is unable to convince consumers that they need additional services, it will begin to diversify into other areas, such as finance or high technology. In addition, the voluntary sector has been experimenting with quasi-corporate, hybrid organizational forms that appear to be competitive with their for-profit counterparts. All things being equal, innovative nonprofit organizational forms have one advantage over for-profit firms—surplus can be plowed back into the organization since they do not have to generate a profit. Finally, government is likely to exert some regulatory control over human service corporations if the public balks at escalating costs that are borne primarily by government. The most recent example of this is the Diagnosis Related Group/Prospective Payment System instituted by Medicare to control public health care costs. Without substantial governmental subsidies, the corporate sector may not be willing to serve particular populations, essentially leaving some social problems to the governmental and voluntary sectors. Thus, the policy environment of the future may not be as favorable toward the corporate sector as it has been to date. For the moment, though, the corporate sector appears to be increasing its command of portions of the welfare market and consolidating its influence.

Dual Welfare Systems

Favored by the Left, this scenario suggests that the private organizations of the voluntary and corporate sectors will continue to cream the client populations of welfare programs, leaving only the most destitute and multi-problem cases for governmental programs. According to this scenario, the private nonprofit agencies have historically preferred clients who are better off, and the human service corporations replicate this tendency more efficiently and on a greater scale. As the corporate sector pushes the voluntary sector aside, it cultivates the allegiance of the middle class which begins to define human services within a corporate context. This weakens political and economic support for governmental programs which serve those unable to gain access to corporate human services. As resources dry up, government programs wither and become more stigmatic.

The dual welfare system scenario is correct in one respect, but errs in another. Recently, a substantial homeless population with a variety of serious problems has emerged in the United States. Several social and economic indicators show that lower status groups are faring much worse than they have in the past. When already vulnerable populations are further disadvantaged by punitive social policies that are promoted by organizations associated with the corporate community, it seems clear that public welfare is being sacrificed for private gain. However, portraying the corporate sector as detrimental to the social welfare needs of the nation is not a particularly accurate depiction of the role of the business community in American social welfare. Human service corporations are already meeting the service demands of millions of people, a fact that is likely to become only more incontrovertible in the future.

Given the existence of for-profit human service firms, a useful question emerges about the "social carrying capacity" of the corporate sector. Critics of for-profit human services must acknowledge the occasional failure of public institutions to provide legally mandated services, even when they have enjoyed a monopoly, as in the case of corrections. In this regard, is it ethical to maintain a dehumanizing public correctional system when, as in the case of Tennessee, a for-profit firm offers to take it over and upgrade facilities? Finally, human service corporations might be put to more socially useful ends if they were managed by social welfare professionals. But social welfare professionals have been inclined to work in the voluntary and governmental sectors; few have elected to work for human service corporations.[27] It seems unlikely that human service corporations would demonstrate much sensitivity to severely disadvantaged groups without the influence of social welfare professionals electing to work in the corporate sector.

Which one of these scenarios—the mixed welfare economy, the corporate welfare state, or dual welfare systems—becomes prominent in American social welfare has enormous implications for clients of social programs and the professionals who work within them. Both clients and professionals stand to gain, or lose, much depending on their involvement in the debates and decisions that ultimately determine the preference of one scenario over the others. In the current period of transition, it is worth remembering that, little more than a half-century ago, a small but committed group of progressives forged the system of governmental programs that came to define the American welfare state of the twentieth century. It remains to be seen if another generation of leaders can demonstrate the same vision and courage necessary to define a social policy for the twenty-first century that assures the social welfare of all Americans.

NOTES

1. Daniel Patrick Moynihan, *Came the Revolution* (New York: Harcourt Brace Jovanovich, 1988), p. 291.

2. R. Erikson, E. Hansen, S. Ringen and H. Uusitalo, *The Scandinavian Model* (Armonk, N.Y.: M. E. Sharpe, 1987).

3. Richard Titmuss, *Commitment to Welfare* (New York: Pantheon, 1968), p. 127.

4. Harold Wilensky and Charles Lebeaux, *Industrial Society and Social Welfare* (New York: Free Press, 1965), p. 147.

5. Mimi Abramovitz, "The Privatization of the Welfare State," *Social Work* 31, no. 4 (July–August 1986), pp. 257–64.

6. Wilensky and Lebeaux, *Industrial Society and Social Welfare*, p. 231.

7. Marc Bendick, *Privatizing the Delivery of Social Welfare Service* (Washington, D.C.: National Conference on Social Welfare, 1985), pp. 1, 6.

8. Quoted in David Broder, "Reagan's Policies Are Standard for Would-Be Successors," *Omaha World-Herald*, January 24, 1988, p. 25A.

9. Michael Sandel, "Democrats and Community," *The New Republic*, January 22, 1988, p. 21.

10. Bruce Jansson, *The Reluctant Welfare State* (Belmont, Calif.: Wadsworth, 1988), Chapter 1.

11. Charles Murray, *Losing Ground* (New York: Basic Books, 1984), pp. 227–28.

12. Irving Howe, *Beyond the Welfare State* (New York: Schocken Books, 1982), pp. 1, 10.

13. Frances Fox Piven and Richard Cloward, *The New Class War* (New York: Pantheon, 1982), pp. x–xi.

14. Robert Morris, *Rethinking Social Welfare* (New York: Longman, 1987).

15. Robert Kuttner, *The Economic Illusion* (Boston: Houghton Mifflin, 1984).

16. Robert Kuttner, "The Welfare Strait," *The New Republic*, July 6, 1987, p. 20.

17. Russell Jacoby, *The Last Intellectuals* (New York: Basic Books, 1987).

18. Wilensky and Lebeaux, *Industrial Society and Social Welfare*, p. 42.

19. Claus Offe, *Contradictions of the Welfare State* (Cambridge, Mass.: MIT Press, 1984), p. 150.

20. Wilensky and Lebeaux, *Industrial Society and Social Welfare*, p. 139.

21. Ibid., p. 140.

22. David Stoesz, "Functional Concept of Social Welfare," *Social Work* 33, no. 1 (January–

February 1988).

23. In this respect, the functional conception of social welfare is akin to the functional school of sociology.

24. Robert Reich, *Tales of a New America* (New York: Vintage, 1987), p. 57.

25. William Lind and William Marshner, *Cultural Conservatism: Toward a New National Agenda* (Washington, D.C.: Free Congress Research and Education Foundation, 1987), p. 80.

26. Yeheskel Hasenfeld, "The Changing Context of Human Services Administration," *Social Work* (November–December 1984), p. 524.

27. David Stoesz, "Human Service Corporations: New Opportunities for Administration in Social Work," *Administration in Social Work* (forthcoming, 1989).

CHAPTER 19

Welfare Reform

This chapter examines welfare reform, a concept that has a relatively narrow meaning in the United States since it is associated with the Aid to Families with Dependent Children (AFDC) program. Since the 1960s, several attempts have been made to reform AFDC, but it was not until 1988 that AFDC was substantially changed. The alterations in the AFDC program illustrate an ideological shift in American culture that is increasingly conservative. Social welfare policy as a whole has begun to reflect conservative values by emphasizing reciprocity, productivity, and familial responsibility. Still, despite the reform of AFDC, a number of important social welfare issues remain unresolved. These are likely to occupy analysts of social policy and advocates of social justice for the next several years.

Welfare reform has been a heated topic in the United States for several decades. Most presidents since John F. Kennedy have either offered welfare proposals, or at least given lip service to the need for reform. Until recently, welfare reform had a liberal connotation since reform proposals usually called for major increases in benefits as well as expanding eligibility for welfare programs. Thus, welfare reform tended to mean some form of a guaranteed annual income for the poor—one component of the classic liberal formulation for social welfare reform which also included national health care and full employment. This liberal orientation to welfare reform was so prevalent that even conservative administrations used it as the basis for welfare reform initiatives. For example, in the 1970s Richard Nixon, a Republican president, proposed a massive overhaul of welfare in the form of the Family Assistance Plan (FAP), a guaranteed annual income program.

By the 1980s, however, this liberal orientation to welfare reform was eclipsed by a conservative vision. This shift in ideology can be attributed to significant changes in the social, political, and economic sectors of American culture. The first of these was the role played by analysts from think tanks in breaking up the hegemony of the federal government in social welfare. Although conservative policy institutes, such as the American Enterprise Institute (AEI) and the Heritage Foundation, have aspired to roll back the New Deal,[1] initial moves in this direction were made by liberal analysts. In 1977 Charles Schultze, a senior fellow at the Brookings Institution and former Chairman of the President's Council of Economic Advisors under Jimmy Carter, wrote *The Public Use of Private Interest* in which he argued that governmental intervention, through higher expenditures and increased regulation, was inferior to market strategies in dealing with social problems.[2] Soon thereafter, another Brookings senior fellow, Henry Aaron, published a critique of the War on Poverty, concluding that the intellectual basis of poverty programs was inherently flawed.[3] Subsequently, analysts from the Urban Institute published *Private Provision of Public Services*, a programmatic evaluation of nongovernmental activities in several areas, including social welfare.[4] When AEI's then-president, William Baroody, Jr., stated his intent to promote a new and post-New Deal philosophy, thus reducing governmental involvement in domestic policy, some of the groundwork had already been done by liberal scholars.

Second, in a development much depreciated by liberal intellectuals, a loose amalgam of religious fundamentalists and conservative populists merged to form the influential "traditionalist movement." Seeking to reinforce basic values—respect for family and country, hard work, freedom and independence—traditionalists challenged welfare programs which were alleged to fracture family life, erode the work ethic, and encourage undesirable behavior. The traditionalist movement flexed its political muscle during the 1980 election which not only brought Ronald Reagan into the presidency, but also placed a Republican majority in the Senate. This provided the Reagan administration with the political clout it needed to alter domestic policy during the early 1980s. Traditionalists also backed George Bush in his successful run for the presidency in 1988. Successes of the traditionalist movement were chronicled in *Back to Basics* by Burton Pines, a vice president of the Heritage Foundation.[5]

Third, a perception emerged in the advanced capitalist nations that welfare expenditures were becoming a drag on their economies. Noting that the problem afflicted even economies with greater commitments to governmental welfare programs than found in the United States, *Time* reported:

> At its present levels, the welfare apparatus has simply become too expensive for most governments—and their taxpayers. Across the [European] continent, social security systems are grappling with fiscal crisis, in part because ponderous, costly bureaucracies have mushroomed to administer a vast array of programs that sometimes neglect the essential to serve up what is merely desirable ... Bloated beyond its architects' intent, welfarism is threatening bankruptcy in some countries.[6]

In the United States, increased expenditures for non-welfare activities, particularly the military, compounded the problem of "runaway welfarism" by creating unprecedented deficits. In response, the Balanced Budget and Emergency Deficit Control Act of 1985 (commonly referred to as the Gramm-Rudman-Hollings Act) limited future expenditures. Although certain provisions were ruled unconstitutional, Congressional leaders used the basic provisions of the act and other methods for making appropriations contingent on meeting targets in reducing the deficit. As a result, $23 billion was cut from government expenditures in 1987, half from domestic programs. In this context, a deficit-driven budget meant that new welfare initiatives that required additional funds were unlikely in the foreseeable future, and that further cuts in social programs were more likely. This relationship between the swelling budget deficit and the limits of social programs did not go unnoticed by Daniel Patrick Moynihan, probably the most influential proponent of welfare reform since the New Deal. Suggesting that the budget deficit was a deliberate contrivance on the part of the Reagan administration to cap popular social programs that had been consistently defended by Congress, Moynihan concluded that the budget deficit was likely to "virtually paralyze American national government for the rest of the decade."[7]

Together, these factors have had an enormous influence on American social welfare. Within a relatively short period the classic liberal trinity of welfare reform—full employment, a guaranteed annual income, and national health care—had virtually disappeared from public discourse. In their place, narrow interpretations of welfare reform prevailed, reflecting a general drift toward conservatism that affected the nation as a whole. The conservative influence on domestic policy was reflected in two ideological developments within the American polity: neoconservatism and neoliberalism.

NEOCONSERVATISM

Prior to the 1970s, conservative thought held that business activity and government programs were essentially independent of one another.

Accordingly, conservatives seemed content to snipe at welfare programs, reserving their attention for areas more in line with traditional conservative concerns: the economy, defense, and foreign affairs. By the mid-1970s, however, younger conservative intellectuals recognized that this classically conservative stance, vis-à-vis social welfare, was no longer tenable: welfare had become too important to be dismissed outright. Consequently, a neoconservative formulation[8] emerged that sought to contain the growth in governmental welfare programs, while transferring as much welfare responsibility as possible from government to the private sector. Explicit in this was an unqualified antagonism toward government intrusion in social affairs. Government programs were faulted for a breakdown in the mutual obligation between groups, the lack of attention to efficiencies and incentives in the way programs were operated and benefits awarded, the induced dependency of beneficiaries on programs, and the growth of the welfare industry and its special interest groups, particularly professional associations.[9]

The Hoover Institution of Stanford, California, proved instrumental in shaping the neoconservative position on welfare. "There is no inherent reason that Americans should look to government for those goods and services that can be individually acquired," argued Hoover's Alvin Rabushka, who listed four strategies for reforming welfare: "(1) let users pay, (2) contract for services, (3) fund mandated services through the state, and (4) emphasize private substitution."[10] Martin Anderson, a Hoover senior fellow and subsequent domestic policy advisor for the Reagan administration, elaborated the neoconservative position on welfare:

1. Reaffirm the need-only philosophical approach to welfare and state it as explicit national policy.
2. Increase efforts to eliminate fraud.
3. Establish and enforce a fair, clear, work requirement.
4. Remove inappropriate beneficiaries from the welfare rolls.
5. Enforce support of dependents by those who have the responsibility and are shirking it.
6. Improve the efficiency and effectiveness of welfare administration.
7. Shift more responsibility from the federal government to state and local governments and private institutions.[11]

Complementing the work of Hoover analysts, AEI commissioned Peter Berger, a sociologist, and Richard John Neuhaus, a theologian, to prepare a theoretical analysis of American society. Berger and Neuhaus's *To Empower People: The Role of Mediating Structures in Public Policy*, identified the fundamental problem confronting American culture as the growth of megastructures (i.e., big government, big business, big labor, and professional bureaucracies), and a corresponding diminution in the value of the individual. The route to empowerment of people, then, was to revitalize "mediating structures"—among them, the neighborhood, family, church, and voluntary association.[12] In a subsequent analysis, an AEI scholar transferred the corporation from a megastructure to a mediating structure, thus leaving the basic institutions of liberal social reform—government, the professions, and labor—as the source of mass alienation.[13]

Based on these preliminary works, conservative scholars began to develop plausible proposals for welfare reform. With the election of Ronald Reagan, a hoary and worn rhetoric about counterproductive welfare programs suddenly gave way to some relatively sophisticated thinking about social welfare. In place of the cliches about welfare cheats, parochial bureaucrats, and bleeding-heart social workers, neoconservatives made serious proposals in the areas of workfare, community development, and child welfare. In a short period, liberal hegemony in social welfare was confronted by a group of scholars who held a vastly different vision of American social welfare.

A handful of works served as beachheads for the conservative assault on the liberal welfare state. George Gilder's *Wealth and Poverty* argued that beneficent welfare programs represented a "moral hazard," insulating people against risks that were essential to capitalism, and then eventually contributed to dependency. Instead of welfare, Gilder concluded, "In order to succeed, the poor need most of all the spur of their poverty."[14] Martin Anderson contended that the poverty line figure should include the cash equivalent of in-kind benefits—Food Stamps, Medicaid, and housing vouchers—that would effectively lower the poverty rate by 40 percent. "The war on poverty has been won," Anderson proclaimed, "except for perhaps a few mopping-up operations."[15] Meanwhile, AEI prepared *Meeting Human Needs*, an anthology detailing how the private sector could shoulder more of the public welfare burden.[16] However, the capstone of the conservative critique of liberal government initiatives was Charles Murray's *Losing Ground: American Social Policy 1950–1980*. An analyst associated with the Manhattan Institute and the Heritage Foundation, Murray alleged that government social programs of the Great Society had actually worsened the conditions of the poor. In *Losing Ground*, Murray advocated no less than a "zero transfer system" that consisted of "scrapping the entire federal welfare and income support structure for working-aged persons."[17] Subsequently, neoconservatives seemed to relish in making proposals to reform welfare; no policy institute from the right of the ideological spectrum had proven its mettle unless it had produced a plan to clean up "the welfare mess." The Heritage Foundation featured *Out of the Poverty Trap: A Conservative Strategy for Welfare Reform* by Stuart Butler and Anna Kondratas.[18] AEI countered with *The New Consensus on Family and Welfare*, the product of a distinguished panel of neoconservative scholars directed by Michael Novak.[19] Not to be outdone, the Free Congress Research and Education Foundation proposed reforming welfare through "cultural conservatism," that is by reinforcing "traditional values: delayed gratification, work and saving, commitment to family and to the next generation, education and training, self-improvement, and rejection of crime, drugs, and casual sex."[20] As a collection, these works provided conservatives with a potent critique of liberal governmental welfare programs. Unlike classical conservatives of an earlier generation who simply refused to deal with welfare policy questions, neoconservatives not only did their homework on social welfare policy, but began to prepare serious proposals for welfare reform.

NEOLIBERALISM

Smarting from the defeat of Jimmy Carter and the loss of the Senate to the Republican party in 1980, many liberal Democrats began to reevaluate their party's traditional position on domestic policy. This reexamination, christened "neoliberalism" by Charles Peters to differentiate the new ideology from liberalism and neoconservatism, attracted a small following in the early 1980s. With the resounding defeat of Walter Mondale—a candidate who symbolized liberal social policy—neoliberalism moved to stage center of Democratic party politics. The defeat of Michael Dukakis underlined the need for Democrats to reformulate their positions on domestic policy. By the late 1980s, several leading Democrats were identified as neoliberal —Richard Gephardt, Charles Robb, Albert Gore, Jr., Bill Bradley, and Tim Wirth. Moreover, the movement rapidly influenced social policy proposals advanced by the Democratic party. Randall Rothenberg charted the influence of neoliberalism on the Democratic domestic policy platform as early as 1982:

The party's June 1982 midterm convention in Philadelphia did not endorse a large-scale federal jobs program, in spite of more than 9 million unemployed. It did not re-propose national health insurance, even though medical costs were still soaring. It did not submit yet again a plan for a guaranteed annual income, although the American welfare system was still not operating efficiently.[21]

In place of liberal proposals of welfare reform—usually calling for an expansion of government effort—neoliberal proposals have tended to reduce governmental costs while encouraging business to assume more responsibility for the welfare of the population. For example, Charles Peters, editor of the *Washington Monthly*, advocated means-testing welfare programs. In defense of neoliberalism, Peters explained that: "We still believe in liberty and justice and a fair chance for all, in mercy for the afflicted, and help for the down and out ... but we no longer automatically favor unions and big government or oppose the military and big business." In reviewing "income maintenance programs like social security, welfare, veterans' pensions, and unemployment compensation," Peters outlined the neoliberal position:

> We want to eliminate duplication and apply a means-test to these programs. As a practical matter the country can't afford to spend money on people who don't need it ... as liberal idealists, we don't think the well-off should be getting money from these programs anyway— every cent we can afford should go to helping those in real need. Social Security for those totally dependent on it is miserably inadequate, as is welfare in many states.[22]

Robert Reich, a Harvard professor and advisor to the Democratic party, advocates investments in "human capital," and thinks these should be adapted to productivity. Restructuring human capital investment, or, in other words, reforming the current welfare apparatus, involves a thorough retooling of virtually every program.

For example, we can expect that a significant part of the present welfare system will be replaced by government grants to businesses that agree to hire the chronically unemployed. . . .

Other social services—health care, social security, day care, disability benefits, unemployment benefits, relocation assistance—will become part of the process of structural adjustment. Public funds now spent directly on these services will instead be made available to businesses, according to the number of people they agree to hire. Government bureaucracies that now administer these programs to individuals will be supplanted, to a large extent, by companies that administer them to their employees.

Companies, rather than state and local governments, will be the agents and intermediaries through which such assistance is provided.[23]

THE NEW WELFARE REFORM INITIATIVE

Out of this conservative climate, anti-welfare sentiment shaped proposals for welfare reform. To no one's surprise, the welfare reform plan proposed by the Reagan administration effectively eliminated, for all practical purposes, a poor mother's entitlement to support from government welfare programs. The administration's Low-Income Opportunity Act would have ended the historical entitlement nature of current benefit programs, allowed states to set benefit levels, and especially, program and eligibility guidelines. This proposal would have authorized statewide or local demonstration projects to test new methods for simplifying existing programs that were designed to assist poor people in getting off welfare and into productive work. Accordingly, the plan would have allowed individual states to streamline existing programs and thus reduce duplicative and inefficient expenditures. Predicated upon the belief that state and local governments could best assess the needs of the poor, the bill was designed to give states wide latitude in program design, eligibility guidelines, benefit levels, and the allocation of program resources. Essentially, the Reagan proposal called for a series of state-sponsored welfare experiments with virtually no assistance from the federal government. Opponents were quick to point out that most of the burden of such a program would be borne by recipients of public welfare programs who were to be the subjects of these experiments.

The bills advanced by Congressional Democrats, in contrast to their welfare reforms proposed in earlier administrations, *were* unusual. Instead of establishing a federal welfare program mandating adequate benefit levels, Congressional Democrats followed the conservative trend in thinking on welfare reform by allowing states to continue to define need, set their own benefit levels, establish (within federal limitations) income and resource limits, and administer the program. Although the welfare reforms proposed by Congress were more conservative than earlier Democratic plans, the Reagan administration threatened to veto any reform bill which did not also include a tough work requirement.

Differences between the moderately conservative Democratic plan and the very conservative Reagan proposal were ironed out in a compromise bill which Thomas Downey, chair of the House subcommittee on public assistance, hailed as the first "significant change in our welfare system in 53 years."[24] Under the proposal $3.34 billion would be allocated over the first five years for states to establish education and job-seeking programs for AFDC recipients. During 1990 and 1991 states would have to enroll at least 7 percent of AFDC parents in "workfare"; and by 1995 the enrollment must rise to 20 percent. Two-parent families are covered in the bill; however, beginning in 1997, one parent will be required to work at least 16 hours a week in an unpaid job in exchange for benefits.[25] Among the more progressive provisions of the plan are the extension of eligibility for day-care grants and Medicaid for one year after leaving AFDC for private employment. The bill also mandates the automatic deduction of child support from an absent parent's paycheck.[26] Dan Rostenkowski, chair of the House Ways and Means Committee that oversees most welfare legislation, estimated that an additional 65,000 two-parent families would receive benefits, that 400,000 people would participate in workfare by 1993, and that 475,000 would be eligible for transitional Medicaid benefits under provisions of the bill.[27] This compromise bill was signed into law by President Reagan in October 1988.

Given these provisions, how much "reform" is in the new welfare reform initiative? The most significant improvements are the extension of child day care and Medicaid for one year after finding employment and the inclusion of two-parent households in the program. These provisions will doubtlessly help parents who are occupationally upwardly mobile; however, the great majority of people on AFDC exhibit a job history in which welfare complements episodic and low-wage employment. In light of this, the new welfare initiative will extend important benefits to the working poor, but it is unlikely to boost people off welfare by itself. Unless wages increase and jobs are more reliable, the working poor will continue to need welfare benefits periodically. On the other hand, some provisions of the bill are clearly punitive and are unlikely to enhance substantially the self-sufficiency of AFDC recipients. Requiring one parent of two-parent households to do make-work in exchange for benefits is unlikely to increase economic independence, and may actually impede it if beneficiaries are forced to do make-work when they could be seeking work in the labor market. Garnishing wages is unlikely to increase economic independence if a parent's wages are so low that such a requirement creates incentives to quit work, instead of paying child support. Feminist policy analyst Mimi Abramovitz observed that for poor men this provision "may be more like squeezing blood from a stone."[28] Finally, the reliance on states to operate workfare programs that are not adequately funded is likely to result in welfare reform that is uneven—relatively wealthy states, such as Massachusetts and California, will expand on generous workfare programs that are already in place, while poorer states, such as Mississippi and New Mexico, will be hard-pressed to deploy programs that are nothing other than punitive.

With limited exceptions, welfare reform in 1988 was clearly a conservative triumph. "By replacing liberal tenets of entitlement, self-determination and Federal responsibility with more conservative notions of contract, compulsion, and states' rights," observed Mimi Abramovitz, "welfare reform erodes some of the fundamental principles that support the U.S. welfare state."[29] Perhaps the clearest example of how regressive welfare reform has become is found in the way income has been reapportioned from poor families to workfare officials. From 1970 to 1988, the median state's AFDC benefit dropped 35 percent in constant dollars as a result of inflation. In other words, had AFDC benefits simply remained constant with inflation, beneficiaries in 1988 would have received $5.88 billion *more* than what they are getting. The 1988 welfare reform initiative proposes to "reallocate" over a five-year span only 57 percent of this lost income ($3.34 billion) back to the poor through compulsory workfare.[30] At the same time, AFDC benefits remained below the poverty level for all states, except for Alaska.[31] For the poor, welfare reform in 1988 represented little more than diverting only a portion of the income supplement lost since 1970 to welfare managers who operated stringent workfare programs. From this perspective, there is little in welfare "reform" that represents a net improvement in the lives of families living in poverty.

REFORMING THE WELFARE STATE

By the late 1980s neoconservatism and neoliberalism had made a clear imprint on social welfare policy. In contrast to ambitious proposals advanced by previous administrations—such as the Family Assistance Plan of the Nixon administration, that proposed a guaranteed annual income, and the Program for Better Jobs and Income of the Carter administration, which proposed a public jobs effort—the welfare reform plans that were to gain serious attention during the late 1980s were comparatively modest. Even groups previously enraged by Reagan administration strikes against welfare, such as the National Governors' Association and the American Public Welfare Association, supported proposals that were quite conservative in contrast to those of the past.

While the concept of workfare might have appealed to many people, by the time the idea was packaged as prospective legislation, it represented anything but *major* welfare reform. The cost of the compromise welfare reform proposal of 1988 paled in contrast to the reforms of the New Deal and the War on Poverty, and did not begin to recover the massive amounts cut from welfare programs in recent years.[32] To have proposed radical welfare reform was simply out of the question. Robert Greenstein, Executive Director of the Center on Budget and Policy Priorities, a liberal think tank in Washington, D.C., observed that the price tag of a major restructuring of welfare "moves outside the realm of what can even be discussed in Congress."[33]

At the moment, the social, economic, and political forces that have propelled conservatism appear likely to influence social policy throughout the remainder of the century. From this conservative direction, three fundamental values emerge that bear directly on the shape of future welfare proposals: reciprocity, productivity, and familial responsibility.

Reciprocity

A growing literature on the American underclass suggests that welfare programs contribute to dependency and dysfunctional behaviors, especially when benefits are not conditional on a standard of conduct expected of recipients. In a convincing argument, Lawrence Mead observed that "the damage [by welfare programs] seems to be done, not by the benefits, themselves, but by the fact that they are *entitlements*, given regardless of the behavior of clients. They raise the income of recipients, but, more important, free them to behave without accountability to society."[34] Consequently, a common feature of welfare reform is likely to be that of employment—or, in the absence of a job, education or job-finding activities—as a condition for eligibility. Although reciprocity is usually advanced as a way to encourage socially desirable behavior by welfare recipients, it also contributes to the public credibility of welfare programs. In introducing his Family Security Act, which includes a workfare component, Daniel Patrick Moynihan argued that:

> Mothers, the custodial parents in most single-parent families, must try to earn income, at least part time, to help support their children. The statistics are a stark testament to the need: 72 percent of all mothers with children between 6 and 18 are in the labor force. Over half of all mothers with children under age 3 are in the labor force.
>
> This marks a great change in the position of women in American life. The only women who have not participated in this change are the heads of AFDC families, of whom fewer than 5 percent work part time or full time.
>
> As a nation, we find a 7 percent unemployment rate barely tolerable. What then are we to think of a system that keeps 95 percent of poor mothers unemployed and out of the labor force?[35]

Productivity

Budget restraints, coupled with conservative values, are likely to make social programs more congruent with economic productivity. There are two ways in which productivity affects welfare reform. First, programs that support the employable—women and minorities—stand a better chance of passage than programs which maintain populations not expected to compete in the labor force—the aged and children. Coupling welfare to productivity can make for some strange bedfellows when it comes to welfare reform. For example, in response to the numbers of mothers in the labor force, Senator Orrin Hatch, an arch-critic of progressive welfare programs, proposed a $375 million child day care program.[36] Second, welfare programs can be used to rebuild deteriorating communities in America. The precedent exists with the jobs programs of the New Deal—the Civilian Conservation Corps, the Works Progress Administration, the Public Works Administration—and more recent examples, such as the California Conservation Corps. The redefinition of relief from association with welfare to association with work carries with it the prospect of using social programs to reconstruct America's deteriorating infrastructure. Allying welfare to productivity draws social programs closer to the American economic system, a strategy that may be necessary to justify greater expenditures for social welfare in the future. Under the rubric of "industrial policy," both conservatives and liberals have advocated for major governmental initiatives to enhance the competitiveness of the American economy vis-à-vis those of western Europe and Japan. As a result, welfare advocates are likely to be more successful if they base the rationale for new social programs on investments in human capital or in community restoration that contributes to the economic vitality of the nation.[37]

Familial Responsibility

Another thread in current welfare reform proposals is the belief that the government should abandon its role as the "rescuer of first resort." Retreating to traditional values, this philosophy decrees that spouses (usually the father, since the mother is most often the custodial parent) have the ultimate responsibility for support of their offspring. The 1988 AFDC reforms call for stringent child support enforcement: after a child support award is granted, states must contact employers and arrange for the money to be automatically withheld from an employee's paycheck. Employers would then forward the withheld wages to state agencies for distribution to the family. In addition, inter-state administrative mechanisms would be developed to expedite the location of a delinquent parent and as a means for forwarding inter-state payments. Since 1981 even impoverished non-custodial parents have been required to pay child support. Perhaps more a principle than a fiscal attempt to gain revenue, this policy reinforces a belief in the responsibility of the parent to physically provide for the child.

TOWARD A NEW WELFARE AGENDA

Current proposals on welfare reform do not merely reflect a series of benign policy initiatives—they represent a fundamental shift away from sweeping notions of universal entitlements toward a strongly residual conception of social welfare. Welfare reform ideologies that stress reciprocity, productivity, and familial responsibility reflect a return to traditional values of self-reliance, independence, individual responsibility, and the limited role of government. For liberals who have advocated expanding federal social programs, this approach embodies a return to a harsh and punitive world that is incongruent with modern civilization. According to these critics, postindustrial capitalism is marked by an interdependence between individuals and government, with human and market needs being inextricably linked. Regional and international economic dislocations can pose significant problems for government, particularly when the cost for dealing with these falls on the public sector. When unplanned capitalist development displaces large segments of workers, it becomes the government's responsibility to sweep up the

human debris. From this perspective, a conservative ideology of welfare reform is not only out-of-sync with the requirements of a postindustrial economy, but also serves to condemn individuals for their own impoverishment, to "blame the victim," and to aggravate social injustice.

If proponents of social justice are to reassert their role in welfare reform, they must begin to rethink social welfare.[38] At the core of resurrecting a progressive welfare agenda lie a series of assumptions. For one, "welfare bashing"—blaming the welfare system for poverty —must be reconsidered. It must be acknowledged that the welfare system does not create poverty; its fault, if indeed there is one, is that despite huge expenditures it cannot compensate for the degree of social and economic dislocation associated with capitalist development. It is more reasonable to realize that the American welfare state has simply been unable to keep up with the increased income and social stratification that marks post-World War II society. Unfortunately, the welfare state has served as the perfect "fall guy" for those who are displeased with government social programs.

Under attack from neoconservatives and neoliberals, the temptation is great for welfare advocates simply to defend programs against further assault. This strategy, regrettably, is often at the expense of a needed reevaluation of the social, economic, and political context in which welfare programs exist, The American welfare state must be reorganized to address the current realities of an increasingly complex economy that is less able to provide a high volume of stable, well-paying jobs and upward mobility for large numbers of its citizens. Although the New Deal welfare state may have been relevant to the economic realities of the 1930s to the 1970s, the changing economic realities of the 1980s make it almost anachronistic. Any welfare system must be tailored to the given economic and social conditions of a society; as those conditions change so must the welfare state. If the American welfare state is deeply flawed, it is because it has failed to keep pace with the new economic realities created by the mobility of international capital, the concentration of corporate power, the decreasing competitiveness of American industry, and the export of relatively well-paying industrial jobs. In short, the current welfare state is grounded in another age—an age of real economic growth, occupational mobility, and an expansion of the industrial base. The task for welfare professionals, then, is to reestablish a welfare state that reflects the economic and social realities of the 1980s and beyond.

Recently, welfare professionals have come to recognize the very real problems of the American welfare state. Neil Gilbert, for example, observed that the welfare state is adrift.[39] Welfare professionals are seriously handicapped without a postindustrial vision of welfare. For many experts, reforms proposals that stress workfare and total economic self-sufficiency are, by themselves, inadequate to address the problem, but they have failed to generate an alternative that departs from the broad New Deal-type social programs that are so familiar to them. Eventual disappointment with workfare will only result in more opprobrium leveled at welfare recipients. In the end, both welfare policy analysts and workfare recipients stand to be held responsible for the consequences of conservative welfare reform.

Current welfare reform proposals are flawed in other ways. In November, 1987, there were 7.1 million unemployed workers; 5.5 million part-time workers who could not find full-time work; and several million working poor who, even though they were working full-time did not earn enough money to escape poverty. If these people are unable to find work, or earn enough from the work they have, how can welfare recipients be expected to become self-sufficient? Moreover, even though unemployment has been reduced to under 7 percent, it is differentially distributed. Relatively well-off sections of the country (e.g., Massachusetts, New Hampshire, California, and so forth) experience

less unemployment while the "rust bowl" of the industrial midwest and the farm states experience high rates of unemployment. Furthermore, unemployment rates tend to differ widely even within states. Vigorous promotion of workfare may thus force poor rural families to move to urban areas where there are job possibilities, a trend that will further impoverish and depopulate already shaky rural areas.

Many economists believe that America will be forced to develop some form of national industrial policy in order to remain competitive with foreign industries. National industrial policy refers to the deliberate, planned, and controlled rebuilding of American industry and infrastructure. An American industrial policy would include the rebuilding and modernization of plants, retooling basic industries, retraining the labor force, and rebuilding highways, schools, bridges, communications, and central cities. Through industrial policy, plans for social and economic development would be formulated by business, government, and labor unions, with the federal government providing the resources for implementation. The fact that from 1980 to 1987, the United States went from the largest creditor to the largest debtor nation in the world gives some immediacy to the proposal.

Social welfare measures could become an integral part of a national industrial policy. Developmental programs for the hard-core unemployed could be initiated, as well as work programs that assured education and training for competitive employment for welfare recipients.[40] Given present trends within the labor market, it must be recognized that income from some kinds of work must be subsidized, in some cases on a long-term basis. A community development program could encourage economic growth within inner cities and other areas in economic decline. Social welfare proposals could also be expanded to the middle classes—as in child day care, health insurance, and student loans—as a way to enhance the productivity of middle-income

Americans. Expanding social welfare programs to the middle class not only makes economic sense in that this population is the backbone of the economy, but it also makes political sense, since this portion of the population is most active politically. Still, it is evident that the middle and upper classes are reluctant to provide additional welfare benefits unless they perceive that these benefits will, at least in part, contribute positively to the national culture. Increasingly, welfare benefits are linked to reciprocity and productivity, values that now serve as the litmus test to determine the plausibility of welfare reform proposals. Thus, any feasible welfare reform proposal must contain elements of traditional values complemented by the current economic reality.

This is clearly a difficult time for the American welfare state. Even after huge expenditures on social welfare services, according to Richard Estes, the United States ranks twenty-third internationally in terms of the adequacy of its social provisions.[41] Given the present trend in which the economy produces vast numbers of service jobs—many of which are part-time, have little, if any, benefits, and pay the minimum wage—long-term welfare benefit packages will likely be required for an increasing number of citizens. How much those income benefit packages will contain, and at what cost, will be a matter for future discourse in public policy. Clearly, the American welfare state is at a juncture: one road leads to restrictive and punitive approaches to welfare, the other road to innovative and far-reaching programs that encompass social reconstruction and a better quality of life for everyone. Which direction the country takes will affect the structure of the American welfare state and the beneficiaries who are dependent on it.

NOTES

1. The clearest example of this is William J. Baroody, Jr., "The President's Review," *AEI Annual Report 1981–82* (Washington, D.C.: American Enterprise Institute, 1982).

2. Charles Schultze, *The Public Use of Private Interest* (Washington, D.C.: Brookings Institution, 1977)—although Brookings's Bruce Smith was to report later that the shift had gone too far right. Bruce Smith, "Changing Public-Private Sector Relations," *The Annals* (March 1983).

3. Henry Aaron, *Poverty and the Professors: The Great Society in Perspective* (Washington, D.C.: Brookings Institution, 1978).

4. Ronald Fisk, Herbert Kiesling, and Thomas Muller, *Private Provision of Public Service* (Washington, D.C.: Urban Institute, 1978). Not long thereafter, the Urban Institute published another title on the subject—Harry Hatry, *A Review of Private Approaches for Delivery of Public Services* (Washington, D.C.: Urban Institute, 1983).

5. Burton Pines, *Back to Basics* (New York: William Morrow, 1982).

6. Frederick Painton, "Reassessing the Welfare State," *Time,* January 12, 1981, p. 32.

7. Daniel Patrick Moynihan, *Came the Revolution* (New York: Harcourt Brace Jovanovich, 1988), p. 153.

8. See Peter Steinfels, *The Neoconservatives* (New York: Simon and Schuster, 1979).

9. Interview with Stuart Butler, Director of Domestic Policy, at the Heritage Foundation, October 4, 1984.

10. Alvin Rabushka, "Tax and Spending Limits," in Peter Duignan and Alvin Rabushka, eds., *The United States in the 1980s* (Stanford, Calif.: Hoover Institution, 1980), pp. 104–6.

11. Martin Anderson, "Welfare Reform," in Peter Duignan and Alvin Rabushka, eds., *The United States in the 1980s* (Stanford, Calif.: Hoover Institution, 1980), pp. 171–76.

12. Peter Berger and John Neuhaus, *To Empower People* (Washington, D.C.: American Enterprise Institute, 1977).

13. Michael Novak, *Toward a Theology of the Corporation* (Washington, D.C.: American Enterprise Institute, 1981), p. 5.

14. George Gilder, *Wealth and Poverty* (New York: Basic Books, 1981), p. 118.

15. Anderson, "Welfare Reform," p. 145.

16. Jack Meyer, ed., *Meeting Human Needs* (Washington, D.C.: American Enterprise Institute, 1981).

17. Charles Murray, *Losing Ground* (New York: Basic Books, 1984), pp. 226, 227.

18. Stuart Butler and Anna Kondratas, *Out of the Poverty Trap: A Conservative Strategy for Welfare Reform* (New York: The Free Press, 1987).

19. Michael Novak, *The New Consensus on Family and Welfare* (Washington, D.C.: American Enterprise Institute, 1987).

20. William Lind and William Marshner, *Cultural Conservatism: Toward a New National Agenda* (Washington, D.C.: Free Congress Research and Education Foundation, 1987), p. 83.

21. Randall Rothenberg, *The Neoliberals* (New York: Simon and Schuster, 1984), pp. 244–45.

22. Charles Peters, "A New Politics," *Public Welfare* (Spring 1983), pp. 34, 36.

23. Robert Reich, *The Next American Frontier* (New York: Times Books, 1983), p. 248.

24. William Eaton, "Major Welfare Reform Compromise Reached," *Los Angeles Times*, September 27, 1988, p. 15.

25. Spencer Rich, "Compromise Reached on Welfare Overhaul," *The Washington Post*, September 27, 1988.

26. Eaton, "Major Welfare Reform Compromise Reached."

27. Spencer Rich, "Panel Clears Welfare Bill," *The Washington Post,* September 28, 1988.

28. Mimi Abramovitz, "Why Welfare Reform Is a Sham," *The Nation*, September 26, 1988, p. 239.

29. Ibid., p. 240.

30. Computations are based on *Background Material and Data on Programs within the Jurisdiction of the Committee on Ways and Means* (Washington, D.C.: U.S. Government Printing Office, 1988), pp. 415, 424.

31. Ibid., pp. 408–10.

32. The Center on Budget and Policy Priorities estimates that $57 billion was cut from federal welfare programs which benefited low-income Americans between 1982 and 1986.

33. Personal communication, September 28, 1987.

34. Lawrence Mead, *Beyond Entitlement* (New York: Free Press, 1986), p. 65.

35. Daniel Patrick Moynihan, *Congressional Record*, pp. S10401–2.

36. Orrin Hatch, *Congressional Record*, September 11, 1987.

37. For a more complete discussion, see David Stoesz, "The Functional Conception of Social Welfare, *Social Work* (forthcoming 1989).

38. See Robert Morris, *Rethinking Social Policy* (White Plains, N.Y.: Longman, 1986).

39. Neil Gilbert, "The Welfare State Adrift," *Social Work* 31, no. 4 (July–August, 1986), pp. 245–49.

40. "Proposed Welfare Reform Bill Would Make Some Go to Work," San Diego *Tribune*, March 19, 1987.

41. Richard J. Estes. *The Social Progress of Nations* (New York: Praeger, 1984), p. 109.

CHAPTER 20

Privatization: Issues for the Voluntary and Corporate Sectors

The fragmentation of consensus about the American welfare state is evident in reductions in governmental social programs and calls for the private sector to assume more of the welfare burden. The movement toward "privatization" of governmental welfare activities has become important in defining the future of social welfare in the United States. One significant question raised by privatization is whether the nonprofit voluntary sector or the for-profit corporate sector should compensate for governmental retrenchment. Among the issues precipitated by privatization are the commercialization of human services, the preferential selection of clients, the efficiency of nongovernmental providers, standardization of service provision, and the emergence of human service oligopolies. As privatization continues to influence social welfare, these issues become more prominent in debates about social welfare policy.

As a function of public dissatisfaction with governmental social programs, increasing reliance on the private sector to finance and deliver social services has emerged as an important theme in American social welfare. "Privatization," as this idea has been termed, addresses the problem of the proper relationship between the public and private spheres of the national culture. In this case, privatization has come to refer to "the idea that private is invariably more efficient than public, that government ought to stay out of as many realms as possible, and that government should contract out tasks to private firms or give people vouchers rather than provide them services directly."[1] That government should not hold a monopoly on social welfare is not a novel idea. Even liberal policy analysts have entertained ways in which the private sector could complement governmental welfare initiatives.[2] Often liberal proponents of welfare programs are willing to concede a viable private sector role—even an innovative one—but insist that government be the primary instrument to advance social welfare. Conservatives, of course, see the proper balance as one where the private sector is the primary source of protection against social and economic calamity, and that government activity should be held in reserve. According to conservative doctrine, government can deploy the "safety net" of social programs, but these should provide benefits only as a last resort.

A clear articulation of the conservative vision of reinforcing the role of the private sector in social affairs appeared in the 1988 *Report of the President's Commission on Privatization*. "In the United States . . . the growth of government has been based on the political and economic design that emerged from the Progressive movement around the turn of this century," noted the *Report*. "The American privatization movement has represented in significant part a reaction against the themes and results of Progressive thought."[3] Specifically, the *Report* targeted government social programs and the professional administrators who manage them as the undesirable consequences of the progressive state of mind which can be corrected by privatization. The implications of this analysis are broad—not only should benefits be removed from government and provided by the private sector, but the administration of social programs should also be removed from public and placed under private auspices, as well. Accordingly, the President's Commission on Privatization identified three "techniques for the privatization of service delivery": (1) the selling of government assets, (2) contracting with private firms to provide goods and services previously offered by government, and (3) the use of vouchers, whereby the government distributes coupons which authorize private providers to reimbursement by government for the provision of goods and services.[4] While all of these methods have been used to restructure welfare programs at one time or another, the *Report* introduces an unprecedented idea into the debate in characterizing the issue as a "zero-sum game," one in which the advantage to one party is at the expense of the other. In this case, proponents of privatization suggest that the private sector should assume more responsibility for welfare, but with the reduction of government social programs. It is this sacrifice of the government's obligation to assure the general welfare that makes the current debate on privatization so important.

A new question in the debate on the balance of private and public responsibility for welfare was introduced with the recent emergence of human service corporations—if government is to divest itself of its welfare obligation, can the business community pick up the slack? If the answer is "yes," proponents of privatization have two options for the private provision of social welfare: the nonprofit, voluntary sector and the for-profit, corporate sector. In the years following President Lyndon Johnson's Great Society programs, government began to experiment with contracting out services through both nonprofit and for-profit providers. The for-profit, corporate sector capitalized on the contracting out provisions of the Medicare and Medicaid programs. Through the "purchase of service" concept introduced in Title XX, nonprofit agencies became contractors providing a range of social services on behalf of public welfare departments. Unfortunately, studies comparing the performance of these sectors have been few and their findings debatable.[5]

In the absence of definitive studies showing the advantages of one sector over another, the privatization debate has become volatile. Advocates of *voluntarization*—reliance on the voluntary sector to assume more of the responsibility for welfare—point to its historical contribution to the national culture, how its agencies are rooted in the community, and the altruistic motive behind its programs. Proponents of *corporatization*—dependence on the corporate sector to provide welfare—argue that it offers more cost-effective administration, it is more responsive to consumer demand, and it pays taxes. Whether voluntarists or corporatists prevail in the privatization debate will rest largely on the ability of each party to manipulate the social policy process in its favor. Whatever the outcome, this process is certain to be lengthy and complex, as one might expect with the remaking of an institutional structure that has become as essential as social welfare is in the United States. Whether voluntarization or corporatization defines the future of American social welfare, privatization has already highlighted several important issues.

COMMERCIALIZATION

For welfare professionals the idea of subjecting human need to the economic marketplace is often problematic. It is hard to condone health care advertising, which reached $1 billion in 1986, when the United States is without a universal program for expectant mothers and infants.[6] When research on the AIDS virus led to a diagnostic test, some private physicians exploited the AIDS panic and charged as much as $300 for each test, while the U.S. Army negotiated a test price of 82 cents.[7] As objectionable as these market-induced practices may be, the commercialization of human services is a reality that welfare professionals cannot simply dismiss out of a sense of moral indignation.

In one of the few treatments of the matter, *The Gift Relationship*, Richard Titmuss explored the differences in the way nations manage their blood banks. Unlike the United Kingdom, blood in the United States is "treated in laws as an article of commerce"; as such, rules of the market affect the supply and quality of blood. Titmuss observed the growth of blood and plasma businesses with alarm because they bought blood from a population that was often characterized by poverty and poor health. Quite apart from the health hazard presented by a blood supply derived from such a population—a hazard highlighted by the AIDS crisis—Titmuss was concerned about how the profit motive would disrupt the voluntary impulses of community life. "There is growing disquiet in the United States," he observed, "with expanding blood programs that such programs are driving out the voluntary system."[8] By 1976, 63.3 percent of blood banks in the United States were commercial.[9]

The commercialization issue is particularly important for financially strapped nonprofit agencies. Faced with declining revenues, some voluntary sector agencies experimented with commercial activities in order to supplement income derived from traditional sources: contributions, grants, and fees. That nonprofit organizations should be allowed to engage in commercial endeavors without restriction, is "unfair competition" according to business operators who note that nonprofits do not ordinarily pay taxes on their income. Limits on the freedom of nonprofit organizations to engage in commercial activities were highlighted in a celebrated case involving the New York University Law School and the Mueller Macaroni Company. Seeking a way to enhance revenues to the law school, enterprising alumni acquired the Mueller Company and reorganized it as a nonprofit organization registered in Delaware. Income from the macaroni company was thus redefined as nontaxable income and diverted to the law school as a charitable contribution. However, this clever arrangement did not go unnoticed by Mueller's competitors, who recognized the possibility of Mueller being able to use its newly acquired tax exempt status to cut prices and drive other macaroni companies from the market. Further, they argued, what was to prevent any well-endowed nonprofit institution from acquiring profitable businesses as a way to supplement income while dodging their tax obligation? The situation soon proved so embarrassing to the law school that it sent no representatives to congressional hearings that deliberated on the ethics of the arrangement. Eventually, the tax code was altered making income from commercial activities that are not related to the service function of the agency taxable.[10]

Since 1950, revenue obtained by nonprofit organizations from commercial activity is taxable under the unrelated business income tax (UBIT). While the Mueller case served as an adequate measure against gross breaches of business propriety, subsequent developments raised further questions around the commerce issue. For example, a nonprofit hospital association in Virginia attempted to maintain its competitive edge by acquiring several commercial ventures, including an advertising agency, two health clubs, an interior decorating firm, a pharmacy, and a helicopter ambulance service—acquisitions criticized by nearby businesses.[11] Even the YMCA has come under fire. In this case, the 1100-member International Racquet Sports Association complained that "Ys" held an unfair competitive advantage over for-profit racquet clubs.[12] These and other conflicts between nonprofit and for-profit organizations were aired during hearings held by the House Ways and Means Committee in 1987.[13]

During the hearings, representatives of the business community complained that nonprofits were engaged in "unfair competition" with for-profit businesses. According to business representatives, their competition occurred in two ways. First, the UBIT failed to distinguish between related and unrelated business activities. For example, the nonprofit hospital's pharmacy is considered related to the hospital's mission and is therefore exempt from paying taxes on income, but the for-profit hospital's pharmacy is part of the business and its income is thus taxable. Second, nonprofit organizations benefit from the "halo effect"; that is, the perception of the public that their services are superior because they do not operate from the profit motive. Thus, health spas complain that the philanthropic image of "Ys" is inaccurate, because "Ys" use business practices such as marketing and advertising to promote their services.

Although complaints of unfair competition by nonprofit organizations appear to be academic, the accusations open the possibility of further restricting the revenue base of voluntary sector agencies. For example, some "Ys" have stopped advertising their programs for fear that local authorities may interpret that activity as commercial and thereby attempt to tax income derived from them. The unfair competition issue presents some very disturbing questions for administrators of nonprofit organizations. If a nonprofit family service agency bills a client's insurance company for a "usual, customary, and reasonable" fee that is comparable to that charged by a private practice group that must pay taxes on such income, should this income remain tax exempt? Should tax exempt income be limited to only charitable contributions? Do program outreach and public education activities constitute marketing and advertising and, as such, be limited if a nonprofit is to retain its tax exemption? Questions such as these strike at the heart of the function of the voluntary sector. How these questions are resolved will be of great concern to proponents of nonprofit community service agencies, particularly those organizations faced with dwindling revenues.

PREFERENTIAL SELECTION

If privatization has implications for program administrators, as evident in the commercialization of human service, it also has significant implications for clients. The application of market principles to client service introduces strong incentives for providers to differentiate clients according to their effect on organizational performance. Such selection can be at variance with professional standards which emphasize the client's need for service over organizational considerations. But the marketplace penalizes providers who are imprudent about client selection, while at the same time rewards providers who are more discriminating. The subtle and blatant practice of choosing clients according to criteria of organizational performance—as opposed to client need—is defined as "preferential selection." Under conditions of the marketplace, providers who do not practice preferential selection are bound to service a disproportionate number of clients with serious problems and with less ability to pay the cost of care, thereby running deficits. On the other hand, providers who select clients with less serious problems and who can cover the cost of care often claim surpluses. Preferential selection could be excused, perhaps, as a benign method through which organizations determine those clients that are likely to be best served—if it were not for the odious practice of client "dumping." Dumping occurs when clients, already being served by an organization, are abruptly transferred to another organization because they represent a drain on institutional resources.

Critics of privatization complain that creaming the client population through preferential selection is unethical and should be prohibited. Simply ruling out the practice is, however, easier said than done. Accusations of preferential selection are not new; private, nonprofit agencies have been accused of denying services to welfare recipients well before proprietary firms became established.[14] Yet, recent reports of dumping when life-threatening injuries are evident have drawn the ire of many human service professionals. In some instances, private hospitals have transferred indigent patients with traumatic injuries to public facilities without providing proper medical care, thus resulting in the patients' death.

Incidents of dumping are related directly to the patient's ability to pay for service, and transfers of poor patients have increased as Medicaid is cut. For example, the transfer of poor patients to publicly owned Cook County General Hospital in Chicago increased from between 90 and 125 per month to 560 patients in August 1981, one month after Illinois instituted cuts in its Medicaid program.[15] In another instance, researchers at Highland General Hospital, the public health care facility in Alameda County, California, examined the transfer disposition of 458 patients over a six-month period. The researchers concluded that "the transfer of patients from private to public hospital emergency rooms is common, involves primarily uninsured or government insured patients, disproportionately affects minority group members, and sometimes places patients in jeopardy."[16] In Denver, where public hospitals have borne heavy deficits for carrying a disproportionate burden of the medically indigent, the problem has become critical. Jane Collins, director of clinical social work for the Denver Department of Health and Hospitals, described public hospitals in the city as becoming "social dumps."[17]

In a market, preferential selection on the part of a large number of providers is likely to be adopted by others who wish to remain in a competitive position. In analyzing the practice in health care, a team of researchers from Harvard University and the American Medical Association noted that, "in the same way that competition from for-profit providers leads to reduction in access, the more competitive the market for hospital services generally, the more likely are all hospitals in that market to discourage admissions of Medicaid and uninsured

patients."[18] In other words, nonprofit providers are compelled to accept the discriminatory practices of for-profit providers in a competitive market, unless the nonprofits are willing, in effect, to underwrite the losses that more costly clients represent for their organizations. "When competitive pressures are great," noted researchers from Yale and Harvard Universities, "the behavior of for-profit and nonprofit institutions often converges."[19]

COST EFFECTIVENESS

Proponents of privatization frequently cite the discipline imposed by a competitive environment on organizational performance as a rationale for market reforms in social welfare. A competitive environment provides strong incentives for firms to adopt cost-effective practices which reduce waste. This claim has led to a handful of studies of for-profit versus nonprofit service providers. In 1981, Lewin and Associates compared 53 nonprofit hospitals with a matched set of for-profit hospitals in the South and Southwest. They concluded that investor-owned hospitals were more expensive than nonprofit hospitals, largely due to higher ancillary (laboratory, radiology services, etc.) and administrative service costs. Also, investor-owned hospitals used fewer full-time equivalent staff to provide care than did nonprofit hospitals.[20] This last finding is unsettling, because lower staff to patient ratios had been associated with higher rates of contagious disease in nursing homes.[21] The Florida Hospital Cost Containment Board released a 1980 analysis comparing 72 proprietary and 82 nonprofit hospitals in that state. With results similar to the Lewin study, the Board reported a 15 percent higher charge for patient care and an 11 percent higher collection rate by investor-owned hospitals over their nonprofit counterparts.[22]

In an ambitious study, researchers from the Western Consortium for the Health Professions compared 280 hospitals which were private voluntary, public, and investor-owned. The Western Consortium researchers reached conclusions that were even less supportive of subjecting health care to the marketplace. For example, they suggested that investor-owned hospitals used emergency services and room and board as loss-leaders, funneling patients into a pricing situation where higher cost ancillary services would be used. Investor-owned hospitals cared for the smallest proportion of patients dependent on Medicaid. The researchers concluded that "the data do not support the claim that investor-owned chains enjoy overall operating efficiencies or economics of scale in administrative or fiscal services."[23] Data from the Health Care Finance Administration of the Department of Health and Human Services confirm these studies. In 1985, the cost for each short-term hospitalization was calculated according to hospital auspice, as noted in Table 20.1.

Significantly, the higher cost of proprietary hospitals could not have been attributed to longer periods of hospitalization, since the average stay at for-profit hospitals, 7.8 days, was (along with government institutions) the lowest of the group.[24] Finally, in the most comprehensive review of the issue, the Institute of Medicine of the National Academy of Sciences concluded that there is "no evidence to support the common belief that investor-owned organizations are less costly or more efficient than are not-for-profit organizations."[25]

While skeptics of market strategies in welfare use such studies to criticize the false economies of the human services market, it appears that practices of for-profit firms are influencing

nonprofit human service organizations. Many nonprofits have adopted features of for-profit firms—bulk-buying, sophisticated information systems, staff reductions—to enhance organizational efficiency. As noted above, when nonprofits compete with for-profit firms in the same market, the adoption of competitive practices is inevitable in order to assure organizational survival. As a result, competitive practices characteristic of human service corporations may become standard organizational procedure, not because they serve the public interest better, but because the rules of the marketplace require their adoption.

The promise of cost containment through privatization has not been borne out, and this presents an enormous problem for the governmental sector. Under a privatized system, government is in a weak position to control the prices charged by contracting agencies, unless the governmental sector is prepared to deploy its own set of public institutions, thereby avoiding the private sector altogether. A good example is provided by the Medicare program through which the government subsidizes health care, most of which is provided by the private sector. In response to runaway Medicare costs, Congress enacted the Diagnosis Related Group (DRG) prospective payment plan in 1983, whereby hospitals are reimbursed fixed amounts for procedures. Three years after the DRG system was in place, the Congressional Budget Office reported that hospitals increased their surplus attributed to Medicare by 15.7 percent during 1985. This surplus occurred despite a reduction in the number of Medicare patients admitted to hospitals.[26]

Proponents of privatization often claim that noncompetitive markets and governmental regulation, as in the case of the DRG prospective payment system, impose additional costs which must be passed on to consumers. Research, however, does not bear this out. In a study of 6000 hospitals sponsored by the National Center for Health Services Research and Health Care Technology Assessment, a re-

TABLE 20.1. Cost for Short-Term Hospital Stay by Auspice

Auspice Of Hospital	Cost Per Stay
Church	$5,453
Other nonprofit	$5,542
Government	$4,429
Proprietary	$5,795

search team found that "hospitals located in areas with 11 or more neighboring facilities within a 15 mile radius—the most competitive type of hospital market—have admission costs and patient day costs that are 26 percent and 15 percent higher, respectively, than corresponding figures for hospitals with no competitors." Significantly, the hospitals were surveyed before 1983, so governmental regulation through the DRG system could not have contributed to increased costs.[27]

STANDARDIZATION

Privatization induces human service organizations into accepting an industrial mode of production where the accepted measure of success is not necessarily the quality of service rendered, but the number of people processed. Organizational surplus, essential for investor-owned facilities, tends to be derived from increasing the intensity of production and lowering labor costs. The logic of the market dictates that the goal of production is to process the largest number of people at the lowest possible cost. Standardization of services is an important method for expediting the processing of people.

Such uniformity of care has become an issue in the nursing home industry. Because Medicaid regulations stipulate standards of care, providers deriving a large portion of their revenues from Medicaid are induced to standardize care for all patients. Consequently, well-to-do patients were unable to purchase better care from a nursing home even though they had the resources to do so. Standardization of care became cause for serious concern among nursing home corporations. Richard Buchanan, professor of business administration at Bowling Green State University, noted the social consequences of standardized care.

> The nursing home industry's identical treatment of everyone creates a one-class social system for all patients. This constitutes a denial

of the affluent person's rights to purchase the quality of life that had been his or hers until stricken with illness or infirmity. This phenomenon represents creeping socialism of a major order, and creates an atmosphere ripe for either legal or market reprisal.[28]

That standardization of care within an industry dominated by for-profit firms would be equated with "socialism" is perhaps the best measure of the severity of the problem.

Under these circumstances, life care—or the continuing care retirement community— has emerged as an attractive alternative to the nursing home for the provision of long-term care. Under life care, residents can purchase cottages or apartments in self-contained communities which include a range of human services. In many respects, the life care community provides more affluent residents an opportunity to purchase a higher level of long-term care. One continuing care facility boasted wall-to-wall carpeting, maid service, and a designed courtyard. "Already, the facility has shown its first in-house movie . . . and soon residents will be soaking up steam in the saunas, relaxing in the Jacuzzi, exercising on the mechanical bicycles, or browsing in the library," noted a visitor.[29] Among the amenities found in the more posh life care community are a cocktail lounge, billiards room, and elegantly furnished restaurants serving continental cuisine, sporty facilities such as these "provide a lifestyle of grace and activity for seniors with the ability to pay for it," observed an industry reporter.[30] "We sell a style of life," explained David Steel, vice president of Retirement Centers of America Inc., a subsidiary of Avon.[31]

Entry into life care communities can be equivalent to purchasing a home. Nationwide, the average entrance fees were $35,000 for a single person and $39,000 for a couple in the early 1980s. Monthly fees for medical care, dining and laundry, recreation, and transportation averaged $600 for a single person and $850 for a couple.[32] In more exclusive communities, one- and two-bedroom units sell from $100,000 to $170,000.[33] By the mid-1980s, 275 life care communities housed 100,000 elders.[34] But this was only the tip of a very large iceberg. Robert Ball, former Commissioner of Social Security, estimated that perhaps 15 million elders could afford this type of care.[35] Despite well-publicized bankruptcies of several life care communities, the prospect of a market of this scale has attracted the interest of several corporations.[36] Beverly Enterprises, the largest nursing home corporation, announced plans to build or acquire several life care communities.[37] Subsequently, Marriott Corporation stated its intent to build a number of life care communities serving between 300 and 400 residents each.[38] Despite the recession of the early 1980s, the interest of brokerage houses in continuing care remained high.[39] By the year 2000, 15 million Americans will need some form of long-term care.[40]

The prospect of extensive proprietary involvement in life care troubles some analysts. Lloyd Lewis, director of a nonprofit life care community, fears that "well-funded proprietary interests" would "drain off the more financially able segment of our older population, widening the gap between the 'haves' and the 'have nots.' "[41] To a significant extent this is already occurring. Robert Ball noted that life care communities operating under nonprofit auspices are beyond the means of "the poor, the near poor, or even the 'low-income elderly.' "[42]

The accommodation of long-term care facilities to the desire for amenities on the part of affluent residents is likely to produce significant change in how the nation cares for its elderly. In 1982, for example, the *New York Times* reported a nationwide shortage of nursing home beds for those "whose nursing care is financed by the government through Medicaid."[43] As human service corporations divert capital to care for those who represent profit margins, economic and political support diminishes for care of those less fortunate. "Those who can-

not gain admission to [a private] institution will be forced into boarding homes ... or bootleg boarding homes," commented Milton Jacobs, vice president of American Medical Affiliates. "These boarding homes will be filled with what are literally social rejects. We're reverting back to the way the industry was in the fifties and sixties."[44] Left unchecked, in other words, long-term care is likely to divide into two clearly demarcated systems: the affluent enjoying the generous care of completely—some would say excessively—provisioned life care communities, the poor elderly dependent on the squalid institutions willing to accept government payment for care. To a great extent, dual systems of long-term care will be attributed to the desire by the affluent to escape standardization of care associated with the economies of privatization.

OLIGOPOLIZATION

The privatization of human services invites the development of oligopolies—the control of a market by few providers—as organizations seek to reduce competition by acquiring competitors. Within the corporate sector, three waves of acquisition can be identified: acquisitions affecting long-term care, acquisitions affecting hospital management, and acquisitions affecting health maintenance industries. Significantly, virtually all of this oligopolization has occurred since the mid-1970s.

Driven by the same competitive pressures, consolidation of proprietary health providers has encouraged nonprofit providers to form franchises. In terms of number of beds, five of the ten largest hospital systems are nonprofit. Of these, three are operated by religious organizations, one—the New York City Health and Hospital Corporation—is a public conglomerate, another—Kaiser Foundation Hospital—is a private nonprofit entity. Increasingly, the nonprofit health providers are having to join together in order to compete with the aggressive proprietary providers, leading to oligopolies within the voluntary sector.[45]

Oligopolization of human services presents a daunting specter since a small number of wealthy and powerful organizations are in a strong position to shape social policy to conform with their interests. Within health care, this development has led Arnold Relman, editor of *The New England Journal of Medicine*, to voice alarm at the growing influence of the "new medical-industrial complex" in defining health policy in the United States.[46] Whether human service corporations presently have enough influence and power to be considered a "human service-industrial complex" is doubtful; but, further privatization of social welfare would make such a development a distinct possibility.

THE CHALLENGE OF PRIVATIZATION

It is difficult for welfare professionals to be sanguine about privatization. For those committed to increasing government responsibility to assure social and economic equality, privatization is simply a retreat from a century of hard-won gains in social programs. Their case is argued cogently by Pulitzer-prize winning sociologist, Paul Starr:

> A large-scale shift of public services to private providers would contribute to further isolating the least advantaged, since private firms have strong incentives to skim off the best clients and most profitable services. The result would often be a residual, poorer public sector providing services of last resort. Such institutions would be even less attractive as places to work than they are today. And their worsening difficulties would no doubt be cited as confirmation of the irremediable incompetence of public managers and inferiority of public services. Public institutions already suffer from this vicious circle; most forms of privatization would intensify it.[47]

For defenders of government social programs, the problems attributed to privatization—commercialization, client creaming, inflated costs, standardization, and oligopolization—make it a poor vehicle for advancing social welfare.

Yet, reliance on the private sector at a time when public social programs are under assault is a reality that must be faced by those concerned about social welfare. In the absence of an effective Left and the diminishing influence of a progressive labor movement, there appears little chance of launching new government social programs. If the public is unwilling to authorize and pay for new governmental social programs, welfare professionals have little choice but to reconsider privatization as a basis for welfare provision. Upon inspection, it could be argued that there are compelling reasons to believe that privatization could be a strategy for promoting social welfare. Through commercial loans and issuance of stock, for-profit organizations have faster access to capital than does the governmental sector (which requires a lengthy public expenditure authorization process) or the voluntary sector (which relies on arduous fund-raising campaigns) for purposes of program expansion. The private sector has also been the source of important innovations in programs and organizational administration, which have often become the exemplars for effective administration.[48] It could be argued further that welfare conscious administrators have missed opportunities for promoting social welfare by ignoring opportunities for professional practice associated with privatization. In this regard, welfare professionals might wonder if patient abuses in the nursing home industry, chronicled in *Tender Loving Greed*, would have been lessened had socially conscious administrators managed long-term care facilities.[49] As it is, human service workers now find themselves in the unenviable position of lobbying for a standard "requiring nursing homes with more than 120 beds to employ full-time at least one [undergraduate] social worker."[50]

Human service professionals will continue to deal with the consequences of privatization in the foreseeable future. The President's Commission on Privatization notes that, "the impact of the privatization movement, broadly understood, is only beginning to be felt. Privatization in this broad sense may well be seen by future historians as one of the most important developments in American political and economic life of the late 20th century."[51] How welfare professionals choose to respond to the challenge of privatization—by reaction or innovation—will be critical for the future of American social welfare. Privatization may come to be a rallying cry for defenders of established programs that have been discredited as being wasteful, inflexible, and currying the favors of special interests, or privatization may ultimately mean discovering new ways to exploit the social carrying capacity of the private sector. As David Donnison has suggested, welfare professionals would be wiser to reconsider their aversion toward the private sector and try to find the "progressive potential in privatization."[52]

NOTES

1. Paul Starr, "The Meaning of Privatization," quoted in American Federation of State, County, and Municipal Employees, *Private Profit, Public Risk: The Contracting Out of Professional Services* (Washington, D.C.: AFSCME, 1986), pp. 4–5.

2. Charles Schultz, *The Public Use of Private Interest* (Washington, D.C.: Brookings Institution, 1977); Donald Fisk, Herbert Kiesling, and Thomas Muller, *Private Provision of Public Service* (Washington, D.C.: Urban Institute, 1978); Harry Hatry, *A Review of Private Approaches for the Delivery of Public Services* (Washington, D.C.: Urban Institute, 1983).

3. *Privatization: Toward More Effective Government* (Washington, D.C.: Report of the President's Commission on Privatization, March 1988), p. 230.

4. Ibid., pp. 1–2.

5. And all of these have been in health care: Lawrence S. Lewin, Robert A. Derzon, and Rhea Margulies, "Investor-Owned and Nonprofits Differ in Economic Performance," *Hospitals* (July 1, 1981); Robert V. Pattison and Hallie Katz, "Investor-Owned Hospitals and Not-for-Profit Hospitals," *New England Journal of Medicine* (August 11, 1983); Robin Eskoz and K. Michael Peddecord, "The Relationship of Hospital Ownership and Service Composition to Hospital Charges," *Health Care Financing Review* (Spring 1985); J. Michael Watt et al., "The Comparative Economic Performance of Investor-Owned Chain and Not-for-Profit Hospitals," *New England Journal of Medicine* (January 9, 1986); Bradford Gray and Walter McNerney, "For-Profit Enterprise in Health Care: The Institute of Medicine Study," *New England Journal of Medicine* (June 5, 1986); Regina Herzlinger and William Kradker, "Who Profits from Nonprofits?" *Harvard Business Review* (January–February 1987).

6. Philip Alper, "Medical Practice in the Competitive Market," *New England Journal of Medicine* (February 5, 1987), pp. 337–38.

7. Patricia Franklin et al., "The AIDS Business," *Business* (April 1987), p. 44.

8. Richard Titmuss, *The Gift Relationship* (New York: Pantheon, 1971), p. 223.

9. Theodore Marmor, Mark Schlesinger and Richard Smithey, "A New Look at Nonprofits: Health Care Policy in a Competitive Age," *Yale Journal of Regulation* 3, no. 2 (Spring 1986), p. 320.

10. W. Harrison Wellford and Janne Gallagher, *Charity and the Competition Challenge* (Washington, D.C.: National Assembly of National Voluntary Health and Social Welfare Organizations, 1987), Chapter IV, pp. 13–15.

11. Michael Abramowitz, "Nonprofit Hospitals Venture into New Lines of Business," *The Washington Post*, February 15, 1987.

12. Todd Gillman, "Health Clubs Hit YMCAs' Tax Breaks," *The Washington Post*, June 30, 1987.

13. Anne Swardson, "Hill Taking New Look at Nonprofits," *The Washington Post*, June 21, 1987.

14. Richard Cloward and Irwin Epstein, "Private Social Welfare's Disengagement from the Poor," in M. Zald, ed., *Social Welfare Institutions* (New York: Wiley, 1965), pp. 628–29.

15. Emily Friedman, "The 'Dumping' Dilemma: The Poor Are Always with Some of Us," *Hospitals* (September 1, 1982), p. 52.

16. David Himmelstein et al., "Patient Transfers: Medical Practice as Social Triage," *American Journal of Public Health* (May 1984), p. 496.

17. Friedman, "The Dumping Dilemma," p. 54.

18. Mark Schlesinger et al., "The Privatization of Health Care and Physicians' Perceptions of Access to Hospital Services," *The Milbank Quarterly* 65 (1987), p. 40.

19. Marmor et al., "A New Look at Nonprofits," p. 344.

20. Lewin et al., "Investor-Owned and Nonprofits Differ in Economic Performance."

21. Jerry Avorn, "Nursing-Home Infections—The Context," *New England Journal of Medicine* (September 24, 1981), p. 759.

22. Reported in Arnold Relman, "Investor-Owned Hospitals and Health Care Costs," *New England Journal of Medicine* (August 11, 1983), pp. 370–71.

23. Pattison and Katz, "Investor-Owned Hospitals and Not-For-Profit Hospitals," p. 353.

24. Michael McMullan, personal correspondence, March 7, 1988; and "Use of Short-Stay Hospital Services by Medicare Hospital Insurance Beneficiaries by State of Provider and Type of Control: 1985" (Baltimore: Health Care Finance Administration, 1985).

25. Gray and McNerney, "For-Profit Enterprise in Health Care," p. 1525.

26. "Hospitals' Medicare Profits Up," *San Diego Union*, March 29, 1987, p. A5.

27. "Competition for Doctors and Patients Increases Hospital Costs," *NCHSR Research Activities* 101 (January 1988), p. 3.

28. Richard Buchanan, "Long-Term Care's Pricing Dilemma," *Contemporary Administrator* (February 1981), p. 20.

29. Ann LoLordo, "Life-Care Centers Offer Seniors Worry-Free Living," *The Baltimore Sun*, June 4, 1984, p. D4.

30. Carol Olten, "Communities Offering Seniors a Graceful Life," *The San Diego Union*, March 13, 1988.

31. Anthony Perry, "North County Housing Boom: A Lucrative Shade of Gray," *Los Angeles Times*, March 6, 1988.

32. U.S. Senate Special Committee on Aging, *Discrimination Against the Poor and Disabled in Nursing Homes* (Washington, D.C.: U.S. Government Printing Office, 1984), p. 8.

33. Perry, "North County Housing Boom."

34. U.S. Senate, *Discrimination Against the Poor and Disabled in Nursing Homes*, pp. 6–8.

35. Ibid., p. 8.

36. The most well-known bankruptcy of a life care community was that of Pacific Homes of California in 1979.

37. "Sun City—With an Add-On," *Forbes* (November 23, 1981), p. 84.

38. Jesse Glasgow, "Marriott to Test Life-Care," *The Baltimore Sun*, June 16, 1984, p. C1.

39. "Merrill-Lynch: Bullish on Health Care," *Contemporary Administrator* (February 1982), p. 16.

40. Anne Somers, "Insurance for Long-Term Care," *New England Journal of Medicine* (July 2, 1987), p. 27.

41. U.S. Senate, *Discrimination Against the Poor and Disabled in Nursing Homes*, p. 25.

42. Ibid., p. 10.

43. Robert Pear, "Lack of Beds Seen in Nursing Homes," *New York Times*, October 17, 1982, p. 1.

44. Quoted in William Spicer, "The Boom in Building," *Contemporary Administrator* (February 1982), p. 16.

45. Donald Light, "Corporate Medicine for Profit," *Scientific American* (December 1986), p. 42.

46. Arnold Relman, "The New Medical-Industrial Complex," *New England Journal of Medicine* 303, no. 17 (1980).

47. Paul Starr, "The Limits of Privatization," in Steve Hanke, *Prospects for Privatization* (New York: Proceedings of the Academy of Political Science, 1987).

48. David Stoesz, "Human Service Corporations: New Opportunities in Social Work Administration," *Social Work Administration* (forthcoming, 1989).

49. Mary Adelaide Mendelson, *Tender Loving Greed* (New York: Knopf, 1974).

50. "'87 Session of Congress Ends in 11th-Hour Win for NASW," *NASW News* (February 1988), p. 1.

51. *Privatization*, p. 251.

52. David Donnison, "The Progressive Potential of Privatisation," in Julian LeGrand and Ray Robinson, eds., *Privatisation and the Welfare State* (London: George Allen & Unwin, 1984).

CHAPTER 21

Issues in Social Service Delivery

This chapter will explore various ways that social welfare policies play out in an organizational context. As such, this chapter will examine the often conflicting goals between professional and organizational responsibilities and, in particular, the inherent problems in the delivery of social services which affect both clients and social workers. In addition, this chapter will investigate issues affecting the structure of social services, including unionization and the collective ownership of human services.

While many of the previous chapters examined macro-level social policy, most social work practitioners also have to reckon with micro-level social policies in their workplace. Often, these organizational policies may run counter to what social workers believe to be in the best interests of their clients, co-workers, and themselves. Policies taking place in the organizational setting have a significant influence on the experience of social workers, and particularly on the overall dilemma of how to fulfill both professional and organizational expectations. The need to accommodate professional responsibilities and organizational commitments may result in a situation fraught with ambiguity and a push-pull between these often conflicting roles. How individual social workers resolve this difficult situation is dependent on the values of the worker and the context in which he or she operates. Because social work ethics are necessarily broad—and often vague—their actual application is usually open to interpretation, and in some measure, is subjective. The two issues presented in this chapter—social service technology and social work unionization—are examples of im-portant current concerns that relate to the tension between professional and organizational responsibilities.

BUREAUCRACY AND THE DELIVERY OF SOCIAL SERVICES

Early social work was a voluntary and philanthropic endeavor with little sense of formal organization. By the 1920s, however, Frederick Taylor and others introduced scientific management, a system which emphasized the most economical use of energy to accomplish a given task. Efficiency became the creed of scientific managers, and each step in the production process was designed to be as efficient as possible. Business leaders who strongly influenced Community Chests—the forerunner of the United Way—attempted to apply those Tayloristic notions to the management of social services. As such, voluntary social services were expected to be efficient enterprises run by professional managers.

Most private and public social services are operated under the auspices of a bureaucratic structure. Although bureaucracy, an organizational structure characterized by a pyramidal design, has received "bad press" in the last 50 years, it remains an efficient way to handle complex tasks and manage an agency structure. In a bureaucratic pyramid, most employees are at the bottom (the widest point), and as the pyramid narrows there are fewer employees, with the top marked by only a few managers and a chief executive. Each level of the bureaucracy is responsible for specific tasks and organizational functions, and each level is accountable to the one directly above it. In an efficient bureaucracy, each level is intimately aware of the tasks, goals, and effectiveness of the level beneath it. The main job of the chief executive is to manage the bureaucracy. An "ideal" form of bureaucracy (rarely found) exists in a symbiotic relationship with its parts. Although some of the major attributes of bureaucracy—efficiency, impersonality, hierarchy, and centralization—seem to run counter to the key social work values of democracy, professional autonomy, and individualized client service, most social service agencies have adopted bureaucratic forms of organization because of the scope, complexity, and size of their operations.

Problems in the Delivery of Social Services

Social service delivery systems include the form, process, and content of social services. In other words, social service delivery refers to the way social services are made available and administered to clients. Neil Gilbert and Harry Specht define social service delivery systems as "the organizational arrangements among distributors and between distributors and consumers of social welfare benefits in the context of the local community."[1] As they have evolved, however, social service delivery systems have become plagued by four major problems: (1) fragmentation, (2) discontinuity, (3) unaccountability, and (4) inaccessibility. Gilbert and Specht provide an interesting description of these four problems:

> A man in an automobile accident is rushed by ambulance to ward "A" where he is examined; he is next taken to ward "B" for medical treatment, and then moved to ward "C" for rest and observation. If wards "A," "B," and "C" are in different parts of town, operate on different schedules, and provide overlapping services— that's *fragmentation*. If the ambulance disappears after dropping the patient at ward "A"— that's *discontinuity*. If the distance between the accident and ward "A" is too far, if there is no

> ambulance, if our patient is not admitted to the ward because of his social class, ethnic affiliation, or the like, or if he is taken to a ward for mental patients—that's *inaccessibility*. When any or all of these circumstances exist and our patient has no viable means of redressing his grievances—the delivery system suffers from *unaccountability*.[2]

A critical examination of the social service delivery system in the U.S. suggests that it may suffer from all of the above difficulties.

In social work, as in most other professions, catchwords like efficiency, accountability, system rationality, and austerity have become part of the daily vocabulary of professional life. Moreover, time and motion studies, sophisticated evaluation research, quantitative measures of client contact, and clinical proof of success are becoming increasingly common under the general rubric of accountability. These evaluative technologies represent a growing demand for the rationalization of social services, a demand fueled by dwindling fiscal resources earmarked for social welfare, the intense competition for capital between the social welfare state and the military-industrial complex, concerns about increases in taxation, and federal deficit spending which has reached catastrophic proportions.

Concomitant with fiscal austerity is an apparent increase in job dissatisfaction among private and public agency social workers, many of whom are reporting severe problems in relation to "burnout" and low agency morale.[3] Perhaps not surprisingly, this job dissatisfaction comes on the heels of the adoption of highly sophisticated management technologies including scientific management (e.g., management by objectives, goal attainment scaling, and so forth), attempts at greater quantification of client-worker contact hours, a plethora of designs used to evaluate and measure how worker time is spent, and so forth. Given the recent fiscal constraints in both public and private social welfare agencies, it can be anticipated that greater economic rationalization through increased technological monitoring and the downward reclassifying of social work positions is likely in the future.[4]

The response of many social welfare managers to diminished funding has focused on the development of more sophisticated technologies. Charles Perrow defines technology as

> . . . the actions that an individual performs upon an object, with or without the aid of tools or mechanical devices, in order to make some change in that object. The object, or "raw material," may be a living being, human or otherwise, a symbol, or an inanimate object. People are raw materials in people changing or people processing organizations; symbols are materials in banks, advertising agencies, and some research organizations; the interactions of people are raw materials to be manipulated by administrators in organizations; boards of directors, committees, and councils are usually involved with the changing or processing of symbols and human interactions, and so on.[5]

In this chapter, the authors define technology as "how the work is done," i.e., the machinery, the styles and philosophies of management, and the general design, organization, and execution of agency work.

The engine that drives technology is the desire to cut costs, usually the costs of labor. Utilizing technology optimally results in higher productivity—an increase in the quantities produced. (In human service organizations the "quantity" produced is the number of clients processed.) The overall goal of human service technology is to process the greatest number of clients at the least possible cost.

Standardizing the mode of production requires that raw materials be perceived in a normative fashion, that clients and workers have attributes that are replicable, that there be predictable behavior in the roles of each, and that exceptions to the production process must be overlooked or rejected. In short, the production process must become normative for the system to achieve rationalization.

While this system ensures that production is achieved at the least possible cost, it also provides ethical dilemmas for trained social workers. For example, professional training emphasizes that clients be seen as individuals who possess unique attributes and thus are entitled to receive individualized service. Moreover, clients are perceived as possessing self-determination. The wholesaling of problems that mark technological approaches to service delivery run counter to professional social work norms, and the processing of clients based solely on their classifiable problem is antithetical to the objectives of professional training. Moreover, social work training emphasizes individualized approaches to client problems, while technological approaches to social service delivery require meeting the needs of clients as the agency defines those needs. Unfortunately, this situation can aggravate the alienation that a client may already be feeling, and thus social services may perpetuate rather than alleviate a problem.

On the other hand, the social worker must operate within the context of service defined by the organization. Obviously, the social worker cannot promise the client more than the agency can deliver, and if the social worker circumvents the agency's authority, he or she risks termination. In a large bureaucracy the individual social worker often has little direct control over policies involving the services offered and how they are delivered. This tightrope between professional ethics and real-world constraints often leads to role confusion and value conflicts.

The De-Skilling of Social Workers

The values, philosophy, and culture of social work are often at odds with the values of technological rationalization. Particularly, social work places a high premium on human interaction and process, is labor-intensive, and has a non-linear view of the world. When complex technology contradicts the "terrain" (the actual work duties) of social services, social work skills can become devalued, and the professional currency of social workers diminished.

Technocrats attempt to conform the production process to fit the strengths and needs of a particular technology. Therefore, social service technologies will try to conform social work practice into a system which can be rationalized, measured, and evaluated. Because evaluative criteria are inherent in the technology, if social work fails in its quantitative goals (e.g., numbers of people receiving service) it is evaluated as ineffective. In that sense, technology determines practice. The confusion about means and ends can make social work practice rigid and, in the end, evaluative technology drives social work rather than the other way around.

Social service technology fits under the aegis of industrial production in several other ways. Both industrial and social agency production demand standardization of the raw materials of production (clients and workers).[6] Adherence to the industrial model of production can force social work, a non-routinized type of work, into a routinized and standardized framework. For example, the objective of operations research, at least as used in social work, is to develop an unobstructed and continuous assembly-line process which is devoid of organizational and production obstacles.[7] In short, the principle inherent in routinized work tasks[8] suggests that if clients are stable and uniform, and if much is known about the process of treatment, a routine work flow will follow.[9]

Routinization exacerbates the present division of labor in social work, and helps to locate the agency's decision-making functions within an insulated context. If a social worker's job is routinized—to be routine, tasks must be particular, specific, and measurable—he or she can only make decisions related to a small task. Moreover, the more routine the task the less the social worker knows about the overall functioning of the agency, and thus, is not well enough informed to have significant input into agency decisions. Even within the context of their routinized task, social workers may not be allowed to control the decision-making aspects of their job. Thus, routinized tasks allow for a division of labor which centralizes decision-making within an administrative cadre.

Unique problems arise when routinized tasks are introduced into the social service field. According to Eliot Friedson, professionalism is the quality of being free, self-directed, and autonomous.[10] A professional regulates his or her work. Conversely, according to Friedson, an occupation that cannot direct or control the production and application of knowledge and skill to the work it performs is not a profession.[11] The routinization of social service delivery is problematic for the social worker who, as a result of educational training, believes professionalism to be a central mandate of social work. Friedson sums up the dilemma:

> It has been felt by many writers that the worker, as well as the client, suffers from the bureaucratization of production by a monocratic administration. Lacking identification with the prime goals of the organization, lacking an important voice in setting the formal level and direction of work, and performing work which has been so rationalized as to become mechanical and meaningless, functioning as a minute segment of an intricate mosaic of specialized activities which he is in no position to perceive or understand, the worker is said to be alienated.[12]

As a consequence of the need to increase efficiency, productivity, and profits, the tasks of social workers may be reduced to simple routines. Social workers may lose some of the qualities of autonomous practice and run the risk of being defined as mere "factors of production." This situation removes the essence of dignity and worth from social workers.[13] Social work practice is at risk of becoming routinized, its tasks mechanized, and its final mission made more fully automatic.[14]

The discounting of social work skills may lead less qualified people to operate social services. Hence, with the downward reclassification of social work positions, a reduction in the value of professional social work may become more widespread. The caseworker whose skill is not clearly defined in the terms used by the technology, is devalued. Because technology must measure, and what is not quantifiable cannot be measured,[15] behavioral change may become the sole barometer of effective casework.

When a sophisticated technology does not pay attention to the organization of social work, and when that technology is mastered by only a few, severe workplace dislocation and stratification can occur. In particular, social workers who lack the skills to compete in the technological arena are at a disadvantage. Thus, workplace relations become transformed into a stratified system of power relationships. In effect, less technologically adept social workers are relegated to lower positions of power. The value of social workers and their ability to decide on the fundamental questions that affect their practice are diminished in light of the newly emerging power relationships.

The adoption of complex managerial techniques may lead to the importation of technologically trained non-social work managers, often MPAs or MBAs. This importation can result in the domination of social work by other professions, since these managers often have little understanding of the terrain of social work practice.

The de-skilling cycle nears completion when the social worker doubts his or her own skills. With that devaluation comes a subsequent decline in self-concept and a diminution in the purpose of work.[16] In other words, technology dissolves the labor process as one conducted by workers and reconstitutes it as a process controlled by management.[17]

To the extent that it stands to become a permanent fixture of the profession, the rationalization of social work is already evident in social work practice and administration. In the end, powerful technologies used exclusively in the service of economic rationalization may create electronic sweatshops, particularly in the area of public welfare. When social work skills are evaluated on a piecework basis, and when the art of social work is dismembered into tiny components for the purpose of positivist-based evaluation, the value of the profession and the quality of services offered to clients are reduced.

The following recommendations suggest some alternative ways of rationalizing social services:

1. The current notion of productivity should be reassessed, and in its place there must be a modified form of production based on human rather than machine needs. Productivity must be redefined to reflect the best interests of clients and workers, and alternative means of measurement and evaluation should be created.

   Appropriate technology for the social welfare field must be developed and utilized. The concept of appropriate technology presupposes the need to redefine efficiency in human rather than technological terms, with this redefinition hinging on reevaluating the goals of social service. Social service planning should be based on the needs of workers and clients and flow from a humanistic framework. This assumes a reassessment of the needs of workers and the creation of an alternative ideology around the role of work in modern life.

   Technological assessments should be based on a "regional" approach to evaluating the various sectors (i.e., child welfare, mental health, etc.) of the profession. Each "region" must develop its own specific form of technology that evaluates its locality (practice area of social work, e.g., casework, group work, etc.). The exclusive use of one evaluative technology will compromise the profession, and attempts to homogenize the terrain by superimposing a nonindigenous technology will only make social services appear ineffective.

2. Social service organizations need less rigid bureaucratic models and more humane and democratic organizational forms. Hierarchical organizations which pit worker against supervisor and center decision making on a select few should be replaced by more collegial work formats that allow for greater initiative and worker control.

3. Social service technology should be easily understood by those expected to implement it. This does not suggest utilizing only rudimentary and crude forms of technology, but instead, forms of technology should be used that can be mastered by practitioners with social work training. Technologies must also be flexible and open to input by social work personnel. Lastly, new technologies should be dynamic and easily altered to the changing conditions of social work practice.

Although in many ways the above scenario represents a worst-case problem, most social workers are affected by both technology and bureaucratization in varying degrees. The role conflict engendered by rigid and often highly bureaucratized agency policies has resulted in a wide range of responses by social workers. Some social workers have lobbied both internally and publicly for changes in agency policies, other workers have chosen to leave social work, others have acquiesced or tried to accommodate to the agency, others have gone into administration in hopes of changing unjust policies, and still others have chosen to join unions and other professional associations to collectively struggle for both their own interests and those of their clients.

SOCIAL WORKERS AND UNIONS

Public employee unions represent a wide-ranging segment of the public work force, of which social work is only a small part. Unlike teachers (e.g., the National Education Association and the American Federation of Teachers), social workers in most places do not have exclusive unions.

The unionization of social workers has grown despite a decline in the overall percentage of unionized workers in the labor force. Although the exact number of social workers affiliated with unions is difficult to determine, the four largest public sector unions claim over 125,000 social work members (American Federation of State, County, and Municipal Employees (AFSCME), 70,000; Service Employees International Union (SEIU), 40,000; Communications Workers of America (CWA), 10,000; and the National Union of Hospital and Health Care Employees (NUHHCE), 10,000).[18] This number represents a significant increase from a decade earlier.[19]

The causes for the growth in social work unionization are related to declining employment security for technical/professional workers in health care and government services (i.e., the impact of DRGs, the declassification of social work positions in many states, and public welfare layoffs), the passage of more liberal public sector labor laws (e.g., AFSCME gained 40,000 new members after Ohio passed new public sector labor statutes), and broader scope of bargaining issues which include quality of work life, training and career development, pay equity, stress reduction, day care, and job safety.[20] Despite its steady growth, the impact of unionization and collective bargaining has received only sporadic coverage in the social work literature.[21]

The Background
of Social Work Unionization

Any examination of organized labor and social work must be reduced to a fundamental question: Are unionism and professional social work compatible? Questions about the compatibility of labor and social work have been salient since the 1930s, and in a controversial paper delivered at the 1934 National Conference on Social Work, Mary van Kleeck, an important figure in social reform, observed that:

> ... the immediate common goals of labor and social work ... [are] maintenance of standards of living, both for individuals and for the community. Social work, particularly in these last few years, has repeatedly declared that it is ... representative of the common good will of those who seek to bring expert knowledge to bear upon ... the whole program of social legislation and public services....
>
> The labor groups have had the same general aim. They have sought to maintain the standards of living of the workers; to ask that the return in the pay envelope bear some proportion to the productivity of labor; to ask that there be leisure, growing also out of the increased productivity of labor.[22]

Van Kleeck saw the potential for a partnership between social work and labor unions, whereby both groups could help forge a new society. An idealist, van Kleeck saw the goals of social work and labor as the common goals of humanity. Van Kleeck's positive view of labor unions was shared by the nascent group of social work rank and filers of the early 1930s. Concerned with fusing professional social work values with trade union values, this group maintained that "any cursory examination of the program and demands of the trade union reveals their goals to be as clear and direct as those of the professional society—high standards of service and high standards of employment practices."[23] While a full account of the rank and file movement of the 1930s is beyond

the scope of this chapter, it is fair to say that it helped allow later social work unionization to take root.[24]

Although the rank and file movement and its unofficial organ, *Social Work Today*, had all but vanished by 1947, the idea of union membership had already gained widespread acceptance.[25] A 1947 article in the *Social Work Yearbook* observed that "labor and social work make contact at many points and have much in common."[26] The article stated that "The ultimate goal of organized labor has always been improvement in the standards of living among the workers of the nation.... Social Work, too, is concerned with action for long-range social progress."[27]

Apart from the important inroads made by the rank and filers of the 1930s, the relationship between professional social work associations and unions can be traced to organized labor's involvement in the public and private network of social services. Although the social welfare experiences of displaced workers in the 1930s was by and large negative, the ordeal taught labor leaders that social services potentially affected more than just a small segment of society. The interest of organized labor in social services—often private, nonprofit agencies involved with the Community Chests—brought unions and social workers into closer contact. According to Wilbur F. Maxwell, this contact allowed social workers to "become aware of the labor movement as something other than merely a force dealing with economic and wage problems," and for unions to see "social work as something other than merely an agency for dispensing 'charity' and relief."[28]

Despite the absence of a formal nexus, the relationship between labor and social work led in 1967 to the adoption of a policy that reaffirmed the right of NASW members to "participate in the formulation of personnel policies and procedures through whatever instruments they choose." Revised in 1971 and 1975, this policy statement advises management to "accept and work with whatever means of representation is chosen by the employee group."[29]

By the 1960s public sector unions were no longer the fledgling unions they were in the 1930s. Moreover, these unions were characterized by business unionism, and were part of the AFL-CIO network, long considered by many critics a conservative bastion. Nevertheless, by the 1970s many progressive social workers began to reconsider established institutions, especially trade unions. The creation of the Bertha Capen Reynolds Society and the beginning of a new journal, *The Catalyst*, were indicative of a reconsideration of the relationship between labor and social work.[30]

Common Goals of Labor and Social Work

Although there appears to be little formal association between the NASW and public sector unions on a national level,[31] they do nominally interact through the Coalition of American Public Employees (CAPE). CAPE, an organization which includes NASW as well as the major public sector unions, lobbies on issues surrounding national public welfare. At the local level, however, there have been several examples of active collaboration between professional social work associations and unions, often around issues of social service cuts and other domestic concerns.[32]

In an attempt to encourage a better relationship with professional social workers, Jerry Wurf, former AFSCME President, wrote an article for the *NASW News* in which he maintained that:

> AFSCME's involvement with . . . [social issues] . . . is part of a larger commitment to improving public services and programs. But more importantly, these vital efforts prove the true mission of a labor organization to be closely linked to that of social work. AFSCME's growth in the last decade was due in large part to its role as a social missionary. This precious pursuit has undoubtedly been enhanced by the growing number of social workers in our ranks.[33]

Since both organizations are politically liberal in their outlook, it is not surprising that the scorecard of agreement on domestic issues is nearly perfect. For example, both AFSCME and NASW endorsed the Federal Pay Practices Act of 1985. NASW and AFSCME are also concerned about the effects of the Gramm-Rudman-Hollings bill on social welfare financing,[34] and both groups agree on the necessity to re-fund the Title XX Social Services Block Grant to its higher pre-1981 levels.[35] Other AFSCME issues where NASW support is expected include opposition to cuts in Medicaid and the expansion of the program to cover all pregnant women, modification in the diagnosis related groups to make them more sensitive to the severity of illness, continued funding and expansion of the WIC program, the elimination of Food Stamp cuts, and an increase of AFDC payment standards to 80 percent of the poverty level.[36]

Welfare reform represents another issue of potential agreement between AFSCME and NASW. For example, NASW endorses providing welfare recipients with voluntary employment and adequate pay, opportunities for meaningful long-term work, and health insurance for children and adult family members. NASW is opposed to forced work programs, and advocates the creation of a full employment policy, an increase in the minimum wage, elimination of all discrimination in hiring, a national minimum benefit level for AFDC (indexed for inflation), and the provision of adequate support services for working parents.[37]

The AFSCME program for welfare reform is almost identical to NASW's. For example, AFSCME supports voluntary work and training programs and, like NASW, AFSCME proposals call for a substantial commitment of resources. In addition, AFSCME argues for strong support services in the areas of child care, health care, and transportation. And lastly, like NASW, AFSCME calls for an increase in the minimum wage, a policy of high employment, and an end to employer discrimination practices.[38]

A final area of agreement between public sector unions and NASW involves the issue of defense spending. In testimony given before the budget committee of the U.S. House of Representatives, NASW officials stated that: "NASW has two major concerns about the military budget: (1) it cannot be allowed to expand at the cost of domestic programs, and (2) the allocation of funds within the military should favor personnel needs and preparedness rather than strategic and nuclear weapons."[39] In substantial agreement with NASW, one AFSCME resolution called for an end to "the unwarranted, inflationary, and unjustified defense buildup proposed by the Reagan Administration."[40] Going one step further, the resolution demanded an "orderly, planned economic conversion," which entails "alternative uses for defense installations and plans for the redevelopment of communities adversely affected by such closings."[41] Although NASW and public sector unions have some differing viewpoints on national policy, for the most part, a substantial level of agreement prevails.

Anti-Unionism in Social Work

Despite the common goals of public sector unions and social work associations, opposition exists in several sectors of the profession. In general, opponents of unionism maintain that (1) unions cost employees money, (2) strike losses are never retrieved, (3) union members have little voice in union affairs and are often purposely kept ignorant, (4) bureaucratic union hierarchies control the economic destiny of employees, (5) union corruption is rampant, (6) the consistent opposition of unions to increases in productivity arrests organizational growth, (7) union "featherbedding" results in unneeded employees and unnecessary payroll expenses, (8) union membership campaigns foster conflict rather than collaboration, (9) the right of managers to strive for greater produc-

tivity is curtailed by union rules, and (10) unions have little consideration for the effects of increased wages on future employment, inflation, and tax increases.[42] In short, the anti-union bias in social work is tightly focused around issues of professionalism and bureaucracy.

Writing in *Social Work*, Dena Fisher examined a 1984 strike by Local 1199 of the Retail Drug Employees Union. This strike involved over fifty institutions and virtually all the social work staff in hospitals and nursing homes covered by the union. Fisher concluded that:

> Standards for professional practice conflict with the [NASW] Code of Ethics with regard to behavior during a labor strike when the prescribed behavior includes withholding service, failing to terminate clients properly, and picketing activity directed toward consumers of health care.... The problem is that participation in a strike is a nonprofessional activity.... Standards of professional behavior conflict with union membership requirements....[43]

Apart from fears that clients will be endangered by strikes, apprehension about the impact of unionism also centers around an uneasiness that when organized, social workers will become like other organized workers; that is, professional concerns will become subordinated to union issues. A belief in the "exceptionalism" of social work forms a superstructure underlying the debate on professionalism. This "exceptionalism" implies that tasks performed by social workers are more important than those performed by many other workers—especially, nonprofessionals—and therefore normal labor relations principles are not applicable.

Another concern of the anti-union forces revolves around the issue of bureaucracy. Although most social workers operate within the context of a bureaucratic setting, that same setting is often seen as interfering with professional autonomy by introducing rules, regulations, and an administrative hierarchy which superimposes authority of office over authority of expertise.[44] In the eyes of many people, including social workers, bureaucracies are associated with rigidity and authoritarian procedures. It is therefore not surprising that some social workers view unions as representing the same bureaucratic constraints that they despise in their organizational life. This situation is exacerbated when the union is not seen as part of an existing bureaucracy, but instead, as a new bureaucratic mechanism introduced into the workplace which further diminishes professional autonomy.[45] Ernie S. Lightman summarizes the dilemma: "The norm of altruistic service is challenged not only by the general bureaucratic context but also by the overt goals of personal gain and the language of confrontation which are assumed to characterize the union."[46]

Although rarely mentioned, opponents of unionization harbor a concern regarding management prerogatives. Early social work unions promoted two ideals: (1) to better the salaries and working conditions of social service workers, and (2) to improve benefits and services offered to clients. This approach implies that social workers function as employees championing their own self-interest and as advocates for their clients,[47] a situation unique among trade unions and possibly forming the basis for much of management's resistance to unionization. A statement by Fred Steininger, former official of the Department of Health, Education and Welfare, summarizes the dilemma of management:

> Employee unions have argued for a voice in management. Management has stood on its prerogatives. Some administrators have been seduced by the union's cause when it argued for decent housing, respect for the individual, and opportunity for the hopeless. They have backed the union only to find that they came to a parting of the ways when the employees' voice in management seemed louder than their own.[48]

The NASW Position on Unionism

As long as 30 years ago, NASW established that "employees have a right to belong to a union of their choice for purposes of collective bargaining."[49] Ernie S. Lightman maintains that NASW views collective bargaining as "one means of providing a rational and coherent method of solving problems, but the NASW fails to denote trade unionism explicitly as a preferred alternative, and by implication suggests that other approaches may be more desirable."[50] According to Lightman, the NASW position on social work unionization can be best described as neutral. By explicitly stating in the *Code of Ethics* that social workers' primary responsibility is to clients, NASW has inadvertently indicated that the service norm must take precedence over all bureaucratic processes and goals.[51]

The NASW is caught in a philosophical bind. Because it aggressively endorses the right of clients to self-determination, how can it allow that right to be denied social workers? Moreover, social work values such as advocacy, empowerment and self-determination cannot be endorsed for clients while at the same time being abridged for those who serve them. Such philosophical arguments require that NASW accept—if not actively support—social work unionization.

Are Unionization and Professionalism Compatible?

Although relatively few studies have examined the compatibility of unionism and professional social work, all have found that most unionized social workers perceive little incongruity between the two loyalties.[52] For example, Leslie Alexander et al. studied 84 MSW-degreed union members and found that "they view their work as solidly professional and, for the most part, do not see unionism and professionalism as incompatible."[53] Lightman had similar findings when studying 121 randomly chosen professional social workers in Toronto. According to Lightman, "the vast majority saw no incompatibility; indeed, many felt unionization may facilitate service goals, offsetting workplace bureaucracy."[54] And lastly, reporting on exploratory research using two child welfare agencies, one in Pennsylvania and the other in Illinois, Gary Shaffer found that "workers did not find unionism incompatible with their educational or professional goals."[55]

While the above research suggests the majority of organized social workers perceive little incongruity between being a professional social worker and a union member, the studies also hint at a bifurcated attitude toward unions and professional associations. For example, Alexander et al. found that social workers clearly preferred a job-conscious or instrumental form of unionism over an approach that stressed professional or political concerns.[56] A similar finding was reported by Lightman.[57]

It thus appears that unionized social workers may separate their professional and workplace concerns: unions are viewed by these social workers as best representing their workplace interests, i.e., pay, seniority, and job security issues, while professional associations are seen as embodying their professional concerns. This perspective is not surprising, since professional social work associations possess little actual clout in the workplace. For example, although NASW can censure an agency and publish its name in the *NASW News*, it has no other power of enforcement. On the other hand, unions can pursue grievance procedures, National Labor Relations Board (NLRB) hearings, law suits, and other remedies in pursuit of an employee's rights.

The Compatibility of Labor and Social Work

Although unionism and professional social work may be compatible, there remains a need for change and compromise on the part of both professional associations and labor unions. Traditional notions of trade unionism often fail to address many of the concerns of professional social workers. Unions must recognize that although bread-and-butter economic issues are important to social workers, this group is also concerned with professional issues that bear directly on their ability to serve clients. In that sense, unions must fuse traditional unionism with the professional concerns of social workers,[58] as well as find ways to actively address the service goals of social workers. The problem of union insensitivity to professional concerns is heightened by the influx into the public sector of various unions, many of whose only experience has been with private sector labor relations.

Obstacles to compatibility also involve professional organizations. For example, professional social work associations must understand that collective bargaining bespeaks dignity rather than charity, representing a means for turning begging into negotiations. Moreover, collective bargaining fits well within the context of self-determination, one of the most cherished of social work values. In its pure form, collective bargaining is a mainstay of democracy—it represents a meeting of minds as opposed to a decision rooted in capricious rules and regulations. In sum, the underlying philosophy of collective bargaining is congruent with social work's emphasis on democracy.

Public sector unions appear to be durable, and as Jerry Wurf, former president of AFSCME, observed:

> We've come a long way, and it hasn't been easy. In state after state, governors aspiring to strengthen or reinstate political patronage have attempted to crush public employee unionism . . . we've taken the worst public management has thrown at us—and we're still there.[59]

Regardless of the ambivalence felt in some quarters, the union movement in social work is entrenched. As such, professional social workers will continue to be unionized in significant numbers—some will become ardent trade unionists, others will be uninvolved in union matters, and still others may assume important positions within the union hierarchy.

Issues involving the compatibility of social work and unionism—often based on views of social work exceptionalism—are problematic. Although professional social work encompasses ideals of autonomy and self-directed practice, most social workers are employed by bureaucratic structures which relate to them as workers. Moreover, notions of professionalism do not function as effective forms of protection in workplace disputes over wages and working conditions. In the final analysis, social workers are as vulnerable to unfair employment practices as other workers.

Despite obvious differences, an overall compatibility appears to exist between the goals of public sector unions and professional social work. However, unions have not adequately addressed the problems of social service delivery, the effects of technology in the workplace, and the quality of services for clients. If—apart from wage and benefit demands—unions are to better respond to the professional needs of social workers, they must have more sensitivity to issues of professionalism. That may occur through more involvement in union affairs by organized social workers, a better relationship between professional social work associations and public employee unions or, more likely, by a combination of the two. In the end, public employee unions may well have the ability to further the social goals and mission of professional social work.

SELF-DETERMINATION IN THE SOCIAL SERVICE WORKPLACE

Traditional forms of unionism represent only one avenue for social workers to cope with often problematic agency policies, and to achieve the same level of self-determination in the workplace as they encourage clients to achieve in their personal lives. Nevertheless, an alternative to traditional unionism is what Leslie B. Alexander calls hybrid unionization. According to Alexander, the hybrid model:

> . . . assumes that when unions and professionals interact over time, each begins to assume some of the characteristics of the other; new forms emerge that borrow from, but do not entirely conform to, either the traditional union or the traditional professional model. The result might be one new form that combines the functions of a union and a professional association, or it might be two parallel forms. . . .
>
> When the structure and style of existing professional unions are examined, it becomes clear that unions of professionals are comparable to neither traditional professional associations nor traditional unions. Rather, a process of diffusion takes place. A new hybrid form of organization develops, drawing from, yet different from, both unions and professional associations in the classic sense.[60]

Given that the bureaucratic edifice of the industrial era may not be an adequate structure for the human service sector of a post-industrial economy, traditional and nontraditional forms of unionization demand greater scrutiny. Although unions could be instrumental in pioneering innovative service delivery organizations which better meet the needs of social workers, their clients, and the community, they do not radically alter the structure by which human services are delivered. An alternative proposal was made several years ago by one of the authors in which he advanced a model for mental health services—the Family Life Center—based on the logic that generated Employee Stock Ownership Plans and other forms of worker ownership.[61] According to this proposal, workers would own their own agencies and thus the means of service delivery. With the recent exception of private practice, social workers have always worked under conditions established by others. The popularity of private practice suggests that this is no longer acceptable for younger professionals. An organizational model in which social workers manage their own work—similar to a co-operative—would be attractive to many social workers. Professional social workers collectively owning and managing their own social service agency would help address social service delivery problems, as well as the value and role conflicts that these problems breed.

Whatever the solution—unionization, collective ownership, or some other strategy—serious problems exist in the delivery of social services which must be confronted. New organizational forms must be developed which address the quality of services to clients, client accountability, worker "burnout," de-skilling, and the often fierce rationalization of the social service workplace.

NOTES

1. Neil Gilbert, Harry Specht, *Dimensions of Social Welfare Policy* (Englewood Cliffs, N.J.: Prentice-Hall, 1974), p. 119.

2. Ibid., p. 121.

3. See, for example, Srinika Jayaratne and Wayne E. Chess, "Job Satisfaction, Burnout, and Turnover: A National Study," *Social Work* 29, no. 5 (September–October 1984), pp. 442–52; Herbert Freudenberger, "Staff Burnout," *Journal of Social Issues* 30, no. 2 (Winter 1974), pp. 459–65.

4. On the relationship of declassification to the future of social service, see Peter J. Peccora and Michael J. Austin, "Declassification of Social Service Jobs: Issues and Strategies," *Social Work* 28, no. 6 (November–December 1983), pp. 421–26; and H. Jacob Karger, "Reclassification: Is There a Future in Public Welfare for Trained Social Workers?" *Social Work* 28, no. 6 (November–December 1983), pp. 427–34.

5. Charles Perrow, "A Framework for the Comparative Analysis of Organizations," *American Sociological Review* 36, no. 2 (April 1967), p. 195.

6. Ibid., p. 196.

7. The development of an assembly-like process is clearly applicable to social service organizations. For example, see Jerald Hage and Michael Aiken, "Routine Technology, Social Structure, and Organizational Goals," in Yeheskel Hasenfeld and Richard A. English, *Human Service Organizations* (Ann Arbor: University of Michigan Press, 1974), p. 298.

8. Routinized tasks are similar to what Eugene Litvak refers to as uniformity of tasks. See Eugene Litvak, "Models of Bureaucracy Which Permit Conflict," in Hasenfeld and English, *Human Service Organizations*, pp. 400–21.

9. Ibid., p. 419.

10. Eliot Freidson, "Dominant Professions, Bureaucracy, and Client Services," in William R. Rosengren and Mary Leyton, eds., *Organizations and Clients: Essays in the Sociology of Service* (Columbus, Ohio: Charles E. Merrill, 1970), p. 74.

11. Ibid., p. 75.

12. Ibid., p. 81.

13. David Gil's assessment of the violence inherent in the workplace is interesting, although not directly related to social work practice. See David G. Gil, "Reversing Dynamics of Violence by Transforming Work," *Journal of International and Comparative Social Welfare* 1, no. 1 (Fall 1984), p. 7.

14. Lewis Mumford's analysis of the criteria for machine technologies is interesting, although not directly related to social work. See Lewis Mumford, "The Machine Culture," in Eric and Mary Josephson, *Man Alone* (New York: Dell, 1966), p. 118.

15. A good example of an exaggerated position in the technological debate is evident in Walter Hudson's "First Axioms of Treatment," *Social Work* 23, no. 1 (January 1978), p. 65. Hudson maintains that "if you cannot measure the client's problem, it does not exist," and "if you cannot measure the client's problem, you cannot treat it."

16. For an analysis of the symptoms and causes of alienation in public welfare, see Howard J. Karger, "Burnout as Alienation," *Social Service Review* 42, no. 2 (June 1981), pp. 271–83.

17. See Stanley Aronowitz, *False Promises* (New York: McGraw-Hill, 1973).

18. Gary Shaffer, "Professional Social Worker Unionization: Current Contract Developments and Implications for Managers," National Association of Social Workers, Annual Conference, *Management Conference*, New Orleans, La., September 12, 1987, p. 1.

19. Ibid., p. 2.

20. Ibid.

21. See Howard J. Karger, ed., *Social Workers and Labor Unions* (Westport, Conn.: Greenwood Press, 1988). See also Milton Tambor and Gary Shaffer, "Social Work Unionization: A Beginning Bibliography," *Catalyst* 5, nos. 17–18 (November 1985), p. 132; and Gary L. Shaffer, "Labor Relations and the Unionization of Professional Social Workers: A Neglected Area in Social Work Education," *Journal of Education for Social Work*, 15 (Winter 1979), pp. 80–86.

22. Mary van Kleeck, "The Common Goals of Labor and Social Work," *Proceedings, National Conference of Social Work, 1934* (Chicago: The University of Chicago Press, 1935), p. 295.

23. Quoted in Milton Tambor, "The Social Worker as Worker: A Union Perspective," in Simon Slavin, *Managing Finances, Personnel, and Information in Human Services* (New York: Haworth Press, 1985), p. 267.

24. For an account of the rank and file movement of the 1930s see Jacob Fisher, *The History of the Rank and File, 1931–6* (New York: New York School of Philanthropy, 1936), and *The Response of Social Work to the Depression* (Boston: Schenkman, 1980); Howard Jacob Karger, "The Early Unionization Movement in Social Work, 1934–1947," *Social Development Issues* 8, no. 3 (Winter 1984), pp. 73–78; Leslie B. Alexander, "Organizing the Professional Social Worker: Union Development in Voluntary Social Work, 1930–1950," Doctoral Dissertation, Bryn Mawr College, 1976; and Alexander and Milton Speizman, "The Union Movement in Voluntary Social Work," in the *Social Welfare Forum, 1979* (New York: Columbia University Press, 1980), pp. 179–87; and John Earl Haynes, "The Rank and File Movement in Private Social Work," *Labor History* 16, no. 1 (Winter 1975), pp. 78–98.

25. Although the causes for the demise of the rank and file movement and *Social Work Today* are not fully understood, there is some belief that the movement vanished for several reasons, including a dwindling of interest of the principals, the relative growth in the economy during the preparation for World War II, and the overshadowing of social justice concerns that marked the war period. Perhaps because of the McCarthy probes and the general anti-progressive views that marked the 1950s, the rank and file movement did not reemerge after WW II. For a more detailed analysis see Fisher, Alexander, Karger, and Haynes.

26. Wilbur F. Maxwell, "Labor and Social Work," in *Social Work Yearbook, 1947* (New York: Russell Sage, 1947), p. 277.

27. Ibid., p. 278.

28. Ibid.

29. Elma Phillipson Cole, "Unions in Social Work," *Encyclopedia of Social Work* (Silver Spring, Md.: NASW, 1977), p. 1559.

30. Bertha Capen Reynolds, a well-known early social worker, was also a strong supporter of unions. See Bertha Capen Reynolds, *An Unchartered Journey* (New York: Citadel Press, 1961). The *Catalyst*, a socialist journal addressing social welfare issues, also champions social work unionization.

31. The lack of sustained formal contact between NASW and public sector labor unions was affirmed in telephone conversations with Thomas Gauthier, Senior Staff Associate, NASW, on November 10, 1986, and with Albert Russo, Community Services Department, AFSCME, November 12, 1986.

32. Leslie B. Alexander, "Unions: Social Work," *Encyclopedia of Social Work* (New York: National Association of Social Workers, 1987), p. 798.

33. Jerry Wurf, "Labor Movement, Social Work Fighting Similar Battles," *NASW News* 25, no. 12 (December 1980), p. 7.

34. Resolution on Gramm-Rudman-Hollings Bill, AFSCME, 27th International Convention, June 23–27, 1986, Chicago, Illinois, n.p.

35. See "Legislative Agenda, 1986," National Association of Social Workers, Silver Spring, Maryland. Also see Resolution, "Funding

of Social Services," AFSCME, 27th International Convention, June 23–27, 1986, Chicago, Illinois. See also National Association of Social Workers, "Testimony Before the Committee on the Budget of the U.S. House of Representatives on *The Fiscal Year 1988 Federal Budget*," February 19, 1987.

36. Resolutions, AFSCME, 27th International Convention, n.p.

37. Dorothy V. Harris, President, NASW, "Testimony before the Committee on Finance of the United States Senate on Welfare Reform", National Association of Social Workers, Silver Spring, Maryland, February 2, 1987, p. 3.

38. Gerald W. McEntee, International President, American Federation of State and County Municipal Employees, Testimony Before the Subcommittee on Social Security and Family Policy of the Senate Committee on Finance, "Welfare: Reform or Replacement?" February 23, 1987.

39. Testimony on the *Fiscal Year 1988 Federal Budget*, p. 5.

40. Resolution, AFSCME, Defense Spending, 27th International Convention, n.p.

41. Ibid.

42. See Rene Laliberty and W. I. Christopher, *Health Care Labor Relations: A Guide for the '80s* (Owing Mills, Md.: National Health Publishing, 1986), p. 57.

43. Dena Fisher, "Problems for Social Work in a Strike Situation: Professional, Ethical, and Value Considerations," *Social Work* 32, no. 3 (May–June 1987), pp. 253–54.

44. See Ernie S. Lightman, "Professionalization, Bureaucratization, and Unionization in Social Work," *Social Service Review*, 56, no. 1 (March 1982), p. 131.

45. Ibid., p. 132.

46. Ibid.

47. Milton Tambor, "Unions and Voluntary Agencies," *Social Work*, 18 (July 1973), pp. 41–47.

48. Fred H. Steininger, "Employee Unions in Public Welfare." Paper presented in the National Conference on Public Administration, American Society of Public Administration, Boston, Massachusetts, 1968. Quoted in Elma Phillipson Cole's "Unions in Social Work," *Encyclopedia of Social Work* (New York: National

Association of Social Workers, 1977), pp. 1560–61.

49. Quoted in Helen Rehr, "Problems for a Profession in a Strike Situation," *Social Work* 5, no. 2 (April 1960), pp. 24–25.

50. Ernie S. Lightman, "An Imbalance of Power: Social Workers in Unions," *Administration in Social Work* 2, no. 1 (Spring 1978), p. 76.

51. Lightman, "Professionalization, Bureaucratization, and Unionization in Social Work," pp. 133–34.

52. See, for example, Leslie B. Alexander, Philip Lichtenberg, and Dennis Brunn, "Social Workers in Unions: A Survey," *Social Work* 25, no. 3 (May 1980), pp. 216–23; Gary L. Shaffer and Kathleen Ahearn, "Current Perceptions, Opinions, and Attitudes Held by Professional Social Workers Toward Unionization and the Collective Bargaining Process," unpublished paper, School of Social Work, University of Illinois, Urbana-Champaign, 1982; Ernie S. Lightman, "Professionalization, Bureaucratization, and Unionization in Social Work"; Ernie S. Lightman, "Social Workers, Strikes and Service to Clients," *Social Work* 28, no. 2 (1983), pp. 142–47; and M. L. Kirzner, *Public Welfare Unions and Public Assistance Policy: A Case Study of the Pennsylvania Social Services Union*, unpublished doctoral dissertation, University of Pennsylvania, 1985.

53. Alexander et al., "Social Workers in Unions," p. 222.

54. Lightman, "Professionalization, Bureaucratization, and Unionization in Social Work," p. 130.

55. Gary Shaffer, "Labor Relations and the Unionization of Professional Social Workers: A Neglected Area in Social Work Education," *Journal of Education for Social Work* 15, no. 3 (1979), pp. 80–86.

56. Alexander et al., "Social Workers in Unions," p. 222.

57. Lightman, "Professionalization, Bureaucratization, and Unionization in Social Work," pp. 136–40.

58. See Leslie B. Alexander, "Professionalization and Unionization: Compatible After All? *Social Work* 25, no. 6 (November 1980), pp. 476–82.

59. Jerry Wurf, "Union Leaders and Public Sector

Unions," Center for Contemporary Studies, *Public Employee Unions: A Study of the Crisis in Public Sector Labor Relations* (San Francisco: Institute for Contemporary Studies, 1976), pp. 176–77.

60. Alexander, "Professionalization and Unionization: Compatible After All? p. 481.

61. David Stoesz, "The Family Life Center," *Social Work* 26, no. 5 (September 1981).

CHAPTER 22

Social Work and the Future of American Social Welfare

Since industrialization, social workers have recognized the importance of social policy for social welfare and have been involved in politics. During the modern era, social welfare professionals have won elected office at the national, state, and local levels. Welfare professionals have also worked within policy institutes to advance social programs for disenfranchised populations. Other social workers have found that the American policy process does not adequately address the needs of some groups and have been active in radical social work. If social welfare professionals are to continue to be influential in shaping social welfare policy, they will have to be involved in social policy along several fronts.

The formulation of social welfare policy in the United States is a complicated and often arduous process. Much of this can be attributed to the nature of American culture—to the competing interests that contribute to a pluralistic society, to the federal system of government that delineates decision making on several levels at once, to the public and private bureaucracies that serve large numbers of consumers, to economic and technological developments that lead to specialization. Under these circumstances, the prospect of changing social welfare policy toward preconceived ends that improve the circumstances of disadvantaged groups can be a daunting task. Regrettably, few welfare professionals consider social policy an enterprise worthy of undertaking. Most social workers prefer direct service activity where they have little opportunity for direct involvement in social welfare policy. Some

social workers have attained important positions in federal and state human service bureaucracies and are much closer to the policy process. Unfortunately, these managers are often administering welfare policies that have been made by legislatures which do not necessarily represent either clients or human service professionals. Perhaps most troubling, the involvement of social workers in the formulation of social policy has been diminishing in recent years. In a provocative statement, June Hopps, Dean of the Boston College School of Social Work and Editor-in-Chief of *Social Work*, acknowledged that "since the late 1960s and early 1970s, the [social work] profession has experienced a dramatic loss of influence in the arenas where policy is shaped and administered."[1]

If an indicator of good social policy is the correspondence between the policy and the social reality of its intended beneficiaries, then social welfare policy should be enhanced by the input of social workers. However, social workers have left much of the decision making about social welfare to professionals from other disciplines. "There are increasing numbers of non-social workers, including psychologists and urban planners," observed Eleanor Brilliant, "taking what might have been social work jobs in service delivery and policy analysis."[2] The consequences of welfare professionals opting to leave social policy in the hands of others have important implications. For direct service workers, it can mean having to apply eligibility standards or procedures that, while logical in some respects, make little sense in the social context of many clients. For the public, it may mean a gradual disenchantment with social programs that do not seem to work. While the causes of the retrenchment affecting social programs since the late 1970s are complex, it is worth noting that public dissatisfaction with social programs has escalated as welfare professionals have retreated from active involvement in social welfare policy.

For welfare professionals to reassert their voice in the formulation and execution of social policy will take concerted effort. Individual leadership is a necessary, but no longer sufficient, precondition for achieving this objective. Essential to the undertaking is the ability to understand and manipulate complex organizations and programs. In fact, this skill may be the most critical for welfare professionals to acquire if they are to advance social justice, for it addresses a question central to the postindustrial era. During the industrial revolution, Karl Marx suggested that the central question was "Who controls the means of production?" A mature industrial order and the expansion of civil bureaucracy led Max Weber to ask, "Who controls the means of administration?" The evolution of a postindustrial order where primary economic activity occurs in a service sector dependent on processed information raises another question: "Who controls the means of analysis?" If social workers are to shape social policy as effectively as they have in the past, they will have to learn to control the means of analysis. This means conducting research on social problems, surveying public opinion about welfare programs, analyzing existing social policy for opportunities to enhance welfare provision, and winning elected office in order to make decisions about proposed social welfare policies.

LEADERS IN SOCIAL WELFARE

Throughout the history of American social welfare, advocates of care for vulnerable populations have been instrumental in shaping social policies. If one looks beneath the surface of policy statements, one finds a rich and often exciting account of the skirmishes fought by advocates for social justice. In some respects, social policy innovations are nothing more than individual and collective biography written in official language. In an age of mass populations, often manipulated by private and public megastructures, it is easy to forget how powerful some individuals have been in shaping American social welfare policy. Many of these leaders are known because they have achieved national prominence; yet, some of the more heroic acts to advance social justice are performed by individuals who are less well-known. Not to be forgotten in this regard is Michael Schwerner, a social worker, who was murdered while working in a voter registration drive in the South during the Civil Rights Movement.[3]

Early social welfare leaders emerged during the Progressive Era, a period when educated and socially conscious men and women sought to create structures that would advance social justice in America. The settlement house gained a reputation as the locus for reform activity, leading one historian to conclude that "settlement workers during the Progressive Era were probably more committed to political action than any other group of welfare workers before or since."[4] From this group, Jane Addams quickly surfaced as a leader of national prominence. Through her settlement home, Hull House, she not only fought for improvements in care for slum dwellers in inner-city Chicago, but also for international peace. Social work for Jane Addams *was* social reform. Instead of focusing solely on restoration and rehabilitation, Addams claimed there was a superior role for the profession: "It must decide whether it is to remain behind in the area of caring for the victimized," she argued, "or whether to press ahead into the dangerous area of conflict where the struggle must be pressed to bring to pass an order of society with few victims."[5] In that struggle, Addams served nobly, receiving an honorary degree from Yale University, and serving as president of the Women's International League for Peace and Freedom. In 1931, Jane Addams was awarded the Nobel Peace Prize, a suitable distinction for a social worker who once had herself appointed a garbage collector in order to improve sanitation in the slum around Hull House.

Hull House proved a remarkable institution, attracting young Progressives who used their residence there to gain first-hand knowledge about social conditions of the disadvantaged and experience in social change strategies. In fact, the tenants of Hull House accounted for much of the vision and leadership of the New Deal:

> Edith Abbott, president of the National Conference of Social Welfare, Dean of the University of Chicago School of Social Service Administration, and participant in the drafting of the Social Security Act of 1935;
>
> Grace Abbott, organizer of the first White House Conference on Children, director of the U.S. Children's Bureau, and participant in the construction of the Social Security Act;
>
> Julia Lathrop, developer of the first juvenile court and the first child mental health clinic in the United States, and the first director of the U.S. Children's Bureau;
>
> Florence Kelley, director of the National Consumer League, cofounder of the U.S. Children's Bureau, and a member of the National Child Labor Committee; and
>
> Frances Perkins, director of the New York Council of Organizations for War Services, director of the Council on Immigrant Education, and the first Secretary of Labor.[6]

But the activity around Hull House was not limited to those with a narrow view of reform. A regular participant in the settlement was John Dewey, in his time "America's most influential philosopher, educator, as well as one of the most outspoken champions of social reform."[7]

Settlement experiences crystallized the motivations of other reformers, as well. Harry Hopkins, primary architect of the New Deal and the social programs that comprised the Social Security Act, had resided at New York's Christadora House Settlement. Ida Bell Wells-Barnett led the Negro Fellowship League to establish a settlement house for blacks in Chicago. And Lillian Wald, with Florence Kelley, a cofounder of the U.S. Children's Bureau, had earlier established New York's Henry Street Settlement, an institution to achieve distinction within the black community. Under the guidance of Mary White Ovington, a social worker, the first meetings of the National Association for the Advancement of Colored People were held at the Henry Street Settlement.[8]

Early social welfare leaders championed causes that improved the conditions of children and immigrants, but they did not forsake blacks. When it became apparent that Booker T. Washington's "industrial education" was unable to contend effectively with ubiquitous racial discrimination, social reformers—Jane Addams, Ida Bell Wells-Barnett, and John Dewey—joined W. E. B. Du Bois in the Niagara Movement. The early organizations spawned by the Niagara Movement were later consolidated into the National Urban League, with George Edmund Haynes, a social worker, one of its codirectors. In 1910, Haynes had been the first black to graduate from the New York School of Philanthropy, so it is not surprising that an important Urban League program was the provision of fellowships for blacks to the school.[9] Later, during the height of the Civil Rights Movement, the National

Urban League, under the direction of social worker Whitney Young, Jr., collaborated in organizing the August 28, 1963, "March on Washington," memorialized by Martin Luther King, Jr.'s ringing words, "I have a dream!"[10]

If the New Deal bore the imprint of social workers, the Great Society was similarly marked some thirty years later. Significantly, a leader of the War on Poverty was Wilbur Cohen, a social worker who had been the first employee of the Social Security Board created in 1935. Eventually, Cohen was to be credited with some sixty-five innovations in social welfare policy, but his crowning achievement was the passage of Medicare and Medicaid in 1965. The Secretary of Health, Education and Welfare during the Johnson administration, Cohen was arguably the nation's most decorated social worker, receiving 18 honorary degrees from American universities.[11]

POLITICAL PRACTICE

Although many welfare professionals began their careers advocating social welfare policy, then assuming administrative positions managing social programs, others used elected office to advance social reform. The first woman elected to the House of Representatives was Jeannette Rankin, who won a seat in 1916 running as a Republican in Montana. As a social worker who had studied under Frances Perkins, Rankin voted for early social welfare legislation and against military expansion. More recently, social workers in political practice include Maryann Mahaffey, a member of the Detroit City Council (and coeditor of *Practical Politics: Social Work and Political Responsibility*) and Ruth Messinger, a member of the New York City Council. Other social workers became mayors of major American cities. Sidney Barthelemy earned his Master of Social Work degree and directed the New Orleans City Welfare Department. In 1974, Barthelemy became the first black elected to the Louisiana

State Senate since Reconstruction. After serving on the New Orleans City Council, he was elected mayor in 1986.[12]

After receiving his Master of Social Work degree in Florida, Art Agnos moved to San Francisco. Agnos's experience as a staff person for state officials paid off with his election as mayor in 1987, an election in which he claimed 70 percent of the vote.[13]

By the late 1980s, three social workers had attained national office. Ronald Dellums, a Marine Corps veteran, earned his Master of Social Work degree, then served on the Berkeley (California) City Council from 1967 to 1971, when he was elected to Congress. Since then he has proposed an alternative military budget based on arms reduction, fought for greater employment opportunities for minorities, and sought services for the homeless. Dellums is perhaps best known for his proposed National

Sidney Barthelemey

Art Agnos

Health Service Act, "the most comprehensive health care legislation ever introduced in Congress."[14]

Barbara Mikulski received her Master of Social Work degree in 1965, served on the Baltimore City Council and in the United States House of Representatives. In 1986, Mikulski became the first Democratic woman to be elected to the United States Senate in her own right. Through appointments in the powerful Appropriations Committee and the Labor and Human Resources Committee, Mikulski is well positioned to advocate programs in health and human services.[15]

Edolphus "Ed" Towns received his Master of Social Work degree in 1973. Elected as the Democratic State Committeeman and then the first black Deputy Borough President in Brooklyn's history, Towns was elected to serve as the Representative of the 11th Congressional

Ron Dellums

Barbara Mikulski

Edolphus "Ed" Towns

District of New York in 1982, with 90 percent of the vote. Towns's appointments on committees overseeing government operations, public works, and narcotics directly address the primary concerns of his inner-city constituents.[16]

ADVOCACY ORGANIZATIONS

In order to be successful in an increasingly complex political climate, social reformers must be able to take advantage of sophisticated advocacy methods. In social work, the organization which provides assistance to candidates is PACE, "the political action arm of the National Association of Social Workers." PACE uses a variety of tactics "to expand social workers' activity in politics," including

voter registration, support in political campaigns, and analysis of incumbents' voting records.[17] In 1986, PACE donated $110,000 to candidates running for national office; and 39 NASW chapters supported candidates for state and local office.[18] According to Toby Weismiller, NASW Staff Director for Political Affairs, PACE encourages social workers to view holding public office as a practice option. In her summary of the 1986 election, Weismiller noted that social workers who have "learned how to solve problems by working within the community" can use this to great political advantage, as did Barbara Mikulski.

THE NEW WELFARE INSTITUTES

While PACE attempts to influence social welfare policy by sponsoring candidates for public office, other organizations focus on the policy process itself. Policy analysis organizations have been instrumental in shaping social policy from as early as the New Deal period. Subsequently, policy institutes have had liberal or conservative labels ascribed, with the liberal organizations achieving dominance up until the late 1970s, when conservative institutes became more influential. The failure of government social programs to expand during the Carter presidency, followed by the profoundly negative impact of the Reagan administration, led social reformers to look to the traditional policy institutes—the Brookings Institution and the Urban Institute—for leadership. But, the inability of these organizations to shape the debate on American social welfare compelled impatient reformers to establish a new group of policy analysis organizations.

Children's Defense Fund

Begun by Marian Wright Edelman in 1974, the Children's Defense Fund (CDF)[19] sought to address the health, educational, and income needs of the nation's children. By the mid-

1980s, CDF had become a major voice in children's policy and had successfully advocated programs at the federal and state levels. CDF helped pass the Child Health Assurance Program in 1984 which expanded Medicaid eligibility to poor pregnant women, and to children. Following federal devolution of social programs to the states, CDF deployed field offices in five states and provided services to groups in many more. Notably, CDF has not winced at championing groups which have benefited least by welfare programs. Recently, CDF established the Adolescent Pregnancy Prevention project, an imaginative initiative relying on local groups to identify resources for teens.

In less than a decade, the CDF budget had grown to more than $4 million, with staff exceeding seventy. Contributions have been received from important foundations, and support secured from influential persons. In addition to distributing educational packets to poor mothers, CDF regularly sends editorial packets to 200 newspapers across the nation. CDF also printed eye-catching posters and a number of publications for public education purposes. Its annual *Children's Defense Budget* is an authoritative compendium of issues and programs about children.

Independent Sector

In 1978, former Secretary of Health, Education and Welfare John Gardner and philanthropic executive Brian O'Connell merged the Coalition of National Voluntary Organizations and the National Council on Philanthropy to enhance the capacity of the nonprofit sector to deal with social problems. An organizing committee comprised of Gardner, O'Connell, John Filer (Chief Executive Officer of Aetna Insurance Company and Chair of the Commission on Private Philanthropy and Public Needs), and Richard Lyman (President of the Rockefeller Foundation) chartered Independent Sector (IS) in 1980 to further voluntary sector activities.

By 1986, IS had cultivated a Board of Directors numbering 40 and representing influential corporations and nonprofit organizations. From the dues of its 650 institutional members and from contributions, IS boasted a budget exceeding $4.5 million in 1986.[20]

IS quickly became an influential voice for the nonprofit sector, occupying a suite of executive offices in Washington, D.C. In addition to annual seminars on policies affecting nonprofit organizations, IS has sponsored seminal studies of the contributions of nonprofit organizations to the national culture. In an effort to extend the scope of its activities, IS has helped establish research centers in major universities, such as the Mandel Center for Nonprofit Management at Case Western Reserve University.[21]

The Center on Budget and Policy Priorities

Established in 1981 by Robert Greenstein, former Administrator of the Food and Nutrition Service in the Agriculture Department, the Center on Budget and Policy Priorities (CBPP) has fought to defend social programs for low-income people against budget cuts. With a modest staff of 15, CBPP distributes its analyses to congressional staffs, the media, and grassroots organizations. Despite its small size, CBPP provided much of the program analysis to refute arguments presented by officials of the Reagan administration to cut means-tested social programs. Significantly, CBPP and CDF have developed a close working relationship. CBPP regularly provides data to CDF on the health and income status of children, an Greenstein is a regular contributor to CL reports.[22]

The National Center for Social Policy and Practice

In the early stages of development, the Center for Social Policy and Practice originated with the National As Social Workers (NASW). In launc

NASW sought an institute which would serve as an advocate for a more just and equitable society through analyses of social problems, policy, and social work practice. Toward that end, NASW commenced a capital campaign to raise $10 million, and began a series of symposia designed to inform human service professionals about NCSPP and solicit their financial support. In the fall of 1986, Karen Orloff Kaplan, a clinical social worker with expertise in health policy and extensive legislative experience, was named director of NCSPP. Among the projects begun by NCSPP are a survey of benefits for employees of corporations that cover catastrophic illness and long-term care, an AIDS ethics forum, and a policy statement on welfare reform. Located near Washington, D.C., NCSPP is well-positioned to influence social welfare policy, once the institute is fully operational.[23]

SOCIAL WORK AND THE FUTURE OF SOCIAL WELFARE POLICY

The capacity of social workers to reassert their role in social welfare policy depends on the willingness of individuals to consider public office as a setting for social work practice and the ability of the new policy institutes to prepare sophisticated policy analyses. Despite the openness of the American political system, only the naive would ignore the very real obstacles to progressive social reform. Corporate ntributions to candidates for federal office, 9 million in 1983 and 1984[24], far exceed the W-PACE effort. Without a strong economic base, new candidates for national office are likely to be successful in elections where campaign "war chests" are a prerequisite office. The development of the new policy institutes is an encouraging development, CDF an the more prominent of these— half the are operating on budgets one-organizat the more established policy s, the optimism inspired by

Ron Dellums, Barbara Mikulski, Ed Towns, and the NCSPP must be tempered with the reality of what is often an inhospitable political climate.

Perhaps the best indicator of social work's future influence on social policy appears at the local level. Social workers have lobbied successfully on behalf of nonprofit agencies facing threats to their tax exempt status,[25] encouraged students to engage in election campaigns to become more knowledgeable about politics,[26] and managed a campaign for the election of a state senator.[27] In each of these instances, social workers were gaining experience that is essential to political involvement at higher levels.

A good example of what social workers can accomplish at the local level can be found in Tim Dee, the alderman from St. Louis's Seventeenth Ward from 1977 to 1987. Early in his tenure as alderman, Dee documented that the Seventeenth Ward had lost about one-third of its population during the 1970s, a demographic hemorrhage he attributed to the absence of employment opportunities in the inner-city political district. Using a little-known state law that provided for the creation of enterprise zones, Dee created legislation establishing the Seventeenth Ward as an enterprise zone which allowed businesses tax abatement and other advantages if they located in Dee's ward. The strategy paid off. In a few years following the creation of the enterprise zone in September 1983, the Seventeenth Ward boasted some fifteen new businesses and 1200 new jobs, and Dee's enterprise zone was noted as one of the ten best nationally. But Dee was not content to allow his district to be manipulated by businesses seeking concessions from local government as a justification for relocation. In order to make the enterprise zone responsive to the needs of local residents, Dee built into the enabling legislation an intriguing provision that established an enterprise zone commission, representing business and residents, to oversee the economic development of the area. It is difficult to imagine a better example of a social worker using the local political process to improve the conditions of so many disadvantaged people than Tim Dee's innovative work as an alderman in St. Louis.[28]

Social workers disinclined to engage in high-visibility activities such as campaigning for public office could make their imprint on politics through "constituent services." Writing of new developments in Congress, Pulitzer Prize-winning journalist Hedrick Smith observed that members of Congress are increasingly relying on constituent services in place of "pork barrel" projects as domestic expenditures dry up. Using a term familiar to most social workers, politicians call constituent services "casework—having your staff track down missing Social Security checks, inquire about sons and husbands in the armed services, help veterans get medical care, pursue applications for small-business loans."[29] The importance of political casework has been noted by political scientists who attribute up to five percent of the vote to such activities, a significant amount in close elections. David Himes of the National Republican Congressional Committee claimed that "our surveys have shown that constituency service—especially in the House—is more important than issues."[30]

RADICAL SOCIAL WORK

When the established policy process remains unresponsive to the needs of disadvantaged groups, some welfare advocates have resorted to radical methods to advance social justice. For radical social workers "the system" is not the solution, but rather the problem. Accordingly, true social change occurs from pressure brought on the system from the outside, not from incremental adjustments won from bargaining within the system. Of course, many advocates of social justice are willing to consider both conventional and radical tactics,

depending on what might seem effective in a given situation.

Radical social work has enjoyed relatively wide popularity during the labor movement and New Deal period of the 1930s and the Civil Rights and student movements of the 1960s. Among the leaders associated with radical approaches to social welfare was Bertha Capen Reynolds, a social worker who taught at the Smith College School of Social Work and later organized workers for the National Maritime Union. Reynolds believed that organizing workers and communities was essential for a vital democracy and that class divisions fostered by capitalism created many of the social problems that social workers were confronted with. A Marxist, Reynolds protested the violations of civil liberties perpetrated by Senator Joseph McCarthy during the 1950s. After World War II, Saul Alinsky began to build a reputation as a community organizer, first in Chicago and later in Rochester, New York. Alinsky's *Rules for Radicals* quickly became a classic in the radical literature and served as a manifesto for radical social workers.[31] A student of Alinsky, Cesar Chavez organized agricultural workers in the Southwest, founding and becoming president of the United Farm Workers Union. Within academic circles, Frances Fox Piven and Richard Cloward wrote a series of books— *Regulating the Poor*, *Poor People's Movements*, and *The New Class War*—which provided a radical analysis of American social welfare.[32] A social worker, Jeffry Galper applied a radical analysis to social welfare programs as well as social work practice.[33]

Radical social work is associated with the political mobilization of disenfranchised groups and their demands for civil rights and essential benefits. Since 1980, as a result of policies of the federal government that have dramatically worsened the circumstances of many groups, radical social work has enjoyed renewed popularity. When reductions in social programs drove many of the poor into the streets, advocates for the homeless conceived of radical tactics to draw public attention to the problem. Groups such as Mitch Snyder's Washington D.C.–based Community for Creative Non-Violence (CCNV), used guerilla tactics to extort concessions from governmental agencies. When some of the homeless died of exposure during the winter, CCNV constructed a symbolic cemetery across from the White House with the names of those who had died painted on crosses. Following the example of Gandhi, Snyder engaged in several hunger strikes, eventually extracting benefits from a previously intransigent Reagan administration.

Radical social workers have also protested governmental policies in areas not usually considered as social welfare. In the spring of 1988, Glen Remer-Thamert, a Lutheran minister and social worker who was active in the Sanctuary Movement, was fired from his job and indicted for assisting two pregnant women who were refugees from E1 Salvador.[34] During the same period several social workers were among the 1200 people arrested during a peace and disarmament rally held at a Nevada nuclear testing site.[35] Social workers have also used radical tactics to advance the interests of women and homosexuals, as well as to protect the environment.

CONCLUSION

The cultivation of practice skills in the political arena at the local level offers perhaps the most promise for social workers to regain influence in social welfare policy. Such activity can be undertaken by virtually any professional interested in the opportunity. On a volunteer basis, social workers would find few politicians willing to turn down their professional assistance in the provision of constituent services. With experience, enterprising social workers might find that political practice can be remunerative, providing they possess the skills—conducting surveys, maintaining data banks of contributors, organizing public meetings, and

keeping current on legislation important to constituents—important for elected officials. From another perspective, however, the prospect of political practice should be taken seriously indeed. If social workers are sincere about making essential resources available to their clients—a responsibility stated in the *NASW Code of Ethics*—then some form of political practice is a professional obligation. "To do less," noted Maryann Mahaffey, "to avoid the political action necessary to provide these resources, is to fail to live up to the profession's code of ethical practice."[36]

NOTES

1. June Hopps, "Reclaiming Leadership," *Social Work* 31, no. 5 (September—October 1986), p. 323.
2. Eleanor Brilliant, "Social Work Leadership: A Missing Ingredient?" *Social Work* 31, no. 5 (September–October 1986), p. 328.
3. Maryann Mahaffey, "Political Action in Social Work," *Encyclopedia of Social Work*, 18th ed. (Silver Spring, Md.: National Association of Social Workers, 1987), p. 290.
4. Allen Davis, "Settlement Workers in Politics, 1890–1914," in Maryann Mahaffey and John Hanks, eds., *Practical Politics: Social Work and Political Responsibility* (Silver Spring, Md.: National Association of Social Workers, 1982), p. 32.
5. Allen Davis, *American Heroine: The Life and Legend of Jane Addams* (New York: Oxford University Press, 1973), p. 292.
6. Biographical information is derived from *The Encyclopedia of Social Work*, 18th ed. (Silver Spring, Md.: National Association of Social Workers, 1987), except as noted otherwise.
7. Richard Bernstein, "John Dewey," *Encyclopedia of Philosophy*, vol. II, Paul Edwards, ed., (New York: Macmillan and The Free Press, 1967), p. 380.
8. Maryann Mahaffey, "Political Action in Social Work," p. 286.
9. John Hope Franklin, *From Slavery to Freedom: A History of Negro Americans* (New York:

Knopf, 1980), p. 319–21.

10. Ibid., pp. 471–72.

11. Charles Schottland, "Wilbur Joseph Cohen: Some Recollections," *Social Work* 32, no. 5 (September–October 1987), pp. 371–72.

12. "Biographical Profile," courtesy of the Office of the Mayor, New Orleans, n.d.

13. "Art Agnos, Mayor of San Francisco," courtesy of the Office of the Mayor, January, 1988.

14. "Biographical Sketch," courtesy of Congressman Dellums's Office.

15. "Biographical Sketch," courtesy of Senator Mikulski's Office.

16. "Congressman Ed Towns," courtesy of the Congressman's Office, n.d.

17. Interview with Toby Weismiller, NASW, Washington, D.C., January 11, 1988.

18. National Association of Social Workers, *Annual Report 1987* (Washington, D.C.: NASW, 1987), p. 23.

19. For detail on CDF, see Joanna Biggar, "The Protector," *The Washington Post Magazine*, May 18, 1986; and *The Children's Defense Fund Annual Report 1984–85* (Washington, D.C.: Children's Defense Fund, 1985).

20. "CONVO: Background information and initial statements by John Gardner and Brian O'Connell" (Washington, D.C.: Independent Sector, n.d.); *Annual Report 1986* (Washington, D.C.: Independent Sector, 1986).

21. Brian O'Connell, *Philanthropy in Action* (New York: Foundation Center, 1987), pp. 103–4.

22. Information on CBPP was obtained from an interview with David Kahan at CBPP on March 12, 1984.

23. Interview with Karen Kaplan on January 11, 1988, at NCSPP; *National Association of Social Workers, Annual Report 1987* (Silver Spring, Md.: NASW, 1987), p. 18.

24. Steven Lydenberg et al., *Rating America's Corporate Conscience* (Reading, Mass.: Addison-Wesley, 1986), p. 39.

25. Elliot Pagliaccio and Burton Gummer, "Casework and Congress: A Lobbying Strategy," *Social Casework* (March 1988).

26. Grafton Hull, "Joining Together: A Faculty-Student Experience in Political Campaigning," *Journal of Social Work Education* (Fall 1987).

27. William Whitaker and Jan Flory-Baker, "Ragtag Social Workers Take on the Good Old Boys and Elect a State Senator," in Maryann Mahaffey and John Hanks, eds., *Practical Politics: Social Work and Political Responsibility* (Silver Spring, Md.: National Association of Social Workers, 1982).

28. Telephone interview with Tim Dee, March 20, 1988.

29. Hedrick Smith, *The Power Game* (New York: Random House, 1988), p. 124.

30. Ibid., p. 152.

31. Saul Alinsky, *Rules for Radicals* (New York: Vintage, 1946); see also *Reveille for Radicals* (New York: Vintage, 1969).

32. Frances Fox Piven, *Regulating the Poor* (New York: Pantheon, 1971); *Poor People's Movements* (New York: Pantheon, 1977); and *The New Class War* (New York: Pantheon, 1982).

33. Jeffry Galper, *The Politics of Social Services* (Englewood Cliffs, N.J.: Prentice-Hall, 1975); and *Social Work Practice: A Radical Perspective* (Englewood Cliffs, N.J.: Prentice-Hall, 1980).

34. "Social Worker Indicted for 'Sanctuary' Activity," *NASW News* (April 1988), p. 13.

35. "Social Workers Arrested During Nuclear Protest," *NASW News* (May 1988), p. 11.

36. Maryann Mahaffey, "Political Action in Social Work," p. 284.

Glossary

Absolute Poverty. A measurement and classification of poverty that is based on an unequivocal material standard of living necessary for survival.

Affirmative Action. Programs designed to redress the past or present discrimination of minorities (including women) by providing criteria for employment, promotion, and educational opportunities which give these groups preferential access to these resources or opportunities.

Ageism. Age-based discrimination against elderly persons.

Alleviative Approach to Poverty. Strategies designed to ease the suffering of the poor rather than to eliminate the causes of poverty. Examples include AFDC, SSI, and Food Stamps.

Almshouse. A historic institution that was used to maintain the poor. Almshouses, or poor houses as they were sometimes called, were in common use in Great Britain and the United States from the seventeenth through the nineteenth centuries.

Area Poverty. Refers to geographic regions which are economically depressed.

Block Grant. A method of funding social programs through which the federal government makes monies available to states for a wide range of service needs, including social services.

Brown v. Board of Education of Topeka, Kansas. A 1954 landmark U.S. Supreme Court decision which ruled that separate but equal facilities in education were not equal.

Bureaucratic Disentitlement. The denial of benefits to eligible recipients by agents of public agencies.

Bureaucratic Rationality. The ordering of social affairs by governmental agencies.

Capitalism. An economic system where the majority of the production and distribution of goods and services occurs under private auspices.

Capitation. A method of financing services whereby a fixed amount, based on a total amount available for care divided by the number of beneficiaries, is payable to a provider.

Categorical Grant. A method of funding social services through which the federal government makes available to the states monies which must be spent for very narrowly specified service needs.

Charity Organization Society (COS). A voluntary organization in the late nineteenth and early twentieth centuries which attempted to coordinate private charities and promote a scientific approach to philanthropy.

Chronic Unemployment. The rate of unemployment attributable to persons who have persistent trouble finding work due to the absence of low-skilled jobs or because they have severe deficiencies in basic social and work skills.

Circuitbreaker Programs. Tax rebate programs designed to relieve the low-income, elderly, or disabled homeowner or renter from the burden of property or utility taxes.

Clinical Entrepreneurs. An interest group within American social welfare which is associated with private practice and the provision of social welfare in the private marketplace.

Commercialization. The consequence of subjecting social welfare to the marketplace, including advertising for services, marketing services, and pricing services.

Commonweal. The general good, or the public welfare.

Comparable Worth. The idea that workers should be paid equally when they do different types of work that require the same level of skill, education, knowledge, training, responsibility, and effort.

Conservatism. A primary American ideology which emphasizes the role of the marketplace and the private sector in meeting both human and social welfare needs.

Corporate Sector. That part of the mixed welfare economy consisting of large, for-profit human service corporations.

Corporate Social Responsibility. The concept that

corporations should be held accountable for practices and decisions that adversely affect those communities in which they do business. In addition corporate social responsibility also refers to the responsibility that corporations have in promoting the general well-being of society.

Cost of Living Adjustments (COLAs). COLAs are adjustments that are designed to keep income maintenance and social insurance benefits in line with inflation. COLAs are used in Food Stamps, Social Security, and SSI benefits.

Culture of Poverty. A theoretical school which maintains that poverty is transmitted intergenerationally, and that certain of its traits are found in diverse cultures and societies.

Curative Approach to Poverty. An approach designed to rehabilitate the poor through attacking the causes of poverty, e.g., illiteracy, poor nutrition, lack of employment, and so forth.

Cyclical Unemployment. The rate of unemployment attributable to swings in economic performance, such as recessions.

De Facto Segregation. Racial segregation which is not legally mandated.

Deinstitutionalization. Refers to a trend established in the late 1960s where many mentally ill and mentally retarded patients were removed from state institutions and, where possible, put into community settings.

Deliberate Misdiagnosis. The intentional distortion of a diagnosis in order to avoid labeling a client, or for the purposes of collecting insurance payments.

Democratic-Capitalism. The type of political-economy applicable to the United States, characterized by a democratic polity and a capitalist economy.

Diagnostic Related Groups (DRGs). A prospective form of payment for Medicare incurred charges. Specifically, DRGs are a classification scheme whereby hospitals are reimbursed only for the maximum number of days an illness or surgical procedure is designated to take.

Discouraged Workers. Those who have stopped seeking work based on their frustration with their poor employment prospects.

Donaldson v. O'Connor. The court decision stating that mental patients could not be confined unless they were dangerous to themselves or others. They should also not be confined unless they are being treated and cannot survive without hospitalization.

Dual Labor Market. A theory that divides workers into two groups: the primary and secondary labor markets. (See Primary Labor Market and Secondary Labor Market.)

Employee Assistance Programs. Social services provided by companies for their employees in recognition that many personal problems are either directly related to, or have impact upon, the workplace.

Entitlements. Governmental resources (cash or in-kind) to which certain groups are entitled, based on their ability to meet the established criteria.

Equal Rights Amendment (ERA). An act which would give women the same equality of rights under the law as men.

Feminization of Poverty. A social trend marked by the increasing frequency of poverty among women. This tendency toward poverty is thought to be related to the high incidence of women relying on governmental aid, the low wages that characterize traditional female employment, and occupational segregation.

Freedmen's Bureau. An agency set up after the Civil War by the U.S. government to ease the transition of blacks from slavery to freedom. Formally called the Bureau of Refugees, Freedmen and Abandoned Lands.

Frictional Unemployment. The rate of unemployment, usually about 3 percent, considered inevitable for a viable economy.

Functional Welfare. A social-welfare-related concept that holds that social service benefits should be justified in relation to productivity. Usually a standard of conforming conduct is required on the part of recipients in exchange for benefits.

Gentrification. Resettlement of existing low-income neighborhoods by middle- and upper-class homeowners or investors. This development can result in forcing poor and indigenous residents out of their neighborhoods.

Governmental Sector. That part of the mixed welfare economy consisting of social programs administered by government, particularly the federal government.

Great Society. Formerly called the War on Poverty, the Great Society was a series of social welfare programs (e.g., community development, training and employment, health and legal services, etc.) that was enacted from 1963 to 1968, during the administration of President Lyndon Baines Johnson.

Gross National Product. The sum total of all goods and services produced in a society.

Halderman v. Pennhurst. The court decision stating that institutionalized patients were entitled to treatment in the least restrictive environment.

Health Maintenance Organizations (HMOs). Membership organizations which typically provide comprehensive health care. Members usually pay a regular fee and are thus entitled to free (or minimal cost) hospital care and physicians' services.

Homework. The economic system of production in common use during the late nineteenth and early twentieth centuries whereby workers were paid on a piecework basis for work done at home. This system was frequently used in the garment trades.

Homophobia. The fear of (and subsequent discrimination against) homosexuals based solely on their sexual preference.

Housing Starts. Number of new houses begun in a given period.

Housing Stock. The number of presently available houses.

Human Capital. Refers to the market value of an individual (the salary he or she is able to command) based on his or her education, training, skills, experience, and knowledge.

Human Service Executives. An interest group within American social welfare which is associated with human service corporations and advocates the provision of social welfare through large-scale for-profit programs.

Human Services. A recent concept which is equivalent to "social welfare."

Iatrogenic Diseases. Diseases which are directly caused by medical intervention.

Ideological State Apparatus. The methods, i.e., education, the print media, the family, television, and tradition, by which the primary ideology of a society is promulgated and maintained.

Ideology. A set of socially sanctioned assumptions, usually unexamined, that explains how the world works, as well as general methods for addressing social problems.

Income Distribution. The pattern of how income is distributed among the various socioeconomic classes in a society.

Income Inequality. The unequal distribution of income across socioeconomic classes.

Income Maintenance Programs. Social welfare programs designed to contribute to or supplement the income of an individual or family. These programs are usually means-tested and thus based on need.

Income Stratification. Refers to the unequal distribution of income across socioeconomic classes.

Indian Child Welfare Act of 1978. Among other things, this Act restored child-placement decisions to the individual tribes.

Indoor Relief. A historic term used to designate relief services offered in an institutional setting.

In-Kind. Non-cash goods or services provided by the government that function as a proxy for cash, e.g., Food Stamps, Section 8 housing vouchers, Medicare, and so forth.

Institutional Welfare. A conception of welfare holding that governmental social programs that assure citizens of basic needs for food, housing, education, income, employment, and health are essential to an advanced economy. Such programs are considered a right of citizenship.

Keynesian Economics. An economic school which proposes government intervention in the economy, through such activities as social welfare programs, in order to stimulate and regulate economic growth.

Liberalism. A primary American ideology which justifies government intervention in the market in order to assure the provision of basic goods, services, and rights to disenfranchised populations that are unable to obtain these otherwise.

Libertarians. A small but influential group which advocates more individual responsibility and a very limited role for government in social affairs.

Licensed Certified Social Worker. A social worker holding the Master of Social Work degree, who has practiced for two years under supervision, and who has passed an examination. Twenty-nine states license social workers.

Market Rationality.   The ordering of human affairs by corporate institutions within the marketplace.

Means Test.   Income and asset tests designed to determine whether an individual or household meets the economic criteria necessary for receiving governmental cash transfers or in-kind services.

Milford Conference Report.   An important report issued in 1923 which addressed professional social work issues.

Milliken v. Brady.   A 1974 U.S. Supreme Court decision which ruled that school busing across city–suburban boundaries to achieve integration was not required unless segregation had resulted from official action.

Mixed Welfare Economy.   Refers to the coexistence of governmental, private nonprofit, and private for-profit providers of social welfare within the same society.

National Association of Social Workers (NASW).   The major national organization of professional social workers.

National Health Insurance.   Various insurance-based proposals that incorporate comprehensive health coverage.

Neoconservatism.   A recent American ideology, based on conservatism, which recognizes the necessity for social welfare but designs social programs so that they are compatible with the requirements of a market economy and traditional values.

Neoliberalism.   A recent American ideology, based on liberalism, which assumes that universal social programs, such as those advanced by liberals, are implausible because of current social, political, and economic limitations. Neoliberals opt for more modest changes in social welfare programs.

New Deal.   The name given to the massive Depression-era social and economic programs initiated under the presidency of Franklin Delano Roosevelt.

Occupational Segregation.   Usually refers to low wage sectors of the labor market which are principally dominated by a minority group. For example, women are thought to be occupationally segregated in "pink collar" jobs, e.g., secretaries, receptionists, typists, and so forth.

Office of Economic Opportunity (OEO).   The federal agency that was charged with the responsibility for designing and implementing the Great Society programs.

Oligopolization.   The process through which a small number of organizations effectively control a market.

Outdoor Relief.   A historic term used to designate relief services offered in the home of a client.

Per Capita Income.   A determination of income based on dividing the total household income by the number of family members.

Permanency Planning.   A strategy for helping foster children live in families that offer continuity of relationships and the opportunity to establish lifetime relationships.

Plessy v. Ferguson.   The U.S. Supreme Court decision in 1896 which formally established the "separate but equal" doctrine in race relations.

Policy Framework.   A systematic process for examining a specific policy or a set of policies.

Political Action Committees (PACs).   Organizations, usually associated with special interest groups, which divert campaign contributions to candidates running for public office in order to influence indirectly their later decisions on public policy.

Political Practice.   A method of social work practice through which social workers advance their priorities either by assisting those in political office or by running for office themselves.

Poverty Line.   A yearly cash income threshold (based on family size) set by the federal government to determine if an individual or household can be classified as poor. Sometimes called the poverty threshold or poverty index.

Pluralism.   Refers to a society which is heterogeneous and thus has many competing interest groups helping to shape social policies.

Policy Institute.   A private organization, funded by contributions and government contracts, which researches social problems and proposes social policies.

Political-Economy.   The interaction of institutions defining the political and economic processes of a society.

Preferential Selection.   The selection of clients for treatment according to the organizational needs of the provider as opposed to the needs of the client—usually used to describe the practice of private providers who prefer insured clients with less severe problems.

Pre-Transfer Poor. Individuals or households which are under the poverty line because they lack adequate income from private market sources (employment).

Preventive Approach to Poverty. Social welfare strategies designed to prevent people from becoming poor, e.g., social insurance programs.

Preventive Commitment. The institutionalization of persons who do not meet the requirements for involuntary hospitalization but are likely to deteriorate without in-patient care.

Primary Labor Market. Those full-time jobs which provide workers with an adequate salary, a career track, and benefits.

Primary Prevention. Efforts designed to eliminate the origin of social problems.

Private Practice. The provision of clinical services through the marketplace by individual practitioners or small groups of practitioners.

Privatization. Refers to the ownership or management of social services by the private sector, either by nonprofit agencies or proprietary corporations.

Professional Monopoly. The right to exclusive practice granted an occupational group in exchange for its promise to hold the welfare of the entire community as its ultimate concern.

Progressive Movement. A social movement that was popular in the U.S. from the late 1800s to World War I. Progressives stressed the need for morality, ethics, and honesty in all social, political, and economic affairs.

Proprietary. A social welfare organization which provides services on a for-profit basis.

Public Choice School. A school of political-economy which suggests that interest group demands inevitably lead to budget deficits, and government should therefore limit concessions to these groups as much as possible.

Public Transfer Programs. Programs such as AFDC, SSI, and Social Security, which transfer money from the governmental sector to families or individuals who are either entitled to it or have earned it.

Racism. The discrimination and prejudicial treatment of a racially different minority group.

Radical Social Work. Adherents believe that the political-economy is incapable of incremental reform and that the system must be challenged through various means to advance social justice.

Rationalization. Measures designed to make an organization or agency as efficient and cost-effective as possible.

Redlining. In the area of housing, redlining refers to the refusal of mortgage or insurance companies to provide services in selected neighborhoods thought to be high-risk areas for defaults or excessive claims.

Reciprocity. The requirement that a specific activity or standard of conduct be demonstrated in order to obtain welfare benefits.

Relative Poverty. A measurement and classification of poverty which is based on the relative standard of living enjoyed by other members of a society.

Repressive State Apparatus. The set of societal institutions—the police, courts, jails—which intervene to control dissidents when they threaten social stability.

Residual Welfare. A conception of welfare holding that the family and the market are the individual's primary source of assistance, but that governmental "safety net" programs may provide temporary help.

Secondary Labor Market. Those jobs which are characterized by irregular, seasonal, or part-time employment, at a relatively low hourly wage, which do not provide benefits, and which do not have a career track.

Secondary Prevention. Early detection and intervention to keep incipient problems from becoming more debilitating.

Self-Reliance School. A relatively new school of political-economy advocating low-technology and local solutions to social problems.

Settlement Houses. Still in existence, these organizations began in the late nineteenth century as an attempt to bridge the class differences that marked American society. Based on the residence of middle-class volunteers in immigrant neighborhoods, settlement houses emphasized the provision of social services as well as reform activities.

Sexism. The discrimination against women based solely on their gender.

Social Darwinism. A social theory which maintained that Charles Darwin's theories on the laws of nature, i.e., survival of the fittest, also pertain to social life. Some of the main proponents included Herbert Spencer and William Graham Sumner.

Social Gospel Movement. A progressive movement in late nineteenth and early twentieth century America which attempted to merge Christianity with a concern for social justice.

Social Insurance. A system which compels individuals to insure themselves against the possibility of indigence. Similar to private insurance, social insurance programs set aside a sum of money which is held in trust by the government to be used in the event of a worker's death, retirement, disability, or unemployment. Individuals are entitled to social insurance benefits based on their previous contribution to the system.

Socialism. A school of political-economy which attributes the need for social welfare to social problems caused by capitalism. Socialists advocate restructuring the political-economy—in the American case, capitalism—as the most direct way to promote social welfare.

Social Justice. Connotes equity and fairness in all areas of social, political, and economic life, as well as the provision of basic needs to all without regard to their participation in the market, an objective of liberals and progressives.

Social Stratification. The vertical segmentation of the population according to income, occupation, and status.

Social Welfare Policy. The regulation of the provision of benefits to people who require assistance meeting basic needs in living, such as employment, income, food, health care, and relationships.

Sociopolitical Planning. Methods for anticipating program needs which are interactive, involving groups likely to be affected by a program.

Spells of Poverty. Refers to periods of time (often limited) in which individuals or families fall below the poverty line.

Standardization. The reduction of services to a common denominator in order to lower provider costs.

Structural Unemployment. The rate of unemployment attributable to long-lasting and deep maladjustments in the labor market.

Supply-Side Economics. A school of political-economy which proposes reductions in social programs so that tax dollars can be reinvested in the private sector to capitalize economic growth.

Swann v. Charlotte-Mecklenburg Board of Education. A 1971 U.S. Supreme Court ruling which approved court-ordered busing to achieve racial integration in school districts which had a history of discrimination.

Tardive Dyskinesia. Permanent damage to the central nervous system, evident in involuntary movements, caused by psychotropic medication.

Techno-Methodological Planning. Methods of anticipating program requirements using data bases from which projections of future program needs can be derived.

Tertiary Prevention. Efforts to limit the effects of a disorder after it has become manifest.

Think Tank. Policy jargon for a policy institute.

Traditionalists. A social movement that gained increased strength during the 1970s. Traditionalists seek to conform social policy to conservative social and religious values.

Traditional Providers. An interest group within American social welfare associated with voluntary nonprofit agencies which promotes local institutions as a preferred method to solve social problems.

Usual, Customary, and Reasonable (UCR). That fee established by a majority of practitioners in a given community for a given procedure. The UCR is defined by insurance companies to determine the proper level of payment for covered procedures.

Underclass. Refers to the lowest socioeconomic group in society. The underclass is thought to be chronically poor; that is, its members are poor regardless of the economic circumstances in the general society.

Underemployed. Individuals who are working in jobs in which their skills are far above those required for the position. It may also connote those who are employed part-time when their desire is to be employed on a full-time basis.

Unemployment. Unemployed people are those individuals who are over 16 years of age and looking for work.

Voluntary Sector.   That part of the mixed welfare economy consisting of private, nonprofit agencies.

War on Poverty.   See the Great Society.

Welfare Bureaucrats.   Interest groups within American social welfare associated with governmental social programs which advocate the provision of social welfare through large-scale public social programs.

Welfare Capitalism.   An advanced system of social welfare that exists in progressive capitalist countries.

Welfare Dependency.   The economic dependence of a family or individual on the provision of governmental welfare services, especially cash grants.

Welfare State.   The government social programs that assure citizens of basic protection against poverty, sickness, homelessness, unemployment, and malnutrition. The American welfare state has its roofs in the Social Security Act of 1935.

Workfare.   Originally begun in the late 1960s, workfare is a system whereby AFDC or AFDC-UP recipients are required either to work or to receive work training (sometimes in the form of higher education). The concept of workfare underlies the new welfare reform bill passed in 1988.

Working Poor.   Those families or individuals who are in the work force (full- or part-time) and are still at or below the poverty line.

Worthy Poor.   A belief that there are groups of people who are poor by no fault of their own—e.g., the handicapped, children, widows—and thus deserve charity. Conversely, the unworthy poor are those people who are ablebodied—vagrants, the idle, drunkards—but refuse to work. This classification formed part of the basis of the English Poor Laws of 1601, and can still be seen in modern social policies.

Wyatt v. Stickney.   The court decision requiring states to provide adequate levels of treatment to hospitalized mental patients.

YAVIS Syndrome.   The tendency for clinicians to prefer clients who are Young, Attractive, Verbal, Intelligent, and Successful.

Index

Aaron, Henry, 298

AARP [American Association of Retired Persons], 60, 85

Abbott, Edith, 41, 339

Abbott, Grace, 41, 339

Abramovitz, Mimi, 303, 304

Abramson, Alan, 116

Academia, 290

ACSW [Academy of Certified Social Workers], 157

Action for Mental Health [NIMH], 218

Addams, Jane, 41, 42, 45, 232, 338–339

Adolescent Pregnancy Prevention project [CDF], 343

Adoption, 231, 232, 235–238

Adorno, Theodore, 87

Advocacy groups, 15, 18–21, 29, 58–60, 63, 64–66, 132, 292, 342–344. *See also name of specific group*

AFDC [Aid to Families with Dependent Children]: assumptions underlying, 64, 181–182; benefit levels of, 168, 178, 183–188, 304, 328; and child welfare policies, 64, 180, 240, 305–306; and the common goals of social work and labor, 328; and conservatism, 176, 178, 179; controversy about, 176, 178, 181–182, 188; and day care, 180; and dependency, 183; eligibility for, 180–181; and employment policies, 179–180, 183–184, 276, 278–280, 303, 305; expenditures for, 178; and the Food Stamp program, 262; and fraud/cheating, 183; and the functional conception of social welfare, 292–293; funding of, 180–181; history of, 178–180; and the homeless, 256; as an income maintenance program, 169, 176,

178–188; and the invasion of privacy, 188; as the largest public assistance program, 178; and liberalism, 176, 178, 179; and the man-in-the-house rule, 179; and Medicaid, 180, 194–197, 303; myths about, 181–184, 188; and the Nixon administration, 188; and poverty, 96, 184; purpose of, 176, 178–179; and race, 70, 183; and the Reagan administration, 179; recipients of, 70, 179, 188; rights of recipients of, 188; and the Social Security Act [1935], 48; as a social welfare policy, 4; and welfare reform, 298, 303, 304, 305–306. *See also* AFDC-UP

AFDC-UP [Aid to Families with Dependent Children-Unemployed Parent], 173, 178, 180, 194, 196

Affirmative action, 76–77, 86, 130, 131

AFL-CIO, 328

AFSCME, 328–329

Ageism, 84–85

Agnos, Art, 340

AIDS, 84, 118–119, 210–211, 225, 311–312

Aid to the Blind [AB], 188

Aid to Dependent Children [1935], 233

Aid to Families with Dependent Children. *See* AFDC

Aid to the Permanently and Totally Disabled [APTD], 188

Alcohol abuse, 74, 122, 223–226

Alexander, Leslie B., 330, 331, 332

Alinsky, Saul, 118, 345

Allison, Graham, 133

Althusser, Louis, 8–9

American Association of Retired Persons, 292

American Bankers Association, 264

American Civil Liberties Union, 234

American Dietary Association, 263

American Enterprise Institute, 58, 115, 133–135, 137, 138, 298, 300, 301

American Medical Association, 212, 218

American Public Welfare Association, 60, 241

Amidei, Nancy, 137–138

Anderson, Martin, 300, 301

Anshen, Melvin, 130

Association for the Promotion of Profit Sharing, 128

AT&T, 133

Atherton, Charles, 7, 170, 175

Atlantic Richfield, 133

Auletta, Ken, 278, 280

Authoritarian personality theory, 87

Back to Basics [Pines], 135–136, 299

Bakke, Alan, 76

Balanced Budget and Emergency Deficit Control Act [1985], 299, 328

Ball, Robert, 148, 317

Balzano, Michael, 135

Bane, Mary Jo, 280

Banfield, Edward, 103, 104

Barker, Robert, 20, 159

Baroody, William J., Jr., 133–134, 135, 298

Barthelemy, Sidney, 340

Bassuk, Ellen, 256

Battered child syndrome, 233

Battered women, 118–119

Beasely, Tom, 147–148

Beers, Clifford, 217

Bell, Jim, 234

Bell, Winifred, 98

"Beltway bandits", 62

Bendick, Marc, 288

Benefits, 4, 6, 19, 25. See also name of specific type of benefit or program

Berger, Bridgette, 235

Berger, Peter, 134–135, 235, 300

Bergland, Bob, 264

Berkowitz, Edward, 129

Bernstein, Joan, 171

Besharov, Douglas, 234

Bethlehem Steel, 134

Black associations, 41–42

Blacks, 68–72, 86, 87, 94, 95, 96, 105, 237, 262, 271, 339

The Black Underclass [Glasgow], 280

Block grants, 116, 202, 223–224

Blood banks, 312

Boarding homes, 317

Boorstin, Daniel, 17

Born, Catherine, 146–147

Brace, Charles Loring, 36, 39, 232

Bradley, Bill, 301

Bredesen, Philip, 146

Brenner, M. Harvey, 274

Brilliant, Eleanor, 337

Britain, 32–33, 127, 204–207, 211, 312

Brookings Institution, 58, 132, 138, 298, 342

Brown v. Board of Education of Topeka, Kansas [1954], 75, 77

Buchanan, James, 15

Buchanan, Richard, 316

Budget deficits, 15, 287

Bullock, Bruce, 265, 268

Bureaucracies, 55–56, 64, 326, 329–330

Bureaucratic disentitlement, 64

Bureaucratic rationality, 55–56

Bush administration, 12, 58, 115, 135, 299

Business. See Corporate sector

Busing, 75

Butler, Stuart, 135, 301

California, 219, 227–228

Calvin, John, 37–38

Canada, 211

Capitalism, 56, 127, 135, 139, 306

Caremark, 147

Carnegie, Andrew, 128–129

Carter [Jimmy] administration, 137, 219, 249, 342

Casework: as dominant form of social delivery, 18; political, 340–342, 345, 346

Casework agencies, 18, 42–44

Cash benefits, 4

Catastrophic illness, 197, 199–200, 210, 212

Catholic Charities, 263

Cato Institute, 60, 135

CBO [Congressional Budget Office], 62, 98

Center on Budget and Policy Priorities, 58, 72, 343

Center for Participation in Democracy, 64

CETA [Comprehensive Employment and Training Act], 49, 276

Chamber of Commerce, United States, 132

Charitable contributions, 116–117, 122–123, 137, 312

Charity: socialization of, 18, 43–44

Charity Organization Societies [COSs], 38–39, 43–44

Chase Manhattan Bank, 134

Chavez, Cesar, 118, 345

Chevron Corporation, 133

Child abuse, 6, 233–234, 235, 236

Child care, 122, 146–147, 238, 261. *See also* Day care

Child Care Food program, 261

Child Care Services Improvement Act [1986], 238

Child Health Assurance Program [1984], 343

Child labor, 232–233

Child Protective Services, 6

Children: aid societies for, 39, 232; in colonial America, 33; and the COSs, 39; and health care, 194, 196, 209–210, 238–240, 241, 343; homeless, 254, 256; indentured, 33; and labor reform, 48; and poverty, 94, 96, 102; rights of, 234–235; social workers as champions of, 339; and the voluntary sector, 119, 122. *See also* Child welfare policy; *name of specific program or organization*

Children, White House Conference on, 232

Children's Aid Society, 39

Children's Bureau, 232, 233

Children's Defense Fund, 58, 198–199, 210, 238, 241, 342–343, 344

Child support, 78–79, 180, 303, 305–306

Child Welfare League of America, 60, 231

Child welfare policy: and adoption, 231, 232, 236–238; and children's rights, 234–235; and child welfare personnel, 234; components of, 231; controversial nature of, 231; cost of, 235; emerging issues in, 238–240; expenditures for, 234; and the family, 231, 241; and foster care, 231, 232, 234, 235–236; funding of, 234; future of, 241; and health care, 238–240, 241; history of, 231–233; and parental rights, 234–235; and permanency planning, 235–236, 237; and poverty, 241; and progressivism, 232; and protective services, 6, 231, 232, 233–235; and the Reagan administration, 232; and the Social Security program, 48, 233, 236, 238; and state government, 233–235

Christian Socialism, 41

Chu, Franklin, 159

Churches. *See* Religion

Circuit breaker programs, 248–249

Citizens for Tax Justice, 126

Civilian Conservation Corps [CCC], 47–48, 274–275

Civil Rights Act [1964, 1968], 19, 54, 75–76, 77, 83, 291–292

Civil Rights Movement, 9, 64, 75, 339–340, 345

Civil war era, 34–35

Civil Works Administration, 274–275

Class. *See* Social stratification; *name of specific class*

Clinical entrepreneurs, 19–20, 21

Cloward, Richard, 8, 13, 289–290, 345

CMHC. *See* Community Mental Health Centers

Coalition of American Public Employees [CAPE], 328

Code of Ethics [NASW], 155, 329, 330, 346

Cohen, Sidney, 225

Cohen, Wilbur, 340

Colonial America, 33–34

Combined Federal Campaign, 122

Commercialization, 161–162, 311–313

Commodity Credit Corporation, 266, 269

Commodity Distribution program, 261

Commonwealth Fund, 129

Community Action Program [CAP], 49, 63

Community for Creative Non-Violence [Washington, D.C.], 345–346

Community Health Centers, 210

Community Mental Health Centers, 6, 19, 216, 218–219, 221, 222–223, 291–292

Community mental health movement, 216, 218, 219

Community and Migrant Health Centers, 202

Community Reinvestment Act [1977], 244

Community sanction of professions, 153

Community Work Experience Program [CWEP], 279–280

Company towns, 128

Comparable worth, 82–83

Compensatory education, 105

Comprehensive Child Care Act [1971], 81

Comprehensive Employment and Training Act [CETA, 1973], 49, 276

Compulsory treatment, 225–226

Condominiums, 249–250

Conference Board, 123

Congregate Dining programs, 261, 263

Congress, 58–60, 62, 216, 312–313, 345. *See also name of specific committee or person*

Congressional Budget Office, 62, 98

Conservatism: and AFDC, 176, 178, 179; and the corporate sector, 132, 133, 135–137, 138, 139; cultural, 293, 301; and employment policies, 275–276; and family issues, 137, 298, 299; and the functional conception of social welfare, 292–293; and housing policies, 257; as an ideology, 7–9; and Medicaid, 210; and the Nixon

Conservatism *continued*
  administration, 50; and PACs, 60; and policy
  institutes, 132, 133, 135–137, 138; and the
  policy process, 63; and the private sector, 3, 310;
  in the Progressive Era, 45; and the public choice
  school, 15; and religion, 38; and social insurance,
  169, 170; and the Social Security program, 170;
  and supply-side economics, 13; and the
  traditionalist movement, 299; and the voluntary
  sector, 17, 115; and welfare reform, 21–22, 298,
  299, 304, 306; and welfare state, 287, 288–289,
  291. *See also* Neoconservatism
Constituent services, 345, 346
Consulting firms, 62
Consumer rip-offs, 130
Continuing care retirement communities, 148,
  316–317
Control Data Corporation, 131
Coors family, 135
Corporate foundations, 126–127
Corporate sector: and advocacy groups, 132; and
  affirmative action, 130, 131; charitable
  contributions of the, 137; and conservatism, 132,
  133, 135–137, 138, 139; and consumer rip-offs,
  130; criticisms of the, 126–127, 130, 132, 139;
  and the Depression, 129; and dual welfare
  systems, 295–296; and environmental pollution,
  130; and equal opportunity, 131; and the farm
  crisis, 267, 268–269; fringe benefits in the,
  129–130, 137; and the functional conception of
  social welfare, 294; future involvement in social
  welfare of the, 137–140; and government
  assistance/partnership, 138–139; and health
  care/insurance, 127, 129, 130; history of the,
  127–130; and industrial policy, 138–139;
  influence of the, 126, 127–130, 132–137,
  294–295; and Keynesian economics, 10–11; and
  labor, 127–128, 137, 140; and liberalism, 132,
  138; and minorities, 130, 131; and the mixed
  welfare economy, 127, 294; and the New Deal,
  129; and PACs, 60, 132; pension fund
  contributions of the, 130; and policy institutes,
  126, 132–133, 134, 138; and privatization, 127,
  310, 311, 317–318; and progressivism, 126; and
  public image, 130–131; and social responsibility,
  126, 130–132; and the Social Security program,
  129; social work within the, 140; societal abuses
  by the, 126–127; as a source of funding,
  116–117, 123, 126–127; and South Africa issues,
  131, 137–138; and theology, 135; and urban
  blight, 130; and the voluntary sector, 116–117,
  123, 137, 140; and welfare capitalism, 139; and
  welfare reform, 302
Corporate social welfare policy, 5
Corporate welfare state, 294–295
Correction Corporation of America, 147–148
Corrections, 147–148
Cost containment, 201, 203, 211, 315
Cost-of-living adjustments [COLAs], 171
Council on Economic Priorities, 130–131
Covington, Mary White, 42
CRS [Congressional Research Service], 62
Cuban-Americans, 72
Cultural conservatism, 293, 301
Culture of poverty, 103–104
Cyclical unemployment, 273

Danziger, Sheldon, 96
Darwin, Charles, 37
Day care, 81–82, 180, 238, 303, 305. *See also*
  Child care
Decency Principles [Amidei], 137–138
Decision making, 54–56. *See also* Policy process
DeFunis, Marco, Jr., 76
Deinstitutionalization, 219–221, 226, 254, 280
"Deliberate misdiagnosis", 160
Delivery of services: and bureaucracies, 321–326;
  as a current issue, 287; definition of, 322; and
  the de-skilling of social workers, 323–326; and
  efficiency, 321, 324, 325; problems in the,
  322–323; and productivity, 324, 325–326; and
  profits, 324; and routinization, 324–325; and the
  self-determination of social workers, 332–333;
  and standardization, 322, 323; and technology,
  322, 323–326; and unions, 326–332
Dellums, Ronald, 213, 340–341, 344
Demand, 56
Democratic capitalism project, 135
Democratic party, 21, 115, 287, 289, 301–302, 303
Demonstration Cities and Metropolitan Development
  Act [1966], 243–244
Dependency, 70, 183
Depression, 45–48, 129, 169, 266, 274–275, 291
Deserving/undeserving poor, 32–33, 38
De-skilling of social workers, 323–326
Dewey, John, 339
Diagnostic Related Groups [DGRs], 200–202, 210,
  295, 315
Dies, Martin, 48
Disabled, 48, 85–86, 102, 170
Disadvantaged, 7, 21, 276. *See also* Blacks;
  Hispanics; Indians; Racism

Discouraged workers, 273, 281
Discrimination, 83–88, 250. *See also* Racism; Sexism
Dix, Dorothea, 34, 216, 218
Doeringer, Peter, 277
Dolbeare, Cushing N., 253
Dollard, J., 87
Domestic Policy Council Low-Income Opportunity Working Group, 182–183
Domestic Violence bill, 137
Donaldson v. O'Connor, 220–221
Donnison, David, 319
Downey, Thomas, 303
DRGs [Diagnostic Related Groups], 200–202, 210, 295, 315
Drug abuse, 122
Drug-Free America Act [1986], 225
Drugs: prescription, 207–208, 212
Dual labor market, 277–278, 281
Dual welfare systems, 295–296
Du Bois, W. E. B., 41, 42, 339
Dugdale, Richard, 104–105
Dukakis, Michael, 208, 301
Dumping, 4–5, 221, 313–314
Dunbar, Ellen, 161–162
Duncan, Greg, 102, 183, 184
Dunphy, Dexter, 54

Economic Development Act [1965], 49
Economic Development Administration, 61, 135
Economic feasibility, 28–29
Economic instability, 8–9
Economic Opportunity Act [1964], 5, 19, 49, 291–292
Economic Policy Institute, 122–123
Economics: and discrimination, 87, 88; and the diversity of social welfare, 16; Keynesian, 10–11; supply-side, 11–13; and the welfare state, 290–293
Edelman, Marian Wright, 342
Education, 70–72, 73, 74, 75, 76, 83, 86
Educational Amendments [1972], 83
Efficiency, 29–30, 321, 324, 325
Elderly, 84–85, 95, 102, 122, 135, 170, 254, 263, 264. *See also name of specific program*
Elementary and Secondary Education Act [1965], 19, 291–292
Ellwood, David, 280
Employee Assistance Plans, 126, 139–140, 143
Employment: of blacks, 72; of the disabled, 86;

discrimination in, 83; of the elderly, 85; and poverty, 102–103; and women, 78, 80–83
Employment policies: and AFDC, 173, 179–180, 183–184, 276, 278–280, 303, 305; and child welfare policies, 241; and the Civil Rights Act [1964], 83; and conservatism, 275–276; and cyclical unemployment, 273; and the disadvantaged, 276; and discouraged workers, 273, 281; and the distribution of unemployment, 307; and dual labor markets, 277–278, 281; and frictional unemployment, 273, 274; and the functional conception of social welfare, 294; and health care, 194, 202, 207–209; history of, 274–276; and job training programs, 276–277; and labor unions, 278; and liberalism, 276; and the minimum wage, 275–276, 281; and the New Deal, 274–275; and the Reagan administration, 273, 276–277, 279; and the service sector, 278; and structural unemployment, 273; and the underclass, 280–281; and the underemployed, 273, 281; and the unemployment rate, 274; and the War on Poverty, 276; and welfare reform, 299, 303, 305, 307. *See also* Workfare; *name of specific legislation*
England, 32–33, 127, 204–207, 211, 312
Enterprise Foundation, 131
Entitlements, 176, 306
Entrepreneurialism, 123–124, 159
Environmental pollution, 130
Equal Credit Act [1975], 83
Equal opportunity, 76, 131
Equal Pay Act [1963], 83
Equal protection under the law, 75, 76
Equal Rights Amendment, 82–83
Estes, Richard, 308
Ethics, 153, 155, 161, 322. *See also* Code of Ethics [NASW]
Etzioni, Amitai, 54
Eugenics, 104–105, 217
Evaluations, 62–63
Expenditures: for child welfare policies, 234, 235; for the Food Stamp program, 262; for general assistance, 190; for health care, 143, 192, 198, 200–201, 207, 211, 214, 287; for hospitals, 192; for income maintenance programs, 168; for Medicaid, 198; for Medicare, 200–201; for mental health policiess, 220; for nursing homes, 192; for physicians' services, 192; for social insurance, 168; for social welfare, 9, 50, 143, 299
Exxon Corporation, 133, 134

Fair Labor Standards Act [1937, 1938], 48, 275
Families: and adoption, 237–238; and child welfare
  policies, 231, 241; composition of, 70, 102,
  237–238; and conservatism, 137, 298, 299;
  contributions to the voluntary sector of, 122–123;
  deterioriation of black, 68–69; and the farm
  crisis, 267; and liberalism, 137; and poverty, 102;
  and racism, 70; and the residual conception of
  social welfare, 291; and welfare reform, 298,
  305–306; White House Conference about, 137
Family Assistance Plan [FAP], 49–50, 188, 298
Family Life Center, 332–333
Family Planning Program, 202
Family Protection Act, 137
Family Security Act/Plan, 135, 305
Farm Act [1987], 270
Farm crisis, 264–271
Farmers: in the Depression, 46
Farmers Home Administration, 244, 253, 264
Farm Security Administration, 48
FDIC [Federal Deposit Insurance Corporation], 47
Feasibility of policy, 27–30
Federal Dependent Care Tax Credit, 238
Federal Emergency Relief Administration [FERA],
  47, 274–275
Federal Employees Retirement program, 168
Federal government: and the corporate sector,
  138–139; and corporate welfare state, 294–295;
  and dual welfare systems, 295–296; employees of
  the, 62; and the future of the welfare state, 294;
  and housing policy, 244–245, 250–254, 257, 258;
  and human service corporations, 144; influence
  on social policy of, 17; and the institutional
  conception of social welfare, 291–292, 294; and
  Keynesian economics, 10–11; and mental health
  policies, 216, 218; and the mixed welfare
  economy, 294; and Poor Laws, 32–33; and
  private practice, 153; and the public choice
  school, 15; and racism, 76; and the residual
  conception of social welfare, 291, 294;
  responsibility for poor of the, 34; role in New
  Deal of, 16; and supply-side economics, 11–13;
  and the traditionalist school, 14; and the
  voluntary sector, 116, 117, 122; and the welfare
  bureaucrats, 18–19; and welfare reform, 21–22.
  *See also name of specific branch, agency,
  program, or ideology*
Federal Housing Administration, 48
Federalizing meals on Wheels [Balzano], 135
Federal Surplus Relief Corporation, 261
Fees: in private practice, 155–156, 157–158,
  159–160; UCR, 156, 159–160; in the voluntary
  sector, 117, 123–124
Feldstein, Donald, 158
Felix, Robert H., 218
Feminization of poverty, 77–83
Ferrara, Peter, 135
Fetal Alcohol Syndrome, 225
Filer, John, 123, 137, 343
Filer Commission, 123
Fisher, Dena, 329
Flexner, Abraham, 43, 153
Food policy, 119, 261–271. *See also* Food Stamps
Food and Security Act [1985], 269
Food Stamp Act [1964], 19, 291–292
Food Stamps, 118, 227, 257, 261–271, 278, 328
Ford Foundation, 118, 131–132
Ford [Gerald] administration, 134, 219
For-profit organizations, 5, 16, 20–21, 295–296,
  310, 311, 312–314, 315, 318. *See also name of
  specific type of organization*
Foscarinis, Maria, 257
Foster care, 231, 232, 234, 235–236
Foundations, 116–117, 129. *See also name of
  specific foundation*
Fouraker, Lawrence, 133
Fourteenth Amendment, 75, 76
Fox Piven, Frances, 8, 13, 289–290, 345
Framework for social policy analysis, 24–31
France, 81
Fraud, 183, 278
Free Congress Research and Education Foundation,
  293, 301
Freedmen's Bureau, 34–35, 291
Frictional unemployment, 273, 274
Friedson, Eliot, 154, 324
Friendly visitors, 39
Fringe benefits, 129–130, 137
Frustration-aggression hypothesis, 87
Full Employment and Balance Growth Act [1978],
  19, 274, 291–292
Functional conception of social welfare, 292–293,
  294
Fundamentalism, 21–22
Funds for Parents Act [1911], 233

Galbraith, John Kenneth, 107
Galper, Jeffry, 13, 345
Gans, Herbert, 103
GAO [Government Accounting Office], 62
Gardner, John W., 118, 343
Gays. *See* Homosexuality

Gender issues, 80–81, 94, 95, 152. *See also* Women
General assistance, 189–190
General Electric Corporation, 131
General Motors Corporation, 133
Gentrification, 249, 254
Gephardt, Richard, 270, 301
Ghetto culture, 280–281
G.I. Bill [1944], 19, 291–292
Gil, David, 6–7, 106–107
Gilbert, Neil, 127, 322
Gilder, George, 301
Giovannoni, Jeanne, 231
Glasgow, Douglas, 280
Goddard, Henry, 105
Gordon, David, 277
Gore, Albert, Jr., 301
Governmental social welfare policy, 5, 64
Government. *See* Federal government; State government; Welfare state
Gramm-Rudman-Hollings Act. *See* Balanced Budget and Emergency Deficit Control Act [1985]
GrandMet USA, 144
Great Society, 49, 107, 109–110, 340
Greenstein, Robert, 304, 343
Greenwood, Ernest, 153
Grey Panthers, 85
Griffith, Elsie, 147
Group practice, 153
Guaranteed income, 21, 49–50, 188, 298, 299
Gueron, Judith, 279, 280
Guttman, Herbert, 69

Halderman v. Pennhurst, 220
Handicapped. *See* Disabled
Harkin, Tom, 270
Harrington, Michael, 48–49, 170, 263, 264, 290
Hartman, Chester, 246, 257
Hatch, Orrin, 238, 305
Haynes, George Edmund, 42, 339
Head Start, 49, 108
HealthAmerica, 146
Health care: administration of, 211; and AIDS, 210–211; and blacks, 69–70; in Britain, 204–207; and catastrophic illness, 197, 199–200, 210, 212; and children, 194, 196, 209–210, 238–240, 241, 343; components of, 192–193; and the corporate sector, 127; and cost containment, 201, 203, 211, 315; crisis in, 207–214; and the elderly, 85; and employment policies, 194, 202, 207–209; expenditures for,

143, 192, 198, 200–201, 207, 211, 214, 287; and Hispanics, 73; and the homeless, 257; inadequacies in, 210; and Indians, 74; and industrialization, 127; and the maldistribution of facilities, 209; and national health insurance, 212–213; and a National Health Service, 213–214; and the organization of medical services, 192–193; and race, 210; and the Reagan administration, 198–199, 210; in Scandinavia, 202–204, 206–207; and the Social Security Act, 193–194; and technology, 206, 211; and welfare reform, 299. *See also name of specific type of service or program*
Health and Human Services, U.S. Department of, 5
Health Maintenance Organization Act [1973], 143, 146, 202
Henry Street Settlement, 339
Heritage Foundation, 58, 60, 133, 138, 298, 301
Herrnstein, Richard, 105
Himes, David, 345
Hirschman, Albert O., 61
Hispanics, 54–55, 64, 72–74, 94, 95, 262, 271
HMOs [Health Maintenance Organizations], 146, 202, 212, 317–318
Hoffman, Saul, 183, 184
Hofstadter, Richard, 36
Home care, 147
Homeless, 50, 118–119, 221, 226, 241, 243, 254–257, 287, 295
Home Mortgage Disclosure Act [1976], 244
Home ownership, 69, 245, 253
Homestead Acts, 266
Homosexuality, 83–84, 87–88
Hoover, Herbert, 45–46, 233
Hoover Institution, 137, 300
Hopkins, Harry, 19, 339
Hopper, Kim, 257
Hopps, June, 337
Hospital Corporation of America, 144
Hospital management, 145–146
Hospitals, 192, 202, 203, 207, 314–316
House of Representatives, U.S., 59, 312–313
House Un-American Activities Committee, 48
Housing Act [1937, 1949, 1954], 19, 243, 291–292
Housing and Community Development Act [1974], 243–244
Housing policy: and Civil Rights Act [1968], 76; and condominiums, 249–250; and conservatism, 257; and discrimination, 250; and the federal government, 244–245, 250–254, 257, 258; and free-market policy, 257–258; and gentrification,

Housing policy *continued*
   249, 254; history of, 243–245; and home ownership, 245, 253; issues in, 245–254; and liberalism, 258; and low-income housing, 48, 243, 244, 247–254, 257, 258; and mental health, 254–255; and the middle-class, 258; and mortgages, 246–247; and poverty, 247–250, 257, 258; and property taxes, 248–249; and the quality of housing stock, 245–246; and racism, 250; reform of, 257–258; and rental housing, 250–254, 257–258; and revenue sharing, 244; and tax policies, 253; and urban renewal, 243, 250; and utility rates, 249; and the welfare state, 287. *See also* Homeless
Housing and Urban Development, U.S. Department of [HUD], 244, 253
Howe, Irving, 289
Hudson Institute, 123
Hull House, 338–339
Human service corporations:
   advantages/disadvantages of, 148, 150; and child care, 146–147; and the corporate welfare state, 294–295; and corrections, 147–148; criticisms of, 150; and dual welfare systems, 295–296; funding of, 148; and government intervention, 144; and health care, 143, 144–146, 147, 148, 149; influence of, 150; and innovation, 149; and mental health policy, 228; and the NASW, 148; new markets of, 145–148; and privatization, 311, 318; and professional social workers, 148–150, 228, 296; regulation of, 295; revenues of, 144; scope of, 144–145. *See also* For-profit organizations
Human service executives, 20–21
Human services: definition of, 5
Humphrey, Hubert, 289
Humphrey-Hawkins bill. *See* Full Employment and Balance Growth Act [1978]
Hungary, 81
Hunger in America [Physician Task Force], 238, 264
Hunger. *See* Food policy; Food Stamps
Huttman, Elizabeth, 183

IBM [International Business Machines], 131
Ideological State Apparatus [ISA], 8–9
Ideology, 7–9, 21, 27. *See also* name of specific ideology
Illiteracy, 119
Immigration, 5, 16, 35–36, 61, 73–74, 339
Immigration Reform and Control Act [1986], 5, 54–55, 73–74
Implementation of policy: and, 27, 29–30, 60–62
Income: of blacks, 69, 72; of the disabled, 86; distribution of, 48, 92, 97–101, 105; and the farm crisis, 267; and Food Stamps, 262; of Hispanics, 72, 73; of Indians, 74; and the New Deal, 48; and poverty, 92, 97–101, 105; of women, 78–79, 80–81
Income maintenance programs, 167, 168, 176, 188–190, 302. *See also* name of specific program
Income security, 135
Income taxes, 101, 312–313
Income test, 168
Indentured children, 33
Independent Sector [voluntary organization], 115, 123, 343, 344
Indians, Native American, 74–75, 237, 271
Industrial Areas Foundation, 118
Industrialization, 32, 35–45, 127, 288
"Industrial policy", 138–139, 305, 307–308
Inequality, 97–101
Infant mortality, 69–70, 73, 74, 208, 210, 233, 239
Inflation, 92, 262
In-kind benefits, 4
In Search of Excellence [Peters and Waterman], 149
Institutional conception of social welfare, 291–292, 294
Institutional racism, 68–75
Insurance programs, 123–124, 127, 129, 130, 155–156, 159–161
Integrated Service System [ISS], 227–228
Interest groups. *See* Advocacy groups
International Racquet Sports Association, 312–313
Invasion of privacy, 188
Involuntary sterilization, 217
IQ [intelligence quotient], 105
IRAs [individual retirement accounts], 135
ISS [Integrated Service System], 227–228

Jackson, Jesse, 66
Jacobs, Milton, 317
Jacoby, Russell, 290
Jayaratne, Srinika, 152
J.C. Penny, 134
Jensen, Arthur, 105
Job Corps, 49, 118, 276
Job training programs, 276–277
Johnson, Alice, 255–256
Johnson, Leonard, 42
Johnson [Lyndon] administration, 49, 219. *See also*

Great Society; War on Poverty
Jones, Reginald H., 138

Kahn, Alfred, 7
Kaiser Foundation Hospital, 317–318
Kaiser-Permanente, 146
Kammerman, Sheila, 81
Kaplan, Karen Orloff, 344
Kaus, Mickey, 281
Kelley, Florence, 232–233, 339
Kellogg, Paul U., 45
Kemp, Jack, 11, 135
Kempe, C. Henry, 233
Kennedy, Edward, 212, 289
Kennedy [John F.] administration, 218, 261
Kerr-Mills Act [1957], 193–194
Keynes, John Maynard, 10–11
Keynesian economics, 10–11, 12, 21
Kinder-Care, 147
King, Martin Luther, Jr., 75
Kirk, Stuart, 160
Kleeck, Mary van, 327
Kondratas, Anna, 301
Kramer, Ralph, 124
Kreuger, Larry, 255–256
Kristol, Irving, 132, 134
Kutchins, Herb, 160
Kuttner, Robert, 290

Labor, 48, 60, 127–128, 132, 212, 326–332. See
    also Unionization; name of specific legislation
Laissez-faire economics, 170
Larson, Magali, 155
Lathrop, Julia, 41, 232, 339
Laws of settlement, 33
LCSW [Licensed Certified Social Worker], 157–158
Leaders in social welfare, 338–340. See also name
    of specific person
Lebeaux, Charles, 288, 290
Legal Services Corporation, 49
Lemann, Nicholas, 281
Lesbians. See Homosexuality
"Less eligibility" principle, 33
Levenstein, Sidney, 154
Lewis, Lloyd, 317
Lewis, Oscar, 103–104
Liberalism: and AFDC, 176, 178, 179; and
    affirmative action, 77; and the corporate sector,
    132, 138; and employment policies, 276; and
    family issues, 137; and the functional conception
    of social welfare, 292–293; and government, 287;

and housing policy, 258; as an ideology, 7–9; and
    the institutional conception of social welfare, 292;
    institutionalization of, 19; and the private sector,
    310; and the Progressive Movement, 45; and the
    voluntary sector, 115; and welfare reform, 21–22,
    298–299, 306; and the welfare state, 287,
    288–289. See also Neoliberalism
Liberation Theology, 38
Libertarians, 14
Licensed Certified Social Worker [LCSW], 157–158
Licensing, 155, 156, 157
Life care communities, 148, 316–317
Lightman, Ernie S., 330–331
Lindblom, Charles, 54
Linowes, David, 132
Lipsky, Michael, 64
Lobbyists, 60
Local governments, 46, 99–101
Local Initiatives Support Corporation, 131–132
Local level: social welfare at the, 344–345
Long-term care, 149, 228. See also name of
    specific type of facility
Losing Ground [Murray], 135, 289, 301
Lowell, Josephine Shaw, 39
Lower class, 54
Low Income Home Energy Assistance Program, 249
Low-income housing, 48, 243, 244, 247–254, 257,
    258
Low-Income Opportunity Act [proposed], 302–303
Luther, Martin, 37–38
Lyman, Richard, 343

McGovern, George, 289
McIntyre, Robert, 98–99
McLuhan, Marshall, 53
McQuaid, Kim, 129
Mahaffey, Maryann, 340, 346
Manhattan Institute, 135, 301
Manpower Development Research Corporation
    [MDRC], 278–280, 281
Manpower Development and Training Act [1962],
    276
Margolin, Harold, 148
Market rationality, 55, 56
Marriott Corporation, 148, 317
Marx, Karl, 53, 337
Marxism, 105
Massachusetts Health Security Act [1988], 208–209
Massey, Jack, 147–148
Maternal health, 202, 233, 238–240, 241
Maternity and Infancy Act [1921], 233

Maternity leave, 81
Maxwell, Wilbur F., 327
Mead, Lawrence, 305
Meals on Wheels, 261, 263
Means test, 4, 64, 168, 176, 188, 194, 302. *See also name of specific program*
Mechanic, David, 218
Mediating structures project, 134–135
Medicaid: administration of, 194; and AFDC, 180, 194–197, 303; budget for, 194; and catastrophic illness, 197; and children, 194, 196, 343; and the common goals of social work and labor, 328; and conservatism, 210; contracting out of, 311; coverage of, 194, 196, 197; criticisms of, 198–199, 210; eligibility for, 194, 197; and employment policies, 194, 278; enactment of, 143; expenditures for, 198; funding of, 210; and human service corporations, 143; impact of, 198; inadequacies in, 197–198; as the largest public assistance program, 194; as a major health care program, 193–199; means test for, 194; Medically Needy component of, 196–197; and mental health policies, 227, 228; and national health insurance, 212; passage of, 19, 194, 291–292, 340; and physicians' services, 198; and poverty, 197–198; and privatization, 311, 314, 315, 316, 317; recipients of, 194; and reimbursements, 194; as a social insurance program, 169; and SSI, 194, 197; and the voluntary sector, 118; and welfare reform, 303
Medicare: attitudes about, 64; and catastrophic illness, 199–200; contracting out of, 311; and the corporate welfare state, 295; and cost containment, 201; coverage of, 199–200; and the Diagnostic Related Groups [DGRs], 200–202, 210, 295; enactment of, 143; expenditures for, 200–201; funding of, 199, 200, 210; and HMOs, 202; Hospital Insurance portion of, 199, 201; and human service corporations, 143; inadequacies of, 200; as a major program, 199–202; and mental health policies, 228; and national health insurance, 212; passage of, 19, 194, 291–292, 340; and physicans, 201; and privatization, 311, 315; purpose of, 199; and the Reagan administration, 210; recipients of, 200–201; and reimbursements, 201; as a social insurance program, 169, 170; Supplemental Medical Insurance portion of, 199
Meeting Human Needs. See American Enterprise Institute
Memphis Firefighters v. Stotts [1984], 76

Mencken, H. L., 43
Mental health: as a social problem, 6
Mental Health Act [1946], 217–218
Mental health policy: and alcoholism, 223–226; and the Community Mental Health Centers, 6, 19, 216, 218–219, 221, 222–223, 291–292; and congress, 216; and deinstitutionalization, 219–221, 226; and eugenics, 217; expenditures for, 220; and the federal government, 216, 218; and Food stamps, 227; funding of, 219, 222–224, 227–228; future of, 226–228; and the homeless, 221, 226, 257; and housing policies, 254–255; and ISS, 227–228; and long-term care, 228; and Medicaid/Medicare, 227, 228; and the nursing home industry, 228; and preventive commitment, 226–227; and professional social workers, 228; and the Progressive era, 217; and psychotropic medication, 221, 227; and the Reagan administration, 222–223; reform of, 217–218; and reimbursements, 227–228; and the revolving door, 221, 226; and the rights of mental patients, 216, 219, 226–227; and substance abuse, 223–226; and Supplemental Security Income, 227; and Title XX, 227; and welfare state ideology, 287
Merton, C., 171
Messinger, Ruth, 340
Methadone, 29
Mexican-Americans, 72–74
Middle class, 54, 106, 258, 295–296, 307–308
Migrant workers, 54–55, 73
Mikulski, Barbara, 341, 342, 344
Milford Conference [1923], 18, 43, 44
Milliken v. Brady [1974], 75
Minimum wage, 102, 275–276, 281
Minorities, 130, 131, 280. *See also name of specific minority*
Mixed welfare economy, 127, 294
Mobilization for Youth, 118
Model Cities Program, 49, 243–244
Montgomery, Alabama, 75
Moral Majority, 14
Morehouse College, 42
Morris, Robert, 290
Mortality: infant, 208, 210, 233, 239; maternal, 233
Mortgages, 246–247
Moynihan, Daniel Patrick, 17, 68–69, 289, 299, 305
MSW [Master's in Social Work], 152, 157
Mueller Macaroni Company, 312

Murray, Charles, 135, 289, 301

NAACP [National Association for the Advancement of Colored People], 42, 60, 292, 339
NASW [National Association of Social Workers]: and the ACSW, 157; censures by the, 331; and clinical entrepreneurs, 20; Code of Ethics of the, 155, 329, 330, 346; and human service corporations, 148; and licensing, 156, 157; and lobbyists, 60; and the National Center for Social Policy and Practice, 343–344; and PACE, 59–60, 342; and PACs, 60; and private practice, 152, 156; and the unionization of social workers, 327–329, 330, 331; and vendorship, 156
National Assembly of Voluntary Health and Welfare Associations, 60
National Association of Manufacturers, 132
National Association for Mental Health, 217
National Association of Social Workers. See NASW
National Center for Child Abuse and Neglect, 233–234
National Center for Social Policy and Practice, 58, 343–344
National Committee for Prevention of Child Abuse, 236
National Conference of Charities and Correction [1915], 43
National Conference on Social Welfare, 60
National Consumer League, 232–233
National health care, 21, 212–213
National Health Service, 213–214, 340–341
National Institute of Mental Health [NIMH], 217–218, 219
National Labor Relations Act [1937], 48
National Low-Income Coalition, 258
National Medical Enterprises, 144, 145
National Recovery Act, 47
National Rifle Association, 122
National Urban League, 42, 60, 339–340
National Welfare Rights Organization [NWRO], 179
National Youth Administration, 47–48
Neighborhood Youth Corps, 49, 276
Neil Gilbert, 307
Nelson, Nelson Olsen, 128
Neoconservatism, 8, 293, 299–301, 304
Neoliberalism, 8, 21, 293, 301–302, 304
Neuhaus, Richard John, 134–135, 300
New Deal, 16, 19, 129, 212, 274–275, 289, 340, 345. See also Depression; name of specific agency or legislation
New Harmony, Indiana, 127

New Lanark, 127
The New Consensus on Family and Welfare. See Novak, Michael
New York Society for the Prevention of Cruelty to Children, 232
New York University, 312
Niagara Movement, 42, 339
Nixon [Richard] administration, 49–50, 62, 81, 188, 219, 298
Noncash benefits, 93
Nonprofit agencies, 5, 16, 119–122, 295–296, 310, 311, 312–314, 315 See also Voluntary sector; name of specific organization
Normative-cultural theory, 87
Norway, 202–203, 206–207
Novak, Michael, 134, 135, 138, 301
NOW [National Organization for Women], 60
Nursery for Children of Poor Women, 81
Nursing homes, 145, 192, 197, 200, 212, 228, 316, 317, 318

Oakland, California, 61
OASHDI. See Social Security program
O'Connell, Brian, 343
Offe, Claus, 291
Office of Economic Opportunity, 49, 276
Oklahoma City Board of Education v. the National Gay Task Force, 84
Olasky, Marvin, 132
Old Age Assistance program, 168, 188
Old Age and Survivors Fund, 171
Older Americans Act [1965], 85, 135, 291–292
Oligopolization, 317–318
OMB [Office of Management and Budget], 62
Omnibus Budget and Reconciliation Act [1981], 219, 279
Oppression, 87–88
Ortiz, Elizabeth, 148
"Overdiagnosis", 160
Ovington, Mary White, 339
Owen, Robert, 127

PACE [Political Action for Candidate Election], 59–60, 342
PACs [Political Action Committees], 59–60, 132
Parental rights, 234–235
Pareto Optimality, 7
Parity Farm Program, 266–227
Paternalism, 45
Payment-in-Kind [PIK], 269
Pension plans, 130, 176

Pepper, Claude, 60

Perkins, Frances, 41, 339

Permanency planning, 235–236, 237

Perrow, Charles, 322

Peters, Charles, 58, 149, 301, 302

Phillips, Kevin, 139

Physicians, 192, 198, 201, 203, 204–207, 238, 264

Physicians' Task Force on Hunger in America, 238, 264

Pines, Burton, 135–136, 299

Piore, Michael, 277, 278

Planning, 56

Plessy v. Ferguson [1896], 75

Policy institutes [think tanks], 57–58, 126, 132–137, 138, 298, 342–344. *See also name of specific institute*

Policy process: and advocacy groups, 58–60; and aspects of decision making, 54; in Congress, 59–60; cost of influencing the, 60; evaluation as a stage in the, 62–63; formulation as a stage in the, 56–58; and the implementation of policy, 60–62; implications for social welfare of the, 63–66; institutional role in the, 57–58; legislation as a stage in the, 58–60; overview of the, 54–56; and public support of programs, 61–62; and sexism, 83; stages of the, 56–63; and voter registration, 64, 66. *See also* Social policy

Political action, 287, 337, 340–342, 344, 345, 346

Political Action for Candidate Election [PACE], 59–60, 342

Political economy, 9–15, 154–156

Political feasibility, 28

Political machines, 36

Political practice, 340–342, 345, 346

Poor Laws, 32–33, 127

Poverty: in the 1950s, 48–49; absolute, 92; and AFDC, 96, 184; and AIDS, 211; area, 107–110; and blacks, 69–72, 94, 95, 96; case, 107–110; causes of, 102, 103, 107; characteristics of, 102; and children, 94, 96, 102, 241; in colonial America, 33–34; culture of, 103–104; cycle of, 107, 280; definition of, 92, 105; demographics of, 94–96; and the disabled, 102; and discrimination, 88; and education, 70–72; and the elderly, 95, 102, 170; and employment, 96, 102–103; and eugenics, 104–105; and family composition, 102; feminization of, 77–83; and food policy, 261–271; functions of 105–106; and gender, 94, 95; and general assistance 189–190; and Hispanics, 72–74, 94, 95; and housing policy, 247–250, 257, 258; and income

distribution, 92, 97–101, 105; and Indians, 74–75; and inequality, 97–101; inevitability of, 138; and inflation, 92; long-term nature of, 280; and Medicaid, 197–198; and the middle class, 106; and migrant workers, 73; and minorities, 280; as a moral failing, 37–38; and policy institutes, 138; as a political issue, 109–110; and race, 94; and radicalism, 105–107; and the Reagan administration, 50, 96, 109; relative, 92; religious aspects of, 37–38; responsibility for, 33; rural, 270–271; and social class, 106–107; and the Social Security program, 95, 107; and social stability, 106; and stigma, 68; strategies to combat, 107–110; and tax policies, 98–101; theoretical formulations about, 103–107; and welfare reform, 301, 306; and who are poor, 93–96; and work, 102–103, 105–106. *See also* Homeless; War on Poverty

Poverty index, 92–93, 109–110, 184, 189–190

Preferential selection, 159, 313–314

Prejudice, 88

Presidential Executive Order 11375 [1972], 83

President's [Reagan] Commission on Privatization, 310–311, 318–319

Pressman, Jeffrey, 61

Preventive commitment, 226–227

Prigmore, Charles, 7, 170, 175

Private capitalization, 12

Private Industry Councils, 276–277

Private practice, 19–20, 152–162, 332–333

Private Provision of Public Services [Urban Institute], 298

Private sector: as the basis of welfare, 3; and conservatism, 3, 310; and the diversity of social welfare, 16; and dual welfare systems, 295–296; and liberalism, 310; during the New Deal, 19; and preferential selection, 313–314; and privatization, 313–314, 318; in the Progressive Era, 45; and supply-side economics, 11–13; and welfare reform, 301; and the welfare state, 291. *See also name of specific type of organization*

Privatization, 127, 132, 135, 156, 206, 287, 310–319

Privatization, Report of the President's Commission on [1988], 310–311, 318–319

Productivity, 298, 302, 305, 306, 307–308, 324, 325–326

Professionalism: characteristics of, 324; and community sanction, 153; and private practice, 153–154; of social work, 43; sociology of, 153–154; and unionization, 329, 330–332

Professional monopoly, 154–155, 156
Professional organizations, 157, 331. *See also name of specific organization*
Progressive Era, 44, 217, 338–339
Progressive Movement, 44–45
Progressivism, 126, 169, 232, 290
Prohibition, 25
Property taxes, 248–249
Proposition 13 [California], 276
Protective services, 6, 231, 232, 233–235
Protestant ethic, 37–38
Psychoanalytic theory, 88
Psychotropic medication, 221, 227
Public accommodations, 75, 76
Public assistance, 33, 79–80, 107, 109–110, 167–168, 278. *See also name of specific program*
Public choice school, 15, 21
Public health services, 48, 192–193
Public interest organizations, 132–133
Public investment, 12
Public policy: cyclic nature of, 61–62; definition of, 4. *See also* Policy process; Social policy
Public sentiment, 29, 43, 61–62
Public Works Administration, 47, 274–275
Puerto Ricans, 72–74
Pullman Company, 128
Purchase of service, 311

Rabushka, Alvin, 300
Race, 94, 95, 183, 210. *See also name of specific race*
Racism, 68–77, 87–88, 250
Radicalism, 105–107, 289–290, 295, 345–346
Rainbow Coalition, 66
Rankin, Jeannette, 340
Rating America's Corporate Conscience [Council on Economic Priorities], 131
Rationality, 55–56
Reagan administration: and advocacy groups, 60; and AFDC, 179; and affirmative action, 76–77; appointments in the, 62; and child welfare policies, 232; and the common goals of social work and labor, 329; and day care, 81; and the devolution of welfare, 16; and employment policies, 273, 276–277, 279; and the farm crisis, 268, 269; and food policies, 262, 263, 268, 269; and the future of social welfare, 346; and health care policies, 198–199, 210; and housing policies, 253–254, 257; and the implementation of public policy, 62; and mental health policies, 219, 222–223; and policy institutes, 58, 134,

135, 342; and poverty, 50, 96, 109; and social insurance, 169; and the Social Security program, 60, 169; and supply-side economics, 11; and urban development, 135; and the voluntary sector, 115, 116; and welfare bureaucrats, 19; and welfare reform, 299, 302–303, 304; and the welfare state, 50, 287–288, 289. *See also* Privatization
Reciprocity, 298, 304–305, 306, 308
Redistribution of resources, 4, 13
Redman, Eric, 58
Reform. *See* Welfare reform; *name of specific program*
Regulation, 20, 153, 154–155
Rehabilitation Act [1973], 86
Reich, Robert, 17, 138–139, 302
Reich, Wilhelm, 87
Reimbursements, 155–156, 159–160, 194, 201, 202, 203–204, 205, 227–228
Reischauer, Robert, 280
Religion, 14, 16–17, 32, 35, 37–38, 135, 287, 299
Relman, Arnold, 318
Remer-Thamert, Glen, 346
Rent subsidies, 250–254
Report of the President's Commission on Privatization [1988], 310–311, 318–319
Repressive State Apparatus [RSA], 8–9
Republican party, 132
Residency requirements, 33
Residual conception of social welfare, 291, 294, 306
Revenue sharing, 244
Reverse discrimination, 76
Revolving door, 221, 226
Reynolds, Bertha Capen, 345
Rights: of AFDC recipients, 188; of children, 234–235; of mental patients, 216, 219, 226–227; of parents, 234–235
Riis, Jacob, 36
Robb, Charles, 301
Rockefeller, John D., 128, 129
Rockefeller Foundation, 129
Rooney, Ronald, 236
Roosevelt, Franklin Delano, 47–48, 169
Roosevelt, Theodore, 45
Rostenkowski, Dan, 303
Roth, William, 86
Rothenberg, Randall, 301–302
Rouse, James, 131
Routinization, 324–325
Runaways, 241, 254

Rural poverty, 270–271
Ruth Massinga v. L.J. et al., 234

Safety nets, 176, 189, 291, 310
Sage [Russell] Foundation, 129
Salamon, Lester, 116
Salaries: in private practice, 152, 157–158, 161
Sales taxes, 99–101
Salvation Army, 263
Sandel, Michael, 289
Sanitary Commission, U.S., 34
Scandinavia, 288
School Lunch and Breakfast programs, 261, 262–263, 264
Schultze, Charles, 298
Schwerner, Michael, 337
Scientific inquiry, 25
Scientific management, 321, 322
Sectarian agencies, 17
Section 504 [Rehabilitation Act, 1973], 86
Segregation, 75–76
Self-determination of social workers, 332–333
Self-regulating economy, 11
Self-reliance school, 14–15
Selma, Alabama, 75
Senate, U.S.: committees of the, 59
Seniority rules, 76
Separate but equal, 75
Service contracts, 116
Service delivery models, 44
Service sector, 278
Settlement: laws of, 33
Settlement houses, 39–41, 43–44, 45, 338–339
Sexism, 77–83, 87–88
Shaffer, Gary, 331
Sherraden, Michael, 273
Shockley, William, 105
Siegrist, Richard, Jr., 145–146
"Signing off", 160–161
Sixth Omnibus Budget Reconciliation Act [SOBRA, 1986], 196, 197
Smith, Hedrick, 345
Snyder, Mitch, 345–346
Social altruism, 6
Social contract, 13, 53, 295
Social control, 6, 13, 39
Social Darwinism, 37, 39, 88
Social Gospel, 38
Social instability, 8–9, 106
Social insurance, 4, 167–172, 175–176. *See also name of specific program*

Socialism, 13, 21
Socialization, 87
Socialization of charity, 18, 43–44
Social justice, 4, 118–119, 161–162, 306
Social policy: analysis of, 24–31, 337, 344; assumptions about, 63–64; definitions of, 4–5; primary players in determining, 63; as private policy, 4; as public policy, 4; purposes of, 6; redistribution of resources as basic theme of, 4; and social problems, 5–6; and social stratification, 63–66; values within, 6–7. *See also* Policy process; Public policy; *name of specific sector of society*
Social problems, 5–6. *See also name of specific problem*
Social reform, 19, 41, 45. *See also* Welfare reform
Social responsibility, 126, 130–132
Social sciences, 37
Social Security Act [1935, 1975, 1983]: and child welfare policies, 233, 236, 238; and the corporate sector, 129; and health care, 193–194, 212; and the institutional conception of social welfare, 291–292; passage of the, 5, 19, 48; provisions of the, 48; as a radical departure from the status quo, 54; as a social insurance program, 167, 169; as a solution to a social problem, 5; and the voluntary sector, 116; and the welfare bureaucrats, 19. *See also* Social Security program; Title XX; *name of specific program*
Social Security Administration, 92
Social Security Disability Insurance program, 85
Social Security program: administration of the, 169–170; advantages/disadvantages of, 170–171; attitudes about, 64; benefits of the, 170; and conservatism, 170; and the corporate sector, 129; and cost-of-living adjustments, 171; coverage of the, 170; eligibility for the, 170, 175–176; funding of the, 170, 172; future of the, 172; implementation of the, 170; importance of the, 176; and income redistribution, 167; issues concerning the, 171–172, 175–176; and laissez-faire economics, 170; and policy institutes, 135; principles of the, 170; and private pension plans, 176; and public welfare, 175; and race, 95; and the Reagan administration, 60, 169; and sexism, 79–80; as a social insurance program, 167, 168, 169–172; Swope's influence on the, 129; and tax system, 172, 175–176. *See also* Social Security Act; *name of specific program or topic*
Social services: definition of, 4

Social Services Block Grant, 116

Social stability/instability, 8–9, 106

Social stratification, 53–54, 63, 66

Social welfare: at the local level, 344–345; as big business, 3; complexity of, 21–22; conceptual bases of, 290–293; cultural influences on, 15–16; diversity in, 3–4, 15–17, 21–22; expenditures for, 9, 50, 143, 299; future of, 337–346; ideologies within, 21; leaders in, 338–340; political-economy of, 9–15; recent changes in, 21–22; and social control, 6, 13, 39

Social welfare policy. See Public policy; Social policy

Social workers: burnout of, 64; de-skilling of, 323–326; and dual welfare systems, 296; and the future of social work, 337–346; and human service corporations, 148–150, 228, 296; job dissatisfaction among, 322; licensing of, 155–157; and mental health policy, 228; morale of, 322; norms for, 322; and political action, 287, 337, 340–342, 344, 345, 346; and privatization, 318; role confusion of, 322; self-determination of, 332–333; and the social policy process, 63, 64; and technology, 323–326; unionization of, 326–332; and the voluntary sector, 296; and welfare reform, 307; and welfare state ideology, 288–289. See also NASW; name of specific topic

Social work [profession]: anti-unionism in, 329–330; commercialization of, 161–162; criteria for, 153; domination by other professions of, 325; and labor, 328–332; privatization of, 156; professionalization of, 43; regulation of, 20; scientific base of, 43; within the corporate sector, 140. See also Social workers

Society for the Prevention of Cruelty to Animals, 232

Sociopolitical planning, 56

South Africa, 131, 137–138

Southwest Voter Research Institute, 64, 66

Specht, Harry, 322

Special interest groups. See Advocacy groups; name of specific group

Special Milk program, 261

SSI. See Supplemental Security Income

Standardization, 316–317, 322, 323

Starr, Ellen Gates, 41

Starr, Paul, 212, 318

State government, 15–16, 99–101, 216–228, 233–235, 302–304. See also Medicaid; name of specific program

"Stat wars", 63

Steel, David, 316

Stein, Herbert, 134

Stein, Theodore, 236

Steininger, Fred, 330

Stewart B. McKinney Homeless Assistance Act [1987], 257

Stigma, 68–75, 87–88, 264, 291. See also Discrimination; Racism; Sexism

Stock market crash [October 1987], 287

Stone, Alan, 220–221

Straussner, Shulamith, 139

Stretch, John, 255–256

Structural unemployment, 273

Substance abuse, 223–226

Suffrage movement, 45

Sullivan, Leon, 131

Sullivan principles, 137–138

Summer Food program, 261

Supplemental Security Income [SSI, 1974, 1975], 19, 50, 168, 169, 188–189, 194, 197, 227, 291–292

Supply and demand, 56

Supply-side economics, 11–13, 21, 99

Swann v. Charlotte-Mecklenburg Board of Education [1971], 75

Sweden, 81, 202–204, 206–207

Swope, Gerald, 129

Talladega College, 42

Tax policies: and charitable contributions, 122–123; and housing policy, 253; and the libertarians, 14; local, 99–101; and poverty, 98–101; and the Social Security program, 172, 175–176; and the voluntary sector, 116. See also name of specific type of tax

Tax Reform Act [1986], 123

Taylor, Frederick, 321

Technology, 14–15, 56, 206, 211, 287, 322, 323–326

Techno-methodological planning, 56

Teenage pregnancy, 70, 119, 238, 239–240, 241, 343

Tennessee Valley Authority, 48

Theology, 87–88, 135

Thrifty Food Plan, 93

Thurow, Lester, 138

Title V [Maternal and Child Health Block Grant], 202

Title V [Rehabilitation Act, 1973], 86

Title V [Social Security Act]. See AFDC

Title VII [Civil Rights Act, 1964], 83

Title IX [Educational Amendments, 1972], 83
Title X [Family Planning Program], 202
Title XVIII [Social Security Act]. *See* Medicaid
Title XIX [Social Security Act]. *See* Medicare
Title XX [Social Security Act, 1935, 1975], 19, 81, 116, 227, 236, 238, 291–292, 311, 328
Titmuss, Richard, 4, 288, 312
Tocqueville, Alexis de, 35, 118
To Empower People [Berger and Neuhaus], 134–135
Toffler, Alvin, 53
Toren, Nina, 154
Toward a Theology of the Corporation [Novak], 135
Towns, Edolphus, 341–342, 344
Townsend, Francis, 169
Traditionalist movement, 299
Traditionalist school, 14, 21
Traditional providers, 18, 21
Trans-Africa, 137
Transcultural adoption, 237–238
Transfer programs, 79
Treatment: compulsory, 225–226
Trotter, Sharland, 159
Truman, Harry, 212

UCR fees [usual, customary, and reasonable], 156, 159–160
The Underclass [Auletta], 278, 280
Underemployed, 273, 281
Unemployment, 47, 48, 64, 96, 102, 169, 172–173, 275, 291. *See also* Employment; Employment policies; *name of specific program*
Unionization, 137, 140, 278, 326–332
United Kingdom, 32–33, 127, 204–207, 211, 312
United States Employment Service, 275
United Way, 18, 119, 122, 123, 263
Universities, 62
Unrelated business income tax [UBIT], 312–313
Upward Bound, 49
Urban development, 130, 135, 243, 250
Urban Institute, 298, 342
Urban migration, 32
U.S. Conference of Mayors, 254, 255
Utopian plans, 127

Values, 6–7, 14, 26, 27
Vaughan, David, 145
Velasquez, Willie, 64, 66
Vendorship, 155–156
Veterans Administration Hospitals, 202
Veterans of Foreign Wars, 292
Victims, 306

VISTA [Volunteers in Service to America], 49
VOCAL [Victims of Child Abuse Laws], 234–235
Voluntary sector: before 1920, 42; benefits of, 18; and blacks, 42; and the Bush administration, 115; charitable contributions to the, 116–117, 122–123, 137; and commercialization, 312; composition of the, 116; and conservatism, 17, 115; and the corporate sector, 116–117, 123, 137, 140; and the corporate welfare state, 295; in the Depression, 46–47; and dual welfare systems, 295–296; and entrepreneurialism, 123–124; expenditures of the, 122; fees of the, 117, 123–124; as the "forgotten sector", 115–118; and the functional conception of social welfare, 294; functions of the, 118; funding of the, 116–117, 122–124; future of the, 124, 294; government assistance to the, 116, 117, 122; historical role of the, 17; as an initiator of programs, 118–119; and the institutional conception of social welfare, 294; and insurance programs, 123–124; and liberalism, 115; and the local community, 124; and the mixed welfare economy, 294; and the number of volunteers, 116; and privatization, 310, 311, 312, 318; and professional social workers, 296; and the Reagan administration, 115, 116; and service contracts, 116; and the socialization of charity, 18; and social justice, 118–119; and the Social Security Act, 116; tax-exempt status of the, 116; traditional role of, 3, 18; and welfare reform, 21; and the welfare state, 35–45, 115–116, 294. *See also* Nonprofit organizations
Voluntary social policy, 5
Voter registration, 64, 66, 76
Vouchers, 311

Wagner-Peyser Act [1933], 275
Wald, Lillian, 45, 232, 339
War on Poverty, 5, 49, 63, 107, 109–110, 118, 135, 276, 290, 298
Washington, Booker T., 42, 339
Wasserman, Fred, 146
Wattenberg, Ben, 134
Wattenberg, Esther, 237
Weber, Max, 53, 55, 337
Weismiller, Toby, 342
Welfare bureaucrats, 18–19, 21
Welfare capitalism, 127, 139
Welfare mess, 4
Welfare programs: allocations for, 117; federal expenditures for, 116. *See also name of specific program*

Welfare reform, 287, 298–308, 328–329, 338–339, 340–342. *See also name of specific program*
Welfare Reform Act [1988], 180
Welfare state: and the anti-welfare reaction, 48–49; and black associations, 41–42; and casework agencies, 42–44; and conceptions of social welfare, 290–293, 294; and conservatism/neoconservatism, 287, 288–289, 291, 304; corporate, 294–295; and the Depression, 45–48; and the economy, 290–293; and food policy, 261; formation of the, 16; future of the, 293–296; and government, 287; and housing policy, 287; ideology and the, 7–9; incompleteness of the American, 17; and industrialization, 35–45; and the Johnson administration, 49; and liberalism/neoliberalism, 287, 288–289, 304; and mental health policy, 287; origins of the, 32–50; and the private sector, 291; and professional welfare people, 288–289; and the Progressive Movement, 44–45; and radicalism, 289–290; and the Reagan administration, 50; reforming the, 304–306; and religion, 287; in Scandinavia, 288; and settlement houses, 39–41; transformation of the, 287; and the voluntary sector, 35–45, 115–116; and welfare reform, 306
Wells, Ida B., 42
Wells-Barnett, Ida Bell, 339
West, James E., 232
West Germany, 81

Wheeler, Etta, 232
White, David, Sr., 42
White House Conference on Children, 232
White House Conference on Families, 137
WIC [Special Supplemental Program for Women, Infants, and Children], 239, 261, 262, 263, 328
Wildavsky, Aaron, 61
Wilensky, Harold, 288, 290
Wiley, George A., 179
Wilson, William Julius, 77, 281
Wilson, Woodrow, 45
WIN [Work Incentive Program], 180, 276
Wirth, Tim, 301
Wisconsin, 227–228
Women, 45, 78–83, 87, 88. *See also* Sexism
Workers' Compensation, 175
Work ethic, 299
Workfare, 12, 64, 179–180, 184, 273, 278–280, 281, 303–304, 307
Workhouses, 33–34
Working poor, 303
Works Progress Administration [WPA], 47, 48, 274–275
Wurf, Jerry, 328, 331
Wyatt v. Stickney, 220

YAVIS syndrome [young, attractive, verbal, intelligent, and successful], 159
YMCA, 312–313
Young, Whitney, Jr., 339–340